CANADA

MAINE

VT.

N.H.

NEW YORK

Buffalo

MASS.

Boston

CONN.

R.I.

PENNSYLVANIA

Cleveland

N.J.

OHIO

Gettysburg

Baltimore

DEL.

Harper's Ferry

OHIO R.

Washington

MD.

Cincinnati

WEST VIRGINIA

ATLANTIC OCEAN

Louisville

Fredericksburg

JAMES R.

UCKY

Richmond

Ft. Monroe

MBERLAND R.

VIRGINIA

ROANOKE I.

NORTH CAROLINA

CAPE HATTERAS

SSEE R.

CAPE FEAR R.

Beaufort

Chattanooga

Wilmington

SOUTH CAROLINA

Atlanta

Charleston

GEORGIA

Savannah   *Ft. Pulaski*

A

Fernandina

la

FLORIDA

St. Marks   *Ft. Marion*

ICO

DRY TORTUGAS •   • *Key West*

THE ARMY'S NAVY SERIES

Volume II

Assault and Logistics

Union Army Coastal and River Operations
1861 - 1866

by Charles Dana Gibson with E. Kay Gibson

Published by Ensign Press
PO Box 638; Camden, Maine 04843

Printed in the United States of America

Library of Congress No. 95-060239

ISBN: 0-9608996-3-4   Library Binding (hardcover)

ASSAULT AND LOGISTICS: Union Army Coastal and River Operations, 1861 - 1866
Gibson, Charles Dana   1928 -
   1. United States -- History, Military.   2. Civil War -- Union, Army amphibious operations.
   3. Military Logistics.   4. Maritime -- United States

The paper on which this book is printed meets the minimum requirements of American National
Standard for Information Science-Permanence of paper for printed library materials.
ANSI Z 39.48-1984.
Additionally, the paper on which this book is printed meets and exceeds all NASTA specifications.

Main text typeset in Times New Roman 12

Dedicated

To Those Who Served

TABLE OF CONTENTS

II: *WESTERN THEATER OF OPERATIONS: INITIAL PHASE*

III: *THE EASTERN THEATER NORTH OF HATTERAS*

IV: *CAMPAIGNS IN TENNESSEE AND KENTUCKY AUGUST 1862 - FEBRUARY 1863*

V: *FURTHER EVENTS ON THE WESTERN RIVERS*

VI: *UPDATE ON THE WAR SITUATION, ALL THEATERS*

VII: *CONCLUDING THE WESTERN RIVERS AND THE GULF OF MEXICO*

VIII: *THE EASTERN THEATER, 1864 - 1865*

IX: *AFTER THE SURRENDERS, 1865 - 1866*

X: *APPENDICES*

ILLUSTRATIONS

FRONT END PAPERS: Map depicting coastlines of the Atlantic and Gulf of Mexico

BACK END PAPERS: Maps depicting the Chesapeake Bay and the Mississippi Corridor

The silhouette which appears on the cover of this volume is
the transport *GEORGE PEABODY*.

Commentary on Civil War Maps

The average reader of this volume should find that the maps and terrain sketches which we have included are sufficient to follow the trends of operations. For some readers, however, there may be a desire for more finite detail so as to pinpoint obscure locations or to follow the progress of those land campaigns which, because of the special subject matter of this work, have only been peripherally discussed. There are literally scores of available map publications which relate to Civil War operations. Some of these are excellent and some less so. From our experience gained in the writing of this volume, we would selectively recommend the following.

For a generalized overview of all theaters of operations: National Geographic's *Battlefields of the Civil War*. This is a large, flat map printed on both sides in color with battle and campaign dates overlayed. Available directly from National Geographic Society; Washington, DC

For those whose interest lies in well organized graphic presentations of the war's major campaigns and the progress of battles: *Atlas for the American Civil War*. West Point Military History Series. Published by Avery Publishing Group, Inc.; 120 Old Broadway; Garden City Park, NY 11040. ISBN 0-89529-302-1.

To locate obscure place names and for excellent topographic detail as it existed during the 1860s: *The Official Military Atlas of the Civil War*, published in 1988 by Fairfax Press; distributed by Crown Publishers, Inc.; New York. ISBN: 0-517-415666. This is a facsimile of the *Atlas to Accompany the Official Records of the Union and Confederate Armies in the War of the Rebellion* produced by the Government Printing Office between 1891-1895. It is unsurpassed in cartographic information and is well indexed.

PREFACE

During a 1994 interview with the editor of a popular history magazine, a narrative historian of the Civil War was asked whether he felt there were gaps remaining in the telling of Civil War history. The historian responded, *"Not really...I think the gaps are filled."* Our own reaction to that statement is that nothing could be farther from the truth. While it is true that reams of material have been published dealing with the war's strategy and the tactical aspects of the various campaigns, the story of the supply side of the war is far from complete. For instance, little treatment has been given to the role that Army Quartermaster Department shipping played in the movement of men and materiel.

The American Civil War was the first major conflict wherein the conduct of military operations depended upon steam-powered transportation, meaning in that context, the military employment of the railroad and the steamboat. Both sides were heavy users of rail transportation; but it was the Union, with its wider accessibility to coastwise and river routes, which employed the steamboat to its maximum advantage. At certain times, the steamboat was part of the transportation matrix with the railroads playing the major role. In other campaigns, the steamboat was the primary form of transport. To give a few examples:

. The many amphibious assaults made against the southern coastlines, prominent among which were: Thomas W. Sherman's expedition to Port Royal Sound, South Carolina, in 1861; Ambrose Burnside's expedition to secure the North Carolina Sounds during 1862; the separate assaults against Fort Fisher at Cape Fear by Benjamin Butler in November-December of 1864, and by Alfred H. Terry in January of 1865. In all of these expeditions, as well as many other coastal operations, troops and their supplies were carried south aboard the transports of the Quartermaster.

. The campaign(s) against Vicksburg during 1862 and 1863 wherein huge bodies of troops were shifted up and down the Mississippi by steamboat through a region largely devoid of railroad facilities.

. In Tennessee during 1863, a Union army garrisoning the city of Chattanooga became totally cut off from its supply. The railroad tracks leading into the city had been destroyed, and all incoming wagon roads were impassable seas of mud, miring down the Army's draft animals which died by the hundreds while still in their traces.

The only remaining avenue for supply into Chattanooga was the Tennessee River; but there were no available steamboats then on the upper reaches of that river, and navigation there was inordinately difficult. A number of small steamers were hurriedly constructed while others were salvaged. With the help of some innovative engineering, these vessels carried supplies to Chattanooga in time to save that strong point from a forced evacuation. By that effort, the war was shortened many months.

. On the east coast, McClellan's Virginia campaign of 1862 was completely dependent on shipping. When McClellan was ordered to retire from the peninsula following a series of Confederate successes, the evacuation of his army -- in fact the very survival of that army and with it the fate of the Union -- was dependent on the steamboat.

. Marine transportation became the only means of supply during the Richmond-Petersburg campaign when in mid-1864 Grant brought the Army of the Potomac across the James River to join with Butlers' Army of the James. Once he crossed the James, Grant had severed his overland lines of communication. From then on through to the Confederate surrender at Appomattox in April of 1865, everything going to the Union Army in southern Virginia and everything coming from it was carried aboard vessels of the Quartermaster's fleet. Maintaining the Union Army's presence in front of Petersburg-Richmond was a logistical feat which would remain virtually unsurpassed in the volume of individual ship movements until the events at Normandy seventy-nine years later.

. When Sherman arrived at Savannah in December of 1864 following his march to the sea from Atlanta, his army's rations were down to an estimated fourteen day's supply, and the men's boots were wearing out. Before Sherman could begin his northern sweep through the Carolinas, his replenishment had to come by sea. An armada of ninety-nine vessels, many of them remaining on continuous shuttle duty from northern ports, brought down everything from rations to railroad locomotives.

Although historians have not totally overlooked the existence of the Ellet Ram Fleet on the Mississippi, or the subsequently established Mississippi Marine Brigade, nothing comprehensive has been published since 1907 on either organization's operations or the personalities who were directly involved. The story behind their commanders' stormy and rivalrous relationships with the Navy has also been neglected. The same lack of historical overview is evident concerning the development and manning of the Army's Western Gunboat Flotilla which, although largely Navy officered, was essentially an Army outfit up to the time of its transfer to the Navy in October of 1862. Also absent, creating such an informational void that many have never even heard of their existence, are the stories of the Army's light gunboats and its armed assault transports which operated within the coastal zones of Virginia, the Carolinas, and Georgia.

The officers who orchestrated the sea and river movements and the civilian seamen and rivermen who manned the Quartermaster's vessels have largely gone unsung. Brigadier General Lewis B. Parsons, a Union quartermaster who helped bring order out of the shipping chaos of the war's early months, put into place methods of procurement and utilization which in part are being employed by our military even to this day. Yet Parsons's name is rarely mentioned, even in those studies which have encompassed the subject of Civil War logistics.

~

When planning the scope and organization of this volume, we decided at the onset that if the work was to examine the significance of Union Army shipping and its relative importance to the conduct of the war, our major challenge would be to discuss vessel operations in a relationship which was proportionate to the total military (and at times political) scenario. To accomplish that, we felt it was vital to place the role of Quartermaster shipping into the overall framework of the Union effort rather than view it as something separate and apart. Our other self-imposed discipline was to relate the steamboats' interrelationship with the nation's railroad systems and to look at how the Army's Quartermaster Department advantageously integrated the functions of both modes of transportation. We believe we met those challenges with adequate balance.

The reader will discover from our footnotes, that a major reliance has been placed on primary sources, especially those that were composed during or close to the times of the actual happenings. In the instances where we have utilized secondary source material, we did so only with considerable discretion. The same tack was applied to reliance on newspaper accounts. When comparing official records against news stories of the day, we soon discovered that most reporters' accounts written allegedly "at the scene," more often than not presented narrow perspectives and that on average they were of poor analytical content. Consequently, we only used newspaper reports in the most ancillary sense. We also applied discretion to our reliance on memoirs. Some memoirs, particularly those which were written long after the events, are short on fact and on occasion are overly self-serving. David D. Porter's *The Naval History of the Civil War* is a good example of the last. On the other hand, William T. Sherman's memoirs are both accurate in tone and self-critical.

Our most valuable sources for this book were the materials within the Quartermaster records maintained by the National Archives as well as the reports and correspondence to be found within the volumes of *The War of the Rebellion, Official Records of the Union and Confederate Armies* and the *Official Records of the Union and Confederate Navies*. In our mining of the 157 separate bindings which comprise the *Official Records...*, we took pains to search out the full spectrum of materials dealing with each pertinent operation. When working with the viewpoints as set down by various army as well as naval officers, there are often conflicting versions, some so opposing that they become difficult to reconcile, the Battle of Memphis being a strong case in point. In such instances we took pains to reflect the conflicting points of view.

Whenever directly employing a participant's description of an operation, we have in most such cases done so by utilizing those accounts as direct quotations. We believe that this method, rather than our narration, has provided the reader with a period flavor which only a personality of the 1860s who was himself part of that history can accurately portray.

In our use of place names as well as descriptive terminology, we have for the most part elected to employ the usage and spelling which was in force during the 1860s. In cases of confusion over the spelling of place names, the *Atlas of Official Records...Armies* became our final authority. For the spelling of the names of Army vessels, we relied on *Official Records...Armies*. For the spelling of naval vessels, *Official Records...Navies* became our authority.

When identifying vessels with military significance, we have adhered to the following practice. Army supply or combatant vessels, whether Union or Confederate, or whether owned or chartered, are never prefixed. Conversely, commissioned naval vessels of both sides are prefixed, i.e., "USS" for Union Navy and "CSS" for the Confederate Navy. The reader will note our handling of gunboats of the Western Gunboat Flotilla. While under Army jurisdiction prior to October of 1862, the gunboats' names have not been prefixed; following October 1862, when those gunboats were transferred to the Navy, the prefix "USS" was applied.

One of the vexing problems we encountered inherent to the proper identification of vessels employed by the Quartermaster before or during the Civil War was caused by the absence of an exact means by which a vessel can be traced. Prior to 1867, there was no official system which assigned identification numbers to commercial vessels. Consequently, dealing with what were then commonplace names such as *DELAWARE,* or *GENERAL BURNSIDE,* or *DANIEL WEBSTER,* or *MAYFLOWER* can be a trying task. Many different vessels with the same name and of the same type were often employed within the same geographic area. This was especially common for schooners plying the coasts and for riverboats in the west. Identification was not a problem when ownership was shown on sale or charter records. Unfortunately, though, such information was not consistently recorded and often was not recorded at all. Confusion was further abetted by variations in spelling, the same vessel's name variously represented as ending in "i.e." or "y", etc. Quartermaster clerks and authors of operational reports often omitted first names entirely or elected to use abbreviations. One vessel which stands out as an example is a tug which appears variously in both Quartermaster and operational records as *ALFRED CUTTING; ALF CUTTING; A. CUTTING; CUTTING; ALPH CUTTING.* Although tonnage comparisons can be a clue, the standard method used in arriving at tonnage was changed during the Civil War period. As a result, most vessels of that period sport at least two different gross admeasurements. To compound the tonnage puzzle, quartermasters at the various ports often devised their own methods for evaluating a vessel's value as a troop or cargo carrier. They did this by measuring the vessel's cubic capacity which they then converted into net tons to rate the vessel. Later, another quartermaster at another port, and with a similar goal in mind, might have performed a like exercise, employing a measurement method of his own particular design. It is not unusual, therefore, to discover within the charter records the name of a vessel represented by as many as four different tonnage descriptions with no hint as to whether they refer to net or to gross tonnage. The conundrum sometimes presented to the researcher is whether such multiple entries relate just to one vessel or to a number of vessels carrying the same name. Toward dealing with such situations, we created during the formative stage of *Assault and Logistics* a working inventory which we added to as we encountered vessels within the various charter records, operational accounts, etc. The cross-checking which we could do by having such an inventory has enabled us to definitively identify individual vessels in a manner which would have been impossible otherwise. Where there are still certain remnant uncertainties, we have notated them following the operational lists which appear in *Assault and Logistics.* The product of the working inventory is an accounting of over 3,500 separate vessels which during 1995 is to be published as part of *THE ARMY'S NAVY SERIES* under the title *Dictionary of Transports and Combatant Vessels, Steam and Sail, Employed by the Union Army, 1861 - 1868.* The *Dictionary* is annotated and cross-indexed with operational notes on each vessel that was either owned, chartered, or otherwise hired and which served the Union Army's Quartermaster Department on coastal or river routes during the Civil War and during the subsequent period of reconstruction.

~

It is impossible to put together a work of this magnitude without a good deal of advice and encouragement. In acknowledging that assistance which has been forthcoming to us over a span of nearly eleven interrupted years which the preparation of this volume has consumed, our greatest debt is owed to Kenneth Hall, now retired, who was previously with the Civil Branch of the National Archives. Hall, who is known as the dean of merchant ship historians, first pointed out to us the existence of a Quartermaster General's Report which was prepared following the war. That report enumerated the bulk of ocean and river class vessels which served the Union Army in the period between 1861 and 1868. Seeing the enormity of that list, provided us with the insight as to the scope of the Army's involvement in shipping, and it reinforced our determination that this was a story that needed telling.

For assistance with research, we gratefully acknowledge the help and advice given so generously over the years by the many archival specialists from the National Archives, the Center for Military History, the Center for Naval History, and the Military History Institute. Additionally, the Library of Congress as well as private institutions such as the Naval Historical Foundation were most helpful in searching their files for ship photographs even though, as we were to discover, there is a paucity of images dealing with Quartermaster shipping in the 1860s. For advice in dealing with questions of ship registry and enrollment, as well as a number of other important facets, we turned to the research librarians at G. W. Blunt White Library at Mystic Seaport Museum in Mystic, CT; the Mariners Museum in Newport News, VA; and the Maine Maritime Museum in Bath, ME -- all of whom were most helpful. Our thanks also to the librarians at the Camden Public Library, Camden, ME whose interlibrary search facilities are always of great help and to Ken Gross who designed most of the maps and the cover layout.

AND A BIG THANK YOU to the many individuals, both within and outside the academic and governmental communities, whose sound research and editorial advice has contributed in so many ways to this writing.

CDG and EKG
Camden, ME 1995

INTRODUCTION

Secession

On December 20, 1860, the state of South Carolina voted to secede from the United States. Seven days later, troops of South Carolina seized the abandoned, but still federally owned, Fort Moultrie and Castle Pinckney in Charleston harbor. The next act of open rebellion took place on January 3 of the new year, when the state of Georgia took over Fort Pulaski on the Savannah River. That was followed shortly by Georgia's secession; Louisiana seceded that same month. On February 4, representatives from all the states, which up to that point had left the Union (South Carolina, Georgia, Louisiana, Alabama, Florida, and Mississippi) met at Montgomery, Alabama, and formed the Confederate States of America. Jefferson Davis of Mississippi was elected President. On February 23, Texas joined the Confederacy. During April and May, Virginia, Arkansas, and North Carolina joined. The Confederate States of America now included ten states, with Tennessee forming a military alliance by vote of plebiscite.

The Origins of Union Strategy

By the spring of 1861, it had become apparent that there was little hope of bringing the South back into the Union without military coercion. Winfield Scott, General in Chief of the Army since the war with Mexico, had already briefed President Abraham Lincoln on how the Confederacy might be brought to heel with but a minimum of force. Scott reasoned that a tight blockade could do a good part of the job. This could be accomplished by sealing off Virginia from its access to the commerce of Chesapeake Bay and by closing all Southern ports bordering on the Atlantic and the Gulf of Mexico. The western approaches to the Southern states could be blocked by a Union occupation of the corridor of the Mississippi from St. Louis southward to include the Mississippi passes. In this way, the South would be denied trade interaction not only from overseas but from those domestic areas bordering to the west and north.[†]

[†] For an understanding of the import of the western river systems to the strategy of envelopment, it may be helpful for the reader to review the history of those systems prior to 1861. Appendix O is a summarization of the geographic importance of those systems for both the transport of people and commodities.

Apart from establishing some bases on the Atlantic coast considered necessary in order to provide support facilities for the Navy's blockading fleet, any territorial penetration of the South was to be limited to occupation of a narrow corridor of land bordering the Mississippi River. The forecast was that once the South was tightly blockaded, the individual Southern states, one following the other, would fall away from the Confederacy like collapsing dominoes, each suing independently for readmission to the Union. To effect that reaction, care would have to be taken not to antagonize Southern opinions by any impression of military conquest. The most persuasive argument Scott made for his plan, and one which made it especially attractive to Lincoln, was that the bitterness of bloodshed could be largely avoided, thus the eventual reuniting of the nation would be easier to bring about in the end.

A strong ally of Scott's theory was Captain Samuel F. DuPont of the Navy. These two officers, on the go-ahead from Lincoln, set about supervising the finite planning. Scott's and DuPont's product came to be christened "Anaconda," a name coined in reference to the tropical water snake which, utilizing water as its medium of operations, strangles its prey through a crushing envelopment.

Scott proposed the Ohio River as a military defense line -- that line to begin at the Ohio's junction with the Mississippi and to follow the river's course eastward to the foothills of the Allegheny Mountains. The western counties of Virginia were located where the Ohio met the mountains. The population of those counties was largely non-slave holding, and the people held little in common -- politically, economically, or socially-- with the populace of Virginia's slave-holding counties to the east. In fact, western Virginia was almost universally unsympathetic toward secession. Scott believed that it was essential to bring these western counties into a working alliance with the Union; otherwise, the concept of Anaconda would be endangered. The main reason for that worry was that the rail line of the Baltimore and Ohio (B & O) ran through the area. Without the B & O tracks securely in Union hands, the essential connection between the central Atlantic states north of Virginia and Union forces operating in the west would be severed. If that happened, not only would it be difficult to launch a coordinated campaign for control of the Mississippi corridor, but it would be virtually impossible to seal off the Confederacy from illegal trade interaction with Indiana and Ohio.

Western Virginia remained a political question mark until August. In that month, representatives of the twenty-six western Virginia counties -- those counties west of the Alleghenies -- convened at Wheeling and created the new state of Kanawha, a state which as such was to remain neutral. During May of 1862, Kanawha, its name formally changed to West Virginia, requested admission to the Union, that act removing all doubt as to how West Virginia stood.[‡] For the time being, the B & O was secure for Union use.

The state of Kentucky, which lies in its entirety south of the Ohio River, was south of Scott's military line of defense. Scott envisioned Kentucky as a buffer zone between North and South. At first, Kentucky performed to expectation, holding to a neutral stance; but internally its politics were mixed, its people torn as to which

---

‡   By an act of Congress, West Virginia was admitted to the Union in June of 1863.

way to lean. This uncertainty was one of the reasons why Scott had chosen the Ohio as Anaconda's northern line.

Things began changing rapidly when on September 3, 1861, Kentucky's neutrality was violated by a Confederate Army led by Major General Leonidas Polk. The Ohio River, by Polk's action, had now become more than just an arbitrary line. It had also become a geographic moat to be defended against a Confederate Army seemingly on the offensive. The Administration's concern about violating Southern territory no longer seemed to hold much sanctity. After all, Polk's invasion of what had been neutral ground was indicative of the other side's aggression, was it not?

Although some writers seem fond of believing that the Anaconda theory ended with the retirement of General Winfield Scott in November of 1861, we find this hard to accept. What developed after Scott left the policy-making scene, indicates that his ideas continued to play a part well into 1862. The first noticeable dilution of the original strategy took place in mid-1861 when Union forces penetrated into northern Virginia. That movement was the first of many such penetrations, some successful, some failures. It was not, though, until 1864 that Scott's concepts were totally abandoned, to be replaced by a policy of all-out war.

Confederate Strategy at the Onset of War

From the viewpoint of the Confederacy, the original objective of Jefferson Davis and General Robert E. Lee, his chief military advisor, was the preservation of Southern boundaries. Foraying beyond those boundaries to beat back Union concentrations threatening to move southward was acceptable, but that was as far as incursions to the north should go. Davis and Lee believed that to hold onto Confederate territory would be sufficient to achieve victory. The North would soon realize that the determination of the South to remain separate was final. The Confederate invasion of Kentucky, although certainly to be considered a territorial expansion, was excused at the time by Davis who used the questionable rationale that Kentucky was an area of strong Southern allegiance.

Few in the Confederate government appreciated the ideological steadfastness of the Union leadership, which on an almost across-the-board basis, held to the belief that the Union must be put together again -- regardless of what it might cost in blood and money. This lack of understanding by the South led to many Confederate misjudgments.

Had the leadership of either side been able to foresee the horror of the next four years, it is doubtful that either would have been as strong in resolve as they were in that fateful spring of 1861.

PART I

THE EARLY MONTHS

THE MILITARY AND NAVAL SITUATIONS:
ATLANTIC AND GULF COASTS

Charleston, South Carolina

In December of 1860, the officer in command of Federal defenses at Charleston was Major Robert Anderson. Anderson, under orders to hold his presence there, realized that Fort Moultrie and Castle Pinckney were untenable; consequently, he had withdrawn his entire command to Fort Sumter located in the outer harbor. Once there, he received a demand to immediately surrender to South Carolina state forces. He adamantly refused. In January 1861, an attempt was made to bring in additional Federal reinforcements aboard the merchant ship *STAR OF THE WEST*. The ship was fired upon by South Carolina artillery and forced to withdraw. On March 1, 1861, Confederate military forces relieved Carolinian militia then threatening Anderson at Fort Sumter. Tensions mounted.

General Winfield Scott informed President Abraham Lincoln that reinforcing Fort Sumter would require a fleet of war vessels to convoy transports from the north carrying twenty thousand Federal troops, this being the estimated number of men needed to accomplish Anderson's continuous presence at Charleston harbor.[1] Not having the troops available, and still hoping to placate the threat of war, Lincoln decided to try to reinforce Anderson but only with just enough troops to comfortably fit within the restricted confines of Fort Sumter.

Finally in March, after much debate within the administration, a relief force of eight ships was put together as an Army- Navy joint operation and sent south to strengthen Fort Sumter's garrison. Under the command of the Navy's Gustavus Vasa Fox (who later in the war would become the Assistant Secretary of the Navy), the expedition set sail but arrived too late. The bombardment of Fort Sumter had begun. On April 14, the garrison surrendered. One of the transports, the *BALTIC*, took aboard Anderson and his troops and transported them to New York to a welcome for heroes.

In Florida

To prevent a Southern takeover at Key West, Federal troops were moved there to establish a fortified garrison. Another contingent of troops reinforced Fort

Jefferson, then an operational Army post on the remote Dry Tortugas at the geographic end of the Florida Keys.

Under threatening pressures, the Federal Army garrison at Pensacola was evacuated to Fort Pickens, a battlement located on Santa Rosa Island offlying Pensacola Bay. Reinforcements were immediately sent down to Fort Pickens from New York while yet another backup force was ordered to make ready for transportation south. Toward the goal of maintaining Union control of the northern Gulf of Mexico, Fort Pickens was considered to be of strategic importance; it would be held.

Ship Island, off Mobile Bay

On January 20, 1861, Mississippi state troops took over what was known as Fort Massachusetts located on Ship Island. This was an unexpected development, and it came as a blow to Samuel F. DuPont of the Union Navy Blockade Board. The island, with its relatively sheltered anchorage, had been thought of by DuPont's planning group as a base for a blockading squadron which was soon to go into deployment off the Mississippi Passes.

Possession of the island by the Mississippi troops was not to last. In September the island was reoccupied by Federal troops. Defenses were strengthened with the intention of using the place as a naval operational base along the lines which Admiral DuPont had envisioned and as a launching platform for a military invasion of the lower Mississippi.

Texas Coast

From February to April 1861, all Federal Army posts, both inland and along the coast, were surrendered to Texas state troops.

In March, the *STAR OF THE WEST*, which in January had been chartered to reinforce Fort Sumter, but which had failed to do so after receiving heavy fire from Carolinian batteries, was rechartered. Her assignment, this time, was to repatriate Federal troops then in Texas who had been paroled until exchanged. Despite what seems to have been her cartel-like status, upon arrival at Indianola, Texas, the *STAR OF THE WEST* was captured and condemned as a Confederate prize. The paroled prisoners were then loaded aboard the small schooners *HORACE* and *URBANA*, and the brig *MYSTIC* on which they were transported to New York.[2]

Naval Blockade; Privateers

On April 17, 1861, President Lincoln issued a proclamation stating that a naval blockade had been placed in force against the Confederate States of America. On the same day, from the temporary capital of the Confederacy at Montgomery, Alabama, Jefferson Davis inserted notices in coastal city newspapers stating that applications for letters of marque authorizing privateering against Union shipping would be accepted. This caused an immediate protest in the north, resulting in the warning that Southern privateer crews taken by Union naval forces were to be handled as pirates.[3] The crews of three Confederate privateers had been captured earlier and indicted on piracy charges by a federal admiralty court; but before the trial, the Confederates let it be known that if any execution was carried out, then a like number of Union Army officers then being held in Southern prisons would face the same fate. The result was that the charges were eventually dropped. The captive privateers were thenceforth handled as legitimate prisoners of war, being later exchanged.[4]

On the Chesapeake

Reinforcements sent to protect the capital had started coming in as early as April (1861) when the 6th Massachusetts Infantry Regiment left its home state by rail for duty in the defense of Washington. The specter of the capital becoming isolated by hostile forces was put into a political focus at Baltimore. The 6th Massachusetts Infantry had been scheduled to transfer trains there. Doing this necessitated that the troops make a short march through the city in order to board a direct spur line to Washington. While marching between stations, the troops were attacked by a mob with Southern sympathies. It was an ugly scene with injury to both troops and members of the mob. This incident led to Lincoln's immediate decision not to force the political situation in Maryland's capital by the presence there of Federal troops, even if only passing through. Baltimore was to be by-passed. In the future, incoming troop contingents traveling by sea from Boston or New York would go to Annapolis where they would be entrained for Washington City. Those coming by rail would go as far as Philadelphia where they would be embarked onto bay steamers for transit to Annapolis via the Chesapeake and Delaware Canal. At Annapolis, they would entrain for Washington. At this time, Chesapeake Bay was considered safely under the control of the Union Navy, but that was to prove short lived.

The security of Chesapeake Bay had its most serious threat on April 18 when, for no rational reason other than panic on the part of its commander, the Union naval base at Norfolk, Virginia, was evacuated. The departing Federals destroyed most of the naval yard facilities and scuttled nine Union naval vessels at dockside before they hastened to Fortress Monroe at Hampton. One of the scuttled vessels was the *USS MERRIMAC*, later to be salvaged by Confederate naval forces, repaired, and renamed as the ironclad *CSS VIRGINIA*. This ironclad would soon come uncomfortably close to tipping the balance of naval supremacy on the Chesapeake. A sizable quantity of naval guns were also left at Norfolk; few of them were spiked before they were abandoned. These unspiked guns would later be used to equip many of the Confederate batteries throughout the south. The unnecessary evacuation of Norfolk represented a dark hour for the Union -- one for which even the kindest hindsight can find no justification.

Chesapeake Bay, as well as the rivers emptying into it, allowed a ready access to Virginia from the sea. The Anaconda strategy included Union control of that access. Even if the blockade of the Chesapeake's southern shore had not been a key factor in the containment plan called for by Anaconda, the control of the Chesapeake went hand in hand with the Union's own security, both physically and politically.

Primarily the safety of the capital at Washington, as well as the entire Delmarva Peninsula, depended on the control of Chesapeake Bay. The psychological impact, if Washington had been lost, would have been far greater than either the city's territorial or material value.

Although the thinking in the Southern camp was not toward waging a large scale aggressive war, these thoughts were not known to Lincoln or to his generals. An invasion aimed at taking Washington appeared the more likely.

It would become evident during the war's early months that Jefferson Davis held little hesitation when it came to closing off key Union points along the Potomac, particularly those which might offer a springboard for Union Army movements into northern Virginia. Nor would Davis or his advisor Robert E. Lee hesitate whenever the opportunity arose to close off Union supply lines when such lines were in proximity to Confederate territory. It was that last which led to the Confederate seizure of Harper's Ferry on the upper Potomac, and with it, the bridge of the Baltimore and Ohio (B & O) Railroad where it crossed the Potomac at that point. The first major Union incursion into northern Virginia was in connection with an attempt to retake Harper's Ferry and thus regain the use of the B & O. That action resulted in the first large battle of the Civil War.

First Bull Run

The Union movement into Virginia had two strategic rationales. The first, as stated, was to resecure Harper's Ferry and the Union's use of the B & O. The second was to sever another railroad system which was in use by the Confederates. In Confederate territory west-southwest of the city of Washington, the interlock of two important railroads was at a place called Manassas Junction. One of these railroads ran southwesterly to Charlottesville and then on to Lynchburg. The other, the Manassas Gap Railroad, ran northwesterly to the northern end of the Blue Ridge Mountains, giving access to the rich agricultural production of the Shenandoah Valley. The Manassas Gap line had tremendous importance to the supply of Confederate armies operating in northern Virginia. If the Union could take and hold Manassas Junction, Confederate logistics would be dealt a serious blow. An added advantage of such an action would be that it would pinch off any direct rail approach for the Confederates in any move contemplated against Washington.

The Union plan called for occupying Manassas Junction and then swinging north to retake Harper's Ferry. Campaign plans were never a well kept secret during the Civil War; this time was not to be an exception. A Mrs. Rose Greenhow, late of Richmond and now living in Washington, was busily acting as a Confederate informer. It was she who would inform Richmond as to what was in the wind. Even without Greenhow's spying, a thorough reading of the northern press would have provided Jefferson Davis with ample warning. The press in Washington not only did its reporting of events without censorship, but going beyond straight news, went so far as to write up every rumor emanating from military circles. In light of that intelligence, a Confederate force, consisting of twenty-two thousand men under Brigadier General

P. G. T. Beauregard, moved to protect Manassas Junction against the heralded Union attack.

On July 11, 1961, a Union Army under Brigadier General Irvin McDowell marched out of Washington toward Manassas Junction. McDowell's force consisted of thirty-five thousand men, most of whom were short-term enlistees who had been in the Army but a matter of weeks. He had with him a few regulars and a few of the Navy's marines; but in largest part, the last were as green to soldiering as were the short-term volunteers. A separate Union force was established at this time in defensive positions at the Pennsylvania - Virginia border near the northern end of the Shenandoah Valley. That force, although placed there only in a passive mode, was thought by the Confederates to pose a threat as invaders into the Shenandoah Valley. This is what General-in-Chief Winfield Scott had hoped the Confederates would believe, thus holding any Confederate force in the northern Shenandoah, and keeping them from crossing over the Blue Ridge to assist Beauregard at Manassas Junction.

On July 21, the Beauregard and McDowell armies met in an action which has often been likened to the clashing of two armed mobs. What had originally been a parity in the strength of the two forces, with some minor advantage given to McDowell, had been rectified but hours before the battle by a Confederate force coming from the Shenandoah. This was the same force which had supposedly been occupied in place by the threat of Union troops aligned at the Pennsylvania - Virginia border. Scott's hopes in that respect had not been fulfilled. Instead, the Confederates had moved out, screened by a brigade of cavalry which remained in front of the Union positions. Unbeknownst to the Union pickets, these twelve thousand Confederate infantrymen had moved over the mountains via the Manassas Gap Railroad. For the first time in warfare, infantry had crossed the threshold from shoe leather to iron rail.

With the arrival of the Confederate reinforcements, the two forces facing one another at Manassas (near a little river called Bull Run) were now almost equal in numerical strength. The Confederates had one advantage. They held defensive positions; and as "Johnnys-on-the-spot", they had already gained some knowledge of the terrain and with it, a certain confidence. This understanding of the land became a paramount factor once the battle started.

Within McDowell's army, there was a lack of noteworthy organization, at least beyond the regimental level. There was also little in the way of communication ability between regimental units. This lack of command network soon developed into confusion. Once the firing became heavy, the confusion turned to panic. McDowell's army began disintegrating and started a rout toward the safety of Washington. Had it not been for the equally disorganized Confederates which prevented Beauregard from taking advantage of the Union panic, McDowell's army probably would have been destroyed, then and there. As a result, the Civil War might have been over, with the South emerging victorious. But such was not to be. Instead, the First Battle of Bull Run (as it came to be known in the North) or the First Battle of Manassas (as the South would term it) marked the point when Lincoln and his generals became painfully aware of a long struggle which now seemed to lie ahead of them.

The defeat at Bull Run was an immediate impetus in the establishment of a defensive philosophy by the Union generals -- a philosophy shared by Lincoln and his cabinet. This translated into the creation of three defensive perimeters, all of them tight into the outskirts of the capital.

Lincoln frantically called for reinforcements. The city of Washington, if not the outcome of the war itself, was at serious risk. The tidewaters of the Potomac River were still controlled by the Union Navy; but before long, even those waters would fall into an uneven balance when Confederate artillery went into position on the southern bank of the river just downstream from the city.

HATTERAS EXPEDITION
(August - September 1861)

A Foothold

As a reaction to the declaration by President Lincoln of a naval blockade, the Confederacy quickly established defensive installations at key entry points which could be of use to Southern blockade runners. Because of the access it gave to the Albemarle and Pamlico sounds of North Carolina, Hatteras Inlet (on the outer Carolina Banks) had become one of the more important points of access. Hatteras Inlet was defended by two Confederate installations, Fort Hatteras and Fort Clarke.

The man who would be chosen by Lincoln to take those defenses was Benjamin F. Butler, the first major general to be appointed by President Lincoln into the new Union Army of volunteers. Butler, a powerful politician from Massachusetts, had been commissioned solely on political grounds. He had no background in military matters other than some militia participation; certainly nothing which could qualify him for a command of such magnitude. Perhaps this lack of familiarity with the military is why Butler by-passed normal military channels when he proposed directly to Lincoln that an expedition be launched to attack Hatteras Inlet. Once taken, it was to be closed against further Confederate use. The plan that developed from this proposal was for a landing force of 860 troops, with Butler in command, to be put ashore near Hatteras Inlet under the protection of naval bombardment. Once ashore, Butler would storm the forts. With the forts taken and their battlements rendered impotent, he would then withdraw his force.

The need for shelter for the naval blockading force then operating in the dangerous offings of Cape Hatteras resulted in a joint Army- Navy decision which modified the original Butler proposal. It was decided that once Hatteras Inlet had been captured, it was to be held, not just for the Union Navy's use, but as a place from which hit-and-run amphibious operations could be conducted against the Carolina mainland. Both the Army and the Navy felt that possession of the barrier islands -- that is those islands located immediately to each side of Hatteras Inlet -- could provide a base for control not only of the Albemarle Sound, but also of the southern approaches to the Albemarle and Chesapeake Canal. Since that canal led to Norfolk, this would mean the total isolation by water of that Confederate-occupied city.[5]

On his end of the expedition's planning, the novice Butler had not thought to make early arrangements to obtain the necessary transports. At the last minute, this rather essential detail came to rest with the Navy, with direct responsibility for finding and chartering needed merchant ships being placed with Commander H. S. Stellwagen. Stellwagen decided to follow the procedure then being used by the Navy in its own employment of merchant vessels which had been acquired to support the fleet. This method involved chartering the vessels, fully found with master, officers, and crew.

As the naval escorts, bombardment vessels, and transports were being formed to leave the Chesapeake, a telegram (dated August 27, 1861, from the Confederate Army commander at Norfolk) was sent to Richmond.

> The enemy's fleet -- two steam frigates, two transport steamers, eight smaller steamers with boats in tow, and a body of troops -- left last evening; passed out of the Capes and steered south, I think to coast off North Carolina. No news of him this morning.
>
> Benjamin Huger, Brigadier General[6]

The Confederate appraisal of destination proved to be accurate. On August 28, a naval bombardment of the Hatteras Inlet forts began, followed shortly by a landing attempt on the part of Butler's infantry. After two of the boats in the first wave were swamped in the surf, the landing operations were stopped until the weather moderated.[7] The troops from those boats which had swamped managed to get ashore and dig into place. In a few hours, the weather had laid down sufficiently to resume landing the infantry reinforcements, together with a small contingent of marines. On seeing this second force come ashore, the Confederates abandoned one of their forts, retreating into a second one from which they commenced directing heavy cannon fire against the Union fleet. The fleet reciprocated. The bombardment from the sea continued that afternoon until dusk and resumed the next morning. Shortly after day break, Butler sent the remainder of his troops onto the beach. The sight of the landings was enough to motivate a Confederate surrender. Six hundred and fifteen prisoners fell into Butler's hands. Casualties on the Confederate side were found to be light, with only seven dead and twenty-four wounded. Union casualties were even less.

With Hatteras Inlet now in Union hands, it was decided not to proceed farther until reinforcements could arrive from the Chesapeake. Operations could then be extended northward toward Roanoke Island, which if occupied, would be taken and used as a base for an expedition to seal off both the Dismal Swamp Canal and the Albemarle and Chesapeake Canal. Both of these canals led north through their respective cuts to Confederate held Norfolk. Because swampy terrain precluding wagon traffic covered the area between the sounds and Norfolk, sealing off the two canals at their southern ends would effectively prevent the threat of Confederate forces operating from Norfolk. At the same time, sealing the canals would block any Confederate communications which the canals had afforded to date.

The officer Butler left in charge at Hatteras Inlet was particularly worried about the protection of his flanks from Confederate raids which might originate from north of the inlet. To protect the northern approaches to Hatteras Inlet, Butler had established a company-strength garrison of infantry on Chicamacomico Island. (This island was directly opposite Roanoke Island, then being strongly held by Confederates.) The Chicamacomico garrison was to watch for any threatening enemy activity. On October 1st, it was scheduled to receive reinforcements and supplies coming up from Hatteras Inlet aboard the armed Army tug *FANNY* which was to proceed there by way of Pamlico Sound. That night, the *FANNY*, at an anchorage off Chicamacomico Island, was captured by a Confederate raiding party. This event, although rather insignificant insofar as any impact it had on operations, did represent the first direct attack of the war against a vessel flying the banner of the Union Army's Quartermaster Department.[8]

Blockship Operations

Before Butler's withdrawal, it was planned that the Navy would sink stone-laden hulks within Hatteras Inlet to block it against further navigation. The sinking of the hulks as an effective blocking device was immediately brought into question by Flag Officer S. H. Stringham, through a letter to the Secretary of the Navy dated August 6, 1861. Stringham reported his conversation with two merchant marine captains who had a familiarity with that part of the Carolina coast. Both men had stated to him that Hatteras Inlet had practically the worst current conditions the coast could offer and that if blocked, a new inlet would soon appear either north or south of any impediment that was placed in the existing channel. As time would tell, this was sound advice which was not heeded.[9]

At about the same time that *FANNY* had been captured by the Confederates, a fleet of old schooners, heavily laden with stone, was sent south from Hampton Roads. According to the plan, they were destined to be sunk at Oregon, Loggerhead, and Ocracoke inlets. Hatteras Inlet was selected to remain open for Union use, both as a storm shelter for the offshore blockading patrol and as a point of entry for the reinforcing troops and the gunboats which would be required to fulfill Butler's goal of securing Albemarle and Pamlico sounds. Despite Flag Officer Stringham's earlier research which had resulted in a poor prognosis for blocking the Outer Banks' inlets with hulks, it was to be attempted anyway. At the very least, blocking the three inlets which had been selected would serve as a temporary restriction against Confederate use until the adjacent islands could be garrisoned. To transport the stone ships to the Hatteras inlets the plan was that the more seaworthy of them would be sailed to the locations by merchant marine crews hired especially for the job. The less seaworthy were to be brought south under tow. Once off the inlets, teams working from tugs were to maneuver the hulks into position for the sinkings.[10] A problem arose when Confederate outposts were discovered at both Oregon Inlet and at Loggerhead Inlet, making it too dangerous for the teams assigned to the positioning tasks. It was then decided that only Ocracoke Inlet would be blocked, but whether that inlet was ever actually blocked remains even today an unanswered question.[11]

The blocking of other Confederate harbors to the south by a separate fleet of stone ships (mainly laid-up whalers) occurred some weeks later. That operation proved to be temporarily successful. However, the advantage first gained by using these stone laden hulks to restrict the use of the ports by the Confederates later backfired since the hulks also badly hampered Union ships attempting to enter the harbors on raids.[12]

The employment of blockships by Union forces was applied throughout the war. The use of stone ships for blocking purposes occurred all along the east coast and, to a significant degree, within the Virginia rivers draining into the Chesapeake Bay.

Experience Gained

Apparently the Navy began feeling overtaxed as a result of the responsibility it had shouldered for troop transportation during joint Army- Navy expeditions. With the task of the blockade, the Navy felt it had enough to handle. This was made evident during September 1861 in a letter addressed to the Assistant Secretary of the Navy by Flag Officer S. H. Stringham. In that letter, Stringham represented the official viewpoint of the Navy in regard to the moving of the Army's men, supplies, or equipment by sea. He stated that the Navy wished to divest itself of such responsibility lest the task became accepted as a normal Navy function. He cited the Hatteras Inlet Expedition as a strong case in point as to why responsibility for troop movement by sea should remain with the Army. In discussing future transportation for coastal assaults, Stringham wrote:

> Transports would also have to be provided for the troops which, together with the providing of surfboats, more properly belongs to the Army; but I call your attention to them, because when ready to leave this place for the Hatteras Expedition, I was informed no such provision had been or was to be made by the Army, and I was therefore compelled to hunt up and take such as I could find on the spot, which were very imperfect.[13]

When summarizing the benefits gained by the Hatteras Expedition and the effect it had on the war, the major advantage was that it tied down Confederate strength that could have been used elsewhere. To a small degree, it also hampered blockade running on that part of the coast. From the Navy's viewpoint, it provided limited storm shelter for those Union naval ships operating directly off Cape Hatteras. It did not, however, bring the Albemarle and Pamlico sounds under Union control; nor did it establish, as Butler had hoped, a launching pad for Union raids to be carried up the rivers which fed into the sounds. The reason for this was two-fold:

1) The expedition was not immediately reinforced as Butler had initially envisioned it should have been.
2) As long as Roanoke Island was held by the Confederates, there was no way for the Union to have complete control of the waters of the Carolina sounds. Without that control, any operation within the sounds would be highly vulnerable from the rear.

The importance of Albemarle and Pamlico sounds was described by David D. Porter shortly after Butler had taken Hatteras Inlet:

> The principle entrances into the sounds of North Carolina were secured, but the Confederate had still the means, not only of annoying the coastwise commerce daily

before the inlets, but also of supplying their armies through the intricate and numerous channels belonging to the several sounds, and known only to themselves.[14]

By now, it was early October (1861). Another three months would pass before the tenuous hold that the Federals had at Hatteras Inlet would be strengthened. (Reinforcements under the command of Brigadier General Ambrose E. Burnside would arrive in considerable strength in January.) Before anything else could be accomplished at Hatteras, the Union high command would place priority on taking possession of another enclave farther to the south.

EXPEDITION TO PORT ROYAL SOUND, SOUTH CAROLINA
(October 1861 - March 1862)

In order to put into effect that part of the Anaconda plan which dealt with the blockading of the Atlantic and Gulf coasts, the Navy had long considered it essential that at least two seaport bases be secured for Union use along the southeastern coast. These ports were then to be held as coaling stations and were to be kept supplied by merchant marine colliers contracted for that purpose. It was planned that the blockading warships would load directly from the colliers which were to be anchored in the harbors' shelter. When emptied, each collier would then sail for a northern port to take on more coal for return to the southern harbor to which it had been assigned.

Bull Bay (north of Charleston) and Fernandina (in northern Florida) were the ports originally selected. An assault was to be launched simultaneously against each place so as to tie up any mobile defense force which the Confederates might bring to bear. The first change made in this plan was a switch from Bull Bay to Port Royal Sound just north of Savannah. But the plan was again altered, this time on the theory that a divided force might not be as successful as one large force delivering a single punch. That single attack was now to be against Port Royal Sound. If it was successful, a follow-up expedition would be launched against Fernandina.

The Navy's responsibility in carrying out the assault against Port Royal Sound was delegated to Flag Officer Samuel F. DuPont who would use the Navy's ships-of-the-line plus a number of steamers converted into warships. With the exception of a small detachment of marines supplied by the Navy, the assault force to go ashore was to be composed entirely of Army troops led by Brigadier General Thomas W. Sherman. Unlike the earlier attack against Hatteras Inlet, this time the Army was to arrange for its own transports as well as for the supply ships to service its needs once ashore. For troop carrying purposes, the Army chartered thirty-two vessels. The Navy hired one, the *GOVERNOR*, to be used to transport a battalion of marines.

Some serious thought had been given, by both the Army and the Navy, as to the means by which troops were to be ferried ashore from the transports. In September, the Secretary of the Navy, upon the recommendations of Flag Officer

Stringham, had ordered construction of a quantity of landing boats to be patterned after those which had been so successfully employed at Vera Cruz in 1847. The responsibility for the procurement of these landing boats remained with the Navy.

When planning the Port Royal Expedition, lessons learned during the Mexican War seem to have been taken into some account. This appears reflected by an order which was dated October 15, signed by L. H. Pelouze, Acting Assistant Adjutant General. The order gave rather explicit instructions for the responsibility and behavior of the troops at sea, such as their assignments to shipboard guard duty and other chores. It gave guidance as to the relationship of troop officers toward masters of transports. It even included a prohibition against "fancy cooking," such as frying meat in fat, explaining that it was deleterious to the health of troops at sea.[15]

Regarding specific troop assignments, general orders were issued by instructions of Brigadier General Thomas W. Sherman. These listed the transports in the matter of loading troops, livestock, and general supplies:

HEADQUARTERS, EXPEDITIONARY CORPS,
Annapolis, Maryland., October 17, 1861.

General Orders No. 15

The embarkation of the troops of this division will commence immediately and in accordance with the following order and assignment:

I. First Brigade, Brigadier General Viele, commanding.
    3d Regiment New Hampshire Volunteers to steamer *ATLANTIC*.
    46th Regiment New York Volunteers to steamer *WEBSTER*.*
    47th Regiment New York Volunteers to steamer *ROANOKE*.
    48th Regiment New York Volunteers to steamer *EMPIRE CITY*.
    80th Regiment Maine Volunteers to steamer *ARIEL*.
    The horses and wagons pertaining to the First Brigade are assigned to the steamers *BELVIDERE* and *PHILADELPHIA*.

II. Second Brigade, Brigadier General I. I. Stevens, commanding.
    Roundhead Regiment Pennsylvania Volunteers to steamer *OCEAN QUEEN*.
    Five companies of the 50th Regiment Pennsylvania Volunteers to steamer *OCEAN QUEEN*.
    Five companies of the 50th Regiment Pennsylvania Volunteers to steamer *VANDERBILT*.†
    8th Regiment Michigan Volunteers to steamer *VANDERBILT*.†
    The horses and wagons pertaining to the Second Brigade are assigned to the steamer *BEN DE FORD*.

III. Third Brigade, Brigadier General H. G. Wright, commanding.
    4th Regiment New Hampshire Volunteers to the steamer *BALTIC*.
    6th Regiment Connecticut Volunteers to the steamers *MARION* and *PARKERSBURG*.
    7th Regiment Connecticut Volunteers to the steamer *ILLINOIS*.
    9th Regiment Maine Volunteers to the steamer *COATZACOALCOS*.
    The horses and wagons pertaining to the Third Brigade are assigned to the steamer *BALTIC*.

IV. Hamilton's light battery to steamer *ERICSSON*.

V. The Battalion of Volunteer Engineers (now at Fortress Monroe, Virginia) to the steamer *CAHAWBA*.

VII.   Division headquarters to the steamer *ATLANTIC* and the horses pertaining thereto to the steamer *ERICSSON.*

VIII.   Each brigade commander will select from the transports assigned to his brigade the one upon which the headquarters will embark, the name of the transport thus selected to be reported to these headquarters.

IX.   The horses and equipment of mounted officers will, as far as practicable, be so placed as to be disembarked at the shortest notice.

X.   Brigade commanders will issue and enforce such orders as will effectually prevent any person not belonging to the military organization from embarking on their transports, and will prevent any stores from being shipped but the necessary provisions and supplies, including the authorized allowance of camp and garrison equipage.

XI.   No sutler but the one appointed by the Secretary of War will be recognized in any manner or received on board the transports belonging to this command.

By order of General T. W. Sherman:

        L. H. Pelouze, Captain, 50th Infantry, Acting Assistant Adjutant General[16]

* Possibly *DANIEL WEBSTER NO. 1.*
† *C. VANDERBILT*

On October 29, the expedition's ships, consisting of Army transports and supply vessels as well as the naval transport *GOVERNOR* began weighing anchor. The invasion armada readied to head down the bay in three columns. As the transports formed up, Flag Officer DuPont's seventeen naval vessels joined them in escort. Twenty-five sailing colliers had preceded the invasion fleet by a day; they were to provide an immediate coaling service to the transports and naval craft once Port Royal had been taken.[17]

It had been forecast that the expedition against Port Royal Sound would face serious difficulty at the entrance to the sound. At the seaward head of the sound (on its south side) was Hilton Head Island; Fort Walker, boasting a reported twenty-three guns, was at Hilton Head Island's northern tip. Directly across the sound's entrance was Fort Beauregard, itself mounting twenty guns. While forcing an entrance past these forts, the Union fleet would also have to contend with an undetermined number of Confederate naval craft -- a worry despite the fact that their reported quality and fire power was not deemed to be especially threatening. Apprehensions of strong resistance were put to rest soon after the Union fleet opened fire against the Confederate battlements. Although Confederate return fire directed against DuPont's ships was heavy, it was largely ineffective and soon ceased entirely when the garrisons of both forts abandoned their works. The enemy fleet also proved less menacing than was first anticipated. It was found to consist of only one river steamboat in company with two or three "gunboats," the latter hastily improvised from harbor tugs. Total casualties to the Union invasion force were eight killed and twenty-three wounded, a surprisingly small number for what had been gained. The records point to but few Confederate casualties, those all having occurred at the opening of the bombardment before the forts were abandoned.

The actual taking of Port Royal, negligible in cost to the attackers, contrasts to the havoc that occurred on the voyage down the coast from Hampton Roads. Heavy weather had struck the fleet off Cape Hatteras, scattering it in all directions. The Navy's transport *GOVERNOR* was the first lost, fortunately staying afloat long enough for the marines she carried to be rescued by heroic effort of the crew of the *USS SABINE*.[18] The *PEERLESS*, an Army transport loaded with supplies (including live cattle) was discovered to be sinking. Her crew was rescued, but the cattle went to the bottom. The Army troop transport *ROANOKE* and the supply ship *WINFIELD SCOTT* were both forced to jettison a good portion of their stores and cargo or they, too, probably would have foundered. Two Army supply vessels, the *UNION* and the *OSCEOLA*, went ashore on Cape Hatteras. The *OSCEOLA's* crew, which had taken to the boats, landed near Georgetown, South Carolina, in sight of a Confederate patrol which captured all hands.[19] In total, the Army lost three of its transports; the Navy lost one -- all victims of the weather. The most serious loss of cargo involved the *GOVERNOR* which was carrying a number of the special landing boats which were to have been put to use in ferrying the troops ashore once at Port Royal Sound.

On November 8, the day that the Port Royal Sound environs were secured, a hurried reconnaissance up the Beaufort River disclosed no further Confederate presence in the immediate area. With Port Royal Sound in Union hands, two things had been accomplished: First, a coaling station was now a reality. This tremendously increased the effectiveness of the offshore naval blockade as long trips to Hampton Roads for recoaling of individual vessels of the naval blockade force were no longer necessary. Accordingly, fewer naval vessels would be required, as those on station could remain in place with but short interludes spent coming into Port Royal Sound to lay against the colliers. Secondly, by using Hilton Head as a base, attacks could be easily launched against other Confederate points along the nearby coastline -- Fernandina being the first to be scheduled for such attention. Before that could occur, there was the matter of Beaufort at the head of Port Royal Sound. That place would have to be taken before Union presence on Hilton Head Island could be considered secure. Beaufort was occupied after only a token resistance. A map was found there at what had been the headquarters of Confederate Brigadier General Thomas F. Drayton. All enemy gun emplacements on that part of the southern coast were marked in red on the map.[20]

Vessels Chartered for Expedition to Port Royal

Vessels chartered by the Quartermaster Department for the expedition to Port Royal Sound were enumerated in a list the Quartermaster General supplied on request of Congress's Joint Committee on the Conduct of the War. Captain Rufus Saxton, the officer who prepared the list was the person in charge of chartering at both Boston and New York City over a period from October 1, 1861, through to March 31, 1862. For the reader's convenience, we alphabetized Saxton's list which appeared in the *Report of the Committee on the Conduct of the War*.[21]

Vessel Name	Class	No. of Days	Amount Paid
ALEXANDER YOUNG	Schooner	53	1,431.00
ARIEL	Steamship	84	92,400.00
ATLANTIC	ditto	182	$273,000.00
AZALIA	Schooner	14	270.97
BALTIC	Steamship	46	69,000.00
BELVIDERE	ditto	169	109,850.00
BEN DE FORD	ditto	168	126,000.00
BLACKBIRD	Schooner	46	920.00
CAHAWBA	Steamship	87	113,100.00
COATZACOALCOS	ditto	39	50,700.00
DANIEL WEBSTER [5]	ditto	74	66,600.00
EMPIRE CITY	ditto	82	82,000.00
ERICSSON	ditto	47	56,400.00
F. P. SIMPSON	Schooner	57	1,282.50
FANNY KEATING	ditto	97	3,880.00
GOLDEN EAGLE	Ship	133	33,250.00
GREAT REPUBLIC	ditto	63.5	31,750.00
HONDURAS	Steamship	48	19,200.00
ILLINOIS	ditto	52	78,000.00
J. B. MYERS [4]	Schooner	19	608.00
J. P. ELLICOTT	Brig	61	1,830.00
JAMES G. STILLE [3]	Schooner	59	1,003.00
JAMES M. HOLMES	ditto	64	1,920.00
JOHN GUYANT	ditto	66	990.00
JOHN ROSE	ditto	10	250.00
LOCUST POINT	Steamship	173	60,550.00
MARION	ditto	78	78,000.00
MAYFLOWER	ditto	138	55,200.00
N. STOWERS	Brig	44	1,320.00
OCEAN EXPRESS	Ship	99.5	34,825.00
OCEAN QUEEN	Steamship	54	108,000.00
PARKERSBURG	ditto	178	89,000.00
PHILADELPHIA	ditto	74	74,000.00
POTOMAC	ditto	173	60,550.00
R. J. MERCER [2]	Schooner	44	880.00
RACHEL S. MILLER	ditto	11	330.00
REINDEER	ditto	10	160.00
ROANOKE	Steamship	87	65,250.00
STAR OF THE SOUTH	ditto	75	56,250.00
VANDERBILT [6]	ditto	92	184,000.00
VIRGINIA PRICE	Schooner	25	750.00
WILLIAM G. AUDENRIED	ditto	54	1,382.40
ZENAS COFFIN [1]	Ship	94	9,400.00

[1] Received additional compensation of $2,080 for carriage of 520 tons of coal at $4 per ton
[2] ROBERT J. MERCER
[3] JAMES G. STELLE
[4] JOHN B. MYERS
[5] Possibly DANIEL WEBSTER NO. 1
[6] C. VANDERBILT

Other vessels which were not within Saxton's report but which were known to have been chartered by Army quartermasters for the Port Royal Expedition follow.[22]

AID, schooner	*LEWIS CHESTER*, schooner
CHARLES M. NEAL, schooner	*N. E. CLARK*, schooner
COSMOPOLITAN, steamship	*OSCEOLA*, steamship
DANIEL MALONEY, brig	*PEERLESS*, steamship
E. J. ALLEN, schooner	*SARAH CULLEN*, schooner
EFFORT, schooner	*SARAH J. BRIGHT*, schooner
ELIZABETH ENGLISH, schooner	*SARATOGA*, schooner
J. FRAMBES, schooner	*SNOW FLAKE*, schooner
JAMES M. VANCE, schooner	*SUSAN F. ABBOTT*, schooner
JAMES S. HEWITT, schooner	*WILLARD SAULSBURY*, schooner
JANE SATTERTHWAITE, schooner	

Operations Conducted from Port Royal

Considerable discussion developed within quartermaster circles over the handling of the transports which were lying inactively at anchor off Hilton Head. The charter arrangements originally made with the vessels' owners stated that the vessels were to be released roughly fifteen days after the date of their hire commencing at northern ports.[23] This was becoming a difficult clause with which to comply since some of the ships were now being used for troop barracks as there were no adequate facilities ashore.

There were other problems as well. Considerable ship to shore traffic -- most of it unauthorized -- was taking place through the use of small boats from the transports and two former New York ferryboats which the Army had chartered for troop lightering. The troops crammed aboard the transports were not of the best quality in the first instance, and the discipline practiced over them was more often than not of a slack nature. A consequence to all this was that looting on Hilton Head Island soon became widespread, not only against abandoned Confederate property, but also against Union Army property being stockpiled at depot sites on the island. It was only following a number of courts-martial (which resulted in some sentences of execution) that an end was put to the depredations. Meanwhile, as the troop laden transports swung idly at anchor, the fifteen days' demurrage allowed under the charters stretched to seventeen -- then twenty extra days representing high penalty charges -- before the troops were all brought ashore, and the majority of the chartered ships could be returned to their owners. That experience over demurrage made the Army aware that it was far more cost effective and certainly more feasible to either begin operating its own troop and supply transports under the house flag of the Quartermaster General, or failing that, to draw a more satisfactory charter instrument allowing the Army to extend a charter without the imposition of demurrage.

Movements against Fernandina and elsewhere on the nearby coast required the use of a number of shallow draft transports. Brigadier General Sherman believed that the envelopment and taking of the strong points expected at Fernandina could only be brought about satisfactorily if the attacking force approached simultaneously from seaward and from the interconnecting waterways of the rivers and sounds located to the north of the town. When the Army started out from Hampton Roads, only four of the initially chartered ships were of a draft shallow enough to allow them to negotiate the inland waterway channels which reconnaissance of the Georgia sounds had shown to be navigable. During the storm, on the trip south from the Chesapeake, it was these same four shallow draft vessels which had taken the worst beatings. Two of the original four, *PEERLESS* and *OSCEOLA*, had been lost. The remaining two were so battered that they could not be used again until repairs were made. With but only limited repair facilities available at Port Royal Sound, this would waste a lot of precious time. The solution was to bring in from the north more shallow draft vessels. While Sherman and DuPont awaited their arrival, a number of probing forays were made both north and south of Port Royal Sound. Those reconnaissance probes were supplemented with intelligence supplied by Negroes living in the coastal communities as well as by captured documents, including some not overly discreet Southern newspapers. Together they gave a relatively good picture of the situation. It appeared that only around four thousand Confederate troops were stationed in the entire coastal strip stretching from the Florida line northward to Charleston.

At the onset of war, the Confederate command structure for the coastal regions of the Carolinas and Georgia had been split between the state militias and the Confederate States Army. Seeing the danger with such a disjointed and weak arrangement, Confederate President Jefferson Davis had sent Robert E. Lee to evaluate the military situation. Lee recommended, given the lack of intercommunication and the rail transport at hand, that to hold the entire coast would be a hopeless task. Only Charleston, Savannah, and Wilmington seemed at all defensible. Furthermore, Lee believed that the territory along the coastline between Savannah and Charleston was of no real strategic importance. Lee's recommended strategy was to maintain a single highly mobile defensive force which would have as its primary responsibility the retention of the rail connection between Charleston and Savannah. Strong points consisting of artillery well dug into fortifications were to be maintained wherever the railroad right of way crossed rivers which were navigable from the sea and which were therefore within reach of Union gunboats. Downstream from such bridge crossings, a light Confederate presence would be maintained, usually in the form of emplacements of one or two cannon with supporting infantry units of company strength. Their function would be to harass and get the attention of Union forces which might otherwise be concentrated and free for large scale offensive operations.

There was north of Charleston a suitable port which gave the Confederates open access to the sea. This was Wilmington, North Carolina, lying upstream on the Cape Fear River. Lee had placed his reliance for holding Wilmington on Fort Fisher, a fortification on the outer beach located so as to overlook the channel leading to Wilmington. Lee thought it could be strengthened so as to be difficult to take by assault. He had decided that Wilmington could be held, given any determination on the part of Fort Fisher's defenders. Another port open to deep draft vessels was Beaufort -Morehead City, a twin port in North Carolina; but that was deemed to be a difficult place to defend. South of Savannah, the ports of Brunswick, Georgia, and Fernandina, Florida, were to remain fortified, but only to prevent an easy Union occupation. Should an attack in force come against either of these two places, it was not to be heavily resisted. As circumstances might change, and time allowing, Brunswick and Fernandina could receive heavier fortifications and with them a firmer commitment toward their defense. The Union command did not of course know Lee's thinking; but the lack of troop presence at most places made it clear that much of the southern coast lay open to capture.

On November 24, a Union naval patrol made a reconnaissance of the approaches to the city of Savannah. The earthworks guarding the Savannah River entrance were discovered to be abandoned. Simultaneously, another reconnaissance was taking place to the north at Saint Helena Sound. There, a number of Confederate emplacements were discovered with guns in place; but the gunners had vanished. There seemed little question that intelligence estimates predicting that the Confederates were going to move inland from their outer defenses were correct. The white coastal population had already disappeared. The only persons discovered on these reconnaissance probes were slaves who had managed to avoid the exodus of their masters. These Negroes, whenever encountered, begged to be evacuated north. They feared recapture by their owners and the ensuing punishment. This was the first experience that Union occupiers had with the refugee problems soon to be encountered in volume. This was to be brought into full focus as more and more Negroes began crossing into the Union lines. At this early point in the war, the Negroes were thought of by most Union commanders as "contrabands," and therefore were usually considered as prizes of war. The Lincoln Administration concurred in this informal attitude, but no real policy existed -- that is until July 1862 when military commanders were given official authorization to impress as military laborers any fugitives found within their lines. As such, the contrabands were to be subsisted, being paid minimally for their labor. This was a far cry from complete freedom, but at least it would provide them with a means for existence. The general impressment order of July 1862 had been preceded by authority issued by the War Department dated October 14, 1861, which specifically allowed the Port Royal Expedition to employ fugitive slaves "as soldiers;" however, through a clause somewhat contradictory to the true meaning of "soldier", the order prohibited their being armed. Obviously, a gimmick had been invented which allowed Negroes to become labor troops, subject to military discipline, and thus prohibited from refusing to work.[24] The refugee population consisted of men, women, and children -- all in desperate need when they came into Union lines. A refugee compound estimated to be able to accommodate over one thousand inhabitants, was established at Edisto Island under Union Navy protection. There were other encampments as well, although none as large as the one on Edisto. For these former slaves, freedom was at this time more hope than fact. It would not be until September 1862 that Negroes in areas occupied by Union forces were declared truly free. (In January 1863 full emancipation would be declared. The Negroes would subsequently be notified of their eligibility for enlistment as soldiers in the Armed Forces of the Union whereby they were at long last to receive arms. However, even after that emancipation, Union Army commanders would not be above impressing escaped slaves into labor gangs when the situation presented a need.)

As early as September 25, 1861, the Navy Department began enlisting Negroes into the Navy at the rating of "boy" with wages limited to $10 a month.[25] This same wage rate was applied to Negroes and "light colored" signed as crewmen on vessels operated by the Union Army Quartermaster Department. Such persons were usually employed as deck hands, stokers, or laborers to handle cargo.[26]

Second Probe of the Savannah River

On January 26, 1862, a Union expeditionary force left Port Royal Sound bound toward Wassaw Sound. Wassaw Sound (then, and still) is a shallow roadstead with its entrance about ten miles south of the ship channel of the Savannah River. From Wassaw Sound two small rivers allowed access into the Savannah River at points which by-passed the Savannah's main ship channel which was then being guarded by Confederate-held Fort Pulaski. The expedition's naval element consisted of shallow draft men-o-war and two armed launches, all under the overall command of Fleet Captain Charles H. Davis. The Army's contribution to this expedition consisted of twenty-four hundred troops under the command of Brigadier General H. G. Wright. During the evening prior to departure, most of Wright's troops had been loaded onto the Quartermaster chartered transports *COSMOPOLITAN*, *DELAWARE*, and *BOSTON*. Two specially selected assault companies were aboard the Navy's gunboats *USS OTTAWA* and *USS SENECA*. These gunboats had been selected to carry the two assault companies on the theory that both were of shallow draft and highly maneuverable, thus being able to get into narrow places which the transports might not be able to reach.

The *USS OTTAWA* and *USS SENECA* crossed Wassaw Sound bar, entered the Tybee River, and traveled unopposed to within sight of the Savannah River channel. Meanwhile, the second element of naval vessels, along with the Army transports, worked their way down the inland passages leading from Hilton Head Island to the Wright River. (The Wright River flowed into the Savannah at a point slightly above Fort Pulaski.) Entering into the Savannah River, the transports landed a force which set up a battery of guns at Venus Point (four miles upriver from Fort Pulaski).

The Savannah River was now completely sealed from Confederate use. For the time being, Union attention to the approaches to Savannah had been satisfied. Fort Pulaski remained in Confederate hands, but it was isolated from supplies and from any support which otherwise would have come downriver to it from the city of Savannah.

The expedition retired to Port Royal Sound, leaving behind the men manning the battery at Venus Point. For them, it must have been a lonely experience promising a boring time ahead. However, the boredom was not to be prolonged. On February 14, four Confederate gunboats (armed tugs) tried forcing passage for a supply boat trying to reach Fort Pulaski from Savannah. The guns at Venus Point drove the tugs hurrying back upriver, but not until one of the tugs was seriously damaged.[27] The isolated tour for the Confederates at Fort Pulaski was to be relatively short-lived.

Expedition to Fernandina

On February 23, 1962, the Confederate officer in charge of the military district which included Fernandina received orders from General Robert E. Lee that the guns at Fernandina were to be dismantled and the garrison was to be withdrawn inland. (Fernandina was Florida's northern most port town. It is located on Amelia Island.) On February 27 while those orders were being carried out, a Union force of seventeen naval vessels -- mostly gunboats -- in company with six Army transports, entered Saint Andrew's Sound, a body of water lying north of Cumberland Island. By the time the Union force was discovered entering the passage to the west of Cumberland Island, most of the Confederate guns on Fernandina had already been sent by rail onto the mainland. Those which were left were dismantled and packed and were ready to go out. The rail tracks leading off Amelia Island closely paralleled the tidal river passage which ran along the island's western side and which served its small port complex. This track was therefore in full sight from that inland waterway. Just as the last train was preparing to pull out of the station, the Union gunboat *USS OTTAWA* pulled up, as it were, alongside. Only a narrow strip of mud flat beach separated the gunboat from the locomotive. Fortunately for the railroad men and the train's passengers, steam was already up. The train's departure was immediately accelerated as the locomotive's fireman frantically fed wood to the boiler. The Union gunboat opened fire. The train, now racing hell-bent, crossed the trestle to the mainland and was soon out of range of the gunboat's cannons.[28] Except for the jangled nerves of those who rode the train, there were no personnel casualties on either side during the taking of Fernandina.

On the same day that Fernandina was captured, the Saint Mary's River was ascended by Union gunboats, and the town of Saint Mary's, Georgia, was occupied. At about the same time, Confederate gun emplacements on both Jekyll Island and Saint Simon's Island, Georgia, were discovered to be abandoned. Union troops were installed as occupation garrisons at both of those places.[29]

Saint Augustine; Saint John's River; Savannah River

On March 8, a naval force under the direct command of Flag Officer DuPont anchored off Saint Augustine. The Confederate garrison there immediately surrendered, and soon after, a Union occupation force was established at the mouth of the Saint John's River at what is now Mayport, Florida. On April 10, 1862, a naval bombardment began against Fort Pulaski on the Savannah River. The following day, the Confederate flag was lowered in surrender of that works.

With the exception of the area near Charleston, South Carolina, the coastline from Saint Augustine northward to the southern boundary of North Carolina could for all practical purposes now be considered under Union control even though Federal presence was spotty. There would be occasional disruptions by Confederate raiding forces; but in general, control of the coast in this stretch would remain vested with the Union for the remainder of the Civil War. Except for that part of the outer banks on which Butler's force had established a presence, the coast of North Carolina remained in Confederate hands.

THE BURNSIDE EXPEDITION
(February - July 1862)

Creation of a Coast Division

The Army of the Potomac which came under the command of Major General George B. McClellan in July of 1861 was considered as constituting all Union Army troops employed south of the Chesapeake including the occupied sections of Virginia and coastal North and South Carolina. By way of departmental jurisdiction, the authority held by McClellan therefore encompassed any expeditions which might be launched against the Carolinas as far south as the South Carolina - Georgia line. Brigadier General Ambrose E. Burnside approached McClellan with the idea for a "Coast Division" which would act as an amphibious strike force and which would later serve as garrisons for any Union enclaves taken by that force. As he described it in an article he later wrote for *Battles and Leaders of the Civil War,* Burnside claimed that he initially hit on the idea for such a division during October of 1861 following Butler's Expedition to take Hatteras Inlet.[30] Burnside believed that such a Coast Division, should muster between twelve thousand and fifteen thousand officers and men -- their mobility to be provided by a fleet of light draft steamers and sailing vessels in conjunction with whatever else might become necessary in the way of tugs and barges. As Burnside envisioned, the enclaves which the division would seize would serve as "jump-off" bases from which detachments could move out rapidly to strike the enemy inland of the coastal sounds and as far up the rivers as feasible. Ideally, the division, including its fleet, would be entirely self-contained. In addition to assault craft, supply vessels would also be part of the division's organization, but only to the extent that such vessels could be constantly employed. Beyond the point which would allow a steady vessel utilization, merchant vessels would be chartered to serve special operations requiring heavier than normal sealift capability. Burnside's idea was to crew as much of the division's fleet as practicable with military personnel. Recruitment was to take place at New York and in the seacoast towns of New England where mariners familiar with the coasting trade could be obtained. If enough of these men could not be enlisted, then, at least for the time being, the division's vessels would be crewed with civilians supported by Army gunners. McClellan liked the idea, and with Burnside, he presented the scheme to the Secretary of War who approved it. Burnside immediately set to work to assemble the men and the vessels. Finding suitable vessels was, though, to be the first major challenge. Even at this early point in the war, the coast had been scoured for just about anything that floated, the Navy having taken the cream and more. Those quartermasters Burnside placed in charge of procurement were told to find small seaworthy craft capable of weathering the winter storms along the coast while at the same time having a limited enough draft to allow them access into the shallow sounds of the Carolinas and Georgia. The problem was that the quartermasters were looking for exactly the same type of vessel that was in demand by the Navy for inshore use in the support of its own coastal blockade squadrons. Whenever possible, Burnside wanted to buy vessels, but the market did not constitute a buyer's climate. Ship owners were more than happy with the by-now over-priced charter market, and few of them wanted to rid themselves of vessels which had become valuable investment properties. Despite the many difficulties, and through a combination of purchase and charter, Burnside's people did obtain enough of them to make a maritime oriented division reasonably mobile; but the quality of the fleet he ended up with was not what he had originally hoped for.

In order to arm the vessels, it was necessary to seek cooperation from the Navy. By this means, enough guns were found to equip both the purchased vessels as well as some of those which had been acquired through charter. Twenty years later, Burnside would admit in writing, "It was a motley fleet."[31]

That part of the Burnside fleet which had been purchased included a number of Hudson River barges which the quartermasters ordered strengthened through means of transverse bulkheads placed in such a way as to create watertight compartments in case of hull penetration through shellfire. Further strengthening and protection was accomplished by the use of double planking laid from deck level to the turn of their bilges. Bracing timbers were put on the barges' decks. This strengthening would accommodate the later construction of parapets (to consist of sand bags) to be placed so as to protect from enemy fire those troops on the barges' decks during beach assaults and during penetrations up southern rivers. It was in the planning to use these barges as gun platforms once the Carolina sounds were reached. While at sea or crossing exposed sounds, the barges were to be left unmanned and taken under tow, either by transport steamers or by tugs specially employed for that duty. Sailing vessels of the coasting type had also been purchased. These were to be fitted out with protection similar to that which was on the barges, but with less topside weight involved in the refit. The sailing vessels, in addition to carrying supplies and troops, were, when at sea, to carry as deck cargo those guns which were to be fitted on the barges once sheltered waters had been reached. For open ocean troop carriers, Burnside's quartermasters gathered as many large steamers of the coasting types as they could find. A few were purchased; but most were obtained through charter. Originally the plans called for a fleet which had the ability to carry at one lift fifteen thousand men with their full equipment and necessary baggage, plus six hundred thousand field rations, as well as a reserve of artillery shells and animal forage. Because of the shortage of vessels, the Navy's recommendation to the Quartermaster concerning the troop capacity of each vessel was stretched. A number of vessels would end up carrying twice as many troops as they should have comfortably or safely accommodated.

In addition to the fleet that would be used to get the division to its destinations, there was to be a follow-up fleet consisting of chartered sail vessels. Some were employed to carry building materials to be used for barracks, warehousing, and bridging. Some were designated as colliers, the plan being to bring in a total of five thousand tons of coal to rebunker the original assault fleet. Others would carry replenishment supplies including horses and beef animals on the hoof. One or two of the sailing vessels were to be assigned to carry small lighters for transporting both troops and supplies over shallow landing places.

The original scheme was to have Army officers and enlisted men crew those shallower draft vessels which were to become the division's permanently assigned fleet; however, that idea never seemed to materialize except in some isolated cases. According to crew lists located for seventeen of the purchased vessels, civilians made up the entirety of their operating crews during 1862.[32]

Operational Planning

While his quartermasters were busy putting this collection of shipping together, Burnside and his operations staff, working in close liaison with McClellan, were busy with the military planning for the division's initial mission. An independent suggestion had been put forth by Brigadier General Rush C. Hawkins (he had been a regimental commander in Butler's Expedition) that Roanoke Island offered the maximum advantage for developing an initial presence within the sounds. Other occupations should follow closely. Hawkins laid out for consideration the sequence and the reasons for each occupation.

> First. Roanoke Island, which commands the Croatan Channel between Pamlico and Albemarle sounds, should be occupied at once. It is now held by the rebels. They have a battery completed at the upper end of the island and another in course of erection at the southern extremity. Second. A small force should be stationed at Beacon Island, which is in the mouth of Ocracoke Inlet and commands it. Third. Two or three light draught vessels should be stationed between the mouths of the Neuse and Pamlico rivers. This would shut out all commerce with New Berne and Washington [North Carolina]. Fourth. There should be at least eight light draught gunboats in Pamlico Sound. Fifth. Beaufort should be occupied as soon as possible. [Editor's Note: This is Beaufort, North Carolina, near Beaufort -Morehead City; readers should not confuse it with Beaufort, South Carolina, a town up the Port Royal Sound above Hilton Head.] All of these recommendations should be attended to immediately. Seven thousand men judiciously placed upon the soil of North Carolina would, within the next three weeks, draw twenty thousand Confederate troops from the State of Virginia.
>
> I wish, if you agree with me and deem it consistent with your duty, that you would impress upon the Government the importance and necessity of immediate action in this department.[33]

Both Burnside and McClellan, upon being consulted on Hawkins's proposal, concurred. It was decided that the first stage of the expedition would take place from Hatteras Inlet where the fleet would assemble before moving into Pamlico Sound. Once into the sound, the assault force would proceed northward to Roanoke Island. Hawkins had written his proposal on September 6. Since that time, the island was believed to have been reinforced by the Confederates, with an undetermined number of gunboats placed in support. A fight of more substance than that experienced at Hatteras Inlet was clearly expected. Burnside, in referencing Hawkins's suggestions, proposed to McClellan that once Roanoke Island was taken, it would provide a base from which an expedition could be launched against New Berne. This would put a strong Union force astride the railroad which made a junction at New Berne from the inland towns of Goldsborough and Raleigh, thus allowing rail connection from those places to the twin port towns of Beaufort -Morehead City via New Berne. Morehead City and Beaufort were protected from entry from the sea by Fort Macon which was on the barrier island offlying both towns. The fort was situated so as to command approaches to the inlet, its land side defenses being negligible and thus highly vulnerable. Fort Macon was to be scheduled for attack from its land side.

The importance of Beaufort -Morehead City was that they could provide needed shelter for the Union blockading forces operating in the area offlying Cape Hatteras and Cape Lookout. Hatteras Inlet, although first intended for such shelter purposes, had not worked out too well. The shallow bar guarding the inlet's entrance prevented ships from passing through the inlet except in the most moderate sea conditions. Besides providing a much more suitable shelter for the Union Navy's blockading vessels, Beaufort -Morehead City had become an important entry point for Confederate blockade running. Goods which were being brought in through the blockade were then being carried over the railroad running to New Berne, and from there by rail to Raleigh and Goldsborough to await final distribution. If Burnside could first take New Berne, to be followed by the capture of Fort Macon which guarded the Confederate holdings of Beaufort -Morehead City, those accomplishments could be followed by a strike inland from New Berne along the railroad right of way toward Goldsborough. As planned, the attack against New Berne was to have the support of gunboats which would pace the infantry advancing toward the town along the banks of the Neuse River.

Transports carrying the troops and supplies of the Coast Division, were to assemble at Annapolis where they were to take on the troops. From there, the fleet was to proceed down Chesapeake Bay to Fortress Monroe to rendezvous with the vessels assigned to carry supplies. Burnside intended to make sure that everything and everybody was present and in ample quantity before he left the mouth of the Chesapeake, bound for Hatteras Inlet[34].

At Annapolis the transports were to take aboard a total of ten thousand two hundred officers and men. A review of the actual numbers each vessel carried indicates extreme crowding for ships of their size. The transport *S. R. SPAULDING* (chartered) had assigned to it four hundred troops; the *GUIDE* (purchased) had seven hundred troops; *COSSACK* (purchased) had seven hundred troops; *GEORGE PEABODY* (chartered) had eight hundred troops; the *NORTHERNER* (purchased) had one thousand troops; *NEW BRUNSWICK* (chartered) had seven hundred troops; the *CITY OF NEW YORK* (chartered) had seven hundred troops; the *VIRGINIA* (chartered) had five hundred troops; the *EASTERN QUEEN* (chartered) had eight hundred seventy-five troops; the *JOHN TRUCK* (chartered) had seven hundred troops; the *DRAGOON* (purchased) had three hundred troops. Of the troop transports, all but the *JOHN TRUCK* and the *DRAGOON* appear to have been steamers. None of the larger transports were armed, since Burnside did not plan to use them in the direct assault against Roanoke Island, rather intending to use lighter draft vessels for that purpose once the expedition came in proximity to the landing beaches.

Another group of steamers, these all armed and of the shallow draft type, were selected to carry troops in toward the beaches. They were: the *CHASSEUR* (purchased), four hundred troops; the *VIDETTE* (chartered), three hundred troops; the *PIONEER* (purchased), four hundred troops; the *RANGER* (purchased), four hundred fifty troops; the *HUSSAR* (purchased), four hundred troops; the *LANCER* (purchased), four hundred fifty troops; the *SENTINEL* (purchased), four hundred fifty troops; and *ZOUAVE* (purchased), unknown number of troops. The shallow draft group had been laid out and equipped to also function as gunboats -- their hulls having been accordingly strengthened.

The *PICKET*, a small steamer converted into a gunboat, was originally intended to carry troops. But before departure, she was chosen by General Burnside as his headquarters vessel, a choice he made solely because it was the smallest steam vessel in the fleet and by all outward appearances looked to be the most unseaworthy. Before the fleet left Annapolis, Burnside had come under criticism that some of the vessels were too small and therefore unsuitable for open ocean passage. He had hoped to put this criticism to rest by selecting what was apparently the least safe of the whole lot for his personal transportation.

Transports selected exclusively for supply (all of which were obtained through purchase) were the sailing vessels *CADET*, *GORILLA*, *HIGHLANDER*, *RECRUIT*, *SCOUT*, *SKIRMISHER*, and *VOLTIGEUR*. All but *CADET* were provided with cannon. Barges that were to be towed south (they had been purchased and reconstructed as floating batteries) were the *BOMBSHELL*, *GRAPE SHOT*, *GRENADE*, *ROCKET*, and *SHRAPNEL*.[35]

Embarkation

On January 4, 1862, the troops of the division were all assembled at Annapolis, Maryland; loading commenced the following day. The division at this point in time consisted of five regiments of Massachusetts infantry; three regiments of Connecticut infantry; three regiments of New York infantry; two regiments of Pennsylvania infantry; two regiments of Rhode Island infantry; one regiment of New Jersey infantry; and one company of the 99th New York Infantry.[36] Artillery consisted of two battalions, one regular Army and the other a volunteer outfit raised in Rhode Island. Representing but a small part of the expedition's strength, and not named as part of the troop units just enumerated, was a detachment of the 1st New York Marine Artillery "Naval Brigade" which was referred to in most reports of the operation as the "1st Marine Artillery." This was an outfit that Burnside had originally envisioned as the organization which, once expanded, would supply the gunners who would be carried aboard his gunboats, his armed sailing vessels, and any of the steam transports equipped with cannon. This nucleus would also eventually provide the operating crews for all vessels which were permanently assigned to the Coast Division -- or so it was planned at the time.[37]

By the 7th of January, all troop units were loaded aboard the transports, and the expedition proceeded down Chesapeake Bay to the prearranged rendezvous off Fortress Monroe. The fleet, including naval vessels, when finally assembled at Fortress Monroe totaled almost eighty vessels.

The fleet weighed anchor on January 11, outbound into the open Atlantic. As had been the case with Thomas W. Sherman's Expedition to Port Royal, heavy weather was encountered as soon as it began rounding Cape Hatteras. By dawn, the blow had tapered off; however by sunset, a new gale bore down. Although his later written account of that day does not admit to a problem of discomfort during the blow, Burnside probably began to have reservations concerning the decision he had made to travel aboard the little *PICKET*. Pushing through heavy seas, those vessels in the forefront of the fleet finally came abeam of Hatteras Inlet where a waiting tug started pilot duty by guiding the transports over the entrance bar. Once over the bar and within shelter of the inlet, it was to be discovered that only the very lightest of draft could proceed over a second bar stretching across the swash channel leading into Pamlico Sound.

While assembling the fleet and choosing vessels with appropriate drafts, Burnside's quartermasters had reckoned on fairly recent surveys within Hatteras Inlet; but winter storms had made much of that survey work obsolete.[38] The bar across the inner swash channel was a 2-foot high underwater sand ridge not shown upon the surveys. On the southerly and northerly sides of the basin between the bars were the wind-blown beaches of the outer islands of the Cape Hatteras land chain on which stood Fort Hatteras and Fort Clarke, the forts taken earlier by Butler. The anchorage which was available in the lake-like basin between the bars, although large enough to hold a reasonable number of vessels, could not safely accommodate the amount of shipping now coming into the inlet. The circumstances were exacerbated by a hard packed sand bottom which was not conducive to good anchor holding. The consequences of this combination of too little space and a poor holding bottom soon translated itself into a series of collisions. Vessels dragged their anchors, slamming against their neighbors with splintering crashes. This necessitated a continual shifting around of ships. Merchant ship masters and naval commanders were each independently trying to gain an appropriate position within which to drop their anchors in relationship to nearby ships. Once accomplished, these attempts only developed into subsequent failure as others shifted their positions. While this chaos was taking place, ships were continuing to come in over the outer bar to join in the confusion.

The troopship *CITY OF NEW YORK* never made it in. Instead, she ran hard onto the outer bar, broached sideways, and quickly became a total loss. She remained afloat long enough for the troops which she carried to be rescued by the attending pilot tug. Another trooper which was following in close succession to *CITY OF NEW YORK* also hit the bar, and she too stuck fast. Fortunately, though, she did not broach. The tug which had been leading her in thus had an opportunity to get a hawser attached so the ship could be pulled over the bar and into the basin. The gunboat ZOUAVE also struck the bar but was able to work herself free. A troop transport, the JOHN TRUCK, was too deep in draft to even attempt an entry. Unable to unload her seven hundred troops to small boats in such heavy seas, ZOUAVE steamed back to Annapolis, troops and all. The POCAHONTAS, an animal transport carrying one hundred three horses, never made it even to the Hatteras Inlet, foundering while en route. Information on her fate came to Burnside's attention when some Union sympathizing "outer bankers" reported that the POCAHONTAS had been driven ashore about twenty miles to the north of the inlet. Her crew, with some sixty troops in all, had gotten on to the beach safely; but only nineteen of the horses had survived.

At the inlet, problems were multiplying. None of the supply ships which had been loaded with drinking water had yet arrived. Since the area near the inlet had no wells worthy of the name, all troops had to be put on short water rations. The fate of the expedition now totally depended on the arrival of supply vessels carrying water.

On January 14, yet another gale howled out of the northeast, striking the outer banks before midnight. More anchor dragging. This time ZOUAVE's luck ran out for good. Being one of the smaller vessels in the anchorage, she had been positioned nearer to the inside swash channel which gave her but inches of clearance beneath her keel. It appears that her anchors were bridled, one anchor being run out within the anchorage area, the other run out onto the bar itself. When the gale began to veer in direction, ZOUAVE swung over onto the edge of the bar, coming down hard on the upper fluke of her own second anchor. This holed her, and she promptly sank.[39]

When the wind decreased and the sea finally began to lay, a number of the shallower draft vessels, including almost all of the Navy's gunboats, were able to cross the swash bar into Pamlico Sound without touching. This was thanks in great part to the higher than normal tides which remained for a time in the aftermath of the storm. The larger Army transports still couldn't make it over. One piece of good fortune -- the ships carrying the much needed water had finally arrived.

At high tide, the depth on the swash channel was around 6 feet, this being two feet short of the surveyed depth of eight feet. Six feet was also two feet shy of what most of the transports safely needed in order to pass over into the sound. Burnside later explained how the transport masters were able to resolve the problem.

> [The] vessels were sent ahead, with full steam, on the bar when the tide was running out, and then anchors were carried out by boats in advance, so as to hold the vessels in position. The swift current would wash the sand from under them and allow them to float, after which they were driven farther on by steam and anchored again, when the sand would again wash out from under them. This process was continued for days, until a broad channel of over eight feet was made, deep enough to allow the passage of the fleet into the sound.[40]

The GEORGE PEABODY had been the first large transport to get over into the sound, that on January the 25th. The last transport passed into the sound on February 3, some thirty-one days after the expedition had sailed from Fortress Monroe.

The Confederates at Roanoke Island had had at least twenty-eight days' notice that Burnside was coming.

Assault Against Roanoke Island

Shortly after the expedition started steaming down the sound toward Roanoke Island, a halt had to be called when another howling gale came out of the northeast. The following day, with the wind dropping, the Army gunboats came alongside the transports to discharge their troop passengers so that they would be free to move forward to join the Navy gunboats for the bombardment of the Confederate defenses and to provide covering fire before and during the troop landings.

The assault on Roanoke Island was to be conducted against the island's western shore, the one side served by a navigable channel. That channel was defended by enfilade fire from Fort Barlow (9 guns) and from Fort Forrest (8 guns). In a line running west from Fort Barlow and out into the water, the Confederates had driven pilings deep into the sound's bottom. These obstructions were intermixed with sunken hulks. Fort Forrest on the western end of this barrier seems to have been somewhat of an extemporaneous and shakey affair. According to Daniel Ammen's written description, the fort was "... placed on abandoned hulks buried in the sand."[41] Eight armed Confederate steamers had been anchored in position north of the barrier of pilings and hulks. At first sight, these steamers appeared menacing; but in reality, they were ineffectively armed for any standup fight. As it developed, as soon as the Federals opened fire, the Southern steamers hauled in their anchors and hightailed it northward up the sound. Two or three of the Union gunboats worked past the barrier and gave chase. Most of the Confederate steamers were subsequently scuttled by their crews when it became apparent that capture was imminent.

Although it had not originally been thought of as the best landing place, Ashby Harbor, an indentation in Roanoke Island's western coastline, was selected by Burnside and his staff as the most advantageous location for putting troops onto the island. The landing, preceded by bombardment from the gunboats, was carried out by surf boats operating in shuttles from the offlying transports. Two of the light draft steamers towed the surf boats part way into the beach to the point where the water shallowed. They were then cast loose to proceed in the rest of the way under oars. The shuttling from transports to surf boats continued until nightfall by which time all the troops, less one regiment, had been landed.

The only real opposition in taking the island was encountered about midway up the island's center from a battery of Southern guns supported by infantry. This position was quickly stormed with only light casualties to the attackers. From that point until sunset, it was all downhill for the Confederates who kept moving back, only occasionally putting up a light resistance. Upon reaching the island's northerly point and with only salt water at their feet, they surrendered en masse. Roanoke Island was Burnside's.

New Berne, North Carolina

With Roanoke Island securely in Union hands, Burnside sent his troops into bivouac. For the men, this provided a well deserved rest after what had been a miserable month crammed in tight numbers aboard the transports. For the enlisted men and junior officers, it was a period for relaxing and wondering what was going to happen next. Officers of field grade level and up were the only ones made aware that the next item on the agenda was to be New Berne on the Neuse River and then the cutting of the railroad line which ran between there and Goldsborough.

On the 26th of February, Burnside's infantrymen found themselves (all too soon, in the opinion of the private soldier) returning to the transports. The age-old Army game of "hurry up and wait" again came into play. It was not until the early morning of March 12 that the transports' anchors came clear of the mud. The ships swung out into Pamlico Sound, preparatory to heading southward toward the Neuse. Late that same afternoon, they began arriving at the south bank of the Neuse River near where Slocum Creek enters. (This is about fifteen miles downstream on the Neuse from New Berne.) Gunboat commanders who had returned from farther up the Neuse reported that it had been blocked by pilings and other obstructions. It appeared, at least from a distant observation, that the gunboats could pass through the obstructions. For all anyone knew, though, mines (or torpedoes as they were called in those days) might have been interspersed among the debris. Such would prove to be the case. One gunboat, feeling its way past the barrier, was severely damaged by one of those explosive devices. When that happened, it was decided that the river was unsafe for troop laden transports. The troops were landed near the entrance of Slocum Creek from where they were to march along the river bank until they reached New Berne. The gunboats would pace them and provide fire support if needed. When the gunboats were abreast of New Berne, a barrage would be laid down as cover for an infantry assault against the town.

For the troops, it was a long, hard slog, most of it ankle deep in mud. A series of hot little fire fights developed on the way toward the town, but the advance was not noticeably slowed by this. The day after they started, the Union troops had arrived at the banks of the Trent River across from New Berne. There they stared at two ruined bridges and open water preventing direct access to the town. This problem was solved when two of the gunboats moved up into the Trent to be used as ferries to move the troops over to the New Berne side. The only resistance had been on the approach march during which ninety of Burnside's force were killed and three hundred and eighty wounded.[42]

The capture of New Berne was not the only action to take place on the Carolina sounds that month.

Up the Pasquotank River

During the operation which led to the capture of Roanoke Island, six Confederate vessels managed to escape up the Pasquotank River. There they came to anchor near Elizabeth City under the protection of an emplacement of four heavy guns. On February 10, 1862, a Union naval force under Commander Stephen C. Rowan and to which Burnside had added an infantry guard, proceeded up the Pasquotank and opened fire on these anchored craft. Even at long range, this had its effect. Five of the enemy's six vessels were damaged so severely they were useless for further service.

The day before the Navy's penetration of the Pasquotank, a force of infantry was transported from Hatteras Inlet north to Nags Head with the intent of pushing the enemy completely off the North Carolina outer banks. This proved unnecessary. The day before, the Confederates had retreated northward to the Virginia mainland, leaving to the Union the entirety of the outer banks.

Chowan River Bridges

In late February, a joint Army- Navy amphibious expedition departed from Roanoke Island toward the Chowan River with the intent of proceeding past the town of Winton toward the point where the Chowan River branches into the Nottoway River. Upstream from Winton, crossing both the Chowan and the Nottoway, there were two important bridges of the Seaboard and Roanoke Railroad. These bridges were to become the targets of the expedition. Brigadier General Rush C. Hawkins, who was in command of this foray, did not anticipate enemy opposition of any significance as he had been told that the local population in that section were friendly to the Union. Such, however, did not prove to be the case. When the lead gunboat came into sight of the town, a Negro woman ran down to the river waving a white rag, beckoning them to come in. While proceeding up the river, Hawkins had taken the lookout perch on the mast. From that vantage point, he detected the sun's rays glistening off musket barrels. Then two pieces of artillery in fixed positions suddenly came into view; but before the guns could open fire, Hawkins shouted a warning. The expedition vessels were turned around and brought to anchor below the town, well out of range of its welcoming committee. Hawkins decided to wait until the next day before taking further action. In the morning when he led his infantry force ashore, the Confederates were quickly driven out of town. A subsequent search of some of the buildings revealed that they contained military stores. These buildings were put to the torch.

Not knowing what might greet him farther up the river, Hawkins decided to leave the destruction of the railroad bridges for some time in the future.

The Dismal Swamp Canal

Following the captures of Roanoke Island and New Berne, word reached General Burnside that the Confederates were in the process of building ironclads at Norfolk and perhaps upstream on the Roanoke River as well. If the enemy could get even one ironclad into the Albemarle Sound, then Union domination on the sounds could be in serious jeopardy. Since the intelligence coming out of Norfolk had been accurate up to that time, steps were put in force to block the two routes that led from Norfolk southward to the Albemarle Sound. The first route was through the Dismal Swamp Canal; the second was through the Albemarle and Chesapeake Canal.

The Dismal Swamp Canal route had originally been surveyed by a young George Washington a century before. It ran from Norfolk southward via the Deep Creek River to a set of locks at Deep Creek hamlet. There the dug portion of the route began, continuing in a nearly straight line to locks at South Mills, and thence to the Pasquotank River which ran past Elizabeth City to drain into Albemarle Sound. In order to block the Dismal Swamp route, both Brigadier General Rush C. Hawkins and the senior naval officer who was to participate in the landings agreed on the feasibility of putting ashore an infantry force at Elizabeth City from where a forced march would be made to South Mills.[43] Once the locks at South Mills were destroyed, the Dismal Swamp connection to Norfolk would be severed. Burnside gave his blessing to the mission and detailed the 21st Massachusetts Infantry and the 51st Pennsylvania Infantry to the task under the brigade command of Brigadier General Jesse L. Reno. He detailed the 9th New York Infantry, the 89th New York Infantry, and the 6th New Hampshire Infantry, with artillery backup provided by a company of the Army's 1st New York Marine Artillery Naval Brigade, brigaded under Hawkins. Reno, being senior officer, was given the overall command.

The troops were landed near Elizabeth City, each brigade making a separate approach march to the South Mills Lock. Hawkins's route, which he had expected to be sixteen miles was "short-cut" at the point of departure upon the advice of a local citizen guide. Actually, the "short cut" proved to be a circuitous route almost doubling the distance. In his written account of the events, Hawkins charged treachery on the part of the guide. One would hope that Hawkins made a correct judgment as he ordered the guide taken into the woods and shot.[44]

While the troops under Hawkins and Reno were marching toward the South Mills Lock, the Confederates were preparing their defenses. The Confederate officer in charge described those preparations:

> Colonel [Ambrose R.] Wright moved forward with his three companies.... After advancing three miles from South Mills, a road emerged from the woods, and the field on the right and the left extended 160-180 yards to thick woods and swamp. On the edge of the woods, on both sides of the road, and perpendicular to it, was a small ditch, the earth from which was thrown up on the south side in a ridge upon which was a heavy railed fence. From this point, the road led through a narrow lane for one mile with cleared land on both sides of it. Here, he [Colonel Wright] determined to make a stand. About three hundred yards from the woods ran a deep wide ditch parallel with the one first mentioned and extending to the woods on either side of the road and a short distance beyond it were dwellings and outhouses which would give cover for the enemy. Colonel Wright, therefore, ordered them burned. The large ditch in his front he filled with fence rails and set them on fire, his object being to have this ditch so hot that by the time the enemy came up, they could not occupy it. [This ditch is marked on report sketch as 'Roasted Ditch.'] ...He also threw down the fences for three hundred yards on each side of the road and for three hundred yards in front of the guns, and tossed the rails into the road to destroy the effect of the enemy's ricochet firing and to deprive him of the cover of the fences....The smoke from the burning buildings and fences rolled toward the enemy, thus masking the position....[45]

When the combined Union force which advanced on the defenses came under fire, they deflected to the right so as to outflank the Confederate position. Colonel Wright's small force then retired, thus ending the "Battle of South Mills" or, as it was later to be termed, "The Battle of Camden". While in the process of regrouping to converge on South Mills, information came to Reno that strong Confederate reinforcements were marching against him from Norfolk. Even though he had not yet destroyed or otherwise blocked the locks, he and Hawkins agreed on an immediate withdrawal. The Dismal Swamp Canal remained open with its lock intact, presumably awaiting passage of any force of Confederate ironclads that might be sent south from Norfolk. Actually, such a threat was a hollow one since the width and depth restrictions of the Dismal Swamp Canal would have denied passage to any ironclad which was large enough to be a serious menace to anyone. Although the dimensions of the canal were a matter of open knowledge to be found within a number of publications available to those with a need of that information, neither Burnside nor his staff had thought to search it out.

Closing the Albemarle and Chesapeake Canal: A Naval Mission

During April, the naval gunboats *USS LOCKWOOD*, *USS WHITEHEAD*, and *USS PUTNAM* were ordered to undertake the mission of blocking the southern section of the Albemarle and Chesapeake Canal. This canal also led from Norfolk south toward the Carolina sounds; however, it was more navigable than the older and shallower Dismal Swamp route, and it therefore posed a more realistic threat for the transit of ironclads.

The three Union gunboats were to be accompanied by the naval tug *USS SHAWSHEEN* which would have in tow a schooner filled with sand ballast. The plan was that the schooner would be sunk as a blocking ship close to the canal's southern entrance, but that was but one part of the plan. Riding aboard *USS LOCKWOOD* with Lieutenant C. W. Flusser, the expedition's leader, was a Professor Benjamin Maillefert of the New York Submarine Engineering Company. Maillefert was along to provide the technical know-how so that the closing of the canal would be so thorough that it would take two or three months of heavy labor, plus the use of dredging equipment, to reopen it.

When Flusser arrived at the southern end of the canal, he put fifty armed men ashore on each bank and sent ahead a launch equipped with a 12-pound cannon. The officer in the launch discovered that the enemy had also begun work to block the canal, but no Confederates were sighted. The destruction work then got underway. First, the ballasted schooner was sunk. Then they tossed into the canal "brush, stumps, rails, trunks of heavy trees, and earth, for a distance of about fifty yards above [the entrance]." While this was taking place, the flanking guards, stacked arms and began throwing dirt as far out into the canal as possible. The work was hard and took two days of labor -- labor which Flusser seemed to have considered a waste of effort. In his report to Rowan, Flusser would write, "the rebels have, I think, no thought of using the canal, as they have themselves been obstructing it above and below the bridge."[46]

[1]   Twenty thousand troops seems to have been somewhat of an over estimate unless of course Scott intended to secure the entire city of Charleston. Duncan S. Somerville tells of a plan hatched at the time by two private ship owners to put together a private relief expedition, a plan which received the temporary enthusiasm of General Scott, but which was, according to Somerville, vetoed by the Navy. Colonel Duncan S. Somerville, *The Aspinwall Empire,* (Mystic, CT: Mystic Seaport Museum, Inc., 1983).

[2]   *Official Records of the Union and Confederate Navies in the War of the Rebellion.* (Washington, DC: Government Printing Office, 1894 - 1917), Series II, Volume 1, pp 49, 50.

[3]   Altogether, forty-nine letters of marque were issued by the Confederate government, but only seventeen of the authorized vessels actually saw service as privateers.

[4]   There is a rather full account of the Confederate privateers within Annex I of Appendix II, *Dictionary of American Naval Fighting Ships,* Volume II, (Washington, DC: Naval History Division, 1963; reprinted with corrections 1969). The trial of the crew of the *SAVANNAH* is covered in detail within *Trial of the Officers and Crew of the Privateer SAVANNAH on the Charge of Piracy,* US Circuit Court for Southern District of New York, Judges Nelson and Shipman, presiding, (New York: Baker and Goodwin, 1862).

[5]   *War of the Rebellion: Official Records of the Union and Confederate Armies,* (Washington, DC: Government Printing Office, 1880 - 1900). Facsimile Ed: (Harrisburg, PA: National Historical Society, 1971. Reprint. Historical Times, Inc., 1985), Series I, Volume 4, pp 579-594.

[6]   *ORN,* I, 6, p 127. The names of the "two transport steamers" so reported were *ADELAIDE* and *GEORGE PEABODY.*

[7]   Captain F. A. Rowe, who in 1861 commanded a company of the 99th New York Infantry, years later wrote an account of the landings at Hatteras which appeared in *The History of the Naval Brigade, 99th New York Volunteers - "Union Coast Guard,"* (New York: Regimental Veterans Association, 1905). Rowe stated in his account that the troops which landed in the first wave consisted of men from the 9th New York Zouaves; the 20th New York Infantry; and the 99th New York Infantry. Rowe also claimed that most of the small boats which were involved in bringing the troops through the surf were "unwieldy iron boats" manned by men from the 99th New York Infantry.

[8]   The *FANNY's* crew, all civilians, escaped; but the reinforcement troops she carried aboard were taken prisoner. From the vitriolic and apparently one-sided reports that we have on that episode (all from the civilian crewmembers), it appears that the *FANNY's* defense was not carried out as heroically as it might have been. The civilian crew, which had all ingloriously hightailed it, blamed their lack of defensive action on the military people aboard who, according to the civilians, refused to take defensive action. *ORN,* I, 6, pp 275-278.

[9]   Whenever hulks or other impedimenta appeared in any of the Carolina inlets, current forces created deep swash channels on either or perhaps both sides of the obstructions. There were even certain instances where channels, deeper than the original ones, were created by the constrictive effect of the hulks. *ORN,* I, 6, p 64.

[10]   *ORN,* I, 6, p 268. Although Butler's army command had charge of those blockships which were to be towed south to the inlets, the navy would be responsible for sinking them.

[11]   The Secretary of the Navy reportedly issued a follow-up order which canceled the instructions to block Ocracoke Inlet; but whether that order was received in time to stop the operation is not clear. *ORN,* I, 6, p 162. The fate of the stone laden schooners destined for these inlets is also unrecorded.

[12]   It is of specific interest to the history of Army shipping to note that three of the blockships intended for Charleston harbor, the *COREA, FRANCIS HENRIETTA,* and *GARLAND,* were saved from scuttling; they were instead delegated to the control of the Army Quartermaster for use as storeships. They were probably located for that purpose at Hilton Head, South Carolina.

[13]   *ORN,* I, 6, pp 204, 205.

[14]   Admiral David D. Porter, *The Naval History of the Civil War,* (Facsimile reprint, Secaucus, NJ: Castle, 1984), p 108.

[15]   *ORA,* I, 6, p 178.

[16]   *ORA,* I, 6, 179, 180.

[17]   Daniel Ammen, *The Atlantic Coast,* Campaigns of the Civil War Series, (Wilmington, NC: Broadfoot Publishing Co., 1989), p 14; also Porter, pp, 54, 55.

[18]   *ORN,* I, 12, pp 245, 246.

[19]   Some who in the past have written on the expedition have reported the name of a lost vessel as being the *OCEAN EMPRESS*; however, no record of such a vessel can be found in any of the archival records, either Navy or Army; nor is such a vessel shown in quartermaster reports as being lost while in service to the Army. A vessel of a similar name, *OCEAN EXPRESS,* is mentioned as requiring limited assistance while somewhere in proximity to Port Royal on November 19. *ORN,* I, 12, p 287.

20   It is hard to understand the carelessness of Brigadier General Drayton's staff in leaving behind a map showing gun emplacements all along the southern coast. This proved to be a priceless benefit in the planning for a number of Union raids which lay ahead.

21   Senate Executive Document No. 37, 37th Congress, 2nd Session.

22   These are included in a listing to be found within *ORN*, I, 12, p 229.

23   *ORA*, I, 6, p 171.

24   *ORA*, I, 6, pp 176, 177.

25   *ORN*, I, 6, p 252.

26   Extant crew lists for Army gunboats and supply vessels in the North Carolina sounds enumerate numbers of Negroes (identified by name and color) utilized as permanent labor parties on Army vessels. Such crew lists appear to have been compiled during the fall of 1862. Vessels involved were: *COPACK, CURLEW, DRAGOON, EAGLE, EASTERN STATE, HAZE, HIGHLANDER, HUSSAR, LANCER, NORTH STATE, NORTHERNER, RANGER, RECRUIT, SCOUT, SKIRMISHER, UNION, WILSON*, and *ZOUAVE*. File locations on these lists are: National Archives, Record Group 92 -- 8W2A/3/3/D/Box 6; SW2/34/3/H; 8W2/38/9/H; 8W2/35/25/Λ; 8W2/34/7/ (New Berne, NC, 1 November 1862).

27   *ORA*, I, 6, p 90.

28   Various accounts, such as those by Ammen and Porter, as well as those within official correspondence, differ as to whether the train itself suffered damage.

29   In 1980, Saint Mary's, Georgia, was selected as the site of a nuclear submarine base.

30   General A. E. Burnside, "The Burnside Expedition," *Battles and Leaders*, I, pp 660-669. Burnside's claim that he was the originator of the idea for an amphibious strike force is open to serious question. Some four months before Burnside broached the matter to McClellan, Colonel Washington A. Bartlett was busy recruiting a regiment in New York City. When announcing that regiment's purpose, he stated that it was to be composed mainly of former sailors who were to man light draft gunboats. In a newspaper story, Bartlett explained the regiment's mission which would be to cruise along the coast of the southern states and land and capture installations such as bridges and even towns. Afterward, the regiment would withdraw to its gunboats. On May 2, 1861, the regiment -- which was later to be designated the 99th New York Infantry -- was ordered to report to Fortress Monroe, Virginia, to be mustered into Federal service. Elements of that regiment were with Butler on the first expedition to Hatteras Inlet later that August. Company B of the 99th New York would man two of the gunboats which were to now serve with Burnside on the second expedition to Hatteras Inlet. The 99th New York Infantry -- known at an earlier point as "The Union Coast Guard," and also known for a short time as the "Naval Brigade" -- should not be confused with the 1st New York Marine Artillery "Naval Brigade" which was an entirely separate organization. Both the 99th New York and the 1st New York Marine Artillery "Naval Brigade" saw service in the Carolina sounds.

31   This was agreed to by others as well. Daniel Ammen, when writing of the "Coast Division," said that the ships which were to be used as troop transports were "often unseaworthy." Ammen, p 176.

32   Crew lists are exist for the following of Brigadier General Burnside's Coast Division vessels on North Carolina sounds, 1861-1862: See footnote 26, this section. Other than the crew lists, no specific dates of employment are given within the lists.

33   General Rush C. Hawkins, "Early Coast Operations in North Carolina," *Battles and Leaders,* I, p 636.

34   *ORA*, III, 1, pp 739, 740.

35   The names given the vessels which were purchased were new names assigned by the Army. *ORA*, I, 9, pp 359, 362; also Series III, 1, pp 739, 740.

36   The division was organized into three brigades, the first under Brigadier General John G. Foster, the second under Brigadier General Jesse L. Reno, and the third under Brigadier General John G. Parke. There was good rapport between Burnside and his brigade commanders. They had all been at West Point together, although in different classes.

37   According to Frederick H. Dyer's *A Compendium of the War of the Rebellion,* (Dayton, OH: The Press of Morningside Bookshop, 1978, reprint of original published in 1908), the first units of the 1st New York Marine Artillery "Naval Brigade" were mustered into service in New York City during November of 1861, but only one small detachment was ready to leave in January with the Burnside Expedition. Since the 1st New York Marine Artillery Naval Brigade detachment was assigned as part of the gunboats' crewing complements, it would not have appeared as part of the Burnside Expedition's troop strength. Other companies of that organization were later sent south to Roanoke Island after the island was taken from the Confederates. From fairly sketchy information, it seems that it was not until the early winter of 1862-1863 that men from the 1st New York Marine Artillery "Naval Brigade" became completely assimilated into some of the operating crews of the gunboats then stationed in the Carolina sounds.

[38]   Hydrography had been performed at Hatteras Inlet during 1861 under the supervision of Thomas S. Phelps, Lieutenant, Commanding, assigned as Assistant Coast Survey. *US Coast Survey*, "Preliminary Chart of Hatteras Inlet", Report of the Superintendent, 1862. Senate Document, 37th Congress, Third Session.

[39]   *ORN*, I, 6, p 582.

[40]   Burnside, *Battles and Leaders*, I, p 666.

[41]   Ammen, p 182.

[42]   The list of Union casualties at New Berne includes the roster returns for a unit identified as the "1st New York Marine Artillery". Elsewhere in the action reports, this detachment is referred to as the "1st Marine Artillery Naval Brigade." Another small unit which suffered casualties in the advance on New Berne was the 99th New York Infantry's Company B (also sometimes referred to as "Union Coast Guard"). Both of these units would figure later in the relatively small amphibious operations which would take place in the Carolina sounds and up its rivers. Appendix I is a summarized history of the 99th New York Infantry Regiment.

The 1st New York Marine Artillery "Naval Brigade" would become infamous and later an embarrassment to Ambrose Burnside. Two of its units became involved in mutinies at separate locations. As far as can be ascertained, the cause was a disparity in pay between military and civilian segments of the gunboat crews. Because of the mutinies, that organization was disbanded in March of 1863. Its enlisted men were reassigned to regular infantry regiments.

[43]   The Dismal Swamp Canal is still in operation, substantially unchanged except for some widening and deepening which took place in the 1890s.

[44]   Hawkins, *Battles and Leaders*, I, p 655 (fn initialed R. C. H.).

[45]   Hawkins, *Battles and Leaders*, I, p 656.

[46]   *ORN*, I, 7, pp 260, 261.

MAPS OF THE COAST OF THE CAROLINAS.

Reproduced from *Battles and Leaders*, Volume I.

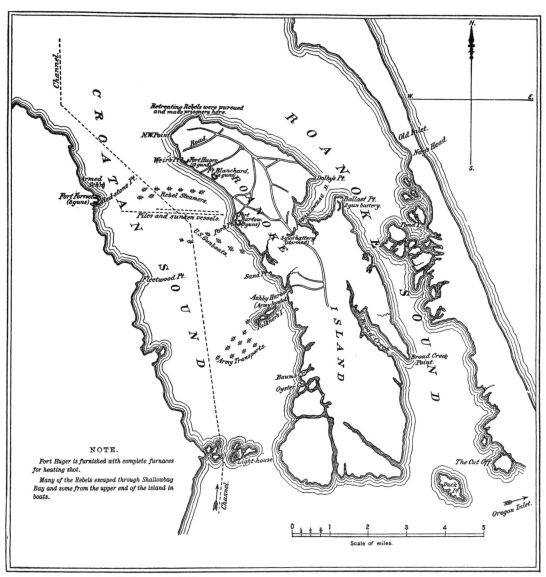

Chartlet of Roanoke Sound and Croatan Sound, North Carolina

Reproduced from *Official Records of the Union and Confederate Navies in the War of the Rebellion*, Series I, 6.

FORT HATTERAS. From collection of the National Archives.

Bombardment of Port Royal. From collection of the Library of Congress.

Major General Montgomery C. Meigs. Union Army Quartermaster General, 1861 throughout the Civil War.
From collection of the National Archives.

Transport CAHAWBA. From collection of the U. S. Army History Military Institute

Transport ARAGO. Deck scene showing gunners, members of the civilian crew at their stations. From collection of the National Archives.

Scene on Pamunkey River, Virginia, in 1862. Chartered steamers are WINONAH and NEW JERSEY. Note barges waiting to discharge their cargo of hay bales.
From collection of National Archives.

Wharf at Alexandria, Virginia, showing facilities for loading and unloading railroad cars and locomotives via the use of ramps shown at end of pier. Note tracks on barges equipped to carry railroad rolling stock. Installation was maintained by the U. S. Military Railroad.

From collection of National Archives.

PART II

WESTERN THEATER OF OPERATIONS: INITIAL PHASE

MANY ENGINEERING CHANGES HAVE IMPROVED NAVIGATION ON THE WESTERN RIVERS SINCE THE MID 1800S. FOR AN UNDERSTANDING OF WESTERN RIVER NAVIGATION AS IT EXISTED IN THE 1860s, READERS ARE URGED TO READ APPENDIX O.

THE LOGISTICAL SIGNIFICANCE OF THE WESTERN RIVERS SYSTEM AS LOOKED AT FROM A MILITARY VIEWPOINT

West of the Mississippi River lay Texas, a place providing a vast reservoir of beef animals which the southern commissary would depend upon from the onset to supply its armies in the field, both for meat and for the leather with which its troops were shod. After the first months of war and following the onset of the Union Navy's coastal blockade -- an activity which was soon to shut off the bulk of incoming commodities to Confederate ports -- the Mexican port of Matamoras became a primary entry point for certain military necessities. From Matamoras, supplies were brought across the border to Brownsville and then transported eastward, either overland, or through the inland waterways which traversed behind the barrier island beaches, finally reaching a rail line which started at Brashear City, Louisiana. This trans-Texas trade included gunpowder and some of the more essential metals. Goods such as shoes, boots, and clothing, were manufactured in the Texas towns of San Antonio, Houston, and Huntsville. From those towns, they found their way eastward. From the Texas towns of Boston, Jefferson, and Tyler, outgoing shipments of other essentials went to Shreveport, Louisiana, and thence down the Red River to the Mississippi and on that river to the rail heads located either at Vicksburg or New Orleans. Nitrate, the product of mines located in Arkansas as well as in Texas, was either shipped directly east as a raw material or was utilized on site for the production of powder and cartridges which were then transported across the Mississippi to the eastern Confederacy. Both Texas and Arkansas were renowned for their horse production, and by the fall of 1861, both states had become a primary source of cavalry mounts.[1]

For the Confederacy, holding the Mississippi River at the Arkansas - Tennessee line was important. But holding the river at Memphis was more than that -- it was vital. From Memphis, an important rail line ran eastward to join with other rail connections coming from both southern Louisiana and Alabama. If those rail lines were to be denied, Confederate Army logistics would suffer badly as the southern armies would be deprived of the material means necessary to bring about direct control of the upper Tennessee Valley. The upper reaches of the Tennessee Valley held the security for the city of Chattanooga. For any Union invader, Chattanooga was the back door approach to Georgia and the Carolinas.

Union strategists considered that the most northern point to be chosen by the Confederates for their defense of the Mississippi would probably be the high bluffs opposite New Madrid. If not there, then the bluffs opposite Osceola, Arkansas; followed by the Memphis area. Finally, if all else failed, the last and strongest bastion could be the bluffs at Vicksburg. If Vicksburg fell, only Port Hudson would remain as a potential strong point. Both Vicksburg and Port Hudson were thought of as "tough nuts," but nuts which would have to be cracked before the Union could claim dominance over the Mississippi River basin.

Before the war, the major trade patterns of mid-America followed the Ohio River and then ran southward on the Mississippi. This route had served a developing industrial base with growth having historically taken place from east to west and from north to south. The 1861-1865 wartime flow of guns, butter, and of course men, were to take similar paths. As it was first envisioned in early 1861, the use of the Mississippi River as an invasion corridor was thought to be of vital strategic importance toward winning the war. Its use had strong political overtones as well, the roots for which went deep into the nation's philosophical and economic soul. This concerned not only those states directly abutting the river but also those states which were indirectly dependent upon it for their commerce. Using that historic basis as well as contemporary intelligence as a rationale, it was argued by Northern strategists that the border states of Kentucky and Missouri were balancing on a fine pivot point between their loyalty to the Federal government and their financial well being which might be better off by an economic marriage with the Confederacy. It was believed that only a federal government committed to taking control of the entire Mississippi system, as demonstrated through direct and early military action, could hold those undecided states to the Union cause.[2]

Major General William Tecumseh Sherman, himself a native of Ohio and a Unionist of very strong conviction, wrote the following words shortly after the capture of Vicksburg in 1863. The sentiments Sherman wrote then were as timely to 1861 as they were when he expressed them later in 1863.

> The valley of the Mississippi is America, and although railroads have changed the economy of intercommunications, if the water channels still mark the lines of fertile land, and afford carriage to the heavy products of it, the inhabitants of the country on the Monongahela, the Illinois, the Minnesota, the Yellowstone, and Osage are as strictly concerned in the security of the lower Mississippi as are those who dwell on its very banks in Louisiana, and now that the nation has recovered its possession, this generation of men would make a fearful mistake if we again commit its charge to a people liable to mistake their title and assert as was recently done, that because they dwelt by sufferance on the banks of this mighty stream, they have a right to control its navigation.[3]

The original idea for waging the war, as it was to be applied to the Mississippi corridor, was to isolate Confederate interests -- east from west -- and from illicit commerce originating in the northern states bordering on the Mississippi. However, the interlocking nature of the western river systems was a factor not completely appreciated by some of those within the Union command until well after hostilities had started.

Accomplishing the final control of the western rivers would be a difficult task for the Union which would extract much in the way of lives and treasure before the job was completed four years later.

OPERATIONS ON THE UPPER WESTERN RIVERS, 1861

At the Outbreak of War

The Anaconda plan which had, at the outbreak of the war, set the basis of strategy for the conquest of the Mississippi corridor should only be considered from the standpoint that it established a broad strategic outline. In actual practice, specific planning for tactical operations was developed as the needs came about. During the early summer of 1861, the development of operations in the Mississippi corridor -- at least as those operations directly or indirectly involved the use of marine transportation and combatant craft -- had its origins with George B. McClellan. This was prior to his transfer to the command of the Army of the Potomac in the summer of 1861. McClellan seems to have been one of those who was fully appreciative of the strategic value of a strong Federal presence at the junction of the Mississippi and the Ohio. The town of Cairo, which is where the rivers come together, was the key defensive point if the Ohio River, the upper Mississippi, and the Missouri River system were all to be held by the Union. From the onset, McClellan was a strong advocate of the use of gunboats, both for the protection of garrisons located on waterways, as well as for prevention of illegal trade. Gunboats would become, therefore, an important part of the defenses at Cairo.

A powerful politician who had backed McClellan on the value of utilizing Cairo as a strong point, as well as looking upon it as an operational base for future penetration of the Mississippi, was a midwesterner named Edward Bates. During the Republican National Convention of 1860, Bates briefly opposed Lincoln for the presidential nomination but then withdrew his own name and threw his support behind Lincoln. Following the inauguration in March of 1861, the now President Lincoln paid his political debt by appointing Bates to the position of Attorney General. Apparently Bates's involvement in the Lincoln Administration went beyond his duties as Attorney General. Bates was probably the first person to propose to Lincoln that the Mississippi be blocked at Cairo. Bates had come to the conclusion that marine equipment, no matter where it was to be employed, should be a matter of naval responsibility. However, the Navy Department, its hands full with the coastal blockade and the threat of Confederate warships and privateers-at-large, begged off from such an all-inclusive involvement and suggested that riverine warfare be the responsibility of the Army. The

Secretary of the Navy did indicate, though, that the Navy would proffer technical advice to the Army if requested. Lieutenant General Winfield Scott seems to have been a direct participant in these early discussions, as it was Scott who first took up on the Navy's offer of technical advice and formally requested that naval assistance be provided. This in turn resulted in an order issued on May 16, 1861, which appears to be the date which marked the beginnings of the Army fleet on the western rivers. The order was addressed to Commander John Rodgers:

> Sir:
>
> You will proceed to Cincinnati, Ohio, or the Headquarters of General McClellan, where[ever] they may be and report to that officer in regard to the expediency of establishing a naval armament on the Mississippi and Ohio rivers, or either of them, with the view of blockading or interdicting communications and interchanges with the states that are in insurrection.
>
> This interior non-intercourse is under the direction and regulation of the Army, and your movements will therefore be governed in great degree by General McClellan, the officer in command, with whom you will put yourself in immediate communication. He will give such orders and requisitions as the case to him shall seem necessary, you acting in conjunction with and subordinate to him.
>
> Whatever naval armament and crew may be necessary to carry into effect the objects here indicated, you will call for by proper requisition. Make your reports to this department.
>
> I am respectfully,
>
> Gideon Welles[4]

A review of the early correspondence dealing with inter-service cooperation on the western rivers makes it quite clear that the Navy's early input into the program was to be restricted to the procurement and/or construction of gunboats as well as the support craft directly involved with those gunboats. Later on, when those gunboats were ready for service, a plan would be worked out giving the Navy operational responsibility for them, but their operations would be conducted under the Army's strategic direction and at the Army's expense. Although the command situation with the western river gunboats would change as the war developed, the transportation of Army personnel and supplies would be a Quartermaster Department function in all of its respects through to the end of hostilities.

The utilization of the western rivers as military transportation avenues would largely depend on the availability of steamboats. That availability, as measured in the time frame of 1861, was overwhelmingly to the advantage of the Union. During the first half of the 19th century, a period which marked the development of steam for river transport, the majority of the ownership of steamboats on the Mississippi system was in the hands of northern entrepreneurs. There were literally hundreds of such small businessmen, few of whom owned more than two or three vessels. Seldom did any corporative alliances bind these owners together for more than the shortest periods of time. As soon as it became apparent that communication was to be cut off with the South, most Northern owners brought their vessels up the Mississippi to Cairo, Illinois, and on into the Ohio system. Because of the disruption of trade caused by the closing off of the lower river systems, these vessels mainly became idle, resulting in a large availability of unemployed shipping on the upper river systems. This was a quartermaster's dream come true. Not only were vessels and crews theirs for the asking, but the types of craft were tailor made for the military needs of the moment. Wartime movements on the rivers would conceivably follow closely along prewar routes, so nothing really new had to be learned by the steamboatmen. It was only the dangers involved that would make it all seem different.

The Totten Report

Commencing with the onset of operations in the midwest, the availability of river transportation was the subject of intense interest to the Quartermaster General. In line with that interest, an initial inventory of all available floating craft was prepared during June of 1861 by Brevet Brigadier General Joseph G. Totten.[5] When Totten was asked to prepare his inventory, it had been requested that he make an analysis of the overall transportation situation on both the Mississippi and the Ohio systems. Although still active in the Army, Totten at the time was 73 years old; his report indicates the energy of a much younger man.[6]

On the Ohio River during the months of May and June 1861, Totten inventoried two hundred and fifty steam passenger vessels, most of which were at the time in a lay-up status. His estimate was that altogether, these vessels could carry seventy-five thousand men in one lift. A separate count was taken at Saint Louis where there were at the time another one hundred and fifty steam vessels, most of them idle, with a total lift capacity estimated at forty-five thousand men. Counted on the Ohio, were one hundred freight barges with a total capacity of two hundred and fifty barrels. About the same number (and capacity) of freight barges were counted as being available at Saint Louis. Additionally, the Ohio had two hundred coal barges with a capacity estimated at two million bushels; at Saint Louis, there was about the same number. Totten's report described how the barges could best be utilized in conjunction with troop movements. Each barge, he wrote, was capable of carrying enough coal for the largest steamer, "all the way to New Orleans." Totten reported that adequate tugs to tow the barges on both the Ohio and the Mississippi were available. The report next discussed the boat building facilities on the Ohio, stating that there were principle yards at Pittsburgh, Pennsylvania; at Wheeling in western Virginia; at Cincinnati, Ohio; and at Madison, New Albany, and Mound City, the latter three towns all in Illinois. At all of those places, except for Mound City, steam engines were reported as being manufactured in addition to "all necessary fittings." Totten concluded his discussion on shipyards by stating his support of the belief circulating in Army circles that the Navy should be included in the design and development of any attack craft that might be built for operations on the rivers. He strongly advised using naval officers in an advisory capacity for the procurement and construction phase of such craft. Attached as an annex were plans for gunboats. These had come from the Navy files of the Chief of the Bureau of Construction, Equipment, and Repairs at Washington, having been hauled out, dusted off, and handed over to Totten.

Totten annexed his recommendations by suggesting that every vessel, attack craft, or transport on the rivers should be supplied with a good river pilot who, in addition to his knowledge of the particular waters being navigated, should possess a grasp of the availability of local resources adjacent to that river. Totten suggested that the scope of such knowledge should include food supplies in the area, sources for drinking water, road access from the river to the interior, and any other items of intelligence which might prove "invaluable to troop commanders when landing troops." Apparently that suggestion was made so as to supplement knowledge already at hand since attached to the report was a table listing information on 121 landing places, all the way from Cincinnati on the Ohio River to Cairo and from Cairo southward to New Orleans. Data for each landing place included availability of coal, slope of the bank (an item of obvious interest in the relationship of the terrain for the landing of artillery and wagons), and any geographic features back from the river which might either aid in or detract from the deployment of troops.

General Scott endorsed Totten's report, passing it along to the Secretary of War, but with the added recommendation that sixteen gunboats, equipped with engines, should be built on the Ohio to be ready for use by the 20th of September (1861). Scott also recommended that the Secretary of War request of the Secretary of the Navy the loan to the Army of experienced naval officers to command each of the gunboats once they were ready for active service.

Official Records...Armies contains correspondence addressed to Totten from "his friend and cousin," Edward D. Mansfield. This is dated June 4, 1861, the day after Totten sent his report in to Scott. It was no doubt passed on later by Totten, probably as an addendum. It is complementary to Totten's descriptions in that it paints for us an even better picture of what the Union quartermasters then had to choose from on the upper rivers.

> First: There are sixty steamboats enrolled in the Port of Cincinnati of which number fifty-three are now in port [presumably laid up]. These boats average over three hundred tons and will doubtlessly carry and accommodate, with baggage, from four to five hundred each, say four hundred-- making twenty thousand.
>
> Second: There are at Pittsburgh, Wheeling, and etc., some forty or fifty more steamboats which are available, discarding the small ones; but if the lower Ohio is to be traversed at low water, then the small stern-wheelers are the best. We might count of the better class some forty more, making fifteen thousand men carriage.
>
> Third: At Louisville [on the Ohio River] and Saint Louis [on the upper Mississippi], there are probably fifty more boats of the largest size. These boats probably average double the tonnage of the others, [those on the Ohio] being boats which cannot pass the locks at Louisville. These large boats, taken together, would probably carry nearly as many as all on the upper Ohio. I should think steamboat accommodations could easily be had to move at one time sixty thousand men. If it were a successful movement, of course the number might be indefinitely increased. In this estimate, I include a considerable number of those which may not be fit for service. The packet-boats are not as desirable except in case of necessity, for they are constructed for a light business.
>
> Fourth: There are in the course of a year about forty towboats (barges) in the Cincinnati trade, a large part of which can no doubt be had...[7]

While discussing navigation problems, Mansfield gave his opinion that there should be close to five feet of water on the lower Ohio until about the middle of July, with the lowest water there being found generally during September and October.

Once past Cairo, heading south down the Mississippi, few problems were to be expected as the water was considerably deeper than in the Ohio. Mansfield qualified himself somewhat by stating that there were dangerous places between Cairo and Memphis and cautioned that he himself had once been at Memphis at lowest water and had found navigation to be rather difficult. Mansfield did not show any real familiarity with the river below Vicksburg.[8] Mansfield then gave his personal opinion of places on the Mississippi which he felt would have particular military value. He described Memphis as being one such place:

> I consider Memphis the most valuable military point on the Mississippi between New Orleans and Cairo -- as a defensible, and, as an aggressor point, more valuable than either of them. It is not only one of the very few high and comparatively healthy places on the river, but [in] its relationship to Arkansas, Mississippi, and Tennessee, it has peculiar advantages. The recent construction of railroads centering at that point has quadrupled its advantages.[9]

By his use of the term "centering" when discussing the railroads, Mansfield was referring to

- the Memphis and Ohio track which ran in a northeasterly direction from Memphis toward the Ohio Valley, and, once there, made its junction with the Baltimore and Ohio system;
- the track of the Memphis and Charleston which ran almost due east from Memphis to Corinth, the latter place being also the junction of the Mobile and Ohio track system which ran south to north.
- the Mississippi and Tennessee's rail line which ran directly from Memphis, south to Jackson, Mississippi, (a place east of Vicksburg) and then continued on to New Orleans.

Mansfield emphasized that Memphis was the only point on the Mississippi from "where you can go directly to Charleston, New Orleans, or through to the valley of the Tennessee." In his opinion, "the holding of Memphis by a military force is the same as the holding of the whole country in the valley of the Tennessee." [10]

The Army's Gunboat Fleet, Navy Manned

It is unclear as to where the idea originated for an amphibious attack force to specifically operate on the Mississippi River system. The most plausible answer is that the idea was planted by Winfield Scott. His original Anaconda plan had called for a fleet of transports to carry Union invaders down the Mississippi. Scott had theorized that these transports would be supported by "from twelve to twenty steam gunboats." It was also Scott who in June recommended the construction of sixteen ironclad gunboats. Clearly, though, the credit for the actual development of the program goes jointly to three men who worked sometimes together, sometimes not, but always toward the same goals. These were: the then military commander on the scene, Major General George McClellan; the Navy's Commander John Rodgers who would serve as construction supervisor for the gunboats; and James B. Eads, the person who would carry out their actual construction.

The two main facets dealing with Union movements on the western rivers -- first, the attack craft, and second, the transport fleet -- were kept organizationally separate right from the beginning. The discussion of how each element came into being must first start with the development phase for the gunboat force, soon to become known as the Union Army's Western Gunboat Flotilla.

The development of the gunboat force on the western rivers started off in May of 1861 with the creation of three "woodclads" which were converted from ordinary river steamers. These were the *A. O. TYLER*, the *LEXINGTON*, and the *CONESTOGA*.[11] Commander John Rodgers, who had been loaned to the Army by the Navy to supervise the conversion of these steamers into gunboats proudly reported on June 8, 1861, that the price of the three boats, taken together, was $97,000 originally paid to their builders, but that he had purchased them for only $62,000. He explained, though, that considerable alterations would have to be made, estimating that the total conversion costs, on top of the purchase price, would be somewhere in the area of $41,000. The projected date for completion of the work had been set by contract for the 27th of June. This same correspondence also referred to the employment of all "necessary pilots, engineers, and firemen here" (meaning the hiring of such people for the gunboats locally at or near Cincinnati).

Apparently Rodgers's report went out to Secretary of the Navy Gideon Welles by telegraph, as *Official Records...Navies* contains communication dated four days later from the Secretary to Rodgers. The Secretary, in a tone of mild reprimand, wired back that the act of buying the boats was a matter not for Rodgers or the Navy, but rather for the local Army quartermaster. The Secretary emphasized to Rodgers that henceforth, any purchases for the gunboat fleet should not be made via purchase orders issued by the Navy; rather all such purchasing was to be undertaken through Army channels. The Secretary further cautioned Rodgers that all recruitment of men for the gunboats, including their operating crews, was a matter to be left strictly for the Army. To his discomfiture, Rodgers was to find himself caught squarely in the middle of a developing misunderstanding between the Navy Department (fearful of getting stuck with the Army's bills), and local Army quartermasters who were jealously on guard as to the prerogatives of their own fiefdoms. Rodgers got more and more upset, not only because of the dilemma he was in, but also because of Welles's tone of censure. After stewing over the injustice of it, he telegraphed back to the Secretary:

> June 12, 1861
> General McClellan has approved the bill for steamboats. The written approval of a superior officer makes an act of purchase his own.
> /s/ John Rodgers, Commander, US Navy[12]

Such a communication sent to the Secretary of the Navy by a relatively junior naval officer was not the kind of thing designed to enhance that officer's standing with the head of his service. Rodgers was to find that out before too long a time had passed.[13]

Supplying crews for the Union gunboat fleet in the west was never to be easy. At the onset, it presented all sorts of new problems which in turn invited all sorts of new solutions. For instance, it was difficult to get local rivermen enthused over serving in what appeared to them to be potential coffins. Consequently, a good portion of the crews ended up being sent out from the east. In an article he wrote after the war, Henry Walke mentions that early in the war five hundred Army enlisted men were dispatched from Washington, DC, where they had been serving as temporary artillerists in the defense of that city.[14] Even after the gunboats were later transferred to the Navy (during the fall of 1862), these men seemingly remained on board. We next hear of them as mentioned in the following general order issued over the signature of David Dixon Porter on July 23, 1863:

> The commanders of vessels having Potomac soldiers on board will discharge them and send them to Cairo by the first opportunity. The soldiers who were temporarily loaned to the Navy will be sent to Vicksburg and delivered over to their respective regiments.[15]

The above order seems not to allude to those Army personnel who volunteered from western regiments. In January of 1862, Brigadier General Ulysses S. Grant had issued a circular to all company and regimental commanders within his jurisdiction on the Ohio and upper Mississippi rivers, calling on these officers to submit lists of those "river and seafaring men who are willing to volunteer to the gunboat service." While later discussing the need for those volunteers, Grant said that such men were absolutely necessary if the gunboats "were going to be used." It seems quite clear that the men volunteering were to transfer as soldiers and would remain soldiers while serving on the gunboats.[16]

The crews were not all Army by any means. One report mentions that "two, or three hundred" seamen of the US Revenue Service were drafted from their eastern ships and stations and sent west to the gunboats. Initially, there were a number of civilian employees hired to serve in assorted capacities ranging from pilots and engineers to deck hands. When the Navy took over the Western Gunboat Flotilla's gunboats in October of 1862, most of the civilians, including some of the pilots, were then militarized.[17]

Despite the Navy's disclaimers of responsibility for the purchase of vessels or supplies for the Army's gunboat fleet, it did agree quite early on to provide armaments considered suitable for installation on the gunboats. The authorization for that was by letter order dated June 17, 1861, from Secretary of the Navy Welles to Rodgers.[18] This order allowed Rodgers to request of the Bureau of Ordnance (Navy) those armaments which could be spared for installation on the Army craft then being made ready on the Ohio and on the Mississippi. Requisitions for the guns were to be funneled by Rodgers through Army channels, to be forwarded for endorsement to the Navy's Bureau of Ordnance. In another letter dated July 19, the Secretary of War expressed his understanding that the War Department would pay for any naval materiel which was furnished. Presumably, this would have also included cannon.

Alfred Thayer Mahan, the great naval theorist, when writing two decades later, tells us something of the guns with which the earliest of the gunboats were equipped.

The armament was determined by the exigencies of the time, such guns as were available being picked up here and there and forwarded to Cairo. The Army supplied thirty-five old 42-pounders, which were rifled, and so threw a 70-pound shell. These, having lost the metal cut away for grooves and not being banded, were called upon to endure the increased strain of firing rifled projectiles with actually less strength than had been allowed for the discharge of a round ball of about half the weight.

Such make-shifts are characteristic of nations that do not prepare for war, and will doubtless occur again in the experience of our Navy; fortunately, in this conflict, the enemy was as ill-provided as ourselves. Several of these guns burst; their crews could be seen eyeing distrustfully at every fire, and when at last they were replaced by sounder weapons, many were not turned into store, but thrown, with a sigh of relief, into the waters of the Mississippi. The remainder of the armament was made up by the Navy of old fashioned 32-pound and VIII [sic] smooth bore guns, fairly serviceable and reliable weapons. Each of these gunboats, when thus ready for service, carried four of the above described rifles, six 32-pounders of 43 CWT, and three VIII [sic] inch shell-guns; total, thirteen.[19]

McClellan was ordered east in July (1861) with orders to take over the command of the Army of the Potomac. His replacement in the west was John Charles Fremont, nicknamed by the press of the day as the "Pathfinder," due to his earlier exploits in western exploration. Fremont would prove to be pathetically devoid of any administrative talents. He also would fail to grasp the strategic picture for the Mississippi.

Initially, Fremont displayed an obsession with a static defense for Saint Louis. He had little appreciation of the reasons for trying to prevent Confederate forces from establishing strong points south of Saint Louis on the Mississippi River. Nor did he seem to appreciate the political disaster then developing throughout Missouri. In Missouri, Confederate partisans, and just plain bandits, were running rampant. It was fortunate for the gunboat program that Fremont looked upon that enterprise as a defensive means for guarding the river approaches to Saint Louis; otherwise, his lack of interest in the role it was really designed to play, that being the eventual conquest of the river corridor, could have resulted in the abandonment of the entire acquisition and construction effort. Coupled with Fremont's lack of strategic savvy was a misunderstanding of the command relationship which he was supposed to have with Commander Rodgers. He took an almost immediate dislike of Rodgers and did his best to undermine him. The antagonism may well have been fanned by Fremont's quartermasters who from the beginning had resented the incursion of a naval officer into their local purchasing programs.

Fremont was basically a political animal, a trait he exhibited in almost everything he did. Using his political contacts, he constantly by-passed normal Army channels of communication. This included his dealings with Rodgers when, in a letter addressed to Lincoln's Postmaster General Montgomery Blair, Fremont wrote:

> It would serve the public interest if Commander John Rodgers were removed and an officer directed to report to me to have command of the operations on the Mississippi. Show this to the President.[20]

By August 1861, recruiting for the gunboat crews had largely become the responsibility of the Navy, but the costs of their salaries were still chargeable to the Army's fiscal account. A report filed by Commander Rodgers and addressed to Secretary of the Navy Gideon Welles, dated Cincinnati, August 9, gave the wage rates for the officers and petty officers. These men were hired in a civilian capacity, but the salaries were based upon the Navy's established rates for naval personnel. Part of a report filed by Rodgers follows.

...I have appointed officers to the boats, taking the naval service as a basis, as follows:

	Salaries per month
One first master	$100.
One second master, as watch officer	80.
One third master	60.
Two pilots	150. each
One assistant surgeon	100.
One acting paymaster	100.
One chief engineer	100.
Three assistant engineers	75. each
One striker	25.
One armorer	30.
One carpenter	30.

The masters are divided in three classes: The first have been captains and the others mates. They have all high reputations for skill, efficiency, and morality, commanding generally by private steamboat owners [wages of] $150 to $200 per month. Mates also received from $60 to $120 per month.

The pilots are highly recommended.

The assistant surgeons are recommended by the medical faculty of the city. They have all enjoyed unusual facilities for acquiring knowledge in their professions by serving in hospitals for long periods.

The engineers were carefully selected.

With these appointments the gunboats are capable of a high degree of efficiency, and with them I hope to do good service.

I have been forced by the rates of wages for pilots on the Southern river to exceed the rates in the East. The pilots here claim and receive from private parties $250 per month. This is the rate fixed by themselves before the war and made obligatory upon them by an association, of which the great majority are members, called the Pilots' Association.

It was only with great difficulty, delay, and reluctance that they consented to take the less wages which I offered.

I have the honor to be, very respectfully, your obedient servant.

[Endorsement]

This whole subject belongs to the War Department.[21]

That the appointments were never considered as temporary commissions or warrants in the Navy is substantiated in a letter written by the Secretary of the Navy to one Joseph J. Davis dated Navy Department, August 12, 1861.

The gunboats on the Mississippi and Western rivers are under the control and direction of the War Department, with which the Navy has no connection either in building or fitting up of boats or officering them...[22]

Commander Rodgers was relieved of command on the western waters in early September, the result of the behind-the-scenes efforts by Fremont. His successor was Captain A. H. Foote, USN. Taken completely by surprise by orders to return east, Rodgers wrote a detailed letter to the Secretary of the Navy, describing the services which he had performed while on the western station. He expressed to Welles his suspicion that the reason he had been relieved was a misunderstanding over the requisitions for which he earlier had been chastised by the Secretary.[23] Rodgers seemed to have no realization at that time of the pressures which had been exerted against him by Fremont. Captain Foote, a friend of Rodgers, and in sympathy to Rodgers's embarrassment over being relieved, wrote a private letter to Assistant Secretary of the Navy, G. V. Fox. In it, Foote praised the work that Rodgers had performed to date in the construction program. This letter, taken together with Fremont's developing reputation for incompetence removed any stigma which may have been applied to Rodgers resulting from his reassignment.[24]

The gunboat fleet made up of converted steamers and newly constructed vessels was developing into something of real substance. The three original "woodclads" were to be joined by seven ironclads constructed from the keel up. This had been no simple task. Foote and the other naval officers working under him had to feel their way along in what was to them a totally strange working environment. In a report Foote sent to the Secretary of the Navy dated November 13, he related how service on the western rivers was contrary to the norm -- in fact totally alien to any naval experience of which he, Foote, was aware. He described in detail to the Secretary that his naval officers were laboring under severe handicap; they lacked standard Navy yard facilities or even the most fundamental access to the specialized equipment and stores required for gunboat service. Nevertheless, they were somehow getting things accomplished, and launchings were reported to be imminent.

As the matter is looked upon in retrospect, a lot of the success in what had so far transpired with the gunboat program was due to the extraordinary character and drive of James Eads who was playing the major role as the contractor for construction. Eads was an engineer and contractor of long experience. Despite overdue payments by the government, Eads took upon himself the fiscal risk, and the building continued without interruption, even under torch light. As the vessels came off the ways, they were quite close to being operationally ready. This was more than could have been reasonably expected under the prevalent conditions.

First Actions with the Gunboats

The *A. O. TYLER*, the *LEXINGTON*, and the *CONESTOGA*, all undergoing conversion at Cincinnati, were threatened with a falling river level. It looked like it might strand them at Cincinnati until the rains of late fall. To prevent that from happening, all three were moved down the Ohio River to Cairo. Although still unfinished, they would provide the newly arrived Foote with a mobility for operations that he had not previously enjoyed. A limited means was now available for a show of force southward on the Mississippi. Reports had been coming in that the Confederates were using the town of New Madrid, located on the west side of the Mississippi near the Kentucky - Tennessee line, as a staging area for disruptive forays into Missouri. Foote ordered Lieutenant S. Ledyard Phelps to take two of the gunboats, enlarge their crews and equipment by drawing from the third boat, and make a show of force in front of New Madrid. Three days following the receipt of that order, Phelps was on his way south.

At Island No. 8, near the town of Hickman, Phelps gave chase to two steamers which he described in his report as being "in the service of the rebels." Apparently, neither of the two were armed, as Phelps's fire was not returned. Phelps did not encounter any enemy fortifications. What was important was that the flag had now been shown south of Cairo.

Above Cairo, on the Missouri side, considerable Confederate activity had been taking place. It was generally in the form of harassment of river traffic and mistreatment of Union sympathizing farmers. No real takeover threat existed against Cairo although partisan activity did present a danger to the city's supply lines. Of even more importance were the political implications of allowing Confederate forces, irregular or not, to operate within what was popularly thought of as Union territory. On the 18th of August, all three gunboats, still in a somewhat unfinished state, moved up the Mississippi from Cairo toward Commerce. That town was reported to be near the center of operations for between eight hundred and one thousand of the enemy's irregulars. At Commerce, widespread fear was afoot, recently made worse by rumors of the kidnapping of young females who were to be used as "camp companions by the partisans." It is probably too complimentary to refer to these armed bands as anything but banditry, composed, as they were in most part, of the riffraff of Missouri, taking advantage of the wartime chaos by posing as Confederate irregulars. Many of them were as young as 12 years of age -- juvenile delinquents of the worst sort who seemed to enjoy themselves mainly by "destroying household property, robbing women and children of their wearing apparel, and carrying off the young girls to their camp." [25]

The gunboat patrol to Commerce proved fruitless. None of the banditry who had been causing trouble were even sighted; but again, the flag had been shown, and that was important in and of itself since it gave a little temporary reassurance to the citizens there. Phelps, in reporting directly to Fremont, said that the inhabitants had appealed to him for some sort of permanent Union garrison. They had stated with considerable logic that without that protection the bandits would be back. Commerce's problem was not a unique one, but neither troops nor the gunboats could be everywhere at once. For the time being, the Union's citizens in Missouri would have to fend for themselves.

Confederate Presence in Kentucky

On September 5, 1861, two gunboats under Phelps which were in escort to three Army transports left Cairo, heading up the Ohio. The transports were loaded with the 9th Illinois Infantry, the 12th Illinois Infantry, and four pieces of light artillery.

The expedition was commanded by Brigadier General Ulysses S. Grant who intended to repress a reported invasion of Confederate forces into neutral Kentucky. On the morning of September 6, Grant's force arrived off Paducah, Kentucky, a river town located at the junction of the Ohio and the Tennessee. Those aboard the transports were itching for a fight; but despite the presence of a considerable number of "secession flags" atop some of Paducah's buildings, not a shot was fired against them, and no enemy was even seen. Grant went ashore with a heavy troop guard and found out from talking with the citizenry that Confederate troops had been encamped within the town; but upon sighting the transports, they had high-tailed it out by road. Grant left most of his force there to hold the place, while he returned to Cairo. From Cairo, he telegraphed the colonel of the 8th Missouri, then upstream on the Mississippi at Cape Girardeau, to bring his command downriver to Cairo where they would board steamers which would take them to Paducah. A Union strong point had now been established on the Kentucky side of the Ohio, and Grant wanted to be sure he did not lose it.

That same month, two other expeditions were launched. The first was a foray by the gunboat *LEXINGTON* down the Mississippi to a point four miles above Hickman where artillery fire from the banks was encountered. Later in the month, a reconnaissance in force was made to Island No. 1. Steamers used as transports on that expedition were the *W. H. BROWN*, *JOHN GAULT*, *ROB ROY*, and the *D. A. JANUARY*.

Expedition to Columbus

In November (1861) a report had come in that the Confederates were establishing artillery batteries on the Mississippi River's eastern shore above Island No. 5. These emplacements were reported on the heights at Columbus across the river from the little town of Belmont, Missouri. Grant was ordered south to make a show of force and, if feasible, to dislodge the enemy from their positions. In escort to the transports that would carry the troops were the gunboats *A. O. TYLER* and *LEXINGTON*. Transports involved were the steamers *CITY OF MEMPHIS*, *CHANCELLOR*, *KEYSTONE*, *ALEX SCOTT*, and *MONTGOMERY*.[26]

Arriving upriver of the Columbus bluffs at dusk, the transports and the gunboats (the latter under the command of Commander Henry Walke) anchored for the night. The next morning, a scout brought in the news that Confederate troops were being ferried across the Mississippi onto the western shore near Belmont. Grant's immediate and correct impression was that these troops were reinforcements on their way into Missouri. This movement had long been anticipated by staff officers who worried that it could bring the troublesome Missouri problem to crisis proportions. Grant had come to the right place at the right time.

Anchors were quickly winched out of the Mississippi's mud, and the transports, with the gunboats taking up the van, proceeded downriver to a point about three miles upstream from Belmont where they were brought hard against the river's western bank. Grant's troops went ashore. The gunboats and transports then moved downriver in a cautious probe aimed at attacking the reported ferries. Confederate fire was opened from the bluffs and directed not at the armored gunboats -- as had been expected by Walke -- but instead, at the vulnerable transports which were bringing up

Walke's rear. When the gunners on the bluffs began making the range, Walke ordered the transports upstream and out of danger. The gunboats also withdrew in order to give covering fire in case the transports were brought under a direct attack from the river's banks. Once the transports arrived in what Walke believed was a relatively safe area, he returned downstream in a second attempt to intercept the ferries. Again, artillery from the bluffs intensified as the gunboats drew near. Although the fire coming from the bluffs was largely inaccurate, it was threatening enough for Walke to pull back. He dared not risk losing even one of the gunboats since the safety of the troops ashore might soon depend on the fire support they could offer. As it was, one round had already gone through the bulwarks of the *A. O. TYLER*, killing one man and wounding two others. The gunboat fleet had suffered its first casualties.

Ashore, Grant had initially gotten the upper hand, having penetrated inland to high ground; but as fresh Confederate forces began to arrive from the other side of the river, the situation started to reverse itself. He could see no alternative other than to retreat toward the transports; but he had no idea where the transports were. It was only by sheer luck that Grant's forward elements broke out onto the river at a point directly opposite from where the steamers were waiting. Their pilots immediately swung in toward the bank and dropped their loading ramps. As the embarkation was taking place, Confederate field guns opened up; but since the steamers as well as the troops waiting to board were under the lee of the bank, no harm resulted. The critical point would come when the transports started to move out into the river. Realizing this, Walke moved the *A. O. TYLER* and *LEXINGTON* in to give covering fire which was started as soon as the transports began to pull away. This kept Confederate heads down, enabling all five transports to get out into the river without suffering hits. But no sooner had they done so than it was discovered that one entire regiment as well as the squadron of cavalry which had been covering them had been left behind. One of the transports moved back toward the bank and again dropped its ramp. The infantry hustled aboard, followed by the cavalry screen. The last of the riders clattered over the gangway as the steamer's pilot jingled for paddle wheels astern.

OPERATIONS ON THE UPPER WESTERN RIVERS, 1862

Fort Henry on the Tennessee River

Fremont had been relieved of command of the western districts in November of 1861, to be replaced by Major General Henry W. Halleck. Foote and Grant, conferring with Halleck, agreed to a move against Fort Henry on the Tennessee River as soon as preparations could be made. The plan was that the fort would be taken under bombardment by the gunboats while Grant's infantry force disembarked on the river bank a short distance downstream from the fort. The infantry would come up to assault the works from the land side. The gunboat fire was not to be lifted until the infantrymen had almost gained the battlements.[27]

Grant had available around six thousand troops which could be utilized for the attack against Fort Henry while still leaving a sufficient force to guard Cairo. More troops were coming into Saint Louis and Cairo daily, and Grant believed that these could be sent forward to him as soon as transports became available to move them up the Ohio and into the Tennessee.

The gunboats assigned by Foote for the bombardment were the *CINCINNATI* (which had become the flag vessel of Foote); the *ESSEX*; the *CARONDELET*; and the *SAINT LOUIS*. These were all ironclads. The three wooden clad gunboats, the *A. O. TYLER*, the *LEXINGTON*, and the *CONESTOGA*, were to stand by as back-ups to remain downstream out of the range of Fort Henry's guns until needed.

The Quartermaster retained twenty-three transports for the operation: [28]

ALEX SCOTT	EMPRESS (armed)	IZETTA
BEN J. ADAMS	FAIRCHILD	MINNEHAHA
BALTIC	FANNY BULLITT	PRAIRIE ROSE
BEE	G. W. GRAHAM	R. M. PATTON
CHANCELLOR	HANNIBAL †	ROB ROY
CITY OF MEMPHIS	IATAN	THOMAS E. TUTT
D. A. JANUARY	ILLINOIS	V. F. WILSON
EMERALD		WHITE CLOUD

† *HANNIBAL* was to be reserved for use as a hospital boat, probably under the aegis of the Sanitary Commission.

The attack against Fort Henry commenced during the first week of February 1862. The gunboats advanced slowly upriver as if to test the effect of the Confederate's return fire until within about six hundred yards of the fort. Then a sustained fire was carried out. The fort's defenders struck their flag almost exactly one hour and fifteen minutes after the gunboats had commenced their bombardment, but by then Grant's infantry still had not arrived, having been delayed by what local inhabitants considered to be a suitable road. It was in actuality a quagmire of mud. Without the presence of the Army, the Confederate works were entered by a landing force from one of the gunboats. Once the men were inside the works, they discovered that the effect of the firing had not been a major factor toward the victory since casualties sustained by the Confederates were light. In fact, the gravest injuries to the enemy were brought on by one of the Confederate's own 24-pounders which burst, killing or disabling its entire crew as well as several other men in proximity to it. The surrender was actually a result of the Confederates' inability to continue any substantive defense.

The only serious damage to the attacking gunboats had occurred on the *ESSEX* which had received a shot directly into her boilers. This caused an explosion which badly scalded many of her crew, killing ten and wounding twenty-three, including her commanding officer, William David Porter, who received a painful scalding. The *CINCINNATI* had been hammered by thirty-one hits but took only one casualty. The *SAINT LOUIS* had received seven hits with no casualties; the *CARONDELET* six hits with no casualties. It was indeed a heady day for officers of the gunboat flotilla. A fixed battlement had surrendered to gunboats -- and this had happened without any troops in support. At least as far as Fort Henry was concerned, armored gunboats used against fixed shore installations had become a proven form of warfare.

As soon as Grant came on the scene, he asked Foote to dispatch a gunboat section up the Tennessee for reconnaissance. While they were upriver, they were to destroy or disable all installations considered to be in support of the Confederate Army as well as all ferries and bridges so as to adversely impact the enemy's transportation. Any steamboats encountered were to be captured and, if feasible, brought downriver under prize crews. Otherwise, they were to be sunk in place. This assignment went to Lieutenant Phelps of the *CONESTOGA* with *LEXINGTON* and *A. O. TYLER* attached.

Phelps's first stop was to be the bridge of the Memphis, Clarksville, and Louisville Railroad. He found the draw closed. A landing party discovered that the machinery for opening the bridge had been deliberately disabled. This proved especially frustrating for the gunboat crews as they had sighted above the bridge several "rebel transport steamers," their wakes fast fading. A repair party was put to work, and in less than an hour, the bridge was open. The *CONESTOGA*, in company with *LEXINGTON*, then headed upstream. Left behind was the *A. O. TYLER*, whose crew was under orders to destroy the railroad tracks in proximity to the bridge's eastern approaches. Once the track was put out of order, *A. O. TYLER* was to follow.[29] Phelps soon overhauled and captured one of the fleeing Confederate craft. By this time, *A. O. TYLER* had come up, her prize lashed alongside. Again leaving *A. O. TYLER* in their wake, *CONESTOGA* and the *LEXINGTON* continued up the river, where their crews captured two more steamers intact. Phelps's appearance on the upper river where no Union warship had been expected caused the crews of six other vessels (ferryboat types) to scuttle before Phelps's men could get aboard. There was enough evidence still left above the water on all of them to indicate that they had been loaded with military supplies which probably had been consigned to Fort Henry. *CONESTOGA* and *LEXINGTON* continued upriver as far as the foot of Muscle Shoals before turning back. For the return trip to Fort Henry, the three prizes, *EASTPORT*, *SALLIE WOOD*, and *MUSCLE*, were taken under tow. The *MUSCLE*, which had been damaged during her capture, began taking on water and had to be abandoned.

Phelps's reconnaissance -- when examined overall -- was a marked success. In addition to the successful captures and the destruction of seven other vessels, valuable intelligence was gained. Phelps would report to Foote that the local population near the banks of the river seemed to be Union to the core. If this was an accurate appraisal of the population as a whole, then Grant could be assured in the future of an active source of support and intelligence which would become useful in any future penetrations of the valley of the Tennessee.

Fort Donelson

With Fort Henry now in Union hands, Grant's next move was to be against Fort Donelson on the Cumberland River. This was an enemy fortification lying about twelve miles eastward from Fort Henry across a strip of high ground which, prior to the Tennessee Valley Authority projects of the twentieth century, divided the Tennessee River from the waters of the Cumberland. Prior to the attack on Fort Henry, the gunboat *CONESTOGA* had made a patrol up the Cumberland and found it clear of obstacles to a point within sight of Fort Donelson. Although it was rumored that the Cumberland River might be mined, the high water conditions then prevailing gave a reasonable assurance that the gunboats and transports would have adequate clearance over any mines which might be moored to the bottom.[30]

Grant sent patrols out from Fort Henry over the two roads which led in the direction of Fort Donelson. One of these roads connected the two forts almost directly. The other, the Dover Road, meandered somewhat before reaching the town of Dover which was located a little distance upriver of Fort Donelson. Grant believed that by using both of these roads for an approach, any Confederates who were attempting to escape from Fort Donelson could be cut off. Meanwhile, Foote moved his gunboats downstream into the Ohio to wait for the transports that were due in from Cairo with additional troops. For one soldier who was making that steamboat trip from Cairo to the Cumberland, the transport "was like an open car loaded with hogs in bad weather going to market."[31]

Fort Donelson proved to be a much tougher proposition than Fort Henry had been. The terrain on the land side of the Confederate works was broken in elevation, so much so as to deny visual communication between any attacking units.[32] Because of the irregular terrain, Grant's army would have to make its approach in column formation which would be risky as it denied adequate flanking protection. When finally in position and ready for the attack, the Union regiments stretched irregularly over hill and dale, most of the regiments being out of sight from one another. To make matters even more difficult, no one had any idea as to any transports the rebels might have in the river above Fort Donelson. Until the river upstream of the fort could be secured, merely blocking the land approaches to Fort Donelson from the south could not prevent fresh troops from reinforcing the fort. Nor could the garrison be prevented from escaping should its commander have a mind to evacuate the place. For this reason, it was decided to delay the attack in hopes that Foote's gunboats could run the Confederate batteries, thus blocking off the river from upstream.

During the waiting period, the weather worsened, and life for everyone became a misery. In this first year of the war, the Union soldiery had not developed the wisdom that comes from long field experience. When Grant's troops had left Fort Henry, the weather had been fine, and only a few of the men had stopped to think that it might not always remain that way. Overcoats, blankets, and even knapsacks had been left behind at Fort Henry. With the weather change, the unprepared troops now became wet and half frozen.

As soon as the gunboats came into proximity of the fort, they opened a heavy fire. This time, it was not to be the one-sided contest that had been the case at Fort Henry. The wheel of the *SAINT LOUIS* and the tiller and the smoke stacks of the *LOUISVILLE* were shot away, both craft being set adrift downriver. Casualties were heavy, especially in the case of pilot house personnel. *PITTSBURG* had begun taking on water, and her commander maneuvered to move her out of range. *CARONDELET*, hugging in close to the fort, kept pouring in a cannonade, but that soon ceased when *PITTSBURG* collided with her. *CARONDELET* was then forced to withdraw. After that happened, the remainder of the gunboats retired downstream and out of range. Since it was clearly apparent that a way past the fort could not be gained by the gunboats, Grant prepared to begin a land attack.

As might have been expected because of the lack of communication between regiments, confusion reigned when the assaulting troops moved forward. Troop commanders were unable to determine what was going on to their right or to their left. Altogether that day, three assaults were made. Each was repulsed. Soon the horror started -- something which happened all too often in Civil War battles. The firing had set underbrush and grass ablaze. The Union wounded, unable to escape the flames, were roasted alive. Their screams did little to enhance the morale of those who waited for orders to again move up against the enemy.

Despite the damage that his artillery had inflicted on Foote's gunboats, Major General Simon Buckner, the Confederate commander of Fort Donelson, realized that it was only a matter of time before he would have to give up. The fort was by this time surrounded on its land side. The one opening Buckner had, namely, the river, was of little benefit without steamers, and he had nothing available along those lines. His only option was to attempt to cut his way out or suffer the loss of his entire garrison through surrender. The two most senior officers under Buckner at Fort Donelson, Gideon J. Pillow and John B. Floyd, were each given their choice as to what to do. Both voted to try and break out. The first attempt punched an opening in the Union line, but the temporary advantage gained was soon lost when the Confederate troop commanders were slow to react to that advantage. Their sluggishness gave Grant time to plug the gap. About twenty-five hundred officers and men were able to escape following this when a contact was finally made with the only two steamers left on the upper Cumberland. A cavalry unit under Nathan Bedford Forrest also managed to get out by wading their horses across a chest-deep swamp which looked so impenetrable that Grant's people had not bothered to guard it.

Meanwhile, the gunboats *SAINT LOUIS* and *LOUISVILLE* came back upriver and began firing against the Confederate works. It was at that point that Buckner made his personal decision to surrender. He asked Grant for terms. In response, he received the famous "unconditional surrender" offer:

> Sir:
> Yours of this date proposing armistice and appointment of commissioners to settle term of capitulation is just received. No terms except unconditional and immediate surrender can be accepted.
> I propose to move immediately upon your works.

To this, Buckner replied:
> The distribution of the forces under my command incident to an unexpected change of commanders and the overwhelming force under your command, compel me, notwithstanding the brilliant success of the Confederate arms yesterday, to accept the ungenerous and unchivalrous terms which you propose.[33]

Before the day was out, Grant's army marched into Fort Donelson. The total loss to the Union Army and Navy: 510 killed, 2152 wounded, and 224 captured or missing.[34] For the Confederate side, the casualty statistics are less clear. In his memoirs, Grant stated that he had asked Buckner what force there was to surrender at Donelson, receiving the reply that the number was uncertain. Later, in his official report sent to Richmond, Buckner claimed that after all escapees, dead, and wounded had been subtracted, there were about nine thousand men which he had left to surrender.[35]

In his report of the attack against Fort Donelson, Foote listed the *SAINT LOUIS*, the *CARONDELET*, the *LOUISVILLE*, the *PITTSBURG*, the *A. O. TYLER*, and the *CONESTOGA* as having taken part in the actual bombardment. He reported heavy damage to the *SAINT LOUIS* and *LOUISVILLE* with both the *PITTSBURG* and the *CARONDELET* having received moderate injury from projectiles penetrating above their water lines. (*CARONDELET* was also damaged from the collision with *PITTSBURG*.) The *SAINT LOUIS* had received fifty-nine cannon shot -- four of them into her hull above the waterline and one taken in the pilot house, this last round having wounded Foote. Aboard the *CARONDELET*, one of the long suspect rifled guns had burst. Altogether in casualties, the gunboats suffered fifty-four killed and wounded. The two most badly damaged of the gunboats were sent back to Cairo for repairs. Two of the gunboats were left to stand guard over the transports while the *A. O. TYLER* was dispatched back to the Tennessee River, there to disable the railroad bridge of the Memphis, Clarksville, and Louisville. (This was the same bridge that Phelps's people had worked on to open during their probe up the Tennessee following the taking of Fort Henry.)[36]

Postmortem of the Fort Henry and Fort Donelson Operations

One Confederate officer's opinion regarding the military value of gunboats was written following the attack against Fort Henry and before the bombardment of Fort Donelson began. The writer was Major Jeremy F. Gilmer, Chief Engineer, Western Department, CSA.

> The attack expected here [at Fort Donelson] is a combined one; gunboats by water and a land force in the rear.
>
> The greatest danger, in my opinion, is from the gunboats which appear to be well protected from our shot. The effect of our shot at Fort Henry was not sufficient to disable them, or any one of them, as far as I have been able to ascertain. This was due, I think, in a great measure to the want of skill of the men who served the guns and not to the invulnerability of the boats themselves.
>
> I saw five gunboats during the attack on Fort Henry, each firing three heavy guns from ports in the bows. It has been reported from various sources that there were seven boats in the Tennessee River at the time of the attack. Only five were engaged at any one time in my opinion.
>
> With the preparations that are now being made here, I feel much confidence that we can make a successful resistance against a land attack. The attack by water will be more difficult to meet. Still I hope for success here also.[37]

Gilmer's assessment was to be countered by the events at Fort Donelson. In a report written the month after his escape from Fort Donelson, the Confederate Gideon J. Pillow described the limitations of gunboats.

> Huntsville, Alabama
> March 3, 1862
>
> My fight with the gunboats at Donelson proves that they cannot withstand heavy metal. To fight them successfully, I suggest as a result of experience, the importance of holding your fire for point blank range; also the importance of having all your shot and shell for rifle well greased with tallow to avoid the danger of bursting the gun. I did it under long and continued fire with perfect safety. [According to Northern newspapers,] the Federal officers admitted at Donelson that their gunboats could not stand the fire of heavy metal. I disabled four of the five whose fire I returned.[38]

The logbook of *PITTSBURG* spelled out the details of what the experience was like during the operation against Fort Donelson.

> Underway -- At Cairo...in company with the *SAINT LOUIS* (flagship) and *LOUISVILLE*, and started up the Ohio River.
>
> Accident to boiler -- ...A bolt came out of the boiler, which should not prevent the boat's running, as, owing to the skill and activity displayed by the chief engineer, the boiler was repaired sufficiently...
>
> Alarm of fire -- While repairs were being made, an alarm of fire was given...bulkhead on starboard side of the engine taking fire from its close proximity to boiler. Prompt action in extinguishing the fire saved us...
>
> Pilot -- At Paducah, we took on board another pilot who remained with us until Saturday... when I allowed him to be transferred to a transport in need of the services of a pilot...

Thursday, the 13th, protection to boilers...Had one hundred bread bags filled with coal and stowed around the boilers as likely to afford some protection... against shot. Subsequently, during the day, increased that protection by adding the men's hammocks to the coal bags.

Anchored two miles from Donelson -- 10:15 p.m., came to anchor during a heavy fall of snow alongside the *CARONDELET*, about two miles this side of Fort Donelson...

2:10 p.m., weigh anchor and start toward the fort, gradually approaching same, in company with the other gunboats...we fired a round of 15-second shell from our three bow guns...Approaching with caution, nearer and nearer to the fort, we continued firing shell, reducing the 15-second to the 5-second fuse...boat was making water, I fell downstream and only kept afloat long enough to get out of the range of enemy's guns by running my guns aft, thus lightening her at the bow, where she had received two large shot between wind and water. That was the termination of my action in that affair... [In addition to the shell damage received, it was at this point that *PITTSBURG* collided with *CARONDELET.*]

Injuries -- The injuries sustained by the boat are numerous, having received at least thirty shots...The next in importance, perhaps, is a 128-pound round shot through the pilot house, in which at the time were the four pilots [civilians], none of whom were injured...

We are unfortunate in having to report but two men severely wounded and not a man killed...

Pumps on board were not sufficient to keep the boat afloat, nor had we material of which to construct others...Remained here until Saturday, 2:15 p.m., when we got underway for Cairo...

Sunday, 16th, 1:35 p.m. -- Got underway again for Cairo...Joint of the safety valve loosened causing steam to escape so fast as to fill the gun deck in a few moments...repaired valve... got underway...arrived at Cairo, [9:50 p.m.], having been absent say 5 days and 14 hours.[39]

The campaign to take Fort Henry and Fort Donelson, and a later movement up the Tennessee River which culminated in the Battle of Shiloh, called for an extremely high volume of troop movements. An essential element in all those actions and in many more to come was the role of transports. The task of gathering together and routing these transports was given to the Union Army's Quartermaster Department. The responsibility for carrying it out came to fall on one man, Lewis Baldwin Parsons. (The part that Parsons played has been largely neglected by historians. Erna Risch, in her fine work *Quartermaster Support of the Army: A History of the Corps, 1775-1939,* delineates Parsons's role, but she neglects the tremendous impact this man had on the efficiency of movement on the western rivers. Appendix B is an examination of the methods used by Parsons in developing a system for the Army's marine transportation on the western rivers.)

The Situation Following Fort Donelson

On February 19, Foote, still ambulatory despite the scalding wounds he received at Fort Donelson, proceeded up the Cumberland to Clarksville with the gunboats *CONESTOGA* and *CAIRO*. On his arrival, Foote discovered the enemy's defenses there to be deserted. The retreating Confederates had burned the bridge belonging to the Memphis, Clarksville, and Louisville Railroad. This bridge had connected the rail line on the west side of the Cumberland River to the railroad junction at Clarksville. From the Clarksville junction, one line of track ran westward to Memphis on the Mississippi. Another line of track ran east to Bowling Green, Kentucky, itself a major rail and road junction. The *A. O. TYLER*, which Foote had dispatched up the Tennessee River, had just burned the railroad bridge crossing that river so all rail transport serving the area from the west was now effectively denied, not only to the Confederates, but to Grant's army as well.

While Foote was upriver at Clarksville, six of the newly constructed mortar boats were being towed into the Cumberland en route upriver to Fort Donelson. Foote and Grant planned to use these in a joint movement against Nashville.

Second Expedition to Columbus, Kentucky

Shortly after the taking of Fort Donelson an amphibious force consisting of four ironclad gunboats, one wooden gunboat, and two mortar boats, all in attendance to five troop laden transports, headed downstream on the Mississippi from Cairo. The date was February 23. The object of this expedition was to capture and hold the bluffs at Columbus which commanded the river at that point.

When the expedition came within sight of the bluffs, the Confederates were seen in the process of evacuating the place. With Fort Henry and Fort Donelson lost, the enemy realized that their position at Columbus had become untenable. The decision had been made to move to positions downriver in the general area of Island No. 10.

Once caught by the Union force in the act of pulling out, the Confederates became highly vulnerable since most of their artillery was already dismounted for transport. The enemy commander's reaction was to try a trick by calling for a parley, alleging as its purpose the desire to obtain permission for families of officers taken at Fort Henry and at Fort Donelson to cross the Union lines to visit their men folk. This deceit worked. The time taken up by the talks was just exactly what the Confederates needed to get the rest of their troops and equipment loaded aboard steamboats. By the time the Union commander awoke to the fact that he had been duped, the last barge load of guns and munitions was safely heading down the Mississippi. A patrol going ashore found the bluffs to be deserted.

The Situation in Kentucky and Tennessee

Sympathy for the Confederacy which had earlier existed in Kentucky was gradually fading away. The Kentucky state government, realizing it could no longer straddle the political fence, ordered all Confederate troops out of the state. The order did not mean an automatic cooperation with the Lincoln Administration, but it did mean that the Confederacy was no longer a tolerated guest nor could it count on logistical assistance from the Kentucky state government.

With their communications becoming increasingly insecure, the Confederate garrison at Bowling Green was evacuated just before the surrender of Fort Donelson. This opened part of the Memphis, Louisville, and Nashville system's right of way for Union use. On the Tennessee River the way was clear for Union gunboats as far upstream as Muscle Shoals, but that was subject to change should the enemy choose to move up out of Alabama.

The Cumberland River was now open for Union shipping to Clarksville. The remaining Confederate presence in northern Tennessee had become narrowly concentrated in the area surrounding Nashville. Nashville had never been thought of by the Confederates as a city to defend; therefore, no battlements of a permanent nature had been established there. Besides that, relationships with the civil population had been discouraging from the onset. This was brought out with clarity when the senior officer of the Confederate Army in Tennessee, Major General Albert Sidney Johnston, suggested blocking the Cumberland River by the use of a huge raft apparatus. His idea had been met with spirited opposition from the locals, most of whom were quite frank in their lack of concern over Confederate military fortunes. The local steamboat interests argued with vigor that a blockage of the river would ruin not only the commercial viability of the immediate Cumberland Valley, but the economy of the entire region along with it. Clearly, dedication toward the South's cause was not a plentiful commodity at Nashville.

The raft issue at Nashville was indicative of the lack of business support the Confederate armed forces faced in most sections of Tennessee as well as within Kentucky. It also came close to reflecting the general attitude of much of the business community throughout the South. During the Civil War, a sort of laissez-faire attitude within the civilian sector of the Confederacy more often than not dominated. In line with Jefferson Davis's personal philosophy, the central government of the Confederacy continually held that private enterprise was not to be interfered with. This policy held sway in a number of scenarios where a subjugation of business interests in favor of military exigency could have had a beneficial effect on military operations. A governmental policy in favor of business freedom continued almost to the end of the Civil War, particularly in regard to the government's use of river shipping and the railroads. More than once in his book *Confederate Supply,* Richard D. Goff brings out that Confederate armies in the field were denied rations and even the means for troop reinforcement because the railroads were permitted to carry commercial and civilian traffic at times when the military badly needed full use.

Federal troops occupied Nashville without opposition on February 26, 1862. Giving up the city meant the loss to the Confederacy of the valuable manufacturing facilities located there. For the Union Army, Nashville had potential value as the location for a quartermaster and commissary depot. Well positioned in proximity to railroad service and to the river systems of both the Tennessee and the Cumberland, Nashville would soon become a vital supply hub from which the Federal armies in the west would expand their operations.

Shiloh

During February and March, Confederate troops had concentrated in great force at the important railroad junction at Corinth, Mississippi which was practically on the line between the states of Tennessee and Mississippi and about fifteen miles west of the great bend of the Tennessee River.[40]

After the capture of Fort Donelson, the casual side of Ulysses S. Grant's personality led him into trouble with his superior, Major General Henry W. Halleck. Exaggerated stories about Grant's drinking, when joined with his carelessness in reporting to Halleck as to what he had been doing and what he planned to do next, resulted in Grant's temporary removal from command.

Properly censured, Grant soon got his army back. Once it was marshaled for movement up the Tennessee River by steamer, Grant scheduled landings on the Tennessee's western bank at a point to the northeast of Corinth. An additional thirty-five hundred Union troops were marching overland to join Grant. These were coming from Nashville and were under the command of Major General Don Carlos Buell.

Foote's gunboats steamed up the Tennessee River in advance of the departure of Grant's transports. Foote had a pretty fair idea of what he could expect upriver. Prior gunboat patrols had established the whereabouts of some spotty Confederate presence along the river, and gunboat skippers had already picked out where troops could be landed on the river with the least difficulty. The area around Pittsburg Landing was tentatively selected as a good point from which troops could move overland toward the Confederate concentrations at Corinth. Pittsburg Landing became the subject of an updated reconnaissance when the place was passed by the gunboat *LEXINGTON* and a white flag was seen flying from the bank. When a party was sent ashore to establish the reason for the flag, no one was to be seen. The *LEXINGTON* then moved downstream to explore Savannah Landing on the eastern side of the river. This was where Buell's troops, marching overland from Nashville, were scheduled to arrive. Savannah Landing was also found to be unoccupied.

On March 8 at Craven's Landing (also called Coffee Landing and about ten miles downstream from Pittsburg Landing), the transport *GOLDEN GATE* put ashore a contingent of troops with the purpose of establishing a patrol sweep along the western bank upstream to Pittsburg Landing. They found the way to be clear. On March 12, under a precautionary covering fire from the *LEXINGTON*, five troop transports put their passengers ashore at Pittsburg Landing. While the area near the river bank was being searched for the presence of the enemy, the *LEXINGTON*, in company with the gunboat *A. O. TYLER*, made an upstream reconnaissance of the river as far as Muscle Shoals. During that patrol, they destroyed everything that looked like it might be used for transporting enemy troops downriver to interfere with the landings.

Intermixed with the fleet of troop transports which were now steaming en masse up the Tennessee toward Pittsburg Landing were supply vessels loaded with all manner of military goods. One of them, the *FORT WAYNE*, came up with pontoon boats which were to be used to bridge the river at Savannah Landing so Buell's troops could cross once they arrived on the Tennessee's eastern bank. No one in the Union command, including Grant himself, seemed to have perceived at this time of the possibility of an aggressive movement by Johnston who now, unbeknownst to Grant, was advancing toward Pittsburg Landing from Corinth. Instead, the anticipation seems to have been that once Buell arrived, the Union Army could simply march unopposed toward Corinth. Early in the forenoon on April 6, that preconception was shattered.

The first indication of trouble came when firing was heard coming from a point inland of Pittsburg Landing. *A. O. TYLER* and *LEXINGTON* were near at hand, and their commanders moved their vessels into position so they could offer covering fire if it was required. It soon was. As early as the noon hour, stragglers and wounded from the Union advance force began coming down to the river bank to report a rapidly deteriorating situation. It seemed that on their arrival at a crossroads called Shiloh Church, Grant's advance force had set up temporary encampments, but no defensive entrenchments or supportive artillery positions had been prepared. The Confederates were now streaming through these tenting grounds, stopping only long enough to dine out of abandoned Union cooking pots.

Buell's column arrived in the nick of time. Prior to that point, the situation had deteriorated to dangerous proportions. Since the pontoon bridge was not yet in place, Buell's people were ferried across the Tennessee by waiting transports. A major obstacle in the effort to get troops inland from Pittsburg Landing to form into a line of battle were the hundreds of stragglers drifting in retreat toward the river from Shiloh Church.

Not all of Grant's army had been forced back. When Buell arrived at the scene, the Union center was holding, and from heavily thicketed cover, it was pouring a withering fire into the Confederate ranks. It was this center upon which Buell's line of resistance anchored itself.[41] One of the Confederates killed by the Union musketry was the enemy commander, Albert Sidney Johnston. He was hit in the leg by a mini-ball which severed an artery, causing him to bleed to death within minutes. His second-in-command, Brigadier General P. G. T. Beauregard, then took over.

The fighting stopped at nightfall. After dark, Union reinforcements came up, and Grant used the hours of darkness to reorganize. With first light the next morning, the battle resumed, soon turning into a slugging match with neither side making inroads against the other. By midday, Beauregard knew he was accomplishing nothing and realized that without adequate reserves, he could not sustain his lines if they were penetrated. He therefore ordered a retreat back toward Corinth.

At the start of the Confederate attack, Grant had been downriver at Savannah Landing on the transport *TIGRESS,* awaiting the arrival of Buell's men. As soon as he heard of the enemy attack, he ordered the *TIGRESS* upriver to Pittsburg Landing. In his report covering the events of that day, Grant would describe what had happened; but in so doing, he glossed over the fact that although victorious in the end, he had allowed his command to become carelessly exposed, opening it to a potential disaster.

> It becomes my duty to again report another battle fought between two great armies, one contending for the maintenance of the best government ever devised, the other for its destruction. It is pleasant to record the success of the Army contending for the former principle.
>
> On Sunday morning [April 6], our pickets were attacked and driven in by the enemy. Immediately, the five divisions stationed at this place were drawn up in a line of battle ready to meet them. The battle soon waxed warm on the left and the

center, veering at times to all parts of the line. The most continuous firing of
musketry and artillery ever heard on this continent was kept up until nightfall, the
enemy having forced the entire line to fall back nearly half way from their camps to
the [Pittsburg] Landing.

At a late hour in the afternoon, a desperate effort was made by the enemy to
turn our left and get possession of the landing, transports, etc. This point was
guarded by the gunboats *TYLER** and *LEXINGTON*, Captains Gwin and Shirk, US
Navy , commanding, four 20-pounder Parrott guns and a battery of rifled guns. As
there is a deep and impassable ravine for artillery or cavalry, and very difficult for
infantry, at this point, no troops were stationed here, except the necessary artillerists
and the small infantry force for their support. Just at this moment, the advance of
Major General Buell's column arrived...an advance was immediately made upon the
point of attack and the enemy was soon driven back. In this repulse, much is due to
the presence of the gunboats *TYLER** and *LEXINGTON* and their able commanders,
Captains Gwin and Shirk....[42]

* A. O. TYLER

If the battle at Shiloh is to be evaluated only on the basis of a body count,
things had come out about equal on each side. Grant lost 1,754 killed; 8,408 wounded
with 2,885 missing and captured. Confederate casualties were 1,723 killed; 8,012
wounded with 959 missing and captured. While Grant had been backed by a
tremendous amount of materiel and fresh troops coming upriver in reserve, Beauregard
had no such support.

Grant's army could not have arrived where it did and in such strength
without the lift capability provided by the multitude of transports. The size of that
armada must have been inspiring to those in witness.

It has generally been claimed that up to 152 transport steamers were
involved at Shiloh, taking part either during the buildup phase, the period of the battle,
or the follow-up support. One source for this claim is T. M. Hurst whose list is
included within an article entitled "The Battle of Shiloh," published in the *Tennessee
Historical Magazine,* July 1919. J. Haden Alldredge, et al, reproduced the Hurst list
within *A History of Navigation on the Tennessee River System* (pp 150, 151) and
added by name another twenty additional steamboats.[43] While the Alldredge work
gave no cite for its additional twenty vessels, the information undoubtedly came from
Official Records...Navies, Volume 22 of Series I. We located within Volume 22,
pp 784, 785, two more vessels which were not mentioned by either Hurst or Alldredge.
The full list totaling 174 vessels is reproduced below. Regarding the Hurst and
Alldredge list: We have used notes to indicate what we believe to be the proper name
representations.

From Hurst List

A. MCDOWELL
ADAM JACOBS
ALEX SCOTT
AMERICUS
ANGLO-SAXON
ARGYLE
ARMADA
ATHY WATHAM
AURORA
AUTOCRAT
BALTIC
BAY CITY
BELLE OF THE WEST
B. J. ADAMS [3]
BEN SOUTH
BLACK HAWK
BOSTON
BOSTONA NO. 1
BOSTONA NO. 2
CHAMPION NO. 2
CHAMPION NO. 4
CHANCELLOR
CHARLEY BOWEN [1]
CHARLEY MILLER [1]
CHOUTEAU [8]
CITY BELLE
CITY OF ALTON
CITY OF MADISON
CITY OF MEMPHIS
CLARA POE
CLARIONET
COMMERCE
COMMERCIAL
CONTINENTAL
CORONET
COUNTESS
CRESCENT CITY
D. A. JANUARY

D. J. TAYLOR [2]
DIAMOND
DUETT
DUNLEITH
E. W. FAIRCHILD [4]
EDWARD WALSH
ELENORA
EMERALD
EMILIE
EMMA
EMMA NO. 2
EMPIRE
EMPIRE CITY
EMPRESS
EQUINOX
EUGENE
EVANSVILLE
FALLS CITY
FANNIE BARKER
FANNY BULLITT
FOREST QUEEN
FORT WAYNE
GLADIATOR
GLENDALE
GOLDEN STATE
GOSSAMER
GRAY EAGLE
HAVANA
HAZEL DELL
HENRY FITZHUGH
HIAWATHA
HORIZON
IATAN
IMPERIAL
INDIANA
IOWA
IZETTA
J. B. FORD

J. B. DICKEY [5]
J. C. SWAN [6]
J. S. PRINGLE
J. W. CHAPMAN
J. W. HILLMAN
J. W. KENNETT
JACOB POE
JAMES H. TROVER
JESSE K. BELL
JEWESS
JOHN BELL
JOHN GAULT
JOHN D. ROE [7]
JOHN RAINE
JOHN WARNER
JONAS POWELL
LADY PIKE
LANCASTER NO. 3
LANCASTER NO. 4
LENI LEOTI
LEONORA
LEWELLYN
LIBERTY
LIZZIE SIMMONS
LOUISIANA
MANHATTAN
MARBLE CITY
MARENGO
MARY E. FORSYTH
MASONIC GEM
MEMPHIS
METEOR
MINNEHAHA
MUSSELMAN [9]
NASHVILLE
NEBRASKA
NEW UNCLE SAM
NIAGARA

OHIO
OHIO NO. 3
ORIENTAL
PHANTOM
PINK VARBLE
PLANET
POLAND
PRAIRIE ROSE
REBECCA
ROCKET
ROSE HAMBLETON
S. W. THOMAS
SAINT CLAIR
SAINT JOHN
SALINE
SALLIE LIST
SCOTIA
SHENANGO
SILVER MOON
SILVER WAVE
SIR WILLIAM WALLACE
SOUTH WESTER
SPREAD EAGLE
SUNNY SOUTH
SUNSHINE
T. J. PATTEN
T. L. MCGILL
TECUMSEH
TELEGRAM NO. 3
TIGRESS
TRIBUNE
TYCOON
UNIVERSE
WESTMORELAND
WHITE CLOUD
WILD CAT
WISCONSIN
YORKTOWN

[1] CHARLIE
[2] DANIEL G. TAYLOR
[3] BEN J. ADAMS

[4] E. H. FAIRCHILD
[5] JOHN H. DICKEY
[6] J. J. SWAN

[7] JOHN J. ROE
[8] HENRY CHOUTEAU
[9] JACOB MUSSELMAN

Additional vessels from Alldredge list:

BELLE CREOLE
CAIRO
DENMARK
FAIRCHILD
GOODY FRIENDS

H. D. BACON
HANNIBAL
HENRY CLAY
JOHN RAMM
LADY JACKSON

LAKE ERIE
METROPOLITAN
NEW ERA
OHIO BELLE
PLATTE VALLEY

SPITFIRE
SUPERIOR
THOMAS E. TUTT
WAR EAGLE
WILSON*

* V. F. WILSON

Additional vessels located by Gibson: *GOLDEN GATE* and *N. W. THOMAS*.

The Taking of Island No. 10

Island No. 10 can be geographically described as one of those transitory land bodies that naturally exist for varied spaces of time in areas of unleveed flat land through which the Mississippi River flows. The shape of the island has changed to a marked degree since the 1860s. In 1862, it was a two-mile long low land mass in the center of a great S-curve bend of the Mississippi. The town of Hickman, Kentucky, was situated at the upstream beginning of that "S" on its eastern side. The town of New Madrid, Missouri, was located below Island No. 10 on the western side of the river at the downstream end of the "S".

Island No. 10 and the town of New Madrid had been heavily garrisoned by Confederate troops. Artillery emplacements had been established both on the island and upon the eastern shore of the river opposite the upstream end of the island, thus providing enfilade for a considerable distance of the river. During the month of March, the number of Confederates there was reduced when part of their number was sent to support Johnston at Corinth. By early April, approximately seven thousand infantry remained to back up the artillery men who were manning the gun emplacements. Island No. 10 was itself difficult to flank from the eastern shore because of the swampy conditions adjacent to the river bank. New Madrid was, however, vulnerable to attack by land via an approach road which led from Belmont, a hamlet twenty-seven miles to the north of New Madrid on the Mississippi's western bank.

Union Brigadier General John Pope devised a plan to take New Madrid and by so doing cut off Island No. 10 from support coming up from the south. The Western Gunboat Flotilla under the command of Foote was to then force its way past the enemy's artillery on Island No. 10 in order to establish a strong Union presence on the river south of the island. As envisioned by Pope, it would then only be a matter of time before the isolated garrison on Island No. 10 would be forced to surrender.

On the 13th of March, Pope's army appeared in front of New Madrid. The Confederate commander in the town, seeing what faced him, evacuated the place that same night, moving his troops across the river by steamer. Meanwhile upriver, Foote's flotilla of six gunboats was preparing to try going below Island No. 10. However, upon the opening of Confederate fire against his lead elements, Foote decided the attempt was too risky and withdrew back upriver and out of range. This was not what Pope had hoped would happen. Even though he now held New Madrid, Pope, by virtue of his location, was totally dependent for supply upon the road from Belmont, a road which might or might not be cut at any moment either by guerrillas or by regular troops coming north out of Arkansas. Pope was in the position of being behind the enemy's main lines and thus denied what should have been his major means of communication -- the river. He would remain highly vulnerable as long as the Confederates on Island No. 10 could prevent Foote's gunboats from passing the island.

Pope was irritated at Foote's failure to run the batteries, but he did not understand at the time the difficulties inherent with such an attempt. As Alfred T. Mahan descriptively brings out in *The Gulf and Inland Waters* the situation with Foote's gunboats at Island No. 10 was exactly opposite of that which had been faced at Fort Henry and at Fort Donelson. There, underpowered and relatively hard to maneuver gunboats had the advantage of working upstream against the current. With the situation as it had existed on the Cumberland and the Tennessee, if a vessel was rendered in any way incapable of maneuver, it could be allowed to drift downstream and out of range of the enemy's guns. At Island No. 10, the heavily gunned enemy fortifications had to be approached from upstream and at a place where the current was particularly strong. Once committed in such a situation, there was no way to extract a disabled vessel from certain destruction since the entirety of the island's western shore had well-emplaced enemy artillery. Having anticipated early-on that the Mississippi campaign would follow along the lines of the type of gunboat assaults that had been used against Fort Henry and Fort Donelson, Foote had ordered maneuverability experiments under heavy current conditions such as might be expected on the Mississippi. One of Foote's commanders, Henry Walke, described those experiments in his writings after the war which were published in *Battles and Leaders*. The experiments were conducted with the gunboat *CARONDELET* after she was repaired (following the damage received at Fort Henry). The test had taken place on the lower Ohio where the current was swift, but of considerably less velocity than the flow which was encountered on the Mississippi at Island No. 10.

> ...She [*CARONDELET*] was ordered to make the experiment of backing upstream which proved a laughable failure. She would sheer from one side of the river to the other, and with two anchors astern, she could not be held steady enough to fight her bow guns downstream. She dragged both anchors alternately, until they came together and the experiment failed completely.

Walke went on to describe the more severe conditions that he later encountered near Island No. 10.

> [There,] the strong and muddy current of the river had overflowed its banks and carried away every movable thing. Houses, trees, fences, and wrecks of all kinds were being swept rapidly downstream.

The current was but one part of the difficulty at Island No. 10. Walke also wrote of the Confederate works to be reduced.

> We were greatly surprised when we arrived above Island No. 10 and saw on the bluffs a chain of forts extending for four miles along the crescent formed shore with the white tents of the enemy in the rear. And there lay the island in the lower corner of the crescent with the side fronting the Missouri shore lined with heavy ordnance, so trained that with the artillery on the opposite shore, almost every point on the river between the island and the Missouri bank could be reached at once by all the enemy's batteries.[44]

After his flotilla's first failed attempt to pass the island, Foote contented himself with mooring the gunboats and his eleven mortar boats in fixed positions on the periphery of what he estimated would be the maximum range of the Confederate artillery. From there, he opened a methodic fire against the downstream forts. Only one Confederate shell struck a gunboat, the *BENTON*. The distance was at the outermost limits of the enemy's range, and little damage was done. The Union gunboats and the mortar boats had a much longer range of fire, and they managed to knock out most of the cannon on the upstream end of the Confederate works. During the bombardment, one of the rifled guns on the *SAINT LOUIS* exploded. As Walke would later write, this was "another proof of the truth of the saying that the guns furnished [to] the Western Gunboat Flotilla were less destructive to the enemy than to ourselves." For the next seventeen days, Foote's gunboats held their positions, firing a few shots now and then but with little new effect.[45]

During what was a period of relative inactivity, a freak accident occurred to the *CARONDELET*. She had been moored at the time against the river bank on the western shore. Current eddies created between the gunboat and the bank undermined some large cottonwood trees. Two of the trees collapsed without warning and fell onto the *CARONDELET*, killing one crewmember, injuring another, and doing considerable damage to the vessel itself.

Meanwhile at New Madrid, General Pope's army, perched on the lower bend of the river's "S" curve, was encountering an impasse. Without steamers, there was no way that the Federals could get across the river to attack the Confederates who were now dug in on the peninsula jutting out from the eastern bank opposite the town. For the Confederates, though, the outlook was much more unpleasant. They had Pope on their front and a difficult swamp at their rear. Anticipating that sooner or later Foote would try forcing his way past Island No. 10, the Confederate commander on the peninsula had established his battery positions so as to cover any river crossing which Pope might contemplate once transports were made available to him. The availability of such transports and the gunboats to afford them fire support was a consideration only for the future and would remain so as long as the river was blocked by the enemy's artillery on Island No. 10. Pope explained those circumstances in a communication addressed to Major General Halleck.

March 23, 1862

Since yesterday, our gunboats seem to have ceased their fire and are waiting for us to reduce the batteries opposite Island No. 10. If I can cross this force [meaning Pope's own troops] it will be an easy matter, as the batteries are only early [sic] parapets, open to the rear -- such works as could be put up in twenty-four hours. The river is very high and rising still, and the current runs so furiously that a rowboat manned by six oarsmen, which I sent out yesterday, was unable to stem it and floated down three miles. It was necessary to haul it back by land.

The river is over a mile wide at every point -- a distance too great for our guns to cover the landing on the opposite side. To cross this Army under such circumstances, in the face of the enemy will be a difficult and dangerous operation, and nothing except the utter failure of our gunboats to achieve what they promise and the imperative necessity of taking the enemy's batteries, now that they have been assailed, would induce me to hazard such an operation with volunteers without positive orders...[46]

The predicament was simply this. Without the gunboats brought downriver past Island No. 10 to New Madrid so as to afford covering fire for a river crossing, Pope realized that there could be no hope of being successful even if he had transports at hand for such a crossing. There had to be some way to get the transports and gunboats past Island No. 10. If not, he and his men could look forward to a long, risk-prone stay at New Madrid. An alternate solution was presented to Pope by one of his officers, Brigadier General Schuyler Hamilton. Hamilton proposed that Colonel J. W. Bissell, who had six hundred engineer troops on hand, should attempt the construction of a canal to provide a means for bypassing Island No. 10. Hamilton suggested that the canal's entrance should be on the western bank of the Mississippi, some distance upriver of Island No. 10. A preliminary survey for the canal called for it to join with Wilson's Bayou which was a natural water course draining the swamp land adjacent to the west bank of the main river. Wilson's Bayou itself dumped into a long flooded slough which had a southward drainage entering into the Mississippi a short distance downstream of New Madrid. The forest cover that separated the Mississippi's channel from Wilson's Bayou was flooded to a depth of approximately 6 feet, so except for cutting through the levy at the river's bank, little actual digging would be required. The major problem would be to saw out the heavy timber which obstructed the first two miles of the planned course. Similar obstructions were present in parts of Wilson's Bayou. Cutting the trees would not be an easy job since the timber was elm, an extremely hard wood. Regardless of the difficulty, Pope saw no alternative and endorsed the idea. Work commenced immediately.

Colonel Bissell described how the cutting operation was performed.

> ...First of all, men standing on platforms on small rafts cut off the trees about eight feet above the water. As soon as the tree was down, another set of men, provided with boats and lines, adjusted about it a line which ran through a snatch block and back to the steam-capstan, and hauled it out of the way; thus a partial cut was made forward, lines always working more than 200 feet ahead of the capstan, so as to leave plenty of room for the saws. It took about four sets of lines to keep pace with twelve saws.
>
> When the space above the stumps allowed sufficient room, a raft about forty feet long was lashed to a stump, and the saw set at work in a frame attached by a pivot and working in an arc... -- two men working the saw at opposite ends by a rope, and a fifth on the farther side of the tree guiding its teeth into the tree. Where the stumps were too close or irregular, three yawl boats were used instead of the raft. No trouble was experienced with stumps a foot or less in diameter. With the larger ones, it was different; the elms spread out so much at the bottom that the saw almost always would run crooked and pinch. If it ran up, we notched the top and set the frame farther in; if down, we put in powerful tackle and pulled the top of the stump over....
>
> It took eight days to cut the two miles. When we reached the bayous, the hard and wet work began. The river had begun to fall, and the water was running very rapidly. We had to get rid of great drift-heaps from the lower side with our machinery all on the upper side....In one of the bayous for about two miles, the current was so swift that all the men who were out on logs [cutting drifts and other obstructions], or in exposed places had safety lines tied around them; during the whole work not a man was killed, injured or taken sick.[47]

With the Bissell route a success, a number of small steamers with barges under tow were brought through the levy into Wilson's Bayou and through the slough to a point in proximity of New Madrid. They were there held out of sight of the Confederates while final arrangements were put into play in readiness for a river crossing. One hitch had developed with the original hopes for the plan. There was a limitation to the route's access, the canal only allowing passage by the shallowest draft transports. Foote's deeper hulled gunboats would not be able to make it through. Foote had consistently refused Pope's request to try another run past Island No. 10, claiming that it would be suicidal. Without the fire support of the gunboats, any transports attempting to cross the main river would be sure to suffer terribly under Confederate fire. In an attempt to substitute for the gunboats, Colonel Bissell was instructed to prepare some of the barges used in the cutting operation so they could be used as gun platforms, the idea being that the barges could be lashed alongside the shallow draft transports to provide floating artillery with which to cover the river crossing from New Madrid to the opposite peninsula. The barges were a little less than one hundred feet in length, but because of their normal use as deck loaded coal barges, they had strongly reinforced decks -- a helpful asset for the mounting of heavy weight guns. Other barges were to be used as transports for the carriage of lighter field guns which would be rolled ashore once the opposite bank was gained. The boilers and engines of the steamers that were to take these barges in tow were to be reinforced against the effects of cannon fire.

Flag Officer Foote, still in pain and discomfort from wounds received on the Tennessee River, and with his general health deteriorating day by day, was not in the most optimistic frame of mind. Yet, spurred on by Pope's preparations, and not wanting the Navy humiliated by any refusal to assist, the flag officer put caution aside and drafted an order which in its essentials is reproduced below:

> US Fleet Steamer *BENTON*
> Off Island No. 10
> March 30, 1862

Commander H. Walke, Commanding *CARONDELET*
Sir:
> You will avail yourself of the first fog or rainy night and drift your steamer down past the batteries on the Tennessee shore and Island No. 10 until you reach New Madrid.
> I assign you this service, as it is vitally important to the capture of this place that a gunboat should soon be at New Madrid, for the purpose of covering General Pope's army while he crosses that point to the opposite, or to the Tennessee side of the river, that he may move his army up to Island No. 10 and attack the rebels in rear while we attack them in front.
> Should you succeed in reaching General Pope, you will freely confer with him and adopt his suggestions, so far as your superior knowledge of what your boat will perform and will enable you to do, for the purpose of protecting his force while crossing the river.
> ...Commending you and all who compose your command to the care and protection of God, who rules the world and directs all things,....
> P. S. Should you meet with disaster, you will, as a last resort, destroy the steam machinery, and if possible escape, set fire to your gunboat or sink her, and prevent her from falling into the hands of the rebels.[48]

Despite Foote's announced change of mind about sending his gunboats downriver, Pope worried over a delay created while Walke waited for the right weather conditions to reduce visibility. In an April 2 telegram to Major General Halleck, Pope outlined his updated plans.

Our boats are in the main bayou and ready to move into the river at a moment's notice. I keep them up the bayou, concealed from the enemy. I am only waiting to finish the floating battery which carries one 8-inch Columbiad and three 32's. It will be finished by tomorrow night, and I think will be impregnable to any batteries the enemy can establish in any reasonable time. I have no hope of Commodore Foote. He has postponed trying to run any of his gunboats past Island No. 10 until some foggy or rainy night. The moon is beginning to make the nights light, and there is no prospect of fog during this sort of weather. We must do without him. I will give you details of the manner I intend to cross by mail.[49]

Although seemingly overlooking any hope of Foote's cooperation in the upcoming river crossing, Pope appears to have still counted on the possibility that the flag officer would be shamed into some immediate action. Whether Foote was at the time aware of Pope's intentions of moving without gunboat support is unclear. In any event, Pope's ability as a forecaster of clear weather proved to be lacking. An approaching weather front soon provided the concealment that Walke needed. On the dark and windy night of April 4, the *CARONDELET* made an attempt to run past Island No. 10. It was spotted while directly abreast of the Confederate batteries; but despite a very heavy fire, it passed unharmed. With the *CARONDELET's* safe arrival at New Madrid, Pope felt more than justified in asking Foote for a second gunboat. The Confederates had just brought more heavy guns up to the river's bank, and conditions across from New Madrid were looking increasingly formidable, and extra fire support to cover the river crossing was now a must. In a telegram dated April 6, 1862, from New Madrid, Assistant Secretary of War Thomas A. Scott, then on the scene with Pope, wired Secretary of War Edwin M. Stanton.

General Pope is progressing well with his plans to execute the most difficult movement of the campaign -- that of crossing the Mississippi in the face of the enemy. He needs another gunboat, but we cannot prevail on Commodore Foote to run the blockade [past Island No. 10]. It can be done with comparative safety any night and might save the lives of thousands of our soldiers. The risk of the boat is trifling compared with that of Pope's army. Can you have it ordered by the Secretary of the Navy today, and thus relieve the Flag Officer from the responsibility which he is not willing to assume?[50]

That request was to be canceled by a second telegram from Assistant Secretary Scott, stating that Pope had just received a dispatch from Foote wherein the latter promised to send another gunboat that very night.

On receipt of Foote's message, Pope sent an advisory memorandum off to Walke.

April 6, 1862

Captain:

I am induced to believe by the report of General [Gordon] Granger and Colonel (J. L. Kirby) Smith that you will be able to silence or take the upper batteries of the enemy on the opposite shore. I mean the batteries immediately opposite our batteries of 32-pounders.

Commodore Foote sends another boat down tonight. I design to attempt the crossing with my force tomorrow, and I desire if it meets your view, that the two gunboats go down as soon as day dawns and silence the batteries specified, and to hold on near the shore until the troops disembark. As soon as you start, I will have the transports brought into the river [from Wilson's Bayou] and loaded with troops, which will cross the river and land near you as soon as the batteries are silenced.

You will doubtlessly have to move close into them, head on, maintain your position, so as to cover the whole ground on the rear of the landing.

Our batteries will be ordered to open as soon as day dawns and will keep up their fire vigorously until the object is accomplished.

I can cross 3500 men at a time. If you can thus silence these batteries in three hours or more, we have the rebels opposite in our hands.[51]

Early the next morning, under cover of a heavy thunderstorm, but with the accompanying lightning unfortunately canceling out concealment, the gunboat *PITTSBURG* started her run past Island No. 10 toward New Madrid. The reception she received from the Confederate batteries as she steamed past the island was hot and heavy. Foote, in a later report to Secretary of the Navy Welles, claimed that *PITTSBURG* had been taken under fire by seventy-three guns. However, their accuracy was not as impressive as their noise. In a message Pope sent upriver that day to Foote, the general announced the gunboat's safe arrival, stating that *PITTSBURG* had been entirely untouched by the Confederate fire.[52]

On the following day, Commander Walke took *CARONDELET*, in company with *PITTSBURG*, against the enemy's batteries across from New Madrid. His report to Pope describes what happened.

> Sir:
> Agreeable to your instructions of the 6th instant, I proceeded down the Mississippi at six-thirty this morning; silenced and spiked all the guns of the rebel batteries opposite your batteries. The lower one made a desperate resistance. It consisted of two 64-pounder howitzers and one 32-pounder mounted on a Navy gun carriage; two were dismounted and the other disabled by a shot. I then captured and spiked, temporarily, two 64-pounders about half a mile above -- and a quarter of a mile above these found a 64-pounder long gun spiked.
> I have brought a man on board, who reports himself to me as being a spy, whom I send to you. The rebels had set fire to their house on the shore opposite.[53]

Pope now made his assault across the river. The resistance he had expected did not materialize. Instead, the enemy folded, both on the peninsula and, shortly following that, at Island No. 10 as well. The entire operation and the part that the gunboats and Pope's army played in it were summed up within the formal report of Pope to Halleck, issued from New Madrid on April 9, 1862.

> The canal across the peninsula opposite Island No. 10, and for the idea of which I am indebted to General Schuyler Hamilton, was completed by Colonel Bissell's engineer regiment, and four steamers brought through on the night of the 6th. The heavy batteries I had thrown up below Tiptonville completely commanded the lowest point of the high ground on the Tennessee shore, entirely cutting off the enemy's retreat by water. His retreat by land has never been possible through the swamps.
> On the night of the 4th, Captain [he held the rank of Commander] Walke of the Navy ran the enemy's batteries at Island No. 10 with the gunboat *CARONDELET*

and reported to me here. On the night of the 6th, the gunboat *PITTSBURG* also ran the blockade.

Our transports were brought into the river from the bayou, where they had been kept concealed, at daylight on the 7th, and Paine's division loaded. The canal has been a prodigiously laborious work. It was twelve miles long, six miles of which were through heavy timber, which had to be sawed off by hand four feet under water. The enemy has lined the opposite shore with batteries, extending from Island No. 10 to Tiptonville -- Meriwether's Landing -- to prevent the passage of the river by this army. I directed Captain [Commander] Walke to run down with the two gunboats at daylight on the 7th to the point selected for crossing and silence the enemy's batteries near it. He performed the service gallantly, and I here bear testimony to the thorough and brilliant manner in which the officer discharged his difficult duties with me, and to the hearty and earnest zeal with which, at all hazards, he cooperated with me.

As soon as he signaled me, the boats containing [Eleanzer A.] Paine's division moved out and commenced to cross the river. The passage of this wide, furious river by our large force was one of the most magnificent spectacles I ever witnessed. By 12 o'clock that night (the 7th) all the forces designed to cross the river were over, without delay or accident.

As we commenced to cross, the enemy began to evacuate Island No. 10 and his pontoons along the shore. The divisions were pushed forward to Tiptonville as fast as they landed, Paine's leading. The enemy was driven before him, and although they made several attempts to form line of battle and make a stand, Paine did not once deploy his column. The enemy was pushed all night vigorously, until at 4 a.m. he was driven back upon the swamp and forced to surrender.

Three generals, seven colonels, seven regiments, several battalions of infantry, five companies of artillery, over one hundred heavy siege guns, twenty-four pieces of field artillery, an immense quantity of ammunition and supplies, and several thousand stands of small arms, a great number of tents, horses, wagons, etc., have fallen into our hands.

Before abandoning Island No. 10 the enemy sank the gunboat *GRAMPUS* and six of his transports. These last I am raising and expect to have ready for service in a few days. The famous floating battery was scuttled and turned adrift with all her guns aboard. She was captured and run aground in shoal water by our forces at New Madrid.[54]

Confederate vessels which were captured or destroyed in the vicinity of Island No. 10 and New Madrid were:[55]

ADMIRAL	*MARS*	*SALLIE WOOD*
DESOTO	*MOHAWK*	*SOVEREIGN*
GRAMPUS	*OHIO BELLE*	*VICTORIA*
JOHN SIMONDS	*PRINCE*	*WINCHESTER*
KENTUCKY	*RED ROVER*	*YAZOO*

ADMIRAL and *MARS* were placed into service by the Army Quartermaster as supply vessels. The others went under the wing of the Western Gunboat Flotilla to be transferred later that year to the Navy's own service. (See Appendix C for further particulars concerning the disposition of Confederate vessels taken at Island No. 10.)

CAMPAIGN AGAINST NEW ORLEANS FROM THE GULF
(Spring of 1862)

A Joint Operation

Once Ship Island, off-lying the coast of Mississippi, was resecured from its Confederate defenders in September 1861, the place entered into the thinking of Union planners as an ideal staging area for a campaign to take over the southern Mississippi. The first hurdle to surmount in such a campaign would be the taking of the fortifications near Head of the Passes where the Mississippi River made its entry into the Gulf of Mexico. Once those fortifications were reduced, operations could begin against New Orleans. After New Orleans came into Union hands, a progression of movements up the Mississippi would be undertaken until, by a joining through physical contact with the Union forces fighting their way downriver, the Mississippi could be made a Union thoroughfare.

The expedition from the Gulf of Mexico into the Mississippi was planned as a joint Army-Navy endeavor. Flag Officer David G. Farragut would command the naval force, and Major General Benjamin F. Butler would command the Army's element. Butler had approximately ten thousand men who would serve as assault troops; they would also be used to garrison various strong points once taken. It was Butler's hope that his strength would later be reinforced since ten thousand men was little enough to hold the ground from Head of the Passes to New Orleans once that ground had been conquered.

The initial movement against Head of the Passes had been scheduled for the spring of 1862. Well before that time, Butler was occupied in putting together troop units and arranging for the transports that were to carry his regiments south from mid-Atlantic ports of embarkation into the Gulf of Mexico. A hefty portion of the troop units which had been authorized for Butler's newest expedition had been with him at Hatteras Inlet during the late summer and fall of 1861.

At the same time that Butler was making his own preparations, Farragut's second in command, Commander David Dixon Porter, was hard at work in the region of Chesapeake Bay and at the port of New York where he was assembling and making ready the gunboats and mortar schooners which were to serve in support of Farragut's ships of the line.[56]

Both the Army and the Navy factions of the expedition began to leave Hampton Roads in staged increments beginning in early February of 1862; the departures continued well into the next month. Most of the Navy ships along with the Army's troop transports and supply vessels were to rendezvous at Key West before leaving for Ship Island.

The trip south to Key West from Hampton Roads was far from routine. While en route, one of the Navy's largest men-o-war, the *USS PENSACOLA*, ran aground. Fortunately, she was refloated without damage. Butler and that part of his command which had sailed with him aboard the Army chartered transport *MISSISSIPPI* had their own sea stories to tell. A planned stop at Hatteras Inlet had been scheduled for the *MISSISSIPPI*. She was to pick up more troop passengers there, but that stop was canceled when the weather began making up. And make-up it did, developing into a heavy gale roaring out of the southwest. The wind then swung into the northeast and rose to hurricane force. Afraid of broaching his ship, the master of the *MISSISSIPPI* headed his vessel into the wind. Even then, and on more than one occasion, green water was taken through the cabin sky lights. Water also entered through the ventilators, partially flooding the engine room. The heavy weather lasted for two more days until the front finally passed. By then, the *MISSISSIPPI* was abeam of Cape Fear, North Carolina. Despite the improved navigating conditions (they were able to sight Cape Fear Lighthouse and its off-lying sea buoy), the master ran the ship aground. At this point, matters of command seem to have become somewhat confused with Butler personally exerting authority over the master -- finally taking over from him. Butler instructed that the surrounding shoals be sounded and that range buoys be prepared for dropping. Those troop passengers with seagoing experience -- and apparently there were a number of such men aboard -- were utilized for both the sounding work and to lay out buoys to mark the deeper water.

While these steps were underway, a sail was seen coming in from the southwest. According to Butler's own account of the matter, "the ensign [of the *MISSISSIPPI*] was hoisted, union down, and [a] signal gun fired." The "sail" proved to be the Navy auxiliary steamship *USS MOUNT VERNON*. The captain of *USS MOUNT VERNON's* brought his vessel in as close to the shoals as he dared -- close enough for his people to get a hawser aboard the *MISSISSIPPI* for a try at pulling her off the shoals. At first, the transport would not budge. Butler then ordered that she be lightened not only of cargo but of some of her troops as well. Stores were thrown overboard, and using small boats, about three hundred soldiers were transferred over to the *USS MOUNT VERNON*. Once the *MISSISSIPPI* was lightened, full steam was ordered in an attempt to run her off under power. The remaining troop passengers were able to pitch the vessel fore and aft by moving at quick time from stern to stem and back again. Finally, the *MISSISSIPPI* began to move ahead slowly. Below decks, another detail of troops was bailing the forward compartments, but they were making slow headway against the incoming water. The baling had to be kept up through the following night. The next day a survey group appointed by Butler reported that in their opinion the *MISSISSIPPI* was safe to proceed to Port Royal under escort of *USS MOUNT VERNON*. The survey team consisted of an Army colonel; the acting sailing master of the *USS MOUNT VERNON* (who had been sent aboard on Butler's request to replace the

MISSISSIPPI's master who by now was relegated to total disgrace); and an Army captain. As a precaution, and before the *MISSISSIPPI* proceeded on her way to Port Royal, a collision mat was run under the ship's stem in way of the leaking hull section. Following this, mattresses were placed inboard in an effort to sandwich over the areas that were leaking; however, this did little good by itself. The leak was eventually stopped by removing the mattresses and applying a cushion of tarred oakum layered over with canvas and sheet rubber. A sheet of iron was put over this and screwed down to the inner hull. A final layer consisting of several barrels of heated resin was poured on over the iron sheet to the thickness of about eight inches.

While en route to Port Royal, Butler had relented and allowed the master to resume his command. But the return of that command was to be of short duration. After arrival at Port Royal, and when shifting docking locations, the master was backing away from the pier when he was assailed by shouts from the deck below, "No! No! You are doing it the wrong way!" This loud advice came from a number of troop officers who, as Butler's aide-de-camp later put it, were "gentlemen of nautical skill." Whether this back-seat driving totally unnerved the captain, or whether the "gentlemen of nautical skill" had been correct in their unsolicited advice, we have no way of knowing. In any event, the master backed *MISSISSIPPI* hard into the bank on the opposite shore, striking the rudder in such a way that the tiller cable parted just before the ship began to move forward again. This caused her to again run hard aground. Attempts to get her off on two successive high tides failed. Finally, on a third attempt, tugs were able to free her. This had been the final straw for Butler who replaced the master with a naval officer detailed from the squadron operating out of Hilton Head.[57] Considering the obvious incompetence of the master, how he had been able to steam as far as Cape Fear before running onto the shoals there seems a matter of some mystery, but probably luck played a great part. The inquiry that was to follow disclosed that even before the storm had hit, the vessel had been run so close to the shoals of the Outer Hatteras Banks that white breakers were seen on each side. Witnesses, presumably the same "gentlemen of nautical skill," had taken soundings. They stated that the vessel was in only 4 fathoms (24 feet) of water at the time. The board of inquiry did not go well for the civilian captain. Before *MISSISSIPPI* left Port Royal, the master, "Captain Fulton", was put under arrest, and by order of Butler, he was to be left at Key West until such time that the charter party on the *MISSISSIPPI* was canceled.

For Butler, the trip south must have been a relaxing distraction from what lay ahead. The concept for the campaign to follow had been laid out within an order developed by Major General George McClellan in cooperation with the Navy Department. As addressed to Major General Butler, that order read:

Washington, February 23, 1862
General:
        You are assigned to the command of the land forces destined to cooperate with the Navy in the attack upon New Orleans. You will use every means to keep your destination a profound secret, even from your staff officers with the exception of your Chief of Staff and Lieutenant Weitzel of the Engineers... This [as enumerated] will make your force 14,400 infantry, 275 cavalry, 580 artillery -- total 15,255 men. The

commanding general of the Department of Key West is authorized to loan you temporarily two regiments. Fort Pickens will probably give you another, which will bring your force to nearly 18,000.

The object of your expedition is one of vital importance -- the capture of New Orleans. The route selected is up the Mississippi River, and the first obstacle to be encountered (perhaps the only one) is the resistance of it by Forts Saint Philip and Jackson. It is expected that the Navy can reduce these works. In that case, you will, after their capture, leave a sufficient garrison in them to render them perfectly secure;....Should the Navy fail to reduce the works, you will land your forces and siege train and endeavor to breach the works, silence their guns, and carry them by assault.

The next resistance will be near the English Bend where there are some earthen batteries. Here it may be necessary for you to land your troops to cooperate with the naval attack, although it is more than probable that the Navy, unassisted, can accomplish the result. If these works are taken, the city of New Orleans necessarily falls. In that event, it will probably be best to occupy Algiers with the mass of your troops; [Algiers lays directly across the river from New Orleans] also the eastern bank of the river above the city. [That being on the same side as New Orleans.] It may be necessary to place some troops in the city to preserve order; but if there appears sufficient Union sentiment to control the city, it may be best, for purposes of discipline, to keep your men out of the city.

After obtaining possession of New Orleans, it will be necessary to reduce all the works guarding its approaches from the east, and particularly to gain the Manchac Pass...[The Manchac Pass was a body of water which was crossed by the railroad line serving New Orleans from the north. It was about twenty-five miles north of New Orleans.] I need not call your attention to the necessity of gaining possession of all the rolling stock you can on the different railways and of obtaining control of the roads themselves. The occupation of Baton Rouge by a combined naval and land force should be accomplished as soon as possible after you have gained New Orleans....Allow nothing to divert you from obtaining full possession of all the approaches to New Orleans...I may briefly state that the general objects of the expedition are, First, the reduction of New Orleans and all its approaches; then Mobile and its defenses; then Pensacola, Galveston, and etc....[58]

Troop arrivals at Ship Island took place over several days. The first troopship to unload (on February 13) was the transport *CONSTITUTION* with a passenger list consisting of two regiments of infantry and a squadron of cavalry. For those going ashore, the conditions found there were far from ideal. The report of Brigadier General J. W. Phelps relates that at the time of his landing on the island, "Recent rains have so flooded part of the island that two regiments cannot be well maneuvered upon it in line without marching through water." It was in this semi-liquid environment that Benjamin Butler was to gather together a force that would, as McClellan had promised, number almost eighteen thousand men. (Butler had by then received the additional troops that he had requested.)

On March 29, General Orders No. 8 was issued by Butler's adjutant. The order called for troops to be loaded aboard the following transports offlying the island: *MISSISSIPPI* (which was to be Butler's command transport), *MATANZAS*, *LEWIS*, *WILD GAZELLE*, and *E. WILDER FARLEY*. While preparations for loading were underway, Butler sent this notification to Farragut by fast courier vessel.

Sir:

I am now ready to put on board six regiments and two batteries, and will be able to be in the 'passes' in twelve hours. I am still of opinion that an effort be made to land aboard [sic] the Fort as soon as you can get the gunboats by. Its moral, not to say actual effect, would aid the attack, if not compel surrender. If the Navy are [sic] not to be ready for six or eight hours, I ought not to sail, as my coal is running short, and I cannot carry more than eight days for sailing. May I ask that you send me word so as to reach me by Tuesday morning, and I will be embarked and waiting. If you prefer, I will be in time to attempt the landing off Isle Breton. If I can aid you in any way, please command me. I shall wait your advice. If it is of importance that you advice me, please do not fail.[59]

On April 10th, General Orders 9, was issued. It ordered further troop embarkations aboard the transports GREAT REPUBLIC, NORTH AMERICA, and additional troops to the MATANZAS and to the E. WILDER FARLEY.[60]

Fort Saint Philip and Fort Jackson

It had been jointly decided by Butler and Farragut that the admiral would send the men-of-war as well as the mortar schooners and the gunboats into the Mississippi through South West Pass. Once into the river, the fleet would proceed thirty-five miles to anchor just out of range of the enemy's guns at Fort Saint Philip and Fort Jackson. Some years before, both of these fortifications had been constructed by the United States Army Engineers. Following their construction, they were garrisoned, but only in a caretaker status. On January 10, 1861, the forts had been taken under occupation by Louisiana state troops.[61] The enemy troops at both of the forts came from a variety of units, and in general, they were poorly disciplined. The choice of such a low caliber garrison was a severe oversight on the part of the Confederate command since the security of the southwestern Confederacy would depend in large part on the courage and abilities of the officers and men who manned the forts on the lower Mississippi.

Besides the firepower that the two forts were expected to bring to bear, another potential problem was presented to Farragut in the form of enemy gunboats. These gunboats were of a quality and quantity not yet fully known. There was also the matter of a chain which the enemy had stretched across the entire river, supporting it by a combination of moored vessels and buoys.

Fort Saint Philip had been constructed of brick, reinforced by earthen revetments. The fort's firepower consisted of four Columbiads and one 24-pounder. In separate but direct support, it had two water batteries -- one upstream and one downstream of the main works. Altogether, the Saint Philip complex could count forty-two guns and six mortars. From its outward appearance, Fort Jackson seemed more sophisticated. It was of pentagon shape and entirely of brick construction. Within the Fort Jackson works there were fourteen 24-pound cannon and ten rifled howitzers together with five Columbiads and thirty-two other cannon, the latter mounted above the others in barbette arrangement. Covering the approaches to Fort Jackson was a supportive water battery consisting of three Columbiads and two rifled cannon. By count, the guns which the Confederates had at both forts would seem to have constituted an impressive firepower; however, Alfred Thayer Mahan opines in *The Gulf and Inland Waters* that they were no match for what Farragut was soon to bring against them. The opposing Confederate fleet over which Farragut had shown concern actually consisted only of two gunboats, one ram, and two lightly armed craft which would prove to be but a minor nuisance.

Initially, the Navy's attempts to enter the Mississippi through South West Pass did not go well. The deep draft ships of the line had trouble getting over the shallow bar at the entrance, and it became necessary to lighten them by offloading guns and stores onto the supply schooners. This was no easy task. Even with that done, it was only after five tries that the largest of Farragut's ships, the *USS PENSACOLA*, was able to get into the river --- and then only at the end of hawsers attached to tugs. David D. Porter, who was a close witness to all of this, later commented that the local pilots who were being relied upon for advice seemed "either nervous or treacherous."[62] While the preparations were being made to get over the bar, Farragut communicated with Butler who was still at Ship Island waiting for the green light to proceed.

> April 1, 1862
>
> Dear General:
> I received your note yesterday and hasten to answer it by the *CALHOUN* [a dispatch vessel]. I have not yet gotten the *PENSACOLA** and the *MISSISSIPPI** over the bar, but hope to accomplish one at least tomorrow, as the water is higher, but the fog is terrible. [The *MISSISSIPPI* named was a naval ship of the line, not to be confused with the Army transport *MISSISSIPPI* which was then part of the transport fleet and General Butler's command vessel.] I think well of your idea of landing above the forts after the gunboats are there, but not before; and I think when the first feat is accomplished, there will be very little difficulty in your doing as you please; that is, we will soon reduce the forts. The difficulty is in passing the forts. They will do all in their power to prevent it, and we must do it in the night or in the fog. But I fear it would be very dull for you here before the ships are over the bar. I am now surveying the coast outside of the forts and will soon know if I can place the bomb vessels [mortar schooners] there. If I can, I think the work will be more easily accomplished. I will let you know the moment the ships are over the bar. I wrote you this morning, but the letter got mislaid, and I have been obliged to write this hasty scrawl in the steamer. Please present me to Mrs. Butler. [Butler's wife was with him at Ship Island.][63]

* *USS*, commissioned Union naval vessel.

Farragut's reference to, "surveying the coast outside of the forts," can only be properly understood if one examines a chart of the area for the 1860s. At that point in time, parts of the Mississippi delta were far different than they are today. The delta on the west bank of the river where Fort Jackson was located was then not very wide, being quite close to an embayment of water open to the Gulf. (That embayment has since filled in.) The east bank of the river on which Fort Saint Philip was located appeared much as the area does today, being located a mile or two over the marshes from Breton Sound, a body of open water lying to the east of the delta. As Farragut's surveyors were to discover, the embayments lying both east and west of the delta, were extremely shallow, therefore effectively precluding their use for any close approach by vessels of any but the shallowest draft. This then meant that any bombardment of either fort would have to be conducted from vessels located on the river, downstream from the forts.[64]

On April 7, Farragut notified Butler that all the naval vessels were by now over the bar and in the river, anchored in proximity to Pilot Town. (Pilot Town was just upstream of the junction of the two main passes of the Mississippi.) Farragut reported that the fleet would be fully coaled and ready in four or five days, and "you can use your own discretion as to when you will come over." Farragut further related to Butler that he had paid "them" a visit at the forts on April 6 in hopes of getting, "...a little fight out of their gunboats." The Confederates fired from the fort, "... but the gunboats would not even venture outside the chain." Farragut concluded by writing, "I shall now go to work to destroy the chain..."

The following week, Farragut was ready to start his attack in earnest. He sent off a fast dispatch to Butler, the latter still waiting with the loaded transports at Ship Island.

> Dear General:
> We hope to get the vessels up tomorrow in the vicinity of Fort Jackson. If you desire to be on here with us, you will be in time by coming directly down. I made a reconnaissance yesterday, and Porter is now getting his positions for his mortar fleet. I have been more fortunate than I had supposed in getting coal. Our vessels are nearly all coaled, and we are only deficient a few hundred tons.[65]

Butler, in a communication addressed to the "Honorary Secretary of War," would soon report:

> Sir:
> I have the honor to report that I am now off the passes with eight regiments and three batteries of artillery of my best troops, under command of Brigadier Generals Phelps and Williams, ready to cooperate with the fleet, who move today or, as I believe, tomorrow upon Forts Saint Philip and Jackson. These are all for which I have possible means of transportation, owing to the circumstances stated in my dispatches of 13 instant, and all that I believe will be needed for the present emergency. You may think that we have delayed, but I beg to assure you that, with the storms and winds and the means at our disposal, we made every haste and are ready as soon as we are needed.
> The health of the command is very good, and their equipment as to arms and provisions abundant.[66]

Porter had ordered his mortar schooners up the river and moored into positions which would afford the best protection from incoming fire while still assuring that their outgoing fire against the forts would have the best effect. With everything in readiness, firing on the forts commenced. At the onset, the Confederate defenders got in some return rounds that proved troublesome. The first day, two of Porter's mortar schooners were hit although neither suffered serious damage. The following day, another mortar schooner was hit; that one sank. The Federal bombardment continued for three more days. On the second night of the bombardment, the enemy sent fire rafts downriver causing considerable excitement, but they had only a minimal effect. Farragut now decided that a long siege was impractical. He would push the issue.

On April 20, under a heavy covering fire, he sent two gunboats up the river with the intent of destroying the chain. In this, they were successful. The river's navigation was now unimpaired except for the enemy cannon at the forts. The following day, Farragut opened the heaviest bombardment yet. Three days later, he successfully ran his men-of-war past both of the forts. Apprised of this success, Butler sent a message to Farragut, suggesting "that I should immediately land troops to cooperate with you at the Quarantine Station and so hem in the forts." When Farragut acquiesced, Butler issued General Orders No. 14.

> The transports *MISSISSIPPI, MATANZAS, LEWIS, SAXON,* and *GREAT REPUBLIC*, with all the troops now on board, will proceed, under convoy of U. S. steamers, *MIAMI** and *SACHEM** and without delay to Sable Island with a view to reach Quarantine Station in rear of Fort Saint Philip...
> Brigadier General Phelps will remain in command of all the troops on board transport ships *NORTH AMERICA* and *E. WILDER FARLEY* and hold himself in readiness to occupy the forts as soon as they shall have been reduced.
> By order of Major General Butler.[67]

* *USS MIAMI* and *USS SACHEM*

The Sable Island mentioned in the above order was part of the Bird Island group located in the sound to the east of the Mississippi's delta. Sable Island was as close to the shore of the main delta as the transports could be brought. From there, ships' boats were to carry in the troops toward the Quarantine Station which was on the same bank of the river as was Fort Saint Philip, but some thousand yards upriver from it.[68]

It was at this juncture, apparently without either objection or concurrence from Butler (none appears to have come down to us through the record), that Farragut decided to proceed up the Mississippi to New Orleans. With Fort Saint Philip and Fort Jackson still in Confederate hands and denying safe passage to the Union troopships, there was no way that Butler's troops could accompany Farragut's movement. Farragut would have nothing in the way of a substantial landing force to send ashore once New Orleans was reached. Consequently, if Farragut took the city, he could not then occupy it.

Following Farragut's departure, Butler described the situation existing on the lower river.

> Off Saint Philip; on the Gulf side
> April 26, 1862
> The fleet passed by the forts on the morning of the 24th instance, but with little loss, leaving the mortar fleet and a few gunboats below without reducing the forts. They have substantially cleared the river of boats above the forts but have left the ram and two rebel boats under the cover of the forts. They [the Confederate ram and the two boats] are proving troublesome to the remnant of our fleet below in the river.
> The flag officer has gone up with twelve vessels of his fleet to New Orleans, leaving us to reduce the forts....[69]

That Farragut went ahead to New Orleans, leaving behind two Confederate forts blocking the Mississippi, seems in retrospect to have been in contradiction of the plan as it had been originally laid out and agreed to by both the War Department and the Navy Department. That plan had specifically called for securing all Confederate rolling stock and other materiel to prevent it from escaping New Orleans. Without troop support, there was no way that Farragut could block that equipment's egress from the city.

Fort Saint Philip and Fort Jackson soon surrendered to Butler, an event which had come about in main due to the mutiny of a large part of their garrisons. The surrender was not, though, soon enough. By the time Butler arrived at New Orleans, the Confederates had removed from the city practically everything of military significance. Naval historian Rowena Reed has been justifiably critical of Farragut:

> During the week between Farragut's appearance [at New Orleans] and the arrival of Butler's troops on 1 May, the Confederates removed almost everything of military value, including all of the rolling stock on the railroads, and most of the river vessels. They even managed to dismantle and bring away their armament factories along with the machinery for making iron plates for their gunboats. Had the forts been taken first in accordance with the original plan, the Army and Navy would have arrived off the city together and the opportunity to destroy or capture all of the enemy's equipment and stores would probably not have been lost. Without the materiel saved from New Orleans, the Confederates would have been hard pressed to fortify any point in the river above the city or to arm local militia for its defense.[70]

Technically, Farragut had taken possession of the city, but this was merely a formality consisting of little else than putting a naval officer ashore with a foot guard of marines and two small boat howitzers. The officer and his party first proceeded to the State House where they hauled down the Confederate flag and ran up the "Stars and Stripes." They repeated the same performance at the Customs House and then immediately reboarded the vessels of the waiting fleet, a fortunate choice since an angry mob was making their stay an unpleasant one. For all practical purposes, once Farragut's landing party left the New Orleans wharf, the city was again back in Confederate hands to do with as the enemy pleased.

~

We will return again to Farragut and his continuation northward on the Mississippi River. But first, we shall cover operations which were transpiring on the upper Mississippi River.

EVENTS LEADING UP TO THE TAKING OF MEMPHIS
(April - June 1862)

Ellet's Ram Fleet

The Civil War on the western rivers had its especially fascinating cast of characters, not the least of which were the members of the Ellet family, a name which became synonymous with the Mississippi Ram Fleet. Paramount to the taking of Memphis was the Ellet fleet of rams under the operational command of Charles Ellet, Jr.

~

Six members of the Ellet family eventually became directly associated with the Ram Fleet and its successor, the Mississippi Marine Brigade. Colonel Charles Ellet, Jr., was originator of the Ram Fleet concept as well as its first commander. He would die of wounds received at the Battle of Memphis. Lieutenant Colonel Alfred W. Ellet took command of the Ram Fleet after the Battle of Memphis, shortly after that being promoted to brigadier general. He was later given command of the Mississippi Marine Brigade which he had organized. Medical Cadet Charles Rivers Ellet would take over command of those vessels of the Ram Fleet which were actively operating on the river systems when Alfred W. Ellet left to organize the Mississippi Marine Brigade at Saint Louis. Charles Rivers Ellet was jumped up at that time to the rank of full colonel (staff). Lieutenant Colonel John A. Ellet became second in command of the rams after the Battle of Memphis. He stayed on when the Mississippi Marine Brigade was organized. When the Mississippi Marine Brigade was disbanded in 1864, John took command of the successor organization, the Consolidated Marine Regiment. Lieutenant Edward C. Ellet was a staff officer of the Mississippi Marine Brigade. Richard C. Ellet was a lieutenant in the cavalry section of the Mississippi Marine Brigade.

~

The elder of the Ellet family, Charles Ellet, Jr., had been a practicing engineer before the war. His engineering talents were broad in scope, encompassing the design and construction of extension bridges and railroads. He had been a prime mover and official with the James River and Kanawha Canal Company and had been a pioneer in the principles of improving river navigation through the use of reservoirs. He had written professional papers which were widely distributed and which included a treatise on flood control in the Mississippi corridor.[71] He is first mentioned in Civil War period War Department correspondence dated March 25, 1862, addressed from Secretary of War Edwin M. Stanton to Major General Henry W. Halleck. This correspondence related to the use of rams. Ellet had written on the subject as early as 1855, and it was that early writing which was referenced by Stanton. Ellet had recently become a technical consultant to Cornelius Vanderbilt regarding Vanderbilt's offer of his namesake vessel, the steamship *C. VANDERBILT*, as a sacrificial ram ship should the *CSS VIRGINIA* venture out for a second time into Hampton Roads.[72] Stanton reiterated to Halleck Ellet's belief that a ram vessel, specially constructed and reinforced, was the only sure way to counter armored gunboats. The Secretary's correspondence ended with the information that Ellet was being immediately sent west to consult on the matter of the Army constructing a ram for service on the Mississippi. Three weeks following this, Ellet -- by then well established in Halleck's confidence -- had progressed from consultant to activist overseer of the ram program. In a report forwarded to Stanton and which was addressed from an Ohio River shipyard, Ellet informed the Secretary that not one ram, but three (the *SWITZERLAND*, the *LANCASTER*, and the *QUEEN OF THE WEST*) were progressing rapidly. These were steam vessels which had been purchased on Halleck's direct orders and which he, Ellet, was now hurriedly converting.[73] A fourth steamer, the *MONARCH*, also destined for conversion, was then on its way to a shipyard in Cincinnati where stocks were being reserved for the necessary work.[74] There was nothing particularly unique or different about the river boats which Ellet had selected for conversion, his only requirements being that they be reasonably well built and that they possess strong machinery and slightly better than average horsepower. Strengthening of the hull structures to withstand the type of impact a ram could be subjected to was the key to Ellet's equation which would turn ordinary vessels into acceptable rams. In correspondence written at that time, Ellet stated that strengthening of river boats did not always result in what a ram should be, explaining that a correct ratio of weight to horsepower was also important. The time needed to build the ideal ram was not available; haste in putting such vessels on the river was what the military situation on the Mississippi now demanded. Ellet did not recommend arming the rams, their defense instead depending on their maneuverability and speed. His contention was that the weight of cannon would result in an undesirable sacrifice of speed. He did, though, recommend that a small force of infantrymen be carried aboard to act as guards and to rebel boarders during actions. (Later, his successor commander would arm the rams, but this was done for a method of warfare which Charles Ellet, Jr. had not originally envisioned.)

Besides those steamers already mentioned, Ellet would soon afterward purchase the *DICK FULTON*, the *T. D. HORNER*, the *LIONESS*, the *MINGO*, and the *SAMSON*. Some of these would be converted to rams while others would become support craft to the Ram Fleet. Almost as a matter of preconceived inevitability, the mantle of command of the Ram Fleet would fall upon its conceiver. Up to this point, Ellet still remained a civilian, and it seems that at least up to late April of 1862, no one had questioned the propriety of a civilian being placed in field command of a combatant element.

At about this time, intelligence reports were coming into the War Department indicating that Confederate shipyards were constructing gunboats as well as rams. On April 27, Ellet received the following telegram from Stanton.

> We have certain intelligence that New Orleans has been captured -- there appears to be no doubt of the fact. Commodore [David G.] Farragut has orders to push up immediately to Memphis, and join Commodore Foote, without waiting at New Orleans. You should loose no time in starting your fleet to the same point. Our squadron was at New Orleans two days ago, Sunday 8 p.m.

Ellet answered Stanton on the following day, also by telegraph.

> Your several dispatches have been received and acted upon. No efforts are spared to get the boats underway. The *MINGO* will leave tomorrow noon; the *LIONESS* tomorrow evening; both with coal barges. The *SAMSON*, I think, will start Wednesday. The tender *DICK FULTON* can overtake the tows before they reach Louisville. The other tender [probably the *T. D. HORNER*] will wait for the sheltering barge, but I think will come up in time. Will the Department supply the clerk who is to act as paymaster, or shall the committee appoint one? Can arrangements be made to enable the wives of the men to draw a part of their pay if they should be detained below? This I find to be important. I will instruct my brother [Alfred W. Ellet] to meet me at Cairo. He will assuredly come rapidly.[75]

It was now that Ellet's role would be officially enlarged to that of a military commander. Ellet seems to have wanted to remain a civilian if allowed to. Apparently Stanton had earlier broached a colonelcy to which Ellet replied:

> ...Personally, I have two points to submit to you. I would prefer not to hold a military rank unless you deem it indispensable, and in that case, even though it will only be a temporary appointment and for a special duty, I would much prefer that it should be a grade higher. To command the military guard and to stand second to myself in command of the fleet, I would ask leave to name my brother, Captain Alfred W. Ellet of the 59th Illinois Volunteers...[76]

In the same letter, Ellet politely objected to Secretary Stanton's instructions that although he was to command independently, he was still to place himself under the overall orders of Commodore Foote, the senior naval officer assigned to the Army's Western Gunboat Flotilla. Stanton had visualized Ellet subordinating himself and his Ram Fleet to Foote at those particular times when the rams and Foote's flotilla were conducting operations as a joint force. His letter to Ellet had expressed the conditions of such subordination. In a telegram dated April 26th, Stanton explained that he had earlier proposed the rank of colonel (of staff) because he thought it important for Ellet to hold a military rank. He then explained that colonel (of staff) was the highest rank he could bestow without action of the Senate which "would have required considerable red tape and time." As to the request from Ellet that his brother Alfred be commissioned as lieutenant colonel (of staff): This Stanton granted, along with the authority for Alfred W. Ellet to transfer from his former regiment the necessary number of soldiers needed to act as riflemen aboard the rams. Stanton finally decided to meet Charles Ellet halfway over the issue of subordinating the Ram Fleet's tactical employment to Commodore Foote's overall guidance. Stanton accomplished this with a heavy laying on of language designed to smooth feelings; but its ambiguity remains somewhat of a classic and was considerably removed from the tone of a normal military order. The Secretary's diplomacy in that regard would become the root cause of future problems between Ellet and the Navy on the western rivers.

> ...The peculiarity of the enterprise which you have undertaken induced the expression of 'concurrence,' instead of placing you distinctly under the command of the naval commander. There ought not to be two commanders on the same element in war operations; but as the service you are engaged in is peculiar, the naval commander will be so advised, and will be desired not to exercise direct control over your movements unless they shall manifestly expose the general operations on the Mississippi to some unfavorable influence; which is not, however, anticipated.[77]

The rather strange relationship which was to take form between Colonel Ellet and Commodore Foote, and around which Secretary of Stanton had danced within his instructions, seems to have been further confused in a later telegram Stanton sent to Halleck dated April 28, 1862. While discussing the departures of the steam rams from the builders' yards, Stanton described an entirely different arrangement from the one he had earlier expressed to Ellet.

> ...They [the rams] are under command of Colonel Ellet, specially assigned to that duty. He will be subject to the orders of Commodore Foote, and will join him immediately.[78]

There is nothing in the Stanton to Halleck correspondence to show that Charles Ellet was copied with the above which in effect would seemingly have updated Ellet's relationship with Foote. The discrepancy between what Ellet had been told by Stanton and Stanton's directions to Halleck (to which Foote and his successor were both made privy) was to become the source of considerable misunderstanding starting on the very day that Ellet joined forces with Foote.

According to a roster submitted by Colonel Charles Ellet, Jr., for the vessels *QUEEN OF THE WEST* and *MONARCH* and which was made up following the action at Memphis on June 6, 1862, as well as a roster sent in by the captain of the ram *LANCASTER* in late July of the same year, the operating crews of the Ram Fleet were civilian in make up. This arrangement included officers and men. Examining the *QUEEN OF THE WEST* and the *MONARCH* rosters, we find that as of July 1862, Colonel Ellet had not yet settled on standardized job titles. For instance, the deck officers of the *QUEEN OF THE WEST* are referred to as "first master," "second master," "third master;" those of the *MONARCH* are referred to as "captain," "first mate," etc.[79] The roster from *LANCASTER* shows a similar inconsistency insofar as job titles. Warren D. Crandall, a ram fleet veteran and its postwar historian, wrote that it was his impression that it was Ellet's original plan to place aboard each ram a military officer to serve as combat commander as soon as the proper people could be assembled.[80]

On April 19, Ellet had written Secretary Stanton, outlining his plans for the policies under which he intended to employ civilians. He would later ask for specific authority to proceed with those suggested policies when hiring. That last request alluded to certain inadequacies which had cropped up in the labor practices he had followed at the beginning.

> ...[request] authority [be granted] to me to engage the crews and to promise them fair current Mississippi River wages in their several departments, with stipulated allowances for extraordinary dangers and enterprise. The engagement will be very short. What we do with these rams will probably be accomplished within a month after starting the first boat...A month's wages is no adequate compensation for the volunteer crew. I propose, therefore, that in addition to their current wages, they all be issued an extra month's pay for every fortified rebel position they pass below; also, as you have suggested, prize money if they capture prizes in accordance with existing regulations; but as the arrangements of this expedition are not favorable to taking and holding prizes but are calculated essentially to destroy the enemy's floating war property and cripple his means of transportation, that for all services of this character which may be rendered, such compensation should be allowed as in the judgment of the Secretary of War is equitable...I propose to furnish each steamer with the military guard of twelve to twenty men under a lieutenant with an officer of higher grade in command of the whole in addition to the ordinary crew of the boat, to do guard duty at all times and assist in the defense of the boats when necessary.[81]

~

Harassed by a multitude of last minute arrangements, Ellet and his rams would not enter on active operations until May 26, 1862. Prior to that time, Island No. 10 would have been taken, and an action at Plum Bend would be fought between Foote's gunboats and a force of Confederate rams.

The Enemy's Fleet on the Western Rivers

The Confederate Mississippi River Defense Service was the enemy fleet with which Foote and Ellet would have to contend. This fleet was first conceived during January of 1862 by Judah P. Benjamin, the Confederate Secretary of War. By letter, Benjamin ordered that Major General Mansfield Lovell, CSA (who then commanded at New Orleans) seize "fourteen steamships," instructing Lovell that the steamships to be seized were to become a fleet of armed vessels in compliance with "two laws, Numbers 344 and 350...providing $1,000,000 for application to floating defenses for the western rivers and authorizing not more than six thousand men..." This force was not to be a part of the Confederate Navy but instead would be subject to the overall command of the military chief of the department in which the fleet would be ordered to operate. The vessels were to be strengthened for use as rams but also were to be armed as their captains saw fit. Captain J. H. Townsend and Captain James E. Montgomery, were named by President Jefferson Davis as two experienced rivermen. Both were mentioned in Benjamin's instructions as having been personally selected by Davis to command two of these boats. The other captains were to be appointed by Davis at a later date. (Montgomery turned out to be the one who made the later selections.) The captains were to serve under Confederate commissions. Each captain was to recruit his own crew. Benjamin did not make it clear to Lovell as to whether the rest of the crews would be military personnel or individuals retaining civilian status. What evidence there is on the subject seems to indicate that the crews were signed on under a form of shipping articles for a given period of obligation.[82] Confederate correspondence written in the spring of 1862, makes it clear that by then Montgomery was officially the fleet commander, that correspondence having been signed by Montgomery as "Commanding, Mississippi River Defense Service." The same correspondence file includes a letter dated the following day and addressed to General Beauregard. That letter was signed by Brigadier General M. Jeff Thompson who therein identified himself as "Brigadier General, Missouri State Guards, Commanding Confederate Gunners." That and other evidence shows that a force of military gunners under Thompson was attached to Montgomery's command but that Montgomery held tactical control of the fleet, subject to any and all orders which might emanate from the chief of the military department in which he would be operating.[83]

By early April of 1862, the Mississippi River Defense Service consisted of the fourteen vessels which Benjamin had called for. All of them had been strengthened to one degree or another to act as rams, and most, if not all of them, were armed with cannon. Eight of these vessels under Montgomery's direct command had been sent up the Mississippi to aid in the defense of Fort Pillow while six of them were retained downriver under a subordinate commander for the defense of the southern approaches to New Orleans.

~

After the capitulation of Island No. 10 which had occurred on April 8, Flag Officer Foote moved the gunboat flotilla downriver to Tiptonville Landing. (Tiptonville, below New Madrid, was upriver from a curve in the Mississippi then called Plum Run Bend. Fort Pillow, the next target for Federal conquest, was just below that bend.) Foote placed his gunboats into line of battle to await whatever the Confederates had in mind. He would not have to wait for long.

The morning following Foote's arrival at Tiptonville Landing, five of Montgomery's vessels came into sight from downriver. They opened fire on the Federal gunboats but then hurriedly turned back downriver. Foote ordered a chase but called it off when he saw that further pursuit would only expose his gunboats to the range of Fort Pillow's cannon. It was still too early for Foote to test the effectiveness of that fort's artillery. The planning for an assault against Fort Pillow called for the use of mortar boats to first soften up the place. Only when the fort appeared to be markedly damaged would a direct attack be attempted. An assault by Pope's infantry, now downriver by transports from New Madrid, would hit the Fort Pillow defenses from the land side. The gunboats, in support of another force of infantry which were landed from Army transports, were to come at the defenses from the river. After Fort Pillow was taken, it was planned that the same tactic would be put into play farther downriver against Fort Randolph.

Pope's men were in encampment at Osceola, a town on the Arkansas bank. They were to remain there while Foote's mortar boats went into action. But no sooner had Pope's troops settled into their tents than orders came from Major General Halleck that Pope was to start reloading them onto transports and proceed back up the Mississippi to Cairo and from there up the Ohio and into the Tennessee to Pittsburg

Landing. From there, Pope and his men were then to march in reinforcement to Grant who was now in front of Corinth after having fought the battle at Shiloh on April 6 and 7. By the 18th of April, thirty transports loaded with Pope's force consisting of fourteen thousand five hundred men with around five thousand horses had left Osceola for the Tennessee. To support Foote in front of Fort Pillow, Pope had left behind at Osceola about fifteen hundred infantry under Colonel Graham N. Fitch -- hardly enough strength to carry out a frontal assault against well defended battlements.

~

While Pope was on his way to the Tennessee to reinforce Grant, a second steamboat movement was taking place from Cape Girardeau (a place north of Cairo on the Mississippi). This movement entailed an 8,000-man force which had previously been engaged in operations within the interior of Arkansas. These troops would also support Grant. Halleck had decided to put all matters on the Mississippi on hold while he marshaled everything available toward the defeat of Beauregard who was expected to hold his defensive positions either at or near Corinth.

~

Indications now seemed to be that whatever happened at Forts Pillow and Randolph would depend on whether Beauregard could hold Corinth and on how the fleet of the Mississippi River Defense Service (now moored just below Fort Pillow) would measure up in a showdown fight against the Union gunboats. If Corinth fell, or if Beauregard abandoned it, there would be little point in the Confederates holding on to either Fort Pillow or Fort Randolph. Even though these forts might be defended in the immediate sense, a defeat of Montgomery's Mississippi River Defense Service would cut off supply to them from downriver. The garrisons would simply be left isolated to wither on the vine for lack of sustenance. At least that was the then current Federal thinking on the subject -- all problematical of course. Foote decided that his best option would be to hold his moored positions and attempt to pound Fort Pillow into submission with the mortar boats.[84]

For the bombardment of Fort Pillow, each morning one or sometimes two mortar boats were towed down the river and into firing positions where they were moored securely to the river bank just out of line of sight from the Confederate gunners at the fort. Each day, one of the gunboats would "ride shotgun" over the mortar boats on firing station so as to guard against any upriver foray on the part of Montgomery's fleet. The only drawback to this system, and one which was soon to be all too readily apparent to Foote and his officers, was the inability to spot any enemy steamers coming from the direction of Fort Pillow, that is until an approaching craft was within less than a mile.

The wound that Foote had received at Fort Donelson was by now causing him acute agony. He feared that the pain was clouding his ability, and he asked the Secretary of the Navy to relieve him of his command, a request which was granted on May 9. Fleet Captain (soon to be Flag Officer) Charles Henry Davis, was assigned as Foote's relief. When Davis arrived to take over, he hardly had a chance to settle in before Montgomery's vessels moved to the attack.

MORTAR BOAT 16, which had the day's firing duty, had been towed downstream at first light and was moored fast against the bank at Craigshead Point. The gunboat escort for the day was *CINCINNATI*. According to one of the accounts, steam was let down on the *CINCINNATI* as soon as her mooring lines had been run out. Crewmen were then put to the work of scrubbing down the decks. While this maintenance activity was taking place, her lookouts sighted steamers at a distance of three-fourths of a mile, coming on fast. The engineers on *CINCINNATI* frantically tossed anything they had, including lubricating oil, into the fire boxes in an effort to get up at least enough steam to allow steerageway toward a shallow bar behind which *CINCINNATI's* commander hoped the Confederate rams could not get at him. Meanwhile, the crews of the *CARONDELET* and *PITTSBURG*, having spotted what was happening, cast off from the bank and at best speed, considering their own low steam pressures, headed downriver in support. Moored across the river from *CARONDELET* and *PITTSBURG* were the *CAIRO* and the *SAINT LOUIS*, both hidden from view by the morning haze. Consequently, their lookouts could not see what was happening. *BENTON* and *MOUND CITY* were both closer to the scene and not affected by the haze.

The young officer on *MORTAR BOAT 16* reduced his powder charges to the shortest range possible, and with fuses cut, fired his mortar so as to burst the shells directly over the oncoming Confederate rams. The entirety of the Mississippi River Defense Service fleet on the upper Mississippi -- eight vessels in all -- was by now in clear view (all appearing to be rams carrying cannon on their bows). The captain of *MOUND CITY* had by now seen what was happening and with his engineers reporting partial steam on the boilers, he ordered the mooring lines off the bank. With the flow of the river acting as an assist, he made for the scene of action. So did the captain of *BENTON*. When within about three-eighths of a mile range, the Federal gunboats opened up against the Confederate lead ram, the *GENERAL BRAGG*, but they had to stop firing when *CINCINNATI* came into line between them and the target. *GENERAL BRAGG* then struck *CINCINNATI* on her starboard quarter and holed her above the waterline. For a time the two steamers held together while *CINCINNATI's* gunners blasted away at point blank range. When *GENERAL BRAGG* finally broke clear, a broadside from *CINCINNATI* knocked out the Confederate vessel's steering gear, eliminating her from the fight. No longer under her helmsman's control, *GENERAL BRAGG* drifted downriver with the current. Meanwhile, *CINCINNATI* started to retreat upriver with two Confederate rams, the *GENERAL STERLING PRICE* and the *GENERAL SUMTER*, in close pursuit. Both of them now struck *CINCINNATI*, putting her into a sinking condition. *BENTON* hit *GENERAL SUMTER* with a lucky shot which severed a steam line, producing some dramatic visual effects; however, the actual damage was slight. Now it became *MOUND CITY's* turn to suffer when she was rammed by a glancing blow from the *GENERAL EARL VAN DORN*. This caused the Federal gunboat to take on water which was incentive enough for her commander to start back up the river. The Confederate rams were now beginning to receive well-directed fire from the remaining Federal gunboats. Because of that, together with the realization that his maneuvers were taking him into shoal waters, Montgomery signaled his captains to withdraw. As the enemy rams began to turn downstream, they were closely followed by the undamaged *BENTON* and the *CARONDELET* which kept up their pursuit until the Confederates were under the protection of Fort Pillow's guns. At that point, the chase was broken off.

Damage to the Confederates was first thought to be heavy; but actually it was quite negligible.[85] According to the reports of Davis's officers, the boilers of *GENERAL BRAGG* and *GENERAL SUMTER* were thought to have exploded, but in fact *GENERAL BRAGG* had suffered only light damage to her steering gear. The damage to *GENERAL SUMTER* was also minor.[86] The Federal flotilla had, on the other hand, taken a real beating. For some time, Davis would lose the services of *CINCINNATI* and *MOUND CITY*. *CINCINNATI* had sunk to the river's bottom with only her super structure showing. She was, however, raised and then patched enough to keep her afloat. *MOUND CITY's* entire bow structure had been wrenched off. She, too, would have sunk had it not been for one of the Flotilla's auxiliaries which, in the nick of time, provided a heavy pump. Both gunboats were towed upriver to Cairo where they underwent repairs.[87]

The action at Plum Run Bend was seen as proof of the effectiveness of rams against armored gunboats. To counter Montgomery in the future, some protective steps would have to be taken. Davis's captains jointly decided in conference on the use of log buttresses to be hung horizontally over the vulnerable areas of the gunboats such as their boilers and powder magazines. Further defense would have to count on the arrival of Ellet and his rams.

From the Confederate viewpoint, the report of Montgomery, as he made it to his superior General Beauregard, was a jubilant one.

> General M. Jeff Thompson was on the *GENERAL BRAGG*; his officers and men were divided among the boats. They were all at their posts, ready to do good service should an occasion offer. To my officers and men, I am highly indebted for their courage and promptness in executing orders.[88]

Montgomery concluded that report by predicting that unless the enemy, "greatly increase[s] their force, they will never penetrate farther down the river." There is no evidence to indicate that Montgomery was at the time aware of the impending arrival, or even of the existence of the Ellet Ram Fleet.

Following the action, Flag Officer Davis reported on the prognosis for the taking of Fort Pillow.

> Sir:
> I have the honor to inform the Department that the result of General Quinby's reconnaissance [the senior Army troop commander then on the scene] is that he considers a greater number of troops than that which he has with him (in the District) necessary for the success of the operations we have had in contemplation.
> He has returned to Hickman with his command where he will wait for reinforcements.
> Since I last wrote the Department, Lieutenant Colonel [Alfred] Ellet has brought down four of the rams, hastily prepared for service. I have no doubt that they will be useful in the event of another engagement.
> The *MOUND CITY* has rejoined the flotilla.
> It is far from my expectation that the rebel gunboats will venture to renew the attack.[89]

Ellet Arrives At Fort Pillow

Charles Ellet, Jr., arrived at Fort Pillow on May 26 shortly after his brother Lieutenant Colonel Alfred W. Ellet appeared on the scene with the first four of the rams. Despite being a novice to the profession of arms, no one could have accused Colonel Charles Ellet, Jr., of being shy about making his presence known to the military professionals. The day after his arrival at Fort Pillow he put before the Navy's Davis a tactical plan of action. Writing to the Secretary of War, Ellet described that first interview with Davis.

> Above Fort Pillow
> May 27, 1862
> I arrived at my fleet yesterday, leaving one of my boats at New Albany, ready to follow in twenty-four hours. The others are all here.
> I visited Commodore [Flag Officer] Davis immediately to obtain his views and offer cooperation. The Commodore intimated an unwillingness to assume any risk at this time, but will communicate with me again, after further reflection touching my proposition to him to run below these batteries [Fort Pillow] and surprise the enemy's fleet and transports before they can escape up the tributaries.
> To me, the risk is greater to lie here with my small guard and within an hour's march of a strong encampment of the enemy, than to run by the batteries and make the attack. I shall, if necessary, repeat the proposition the moment the SWITZERLAND arrives with the barges I have prepared to shelter the boats. I wish to take advantage of the high water.[90]

The barges which Ellet had referred to in his report to the Secretary were to be placed alongside the rams so as to buffer them against enemy shell fire. This arrangement was not just a simple matter of tying a barge alongside. Rather, it necessitated a considerable construction technique which was described by one of Colonel Ellet's officers.

> Over the barge was built a sharp angled roof made of twelve inch square timber formed by securely bolting one end of the plank to the gunwales along both sides of the barge and drawing them together at the top, making the apex of the angle higher than the ram, the sides of the roof presenting a resistance of twenty-four inches of solid timber to the rebel guns. To guard against line shots Colonel Ellet had the angles formed between the side walls of the barge above the gunwales and the slanting timbers filled with draft, wood blocks, etc., making a perfect resistance against all such shots.[91]

Ellet's idea for making a run past the fort was markedly different from the plan which had earlier been developed between Foote and Halleck; but that plan was now on hold and had been since Pope's infantry departed for Corinth. Ignoring the thinking of the professionals who advocated waiting for Pope's return, the impatient Ellet kept pushing Davis for a river dash past the fort. Davis more than once rejected Ellet's suggestions, feeling they were far too risky. In an attempt to guide the colonel into a more military way of doing things, Davis tried to school him on how the Navy believed the rams could best be utilized. He also attempted (by letter) to counsel Ellet as to what the Navy Department believed should be the subordinate role Ellet and his rams should play in a working relationship with the Western Gunboat Flotilla and its designated commander.

> Dear Sir:
>
> I have thought over a great deal the subject of our conversation on Monday morning and have come to the following conclusion: [This was a conversation during which Ellet had proposed that his rams should take the van in any future movement against the enemy's fleet.]
>
> It will be most expedient and proper that the gunboats should take the front rank in a naval engagement with the enemy, and that the rams coming up in the rear, should watch for an opportunity, either to take the enemy in the flank, to assail any straggler, to assist any disabled vessel of our squadron, and to pounce upon and carry off any disabled vessel of the enemy.
>
> The gunboats of the flotilla and the rams bear to each other the relation of heavy artillery and light skirmishers; and to expose the latter to the first brunt and shock of battle would be to misapply their peculiar usefulness and mode of warfare.
>
> It is my wish, therefore, in the event of a naval engagement that the rams under your command should follow in the rear and on the wings of my squadron; particular instructions being given to their captains to profit by every opportunity of assailing a vessel of the enemy's flotilla, or making a prize of one of his disabled boats.
>
> If these directions are agreeable to you, I will thank you to communicate them to the captains under your immediate command; if not, we will confer again upon the subject...[92]

Ellet proved totally unreceptive to Davis's counsel. He wrote the Secretary of War, complaining that he had not received any specific answer to his suggestions made to Davis in that the flag officer join with him in a combined movement to pass Fort Pillow and engage the enemy's fleet below the fort. Ellet concluded by stating that if he did not get Davis's cooperation, he would move downriver on his own.[93] Meanwhile, Ellet kept nagging Davis, bringing his argument to the point of an ultimatum directed by letter on June 1.

Ellet got his answer. It was a decidedly negative one couched by Davis in an angry tone.

> Sir:
>
> I have received your letter of yesterday. I decline taking any part in the expedition which you inform me you are preparing to set on foot tomorrow morning at early dawn.
>
> I would thank you to inform me how far you consider yourself under my authority; and I shall esteem it a favor to receive from you a copy of the orders under which you are acting.[94]

Within what must have been a time span of only minutes from the receipt of Davis's refusal and demand, Ellet penned his reply, stating that he regretted Davis's "indisposition to cooperate in a movement against the enemy's fleet lying within easy reach." He also tersely informed the flag officer that, "I do not consider myself at all under your authority." The next morning, Ellet penned off a follow-up. This contained excerpts of his instructions relative to authority to act independently, at least as he, Ellet, viewed the matter. These excerpts were from the first instructions he had received from Secretary Stanton.[95] Ellet closed by stating to Davis that he would concur with the flag officer's objections only if, "...in your opinion, the success of a general operation will be jeopardized by that which I propose to undertake." That same day, Davis replied in what can only be described as resignation toward Ellet's impulsiveness. While neglecting to state any formal objection, Davis absolved himself of any blame for consequences resulting from whatever Ellet might do on his own hook.

In a telegraph to Secretary Stanton, Ellet outlined what he was about to undertake.

> An exaggerated view of the power of these rebel rams has spread among my fleet from the gunboats, and I feel the necessity of doing something to check the extension of the contagion. I am fully impressed with the hazards of this enterprise; but I deem the object sufficient to warrant the movement. I will take command of the *QUEEN OF THE WEST*. My brother, Lieutenant Colonel [Alfred W.] Ellet will follow with the *MONARCH*, so as to double the chance of reaching the rebel boat... [The "rebel boat" to which Ellet refers was one moored under the protection of Fort Pillow's guns.] [96]

Ellet concluded by stating that he was taking full responsibility for whatever happened and that only volunteers were to go on either of the boats. When the colonel announced to the crew of the *QUEEN OF THE WEST* what he had in mind and asked for volunteers, the response was disappointing to say the least. Nearly the entire civilian crew, including the captain, two out of three of the pilots, the first mate, and all the engineers walked off with their baggage.

Crew attitudes aboard the *MONARCH* were far better, a result perhaps of that crew's perception that Alfred W. Ellet did not have quite the 'succeed or die' type of fatalism which was becoming so apparent within the makeup of Charles Ellet, Jr. *MONARCH's* crew (other than one pilot) volunteered to the man. Meanwhile, the senior Ellet managed to gather together new crewmembers for those positions left vacant on *QUEEN OF THE WEST*. These volunteers were mainly Army enlisted men who had been part of the armed guard detachments posted to the other rams.

The crewing problems on *QUEEN OF THE WEST* were eventually put right as Ellet would later state in a report written on June 16 to Secretary of War Stanton.

> Two weeks ago, a demoralization, proceeding wholly from cowardice began to agitate the [ram] fleet...The crew that left the *QUEEN OF THE WEST* and allowed volunteers to take their place came to me and expressed their humiliation and begged me to give them another chance, promising never to fail me again.[97]

Ellet would come up with a rather unique way to deal with the worst of his reluctant civilian crewmembers. One such individual was Thomas Littell, the pilot of the *MONARCH* and the only person on that ram who refused to stay aboard for the attack against Fort Pillow. Littell had informed Ellet that he did not wish to risk life and limb in the attack. Ellet laid out the consequences for such refusal in a letter dated June 1, 1862, which he addressed to Littell.

Sir:

You have informed me this minute, in presence of Lieutenant Colonel Ellet, second in command [of the Ram Fleet and commander of the *MONARCH*], Captain Dryden, First Master of the *MONARCH*, and Doctor Robarts, surgeon of the fleet, that you came on board the steam ram *MONARCH* a pilot in the expectation that that boat was to be placed in no danger, was not to be exposed to shot, where you would be in no danger of being hurt; and that you are not willing to remain on the boat if she is really to be exposed to the casualties of war.

Under these circumstances, I have concluded to give you a pass to Cairo, where you can show this letter with a copy of the enclosed oath to which you subscribed when you came aboard to Brigadier General Strong, who will inform you whether or not you are entitled to wages, and how you are to proceed to procure them in case you have any just claim.

While you cannot remain longer on board the *MONARCH*. I cannot allow you to have intercourse with anyone in the fleet, beyond which I will place you under no restraint.

Charles Ellet, Jr., Colonel, Commanding Ram Fleet[98]

QUEEN OF THE WEST and *MONARCH* headed for the enemy steamer tied under the protection of Fort Pillow's guns. Hardly had they started out when their crews saw the enemy vessel slip its lines and head downriver to the protection of Montgomery's fleet. Quite wisely, Ellet decided not to follow. In his telegraphed report to Washington in which he discussed that unsuccessful foray, Ellet vented his frustration by informing Secretary Stanton that Davis had not only refused to join with him in a full fleet movement down the river, but had denied him the right to solicit volunteers from the Western Gunboat Flotilla crews.[99]

One positive result of Ellet's run toward the cannon of Fort Pillow was the discovery that only "seven or eight guns" had fired at his boats. This lack of response gave credence to the mounting intelligence being gathered from patrols and deserters that Fort Pillow had been recently evacuated of most of its cannon. The night after Ellet's foray, and again on the next night following, separate and independent reconnaissance patrols were sent out by Ellet and by Colonel Fitch who was the infantry commander then on the scene. These patrols verified that most of the guns and what appeared to be the largest part of the garrison had departed. It looked promising that an attack from the land (even if only in brigade strength) if carried out in combination with supportive fire from the gunboats, could succeed in taking the place. Planning for that assault was begun. On the late afternoon of June 4, deserters came in telling of a total evacuation. Columns of smoke rising above the fort indicated that the enemy was destroying what remained. Colonel Fitch loaded a detachment of his infantry aboard the transport *HATTIE GILMORE* and after sunset proceeded downriver toward the fort, stopping only to inform Davis and Ellet that if his infantrymen found the fort deserted, they would make a signal. Preceded by a small scout force sent in by rowboats, the *HATTIE GILMORE* was eased against the Fort Pillow wharf. The troops disembarked and fanned out toward the battlements. They met no opposition; the place was found to be totally theirs.[100]

With daylight, Colonel Fitch, in company with the Navy's Lieutenant S. Ledyard Phelps, the skipper of the *BENTON*, made a detailed examination of the Fort Pillow works and found that most of the remaining enemy guns were still intact, only a few having been spiked. An attempt had been made to burn the gun carriages, but even that turned out to be a halfway measure. Phelps would report that a considerable effort seemed to have been put into constructing the battlements, but that expertise in military engineering was not evident from the results. He explained that among other things, fields of fire were poorly laid out and that few of the guns could have been depressed sufficiently to bear on vessels passing close in to the river's bank. [101]

Davis, in consultation with Fitch, decided that one company of infantry, together with one gunboat left behind to protect the approaches from the Arkansas side of the river would be sufficient to garrison Fort Pillow. The remainder of the Western Gunboat Flotilla was to be moved downriver toward Fort Randolph, the next Confederate fortification commanding passage on the river. Ellet, impetuous as always, does not seem to have attended this conference but rather had moved downriver on his own cognizance to discover that Fort Randolph had been abandoned.

Corinth Evacuated and Related Confederate Withdrawals

By May 30, the railroad center at Corinth had been evacuated by Beauregard who then moved his force southward to Tupelo, Mississippi. This pullout cut the Confederates off from east to west rail communication with Memphis and consequently removed much of the flank protection that Memphis had previously enjoyed. It seems fairly certain from what can be ascertained from enemy records that the Confederate high command had decided that it would pull all of its land forces (then on the Mississippi) downriver toward Vicksburg. Whether that decision was coordinated with Beauregard's decision to abandon Corinth is not completely clear, but in any case, the enemy's withdrawals took place at about the same point in time. The most apparent reason why the enemy remained at Fort Pillow and Fort Randolph as long as it had was the need to buy time while manufacturing machinery and military materiel were being evacuated from Memphis.

The Confederate commander at Memphis, Colonel Thomas H. Rosser, described the situation at Memphis in a telegraph he sent on June 3 to his regional superior, Brigadier General Daniel Ruggles.

> The GOLDEN AGE passed down this morning from Fort Pillow with troops for Vicksburg. We may have about 200 troops here on whom to depend, and can make no defense except against a very meager force. We shall remain till everything is shipped and as much longer as possible. Nearly everything has been forwarded. Will finish today probably.[102]

There was one Confederate optimist who still held out hope for holding the Mississippi River above Vicksburg. That man was Brigadier General M. Jeff Thompson, the person in charge of the gunners and sharpshooters assigned to Montgomery's Mississippi River Defense Service. In a telegram to Brigadier General Ruggles, Thompson argued that the river could still be held above Memphis.

> If not already done, for God's sake, order the [Mississippi] River Defense [Service] fleet to defend every bend and dispute every mile of river from Fort Pillow

[to] here. I am willing and believe I am able to hold the river if Montgomery will cooperate, which I believe he will.[103]

Thompson's idea of an heroic holding action seems to have been more bluster than any honest intention on his part. Two days following his offer to Ruggles to "defend every bend" of the river, Thompson again wrote Ruggles, this time asking that the troops under his command (which constituted most of the Mississippi River Defense Service's gunners and all of its sharpshooters) be relieved from duty. The reason, as Thompson stated, was their dissatisfaction with the assignment and their inability to get along with Montgomery's crews.[104] Reading between the lines, this second letter (Thompson to Ruggles) seems to have been motivated by Thompson's desire to unseat Montgomery as the senior officer in charge of the Mississippi River Defense Service and have himself placed into that command slot. If that be so, the attempt was at least partly effective since on the following day Thompson received orders that he was now to be in joint command with Montgomery. However, at the time of his being given the joint command, neither Thompson nor any of his men remained with the Mississippi River Defense Service. The very same day that he had requested that his men be relieved of duty with the fleet, but before receiving a reply from Ruggles, he had arbitrarily moved his command ashore. At the time Thompson received the order to take joint command with Montgomery, he and his men were standing by in the railroad depot at Memphis awaiting a train to the south for Grenada. Thompson would later state that he intended to bring his men back out to the fleet (apparently, one could suppose, when it arrived off Memphis) but that the situation at the time had prevented it. Whether that was true is highly debatable; nevertheless, when Montgomery's fleet next met in battle against Davis and Ellet, the Confederate vessels would be devoid of their assigned gunners. Montgomery's civilian crewmembers would have to fill that role as best they could. Following the war, Thompson wrote his memoirs wherein he sloughed over the circumstances of why he had abandoned Montgomery's fleet when he did.[105] As one might look upon the situation with the Mississippi River Defense Service, it was the low state of discipline of both Montgomery's rivermen and Thompson's own troops that motivated Thompson to take his men ashore. A condition of near anarchy within Thompson's command is described in the memoirs.[106]

Battle of Memphis

At noon on June 5, Davis's gunboats pulled away from Fort Pillow, leaving behind the *PITTSBURG* which was to stay there as a guard vessel. The gunboat *MOUND CITY* was to follow behind the rest of the flotilla, acting as shepherd to a convoy of steamers carrying Fitch's main force of infantry. Not long after Davis's departure, the lead gunboat sighted a steamboat downriver. An armed tug was sent ahead to try to capture it. It turned out to be the *SOVEREIGN* which was added to the rapidly building number of auxiliaries of the Western Gunboat Flotilla.

By sunset, Davis had reached a distance of about one and a half miles above Memphis. Strung out close behind in his wake were the flotilla's mortar boats and their towboats along with the ordnance boats and the commissary boats which made up Davis's train. Davis signaled the auxiliaries to tie to the bank of Island No. 44, a mile or two upriver from the gunboats which were by then abreast of Island No. 45.[107] Some miles farther up the river, darkness had overtaken Ellet's rams which were proceeding in company with MOUND CITY and Fitch's troop transports. While there was still light, that assemblage moored to the river's bank.[108]

When the dawn broke on the morning of June 6, Davis saw downstream of his position "rebel rams and gunboats, numbering eight vessels in all." When sighted, the enemy fleet was lying moored to the bank. When they in turn sighted the Federal gunboats, they dropped downriver. This maneuver was not intended for the purpose of escape, but rather was to give Montgomery steaming room for the formation of a line of battle. Seeing what was happening, Davis (on board BENTON) signaled LOUISVILLE, CARONDELET, CAIRO, and SAINT LOUIS to get underway and work downstream in an alignment to afford each of the gunboats the best vantage point for directing fire against the enemy.

At the first glimmer of dawn, Ellet started his rams down the river. He came in sight of the Federal gunboats at about the same time that Davis was ordering them into alignment. Ellet (on board QUEEN OF THE WEST) signaled the other rams -- MONARCH, LANCASTER, and SWITZERLAND -- to move over against the Arkansas shore and hold position. Ellet wanted the opportunity to board a tug which could take him over to Davis on the BENTON for a conference before the action started. Just as the rams were settling up against the Arkansas bank, the Confederate vessels opened fire against the Federal gunboats. Seeing this, Ellet motioned the tug away and ordered "full ahead" for QUEEN OF THE WEST. Waving his hat from the hurricane deck of the QUEEN OF THE WEST, he gestured MONARCH to follow while he steamed straight through Davis's line of gunboats. What the thoughts of Davis and his officers were at that moment is not of record, but the enlisted men seemed to approve of Ellet's aggressiveness, cheering when the two rams passed by.

The scene into which the gunboats and the rams soon became framed was later described by Alfred W. Ellet who had been on the MONARCH. He wrote of a solid wall of black smoke, so dense that a minute or two after the lead boat (QUEEN OF THE WEST) had passed abeam of the line of gunboats, all that the men on MONARCH could see was the top of QUEEN OF THE WEST's smoke stack.[109] Once QUEEN OF THE WEST got clear of the "wall of smoke," Alfred W. Ellet again caught view of his brother, who was now frantically pointing toward the closest Confederate vessel, GENERAL STERLING PRICE, which he apparently wanted Alfred to ram. The senior Ellet then headed his own QUEEN OF THE WEST straight toward the Confederate GENERAL LOVELL. As QUEEN OF THE WEST drew closer on a bow-to-bow collision course, the GENERAL LOVELL's skipper began to lose his nerve, attempting to turn clear; but he had not acted quite fast enough. Ellet drove in. The resulting collision cut the "rebel ram in two, and she disappeared under the dark waters in less time than it takes to tell the story."[110] While Charles Ellet, Jr., was in the act of backing away from the sinking GENERAL LOVELL, the Confederate rams GENERAL BEAUREGARD and GENERAL SUMTER had worked themselves uncomfortably close to QUEEN OF THE WEST. Within the span of two minutes, both of them struck -- one on QUEEN OF THE WEST's starboard side and the other on her port side. The chaos which followed was heightened by the deafening noise of the engines of all three rams. In trying to disengage, each of them were being run astern at full throttle. The noise was heightened by the sound of grinding hulls and shouting men. Ellet, rushing out of his pilot house to get a better vantage of what was taking place, received a bullet in the knee.[111] Falling to the deck, he shouted orders for his pilot to head for the river bank, judging quite logically, because of the force and location of the ramming, that the *QUEEN OF THE WEST* was probably going to sink.

GENERAL STERLING PRICE, the enemy ram that Charles Ellet had first directed the *MONARCH* to attack was sunk. Witnesses of that event who saw things take place from the *GENERAL BEAUREGARD*, and Brigadier General M. Jeff Thompson who saw the action unfold from the Memphis levee, were collectively of the opinion that the damage was self-inflicted. According to both accounts, *GENERAL STERLING PRICE* and *GENERAL BEAUREGARD* had been headed toward *MONARCH*, each on an angled attack of about 45 degrees, one pointed at the Federal ram's starboard bow and the other at the port bow. Each of them, according to the witnesses, missed *MONARCH* by inches with the inevitable result that the Confederate vessels crashed into each other. Crewmembers on *MONARCH* said there was first a glancing collision between *GENERAL STERLING PRICE* and *MONARCH* seconds before the *GENERAL STERLING PRICE* collided with *GENERAL BEAUREGARD*. Conversely, Colonel Charles Ellet, Jr., backed his brother Alfred's claim of having struck *GENERAL STERLING PRICE* by writing in the Ram Fleet's action report that "piles of furniture were precipitated from the rebel steamer upon the forecastle of the *MONARCH* which were found there after the battle." Regardless of who hit who, the *GENERAL STERLING PRICE* then ran hard onto the Arkansas shore, recoiled slightly, and then settled to the bottom.

MONARCH's attention now turned to the *GENERAL BEAUREGARD* which was attempting to escape downriver. *MONARCH* overtook her and rammed the Confederate hard abeam. Members of *GENERAL BEAUREGARD's* crew ran out on deck to surrender, waving an assortment of white towels and other garments.[112] Another of the Confederate rams, the *LITTLE REBEL* (with fleet commander James E. Montgomery aboard) was already banged up so badly from the shellfire of the gunboats that her crew decided to run her ashore. On the way in toward the river bank, *MONARCH* struck a blow to her stern, moments before the *LITTLE REBEL's* keel felt the mud. *LITTLE REBEL* was pushed ashore hard, coming to rest half in the mud and half on the bank with not even a slim hope of being able to get off under her own machinery's power.

Watching all of the confusion, veiled as it was at times by a pall of smoke, were the citizens of Memphis who had lined the bluffs as if they were on some great grandstand. One of those observers, as already stated, was M. Jeff Thompson whose proper place should have been with Montgomery and the fleet. Thompson later wrote to Beauregard that the *LITTLE REBEL* had been completely riddled and that he, Thompson, believed that Montgomery must have been killed. Thompson, wrong about so many other things, was wrong again. Montgomery and a good portion of his crew had managed to scramble ashore and escape.

After Alfred W. Ellet backed *MONARCH* away from *LITTLE REBEL*, he turned his attention to *GENERAL BEAUREGARD* which was then in the process of sinking. His crew got a line on the foundering rebel vessel and towed the hulk onto a sand bar where it settled, to become a total loss.[113] The Federal gunboats were by now coming up, but their arrival was not timely enough to cut off the escape of *GENERAL SUMTER   GENERAL M. JEFF THOMPSON,   GENERAL EARL VAN DORN,* and *GENERAL BRAGG.* All four vessels, with full steam up, were heading downriver, the gunboats now in pursuit. Joining in that pursuit were the rams *MONARCH* and *SWITZERLAND*, the latter having finally caught up with events. The chase resulted in the capture of all but the *GENERAL EARL VAN DORN* which made good her escape.

The *LANCASTER* and *SWITZERLAND*, both of which Colonel Ellet had thought were close behind him, had missed the heat of the action. As Ellet would critique their activity in his report, the *LANCASTER's* skipper as well as her pilot seemed to have "become excited and confused," mixing up signals sent by bell to the engine room. The embarrassing result was that *LANCASTER* was backed hard against the shore, disabling both of her rudders.[114] The skipper of the *SWITZERLAND*, having been in receipt of orders from Ellet to hold in line "a half mile behind the *LANCASTER* during the engagement," decided -- or so the skipper later claimed -- that his duty therefore lay in assisting the *LANCASTER* to safely moor to the bank. The delay created by his solicitous attendance kept *SWITZERLAND* safely out of the fight. As Charles Ellet was to put it, and with considerable bitterness, "the brunt of the fight had fallen upon the *QUEEN OF THE WEST* and the *MONARCH*."

Despite the pain of his wound and the immobilizing fact that his *QUEEN OF THE WEST* was hard aground against the river's bank, Colonel Charles Ellet, Jr. still had that urge to be first at any place which might have a significance. When one of *QUEEN OF THE WEST's* crew sighted a white flag flying above the city, Ellet sent his son, Medical Cadet Charles R. Ellet, ashore to take the surrender. (This occurred at about the same time that the gunboats, together with the *SWITZERLAND* and *MONARCH* were passing downriver in their chase after Montgomery's surviving rams.) Accompanying Ellet's son were an officer and two privates from the military guard off *QUEEN OF THE WEST* -- a not overly impressive landing force under the safest of circumstances. Although the mayor of Memphis met them politely, the reception on the part of the general citizenry was not a cordial one. A day or so later, Colonel Ellet described his son's experience within a report to the Secretary of War.

> The party was surrounded by an excited crowd using angry and threatening language. They ascended to the top of the post office and planted the flag, though fired upon several times and stoned by the mob below, still I believe that this conduct was reprobated by the people of standing in the place.[115]

The four from *QUEEN OF THE WEST*, which must have been a very nervous group, made it back to their vessel without injury. A couple of hours later, Lieutenant S. L. Phelps, the captain of Davis's flagship *BENTON*, was back from the downriver chase. He then was sent ashore by Davis to accept the town's surrender. Phelps was more pleasantly received, the local citizenry seemingly having calmed down after venting their spleen against young Ellet and party. As Phelps would report in writing to Davis:

I carried the demand for the surrender of the city to the mayor, and was saluted
by a number of ladies and passed through the immense crowd without molestation or
evidence of an exasperated or bitterly hating people and saw no scowling women.[116]

A point of humor came out of those duplicated surrender episodes.
Although both Colonel Ellet and Flag Officer Davis later placed great emphasis on their
taking of the surrender -- each of them making a claim that it was his people who were
the first to accept the capitulation -- the honor really belonged to another who went
ashore later, this being Colonel G. N. Fitch. When young Ellet and Phelps had each
paid their respective visits, the mayor, one John Park, told each of them that he did not
possess the authority to surrender to military officers. However, to Fitch, he expressed
his full desire to surrender the city without reservation.[117]

~

One episode which would continue to disrupt relationships between the
Ellets and the Navy's gunboat people involved *LITTLE REBEL*. Although damaged by
gunboat shellfire, she had actually been forced aground by Alfred W. Ellet's *MONARCH*.
Ignoring that aspect, Flag Officer Davis claimed her as a prize of the gunboats, riding
rough-shod over arguments to the contrary. The controversy continued past what was
to be the short command tenure of Charles Ellet, Jr. It lingered on to create
considerable animosity between his successor Alfred W. Ellet and Flag Officer Davis.
As late as August 30th, Alfred W. Ellet wrote Assistant Quartermaster James Brooks,
complaining that Secretary of War Stanton had promised "the late Charles Ellet, Jr.,"
that the men of the *MONARCH* could expect the prize money due them; yet the matter
continued to be ignored by the War Department. In a later letter to a War Department
official, Alfred would state, "If they [the Congress] should in their wisdom conclude to
transfer the Ram Fleet over to the Navy, it will promptly close my services with it. I
never will permit myself to be made subject to Davis, after what has occurred between
us." According to Warren D. Crandall who was adjutant for the Ram Fleet, the
MONARCH crew eventually received a share of the prize money allocated for
LITTLE REBEL.[118]

~

For the Union, the battle of Memphis was of tremendous significance
toward the control of the central portion of the Mississippi corridor. It had been a
victory won with but a minimal cost to the Union in blood and materiel. The
QUEEN OF THE WEST had been damaged, but, as it turned out, not seriously. There
were no immediate deaths of Federal personnel, and only one man out of the entire
attacking force was wounded, that man being Colonel Charles Ellet, Jr. Although
Ellet's wound was at first thought not to be serious, it soon became infected; he would
be dead before the month was out.[119]

Memphis and its environs were now solidly in Union hands. Before the
passage of many weeks, the city would become one of the most important of the
Union's river ports. It soon became an assembly point for amphibious operations up
the White River and the Arkansas River and a marshaling point for troops and supplies
in preparation for future river movements against Vicksburg.

ON THE CENTRAL MISSISSIPPI
EARLY ATTEMPTS AGAINST VICKSBURG

Going Above New Orleans

Back in the early spring (April 25, 1862) David G. Farragut had taken formal possession of New Orleans, but as earlier related, the city was not secured until later when Major General Benjamin F. Butler's troops arrived to occupy it. In the five days between Farragut's arrival and Butler's occupation, the Confederates had been able to evacuate considerable military and industrial materiel. The absence of Federal restraint during those five days also allowed the destruction of a number of Confederate vessels laying alongside the New Orleans wharves. This deprived Union quartermasters of a number of river craft which otherwise could have proven useful in the campaigns to come. Despite his having allowed this to happen, Farragut was lauded for taking the city and was promoted to rear admiral.

~

Conflicting reports were coming in about what was transpiring with Foote above Memphis. Two Negroes who had come down from Memphis told one of Farragut's officers that Fort Pillow and Memphis were now in the hands of Yankee gunboats. This report proved premature considering that it would not be until the end of the first week in June that Memphis was taken. This was typical of the kind of inaccurate intelligence which was burdening Farragut and Butler at the time.

The original planning had called for Farragut to return to the open Gulf after the taking of New Orleans. This had now been replaced with a new plan calling for a 2-directional push against the bastion of Vicksburg. The army, spearheaded by Davis's gunboats, would drive at the city from the north while a naval force under Farragut would come up the river from the south. Of concern to Farragut were reports that the Confederates were setting up heavy batteries at Natchez. If that was true, there would be a serious obstacle facing his ships before they could reach Vicksburg.

~

On May 4, the Army transport *MISSISSIPPI*, loaded down with two thousand troops, went up the river to New Orleans. The rest of Butler's army -- including those which had remained at Ship Island while awaiting the capture of Fort

Saint Philip and Fort Jackson, soon followed. Without stopping over at New Orleans, some of the transports continued on toward Baton Rouge. By May 7, Union troops were in possession of all enemy installations between New Orleans and the outskirts of Baton Rouge. On May 8, the *USS HARTFORD*, with Farragut aboard, anchored off that city. The following morning, a landing force from the *USS IROQUOIS* took possession of the former Federal barracks and arsenal where they were soon joined by some of Butler's men. When the *USS IROQUOIS* left to go upriver, her commanding officer, James S. Palmer, transmitted by messenger a stern warning to the mayor of the city.

> ...War is a sad calamity, and often inflicts severer wounds than those upon the sensibilities. I therefore trust I may be spared from resorting to any of its dire extremities; but I warn you, Mr. Mayor, that this flag must remain unmolested, though I leave no force on shore to protect it. The rash act of some individual may cause your city to pay a bitter penalty.[120]

USS IROQUOIS, together with *USS ONEIDA* and a bevy of escorting gunboats, arrived off Natchez on May 12. The heavy batteries alleged to have been installed by the enemy fortunately turned out to be myths. Reception by the locals there seemed friendly enough. Palmer thought it best not to push things as far as he had at Baton Rouge but rather to leave that decision up to Farragut when he arrived.

Despite the newest orders from Washington to take the fleet beyond Baton Rouge and up to Vicksburg, Farragut had little enthusiasm for the idea, and he had good reason for that lack of enthusiasm. The level of the river was noticeably falling. His ships had been riddled by shell fire from the passage by Fort Saint Philip and Fort Jackson and were in need of repair. His crews were beginning to come down with just about every pestilence familiar to the lower Mississippi in the summer months. As the weather became hotter, health conditions promised an even further deterioration.

Prior to when he had received his new orders, Farragut had sent David D. Porter and the mortar schooners out of the river and back to Ship Island. On the way there, Porter had used the opportunity to swing over and take Pensacola. There had been no enemy resistance, and Union Army troops were now in garrison. One more Confederate port had been sealed. Farragut wanted desperately to take Mobile and Galveston as well, thus further reducing the demands against the Navy's stretched out Gulf of Mexico blockade squadrons. On the other hand, the Washington planners had their own ideas. They felt that opening Vicksburg held the most importance, and those were the views which would hold sway. The high command at Washington believed that Davis and his Western Gunboat Flotilla, together with what few troops Halleck could spare for the job, could not take Vicksburg without help coming from downriver. Acting Secretary of the Navy Gustavus V. Fox explicitly instructed Farragut on May 17 that the fleet was to ascend the Mississippi without delay. Prior to receiving that order, Farragut had sent some gunboats up the river under the command of Commander S. Phillips Lee. On May 18, Lee arrived within sight of Vicksburg, and under a flag of truce he sent a message ashore to the Confederate authorities.

> The undersigned, with orders from Flag Officer Farragut and Major General
> Butler, respectfully demand the surrender of Vicksburg and its defenses to the lawful

authority of the United States, under which private property and personal rights will be respected.

Respectfully yours,

S. Phillips Lee, Commanding, Advance Naval Division[121]

The response Lee received provided a taste of the enemy's determination to hold Vicksburg.

Sir:

As your communication of this date is addressed to 'The Authorities of Vicksburg,' and that you may have a full reply to said communication, I have to state that Mississippians don't know, and refuse to learn, how to surrender to an enemy. If Commodore Farragut or Brigadier General Butler can teach them, let them come and try.

As to the defense of Vicksburg, I respectfully refer you to Brigadier General [Martin L.] Smith, commanding forces at or near Vicksburg, whose reply is herewith enclosed.

Respectfully,

James S. Autrey, Military Governor and Colonel Commanding Post[122]

The communication from Brigadier General Martin L. Smith, which Autrey had referenced, informed the recipient that his orders were to hold Vicksburg and that he intended to do so. On the 21st, Lee wrote to the mayor of Vicksburg, serving notice that since it was impossible to attack the city's defenses without injuring or destroying the town, it would be advisable for the mayor to order women and children evacuated.

Despite Acting Secretary Fox's instructions of May 17 to Farragut to ascend to Vicksburg with his larger men-of-war, Farragut had his serious reservations as to what could be accomplished by such a move. On May 22, he transmitted those thoughts to Butler then at New Orleans.

Dear General:

I received your kind note, together with the mail by the steamer *FOX.* My ship had got off and was about forty or fifty miles below Vicksburg, at Grand Gulf, which is the most dangerous part of the river, and beyond which I am unwilling to risk the large ships.

It appears to be the general opinion here among the officers, General Williams included, that there is very little use in attacking Vicksburg, as the guns on the heights are so elevated that our fire will not be felt by them. As they have so large a force of soldiers here, several thousand in and about the town, and the facility of bringing in twenty thousand in an hour by railroad from Jackson, altogether [I] think it would be useless to bombard it, as we could not hold it if we take it. Therefore, we have determined to blockade it and occasionally harass them with fire until the battle of Corinth shall decide its fate. General Williams is going up the Red River, where he thinks he may be more useful, and I have given him a gunboat to accompany him. I shall soon drop down the river again, as I consider my services indispensably necessary on the seaboard. I am greatly obliged to you for your kindness in towing up my coal vessels. I do not see that I can be of any service here, and I do not see as General Williams will be of any use here with the small force he has. I shall endeavor to get down as soon as possible.

Very respectfully, your obedient servant,

D. G. Farragut, Flag Officer, Western Gulf Blockading Squadron[123]

At the time that Farragut wrote of his hesitations to Butler, Corinth still remained in Confederate hands and many in the Union high command, including Halleck, expected the Confederates to put up a strong fight for that place. As it turned out, they were wrong. Eight days later (May 30), Beauregard would abandon his Corinth entrenchments and start a retreat southward to Tupelo, Mississippi. It would also turn out that Farragut was mistaken in his belief that the fall of Corinth could influence the Confederates to give up Vicksburg.

Stalled In Place Below the Heights of Vicksburg

By the beginning of the last week in May, Farragut had decided to leave the matter of Navy presence at Vicksburg in the hands of Commander Lee while he (Farragut) remained downriver with the larger ships. His instructions to Lee were to keep up a tight river blockade against Vicksburg and while so doing, occasionally throw a shell into the city to let the Confederates know that the Union Navy was still around. Lee was given the added responsibility of assigning roving gunboat patrols to keep an eye on the Mississippi's eastern bank between Vicksburg and Natchez -- this was to counter the possibility that the enemy might mount batteries on the bluffs along the river in order to harass Union shipping. Another responsibility given Lee was to assure that no trains-Mississippi traffic took place between Vicksburg and a rail line which terminated on the De Soto Peninsula directly across the river from the city. (The name of that rail line, the Vicksburg, Shreveport, and Texas Railroad, was somewhat of a misnomer since it was only a short-haul track running eastward from Monroe, Louisiana, a small town on the Washita River.)

Lee's ability to place effective cannon fire into Vicksburg's battlements was challenged by the counter-fire of a number of Columbiad guns estimated as "8 or 10 in number" which the Confederates had recently brought in by rail from either Pensacola or Mobile.[124] The range of that enemy cannon soon forced Lee's gunboats far enough downriver to put Lee's own guns out of effective range.

In late May, fifteen hundred infantry under the command of Brigadier General Thomas Williams came upriver under Navy escort. The original plans had been to have the transports run past the Vicksburg batteries, supported by the protective fire of Lee's gunboats. Once beyond Vicksburg, they were to continue upriver so their troop passengers could join in the assaults on Fort Pillow and Fort Randolph, attacks which had been scheduled for early June. This idea had to be discarded following the installation by the Confederates of their heavy Columbiad cannon. Instead, and after consultation with Commander Lee, Williams had decided to offload the troops onto the De Soto Peninsula south of the city. After first tearing up part of the track of the Vicksburg, Shreveport, and Texas line, Williams's infantrymen settled themselves into fixed entrenchments. The transports which had brought them were placed on moorings downstream, some distance from the peninsula, where they would remain as a means of retreat should a need arise.

Meanwhile below Vicksburg, enemy partisans had taken up the annoying practice of firing at shipping coming upriver with supplies for Lee and Williams. From Farragut's viewpoint, as he reported it to Secretary of the Navy Gideon Welles, the whole situation on the southern Mississippi was taking on an unfavorable complexion. Besides the annoyance caused by the partisans, the river level continued falling, and the disease rate continued to climb. The Navy's larger vessels were obviously unsuited for the present state of the river. To top things off, the local pilots proved untrustworthy and therefore their advice was considered practically useless.

All in all, the outlook for the Navy and the Army conducting operations on the Mississippi that coming summer -- at least on the stretch from New Orleans to Vicksburg -- was clearly negative. At Vicksburg, Williams's troops were already on half rations. Adding to Farragut's worries were reports of an enemy ram nearing readiness somewhere up the Yazoo River system. Line-crossers who told of having seen it described the ram as being practically indestructible. Taken as a whole, the entire situation was driving Farragut toward the brink of despair. Butler, however, seemed undaunted and was preparing to come upriver with seven thousand men -- vowing he could take Vicksburg if Farragut would lend him his cooperation. Farragut's thoughts were elsewhere. In a letter to Navy Assistant Secretary Fox, the flag officer again pleaded his case for leaving the Mississippi, describing in detail the difficulties in safely sending troops farther up the Mississippi, venturing the opinion that the transports could be subjected "to a fire from every bluff once they passed Natchez." He emphasized the seriousness that enemy batteries posed against unarmored transports, writing that where there were bluffs, there were usually bends in the river, and currents at these bends were often so strong that it could take up to an hour for a steamboat to get around them. Farragut maintained that transports would be unable to survive under such circumstances if brought under fire.[125]

By early June, matters had deteriorated still further. Farragut reported that the supply situation with his fleet was bad -- not only on the river, but along the Gulf coast as well. On one of the offshore blockade vessels (*USS SANTEE*), scurvy had broken out among the crew. In the same report, Farragut wrote that disease conditions on the river were debilitating to operational efficiency. Things had become so bad on Lee's gunboats that some of them were incapable of raising steam since most of the engine crews were down sick. Farragut's concerns continued to fall on deaf ears, as those in the Navy Department at Washington remained committed toward the taking of Vicksburg that summer. In reluctant compliance, Farragut ordered David D. Porter's mortar schooners to move from Ship Island into the Mississippi and up to New Orleans. Beyond that point, a schooner under sail could not buck the current. Accordingly, Porter requested the Army's assistance in providing him with extra tugs to tow his schooners up to Vicksburg.[126] That request, which was transmitted to the Army quartermasters through Butler's headquarters, was met with silence. Porter then made a second request, again without results. This led him to levy charges against the local quartermaster at New Orleans. Those charges were sent by Porter to Farragut for endorsement. Farragut forwarded them to the Office of the Secretary of Navy where they were again endorsed for transmittal to the Secretary of War. Within his charges, Porter was critical of the lack of cooperation from the quartermasters and of the corruption which, Porter alleged, was inherent to the Army's control of shipping at New Orleans.

...I don't hesitate to say that there has been a deliberate attempt made to deceive and trifle with me, and whosoever's fault it is should be made known. We have traitors enough to fight against without finding them holding office under our Government at posts of honor which have for a moment become so lucrative that the holders thereof fear to miss the golden opportunity, and intend to make hay while the sun shines....I mention these things to explain the delays and difficulties I have encountered, and intending to have the matter placed on record....I beg leave to state that by law the Army is obliged to comply with naval requisition, an act having passed on purpose to prevent delays to the public service.[127]

Meanwhile At Memphis

Following the destruction of Montgomery's Mississippi River Defense Service fleet, Flag Officer Davis's gunboats remained headquartered at Memphis. It was to be a full three weeks before they would move farther downriver. Davis had felt that this delay was necessary in order to bring the command back up to fighting efficiency and to make repairs where needed. Besides the fact that most of the gunboats needed work, many of the support vessels were in need of some conversion to make them suitable as auxiliaries. One of these support vessels, the *RED ROVER*, had already undergone extensive changeover. It had become a source of particular pride to George D. Wise, the Army's quartermaster officer attached to the Western Gunboat Flotilla who, as such, was the person directly responsible for such conversions. In a letter dated June 12 to Commodore Foote (who was then in Ohio recuperating from his wound received at Fort Donelson), Wise wrote.

> My Dear Commodore:
> I wish that you could see our hospital boat, the *RED ROVER*, with all her comforts for the sick and disabled seamen. She is decided to be the most complete thing of the kind that ever floated, and is every way a decided success. The Western Sanitary Association gave us, in cost of articles, $3,500. The ice box of the steamer holds three hundred tons. She has bathrooms, laundry, elevator for the sick from the lower to the upper deck, amputation room, nine different water closets, gauze blinds to the windows to keep the cinder and smoke from annoying the sick, two separate kitchens for the sick and well, a regular corps of nurses and two water closets on every deck...[128]

In the same letter to Foote, Wise related a pending change in policy (presumably Army thinking then in the development stage) over the type of gunboat thought to be needed in the future on the western rivers.

> ...We think that the gunboats have nearly finished their work, and that a different kind will be required for the future. The old boats will be used as floating batteries, to be stationed at New Orleans, Vicksburg, Memphis, and Island No. 10. Fast boats, with light, powerful armaments, will act as a river police and keep the river open....

Davis, rather than let his most serviceable gunboats idle away their time at Memphis, decided to dispatch up the Arkansas River- White River system the ironclads *MOUND CITY* and *SAINT LOUIS* along with the woodclads *CONESTOGA* and *A. O. TYLER*.

There was a theory in Union circles that after the Confederate ram *GENERAL EARL VAN DORN* made its escape from Memphis, it had gone up into that river system. Sources thought to be reliable reported that the rebel gunboats *MAUREPAS* and *PONTCHARTRAIN* were also somewhere on the Arkansas River. Davis placed Commander A. H. Kilty, the skipper of *MOUND CITY*, in overall charge to head up the search for these enemy vessels. The 46th Indiana Infantry Regiment under the command of Colonel Graham N. Fitch would serve as a landing force for the neutralizing of any fortifications which might be encountered along the way. At the last minute, a switch was made in this expedition's purpose. This came about as a result of a telegram Davis received from Major General Halleck, requesting of Davis that he send gunboats to escort supply vessels which were to proceed up the White River to make contact with Brigadier General Samuel R. Curtis. Curtis, following a success over Confederate forces at the Battle of Pea Ridge (near the Arkansas- Missouri border), was now in Arkansas where he was being hard pressed by two separate Confederate commands converging on him. To escape being pinched between these enemy forces, Curtis was thought to be marching eastward toward the safety of Union lines on the Mississippi River. Curtis's force was thought to be inferior in numbers to the combined Confederate threat, and he required immediate reinforcements as well as resupply. Road transport was out of the question as the conditions in that part of Arkansas were impossible for wagons. Contact with Curtis would have to depend on a linkup with steamboats to take place somewhere on the White River. To add special urgency, the Secretary of War sent off his own note to the Secretary of Navy, asking for quick cooperation from Davis's gunboat group.[129] On June 11, Colonel Charles Ellet, Jr., (his wound by now in the early stages of blood poisoning) reported by telegram to the Secretary of War that he would help by contributing three of his rams. They were to be placed under the immediate command of a junior officer, one Lieutenant George E. Currie who, as Ellet remarked, "...has not yet had a chance to do much, but who I feel sure with opportunity will justify my confidence." The rams that Ellet proposed going with Currie were the *LANCASTER*, *MINGO*, and *LIONESS*. In a memorandum sent to Davis, Ellet laid out what amounted to conditions under which cooperation with Kilty would be extended. Ellet suggested that the rams take "either the advance or the rear, as they [Commander Kilty] may prefer," but "reserving for Lieutenant Currie the privilege of driving his rams against the enemy whenever he gets a chance."[130] Davis answered politely; but from the tone of his reply, it was clear that he was fed up with what he considered Ellet's prima donna attitude. In his reply, Davis explained that divided authority would retard rather than promote the expedition. The next morning, Ellet sent off a dispatch to the Secretary of War, explaining why he had refused aid to Davis except on his own [Ellet's] terms.

June 12, 1862

Sir:

I have received your dispatch informing me of your appointment of Doctor Robarts as surgeon and Doctor Lawrence as assistant surgeon of my fleet, and requesting a detailed report concerning the rams. For the first few days after receiving my wound, my mind was incapable of transacting business. Since then great nervous prostration, with pain and fever, have rendered me entirely incapable of mental labor. I now have the measles superadded. I will prepare the report you ask for as soon as I am able to dictate it, which I hope will be in the course of two or three days. I did not send a detachment up White River to act in conjunction with the gunboats, as Commodore Davis requested, because the commodore was not willing to receive my cooperating unless I placed my vessels under the command of one of his officers. This, of course, I could not consent to do. Our successes at Memphis were gained by acting independently.

Mr. Brooks has arrived with supplies for my fleet.[131]

Four days later, Ellet dictated still another dispatch addressed to the Secretary of War in which he announced that his wounds had so incapacitated him that he was transferring command of the Ram Fleet to his brother Lieutenant Colonel Alfred W. Ellet. In that dispatch, Ellet described the personnel of the rams as occasionally difficult to deal with, but who at the present time were in excellent spirits and all of whom (presumably meaning both the military and civilian elements of the crews) "wanted their share of fame and approbation."

...Whether this confidence amongst such a heterogeneous material can be transferred to another is to be tested. The conspicuous part acted by Lieutenant Colonel Ellet at Memphis will make it easier for him to command it than anyone else.

I do not propose to leave Lieutenant Colonel Ellet any instructions. His own judgment will be a better guide to him than mine now.[132]

Blood poisoning had by now permeated throughout Colonel Charles Ellet Jr.'s system. He died aboard *QUEEN OF THE WEST* while being transported to a base hospital at Cairo.[133]

Expedition up the White River

Unaccompanied by any of the Ellet rams, the gunboats *MOUND CITY*, *SAINT LOUIS*, and *LEXINGTON* departed Memphis for the mouth of the White River. They were closely trailed by the Army transports *WHITE CLOUD*, *JACOB MUSSELMAN*, and *NEW NATIONAL* carrying the troops under Fitch's command. The gunboat *CONESTOGA* acted as rear guard to the transports. Before reaching the mouth of the White River, Kilty's lead gunboat captured a first class steamer named *CLARA DOLSON* which was sent back to Memphis under guard. By June 16, the expedition had reached what was called "the cut." In river distance, the location of the cut was about five miles downstream from Saint Charles, Arkansas. Near the cut, the fleet came to anchor for the night. From the discoveries of an infantry patrol sent ashore by Colonel Fitch, it was discovered that Saint Charles had been fortified so as to block upstream passage.

Kilty ordered anchors weighed at first light. He led the way upriver, expecting any moment to receive hostile fire. He was not to be disappointed. About two miles from Saint Charles, heavy rifle fire was encountered. Fitch's troops were landed, and they soon drove the riflemen into the fortifications. At the same time, the gunboats moved ahead so as to bring their fire directly against the enemy batteries; but before they could get into the proper positions, the lead gunboat, *MOUND CITY*, came hard against one of three sunken hulks which were partially blocking the river.[134] The hulks not only prevented Kilty from bringing his guns to bear at best advantage, but they also forced him to proceed in single file. As a consequence, *MOUND CITY*, which was in the lead, took the brunt of the enemy's cannon fire. One Confederate shell penetrated her casement, going on to puncture the main steam drum, spewing hot steam in every direction. The horror that followed is described within the report of Colonel Fitch who was ashore at the time and who became an angry witness to what followed.

> ...The crew were seen from the shore to spring from the port holes into the river. Scarcely had they done so before a party of the enemy's sharpshooters descended the bluffs from the batteries and, under the cover of fallen timber on the river bank, commenced murdering those who were struggling in the water, and also firing upon those in our boats sent to pick them up. At the same time another party of the enemy, concealed in the timber on the opposite bank of the river, pursued the same barbarous course.[135]

After signaling the other gunboats to hold their fire, Fitch sent out skirmishers to silence the sharpshooters, following which he led the main body of his regiment against the Fort Charles batteries. Within the span of fifteen minutes, the fortification was in Union hands.

The action of the Confederates in firing on the helpless crew of the *MOUND CITY* was despicable, but so was what transpired later aboard *MOUND CITY*. John A. Duble, First Master of the *CONESTOGA*, had gone aboard the *MOUND CITY* to take over command following his receipt of the news that Kilty had been severely scalded by escaping steam. Duble's report of what he encountered there stands as a condemnation of the poor state of discipline existing at that time -- at least on some of the gunboats. It was a scene more descriptive of "Dante's Inferno" than a warship of the United States.

> US Gunboat *MOUND CITY*
> Saint Charles, Arkansas, White River
> June 18, 1862
>
> Sir:
> In prefacing these memoranda, I cannot help speaking of things which presented themselves to me on this vessel before I was appointed to take command of her by Lieutenant Commanding W. McGunnegle, US Navy, during the time of the horrible suffering on board by the scalded. I beheld with extreme disgust a portion of the few men who were uninjured, drunk. A portion of the crew of the *SAINT LOUIS*, a portion of the crew of the *CONESTOGA*, also some of the soldiers of the *NEW NATIONAL* were in the same beastly condition, and while so, acts most scandalous were perpetrated on board. Men while lying in the agonies of death were robbed of their monk[ey] bags, money purses. Rooms were broken open, trunks, carpet sacks, etc., pillaged, and their contents scattered around and destroyed. Watches of the officers were stolen, and quarreling, cursing, and rioting, as well as robbing, seemed to rule. Liquor was put in water casks, with water and ice, for the relief of the wounded, but these men had buckets full, pure, who drank for the purpose of debauch. My duties at the time called me on the *CONESTOGA*, but I went myself with other officers from the vessel and tried to stop it. I repeatedly

called the attention of the first master of this vessel to the condition of things on board, and some men occupying position in this service seemed to lose their senses, for not the first particle of order was observed.

While the *CONESTOGA* was backing the *MOUND CITY* away from under the batteries of the enemy, after being injured, the *NEW NATIONAL* was constantly in our way. First immediately under our stern, then upon our starboard, then upon our port side, and after repeatedly requesting her commander to get out of our way, as he delayed us much, she landed against the port side of the *MOUND CITY* in the steam, and an accidental shot from a wounded, frantic man came very near destroying as much life on her as there was on this vessel. He was standing scalded by his gun with lock string in his hand, and in his fall in the agonies of death, he pulled the lock string with him and discharged the piece. While our doctor and nurses were rendering all relief in their power to the suffering, a portion of the crews of the boats named seemed bent on destruction and theft. I hope never again to be placed in such a position, where I am compelled to see so much misery, such depravity, and so much disorder.

Very respectfully, your obedient servant,

John A. Duble, First Master, *CONESTOGA*[136]

The next day, Duble would supervise the burying of fifty-nine of the *MOUND CITY's* dead. Those burials were only of the bodies found aboard. Over the next few days, as decomposition set in, more bodies rose from the river's bottom. Out of a crew of 175 officers and men, the final tally of casualties from *MOUND CITY* numbered eighty-two killed at the time of the steam explosion or who died shortly after; forty-three shot while in the water; twenty-four, including Commander Kilty, severely scalded or otherwise wounded. The scalded and otherwise wounded, including those of Fitch's command who became casualties during the assault on Saint Charles, were loaded on the *JACOB MUSSELMAN* and taken back to Memphis under escort of the *CONESTOGA*. After recoaling at Memphis, the *CONESTOGA* rejoined, this time in escort to a commissary steamer which was bringing rations, expectant of a rendezvous with Curtis.

By the time *CONESTOGA* returned up the White, the river level was becoming critical and worsening farther upriver. Colonel Fitch had requested from McGunnegle that the gunboats convoy the troop transports to Des Arc, a town more than 130 miles from where the White River entered the Mississippi. (McGunnegle had taken over the overall gunboat command after Kilty had been evacuated.) At this time of year, and under average weather conditions, the town of Des Arc was normally considered the head of navigation. However, the river was now much lower than normal, and McGunnegle feared stranding. He related his fears in writing to Fitch who replied in a memorandum, requesting convoy protection up to Des Arc, and promising that if McGunnegle would escort the transports upriver, then he, Fitch, would undertake to stay at Des Arc while awaiting contact with Curtis. There would, therefore, be no necessity for having the gunboats remain, thus freeing McGunnegle to proceed back downstream to Saint Charles.[137]

At this same time, and unbeknownst to Fitch, Memphis was coming into danger of a direct attack. If Fitch had been cognizant of those circumstances which could have seriously threatened his line of communication, it seems doubtful that he would have been willing to risk being stranded at Des Arc.

AN OVERVIEW OF THE MILITARY SITUATION
(Late June 1862)

If the dangers to Fitch and to Curtis were not enough to worry those in high command on the Mississippi, what was taking place on the eastern seaboard bespoke of whether active operations should be continued within the Mississippi corridor. Casualties and sickness in Virginia had been horrendous, seriously weakening the Army of the Potomac. Tactically, Robert E. Lee clearly had the upper hand, having been able to prevent a drive by McClellan against Richmond. The initiative had gone to Lee, and it would continue that way until the Battle of Antietam, an event still two long months into the future.

For the Lincoln Administration, the outlook in the east was becoming so wrought with the danger of defeat for the Union that serious consideration was being given to the possibility of bringing western troops to the eastern theater. At the end of June, Halleck sent the following telegram to Grant.

> Report immediately the effective force under command at Memphis and vicinity, exclusive of Sherman's and Hurlbut's divisions; also the part of Wallace's division which can be concentrated at Memphis. I don't want comments, but facts.
>
> The defeat of McClellan at Richmond has created a stampede at Washington. I want facts as to position, as to troops, and how they can be concentrated, in order to enable me to answer questions and carry out orders. State precisely how many troops you have transportation to Cairo from Memphis for.
>
> I want facts.[138]

Grant replied the same day, reporting in part that his quartermasters had assured him of being able to ready "seven boats [capable of] carrying five thousand men." Halleck immediately wired back, giving Grant the clear impression that he might soon have to go into a static defensive posture at Memphis.

> Secure the land side of Memphis by entrenchments and batteries as rapidly as possible. You can impress Negroes for that purpose.[139]

To Major General John A. McClernand then at Jackson, Tennessee, Halleck wired:

...The part of General Wallace's division at Memphis will go up the Mississippi and the portion at Grand Junction will follow as soon as relieved. All transports at Pittsburg [Landing] and Hamburg [another landing site on the Tennessee River] will be filled with troops from this place [Corinth].

The entire campaign in the west is broken up by these orders, and we shall probably lose all we have gained. I will do all I can with the few forces left. You go to a new theater. Success attend you.[140]

While the western divisions were being readied to move east, Halleck gave a lengthy appraisal to the Secretary of War stating his concern as to the serious regression in Union fortunes which could result in the west once troop strength was reduced. The prediction he posed was that all of Arkansas and perhaps west Tennessee would go down and that wholesale insurrection would certainly resume in Missouri. With a probably justified grimness, Halleck forecast certain death to any Union sympathizers in those areas which would have to be given up to the enemy.

During the hectic two days following the receipt of the order to stand ready to denude his western command for the support of McClellan, Halleck had sent at least two telegrams directly to the President. In these, he pleaded his case for actively pursuing the western campaigns which, as he explained, could only be carried out successfully provided troop strength remained undiminished.

On July 2, Lincoln wired Halleck from Stanton's office, assuring him that the western commands would remain intact.

Your several dispatches of yesterday to Secretary of War and myself received. I did say, and now repeat, I would be exceedingly glad for some reinforcements from you; still, do not send a man if in your judgment, it will endanger any point you deem important to hold, or will force you to give up or weaken or delay the Chattanooga Expedition. Please tell me, could you make me a flying visit for consultation without endangering the service in your department?

A. Lincoln[141]

The fact that Lincoln made no mention of Vicksburg was probably indicative of a downgraded consideration that the Mississippi corridor was then receiving on the part of the Administration. It now appeared that the previous importance given toward a drive against Vicksburg from the north was being put on temporary hold. The primary concern from Washington was being directed toward holding Robert E. Lee at bay in Virginia. Ancillary to that would be an effort to crack open the back door to the southeastern Confederacy, this being a reference toward the taking of Chattanooga. Vicksburg still remained of importance; but the responsibility for taking it would, at least temporarily, rest with an approach up the Mississippi River from New Orleans.

Halleck's response to the effort of putting into place a movement against Chattanooga had been to send Major General Don Carlos Buell eastward from Corinth. Buell was to depend on the Memphis and Charleston Railroad's right of way for his sustenance until he reached Decatur. As he moved beyond Decatur toward Chattanooga, his supply was to come from Louisville down the Central Alabama

Railroad to where that line connected with the Memphis and Charleston at Decatur. After passing that point, Buell would rely on yet another rail line, this track being the one running south from Nashville to the little town of Stevenson which lay to the east of Decatur. Compared to the support the rail lines offered, the Tennessee River was judged to be of little use at the time as a supply conduit. Once into the late spring, the river rarely had enough water depth to carry steamer traffic much beyond its lower reaches. Buell would be haunted by a serious security problem which existed with the railroads. The rail line coming south from Nashville ran through country which was difficult to protect since the terrain was heavily wooded offering concealment in which Confederate cavalry could easily operate. Regular and partisan cavalry would disrupt Buell's logistics from the beginning, grinding up his line of communication in piecemeal fashion. But that was not all he would have to contend with. A Confederate Army would move against him from the south while a second Confederate Army would strike into Kentucky through the Cumberland Gap. Buell's move that summer against Chattanooga was to result in failure.

~

For most of the summer of 1862, Grant's forces on the Mississippi would remain static arrayed along a line running from Memphis westward to the bend of the Tennessee. The lassitude was the result of Halleck's caution, a caution which governed operations in the west through much of that period. It was also the result of considerable difficulty in maintaining security over the territory which Federal troops already held. It would not be until the fall of 1862 that War Department planners began to again consider a 2-pronged movement against Vicksburg. Only then would Halleck let Grant off the leash. When that happened, Grant would begin moving south by overland route, trailing a supply umbilical connected to Grand Junction. (Grand Junction was a place name of that century for a settlement located slightly to the west of the present town of Saulsbury, Tennessee, close to the Mississippi state boundary line. Grand Junction was also on the track of the Mississippi Central Railroad which had its northern terminus at Columbus, Kentucky.) Well south of Grand Junction at a place named Holly Springs, Grant would establish a large ordnance and quartermaster depot, the concept for it being that it would lessen his dependence on Grand Junction. To a noticeable degree, this would mean a shorter line of communication to defend against enemy raiders.

By the middle of December 1862, Grant's army would be located at Oxford, Mississippi. From Oxford, his plan was to continue south until he reached Jackson, Mississippi. From Jackson, if everything went well, Grant would strike directly at the back side of Fortress Vicksburg. There is an old military adage that "nothing ever goes according to plan," and such would soon prove to be the case.

A LAST ATTEMPT TO CONTACT CURTIS

On the White River during late June, Colonel Graham N. Fitch was becoming vaguely aware of the disintegrating military situation to his east. His own situation was not one that any troop commander would have envied.

When Fitch had requested that McGunnegle escort the Army transports to Des Arc where he hoped to make contact with Curtis, McGunnegle had pointed to the advice of the pilots who cautioned that the river could be expected to rapidly drop in depth, resulting in the stranding of the entire fleet including those vessels remaining at Saint Charles. The chance of the river rising again much before late fall was considered virtually nil. Although Fitch had finally talked McGunnegle into going a bit farther upstream, the naval officer agreed to proceed only as far as Clarendon and then only with the caveat that upon arrival there, he would return to Saint Charles immediately.

The protests of the pilots proved to have been valid ones. The transports and the gunboats went only a mile or so past Saint Charles before the gunboats (drawing more than the transports) began grounding at uncomfortably frequent intervals. Reaching a place called Crooked Point Cutoff, another council was held between Fitch and McGunnegle with the pilots in attendance. The pilots joined in agreement with McGunnegle that the gunboats should not go farther but instead should return that same day to Saint Charles. Fitch decided to hold the transports at Crooked Point Cutoff on the theory that Curtis's line of march would hit the river somewhere near to that place.

When he arrived back at Saint Charles, McGunnegle was informed that MOUND CITY seemed beyond the point of temporary repairs. Only a regular shipyard could put things right. MOUND CITY was sent to Memphis under the tow of CONESTOGA, SAINT LOUIS accompanying in escort. The LEXINGTON and CINCINNATI remained at Saint Charles to act as escort for Fitch's transports once the transports returned downriver.

Fitch's stay at Crooked Point turned out to be brief. The drop in the river level over the next two days became so obvious that even he could not see the wisdom in tempting fate. Fitch brought the transports down to Saint Charles. The banks of the river, both above and below Saint Charles, were by now thickening with enemy snipers. At Saint Charles, it was now worth one's life to be exposed on an open deck. To deprive cover to the snipers in the vicinity of the transport anchorage, Fitch sent troop details ashore to clear away the brush on the river's bank.

Apprehensive of the continually falling river level and what seemed to be an increase in the enemy's presence locally, McGunnegle was finally able to talk Fitch into making a withdrawal to the Mississippi. That withdrawal would, though, only be temporary. Reinforced at the river's entrance by a regiment of infantry, and with the supplies for Curtis reloaded onto the shallowest draft steamers that the quartermasters could find, Fitch headed back up the White River to Clarendon. A recent rain had raised the river's level just enough so that Flag Officer Davis, in agreement with McGunnegle, felt justified in sending along in escort the gunboats *LEXINGTON* and *CONESTOGA*.

During the transit upriver to Clarendon, snipers became so troublesome as to necessitate the use of flanking parties of infantry marching along the bank. The major reason for the proliferation of snipers was the policy of the Confederate district commander who had been busy issuing appointments in the rank of captain, Confederate Army, to anyone who could assemble a partisan group of as few as ten men. Each such group was then placed on full Confederate Army pay so long as it remained active in the field and engaged in the harassment of Federal river traffic. This practice had become known to Fitch through interrogation of captured prisoners, and it resulted in considerable correspondence which took place under flags of truce between Fitch and the person claiming to be the senior Confederate officer along the river. Fitch protested, but to no avail, over the legitimizing of what he felt was nothing but a partisan guerrilla operation and therefore an illegal act of warfare.

Questioning the local farmers around Clarendon brought news that Devall's Bluff (upstream from Clarendon) was being fortified with artillery. A day or so after receiving that intelligence, and hearing firing coming from that direction, Fitch assumed that the sound came from Curtis's troops under attack. Fitch landed a strong force ashore for the purpose of making contact with Curtis, but the source of the firing could not be located. Following this episode, the fleet withdrew downstream to Saint Charles.

In continuing his efforts to discover the whereabouts of Curtis, Fitch sent out wide ranging cavalry patrols. These frequently clashed with detachments of partisans as well as small-sized units of what seemed to be Confederate regulars; but these troops did not appear to have any relationship with units which might be in opposing contact against Curtis.

On July 7, the transports, under escort of one gunboat, again went upriver as far as Clarendon. There Fitch decided to land his troops and make a probe following the course of the Cache River (a tributary of the White River). Shortly after starting out, a small courier launch journeyed up the Cache carrying a message from Grant ordering Fitch to maintain a static presence at Saint Charles and await there the appearance of Curtis.[142] When back at Saint Charles, a scouting party brought in a prisoner who told Fitch that Curtis had recently passed through the small town of Cotton Plant and was en route to Clarendon. Fitch sent a force to meet Curtis, only to discover that Curtis's rear guard had already left Clarendon two hours before. Despite gun signals and a patrol sent out in chase, Curtis had too great a head start. With no reason to remain any longer at Saint Charles, Fitch moved back to the Mississippi.

Curtis and his men safely reached the main river at Helena, Arkansas, arriving there at about the same time as Fitch's transports.

~

In the middle of August, an expedition left Helena, loaded aboard transports with gunboats in escort. Their mission was to break up any Confederate strong points or supply activities which had developed south of Helena along the Mississippi's western bank. The expedition went as far as the mouth of the White River, but nothing substantial in the way of an enemy presence was discovered. Upon reaching the mouth of the White River, a reconnaissance was launched upstream to determine if any signs of enemy supply operations were evident. Other than finding a couple of abandoned flatboats, nothing was seen which would indicate the enemy's use of the river at that time.

EVENTS DURING THE SIEGE AT VICKSBURG
(Summer of 1862)

Pressure was increasing from the administration via the Navy Department for Farragut to make a major showing before Vicksburg. Assistant Secretary of the Navy Fox wired Farragut that the President was becoming concerned that so little activity was taking place. The same pressures were being directed from the War Department against Butler. As a result of the last, thirty-two hundred infantry, with detachments of artillery, were loaded aboard transports and started up the river from Baton Rouge. They were to join the troops which Brigadier General Thomas Williams had earlier landed on the De Soto Peninsula.

Williams shared apprehension with Farragut as to what might happen to the transports while en route. Enemy mobile batteries had recently been reported as being in position at one time or another on almost every piece of high ground on the river between Baton Rouge and Vicksburg.[143] In a report concerning these batteries, Williams described the technique the enemy was employing.

> The rebel method of using their guns from the cliffs is to run the gun forward
> till it projects beyond the cliff, depress it, fire, and run the gun back out of sight, load
> and repeat.[144]

Fortunately, these batteries were not as lethal as first feared, and except for a handful of casualties, the transports carrying the reinforcements made it safely to Grand Gulf, a river port a few miles downriver from Vicksburg. It had been expected that the Confederates had set up permanent artillery emplacements there and that the river might be impassable at that point. But when the Federal troops landed to secure the town, they found that the place had been abandoned. To discourage a reoccupation, Grand Gulf was burned. The troops then reboarded the transports for the remainder of the trip upriver to De Soto Landing where they arrived on June 25.

A Canal Across the De Soto Peninsula; Mounting Problems

Williams issued an order for survey work to begin for the cutting of a canal to bisect the peninsula from De Soto Landing to a position upriver two and a half miles south of Young's Point which was well beyond gunnery observation from Vicksburg. The purpose of the canal would be to allow passage of troop and supply transports upriver of the city without exposing them to the enemy's fixed batteries on the Vicksburg bluffs. During work on the canal, Farragut's fleet was to remain moored and inactive. When Porter and his mortar flotilla arrived from the south, they were to be positioned out of the line of sight of the Vicksburg gunners yet close enough so they could employ their high trajectory shells against the enemy's positions.

The digging of the canal went slowly. Williams's engineers had placed their reliance on the premise that a strata of sandy loam would be reached within the first two feet of digging. The importance of reaching sand was that once the earthen plugs (or barriers) were removed at each end of the cut, the rush of the Mississippi would hydraulically excavate the canal's channel to a depth suitable for passage of transports. Instead, extremely hard clay was encountered close to the surface, and the clay continued down as far as the engineers could probe. Without the presence of a sandy layer, the entire excavation would be left up to the efforts of human muscles. Most of that muscle power was being provided by nearly twelve hundred ex-slaves, all rounded up from the neighboring plantations.[145]

Williams wrote to Farragut expressing a concern that the concentration of naval power near Vicksburg would leave unguarded the approaches to the Red River. He stressed the point that the Red River was the primary avenue for the Confederates to send supplies into Vicksburg from the west. Farragut agreed to put steps in motion to establish a better surveillance of the Red River's entrance.

Throughout the first two weeks of July, Williams sent infantry patrols out to probe all possible approaches from which attacks could be launched against the works at Vicksburg. Indications were that the enemy was daily tightening and improving his defenses. There was considerable debate going on in Union command circles at this time over whether Vicksburg could be taken in 1862. A good part of the doubts were the result of the unimproved situation in the eastern theater. The need to send western troops east to reinforce the Army of the Potomac still remained a possibility. A large army would be required to take Vicksburg, and nothing close to the necessary troop strength was now at hand. Despite the earlier haranguing to Farragut concerning the need to bring Porter's mortar schooners up to Vicksburg, soon after their arrival, new orders came from Washington to have them returned to New Orleans. From New Orleans, they were to proceed to the Chesapeake for use on the James River in Virginia.

Beyond the lack of the needed military resources, the worst handicaps toward accomplishing anything at Vicksburg were caused by the vagaries of the river. Williams's canal diggers could not keep pace with the dropping level of the river. And that was not all. The faster the river dropped, the more nervous Farragut became that his ships would become stranded. He urgently requested advice from Fox at the Navy Department. Should he stay or withdraw back to New Orleans? Equally serious was the inability to coal the gunboats. Contracts let out by the Navy Department clerks Washington had stupidly specified that colliers would deliver their cargoes at New Orleans. But it was not at New Orleans that the coal was needed; rather, it was required where the ships were -- upriver near Vicksburg. It took a lot of angry written words before Farragut's staff arranged to have the coal delivered to the places where it was required. (Gunboats were also stationed at Baton Rouge and Natchez.) There were a host of other problems as well. Supply steamers became increasingly subject to artillery attacks at any number of unexpected locations. These attacks came from the mobile artillery units which Williams had earlier described and which operated like phantoms along the entire length of the river between Baton Rouge and Vicksburg.

Attacks on Western River Traffic Generally

Attacks by hit and run Confederate units were not just restricted to the lower Mississippi. During one of her trips, the *SALLIE WOOD*, a Quartermaster Department transport attached to the Western Gunboat Flotilla, was fired at from four different locations. All four attacks took place south of Memphis and north of Vicksburg. The last attack did her in, and her pilot was forced to run her up on the shores of Island No. 82 (ninety miles above Vicksburg). All but three of her passengers and crew were captured.

Attacks on steamboats traveling from Memphis north to Cairo became so serious that the Army finally had to take retributive action against the local population, a population long suspected of being guilty of provisioning and sheltering the troops and partisans making the attacks. Orders in the form of edicts went out from Sherman's headquarters proclaiming that whenever a steamer was fired upon, buildings immediate to the guilty battery's location would be burned, and ten families living in proximity were to be forced off their farms for each and every incident. Although initially this order only applied to the Memphis District, it was eventually adopted within most of the river's zones. As a practice, the threat to retaliate against local populations was rarely carried out during 1862; however, by 1863, the situation would become so serious as to make incendiary retribution a rather common occurrence.[146]

THE ELLET RAMS MOVE SOUTH TO VICKSBURG
FOLLOWING THE DEATH OF COLONEL CHARLES ELLET, JR.

The change in the command of the Army's Ram Fleet, which had been necessitated by the wounding and subsequent death of Colonel Charles Ellet, Jr., had the effect of ushering in a new spirit of cooperation between the Army and the Navy on the river. A good deal of that change had to do with the more tractable personality of the new commander of the rams, Lieutenant Colonel Alfred W. Ellet. Another factor was the issuance of fresh orders from the War Department which set into more clarity the working arrangements with the Navy's people. These orders were issued to Lieutenant Colonel Ellet in the form of instructions from the Secretary of War dated June 20, 1862, on the eve of Charles Ellet Jr.'s death. The orders left little room for later uncertainty; however, to assure that no doubt remained in anyone's mind, this time the instructions over how the rams were to operate was set into place by the Secretary of War who was acting directly for the President.

> I regret that your brother's illness deprives the Government of his skillful and gallant services, but have confidence that you will supply his place better than anyone else. You will observe that by his instructions the Ram Fleet was placed under the general command of the commander of the gunboat squadron. The President desires you to consider yourself in the same position, believing the cooperative action will be more likely to produce good results than independent action, and that the commander of the gunboats should have chief command. I shall be glad to have full and frequent reports from you.
>
> Edwin M. Stanton, Secretary of War[147]

A change in concept over the best utilization of the rams had already been decided upon by Alfred W. Ellet. His now dead brother had held fixed ideas that the weight of cannon would adversely impact the ratio of weight to speed that he felt was critical for the success of a ram when striking another vessel. Although the weight of cannon would increase a "ram's mass," Charles had reasoned that the extra weight would actually have a negative effect by reducing speed and maneuverability. Alfred W. Ellet's opinion differed. He reasoned that any loss in speed which might occur from adding the weight of cannon would be made up in overall tactical versatility. If mounted with field guns, the rams would be able to respond against shore batteries and concentrations of enemy troops, an advantage they had not previously held, and an advantage which Alfred thought would soon become vital on the rivers. Alfred believed that since the Confederate's Mississippi River Defense Service was now little more than a memory, the future fortunes of the Ellet force would probably rest on its ability to assault enemy troop and artillery concentrations. Cannon were put aboard the rams before they left Memphis.

On June 19th, Alfred W. Ellet started downriver from Memphis with the *LANCASTER*, *MONARCH*, *DICK FULTON*, *MINGO*, and *LIONESS*. In addition to the crews, the five vessels collectively carried aboard three hundred infantrymen from the 53rd and 59th Illinois Regiments who were to act as gunners and sharpshooters. After a layover for the night at the mouth of the Saint Francis River (eighty-five miles below Memphis), Ellet led his rams into that river and steamed upstream for about fifty miles. He expected to encounter Confederate supply boats, but all that was discovered was one burned out barge and a quantity of charred cotton. Back on the Mississippi, *LIONESS* and *MINGO* were detailed to guard the mouth of the Saint Francis while the rest of Ellet's force continued south, capturing en route a suspicious ferryboat near Helena. At one place, Ellet even did some recruiting, bringing along fifteen Arkansas citizens enrolled as sharpshooters, together with a number of contrabands hired to serve as deck hands and stokers.

On June 24, the *LANCASTER*, *DICK FULTON*, and *MONARCH* dropped anchor above the first bend in the Mississippi north of Vicksburg. This was at Young's Point. The Ellet rams were the first of the upper river fleet to arrive there, having preceded Flag Officer Charles H. Davis's gunboats which would come down four days later. Medical Cadet Charles R. Ellet, accompanied by Edward Davis (the son of soon-to-be Rear Admiral Charles Henry Davis) went ashore at Young's Point disguised in civilian clothes, their orders being to cross the De Soto Peninsula and make contact with Flag Officer David G. Farragut. The two messengers returned the next day to say they had found Farragut's fleet and that the officers had initially received them as suspicious characters. For some unexplained reason, none of the naval officers believed that the rams could have made it all the way from Memphis on their own.[148]

Early the following day, Alfred W. Ellet, leading on *LANCASTER* and in company with *MONARCH*, started up the Yazoo River. The trip was to be a reconnaissance to try to locate Confederate supply steamers reported to be operating in the Yazoo basin. The two rams made it upstream past the junction of the Sunflower River to within about twenty miles of the little hamlet of Liverpool without a shot being fired in their direction. Then, while rounding a bend, they suddenly came into full view of the *GENERAL EARL VAN DORN*. With her were the enemy supply steamers *POLK*, *GENERAL CLARK*, and *LIVINGSTON*. The Confederate captains had no doubt been warned of Ellet's approach since all four vessels were burning furiously, having been cast adrift as incendiaries. *GENERAL EARL VAN DORN* was the first in line of drift; but before she had time to come down against the *LANCASTER*, she exploded and sank, her hull nearly blocking the channel. Moving hard in against the bank, the Federal rams managed to escape contact with the rest of the fire boats which drifted by the obstruction created by the *GENERAL EARL VAN DORN* and grounded downstream.

Fortunately for Ellet, the strandings were close to the bank of the river, and they did not obstruct Ellet's passage when he turned to go back down the river.

Before Ellet left, he managed a fast glimpse of what he knew could only have been the much talked of *CSS ARKANSAS*. She was spotted upriver beyond the incendiaries, shielded behind a series of protective rafts. Up to that time, *CSS ARKANSAS's* existence had been only a rumor, but now the sight of its massive proportions bespoke fact. From what Ellet could make out, she appeared to be near to completion.

LANCASTER and *MONARCH* returned into the Mississippi that evening. No incidents were encountered on their downstream passage.

An idea of the speed and maneuverability of the Ellet ram conversions can be deduced from the round trip they made that day up the Yazoo. They had logged a total of one hundred fifty miles steaming the round trip from the Mississippi up the Yazoo and then back again over the same route -- and this through a river course of many twists and bends.

> *Author's Note: As has been previously stated within the Preface, regarding identification of vessels with a military significance, Army vessels, whether combatant or supply, are not prefixed. Commissioned naval vessels, whether of the Union Navy or Confederate Navy, are prefixed respectively as "USS" and "CSS." With this in mind -- The reader will notice in that which follows that the gunboats of the Army's Western Gunboat Flotilla, although commanded by Flag Officer Charles H. Davis, USN, and largely officered by naval officers, are not prefixed, being simply referenced as CARONDELET, A. O. TYLER, etc. On the other hand, the vessels of Flag Officer David G. Farragut's fleet are prefixed with "USS," all being commissioned naval vessels. In a corresponding vein, after the gunboats of the Western Gunboat Flotilla were transferred to the Navy in October 1862, they were thereafter prefixed with the appropriate "USS", having become, as of the date of that transfer, commissioned naval vessels.*

Passing the Vicksburg Guns

On June 28th, Farragut on his flagship *USS HARTFORD*, along with two other of his larger men-of-war and seven of Commander Lee's gunboats, ran northward past the batteries at Vicksburg. They anchored in proximity to Young's Point. In part, Farragut had made the run to be on hand to meet with Davis's gunboats then on their way down from Memphis. The move was timely since on the same day that Farragut arrived at Young's Point, four of Davis's gunboats showed up in escort to six of the Western Gunboat Flotilla's mortar barges.

Great political hoopla followed this joining of forces. The press, encouraged by the Administration, played up the event way out of proportion to its actual significance. Although Union vessels could now claim to have traveled the Mississippi from Cairo to the sea, more realistically, the linkup by Farragut merely proved that armored vessels were able to run past the Vicksburg guns. The enemy guns at Vicksburg still blocked passage on the Mississippi for unarmored vessels, and it would still be many months before a true claim could be made that the Mississippi was open.

Up After the *CSS ARKANSAS*

Ellet's sighting of *CSS ARKANSAS* gave credence to the fear Farragut had that it could be superior to anything the Federals now had on the upper river. Farragut was of the opinion that it was preferable to destroy the *CSS ARKANSAS* before it could be completed. In conference with Davis, it was decided that two gunboats and the ram *QUEEN OF THE WEST* would be assigned to that task. It was thought that little opposition would be encountered in the run up the river to reach the location where the *CSS ARKANSAS* had been sighted by Ellet. At the most, a few pot shots were expected from sharpshooters; at worse, they might experience the fire from light artillery which could have been put in place since Ellet's reconnaissance of two weeks before. But any of that sort of thing could be handled by the armored gunboats.

At 4:30 a.m. on July 15, the *QUEEN OF THE WEST*, and the gunboats *A. O. TYLER*, and *CARONDELET* started up the Yazoo. They left astern on the Mississippi the combined squadrons of Farragut and Davis whose vessels were either at anchor or moored to the river bank a short distance downstream of the junction of the Yazoo and the main river. The ram *LANCASTER* had been stationed as a guard vessel at the mouth of the Yazoo; she was the only one with steam up on her boilers. The other warships lay quietly, few with even their fires lit. The lack of readiness to maneuver if they had to was not a matter of carelessness but rather was in large part due to the shortage of coal. For some, it had been necessary to draw down their fires so their engineers could perform routine boiler cleaning. Apparently no one had expected that any immediate maneuvers would be needed. Certainly, no one had expected the *CSS ARKANSAS* to arrive on the Mississippi that very day.

Not a full twenty minutes passed following the passage of the two gunboats and the ram up the Yazoo when sounds of heavy firing alerted the watch-standers on *LANCASTER*. Racing down the Yazoo into view of the *LANCASTER's* lookouts came *QUEEN OF THE WEST*, *A. O. TYLER*, and *CARONDELET* -- *CSS ARKANSAS* close behind and closing on their wakes. Upon seeing the crew of *LANCASTER* in the act of slipping their mooring, the approaching Confederates opened fire, hitting the *LANCASTER* with no less than eighty-seven rounds of heavy caliber. Two of those rounds penetrated *LANCASTER's* bulwarks, ripping through eight feet of bunkered coal before puncturing her main steam drum. This put *LANCASTER* out of action.[149]

After finishing with *LANCASTER*, the *CSS ARKANSAS*, firing as she came, steamed past the entire line of the Union fleet. Not one of the Union vessels had even a skeleton crew at battle stations. With the guard ram *LANCASTER* now out of the fight, only *QUEEN OF THE WEST*, *CARONDELET*, and *A. O. TYLER* could offer return fire. By the time the rest of the Union fleet had brought their gun crews to full quarters, *CSS ARKANSAS* was well clear and heading for the safety of Vicksburg's protective guns. She had not, however, escaped damage. *LANCASTER*, *QUEEN OF THE WEST*, *CARONDELET* and *A. O. TYLER* had gotten their full measure of revenge. *CSS ARKANSAS's* engine room had been set afire, and her crew had suffered many dead and wounded. When her pilot brought *CSS ARKANSAS* alongside the Vicksburg wharf, the conditions aboard were appalling. Lieutenant George Gift, one of her officers, later described the scene.

> ...Our smokestack resembled an immense nutmeg grater, so often had it been struck, and the sides of the ship were as spotted as if she had been peppered. A shot had broken our cast-iron ram. Another had demolished a hawse-pipe. Our boats were shot away and dragging. But all this was to be expected and could be repaired. Not so on the inside. A great heap of mangled and ghostly slain lay on the gun deck, with rivulets of blood running away from them. There was a poor fellow torn asunder, another smashed flat, whilst in the 'slaughterhouse,' brains and blood were all about. Down below fifty or sixty wounded were groaning and complaining, or courageously bearing their ills without a murmur.[150]

On the Union side, things were little better. The *LANCASTER* was ready for a shipyard; her crew decimated. Of the three vessels which had gone up the Yazoo after *CSS ARKANSAS*, only *QUEEN OF THE WEST* had escaped serious battle damage. *CARONDELET* lay battered and half sunk against the bank of the river. (She would later be salvaged.) *A. O. TYLER* had lost eight killed and double that number wounded. Farragut's and Lee's vessels had also suffered, but to a lesser extent. Five men from the *USS HARTFORD* had been killed, another five wounded. Another of the naval vessels had hull damage from a collision with the passing *QUEEN OF THE WEST*. One of Farragut's gunboats, the *USS WINONA*, was so badly riddled that she later had to be run up on the shore to keep her from sinking. The whole episode was mortifying to the Union side. Farragut's pride told him things had to be put right. He freely admitted what had been his lack of readiness in a note sent by launch that day to Davis.

> ...We were all caught unprepared for him [*CSS ARKANSAS*] but we must go down and destroy him. I will get the squadron underway as soon as the steam is up, and run down in line -- the ships inside in line with your ironclad vessels. We must go close to him and smash him in. It will be warm work, but we must do it; he must be destroyed...We will go down in line of battle, and when passed we will turn and come up again. Be sure to fire into the wharf boat. She is in place where they make their ordnance incendiary preparations.[151]

By the time Farragut's and Davis's warships were ready to start downstream, darkness was upon them. Farragut would later write to Davis, "...when we got off the town, there was nothing to be seen of the ram. I looked with all of the eyes in my head to no purpose. We could see nothing, but the flash of the enemy's guns to fire at..." Farragut, now again below Vicksburg, would remain there. Davis returned upriver to his old anchorage near Young's Point. The fact that this attempt to get at *CSS ARKANSAS* had failed frustrated Farragut even more. He sent Davis another note: "...I will continue to take chances and or try to destroy her until my squadron is destroyed or she is..." In his reply, which was sent across the De Soto Peninsula via courier and then out to Farragut's ship by launch, Davis attempted to put the matter into a more logical perspective.

> US Flag Steamer *BENTON*
> Off Vicksburg, July 17, 1862
>
> Dear Flag Officer:
> Your letter of July 16 was handed to me early this morning. We shall both of us agree entirely as to our responsibility and as to the disastrous results of any neglect of what will be considered our duty on this occasion.

I do not think the destruction of the *CSS ARKANSAS*, without any regard to the consequences to ourselves, would be an object sufficient to justify the abandonment of all the other advantages which have accumulated from the long series of triumphs and successes of patient waiting and of successful contest on the part of the Army and Navy in the Mississippi River during the last five or six months.

We are now in possession of the Mississippi River from its source to its mouth, with the exception of the short interval that separates our two fleets. Across this interval, we have an uninterrupted communication; above and below it we have an efficient blockading squadron, and the intermediate space of land is already bisected by a canal, by means of which we hope, through the recent rise in the upper waters, to separate the city of Vicksburg from the main channel of the river. [He referred to the De Soto Canal.]

Lastly, we have represented to the Government at home that military reinforcements are necessary to capture and maintain possession of Vicksburg, and these reinforcements are probably on their way to join us.

I look to the continued occupation of the river and its free navigation as an object paramount to all others, as an event as influential as any other in restoring domestic peace and preventing foreign war.

The *CSS ARKANSAS* is harmless in her present position, and will be more easily destroyed should she come out from under the batteries than while enjoying their protection.

With all these prudential considerations, however, I am as eager as yourself to put an end to this impudent rascal's existence. I have given a great deal of thought to it to-day. I have even laid down the plan of proceeding. We cannot do anything until the *ESSEX* can get up steam, which will not be until tonight, if then, and we ought to have the *SUMTER* above to do her ramming with effect.

We should have a good prospect of success to justify our staking upon the hazard of a die all that we have gained, and gained with such sacrifices of life and treasure, and especially when the object we aim at will be as effectually obtained without that risk by the patient exercise of vigilance and self-control; in short, by pursuing the course that was adopted at Fort Columbus, Island No. 10, and Fort Pillow.

Very truly, your friend

C. H. Davis, Flag Officer[152]

Farragut did not accept Davis's calm and reasonable view of the situation, arguing petulantly in reply that both his own position and the orders that governed his actions called for an entirely different reaction.

...You say the *CSS ARKANSAS* is harmless in her present position. I cannot think that she will remain harmless for long; as soon as she is repaired and organized she will keep us all on the qui vive, and cause great expenditures of fuel, which I fear, we will have but a poor chance to replenish. As to your fleet, you are all right; you are open to a downstream supply of all stores from above, while mine are obliged to come up against the stream five hundred miles and fight their way past all the bluffs, at the risk of being destroyed. Hence the difference in our feelings, and I suppose it accounts in great measure for the difference in our instructions, for while yours advise the prudential course, mine advise exactly the opposite, 'that great ends are only to be obtained by great risk,' etc.[153]

In a series of communications, Davis kept arguing moderation, explaining to Farragut that besides the need to hold a position in strength above Vicksburg, he,

Davis, was also responsible for protecting and keeping communications open to General Curtis who was by then in garrison in the vicinity of Helena, Arkansas. Davis also described the under-strength condition of Lee's mortar boats which, besides needing the protection of the gunboats in the most normal of circumstances, were now especially vulnerable due to sickness in the crews (reduced by this point in time to twenty-three percent of normal operational strength). The health of the crews on Davis's gunboats was only slightly better, an average of forty percent of their crew down sick.[154] Nevertheless, Davis expressed a willingness to meet Farragut at least half way by finally agreeing to commit the gunboats *ESSEX* and *SUMTER* and the ram *QUEEN OF THE WEST* toward an effort to sink Farragut's nemesis.

Upon notification that *QUEEN OF THE WEST* had been chosen by Davis to go after the *CSS ARKANSAS*, Alfred W. Ellet personally took over her command. The plan of attack as laid out jointly by Davis and Farragut was that Porter's mortar schooners, which were all moored south of the city, were to move up along the western bank of the river to within four thousand yards of Vicksburg's lower gun emplacements preparatory to commencing fire against these batteries. (Porter's mortar schooners had, as of this point in time, not yet left Vicksburg for their new assignment on the James River.) At the same time that the mortar schooners were to open fire, gunboats from Davis's upriver command (*BENTON*, *CINCINNATI*, and *LOUISVILLE*) were to start shelling Vicksburg's upper batteries. Meanwhile the *ESSEX* was to come downriver in a direct line of approach toward the *CSS ARKANSAS*. *QUEEN OF THE WEST* was to follow close behind. As soon as the *ESSEX* and *QUEEN OF THE WEST* came into proximity of the line of fire of the mortar schooners, the schooners were to cease action.[155] Simultaneously, *SUMTER* was to come up from downriver and join *ESSEX* and *QUEEN OF THE WEST* with a direct attack against *CSS ARKANSAS*. The attacks were to commence with close-in fire followed by rammings.

There is confusion inherent within the reports of this action as to exactly what transpired after the attacks began. It seems, though, that when the *ESSEX* started its run toward the *CSS ARKANSAS*, (this according to the *ESSEX's* battle report), the *CSS ARKANSAS's* crew, "...let go her bow line and the current drifted her stem on; the consequence was this vessel [*ESSEX*] only grazed her side, and [then] ran with great force high on the bank,..." While *ESSEX* was perched on the Vicksburg shore, she naturally became the target of heavy shelling from the closest of the city's shore batteries. Ellet, handling the con on *QUEEN OF THE WEST*, was unable to see either the *ESSEX* or the *SUMTER*; his report indicates that he thought he was alone. The scene at that point was almost obliterated by dense smoke from spent gun powder. Ellet's misconception that he was alone would result in his later unfair charge of a lack of support when it was needed at that time.

> ...that owing to a failure upon the part of the parties who were to cooperate with me in the attack, from some cause that is yet unexplained to me, I did not succeed as I expected, in destroying the *CSS ARKANSAS*. I did succeed, however, in striking her a very severe blow, and no doubt inflicted considerable injury upon her, but being unsupported by the *ESSEX* and *SUMTER*, as I had been led to expect, and exposed alone to the united fire of the upper batteries, I was obliged to draw off without accomplishing the full results anticipated.[156]

ESSEX managed to back off from the bank before she received too many damaging hits, and she made it safely back to the covering fire of the supportive gunboats.[157]

Ellet's withdrawal from the scene of attack against the *CSS ARKANSAS* did not lessen the danger to *QUEEN OF THE WEST*. At this juncture of the mission, Ellet would indeed have grounds for complaint that he was not adequately supported. While retreating back upriver, he discovered that the *BENTON*, *CINCINNATI*, and *LOUISVILLE* had pulled back from their assigned positions, leaving *QUEEN OF THE WEST* to take the full onslaught of everything the Confederate batteries could throw at her. Damage to *QUEEN OF THE WEST* from that last cannonade necessitated her being sent upriver to Saint Louis, there to join the *LANCASTER* in a shipyard.

Of the twenty-nine in Ellet's crew that day, twenty-two were civilians, and of those civilians, eight were contrabands. Ellet would write of this polyglot crew with words of praise.

> When the boat was full of steam, and of course so hot as to be scarcely endurable, with shells bursting, one in the pilot house, another in the engine room, with shot tearing the boat on every side, yet unflinching, every man stood to his post. It is with great pleasure that I bear this just tribute to their creditable behavior.[158]

Brigadier General Thomas Williams who was the officer assigned by Butler to hold defensive positions on the De Soto Peninsula, reported that his force, which at the start was at a strength of thirty-two hundred, was now down to eight hundred effectives. This decrease was in the main due to the ravages of malaria. Discouraged by what had all the appearances of a tactical impasse, Williams wrote Davis that he now viewed as nearly hopeless the possibility of taking Vicksburg that summer.[159] That correspondence included with it a copy of instructions which Williams had received from Butler, ordering him to withdraw to Baton Rouge. Those orders were dated July 17.

> General Williams:
> From all I can learn of operations at Vicksburg, your force is at present not so much needed there as it is elsewhere.
> The enemy is concentrating some forces in the neighborhood of Baton Rouge, and it is necessary that something be done on the Red River line. Besides, you are in the geographical department of General Halleck. Therefore, if the state of affairs will permit without serious detriment to the public service, you will withdraw your force and return as soon as possible to Baton Rouge.[160]

Farragut at last received his authorization to return his command to New Orleans. Davis's gunboats were to return to Memphis. The conquest of Fortress Vicksburg would be put on hold.

On the eve of his departure from Vicksburg, Farragut wrote Davis stating that on his way downriver, he would seize all ferryboats and destroy all flatboats in an attempt to prevent the continual "crossing [of] provisions, troops and lead [ammunition] from the western to the eastern shore by means of the ferries and the flatboats."

On July 28, Flag Officer Davis ordered Ellet's rams to accompany the gunboats back to Memphis. By departure time, the malaria pestilence had come uncomfortably close to decimating the crews.

BATTLE AT BATON ROUGE
AND DESTRUCTION OF THE CSS ARKANSAS

Upon arrival at Baton Rouge to where he moved his troops in compliance with Major General Benjamin Butler's request, Brigadier General Thomas Williams began work on defensive positions. Although the high rate of illness of the troops prevented them from doing anything of real substance toward the digging of fortifications, Williams promised to Butler's adjutant that, "I shall take such measures of military security as may suggest themselves to be necessary, avoiding unnecessary exposure or fatigue to the troops." [161]

Butler's prognosis that Baton Rouge would soon be attacked by Confederate forces proved itself correct. The odds of the Federal force being able to hold did not appear favorable. Poised in front of Baton Rouge were around six thousand Confederates while the defender's strength numbered only around two thousand, half of whom were on the sick list. [162]

Major General John C. Breckinridge, the Confederate commander then threatening Baton Rouge, had requested that the *CSS ARKANSAS* be moved down from Vicksburg for the purpose of providing him with fire support from the river side. A secondary purpose was to cut off any attempt by the Union defenders to retreat to their transports.

David G. Farragut, recently promoted to rear admiral, had already withdrawn most of his fleet to New Orleans, so there was little left on the river to hamper the movement of *CSS ARKANSAS*. Breckinridge urged that time was of the essence. Accordingly, the ram's engineers operated at full steam while en route from Vicksburg. In light of the condition of the engines (badly misaligned from the ramming received in front of Vicksburg) the stress of full steam pressure brought on a succession of breakdowns. Despite these delays, the engineers got *CSS ARKANSAS* down to Baton Rouge, but not before Breckinridge began his assault.

Upon arrival, *CSS ARKANSAS's* crew found their old antagonist the *ESSEX* standing river guard. The Confederate ram's officers decided the best results against *ESSEX* could be obtained by ramming. While swinging onto a collision course, and with her helm half over, one of *CSS ARKANSAS's* engines stopped dead, the rudder at a hard angle. Momentum carried the rebel ram onto the shore where she, "jambed [sic] herself on some old cypress stumps." She roosted there until nightfall while her engineers frantically tried to make repairs. Finally, with everything thought to be ready, she was floated off by jettisoning some railroad tracking which had been laid upon her deck as makeshift armor. Within minutes after getting underway, she again broke down. Being close to the bank when this happened, her deck hands managed to get lines over to the shore. The exhausted engineers went to work again, this time manufacturing replacements for broken wrist pins for the piston arms, the latest cause of breakdown. By the time repairs were made, it was close to daylight. With the glimmer of dawn to see by, the *ESSEX* was sighted coming on at full speed. Lines off, and with steam valves open, the *CSS ARKANSAS* turned to fight. But fight she could not. One of the new wrist pins immediately failed, and with the subsequent loss of power to her port wheel, *CSS ARKANSAS* veered into the bank. This time, she was stuck for good. Her crew abandoned the vessel, but not before they had set fires leading to the powder magazine. She blew up -- a total loss.[163]

Meanwhile, in the make-do entrenchments in front of the city, Williams's infantry held against Breckinridge's attack. The Confederates, giving up the attempt, pulled back toward Vicksburg.[164] Union casualties had been high. Among the dead was Brigadier General Thomas Williams. After the battle, the body of Brigadier General Thomas Williams was loaded aboard the transport *LEWIS WHITEMAN*. When leaving its moorings in front of the city, the *LEWIS WHITEMAN* collided with another transport and sank, taking down with her a large number of Union wounded and Williams's body.

~

Although Vicksburg was still in Confederate hands and would be for some time, Baton Rouge remained as a Federal presence above New Orleans, thus protecting New Orleans from what otherwise would almost surely have been a Confederate attempt to reoccupy.

REORGANIZATIONS
(Fall of 1862)

Transfer of the Western Gunboat Flotilla to the Navy

On July 16, 1862, Congress passed a bill transferring the Western Gunboat Flotilla from the War Department over to the full operational jurisdiction of the Navy Department, the transfer to be effective on September 30. During September, paperwork prepared concerning the transfer of this fleet included a number of tallies which dealt with the flotilla's fiscal and operational history while it was under Army management. In September 1863, these tallies were incorporated into formal reports for presentation to the Congress by the Quartermaster General. (Appendix C is a reproduction of the most informative of those reports.)

Coinciding with the transfer of the vessels of the Western Gunboat Flotilla to the Navy's jurisdiction, David D. Porter relieved Charles H. Davis as its commander. With that transfer in command, the rank of rear admiral was bestowed upon Porter. Under the Navy, the Western Gunboat Flotilla now became the "Upper Mississippi Squadron."

This was also a time of reorganization for the Ellet Ram Fleet; that activity will be covered in detail within Part V.

For a Time, Confusion Reigns

Transfer of the Western Gunboat Flotilla to the Navy and the reorganization of the Ellet fleet was not the only command changeover affecting matters in the west. Major General Henry W. Halleck, who had for so long orchestrated matters in the west, was ordered east in July to take over as Lincoln's General in Chief of the Union Army. For the time being, command in the west was to be left largely decentralized. This was not a situation looked upon favorably by Major General William T. Sherman. On November 16, Sherman would write Rear Admiral Porter, expressing his displeasure over the lack of an orderly command structure within the Mississippi theater of operations.

My opinion is that a perfect concert of action should exist between all the forces of the United States operating down the valley; and I apprehend some difficulty may arise from the fact that you control on the river, Curtis on the west bank, and Grant on the east bank. Were either one of you in absolute command, all of course, would act in concert. Our enemies are now also disconcerted by divided counsels; Van Dorn and Lovell are superior in lineal rank to Pemberton, and yet the latter is in command of the Department of Mississippi and Louisiana.[165]

Sherman's concern over the Army's decentralization was justified. In the fall, things improved somewhat over what they had been during the summer. On October 16, what seemed like a really positive step was taken when Halleck gave Grant the command of the Army of the Tennessee, a command which became inclusive of the District of the Mississippi. With that new assignment went the responsibility to take Vicksburg; but clarity for that responsibility was once again clouded over and confused when Lincoln gave an independent command within Grant's jurisdiction to an almost totally inexperienced volunteer officer, Major General John A. McClernand. Under this new scenario, Grant was to continue his operations against Vicksburg by thrusting south toward Jackson, Mississippi. From there, he would come against the fortress city from the east. At the same time, McClernand, with his command, was to move directly against Vicksburg from the north, following along the river corridor. Although McClernand would be operating largely within Grant's operational zone, things were structured, thanks to Lincoln's interference, so that McClernand would be acting independently of Grant's instructions. This did not make a great deal of sense; but political leaders during wartime often make irrational decisions, and Lincoln was no exception. Grant quietly circumvented the problem, at least as best he could at the time, by assigning Sherman to take over at Memphis while McClernand was busying himself putting together volunteer regiments to the north. From Memphis, Sherman was to get the jump on McClernand by making an amphibious advance south on the river; Grant hoped that advance would synchronize with his own overland movement from Jackson. If all went well, Grant and Sherman planned to be in possession of Vicksburg before McClernand could start.

The launching of an expedition by Brigadier General Samuel R. Curtis that fall was one other example of the right hand not knowing what the left was doing. Curtis's troops had been in fixed positions at Helena. Not being privy to the planning which was going on concerning Vicksburg, and wanting to keep his command busy, Curtis had decided (quite independently of consultation with either Grant or McClernand) to launch an expedition to take the Post on the Arkansas, then known to be a Confederate strong point. The Navy agreed to lend him a hand. On November 19, Curtis's deputy, Brigadier General Alvin P. Hovey loaded six thousand infantry and two thousand cavalry on twelve transports. Under escort of the gunboats of the newly named Upper Mississippi Squadron, the expedition left Helena bound for the mouth of the White River. This was the shortcut route to the Post on the Arkansas which was itself located on the Arkansas River. When Hovey arrived at the mouth of the White River, local farmers reported that the height of the river had dropped an amazing five feet over the two days just past. Launch crews which went upstream from the mouth could sound out no more than thirty inches of depth at one cross section of the channel. Since the transports on the average drew between three and four feet, the only option remaining to Hovey was for him to unload his men and horses and move overland to Post on the Arkansas; but before he got all his men ashore, a steamer bearing dispatches overhauled the expedition with a warning for Hovey not to be absent for long as he and his brigade would soon be needed for work elsewhere.[166] Since it was estimated that to march, invest, and then march back from the Post on the Arkansas would take at least eight days, Hovey opted to abort the expedition and return immediately to Helena. The taking of Post on the Arkansas would be a matter left for attention sometime in the future.

THE SECOND MOVE AGAINST VICKSBURG
(November 1862 to January 1863)

Securing the Flanks, Or Trying To

The newest plan to take Vicksburg was in great part premised upon a successful movement by Grant along the Mississippi and Tennessee Railroad Company's right of way as it led toward Jackson, Mississippi. Contingent to Grant's success was the securing of all river approaches to Vicksburg, thus denying the Confederate defenders the succor of resupply. Between the Mississippi and the line of march intended by Grant, lay a huge network of navigable waterways. This network consisted of the Yazoo and Sunflower rivers and their various tributaries. The Yazoo-Sunflower system had once made connection with the Mississippi north of Vicksburg at Yazoo Pass (across the river from Helena, Arkansas). That connection had been blocked off for some years by the building of a levee. In 1862, the Yazoo's merging with the Mississippi occurred just above Vicksburg. Prior to meeting the Mississippi, the Yazoo served the city of Vicksburg from a number of freight landings. As long as the Yazoo- Sunflower system remained navigable for Confederate steamers, the enemy at Vicksburg would have access to the food resources of the Yazoo basin. The Yazoo also allowed the movement of troops to and from Vicksburg, an access which would still be usable even if Grant were to cut the railway connecting Vicksburg with the east.

The job of taking control of the Yazoo from the Confederates was given to Rear Admiral David D. Porter. He asked the Ellet organization to provide one or two rams to accompany a naval gunboat expedition aimed at a preliminary reconnoitering of the Yazoo- Sunflower system. The ram assigned to the operation was *QUEEN OF THE WEST* under the command of Army Captain Edwin W. Sutherland.[167] Porter, by way of laying out the goals for the reconnaissance, wrote to Captain Walke, the naval officer he had placed in command.

> ...I have no means of ascertaining the height of water in the Yazoo, and I think the only way to find out is to go and see. I shall feel better satisfied when I know we cannot get in, for then I shall know that the rebels cannot get out. In the matter of attacking batteries, you must exercise judgment and no doubt by a little consultation with those connected with you on this expedition you will arrive at a just conclusion.

The object is to prevent the enemy from blocking up the approaches to the river with batteries....The object is to get possession of as much of the Yazoo as we can and hold it...

If you find that you can enter the Yazoo, push on and go as far as you can. Keep the communications open behind you. There are a number of fine, large boats up the Yazoo, try and secure them.[168]

On December 11, by way of an advanced probe, Walke sent up the Yazoo the light gunboats *USS MARMORA* and *USS SIGNAL*. The river was down, and he hesitated to chance the grounding of larger vessels. A considerable amount of enemy activity was seen. Barges and scows were everywhere along the banks. They also came upon "torpedo floats" [mines] which when shot at, "usually exploded." After about twenty miles, the two gunboats returned downriver and reported to Walke. That night, thunderstorms were evident in the eastern sky. The heavy rain which followed caused the Yazoo to rise enough so that Walke felt confident in sending up two of his heavy ironclads, the *USS CAIRO* and *USS PITTSBURG*, accompanied by *QUEEN OF THE WEST*. The *USS SIGNAL* and *USS MARMORA* went with them. The group had not progressed any great distance when the *USS CAIRO*, collided with at least "two torpedoes"; she sank in twelve minutes flat.[169] Sutherland managed to get his *QUEEN OF THE WEST* alongside in time to save the *USS CAIRO's* crew. The gunboat had gone down in 36 feet of water which left only the stacks showing. Before leaving the scene, Sutherland, following the wishes of the *USS CAIRO's* skipper, pulled down the stacks so that the gunboat would not be found by enemy salvors.[170]

Following the loss of *USS CAIRO*, the Walke Expedition returned to the Mississippi.

Meanwhile, something else had gone awry -- this time with Grant.

Disaster Strikes Grant's Logistics

According to plan, once Grant reached Jackson, Mississippi, he was to swing west toward Vicksburg. In tactical concert, Sherman was to launch an assault against the city from the Mississippi side. But long before Grant arrived at Jackson, his line of advance was blocked by Major General Earl Van Dorn's infantry, well supported by cavalry. A separate body of thirty-five hundred Confederate troopers was to cut Grant off from his supply line through a series of strikes to his rear.

In order to escape the notice of Federal patrols, the Confederate horsemen had ridden north on a wide arc through New Albany. They had then swung toward Holly Springs, the location of the huge quartermaster and commissary depot upon which further advance by Grant depended. The enemy cavalry had destroyed supplies valued at $1.5 million, leaving behind only ashes as they headed up through Saulsbury. On the way, they wrecked much of the track and all of the bridges of the Memphis and Charleston Railroad. While the enemy cavalry was raising havoc with Holly Springs and its environs, other enemy horsemen under Nathan Bedford Forrest tore up the railroad right of way north of Grand Junction, thereby cutting off the last of Grant's communications to his rear.

The complete destruction of his logistical tail meant that Grant could not advance nor could he hold where he was. His only option was to fall back and realign his army along a new defensive line starting at the curve of the Tennessee River and stretching in a westward arc to Memphis. (This defensive line roughly followed that of the Tennessee state boundary.) Selecting this line as a defensive boundary was an obvious choice since it anchored on the rail junction on the great curve of the Tennessee at Decatur. If the track leading from there to Memphis could be kept safe from damage by the enemy, the valley of the Tennessee would not itself be jeopardized.

As things now clearly stood, Grant's part in any joint offensive with Sherman toward the taking of Vicksburg had come to an end.

Sherman's Movement Against the Bluffs at Vicksburg

On the same day that Grant's supply base at Holly Springs was being destroyed, Sherman, then still located at Memphis, stood totally unaware of what had happened. Due to the enemy's destruction of the telegraph lines, he would remain substantially ignorant of Grant's situation for some days to come.

Before leaving Memphis, Sherman had received some second hand rumors of Grant's pending predicament, but there had not been any real evidence to justify a delay in his push off to Vicksburg. Not being cognizant of Grant's inability to support him, Sherman was making last minute preparations to move his four divisions onto transports which would take them down the river toward Vicksburg. The transports which were to be employed had been assembled by Quartermaster Lewis B. Parsons who had recently been placed in charge of all steamer movements within the western theater. It was hoped that this centralization of quartermaster authority would remove much of the confusion of control which had in the past contributed toward critical shortages. The forthcoming operation was to be a test for the new arrangement.

At the time the request for transports first came to Parsons from Sherman's headquarters, only eight steamboats were immediately available. Parsons had been told that he had only three days within which to assemble the rest. By his reckoning, he would need to locate and have at Memphis, ready to load, at least forty steamers capable of housing troops. That was Parsons's first challenge. The second challenge would be to assemble sufficient vessels to provide a supply lift to support Sherman once he went south. Parsons realized that normal procurement methods were not enough, so he wired Quartermaster General Montgomery C. Meigs in Washington, requesting the authority to commandeer the steamers he would need. That request was granted, putting into play what amounted to a total control of shipping along the main river as well as on the lower Ohio. One communication was typical of this new authority as it was expressed to the quartermasters on the upper Mississippi and on the Ohio.

December 13, 1862

You will please proceed to Cairo at which place you will detain all boats going in any direction, at all suitable for transports for government. Until further orders from this office, you will please see that every preparation is made, according to your judgment, to prepare the said boats for twenty to forty days absence, especially preparing an ample supply of wood and coal -- you will also see that each boat provides itself with at least twenty-four axes for cutting wood, and more if you think necessary.[171]

The 3-day deadline originally set down by Sherman turned out to be totally unrealistic, especially considering the distances from which the needed shipping would be gathered. In all, putting together the required number of vessels was accomplished in a remarkable eight days. On December 20, Parsons confirmed the readiness of that shipping in a status report sent to the War Department.

> We commence loading this morning and the first division...ten boats are just leaving port. I think we have nearly if not quite enough to carry us to Vicksburg, and 66,000 bushels of coal is on the way from Cairo...I shall go down with the fleets, so as to discharge as many boats as possible, as we have left none to do our transportation from Saint Louis.[172]

All told, Parsons eventually gathered together for loading at Memphis seventy-one steamboats. This was a considerable feat. Parsons later stated to this superior, Brigadier General Robert Allen, that nothing adverse had occurred during the entire lift. However, that statement is difficult to believe. If true, this must have been the first large movement the Army ever conducted by water -- before or since -- which went off without a hitch. For his work in getting Sherman south from Memphis, Parsons received a promotion from captain to full colonel of volunteers.

Altogether, sixty transports were used for the initial troop lift. Another eleven would follow later. The transports in the initial lift were loaded in the sequence here listed.[173]

First Division: A. J. Smith

CHAMPION	commissary boat.
CITIZEN	83rd Ohio (or Indiana?) [sic] Volunteers; less two companies.
CITY OF ALTON	108th and 48th Ohio Volunteers; Headquarters Second Brigade.
CITY OF LOUISIANA	Mercantile battery, Iowa; 131st Illinois Volunteers
DES ARC	Division Headquarters.
DUKE OF ARGYLE	77th Illinois Volunteers.
GENERAL ANDERSON	ordnance boat.
HIAWATHA	96th Ohio Volunteers; section of battery.
J. C. SNOW	16th Indiana Volunteers; First Brigade Headquarters.
J. H. DICKEY[1]	23rd Wisconsin Volunteers.
J. S. PRINGLE	67th Indiana Volunteers.
J. W. CHEESEMAN, JR.[2]	19th Kentucky Volunteers.
METROPOLITAN	60th Indiana Volunteers.
OHIO BELLE	Co. C; 4th Indiana Cavalry; two companies 23rd Wisconsin.
ROBERT CAMPBELL, JR.	97th Illinois Volunteers.
IOWA	131st Illinois Volunteers

Second Division: Morgan L. Smith

CHANCELLOR	Division Headquarters and Thielemann's cavalry.
CITY OF MEMPHIS	Batteries A and B; 1st Illinois Artillery and 8th Missouri Volunteers.
EDWARD WALSH	113th Illinois Volunteers.
OMAHA	57th Ohio Volunteers.
PLANET	116th Illinois Volunteers; one section Parrott [guns].
ROBERT ALLEN	commissary boat.
SIOUX CITY	83rd Indiana Volunteers.
SPREAD EAGLE	127th Illinois Volunteers.
SUNNY SOUTH	54th Ohio Volunteers.
UNIVERSE	6th Missouri Volunteers.
WESTMORELAND	55th Illinois Volunteers; Headquarters General D. Stuart.

Third Division: George W. Morgan

BELLE PEORIA	Headquarters Colonel Lindsey commanding Second Brigade; two companies 49th Indiana Volunteers and pontoon train.
CRESCENT CITY	22nd Kentucky and 54th Indiana Volunteers.
DES MOINES	42nd Ohio Volunteers.
DI VERNON	3rd Kentucky Volunteers; pontoon train.
EMPRESS	Division Headquarters.
FANNY BULLITT	Headquarters Colonel DeCourcy; Third Brigade; 16th Ohio; eight companies.
HENRY VON PHUL	114th Ohio; five guns Lanphere's battery; ordnance stores.
JESSE K. BELL	Headquarters Colonel Shelden; commanding First Brigade.
KEY WEST NO. 2	118th Illinois Volunteers.
LADY JACKSON	commissary boat.
NORTHERNER	120th Ohio Volunteers.
PEMBINA	one gun Lanphere's battery.
SAM GATY	69th Indiana Volunteers.
WAR EAGLE	49th Indiana; eight companies; three guns Foster's battery.

Fourth Division: Frederick Steele

ADRIATIC	1st Missouri Artillery.
CONTINENTAL	Division Headquarters and Ohio battery.
D. G. TAYLOR[3]	sixty men and horses; quartermaster stores.
DACOTAH	3rd Missouri Volunteers
EMMA	17th Missouri Volunteers.
GLADIATOR	30th Missouri Volunteers.
IATAN	34th Iowa Volunteers.
ISABELLA	31st Missouri Volunteers.
JOHN J. ROE and NEBRASKA	4th; 9th; 25th; 31st Iowa Volunteers.
JOHN WARNER	13th Illinois Volunteers.
KEY WEST	1st Iowa Artillery.
L. M. KENNETT	29th Missouri Volunteers.
METEOR	76th Ohio Volunteers.
POLAR STAR	58th Ohio Volunteers.
STEPHEN DECATUR	28th Iowa Volunteers.
SUCKER STATE	32nd Missouri Volunteers.
TECUMSEH	26th Iowa Volunteers.
THOMAS E. TUTT	12th Missouri Volunteers.

[1] *JOHN H. DICKEY* [2] *J. W. CHEESEMAN* [3] *DANIEL G. TAYLOR*

Sherman's Vicksburg Expedition was the first Civil War expedition to take place on the western rivers where the needs in regard to medical care were taken into thorough account. The planning for this seems to have originated with Sherman himself who ordered that a supply base for medical provisions be established at

Memphis and that special hospital boats be provided for and equipped by the Quartermaster Department. These hospital boats were to stay in the field until filled and were then to act as medical evacuation vessels carrying the wounded and sick back to Saint Louis.

~

Sherman's tactical plan for the attack against Vicksburg was to enter the Yazoo River and land his army near the northeast end of the Vicksburg bluffs. In moving up into the Yazoo, one section of Rear Admiral Porter's gunboats was to take the van with the rest of the gunboats interspersed in column with the transports. This interspersing of the gunboats was so as to provide immediate reactive fire in the event any enemy batteries had escaped the observation of the advance gunboats.

Preceding the invasion fleet by some hours would be the gunboat *USS BARON DE KALB* followed by two light patrol vessels, *USS SIGNAL* and *USS LAUREL*, together with Ellet's *QUEEN OF THE WEST*. Their collective mission would be to conduct a general reconnaissance in order to locate enemy batteries and to remove torpedoes. The torpedo removal was to be accomplished by row boats sent out in advance of the *USS BARON DE KALB*. The rowboats were to proceed upstream dragging grapnels which were supposed to snag on to any detonation wires which led from the moored torpedoes to trigger mechanisms located along the river's banks. It was suspected that some torpedoes would be moored in suspension between the bottom and the surface while others would be floating but anchored to the bottom. When a suspicious object was sighted, the rowboats were to move in on the object and lasso it. Once the torpedo was lassoed, it was to be dragged into the bank and secured to a tree or some other fixed object. It was then to be detonated by rifle fire from a safe distance.[174] All of the above was predicated upon the rather unrealistic premise that enemy riflemen would allow all this activity to take place without interference. On the day after Christmas, the advance gunboat element entered the Yazoo.

With some waiting time on his hands, Sherman sent a side expedition off to handle what he felt was a potential security threat to his western flank. When Butler had ordered Williams to evacuate the De Soto Peninsula back in July, the Confederates had moved in quickly to repair the track of the Vicksburg, Shreveport, and Texas Railroad Company. This was the line leading from Monroe to the De Soto Peninsula directly across from Vicksburg. (Previously, Williams's men had ripped up that part of the track in proximity to the De Soto Peninsula.) The Confederate quartermasters were once again using this railroad in their supply of Vicksburg. From the termination of the track at the tip of the peninsula, they had established a cross-river steamer shuttle over to the city. Sherman was now going to put the Vicksburg, Shreveport, and Texas out of business for good. To do that job, he dispatched a brigade under Brigadier General Stephen G. Burbridge who had orders to destroy the railroad's track as far west as Delphi, Louisiana. Thirty-six hours later, Burbridge would report back to Sherman that following a lightning march of seventy-five miles, his men had destroyed enough track and demolished sufficient bridges to keep the railroad from resuming operations for some months to come. They had also burned a couple of conveniently located saw mills to assure that lumber for repairing the bridges could not be milled locally. Except for one insignificant skirmish, Burbridge had met no opposition.[175]

While Burbridge was busy ripping up railroad track on the opposite side of the Mississippi, the gunboats working up the Yazoo were cleansing the area of enemy mines; but while doing so, their crews were suffering heavily at the hands of enemy sharpshooters. Nothing was spotted in the way of artillery emplacements until they met with cannon fire coming from Drumgould's Bluff. This line of bluffs was ten miles upstream on the Yazoo -- far enough in for the safety of Sherman's proposed landings which were to take place farther downstream. Sherman could now order in the transports.[176] The Yazoo was not wide enough for transports to steam abreast except in a very few places, so the orders given were to move upriver by single column.

The upriver trip and the landings themselves proved uneventful. Once the troops had been put ashore, Sherman's division and brigade commanders discovered that the terrain over which they were to order their assaults did not resemble that shown on the maps with which they had been provided. Rather than the portrayed flat, cleared ground which seemingly offered wide approach paths to the enemy works, the ground was heavily overgrown and widely interspersed with creeks and swampy sloughs. The Chickasaw Bayou over which a good part of the troops would have to cross presented the worst obstacle, a natural moat -- and one which would have to be surmounted before any assault could begin. Making the situation worse was the forewarning the Confederates had received well in advance of the landings because of the unavoidable time spent in clearing the Yazoo River of its torpedoes. That warning had given Lieutenant General John C. Pemberton, the Confederate commander at Vicksburg, ample time to start bringing reinforcements in from east of the city. (There was no longer any need for Pemberton to retain those troops eastward of Memphis once Grant had begun his retreat back to the Tennessee state line.) Over the next two days, three full brigades of Confederate infantry would transfer from Grenada into the defensive works at Vicksburg. These, when joined with the troops already there, would bring Pemberton's total defensive force to twelve thousand men. This was far less than the thirty-one thousand troops possessed by Sherman; however, numbers could not make up for the excellent defensive positions held by the Confederates or for the deplorable ground over which Sherman's men would have to pass while going against them.

One analysis of the situation facing Sherman's army has come down to us from Brigadier General George W. Morgan who commanded Sherman's Third Division. Morgan, when writing after the war for *Battles and Leaders*, complained of the lack of familiarity with the terrain which he and other officers had held, especially its swampy features.[177] The creeks and sloughs created a need to funnel the assaulting forces into narrowing fronts which could only expose the men to concentrations of enemy fire. Despite the handicaps, Morgan believed in retrospect that some opportunities may have been missed through overlooking weak points that should have warranted exploitation. This same belief was shared by at least one general officer on the Confederate side, Brigadier General Stephen D. Lee, who was the officer in charge of the enemy's defenses which faced on the Chickasaw Bayou. He later described an opportunity of which Sherman had failed to take advantage.

> Had Sherman moved a little faster after landing, or made his attack at the mound or
> at any point between the bayou and Vicksburg, he could have gone into the city. As

it was, he virtually attacked at the apex of a triangle while I held the base and parts of the two sides.[178]

On the second day after the landings, the onset of a heavy fog created an almost zero visibility. Because of it, Sherman's units were visually cut off from contact with other units on their flanks. Later, when visual contact became possible, assaults were attempted at a number of separate locations. The defenders not only held the high ground, but they also had the easy ability to transfer their locations within the defensive entrenchments. Most importantly, the Confederates could communicate from command to command, a luxury not possessed by the swamp-bound and often fog-shrouded blue coats. At one point, Sherman was forced to re-embark Steele's division onto the transports and land them at another point more adaptable for maneuver. Examined as a whole, the terrain was such that there were only four small areas from which the Federal troops could approach the bluffs. Even in those areas, because of the impassable ground separating each of the approaches from the others, attacks could not be coordinated. The Confederate defenders had every approach point well covered by enfilade artillery, and there was no effective way to offer countering fire since the swampy soil made it impossible for Sherman's artillerymen to bring up their guns.

Casualties mounted. Adding to the entire porridge of misery on the night of December 29, rain began falling in torrents, flooding out practically everything. With the start of the rain, the fog lifted, and Sherman went aboard Porter's flag ship to confer on development of a new plan of action. Sherman wanted the gunboats to take the batteries at Drumgould's Bluff under bombardment. Once those batteries had been neutralized, Steele's division, supported by a brigade from Morgan L. Smith's division, would be transported to a landing place near those battery positions. The terrain there was high and dry, and it was an advantageous location from which to envelope the enemy's defenses. Porter agreed to begin the bombardment at once, and Sherman ordered Steele and Smith to start giving the necessary instructions to bring their troops to the river bank and the waiting transports. But no sooner was this started than the fog set in again. It hung on, and the plan was permanently canceled the following night.

Sherman was close enough to the rail line coming from Jackson (the track ran just back of the defended bluffs) to hear "the cars shuttling in." This was an almost certain indication that Confederate reinforcements were arriving from points farther to the east. Sherman still had not heard directly from Grant, but the conclusion was reached that something must have gone awfully wrong.

~

After losing his supply base at Holly Springs, Grant did his best to get word to Sherman that he was moving back north and that the support Sherman was counting on would not materialize; but the chaos which surrounded Grant's situation prevented messages from getting through. The enemy's cavalry had not only cut the telegraph wires, but they had removed large stretches of the wire, making repairs impossible until new wire could be brought in.

Withdrawal From the Yazoo

To Sherman, the situation began to look impossible. With six percent of his command already dead, wounded, or missing, he decided on a full withdrawal. With the transports reloaded and ready to turn back downstream to the Mississippi, a messenger informed Sherman that Major General John A. McClernand was on the west bank of the Mississippi at Young's Point, preparing to take over command. Sherman ordered all transports to hold position while he crossed the river and conferred with McClernand over whether or not to go ahead with the withdrawal. McClernand agreed with Sherman that the situation held no other option.

Before McClernand arrived, Sherman's plan had been to disembark his army at a point a little farther up the Mississippi at Milliken's Bend. There the troops were to go into defensive bivouac. However, the Mississippi Valley's winter weather, which was now at its worst, put a quick end to that idea. Upon inspection, the area at Milliken's Bend had been found to be totally unsuitable for an encampment. It was practically underwater, and there was no way for the sodden ground to be drained. For the time being, the troops would have to remain on the transports.

The taste of defeat had to be rinsed away from an army now close to demoralization. What better way to accomplish this, Sherman rationalized, than to undertake a small scale offensive action where the odds of success would almost certainly be favorable? Sherman wrote to Grant, explaining what he, with McClernand's agreement, had decided to do.

Milliken's Bend, Louisiana
January 4, 1863

Sir:

Since I had the honor to make my official report of the operations of the forces against Vicksburg, under date of the 3rd instant, a change of programme has been determined on, of which I think I should give you notice, lest the change should not reach you through other channels.

On the 2nd and 3rd instant it rained in torrents, and the alluvion at Milliken's Bend, as everywhere in this region, became like quagmire. It occurred to me, if we disembarked our command, we would be literally mud-bound and could be of little or no service.

The river above is surely interrupted somewhere, for boats (gunboats) due for several days are not yet come, and we know that the boat *BLUE WING*, towing two coal barges for the Navy, was captured by the enemy near the mouth of the Arkansas and carried up that river. The *BLUE WING* is known to have had on board a mail, which thus has fallen into hostile hands.

As long as we are unable with present forces to remove the obstructions at Vicksburg, this force on shore could do little good at this time, whereas it might in a few days ascend the Arkansas, whose waters now admit of navigation, and reduce the Post on the Arkansas, a fortified camp of the enemy, 50 miles up, from which he at all times threatens the river. I suggested the idea to General McClernand (who thought it within the scope of his power), and we proceeded in company to the mouth of the Yazoo and had a conference with Admiral Porter, who agreed to cooperate. We are now en route for Montgomery Point, the mouth of White River, where there is a cutoff to the Arkansas. Our whole land force will be used, and some four ironclads and several wood gunboats.

With this force we should make short work; at all events, if we cannot take by storm these field works, made to oppose the navigation of the rivers in the south, the sooner we know it the better. I hope in this case better success will attend our efforts than at Vicksburg.

General McClernand has this day assumed the general command of the forces, under the title of the Army of the Mississippi, dividing the Army into two Army corps -- the first of which to be commanded by General George W. Morgan and the other by myself. Of course I shall give him as cordial a support as possible, and shall not covet any honor or fame he may gather in this magnificent field of operations.

I have not heard a word from you since I left Oxford, and cannot undertake to describe with what painful suspense I listened for the sound of your guns in the distance while we lay in the swamp of the Yazoo. Observing the heavy reinforcements pouring into Vicksburg, and not hearing from you, I was forced at last to conclude that necessity had compelled you to fall back to Holly Springs.

General McClernand being now charged with fashioning and planning events, I can subside quietly into the more agreeable office of a corps commander, and shall endeavor to make it a good one. I miss Morgan L. Smith very much, and need [Benjamin H.] Grierson for cavalry.[179]

~

Sherman's assumption that Grant may have fallen back on Holly Springs was far short of what had actually happened. By the time Grant received Sherman's letter, he was consolidated at the fallback defense line astride the Tennessee state border.

Post on the Arkansas

The Post on the Arkansas, or Fort Hindman, as the entrenchments there came to be called, had certain strategic significance because of its high ground location overlooking the Arkansas River. Fort Hindman not only safeguarded against penetration farther upstream by Union ironclads, but it also offered a secure bastion from which Confederate supply vessels could depart in support of Vicksburg. Fort Hindman might also provide a potential launching place from where Confederate gunboats could foray in downriver strikes aimed against Mississippi River traffic. Some Union military planners -- Grant among them -- had in the past downplayed the importance of Fort Hindman. Its significance as a base for supply vessels routed to Vicksburg would become irrelevant once the Navy's gunboats established a presence on the Mississippi to the south of the entrance of the Arkansas. Nevertheless, a victory of some sort was needed to build troop morale and, as Sherman had put it to Grant, the taking of Fort Hindman would fit that bill with minimal effort or risk. With the new year dawning, some victory -- any victory -- was needed if public confidence in Union fortunes was to be restored.[180] McClernand later described Post on the Arkansas as

...a small village, the capital of Arkansas County, situated on elevated ground, above the reach of floods, and defining for some miles the left bank of the river. It was settled by the French in 1685; 50 miles above the mouth of the river, 117 miles below Little Rock, and surrounded by a fruitful country, abounding in cattle, corn, and cotton.

Fort Hindman, a square, full-bastioned fort, was erected within this village, upon the bank of the river, at the head of a bend resembling a horseshoe.[181]

Not much has been written about the capture of Fort Hindman, the most probable reason being that by Civil War standards, the event was of short duration involving a minimal loss of life to either side. Taking the place consumed little more than three and a half hours as measured from the sound of the opening guns to the Confederate's waving of a white flag. The ease by which it was invested was in some part because the Union troop movements had not been heralded well in advance by the Northern press. The Confederate commander Brigadier General Thomas J. Churchill would write that the attack had come as a total surprise.

> On the morning of the 9th of January, I was informed by pickets stationed at the mouth of the cutoff that the enemy, with his gunboats, followed by his fleet of seventy or eighty transports, were passing into the Arkansas River. It now became evident that their object was to attack the Arkansas Post....[182]

What the Confederates had to resist with was little enough. Churchill emphasized the gap in attacker - defender strengths.

> In no battle of the war has the disparity of forces been so unequal. The enemy's force was fully fifty thousand when ours did not exceed three thousand...[183]

Churchill's estimate of the Union force was not quite accurate. In January 14 correspondence sent to Grant, McClernand stated an aggregate Union strength at the time of about thirty-two thousand men.[184]

Union success was absolute, and the victory came off as Sherman had prophesied -- a morale booster to the Union soldiery. It also served as a needed tonic to the general public. There is no doubt but that it went a long way to temper the pessimism which had been taking root in the northern press over the conduct of campaigns in the west.

On January 13, Grant, who by now had been placed in overall control of operations along the Mississippi, sent an order to McClernand, instructing him to bring his entire force back to the Mississippi. Despite those direct instructions, in a communication dated the following day, McClernand told Grant there would be a delay while he created an overland diversion to threaten Little Rock and Pine Bluff. McClernand had in fact already sent two columns of infantry toward these places by road.[185] Grant stood on his insistence that McClernand return. McClernand, deciding that continued independence could get him into trouble, opted to obey rather than pursue his quest for easy conquests. The troops of McClernand's command arrived at the river town of Napoleon on the 16th of January of the new year of 1863.

~

Before continuing with the operations on the western rivers, we will next go back to March of 1862 and the events which were then transpiring within the eastern theater of operations.

[1]   Richard D. Goff, *Confederate Supply*, (Durham: Duke University Press, 1969).

[2]   At the end of the Revolutionary War, the settlers in the Ohio River basin complex, including those of western Pennsylvania and the general area which was to become the states of Ohio, Indiana, Kentucky, and Tennessee, believed their fiscal well being depended not on trade with the states to the east, but rather on free access to the sea, via the Mississippi River. In the late 1780s, this philosophy was so strongly developed that in Kentucky and Tennessee it was felt that an alliance with the Spanish (who then held New Orleans) was preferable to maintaining allegiance to the young United States. This thinking continued into 1803 when the United States made its Louisiana Purchase and took under its dominion the Mississippi basin and those points westward. The seditious plot of Aaron Burr which followed in 1806 was the result of an intention by Burr and others to forge a new nation from the Louisiana Purchase. It is thought by most historians that Burr's idea for such a nation was that it would encompass the lands bordering the east and the west banks of the Mississippi River. Such an independently ruled area would then control mid-America's access to the sea through New Orleans. Burr had led an expedition of eighty filibusters down the Mississippi, getting almost as far as Natchez before he was betrayed in his intentions by his fellow conspirators. He was captured, indicted for treason, and brought before the Federal Court at Richmond, Virginia. Only a technicality in the law finally got him off. With probably good reason, Burr had felt assured that his scheme for a western empire would be endorsed by many westerners. The bonding of western settlers to the Mississippi River had long been a strong one. In many quarters, that bonding superseded loyalty to the United States which is probably what Burr had been counting on.

[3]   Communication from William T. Sherman to Henry W. Halleck, September 17, 1863.

[4]   *Official Records of the Union and Confederate Navies in the War of the Rebellion,* (Washington, DC: Government Printing Office, 1894 - 1917), Series I, Volume 22, p 280.

[5]   *War of the Rebellion: Official Records of the Union and Confederate Armies,* (Washington, DC: Government Printing Office, 1880 - 1900). Facsimile Ed: (Harrisburg, PA: National Historical Society, 1971. Reprint. Historical Times, Inc., 1985), Series, I, Volume 52, Part 1, pp 164-168.

[6]   Since Totten's report post dates the May 16 order of Gideon Welles in which Welles had authorized Commander John Rodgers, USN, to effectively take over the construction responsibilities for the gunboat fleet, it appears probable that General Scott had assigned Totten to the task when the inter-service conferences dealing with the matter of the western gunboat fleet were taking place.

[7]   *ORA,* I, 52, Part 1, pp 157, 158.

[8]   As the Navy's Flag Officer, David G. Farragut would discover during 1862, the river south of Vicksburg presented severe draft problems during the drier seasons.

[9]   *ORA,* I, 52, Part 1, pp 157, 158.

[10]   As later events would prove out, although it was a key point in the transportation system, Memphis could by no means be considered as "the same as the holding of the whole country in the valley of the Tennessee." .

[11]   See letter, *ORN, I,* 22, p 283, addressed to the Secretary of the Navy from Commander John Rodgers, dated June 8, 1861. Rodgers explains to the Secretary that the *A. O. TYLER* was to have her name changed to *TAYLOR,* a name, Rodgers comments, which was, "a better augury than *TYLER.*" This name change was apparently never made as subsequent operational records all refer to *A. O. TYLER,* never *TAYLOR.*

[12]   *ORN, I,* 22, p 286.

[13]   The confusion over naval officers serving within Army commands and the chain of command difficulties it sometimes caused (as in the case of the Union Army's Western Gunboat Flotilla) does not seem to have existed on the Confederate side. According to correspondence which appears in *ORN, I,* 23, pp 701, 702, there was a provision under Confederate law whereby, "The law allows the assignment of the Navy's officers to duty with the Army and gives the President the authority to confer upon them Army rank." A postscript to that correspondence relates that up to that time (July 1862) the referenced Confederate naval officers had been assigned to duty with the Army with the rank of colonel. In general, it was the practice for the Confederacy to place riverine operations completely under the jurisdiction of the Army; coastal and, of course, ocean operations came under the control of the Confederate Navy.

[14]   Rear Admiral Henry Walke, "The Western Flotilla," *Battles and Leaders,* I.

[15]   *ORN, I,* 25, p 320.

[16]   *ORA,* I, 7, pp 565, 566.

[17]   Appendix E discusses in considerable detail the utilization and status of civilians employed upon those gunboats.

[18]   *ORN, I,* 22, p 287.

[19]   Alfred Thayer Mahan, *The Gulf and Inland Waters,* Campaigns of the Civil War Series. (Wilmington, NC: Broadfoot Publishing Co., 1989), p 14.

[20]   John Fremont, who had taken over command of the Saint Louis area from George McClellan in July of 1861, had little to do with the origins of the gunboat fleet despite his claims to the contrary. In his memoirs of

these early events which he wrote long after-the-fact, Fremont claimed that credit; but clearly that is not substantiated by the facts dealing with the construction program as they are recorded within correspondence written at the time by others. Major General John C. Fremont, "In Command in Missouri," *Battles and Leaders*, Volume I. To his credit, though, it was Fremont who ordered the construction of the first of thirty-eight mortar boats to be used for siege work against Confederate fortifications. These mortar boats were flat barges; each was to carry one heavy mortar. Eight tow boats would be provided to tow the mortar boats into firing position. The tow boats were the subject of a companion contract which was executed on behalf of the government by Fremont's quartermasters. Fremont also purchased *SUBMARINE NO. 7*, ex *BENTON*, a former snag boat which was at the time being used by James Eads as a salvage vessel. Another wooden steamer, the *NEW ERA*, was picked up by Fremont's quartermasters, to be converted into a gunboat. These last two vessels, in addition to being strengthened, were sheathed with iron.

[21]   *ORN, I*, 22, p 298.

[22]   *ORN, I*, 22, p 299.

[23]   *ORN, I*, 22, pp 318-320.

[24]   *ORN, I*, 22, p 320. Rodgers went on to serve in a succession of responsible Civil War commands. Following the war, he reached the rank of rear admiral.

[25]   *ORN, I*, 22, p 301.

[26]   Various reports within *ORN, I*, 22.

[27]   *ORN, I*, 22, p 314.

[28]   *ORN, I*, 22, pp 777-786.

[29]   Lieutenant S. Ledyard Phelps's report of this affair, dated February 10, 1862, is to be found within the *ORN, I*, 22, pp 571-574. That report places the railroad bridge twenty-five miles above Fort Henry. This was either an error in the report or a misprint in the text of the *ORN*. A measurement taken from *Atlas to Accompany the Official Records of the Union and Confederate Armies,* (Washington, DC: Government Printing Office, 1891-1895) discloses that the bridge was actually only about seven miles above Fort Henry. At that time, there was no other bridge on the river short of Tuscumbia.

[30]   From a review of Confederate reports of that period, it does not appear that the Cumberland River had been mined.

[31]   Letter dated March 30, 1862, from Sylvester C. Bishop, 11th Indiana Zouaves, to his mother. See Benjamin Franklin Cooling, *Forts Henry and Donelson: The Key to the Confederate Heartland*, (Knoxville, TN: University of Tennessee Press, 1987), p 312, fn 19.

[32]   Lewis Wallace, gives an excellent description of the terrain difficulties encountered in the approaches to Fort Donelson. See Brigadier General Lewis Wallace, "The Capture of Fort Donelson," *Battles and Leaders*, I, pp 398-428.

[33]   *ORA, I*, 7, p 161.

[34]   Since the Confederates surrendered and therefore retained no prisoners, it is assumed that the Union loss as "prisoners or missing" alludes only to those "missing."

[35]   The prisoners were transported to prison camps at Springfield, Indianapolis, and Chicago on the chartered steamers *DECATUR*, *TECUMSEH*, and *WHITE CLOUD*. Although Grant had been told that the camps were set up to receive the prisoners, it seems that little if any prior planning had taken place insofar as the handling of such large numbers of men. When they arrived at the various destinations, the camp commanders were not prepared to receive them.

[36]   *ORN, I*, 22, pp 584, 585.

[37]   *ORN, I*, 22, p 608.

[38]   *ORN, I*, 22, p 613.

[39]   *ORN, I*, 22, pp 592, 593.

[40]   Corinth is now at the western end of Pickwick Lake, a body of water which was artificially created in the 1950s as part of the Tennessee Valley Authority project. Corinth had been chosen by Confederate General Albert Sidney Johnston as the place to marshal whatever he could make available in the way of troop strength. He was to use those forces to block further Federal movement. If the Union armies were to be prevented from proceeding southward following the eastern side of the Mississippi River corridor, or eastward within the Tennessee River Valley, Corinth would be the best place where those moves could be stopped. The Confederate forces then moving into Corinth to halt the Union advance consisted of ten thousand men under Leonidas Polk. These troops had previously been part of the Confederate garrison at Columbus on the Mississippi. Another five thousand men under Daniel Ruggles had come by train from New Orleans. Soon joining was a mixed force of another ten thousand men which was combined into a corps under Braxton Bragg, these last units having originated from Mobile and Pensacola. Johnston had under his personal command another seventeen thousand

men that he had brought from Bowling Green, Kentucky. Altogether, a force of about forty-two thousand Confederates was ready to stand against advancing Union troops.

[41]   The thicketed area which gave the Union troops such good protection has since come to be known as the "Hornets Nest".

[42]   *ORN, I*, 22, pp 765, 766.

[43]   The list in the Alldredge work seems to enumerate 153 vessels on the Hurst list; however the Alldredge list is incorrectly numbered in that "139" has been omitted. A physical count reveals 152 named vessels.

[44]   Walke, *Battles and Leaders*, I, pp 430-452.

[45]   The fire of the mortar boats at Island No. 10 proved to be more efficient than that of the gunboats. This would be discovered later from examination made of the island's works and from testimony taken from Confederate prisoners.

[46]   *ORA, I*, 8, p 634. Pope's reference in his last sentence to "volunteers" refers to state regiments as against regular Army troops thus alluding, it would seem, to the political sensitivity of incurring heavy casualties among the citizen soldiery at this early time in the war.

[47]   Colonel J. W. Bissell, "Sawing Out the Channel Above Island No. 10," *Battles and Leaders*, I, pp 460-462.

[48]   *ORN, I*, 22, pp 704, 705.

[49]   *ORA, I*, 8, p 657.

[50]   *ORN, I*, 22, p 715.

[51]   *ORN, I*, 22, p 717.

[52]   *ORN, I*, 22, p 719.

[53]   *ORN, I*, 22, p 718.

[54]   *ORN, I*, 22, pp 724, 725.

[55]   *ORA*, III, 5, p 478.

[56]   Commander David D. Porter was the brother of William D. Porter, Foote's second-in-command of the Western Gunboat Flotilla during the action at Fort Henry.

[57]   *ORA, I*, 6, pp 699-702.

[58]   *ORA, I*, 6, pp 694, 695.

[59]   *ORA, I*, 6, p 706.

[60]   It is noted within *ORA* that the transport *LEWIS*, carrying the 9th Connecticut and a section of an artillery battery, was detailed to act in conjunction with the Navy on diversionary demonstrations against Confederate positions at Biloxi and then later at Mississippi City and at Pass Christian. *ORA, I*, 6, pp 707, 708. Also, *ORN, I*, 18, pp 90, 91.

[61]   *ORA, I*, 1, p 491.

[62]   Rear Admiral David D. Porter, "The Opening of the Mississippi," *Battles and Leaders*, II, p 35.

[63]   *ORA, I*, 53, p 518.

[64]   *Atlas, ORA*, Plate CLVI.

[65]   *ORN, I*, 18, p 128.

[66]   *ORA, I*, 6, p 710. We could locate nothing in either *ORA* or *ORN* concerning the text of the dispatches of 13 April.

[67]   *ORA, I*, 6, p 714.

[68]   *Atlas, ORA*, Plate CLVI.

[69]   *ORA, I*, 6, p 714.

[70]   Rowena Reed, *Combined Operations in the Civil War*, (Annapolis: Naval Institute Press, 1978), p 195. Reed takes her basis concerning the evacuation of materiel from New Orleans from the *Proceedings of the Court of Inquiry relative to the fall of New Orleans* held at Richmond during 1864. Reed cites p 592 of those *Proceedings*.

[71]   Ellet's treatise on flood control was published by the Smithsonian Institute in 1851.

[72]   *ORA, I*, 8, p 643.

[73]   *SWITZERLAND* had cost $13,000 and *QUEEN OF THE WEST*, $16,000. *LANCASTER's* price was not mentioned. Letter, Ellet to Stanton, dated April 10, 1862, was reproduced in Warren D. Crandall, *History of the Ram Fleet and the Mississippi Marine Brigade in the War for the Union on the Mississippi and its Tributaries: The Story of the Ellets and Their Men*, (St. Louis: Privately published by the Society of Survivors, 1907), p 25.

[74]   *ORA, I*, 52, Part I, p 240.

[75]   *ORA, I*, 10, Part II, p 138.

[76]   *ORA, I*, 10, Part II, p 127.

[77]   *ORA, I*, 10, Part II, p 131.

[78]   *ORA, I*, 10, Part II, p 138.

79   *ORN, I,* 23, pp 130-132.

80   Crandall, p 37.

81   *ORA,* I, 10, Part II, pp 112, 113. Ellet's brother was to become the overall commander of the guard units.

82   *ORN, I,* 17, pp 160, 161.

83   *ORN, I,* 23, p 57; also *ORN, I,* 23, p 699.

84   Although in all, thirty-eight mortar boats had been constructed for assignment to the Western Gunboat Flotilla, only eleven of them, at least as referenced in the reports contained within *ORN,* seemed to have been with Foote at Fort Pillow. One report refers to "sixteen," but this was without much doubt an error. It is probable that at the time of the bombardment of Fort Pillow, the remainder of the mortar boats were located at various places upriver or else were on the Tennessee and Cumberland systems where other reports mention they were being utilized for mobile defenses.

85   *ORN, I,* 23, p 13.

86   Reports of Montgomery and Thompson, *ORN, I,* 23, pp 53-57.

87   Although *ORN* contains no correspondence specifically critical of the poor state of readiness maintained by the Federal gunboat captains at the time of Montgomery's attack, this should not be taken to mean that their dereliction went unnoticed. Lack of any posted praise in that age of flowery dispatches may also be taken as silent disapproval. Only one individual was mentioned for recognition in the action. That person was the young officer in charge of *MORTAR BOAT 16* who was cited for the effective way he had directed his fire against the approaching Confederate rams.

88   *ORN, I,* 23, pp 56, 57.

89   *ORN, I,* 23, pp 28, 29.

90   *ORN, I,* 23, pp 29, 30.

91   George E. Currie, Norman E. Clarke, Sr., editor, *Warfare Along the Mississippi: The Letters of Lieutenant Colonel George E. Currie,* (Ann Arbor, MI: Edwards Brothers, 1961), p 41.

92   *ORN, I,* 23, pp 33, 34.

93   *ORA,* I, 10, Part II, p 231.

94   *ORN, I,* 23, p 39.

95   *ORA,* I, 10, Part II, pp 130, 131.

96   *ORN, I,* 23, pp 37-42.

97   *ORA,* I, 52, Part I, p 257. It should be taken into consideration that a refusal of duty, as in this case, was not a unique episode during the Civil War. To give but one example: Later that year (December of 1862) over 390 men of the 15th Pennsylvania Cavalry, also known as the "Anderson Cavalry" refused to go into battle at Murfreesborough, Tennessee. These men represented well over half of that regiment. *ORA,* I, 52, Part I, pp 323-330. Refusal of duty and minor acts of mutiny were common in the 15th Pennsylvania Cavalry, even as late as January of 1863.

98   Crandall, p 46.

99   How successful such a recruiting effort among the gunboats would have been is open to question since it surely must have been known that morale was not good among the ram crews. An admission of the low spirits within the Ram Fleet had been made by Ellet when he informed Stanton that he was ready to proceed without the aid of Davis and his gunboats once he, "had first weed[ed] out some bad material..." *ORN, I,* 23, p 44.

100   *ORN, I,* 23, pp 45, 46. In a report which he addressed to Secretary Stanton, Colonel Charles Ellet, Jr., made the claim that his brother, Lieutenant Colonel Alfred W. Ellet, leading a small force in "a yawl," had gone ashore at Fort Pillow in advance of Colonel Fitch's men. The accuracy of Ellet's claim cannot now be definitively assessed, yet it could have happened just as Ellet claimed. Earlier patrols from the Ram Fleet which were launched by the senior Ellet had been undertaken without coordination and apparently even without the knowledge of Fitch. A researcher of the events leading to the occupation of Fort Pillow can only come away concluding that cooperation between Ellet and Fitch was as inadequate as it had been between Ellet and Davis. One would further be led to the conclusion that Charles Ellet was obsessed that his Ram Fleet should be first in every endeavor. Since both the Fitch force and Ellet's party landed in darkness, it is fortunate that they did not fire against each other, one suspecting the other of being an enemy force.

101   *ORN, I,* 23, pp 51, 52.

102   *ORN, I,* 23, pp 58, 59.

103   *ORN, I,* 23, p 57.

104   *ORA,* I, 10, Part II, pp 588, 589.

105   *The Civil War Reminiscences of General M. Jeff Thompson,* (reprint, Dayton, OH: Morningside House, Inc., 1988). In their analysis of Thompson's motives, the reprint editors at Morningside, are of the opinion (fn 38, p 26) that, "'growing jealousy and misunderstanding' between him [Thompson] and Montgomery" was the contributory factor.

[106]   According to Thompson, there had been an understanding that as soon as Montgomery's fleet was ready to go into action, Thompson was to supply the "fighting crew" to act as gunners and riflemen. For that assignment, Thompson had detailed the artillery companies of "Bowman, McDonald, and Harris" together with the companies of "Hedgepeth, Hunter, Walkin, Kelsey, Liles". Thompson also detailed "companies of infantry." Whether the entirety of the units which Thompson listed were actually all on the eight vessels of the Mississippi River Defense Service at any one time is not made clear within Thompson's account.

[107]   *ORN, I*, 23, p 119.

[108]   According to Colonel Charles Ellet, Jr., writing in his official report for that day, the point of tie-up for the rams was eighteen miles upriver from Memphis. However, Lieutenant Colonel Alfred W. Ellet, writing some years later reported it as twenty-five miles above Memphis. Alfred W. Ellet, "Ellet and His Steam Rams at Memphis," *Battles and Leaders*, I, p 455.

[109]   The dense smoke was created by a combination of black powder from Davis's guns and the stack exhausts of the gunboats since the fire boxes had not had sufficient time to fully heat up from the heavy load of fuel fed into them on such short notice.

[110]   Ellet, *Battles and Leaders*, I, p 456.

[111]   Colonel Charles Ellet, Jr., later thought that the bullet which struck him was from a pistol fired from the bridge deck of *GENERAL BEAUREGARD*.

[112]   Flag Officer Davis later claimed Navy credit for the taking of *GENERAL BEAUREGARD*, stating that it was the gunboats' shells that really did her in. While the shells of the gunboats may have caused her to run south, it seems certain that it was the *MONARCH's* ramming which caused her crew to surrender.

[113]   In his post battle report, Alfred W. Ellet stated that he made prisoners of the *GENERAL BEAUREGARD's* crew. In contradiction, the post action report of Flag Officer Charles H. Davis, claimed that a crew from the mortar boat detachment, which was at the time manning a tug, took them prisoner. This conflicting information was typical of the confusion of "facts" which surround the Battle of Memphis.

[114]   *ORA*, I, 10, Part I, p 909.

[115]   *ORN, I*, 23, p 127.

[116]   *ORN, I*, 23, p 136.

[117]   *ORN, I*, 23, p 122.

[118]   A statute entitled *Act for the Better Government of the Navy of the United States* (1862) became the authority under which prize money could be awarded to Army transports and to the Army's combatant vessels. The act contained the provision, "...any armed vessel in the service of the United States which shall make a capture, or assist in making a capture, under circumstances which would entitle a vessel of the Navy to prize money, shall be entitled to an award of prize money in the same manner as if such vessel belonged to the Navy." The argument over prize money and who was qualified to receive it continued well into mid-1863 at which time Secretary of the Navy Gideon Welles made the point of the 1862 act clear within his correspondence. See *ORN, I*, 14, pp 417, 418.

[119]   The day after the Battle of Memphis, Ellet wrote his report of the action. He was but one of many senior officers who wrote reports of the action. Despite the pain he must have been suffering, the report reads with clarity. See *ORN, I*, 23, pp 118-121, 125, 126, 135, 136. In the reports by the naval officers, there seems to have been a tendency to gloss over some of the more significant details. For instance, both Davis and Phelps allude, through what seems to be a purposeful vagueness, that the *GENERAL M. JEFF THOMPSON* and the *GENERAL BRAGG* were captured by Davis's gunboats, but neither actually said as much. The facts seem clear that each of those captures were the direct result of those two enemy vessels having been driven ashore by their crews while being hard pressed by the Ellet rams *MONARCH* and *SWITZERLAND*. Both Confederate vessels were then set afire by their crews which escaped ashore. Through immediate and heroic measures, both were then salvaged by Davis's gunboat crews. The *GENERAL M. JEFF THOMPSON* would later blow up, apparently from a smoldering fire which was initially overlooked by the naval salvors. Lieutenant Colonel Alfred W. Ellet gives a very good analysis of the battle in his article within *Battles and Leaders*, I, pp 453-459. The report of Brigadier General M. Jeff Thompson, Missouri State Guard, who saw the battle from the bank and who was perhaps representative of the throngs who witnessed the action from the bluff of Memphis, is reproduced within *ORN, I*, 23, pp 139, 140. A rather comprehensive account of the battle was written by then Commander, later Rear Admiral Henry Walke and was published some years later within *Battles and Leaders*, I, pp 449-452. Walke was commander of the *CARONDELET* during that battle. Another description was written by a lesser player, Lieutenant W. F. Warren, USV, who was in charge of a detail of sharpshooters on *MONARCH*. Warren's recounting of the events appears in Crandall, pp 80-83.

[120]   *ORN, I*, 18, pp 474, 475.

[121]   *ORN, I*, 18, p 491.

[122]   *ORN, I*, 18, p 492.

123   *ORN, I*, 18, p 507.

124   Report of Flag Officer Farragut, May 30, 1862, *ORN, I*, 18, p 519.

125   *ORN, I*, 18, pp 521, 522.

126   *ORN, I*, 18, p 543.

127   *ORA, I*, 15, pp 528, 529.

128   *ORN, I*, 23, pp 153, 154. According to the *Dictionary of American Naval Fighting Ships, RED ROVER* was the Army's first regularly designated hospital ship. Its first master was a civilian steamboatman, Captain McDaniel of "the Army's Gunboat Service." The surgeon in charge, was the Navy's Assistant Surgeon George H. Bixby. When the Union Navy took over the Western Gunboat Flotilla and its auxiliaries later in September (1862), she was renamed *USS ROVER*. She then became the Navy's first hospital ship.

129   *ORN, I*, 23, p 160.

130   *ORN, I*, 23, pp 162, 163.

131   *ORN, I*, 23, p 209.

132   *ORN, I*, 23, p 211.

133   According to George E. Currie who was one of Ellet's officers and who was with him at the Battle of Memphis, Ellet refused an early amputation which probably would have saved his life, Ellet having said, "Like my country, I prefer death to dismemberment." Currie, p 52.

134   One of the hulks was later discovered to be *MAUREPAS*. This was one of the enemy's gunboats which Kilty had been charged to hunt down.

135   *ORA, I*, 13, pp 104, 105.

136   *ORN, I*, 23, pp 168, 169.

137   *ORN, I*, 23, p 174.

138   *ORA, I*, 17, Part II, p 55.

139   *ORA, I*, 17, Part II, p 56.

140   *ORA, I*, 17, Part II, p 56.

141   *ORA, I*, 17, Part II, p 63. The "flying visit" that Lincoln requested was to be a prelude toward replacing the failed McClellan in the east with Halleck.

142   *ORA, I*, 13, p 112.

143   See Williams to Davis, *ORA, I*, 15, p 26.

144   *ORA, I*, 15, 27.

145   Report of Brigadier General T. Williams, July 4, 1862, from *ORA, I*, 15, pp 26, 27.

146   *ORA, I*, 17, Part II, p 285.

147   *ORN, I*, 23 ,p 218.

148   *ORN, I*, 23, p 242.

149   Casualties on the *LANCASTER*, which resulted from escaping steam plus the effects of the other hits, were high. Killed were her pilot, three engineers, and five white deck hands. Of the forty-three Negro contrabands who had been aboard serving as stokers and deck hands, only six were still fit for duty, the others either wounded or dead. The following day, *LANCASTER* was towed to Memphis for repairs.

150   Account of Lieutenant George Gift. See H. Allen Gosnell, *Guns on the Western Waters: The Story of River Gunboats in the Civil War*, (Baton Rouge: Louisiana State University Press, 1949), p 122.

151   *ORN, I*, 19, pp 7, 8.

152   *ORN, I*, 19, pp 9, 10. It was unknown to Davis at the time that on July 16, 1862, Farragut had been promoted to rear admiral.

153   *ORN, I*, 19, p 13.

154   *ORN, I*, 19, p 15.

155   *ORN, I*, 19, p 48.

156   *ORN, I*, 19, pp 45, 46.

157   The report by William D. Porter, commander of the *ESSEX,* adds an interesting sidelight to the casual arrangements which were often encountered on the western rivers. Porter concluded his report of that Vicksburg action with the sentence, "Permit me to draw your attention to Master Willie Coates, of only fourteen years of age. This young gentleman volunteered to act as my aid; his conduct was, throughout the action, marked by great coolness and bravery. He has no connection with the service, but I hope you will bring to the notice of the Navy Department the conduct of the little gentleman, as I think he has earned, by his loyalty, coolness, and bravery, an appointment at the Naval Academy." *ORN, I*, 19, p 50. The authors have queried the United States Naval Academy Alumni Association as to whether Coates subsequently entered the Naval Academy. Records indicate that no one of that name entered the Academy between 1862 and 1866. (Letter to senior author from US Naval Academy Alumni Association, 17 March 1989; files of authors.)

---

[158]   *ORN, I*, 19, p 46.

[159]   At this juncture, Brigadier General Thomas Williams had lost any hope of the cross peninsula canal being capable of operation. An engineering drawing of the canal as it was laid out on July 4, 1862, and the relationship of it to river levels at various periods can be found in *ORA, I*, 15, pp 30, 31. That report includes correspondence from Williams dated July 17, 1862, which enumerates the many construction problems encountered during that early June and into July.

[160]   *ORN, I*, 15, p 31.

[161]   *ORA, I*, 15, p 33.

[162]   *ORA, I*, 15, pp 39, 40.

[163]   For report of Lieutenant Isaac N. Brown aboard the *CSS ARKANSAS*, see Gosnell, pp 133, 134. .

[164]   The 7th Vermont had panicked and left their positions, making the task of holding the line especially difficult for those who stood fast. Because of their cowardly performance, the 7th Vermont was denied the Baton Rouge battle pennant on its colors.

[165]   *ORN*, I, 23, p 488.

[166]   *ORN, I*, 23, pp 491-93.

[167]   *SWITZERLAND* was also scheduled to go but for some unexplained reason did not end up on the mission.

[168]   *ORN, I*, 23, pp 495, 496.

[169]   The explosive devices which sank *USS CAIRO* were not the same as "torpedoes" as we think of such devices in terms of 20th century warfare, but rather were moored explosive canisters. Destruction of the *USS CAIRO* ushered in moored mines as a weapons system to be seriously reckoned with on the western rivers. *USS CAIRO* was the first gunboat to feel the lethal bite of mine warfare on the Mississippi although on the eastern seacoast, mining had been quite common for Confederate defensive purposes, both at ports and on a number of tidal estuaries. One such example were the defenses encountered in the attack against New Berne following Burnside's taking of Roanoke Island.

[170]   *ORN, I*, 23, pp 548,-554. The location of the *USS CAIRO* remained a mystery for 102 years. She was finally found and salvaged in 1964. *USS CAIRO* is now on display as part of the Vicksburg National Military Park system. An excellent and well illustrated account on this gunboat, its war history, and the story of its salvage can be found within Edwin C. Bearss, *Hardluck Ironclad,* (Baton Rouge: Louisiana State University Press, 1980).

[171]   Schottenhamel cite: Parsons to Captain John Scudder, December 13, 1862, Copy Book 5, Parsons Collection.

[172]   *ORA,*

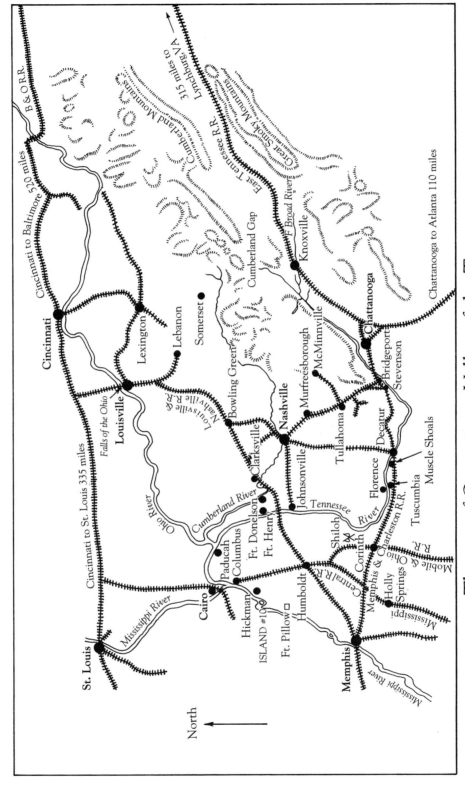

Theater of Operations, Valley of the Tennessee

THE OPENING OF THE LOWER MISSISSIPPI.

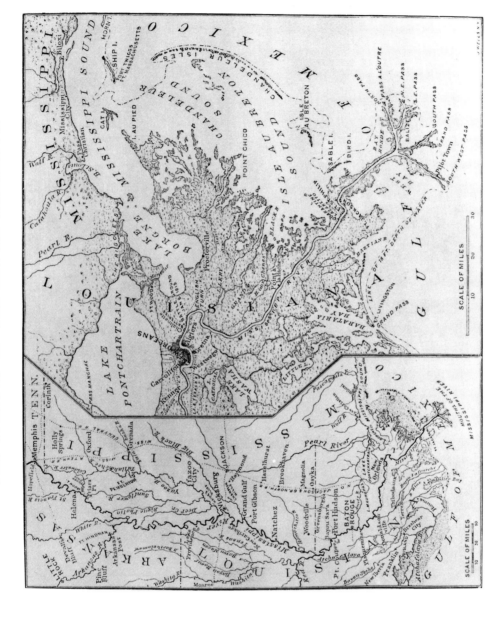

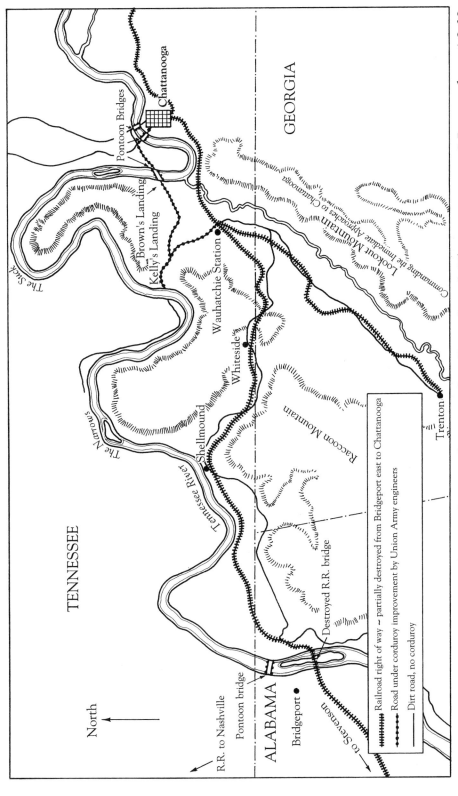

The "Cracker Line" in the Relationship to the Supply of Chattanooga, November 1863

North

TENNESSEE

GEORGIA

ALABAMA

Chattanooga

Pontoon Bridges

Brown's Landing

Kelly's Landing

The Suck

The Narrows

Tennessee River

Wauhatchie Station

Whiteside

Shellmound

Lookout Mountain
Commanding the Immediate Approaches to Chattanooga

Raccoon Mountain

Trenton

Destroyed R.R. bridge

Bridgeport

Pontoon bridge

R.R. to Nashville

to Stevenson

Railroad right of way ~ partially destroyed from Bridgeport east to Chattanooga

Road under corduroy improvement by Union Army engineers

Dirt road, no corduroy

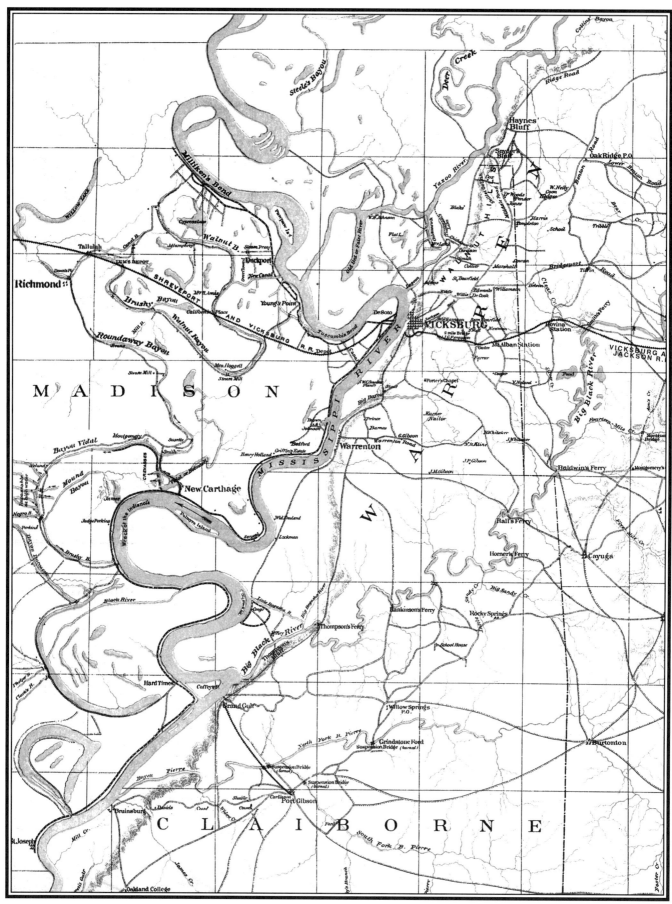

From Atlas, O.R.A.
Plate XXXVI

MAP SHOWING THE ROUTE OF THE LATE EXPEDITION, COMMANDED BY REAR ADMIRAL PORTER, U. S. NAVY, IN ATTEMPTING TO GET INTO THE YAZOO RIVER BY THE WAY OF STEELE'S BAYOU AND DEER CREEK.

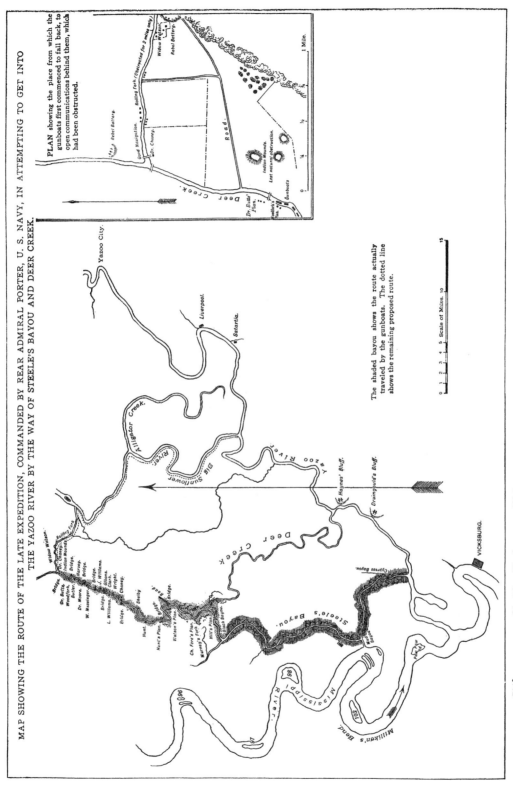

PLAN showing the place from which the gunboats first commenced to fall back, to open communications behind them, which had been obstructed.

The shaded bayou shows the route actually traveled by the gunboats. The dotted line shows the remaining proposed route.

711°—N W R—VOL 24—10.   (To face page 480.)

Reproduced from *Official Records of the Union and Confederate Navies in the War of the Rebellion*, Series I, 24.

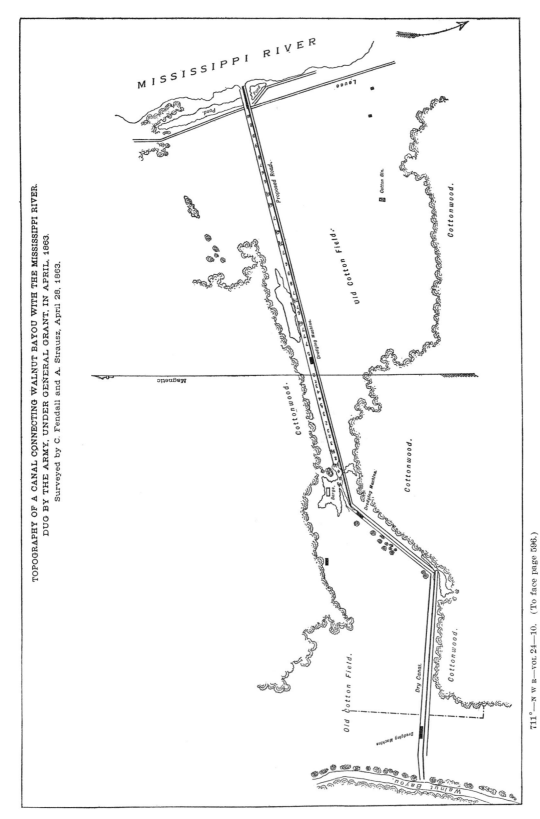

TOPOGRAPHY OF A CANAL CONNECTING WALNUT BAYOU WITH THE MISSISSIPPI RIVER.
DUG BY THE ARMY, UNDER GENERAL GRANT, IN APRIL, 1863.

Surveyed by C. Fendall and A. Strausz, April 28, 1863.

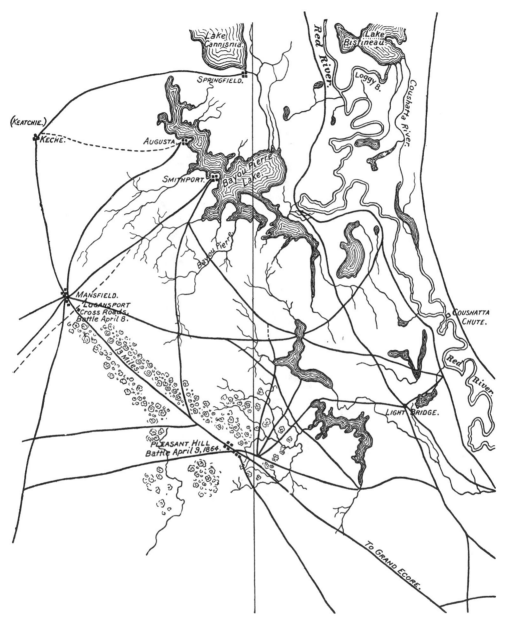

SKETCH OF THE ROADS NEAR THE BATTLEFIELDS OF APRIL 8 AND 9, 1864.

Maj. Le Duc.

Brigadier General Lewis B. Parsons, the officer who would be given charge within the Quartermaster Department of movements by rail and water. From collection of the Library of Congress.

Group 1.   **General Ellet and Staff.**

1—Brig. Gen. Alfred W. Ellet. 2—Capt. Geo. Q. White, A. Q. M. 3—Capt. Jas. C. Brooks, A. C. S. 4—Capt. W. D. Crandall, A. A. G. 5—Lieut. Phillip Howell, A. D. C. 6—Lieut. Ed. C. Ellet, A. D. C. 7—Lieut. Sanford G. Scarritt, A. D. C.

Group 2.   Col. Chas. R. Ellet and Part of M. M. B. Captains.

1—Col. Charles Rivers Ellet, Comdg. Inf. 2—Capt. Thos. C. Groshon, F Inf. 3—Capt. F. V. DeCoster, A Cav. 4—Capt. D. P. Walling, Light Bat. 5—Capt. A. P. Cox, I Inf. 6—Capt. Calvin G. Fisher, E Inf. 7—Capt. Oscar F. Brown, C. Cav. 8—Capt. Jas. P. Harper, H Inf. 9—Capt. Isaac D. Newell, A Inf. 10—Capt. Ed. S. Havens, G Inf.

Reproduced from Warren D. Crandall, *History of the Ram Fleet and the Mississippi Marine Brigade in the War for the Union on the Mississippi and its Tributaries: The Story of the Ellets and Their Men.*

Group 12.   **Group of Marine Boatmen.**

1—Wm. F. Weible, 2d Master Ram Lioness. 2—Almon M. Granger, Master Tug Cutting. 3—John W. Lister, Carp. Queen. 4—Milo M. McLane, 2d Engr. Cleveland. 5—R. E. Ballard, 1st Engr. Horner. 6—Henry W. Granger, Chief Engr. Fleet. 7—John F. Whitney, Master Tug Darlington. 8—Ed. W. Murray, 2d Master Tug Cleveland. 9—Wm. H. Nixon, Landsman Queen. 10—John S. S. Hewes, Mas:er Switzerland. 11—Martin Trimpe, 2d Master Queen. 12—James S. Nixon, Landsman Queen. 13—Ed. R. Loring, Engr. Tug Cutting. 14—Granville P. Robarts, Engr. Ram Fleet. 15—John Wayman, Engr. Monarch.

Mortar boats being constructed for the Western Gunboat Flotilla (1861). From collection of the National Archives.

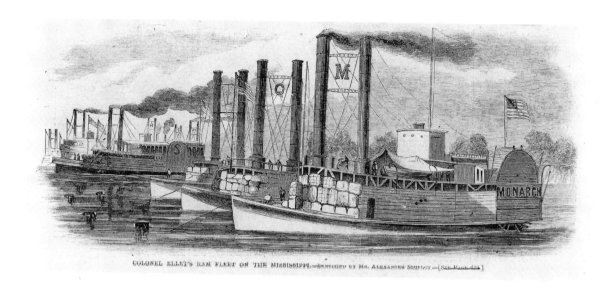

Colonel Charles Ellet's Ram Fleet on the Mississippi. First Fitted out in the Spring of 1862, the fleet consisted of MONARCH, QUEEN OF THE WEST, LIONESS, SWITZERLAND, LANCASTER.
From collection of U. S. Naval Historical Center.

GENERAL STERLING PRICE, sunk by Union forces at Battle of Memphis. Salved and taken into Quartermaster service. Transferred to Navy in fall of 1862. From collection of U. S. Naval Historical Center.

SWITZERLAND. Ellet ram. She carried Colonel Charles Ellet to Saint Louis after his wounding at the Battle of Memphis. The colonel died en route. Reproduced from Warren D. Crandall, *History of the Ram Fleet and the Mississippi Marine Brigade in the War for the Union on the Mississippi and its Tributaries: The Story of the Ellets and Their Men.*

NAVAL BATTLE BEFORE MEMPHIS, JUNE 6, 1862.
Davis Boats at the left, Ellets in Center, Rebels to the right

Reproduced from Warren D. Crandall, *History of the Ram Fleet and the Mississippi Marine Brigade in the War for the Union on the Mississippi and its Tributaries: The Story of the Ellets and Their Men.*

Watercolor Depiction of Ram QUEEN OF THE WEST, 1862-1863. From collection of U. S. Naval Historical Center

Engraving purporting to show Battle of Memphis, Tennessee, on 6 June 1862. At center, MONARCH ramming GENERAL BEAUREGARD. At left are: QUEEN OF THE WEST, GENERAL STERLING PRICE, and LITTLE REBEL. From collection of U. S. Naval Historical Center.

Fighting Marmaduke's Battery at Columbia Bend. The Adams Convoying the Passenger Steamer Henry Ames and Firing Her Bow Guns, While the Monarch Halts to Engage the Enemy.

Convoy support as provided by the Mississippi Marine Brigade. Brigade vessel in background.

Photos this page reproduced from Warren D. Crandall, *History of the Ram Fleet and the Mississippi Marine Brigade in the War for the Union on the Mississippi and its Tributaries: The Story of the Ellets and Their Men.*

METHOD OF CUTTING THE CHANNEL.

SAWING OUT THE CHANNEL ABOVE ISLAND NUMBER TEN.

Reproduced from *Battles and Leaders*. Volume 2.

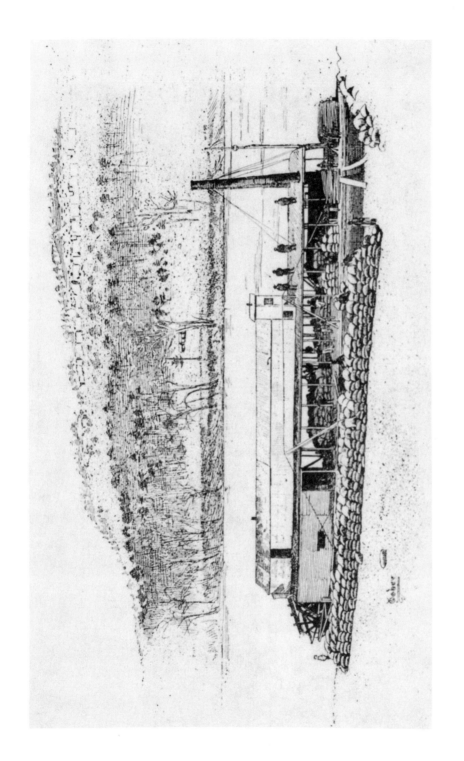

Opening of the Cracker Line.
Reproduced from *Battles and Leaders*, Volume 3.

Sternwheel steamer LOOKOUT. Built by Quartermaster Department at Bridgeport on the upper Tennessee River in 1863 for the supply relief of Chattanooga. Note defensive field gun on bow with soldier gunners. Most of the river steamers operated by the Quartermaster were armed. From collection of National Archives.

MISSIONARY. Built for "Cracker Line" by Quartermaster at Bridgeport on the upper Tennessee. Photo probably taken following the removal of the pontoon bridge at Brown's Landing when steamers began to be warped through "the Suck" and other rapids in order to make it upriver from Bridgeport to Chattanooga. From collection of the National Archives.

B-4866

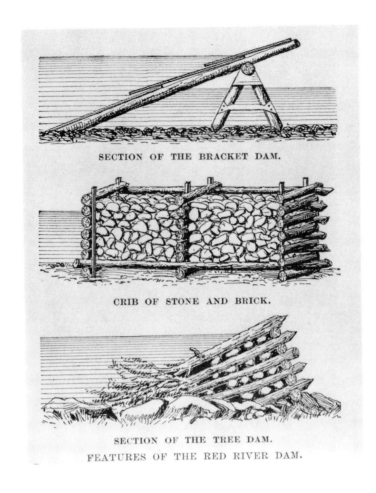

SECTION OF THE BRACKET DAM.

CRIB OF STONE AND BRICK.

SECTION OF THE TREE DAM.

FEATURES OF THE RED RIVER DAM.

THE "LEXINGTON" PASSING OVER THE FALLS AT THE DAM. FROM A WAR-TIME SKETCH.

Both illustrations are reproduced from *Battles and Leaders*, Volume 4.

PART III

THE EASTERN THEATER NORTH OF HATTERAS

ON THE CHESAPEAKE - 1862

The General Situation on the Bay and Tidewaters

Washington was a city under threatened siege. The Potomac River downstream of the capital was already under the domination of Confederate artillery, well dug in on the Virginia side of the river. Upstream, Harper's Ferry was under occupation of a Confederate garrison whose presence there opened the way for the enemy coming at Washington out of the Shenandoah Valley. Most distressing of all was the developing problem of the Chesapeake Bay which up to recently had clearly been a Union body of water but which was now being threatened by a terrifying new weapon, the ironclad *CSS VIRGINIA* (formerly the *USS MERRIMAC*).

On March 8, *CSS VIRGINIA* had administered heavy blows to Union seapower. She had destroyed the *USS CUMBERLAND*, caused the burning of the *USS CONGRESS*, and had badly damaged the *USS MINNESOTA*.[1]

The only hope of stopping this new Confederate menace lay with the North's brand new ironclad, *USS MONITOR*, soon to be en route to Hampton Roads from New York. At the headquarters of the War Department and at the Navy headquarters, the mood was grim. Movement of Union Army troops by water was considered out of the question without the complete Union domination of Chesapeake Bay. It was expected at any moment that *CSS VIRGINIA* would re-enter Hampton Roads and that from there she would foray out to destroy any Union shipping unfortunate enough to cross her bow. All sorts of schemes were being put into motion to try to stop her. They ran the gamut from possible to ludicrous. One of the more practical ideas was already in place, standing by in Hampton Roads. This consisted of two merchant ships which had been taken under Navy charter. Once the *CSS VIRGINIA* again came out, these merchantmen would steer toward her to ram. It was thought that the shear weight of their hulls might be enough to override and sink the rebel ironclad.[2] The names of the sacrificial steamers were *ILLINOIS* and *ARAGO*. A third merchant ship which was chartered by the army a week later and which was to be used for the same purpose, was the *C. VANDERBILT*.

Panic over the *CSS VIRGINIA* went well beyond those situated on the lower Chesapeake, fear having spread to the upper bay as well. Quartermaster General Meigs, in a message to a subordinate officer in charge of transports at Annapolis, cautioned that if the *CSS VIRGINIA* came out again, she might steam up the Bay, shell Annapolis, and perhaps even enter the Potomac. Meigs had his own ideas as to how to handle this new mode of naval warfare.

> Executive Mansion, Washington
> March 9, 1862
>
> Colonel [Rufus] Ingalls, Quartermaster, Annapolis
> Sir:
>
> Should the *MERRIMAC* [now *CSS VIRGINIA*], which did so much damage at Newport News, attempt anything at Annapolis, it is believed that the best defense would be an attack by a number of swift steamers full of men, who should board her by a sudden rush, fire down through her hatches or grated decks, and throw cartridges or shells down her smoke pipe. Sacrifice the steamers in order to retake the *MERRIMAC*.
>
> If an overwhelming force can thus be thrown aboard, there will be little loss of life, though the steamer transports may be destroyed. Of course the steamers should be provided with ladders, planks, and grapples to board with. The *MERRIMAC* has iron sides, sloping above water to a deck about nine feet wide, said to be an iron-grated deck. Promotion, ample reward awaits whoever takes or destroys her. You of course have a swift steamer outside on the lookout.
>
> By order of the Secretary of War.
>
> M. C. Meigs, Quartermaster General[3]

In a telegram dated the same day, sent by McClellan to Major General John A. Dix at Baltimore, McClellan stressed his concern over the necessity to keep troop transports in port as long as the Confederate ram remained at large.

> *MERRIMAC* [*CSS VIRGINIA*] sunk the *CUMBERLAND**; the *CONGRESS** surrendered. *MINNESOTA** and *SAINT LAWRENCE** ran aground approaching scene of contest....Please be fully alert. See that Fort Crandall is placed in a condition for defense as rapidly as possible in case *MERRIMAC* should run by Fortress Monroe. Until further orders, stop passage of any transports passing from Philadelphia to Annapolis and Perryville by canal [Chesapeake and Delaware Canal]. What is condition of Fort Crandall?[4]

* *USS*, commissioned Union naval vessel.

On March 10, *USS MONITOR*, met the *CSS VIRGINIA* in a battle which ended in a stalemate. *CSS VIRGINIA* steamed back into Norfolk. *USS MONITOR* remained on guard in the channel, waiting for *CSS VIRGINIA* to again come out. She was joined there by the three merchant ships designated to act as rams. Unlike the situation prior to the arrival of the *USS MONITOR* when the Union's control of the entire Chesapeake seemed in doubt, the Union ironclad's presence had now neutralized the situation to a marked degree. At this juncture, though, no one knew whether one ironclad could ever destroy another. On May 9, 1862, the Confederates vacated Norfolk. At the time of that evacuation, the *CSS VIRGINIA* was scuttled on order of the Confederate naval commander.

The extent of enemy forces south of Norfolk remained a question that spring. A reconnaissance in force was sent north through the Albemarle and Chesapeake Canal in an attempt to reach Norfolk through that southern doorway. If the approaches to Norfolk through this route proved to be undefended by Confederate forces, then the Albemarle and Chesapeake Canal could become a handy and safe route for the supply of Union forces located within the Carolina sounds.

On May 30, the sidewheel steamer *USS PORT ROYAL* (a Navy gunboat) left Roanoke Island. Aboard her was Brigadier General Rush C. Hawkins and a company of infantry. Hawkins found the entrance to the southern section of the Albemarle and Chesapeake Canal still blocked from the efforts of Lieutenant C. W. Flusser who had performed that work the month before. (See within Part I, "Closing the Albemarle and Chesapeake Canal: A Naval Mission.") Hawkins had selected his approach route to the canal through the shoal strewn Currituck Sound which brought him to a break in the canal route as it traversed open water near Pungo Point. From there, the way seemed clear to Norfolk. No Confederate opposition or even an indication of the enemy's presence was discovered during the trip.[5]

Although free passage of the Albemarle and Chesapeake Canal would provide a direct route for troop reinforcement and supplies between Union-held Norfolk and the Albemarle and Pamlico sounds of North Carolina, it did not noticeably pre-empt the necessity for ocean transport. The shallowness of the Albemarle and Chesapeake Canal, as well as the even shallower depths of the Dismal Swamp Canal, would place severe limitations on the size of vessels which could use these routes. Throughout the rest of the war, most of the supplies sent to Union forces in the coastal North Carolina region had to come from the north on deep draft vessels rounding Cape Hatteras and unloading at the twin ports of Beaufort- Morehead City.

The Union use of the two canal routes did, however, mark the beginning of a Federal military presence along the eastern side of the Virginia tidewater region. Mere presence, however, was not quite the same as a controlled domination. From time to time, there were Confederate challenges, but these had little lasting impact other than to tie up Union forces which could have been used productively elsewhere. The most interesting, albeit minor, episode involving Confederate harassment of the two canals occurred on the southern section of the Albemarle and Chesapeake Canal during May 1863, when two Union mail boats were captured while undertaking regularly scheduled service. The captures had all the ingredients of a wild west stagecoach holdup. The event involved the Union Army mail boat *ARROW* which, when passing through the Coinjock Bridge (then and now a draw bridge), was boarded by Confederate partisans who jumped aboard from the bridge abutments. The raiders seemed to be aware that the *ARROW* normally transferred a part of its mail to *EMILY*, another army steamer, at a point near where the canal emptied into the North River. Arriving at this rendezvous, the *ARROW's* crew was held at gunpoint until the *EMILY* came alongside. Then the raiders took over *EMILY* as well. Both mail steamers were run up the Chowan River into Confederate held territory.[6] The *EMILY* was never to be heard of again. The *ARROW* was recaptured by Union forces in July of 1864.

With the exception of the episode of the *EMILY* and the *ARROW* and some other rather minor instances, the Albemarle and Chesapeake Canal system was a reliable and relatively safe line of shallow draft communication until the end of the war. There were, however, occasional instances of attacks from the banks against shipping, and as late as January of 1865, the army supplied guns and gun crews to vessels regularly transiting the canal.[7] According to the *Tenth Annual Report of the Albemarle and Chesapeake Canal Company* (for the years 1860-1865), it was estimated that 1,297 vessels used the canal in 1862; 950 in 1863; 1,291 in 1864; and 2,617 in 1865. According to that report, steamers were in "preponderance, with 3,844 passages; schooners with 1,690 passages; [along] with other passages including that of sloops, lighters, and barges, rafts and boats." The majority of these craft probably carried military cargoes, but of that there is no specific record. The most significant of the military vessels to transit the Albemarle and Chesapeake Canal during the Civil War was a 32' steam launch. It passed through in October of 1864 under the command of Union Navy Lieutenant William B. Cushing. Cushing had equipped the launch with an explosive spar which he planned to use in a joust with a Confederate ironclad named the *CSS ALBEMARLE*. The *CSS ALBEMARLE* was reported at the time to be ready to leave the Roanoke River to challenge Union naval domination of the North Carolina sounds. Cushing had embarked on what his superiors cautioned was a near-suicidal mission. Perhaps to their amazement, he sank the *CSS ALBEMARLE* and was himself able to escape with all his limbs intact.

~

The Army of the Potomac launched an offensive into Virginia in the spring of 1862 with the direct aim of taking the Confederate capital at Richmond thus forcing an end to the war. At that time, Major General George McClellan was the Union Army's commander in the eastern theater. McClellan's plan was to have his troops transported by ship to Urbana, a small settlement on the southern bank of the Rappahannock River, where they would disembark. From Urbana, McClellan would march overland against Richmond. If the Confederates came in force to oppose him as he neared Richmond, McClellan would move his army across the James River by pontoon bridge, somewhere upstream of City Point, and from there besiege Richmond. Those at least were the plans, but before the campaign could begin, there were a number of matters to be first resolved.

Preparations for Offensive

During the early winter of 1861-1862, McClellan had been busy trying to turn hundreds of disorganized recruits into a disciplined army. President Lincoln, under increasingly intense pressures to come up with a victory, was hopeful that an early offensive into northern Virginia would produce that result. On the other hand, McClellan was worried over moving too fast; Lincoln's own apprehensions weighed into the general's hesitancy. A difference in thinking over how a campaign into Virginia was to proceed had developed between McClellan and some of those in Lincoln's cabinet, McClellan's position being that the campaign should have its beginnings at the line of the Rappahannock River. His plan was to move his army there by water transport rather than by an overland march from Washington. There were some opposing viewpoints among McClellan's subordinate generals, and these arguments naturally leaked to Lincoln's attention -- increasing his apprehension. The only thing on which everyone seemed to be in general agreement was the strategic and political value of taking Richmond. Not only was Richmond the enemy's capital, but it also served the

Confederacy as a center of transportation, being a hub from which road and rail reached out into Virginia's eastern and northern counties. In a military sense, Richmond had, therefore, become the pivot point for the Confederacy's defensive strategy east of the Appalachians.

One of Lincoln's major concerns dealt with the defense of Washington. Lincoln was not alone in believing that it would be politically and militarily foolhardy for the Union Army to move south without full assurance that Washington would remain safe from attack. One factor in the defense of the capital required measures that would prevent an encircling of Washington from the vulnerable northwest. To guard against this happening would mean repairing the railroad bridge and re-establishing possession of the B & O Railroad right of way at the point where that track originally crossed the Potomac at Harper's Ferry, a place now held by Confederate forces. Putting Harper's Ferry and the upper Potomac River back under Union occupation, would create a barrier across the head of the Shenandoah Valley preventing the enemy's use of that valley as an invasion corridor.[8]

Back in December 1861, Major General Nathaniel P. Banks had sent a report to Brigadier General Randolph B. Marcy who was then Chief of Staff to McClellan. At the time, Banks had been assigned the direct responsibility for the defenses of Washington. Banks's report gave detailed suggestions as to how the recapture of Harper's Ferry and the reconstruction of the railroad there should be carried out; but McClellan had put the Banks ideas on hold. Two months later (February 1862) Banks wrote to McClellan urging that the time to move had finally arrived.

> ...The enemy on our front has been unquestionably weakened and demoralized...Not less than fifteen hundred men [Confederates] were disabled at one time by the effects of frost and cold alone, and many amputations were necessary...The enemy was never in a more feeble condition than at this time. His force is chiefly in the vicinity of Winchester and beyond. The reports of large detachments near Charleston (Virginia) and Harper's Ferry are greatly exaggerated in my belief.[9]

McClellan would now issue orders for Banks to immediately occupy Harper's Ferry. Banks's lead elements entered the town and found the place deserted by the enemy which had withdrawn to buttress the Confederate defensive line then building up along the southern bank of the Rappahannock River.

The first thing on Banks's agenda was to put his engineers to work installing a pontoon bridge for bringing horse drawn artillery and supplies over to Harper's Ferry. When McClellan had first issued his orders to Banks to reoccupy the town, he had instructed one of his own staff members to begin the assembly of a group of canal boats. These were to be floated up the Chesapeake and Ohio Barge Canal to a point opposite Harper's Ferry where they were to be hoisted out of the canal and skidded over into the Potomac River. (The Chesapeake and Ohio Barge Canal paralleled the Potomac River from Washington to Harper's Ferry, the Potomac being largely unnavigable above Washington because of rapids.) Once into the river, which was relatively placid opposite Harper's Ferry, the canal boats would be towed to a point where they were to act as anchors for the temporary bridge which was to serve Banks's immediate needs. For some time, the Chesapeake and Ohio Barge Canal's lower reaches had been under the operation of the United States Military Railroad. McClellan had been told by civil engineers attached to that service that the canal's locks lying west of Washington possessed the same construction specifications as the locks within the lower canal near Washington; therefore, floating equipment on its lower end would work equally well on its upper end.[10] Those officials had apparently taken their information from statistics compiled on the nation's canal systems, circa 1830.[11] Much to the embarrassment of all concerned, the United States Military Railroad engineers were totally wrong. The canal boats which McClellan had ordered to be assembled, although fitting nicely through the canal's lower locks, would not fit through those farther up. Banks's people would have to make do with other means by which to bring up the canal boats. When all was in place, Banks's artillery crossed over to Harpers Ferry.

Of immediate importance, and that thanks to Banks's now strong presence at Harper's Ferry, Washington was now guarded at its northwestern quadrant. President Lincoln's concerns on that one score were at last placated. Within a matter of a few short weeks following Banks's occupation of Harper's Ferry, a railroad bridge was again in place affording direct rail connection between the Union armies in the east and those in the west.

Yet one other obstacle had to be taken care of before Lincoln would authorize McClellan to move his army out from the defenses surrounding Washington. During the early winter of 1861-1862, Confederate batteries had been emplaced on the Virginia side of the Potomac, midway between the city and the point where the Potomac empties into Chesapeake Bay. In addition to the military problem that was attached to enemy guns being in such close proximity to the capital, there was an important political significance there as well. Washington was the command center for the Union, both militarily and politically. As such, it was the natural hub for war news radiating out to the nation-at-large. The enemy's presence at the front door of Washington -- especially if it was less than thirty miles from the White House -- became big news. Gossip of enemy fire inflicting damage to vessels en route up the Potomac from the Chesapeake to the capital began making the rounds in early October. The talk was not exaggerated. For all practical purposes, the Potomac had been closed off as an open supply route to the city. Some vessels did make a safe passage upriver, but it was a hazardous affair.[12] A report was filed in December by Lieutenant Colonel George Wells of a Massachusetts regiment which was then assigned to the manning of picket positions across the river from Virginia. Wells related what was probably a representative experience for commercial vessels trying to pass by the enemy batteries during that December.

> I have the honor to report that heavy firing was kept up on the schooners coming up the river. The officer of the day, Captain Chamberlain, reported to me that the vessels were becalmed and not moving. I directed him to take a boat and go to their relief. He reports that he found two schooners which had fouled in the middle of the river and could not proceed, their officers being apparently paralyzed.

The command was given to Captain Chamberlain, who disentangled the vessels and
then towed them up, one at a time, beyond the upper battery. Nearly opposite
Possum Nose Battery he found another schooner at anchor with the crew all below;
he started her off and then went down the river, where he found, nearer the enemy's
shore than ours, a schooner at anchor; she had a shot through the foresail and
immediately on receiving it had hauled down their sails, dropped anchor, and her
crew had gone below, closing the hatch; there was no one to be seen when he
boarded her. Either of these schooners could have been captured or burned by the
enemy with the greatest ease...[13]

No doubt the frightened schooner crews that Wells mentioned in his report
had a tale to tell that night in the bars of Washington. Talk such as that could have
done little to enhance any public illusion that the Union was maintaining control of the
gates to its capital. In March, Lincoln instructed the drafting of a general order relative
to the security of Washington. In that order's second and fourth paragraphs,
instructions were that all enemy gun emplacements on the Potomac should be
eliminated.

March 8, 1862

Ordered, That no change of the base of operations of the Army of the Potomac
shall be made without leaving in and about Washington such a force as, in the
opinion of the General in Chief and the commanders of Army corps, shall leave said
city entirely secure.

That no more than two Army corps (about fifty thousand troops) of said Army
of the Potomac shall be moved en route for a new base of operations until the
navigation of the Potomac from Washington to the Chesapeake Bay shall be freed
from enemy's batteries and other obstructions, or until the President shall hereafter
give express permission.

That any movement as aforesaid, en route for a new base of operations, which
may be ordered by the General in Chief, and which may be intended to move upon
the Chesapeake Bay, shall begin to move upon the bay as early as the 18th March
instant, and the General in Chief shall be responsible that it moves as early as that
day.

Ordered, That the Army and Navy cooperate in an immediate effort to capture
the enemy's batteries upon the Potomac between Washington and the Chesapeake
Bay.

Abraham Lincoln[14]

The northern press had forecast a Federal offensive starting in the near
future, and the gathering of steamers seemed to confirm the rumor that McClellan was
ready to move and that he would probably land his army on the Rappahannock.
Because of this, the Confederates began to organize their defensive line on the southern
side of that river. In order to both reinforce that line and prevent being cut off, the
enemy gunners along the Potomac were ordered to move toward the Rappahannock.
The roads into Virginia had become a quagmire of springtime mud, almost impassable
for heavy wheeled equipment, so the gunners were forced to leave their cannon on the
Potomac. The mud was also the primary reason why McClellan had preferred using
steamers instead of the roads. Through the use of steamers, at least part of an overland
march toward Richmond would be eliminated.

In the eyes of the Lincoln cabinet, McClellan had been looked upon for some time as a foot dragger; but in reality, the time limit of March 18 which Lincoln had imposed upon him had an element of unfairness to it. Despite an early request by McClellan to be given full control over all aspects involved with the forthcoming campaign, that had not been granted. One example of the lack of centralized command had been an order of Secretary of War Stanton regarding assemblage of transport vessels for McClellan's movement. That authority had been taken from the quartermaster general where it formerly belonged and was now placed directly under Assistant Secretary of War John Tucker. Both in theory and in practice, an assistant secretary had command seniority over any military officer, even if the military officer carried the title and the function of "general in chief of operations." The Administration could, therefore, overrule McClellan quite easily on matters of import such as the method and means for procuring the necessary shipping on which the army was to be moved.

If it was impractical for McClellan to make an amphibious move within the time schedule stated by the Lincoln order of March 8, then the alternative was, of course, open to him for a move on Richmond by land. From the President's viewpoint, a move by land would have had the advantage of keeping the capital continuously at the army's rear as it moved toward Richmond. This appears to have been Lincoln's wish from the beginning. Militarily, however, a land move would entail inordinate difficulties with supply, something which the logistically minded McClellan wished to avoid.

A Change of Plan

McClellan's plan for the offensive called for landing his army on the Rappahannock's bank; however, the plan had to be altered due to the enemy's known anticipation of the place of landing. The Confederates had had time to organize a strong defensive line on the southerly bank of the Rappahannock. Since the CSS VIRGINIA was at the time (mid-March) bottled up in Norfolk by USS MONITOR, a troop movement by water down the full length of Chesapeake Bay could now be executed with relative safety. Fortress Monroe, which had remained under the occupation of Union troops since the war began, seemed an excellent staging area for launching the drive against the Confederate capital. It is located on the Chesapeake at the northern entrance of Hampton Roads. Since the land peninsula that leads to Fortress Monroe is bounded by the James River on its south side and by the York River on its north side, a flanking protection was afforded to it by the use of the Navy's gunboats. Landing his army at a place which was controlled on its flanks and which was amenable to access for supply vessels was attractive to McClellan from a variety of standpoints.

~

In order to advantageously supply McClellan's army once it was well established on the peninsula leading from Fortress Monroe, the army's primary quartermaster facility serving the Union armies in the Chesapeake had to be relocated. Back in August of 1861, a major depot for both quartermaster and commissary supplies had been established at Perryville, a river and railroad town located on the upper Chesapeake at the mouth of the Susquehanna River. Perryville had been chosen because it was considered at that time to be safe from direct enemy attack and because there was little danger that the railroad line which served it would be interrupted by sabotage on the part of secessionists then active in and about the city of Baltimore. Besides being a convenient location for movement by rail, Perryville was readily accessible for the direct transfer of goods to ships which were outbound either to Annapolis (where there was a rail spur connecting to Washington) or else directly to the capital via the Potomac River.[15] In March 1862, after Fortress Monroe had been selected as the point for debarkation of McClellan's expeditionary force, the quartermaster general would order that the supply depot at Perryville be broken up. All supplies and equipage then in inventory at Perryville would be sent on to Fortress Monroe. Shipments originating in the northern states and which were consigned to McClellan's army were to be routed directly to the new depot. Once McClellan's army had become firmly established on the Virginia peninsula, supplies and troop reinforcements would then be landed at points to be later designated which were farther up the York River or the James River.

~

True to the timetable as established by Lincoln, the first detachment of McClellan's Army of the Potomac left Washington for Fortress Monroe on March 17. McClellan had requested that fifty thousand troops be transported in the first movement. The ability to move such a large body of troops as well as cavalry mounts and enough equipment and supplies to sustain the army's first echelon was, of course, completely dependent on the number and type of vessels which could be marshaled at one time at the loading sites. Following this first echelon movement, the follow-up requirement called for transporting another sixty thousand men and their supporting artillery and military impedimenta. The enormity of the amount of equipment McClellan required was predicated in part on the assumption that the Confederates would remove or destroy everything in front of McClellan's advance. Assistant Secretary Tucker's report to the Secretary of War relates but a few of the shipping difficulties which were to be overcome.

> I was called to Washington by telegraph on 17th January last by Assistant Secretary of War Thomas A. Scott. I was informed that Major General McClellan wished to see me. From him I learned that he desired to know if transportation on smooth water could be obtained to move at one time, for a short distance, about fifty thousand troops, ten thousand horses, one thousand wagons, thirteen batteries, and the usual equipment of such an army. He frankly stated to me that he had always supposed such a movement entirely feasible until two experienced quartermasters had recently reported it impracticable in their judgment. A few days afterward, I reported to General McClellan that I was entirely confident the transports could be commanded, and stated the mode by which his object could be accomplished. A week or two afterward, I had the honor of an interview with the President and General McClellan, when the subject was further discussed, and especially as to the time required.
>
> I expressed the opinion that as the movement of the horses and wagons would have to be made chiefly by schooners and barges; that as each schooner would

require to be properly fitted for the protection of the horses and furnished with a supply of water and forage, and each transport for the troops provided with water, I did not deem it prudent to assume that such an expedition could start within thirty days from the time the order was given.

The President and General McClellan both urgently stated the vast importance of an earlier movement. I replied that if favorable winds prevailed, and there was great dispatch in loading, the time might be materially diminished.

On the 14th of February you [Secretary of War] advertised for transports of various descriptions, inviting bids. On the 27th February I was informed that the proposed movement by water was decided upon. That evening the quartermaster general was informed of the decision. Directions were given to secure the transportation, and any assistance was tendered. He promptly detailed to this duty two most efficient assistants in his department. Colonel Rufus Ingalls was stationed at Annapolis, where it was then proposed to embark the troops, and Captain Henry C. Hodges was directed to meet me in Philadelphia, to attend to chartering the vessels. With these arrangements I left Washington on the 28th February.

I beg to hand herewith a statement, prepared by Captain Hodges, of the vessels chartered, which exhibits the prices paid and parties from whom they were taken:

113 steamers, at an average price per day $215.10
188 schooners, at an average price per day   24.45
88 barges, at an average price per day 14.27

In thirty-seven days from the time I received the order in Washington (and most of it was accomplished in thirty days) these vessels transported from Perryville, Alexandria, and Washington to Fortress Monroe (the place of departure having been changed, which caused delay) 121,500 men, 14,592 animals, 1,150 wagons, 44 batteries, 74 ambulances, besides pontoon bridges, telegraph materials, and the enormous quantity of equipage, etc., required for an army of such magnitude. The only loss of which I have heard is eight mules and nine barges, which latter went ashore in gale within a few miles of Fortress Monroe, the cargoes being saved. With this trifling exception not the slightest accident has occurred, to my knowledge.[16]

(The 324 vessels listed in a report by Captain Hodges are individually enumerated within this work's companion volume, *Dictionary of Transports and Combatant Vessels, Steam and Sail, Employed by the Union Army, 1861 - 1868.*)

Despite the rosy glow of the Tucker report, considerable difficulties had in fact arisen. This was due in main part to many of the vessels being unsuitable for the task. Another factor not related within Tucker's report but which was a cause of delay and unnecessary confusion was the shortage of quartermaster officers who had experience in waterborne troop movements. The Navy could have helped plug that gap; however, the Navy had justified its failure to participate, citing a preoccupation over holding the *CSS VIRGINIA* in check at Norfolk. An assumption can be gleaned from Tucker's report that he complied with McClellan's request to move "fifty thousand men" in the first troop lift; however, McClellan's own report claimed a lessor number of men in that initial lift.

The initial summary as to number and types of vessels required for the lift of McClellan's army was prepared by Assistant Secretary of War John Tucker and is reproduced in this volume's Appendix P. Tucker recommended 324 vessels; however, this was short of the mark. In the end, the lift required 393.

At Fortress Monroe

As a staging area, Fortress Monroe suffered from serious congestion caused not only by the arrival of so many troops, but from the stockpiling there of a mountain of supplies and equipment. The place definitely had space limitations, and they were being stretched to the extreme.[17] Fortress Monroe simply was not a large enough place to hold everybody and everything being sent there.[18] Because of the crowding at Fortress Monroe and the need to expand the fort's perimeter defenses onto the peninsula, McClellan ordered Brigadier General S. P. Heintzelman, commanding the III Corps, to move two divisions over to Hampton. Heintzelman's orders were to post a division on each of the two main roads leading from the town. The first road led from Hampton to Yorktown via Big Bethal. The other road led directly to Williamsburg. Since Heintzelman was to limit his troop deployments to the peninsula's eastern tip, any reconnaissance of the countryside farther onto the peninsula was to consist only of the lightest of probes. McClellan hoped to give the Confederates a false impression that he would first move by water against Norfolk rather than by land up the peninsula toward Richmond. This was, though, a rather futile farce in light of the scope of information which had already been disseminated in the uncensored Union press, almost all of it prophesying a direct land offensive against Richmond.

By April 2, McClellan had left the Washington scene behind him and had established himself at Fortress Monroe. His account of what he first discovered there was in marked contradiction with the earlier reports made by subordinate commanders in which the state of things had been painted in overly optimistic terms. McClellan was discovering serious inadequacies that could hamper operations.

> ...but a small portion of the cavalry had arrived. The artillery reserve [then offlying Hampton] had not yet completed its disembarkation. I found there the 3rd Pennsylvania Cavalry and the 5th Regular Cavalry. The 2nd Regular Cavalry and a portion of the 1st [Regular Cavalry] had arrived, but not disembarked. So few wagons had arrived that it was not possible to move Casey's division at all for several days, while the other divisions were obliged to move with scant supplies.[19]

Intelligence that McClellan was receiving on enemy strength ran the full gamut in quality. The reports of the officers in charge of the cavalry patrols varied as to reliability depending on the training and experience of the officer doing the reporting. Spy reports obtained through the detective agency of Allen Pinkerton were another primary source of information.[20] The Pinkerton reports were meticulously written; but, as the future would bring to light, they continually over-inflated enemy troop strength. The ambiguity of the information he was receiving only exacerbated McClellan's cautious nature. While part of that caution was the result of the man's ingrained character, much of it was the result of his genuine uncertainty as to what lay in front of him. McClellan had a well-reasoned reluctance to proceed blindly.

Another problem McClellan and his staff faced was terrain analysis. Patrol reports and the reports of spies and line-crossers, when comprehensively examined, portrayed a contradiction between the actual terrain and the maps with which the general's staff officers and the major commanders had been provided. The information shown on these maps, all of which was from rather antiquated data, conflicted with visual observations, the discrepancies being so great as to render the maps virtually useless for planning purposes. This was being rectified as quickly as possible by the Army Topographical Engineers whose officers had started to go out with the patrols. The sketches made by these engineers were immediately distributed to corps and division headquarters as well as to the quartermasters and commissary people responsible for moving supplies.

One of the major advantages used in the argument by McClellan for a campaign on the peninsula was the relative ease of supply by water. If the James River could be rendered free from enemy interference as far up as Bermuda Hundred, then deep draft vessels could move materiel directly to City Point, a landing place which was only thirty-five miles from the urban fringes of Richmond. If the York River was instead selected as a supply route, the distance overland to Richmond would be somewhat more, but not enough to cause any undue problems. Soil type had been another reason for McClellan's selection of the Virginia peninsula as the route to Richmond rather than the overland approach from the Rappahannock. Adaptability of terrain in the handling of artillery and wagon traffic was of paramount consideration during the wet season of the spring. Soils on the peninsula were known to be of a sandy consistency which seemed to McClellan's staff to be an attractive alternative when compared with the more usual Virginia red clay which produced an impassable mud during wet periods. Although the judgments of McClellan's staff were correct regarding the advantage of the peninsula's access by water, their assessment of the soils was not. The sands of the peninsula were of such a fine consistency that when saturated, they resembled quick sand which formed sinks which literally inhaled the hooves of animals and the wheels of wagons. The spring of 1862 was to be an abnormally wet one. More often than not, supply and artillery movement on the roads would come to a standstill as guns, caissons, and wagons sunk to their frames. Even under the best of circumstances and on the better sections of roads, wagon loads had to be limited to not over 1,000 pounds, thereby severely reducing the efficiencies of overland movement.[21] The nearly impassable road conditions which would be encountered and the resultant delays of wagon traffic had a domino effect which adversely impacted the efficiency of water transport. Because of the heavy rains, supplies prone to water damage could not be offloaded for dockside storage since there was almost nothing in the way of covered facilities at the offloading sites. Consequently, shipping was to be held over for abnormally long periods while awaiting the arrival of wagons on which to directly offload.

Another unanticipated need was a requirement for a rather substantial number of vessels to be used as short-haul troop transports as it was found to be quicker to move troops from the York over to the James by steamer rather than march them across the saturated roads. In light of all the various factors which became involved, the quartermasters' first estimate of the number of vessels needed would fall far short as the campaign progressed.

~

During the spring of 1862, as the Peninsular Campaign in Virginia was about to begin, good news from the west and south began reaching Lincoln's ears. On

February 16th, the Confederates at Fort Donelson on the Tennessee River had surrendered to then Brigadier General Ulysses S. Grant. Burnside's presence in the Carolina Sounds meant that the Confederates could ill afford to put the Carolinas in a weakened condition by sending reinforcements to support the Richmond line. On April 6 and 7, the Battle of Shiloh would be fought on the Tennessee; and although costly, it would result in a Union victory.

~

Following McClellan's departure for the peninsula, Washington's northwesterly defenses were left guarded by thirty-five thousand troops under the command of Major General Nathaniel P. Banks. Banks's responsibility was to hold back any movement toward Washington by Confederate forces coming out of the Shenandoah Valley. The enemy force in the Shenandoah consisted of five thousand men under Major General Thomas J. Jackson. Hoping to remove the threat of this force, Banks sent seven thousand of his troops under the field command of Brigadier General James Shields to strike at Jackson. Shields's force marched down the Shenandoah Valley and pushed Jackson southward of the town of Kernstown. At this point Shields halted the pursuit and turned back northward. On March 22, Jackson, who by now had become the pursuer, attacked Shields; but Jackson had badly underestimated Shields's strength. One tally claims that Jackson lost almost forty percent of his force in that action.[22] Even with so high a loss, Jackson had produced a positive result for the Confederacy. His aggressiveness in attacking Shields had convinced both Halleck and Lincoln that such a tenacious enemy in the Shenandoah Valley remained an ongoing threat to Washington's defenses, particularly at the key point of Harper's Ferry. This produced a renewed fear within the thinking of Lincoln and some of the Washington generals. As a consequence, more Union troops would be held bound to the capital's defenses. McClellan would continue to be vexed by a refusal for additional troops to support his campaign on the peninsula.

The Peninsular Campaign Begins: Yorktown and Williamsburg

Despite the fact that the total Union force on the peninsula was not yet fully assembled and that the stockpiles of supplies were not built up to a level which McClellan considered adequate, he started his move from Fortress Monroe in early April. The initial advance carried the Army of the Potomac as far as the Confederate defense line in front of Yorktown. And then down came more rain. Wagons and supply columns became bogged in the fluid sands. For a time, the road leading from Fortress Monroe was made passable by corduroying it with logs; but this process had to be frequently repeated as the logs just kept sinking deeper into the soggy mass. To counter the road problem, steamers started offloading at Cheeseman's Creek which was nearer Yorktown.

It was reported that an army of one hundred thousand strong under General Joseph E. Johnston was moving in to reinforce those Confederates holding the Yorktown defenses. If that news was not bad enough, McClellan was next informed that reinforcements from Major General Irvin McDowell's command, then in reserve in the Washington area and which had originally been scheduled for duty with McClellan on the peninsula, would not be coming. (Fortunately, the report of the one hundred thousand Confederates under Johnston turned out to be false. Some reinforcements did arrive to strengthen the Confederate defenses at Yorktown, but in total these numbered less than thirty thousand.)

Apprehensive of a frontal assault against the enemy works, McClellan decided on a "softening up" through an artillery barrage, to be accompanied by a time-consuming construction of siege line entrenchments. Meanwhile, steps were put into place for an amphibious landing to be made upstream on the York River above the Confederate's positions at Yorktown. A force landed behind the Confederate lines would cut off the enemy's avenue of retreat once the Yorktown works could be breached. Organization and planning for this landing became the responsibility of Lieutenant Colonel Barton S. Alexander. Alexander, an engineer, developed the ingenious idea of converting canal barges into wharfheads. These in turn were to be joined to pontoon bridging leading to the shore. Transports were to come alongside these makeshift wharfheads and offload. In that fashion, troops could be transferred directly from the transports onto the beaches without the need for the use of landing boats.[23] Alexander's fabrications were described in detail within a report he prepared for McClellan's Chief of Engineers:

> By lashing two of the canal barges together, placing the boats [meaning units of lashed barges] some twelve feet apart, and throwing a false or additional deck over the whole, we had an area of some forty feet wide and forty-five feet long, upon which a whole battery of artillery could be placed....Several of these double boats (four I think) were thus prepared, and the men were drilled for two or three days in taking them as near to the shore as they would float and then making a bridge from there to the shore....Experience proved that we could land artillery very rapidly in this way, and when it was landed, each double canal boat became a wharf head, alongside of which our light draft vessels [the smaller transports] could discharge their cargoes. Four of them could consequently give us four wharves as soon as the artillery was discharged...[24]

There would be little wasted motion toward the implementation of Alexander's ideas. Pontoon boats which would bridge the spaces between the canal boats and the shore were to be utilized initially in ferrying to the beach the first assault wave of infantry. Once ashore, that first wave would hold the beachhead until the pier units could be assembled. In practice runs conducted downriver from Yorktown, certain problems cropped up, one in particular being that of getting the first wave of assault troops from the transports down into the pontoon boats. The original plan had been to allow each transport master the option of deciding how this was to be accomplished. However, as Alexander had observed during rehearsals, the troops aboard each of the transports had to clamber over the ships' gunwales and then down into the boats, usually one man at a time, using rope ladders. It was estimated that getting the first wave ashore in this manner would take almost half a day. Such a time-consuming process was clearly unacceptable and could prove disastrous if the landing beaches were found to be defended. In his report, Alexander had explained how he went about quickening the process.

...I deemed it proper, therefore, to make a number of gangplanks so that the men could walk in single file from the deck of the vessel up to the gunwales on either side and down the sides by an easy slope to the boats, the exterior gangplanks being supported from the vessels and extending down into the water, and not resting on the boats, but being entirely independent of them....[25]

On the morning of May 4, the Confederates evacuated their works. By holding at Yorktown, the Confederates had gained the time they required to establish a new line, this one on more defensible terrain. In planning his withdrawal to that new line, the enemy commander had anticipated a swift, easy movement. Instead, he encountered the same difficulties which faced the Union side -- the bad roads. For the pursuing Federals, following on the heels of the Confederates over already churned ground proved even more difficult.

It was at Williamsburg, twelve miles from Yorktown, that the new Confederate defense line was established. One end of it was bounded on the south by an unspanned muddy-bottomed watercourse named College Creek which fed into the James River. This was at a point where high bluffs, in and of themselves, made excellent defensive points. To the northeast of the town, the approaches to that end of the line were protected by a muddy slough called Queen's Creek. Between these natural barriers, the Confederates had prepared gunnery positions to enfilade all possible approaches. McClellan had anticipated that the Confederates would make a major stand at Williamsburg, but in that, he was not correct. Joe Johnston, who had personally arrived on the scene to take over the defense, decided that since the York River was by now under Union control, his left rear was dangerously exposed. Johnston determined that any defense at Williamsburg should only be a holding action to buy some time for a further retrograde toward prior established positions along the Chickahominy River directly in front of Richmond.

The Confederate defenders of the Williamsburg line performed the job they were assigned to, that of fighting off a 2-day probe by Federal forces. At one point, they even sent the Union soldiery reeling backward -- that is until McClellan was able to bring up reserves to stabilize the situation. When the Williamsburg line was abandoned, its defenders quietly moved out as Johnston had planned. They would rejoin the main Confederate force moving toward the Chickahominy River.

McClellan decided to go ahead with a landing behind Johnston's new line at a point farther up the York River. The objective was to come against Johnston from a direction oblique to that of the main line of the Union advance. Alexander remained largely responsible for the planning on how to get the force ashore. The landing force would be of division strength under the command of Brigadier General William B. Franklin. At the site selected for the landing, there was a road (as yet of unknown quality) over which Franklin was to move his division inland.[26] By sunset that same day, Alexander's innovative pierheads were anchored into place, and Franklin managed to get eight thousand men over them, onto the beach, and into line of battle within a total of three hours -- all without mishap. By midnight, all of Franklin's supportive artillery and horses were ashore and being readied to move inland. The next day, more transports arrived, these carrying the division of Brigadier General John Sedgwick. When on the following day the Confederates counterattacked in some strength, this only amounted to a temporary harassment, not upsetting the scheduled plan which was for Franklin and Sedgwick to move their divisions by columns, paralleling the eastern bank of the Pamunkey River.

While Franklin's and Sedgwick's men were moving up the banks of the Pamunkey, Alexander boarded one of the smaller transports and proceeded farther upstream on the lookout for a site which would be suitable for the landing of supplies and accessible to a road leading away from the river. The tiny hamlet of Eltham, located about five miles upstream from the Pamunkey's junction with the York, was selected. A wagon path led from there directly to the road on which Franklin's and Sedgwick's columns were advancing. Two temporary wharves were quickly constructed, just in time to coincide with the arrival of steamers loaded with supplies. Two days later, the place for unloading supplies would be moved upriver to Cumberland. Riding aboard one of the steamers as passengers were two supply officers, Rufus Ingalls and Henry F. Clarke, both men destined to play significant roles in handling the logistics for the campaign to follow. Ingalls was to take temporary charge of the stockpiling and disbursement of all quartermaster supplies coming up the York- Pamunkey system, and Clarke was to take charge of all the incoming commissary goods. Their plan called for depots to be set up on the Pamunkey River which would begin to take over from the depots previously located on the York River.[27]

The reason why the York River, and later its westerly tributary the Pamunkey, were chosen as the supply access in support of the advance toward Richmond was in large part because of Lincoln's standing concern that McClellan should keep Washington at his back. McClellan would, therefore, align his movements on the peninsula so as to come against the Confederate capital from the northeast rather than along the path of the James River. Had he instead used the James River as his logistical tail, he would have created a geographic wedge between his army and Washington, a circumstance that would have been in conflict with Lincoln's wishes.

McClellan's chief quartermaster, in a report that summer to Quartermaster General Meigs, described the transfer of the quartermaster and commissary supply depots from Cheeseman's Creek (near the mouth of the York River) to Yorktown, to be followed again by the establishment of successive depots on the Pamunkey River.

> These depots [Cheeseman's Creek] remained unchanged during the siege of Yorktown, but when the enemy evacuated that place, they were immediately broken up and everything transferred by water at once to Yorktown. As the Army advanced up the peninsula our depots were successively changed from Yorktown to the south bank of York River, opposite West Point, thence to Cumberland, on the Pamunkey, and finally, on the 20th May, they were established at White House, the point where the railroad from West Point to Richmond crosses the Pamunkey River, twenty-three miles from Richmond.
>
> [At White House,] extensive wharves were at once constructed by throwing our barges and canal boats ashore at high water and bridging them over. The railroad bridge across the Pamunkey had been burned by the enemy, and the rolling stock of the road removed. From a reconnaissance in front the railroad was found to be uninjured, with the exception of two or three small bridges, which had been burned. In anticipation of moving along this road toward Richmond, rolling stock for the road had been purchased, and a competent force employed to work it. Working

parties were immediately put on the road and the engines and cars landed and in a few days the road was again in running order, and cars loaded with supplies were constantly running to the front. The real troubles in supplying the Army commenced at this point, owing to the condition of the roads, rendered almost impassable by frequent and long-continued storms....At this point, our large depots remained until the battle of Gaines' Mill, the 27th of June. During this time the Army was in front of Richmond, from fifteen to twenty miles in advance, and all of its immense supplies were thrown forward by the railroad and the large supply trains of the Army. The frequent and heavy rains, by injuring the railroad and impairing the wagon roads, rendered it a matter of great difficulty at times to transport the large amount of necessary material and supplies, but in no instance, I believe, did our department fail in discharging the duty devolving upon it.[28]

At the beginning of the Peninsular Campaign, supplies were forwarded to the Army of the Potomac from warehouse points at Alexandria, Baltimore, and Annapolis. As the campaign progressed into its second month, supply shipments began to be sent directly from Philadelphia and New York.

When McClellan started his advance from Fortress Monroe, he was supported by five thousand wagons and three hundred and fifty ambulances, all of this land transport having been shipped in by vessel. The total number of horses and mules for cavalry and draft purposes would eventually number twenty-five thousand head. It has been estimated by logistics historian James A. Huston that to maintain the Union Army on the peninsula during 1862, the total supply tonnage being moved to the troops on line (given as a daily average) came to around six hundred tons, this figure inclusive of animal forage.[29] All of this material arrived on the peninsula by the one means available -- water -- using steamships, sailing vessels, and barges under tow of steam tugs. If Huston's estimate of average daily needs is accepted as correct, then computed upon the basis of the active period of the campaign which lasted over three months, 54,000 tons of supplies would have been shipped to the peninsula, all on waterborne transport. (As impressive as that figure is, it does not address the tonnage involved in the original movement to Fortress Monroe or the tonnage involved during the evacuation at the end of the campaign.)

The Confederate Abandonment of Norfolk

Following the taking of the Confederate defenses at Williamsburg, the York River was turned into a very busy avenue, not only for army owned and chartered shipping, but also for the Navy's fleet of gunboats and its own supply vessels. During one time frame -- that is, during mid-April 1862 -- the Navy had twenty-three men-of-war operating in support of the Union Army on the York River. The Navy would have had a larger presence except that naval vessels were being held in reserve at Hampton Roads and on the lower James River in case the *CSS VIRGINIA* tried to break out and get past the *USS MONITOR* and its supporting ram vessels.[30]

On May 8, the Union garrison at Newport News received intelligence that Norfolk was being evacuated. To corroborate this, a reconnaissance force was sent the following day to Willoughby's Point. President Lincoln was at the time on an inspection trip to Fortress Monroe. When Lincoln was told of the expedition to

Willoughby's Point, which was seven miles north of the then city limits of Norfolk, he could not resist the opportunity to play a personal part. A newspaper reporter, later claiming to have been a witness to the landing at Willoughby's Point, wrote that Lincoln was one of the first on to the beach and that while standing on the beach, he delighted the men by officially welcoming them to Norfolk as they stepped ashore.[31]

Much of Norfolk had been set afire by the retreating garrison. The timing for the Confederate evacuation had not been announced to all the various Confederate units in the town, and the naval officers at the dock yards appear to have been the last to get the word. When the 67-year-old commander of the *CSS VIRGINIA*, Josiah Tattnall, became aware that the city was fast emptying of its military garrison, he decided to take the ironclad out into Hampton Roads, reasoning that if he could get past the *USS MONITOR* and the other guard ships, he could steam up the James River to find sanctuary at City Point. Tattnall's theory was that if he could get to City Point and base the *CSS VIRGINIA* there, then any closer approach to Richmond by water would be denied to Federal forces. Pilots familiar with the James River advised Tattnall that in order to take *CSS VIRGINIA* that far up the James, it would be necessary to lighten her draft by at least five feet. This meant jettisoning almost everything aboard, keeping only her guns and ammunition. The crew began throwing overboard *CSS VIRGINIA*'s iron ballast, stores, and even some of their personal effects; but no sooner had this been accomplished than the pilots announced that rising westerly winds would almost certainly bring about an even lower water level in the James River, making it impossible to get anywhere near City Point unless the ironclad's draft was reduced even more. Tattnall knew that to further reduce the draft would result in bringing the lower edge of the vessel's armor plate out of the water thus exposing her vulnerable unplated bottom. Rather than invite what he believed would be sure-fire destruction, and no doubt the death of her crew, Tattnall decided to scuttle and ordered that *CSS VIRGINIA* be set afire. When the flames reached the powder magazines, she exploded, her remains settling to the harbor's bottom.

The Confederate naval board of inquiry which was to judge the propriety of Tattnall's decision to destroy *CSS VIRGINIA* would determine that he had been wrong in taking such a drastic action. Part of the board's report stated:

> II. It being clearly of evidence that Norfolk being evacuated and Flag Officer Tattnall having been instructed to prevent the enemy from ascending the James River, the *VIRGINIA**, with very little more, if any, lessening of draft, after lightening her to twenty feet, six inches aft, with her iron sheathing still extending to three feet underwater, could have been taken up to Hog Island in the James River [twenty-three miles upstream from where the James entered Hampton Roads] (where the channel is narrow) and could there have prevented the larger vessels and the transports of the enemy from ascending, the court is of the opinion that such disposition ought to have been made of her, and if it should be ascertained that her provisions could not be replenished when those at hand were exhausted, then the proper time would have arrived to take into consideration the expediency or practicability of striking a last blow at the enemy or destroying her....[32]

* *CSS*, commissioned Confederate naval vessel.

A later court-martial exonerated Tattnall of the early censure, but the question remained as to whether or not he could have effectively utilized *CSS VIRGINIA*. By scuttling the vessel, Tattnall left another question unanswered for the time being: Could one ironclad out fight the other?

In addition to having held the command of the now defunct *CSS VIRGINIA*, Josiah Tattnall had also held overall control of all naval units at Norfolk. Before the abandonment of the city, Tattnall ordered that certain vessels which he referred to as "gunboats" proceed up the James River. In reality these were nothing more than ordinary commercial river craft, armed with odds and ends of cannon. These "gunboats" could have done little in the way of blocking the James River to a Union fleet, and Tattnall seems to have realized that. Something else would be needed to do that job. He accordingly ordered a battery of naval guns put in place behind strong earthworks at Drewry's Bluff above Bermuda Hundred. The position was well chosen even though the number of guns in the battery was not impressive, consisting only of four cannon. Following the scuttling of *CSS VIRGINIA*, the ironclad's crew was assigned to this battery as gunners. To block the river approaches to the battery, the Confederates then sank a few old cargo schooners, but their placement was poorly planned. The battery of four cannons established by Tattnall at Drewry's Bluff was the only significant means the enemy then had to deny passage of the James River, but it would be enough. On May 15, Union Navy gunboats opened a long-distanced bombardment against the Drewry's Bluff battery. The bombardment was kept up for some time, but it had little effect.

With Norfolk now in Federal hands and the *CSS VIRGINIA* a scuttled underwater wreck, Union naval forces which had previously been standing guard were now left free for other employment. The majority of them were reassigned to maintain security on the lower York and James rivers.

On the Chickahominy Defensive Line

The Confederate's defensive line in front of Richmond had been well situated on the Chickahominy River. The Richmond side of that river had most of the commanding terrain. When McClellan's troops arrived in front of that Confederate line, they discovered that they would have to first cross the river and then attack fixed positions with the river at their backs. Breaking the enemy's line on the Chickahominy was not going to be easy.

McClellan's consistent pleas for reinforcements had at last wrung from Halleck the promise that McDowell and I Corps of the Army of the Potomac would move to his support by an overland march from Fredericksburg. While anticipating McDowell's arrival, McClellan ordered his army's right wing to cross over the Chickahominy River to the Richmond side and take up positions anchored on the town of Mechanicsville. With that accomplished, McClellan's right wing would be only four miles from Richmond.

~

Robert E. Lee, situated in Richmond at the Confederate War Department, was by now orchestrating the deployment of all Confederate forces in Virginia. Lee realized that if Richmond's defenses were to hold, McClellan must be denied additional reinforcement. Lee was fully aware of Lincoln's phobia over maintaining a strong defense of Washington. With that in mind, he ordered Major General Thomas J. Jackson, then located in the southern part of the Shenandoah Valley, to strike northward against Federal troops then holding positions in the central section of the valley. Lee hoped that this would be viewed by the Lincoln Administration as a strike against Washington. Jackson forced the Union troops back to Front Royal where they attempted to hold; but on May 23, they were again forced into retreat. In front of Jackson now lay Harper's Ferry, the gateway to the capital. His mission accomplished, Jackson broke off his pursuit of the Union forces.

At least for the time being, Harper's Ferry remained in Northern hands. The whole episode confirmed Lincoln's standing conviction that a strong, permanent troop presence was needed to defend the capital. This meant that McClellan would not be reinforced as had been promised.

~

In position in front of Richmond, but devoid of the assistance of additional troops, McClellan became faced with an immediate emergency. His cavalry patrols had reported a Confederate force on the banks of the Pamunkey River at Hanover Court House, a place about twenty miles upstream from White House. This directly threatened the Union positions near there which had been pointedly situated to block the railroad connecting Richmond with the Shenandoah Valley. If that railroad access was again made available to Robert E. Lee, there would be no way to stop Confederate reinforcements and supplies coming directly to Richmond either from the Shenandoah Valley or from points farther to the west. McClellan would act with decisiveness, ordering V Corps under Brigadier General Fitz John Porter to move out toward Hanover Court House. The twelve thousand men of V Corps found themselves pitted against an inferior enemy force of about only four thousand. The reactive movement was a Union success, and the railroad from the Shenandoah Valley into Richmond was blocked.

McClellan had by now established a strong bridgehead on the Richmond side of the Chickahominy. He was preparing for an assault against the enemy positions when heavy rains washed out the pontoon bridges that the Union Army engineers had constructed over the river. This left McClellan with the enemy at his front and an unspanned river at his back. Replacement pontoon bridges were hurriedly put in place, but the continuing rains promised that those bridges could go at any time. Communications between units was extremely poor as swampy conditions existed along wide stretches of the upper Chickahominy. In most cases, contact between units could only be maintained by wide detours on the part of couriers. Telegraph lines were being used, but this means of communication was constantly interrupted by enemy infiltrators severing the wires.

On May 30, the Battle of Seven Pines was fought by units of McClellan's left flank, the church spires of Richmond visible to them six miles in the distance. The battle was of Confederate instigation, brought about by Joseph E. Johnston who decided to take advantage of McClellan's inability to call on his reserves from across the swollen river. The Chickahominy River was well over its banks, and some of the pontoon bridges had again washed out. Only poor generalship by Johnston in coordinating his attacking units prevented a Confederate victory. Johnston was severely wounded during the battle, and direct command of Confederate troops in the field was taken over by Robert E. Lee.

The next four weeks saw a succession of static artillery duels with little movement on either side. The inactivity was temporarily broken on June 13 when a raid by Confederate cavalrymen under Brigadier General J. E. B. Stuart was launched against Tunstall's Station, a point on the railroad between White House and the Federal front lines. Following the destruction of Tunstall's Station and some of the nearby track, Stuart's horsemen rode a wide arc which, before the ride was over, had completely encircled McClellan's rear. Stuart's sweep included the burning of two "government schooners" which were laying dockside at Garlick's Landing near White House.[33]

Union Pullback

Stuart's audaciousness in taking what amounted to a 100-mile ride through an area which was supposed to be controlled by Union forces was not only an embarrassment to McClellan, but it rekindled some nagging concerns that reliance on the supply line provided by the Pamunkey River and the connection of the Richmond and York River Railroad was becoming tenuous. On June 26, when McClellan received intelligence that a fresh enemy attack was being readied to strike the supply depot at White House, he ordered the immediate evacuation of the depot there. In compliance with that order, Colonel Stewart Van Vliet, Chief Quartermaster of the Army of the Potomac, telegraphed Rufus Ingalls at White House.

> You will have your whole command in readiness to start at any moment. Please consult with Lieutenant Nicholson of the Navy to have his vessels placed in such a position that he can protect our depot. There will be no attempt to turn our flank for a day or two, but from all information we have it is supposed that Jackson will be coming down soon.
> Don't fail to send down into the broad river below West Point [meaning the York River] all the vessels in the Pamunkey that are not required soon. Three or four days' forage and provisions are all that should be retained afloat at White House. This is a precautionary measure entirely, but must be attended to at once.[34]

The fall back of the Union Army's supply system from the Pamunkey River was accomplished on such short notice that it became impossible to gather together sufficient vessels to evacuate all of the wounded who had been hospitalized at White House. Six hundred of these unfortunates would go into Confederate captivity. Besides that human tragedy, a considerable amount of military supplies had to be destroyed before the evacuation was completed.

On the 29th of June, McClellan decided that the prospects for holding his positions along the Chickahominy looked dismal. Accordingly, he ordered loaded supply vessels then standing by in the York River to move into the James River and await further orders. Within hours of that decision, an order was issued for the destruction of all rolling stock on the rail line leading forward from White House. All wagons and livestock were to be moved across the peninsula to Malvern Hill on the James River. Steps were underway to prepare Haxall's Landing on the James River as a new quartermaster and commissary depot. On June 30th, as a result of a further realignment of forces by McClellan, a change in depot location was made to Harrison's Landing, a small wharf complex somewhat farther downstream from Haxall's Landing.

McClellan had decided that the most effective way to re-anchor his defense line would be to center it around the high ground of Malvern Hill. His ability to remain on the peninsula, and perhaps even the very survival of the Army of the Potomac, would depend on holding these new positions. Meanwhile, Lee was devoting his efforts toward preventing McClellan from consolidating his lines.

On July 1, the Battle of Malvern Hill was fought. The Union troops held, imposing heavy casualties on the attacking Confederates.

In response to his most recent plea for reinforcement, McClellan received his answer directly from the President.

> Washington
> July 1, 1862
> It is impossible to reinforce you for your present emergency. If we had a million of men we could not get them to you in time. We have not the men to send. If you are not strong enough to face the enemy, you must find a place of security, and wait, rest, and repair. Maintain your ground if you can but save the Army at all events, even if you fall back to Fortress Monroe. We still have strength enough in the country and will bring it out.
>
> A. Lincoln[35]

Despite the repulse of Lee's attack, McClellan felt his situation was precarious. Not wishing to risk things further, he ordered a shrinking in of the Federal line in order to bring all of his main elements into a more direct contact with the James River. This would lessen the dependence on roads for logistical support, and it would allow a better opportunity for an evacuation if matters should come to that.

Next would follow a period of seven days of close, heavy contact with Lee's army. By the end of those seven days of battle, McClellan had lost what military advantage he had earlier gained at Malvern Hill. He also had lost much of his personal reputation, both as a strategist and as a tactician.

McClellan telegraphed Lincoln, going into considerable detail concerning the circumstances leading to the present compression of his front. In that communication, McClellan exhibited a talent for words, using verbiage that attempted to turn a very near disaster into something sounding like a triumph. The wording throughout the telegram is contradictory and can easily be read as remarks coming from a general trying to cover himself for what might well end in a capitulation.

> ...We now occupy a line of heights about two miles from the James, a plain extending from there to the river. Our front is about three miles long. These heights command our whole position, and must be maintained. The gunboats can render valuable support upon both flanks. If the enemy attacks us in front, we must hold our ground as we best may, and at whatever cost. Our positions can be carried only by overwhelming numbers. The spirit of the Army is excellent. Stragglers are finding their regiments, and the soldiers exhibit the best results of discipline. Our

position is by no means impregnable, especially as a morass extends on this side of the high ground from our center to the James on our right. The enemy may attack in vast numbers, and if so, our front will be the scene of a desperate battle which, if lost, will be decisive. Our Army is fearfully weakened by killed, wounded, and prisoners. I cannot now approximate to any statement of our losses, but we were not beaten in any conflict. The enemy were unable by their utmost efforts to drive us from any field.

Never did such a change of base, involving a retrograde movement, and under incessant attacks from a most determined and vastly more numerous foe, partake so little of disorder. We have lost no guns except twenty-five on the field of battle, twenty-one of which were lost by the giving way of McCall's division under the onset of superior numbers.

Our communications by the James River are not secure. There are points where the enemy can establish themselves with cannon or musketry and command the river, and where it is not certain that our gunboats can drive them out. In case of this, or in case our front is broken, I will still make every effort to preserve at least the personnel of the Army, and the events of the last few days leave no question that the troops will do all that their country can ask. Send such reinforcements as you can. I will do what I can. We are shipping our wounded and sick and landing supplies. The Navy Department should cooperate with us to the extent of its resources. Captain Rodgers is doing all in his power in the kindest and most efficient manner.

When all the circumstances of the case are known it will be acknowledged by all competent judges that the movement just completed by this army is unparalleled in the annals of war. Under the most difficult circumstances we have preserved our trains, our guns, our materiel, and, above all, our honor.

George B. McClellan, Major General[36]

Retreat From the James

Over the next month, McClellan was able to hold; but the odds continued to stack up against him. Lee was being reinforced daily while McClellan kept persisting in his demands for more troops, arguing that the true defense of the city of Washington lay not at the entrenchments before that city but rather with him on the James River. Lincoln just as consistently disagreed. The issue was eventually settled when Halleck ordered McClellan to evacuate the Virginia peninsula. Whether McClellan actually received Halleck's original instructions and then chose to ignore them is not known. In any event, Halleck had to follow up with a second order.

Washington, August 3, 1862

I have waited most anxiously to learn the result of your forced reconnaissance toward Richmond, and also whether all your sick have been sent away, and I can get no answer to my telegram.

It is determined to withdraw your army from the peninsula to Aquia Creek [on the lower Potomac River]. You will take immediate measures to effect this, covering the movement the best you can. Its real object and withdrawal should be concealed even from your own officers. Your material and transportation should be removed first. You will assume control of all the means of transportation within your reach, and apply to the naval forces for all the assistance they can render you. You will consult freely with the commander of these forces. The entire execution of the movement is left to your discretion and judgment.

You will leave such forces as you deem proper at Fortress Monroe, Norfolk, and other places which we must occupy.

H. W. Halleck, Major General, Commanding US Army[37]

This time McClellan acknowledged Halleck, but in so doing argued that to give up his position on the James River could lead to catastrophe. Halleck would not budge. The orders to withdraw would hold.

McClellan's greatest problem lay in bringing out his sick, the numbers of which were aggravated by the heat and by the poor sanitary conditions. Much of the problems with sanitation resulted from the concentration of such a large body of troops along such a compressed front. A telegram sent to Halleck by McClellan on August 3 illustrates the magnitude of the suffering:

...We have about twelve thousand five hundred sick, of whom perhaps four thousand might make easy marches. We have here the means [water transportation] to transport twelve hundred and will embark tomorrow that number of the worst cases. With all the means at the disposal of the medical director, the remainder could be shipped in from seven to ten days...[38]

Getting his sick off the peninsula was but phase one of a tremendous evacuation task. Once the sick had been removed, the rest of his army would follow. Meanwhile, Halleck was developing a mounting suspicion that McClellan was stalling. Accordingly, he laid on the line the reasons for the withdrawal and the necessity to get the army off the peninsula with all haste:

...the old Army of the Potomac is split into two parts, with the entire force of the enemy directly between them. They cannot be united by land without exposing both to destruction, and yet they must be united. To send Pope's force by water to the Peninsula is, under present circumstances, a military impossibility. The only alternative is to send the forces on the Peninsula to some point by water, say Fredericksburg, where the two armies can be united.[39]

Though McClellan may not have agreed with Halleck's reasoning, it appears unlikely that he deliberately forestalled the evacuation. The difficulties faced were enormous and growing worse. McClellan's quartermaster whose responsibility it was to delegate shipping, reported some of these difficulties to him on August 7. McClellan passed that report along to Halleck, with a copy to the President.

I have the honor to return the papers herewith which you sent me with the following remarks:

We are embarking five batteries of artillery, with their horses, baggage, etc., which requires the detailing of most of our available boats, except the ferryboats. The Medical Department has ten or twelve of our largest transport vessels, which, if disposable, could carry twelve thousand men. Besides, there are some heavy-draught steamers at Fortress Monroe that cannot come to this point [due to draft restrictions], but which can carry eight thousand or ten thousand infantry.

I have ordered all up here that can ascend to this depot. They will be here tomorrow evening. As it now is, after the details already made, we cannot transport from this place more than five thousand infantry.

> There are no transports now available for cavalry. From and after tomorrow, if the vessels arrive, I could transport ten thousand infantry. In two or three days a regiment of cavalry can be sent if required. If you wait, and ship from Yorktown or Fortress Monroe after the sick and wounded transports are at my disposal, we can transport twenty-five thousand at a time. The number that can be transported is contingent on circumstances referred to.
>
> Most of the propellers [steamboats] here are laden with commissary or other supplies, and most of the tugs are necessary to tow off sail craft also laden with supplies.
>
> I am, very respectfully, your most obedient servant,
>
> Rufus Ingalls, Chief Quartermaster [in charge of ship movements][40]

Halleck was in no mood for even the best of excuses. He wired McClellan on August 9th, passing the information that the Confederates were amassing to the north. He continued to accuse McClellan of not moving as fast as he might. Such accusations were unreasonable. Halleck not only failed to appreciate the limitations of the vessels which were loading at Harrison's Landing, but he did not understand the physical handicaps of the loading facilities. The small amount of available wharfage -- makeshift at that -- at Harrison's Landing was producing a bottleneck which severely slowed embarkation. In the midst of trying to ship organized troop units to Aquia Creek, McClellan's people were doing their best to send out the sick and wounded. Halleck had not stopped to realize that the larger steamers, meaning those which might bring off sizable contingents of men at one time, were of a draft preventing them from ascending the James River to the point where the army was located. There was also a misunderstanding existing over a fairly large group of transports which Halleck had believed were then present on the James River but which, as late as August 12, had not arrived there, having in fact been assigned to another destination.[41] Other vessels which were then on the James River were heavily laden with supplies and other equipment which had yet to be discharged. McClellan, in a testy tone, tried explaining this last factor to Halleck.

> ...I am sure you have been misinformed as to the availability of vessels on hand. We cannot use heavily-loaded supply vessels for troops or animals, and such constitute the mass of those [vessels] here which have been represented to you as capable of transporting this army.[42]

The prognosis for the time required for total evacuation, as it was gauged by McClellan's staff, was that if the loading continued to take place from Harrison's Landing, then the army could not be transported in its entirety in less time than a full month. The danger of course with such a slowly staged evacuation was that at some point, the reduced force which remained would become too weak to ward off attack. This is what McClellan feared most, and he now took action to prevent that from happening. During August 17 and 18, all embarkation ceased to take place from Harrison's Landing while McClellan ordered two of his corps to march overland, one going to Yorktown and the other to Fortress Monroe. At both places, they would be available for evacuation by the deeper draft transports.[43] All future embarkations would take place either from Yorktown or from Fortress Monroe.

One full corps sailed from Fortress Monroe on the 19th and another from Yorktown on the 20th. By the 23rd of August, Franklin's corps, the last to leave, had left the peninsula, McClellan going with them. The only Union forces left behind on the lower Chesapeake were troops assigned as holding garrisons at Yorktown, Fortress Monroe, Newport News, and at Norfolk.

Diversity of Vessel Control During the Peninsular Campaign: The Quartermaster, Commissary, Medical, and Aeronautics Departments

During the Peninsular Campaign of 1862, the Quartermaster Department was responsible for chartering vessels which carried troops as well as those supplies which were the charge of the Quartermaster Department. The Quartermaster Department also had the responsibility for chartering vessels carrying Commissary Department supplies. A problem often arose after the vessels carrying commissary supplies arrived in a forward area. At such time, the vessels came under the control of the senior commissary officer present in that area. Within his post analysis report of the campaign, the chief commissary officer explained how his department's system worked in relationship to vessels.

> ...During the Peninsular Campaign we [the Commissary Department] assumed control over all vessels laden with subsistence stores, and kept in reserve for emergencies several propellers [steamers] so laden, using them besides for towing purposes when required. In very many cases the officers of the department superintended in person and gave all necessary orders for making up tows and changing the location of vessels from one depot to another.[44]

The result of this arrangement was that on the peninsula, an inordinately large number of vessels were held over for warehousing and other duties, thus removing them from the long haul transport train. This placed a strain on the ability of the quartermasters to keep supplies flowing into the area in an orderly manner. There were also some of the same problems on the peninsula that Colonel Parsons was finding so vexing on the western rivers -- particularly the taking over of vessels by divisional and corps commanders for their own headquarters use. Another detriment to the orderly flow of shipping arose from the assignment of vessels to the Army Medical Director. Once such an assignment was made, the quartermasters lost the use of those vessels.

Thanks to the communication system established by the Army's Military Telegraph Service, a reasonable knowledge of ship arrivals and departures was maintained by the quartermasters. Overall, considering the mix in responsibilities and the high volume of shipping which was needed by the Quartermaster, Commissary, and Medical departments, things seem to have been reasonably well managed during the total 5-month involvement with the campaign.

Although credit for the assembly of transports has commonly been attributed to Assistant Secretary of War John Tucker -- probably because of Tucker's own written accounts of those events -- the individual who in actuality held the initial responsibility for gathering that shipping was Rufus Ingalls who was assisted by

Henry C. Hodges. Ingalls was at the time the deputy to Colonel Stewart Van Vliet, who was Chief Quartermaster for Operations in the War Department. Ingalls had served in that capacity since July of 1861. He had a monumental job. During the height of the campaign, he reported to Van Vliet that the volume of vessels being employed on a constant basis had climbed to seventy-one sidewheel steamers totaling 29,071 burden tons; fifty-seven propeller steamers totaling 9,824 burden tons; one hundred eighty-seven sail schooners, brigs, and barks, totaling 36,634 burden tons. Altogether, this had come to three hundred fifteen self-propelled vessels together with ninety barges -- in all, a total of four hundred five bottoms of 86,278 tons burden.[45] Van Vliet made the interesting comment in his own report of the campaign that although each man consumes "three pounds of provisions a day, every horse [consumes] twenty-six pounds of forage." What he did not explain in his report was that the provisions for the troops were, for the most part, in a concentrated form, e.g., hardtack, coffee, and dehydrated vegetables, none of it taking up an inordinate amount of ship or wagon space. On the other hand, hay was very bulky, and large amounts of it were required to maintain animals in the field. An examination of the logistical problems associated with the maintenance of cavalry units gives the present day student of the Civil War a perspective as to why commanders in most Union Army high commands exhibited a lack of enthusiasm for large units of cavalry. (Appendix L discusses the problems connected with the procurement of hay and its shipment during the Civil War.) It has been estimated that at one point (July 20, 1862) the army on the peninsula counted seven thousand cavalry horses, five thousand artillery horses, and thirteen thousand draft horses and mules. All of these animals had been brought in on vessels, and once on the peninsula, the forage they would consume was also brought in by vessel.

In addition to the hay needs for the horses and mules were the forage requirements for the herds of beef which provided such a large part of a soldier's diet. Until slaughtered, these animals had to be well fed to keep their condition. This required huge quantities of hay, all shipped in by schooner or barge. At one point, McClellan's Commissary Department reported a herd of live cattle numbering 2,518 head.[46] Generally, beef cattle were marshaled at Washington and from there shipped to the peninsula aboard schooners under tow of tugs. The Commissary Department included a division which was devoted solely to managing the herds of beef cattle, beef being as important as hardtack in the diet of the army. As early as May 11, cattle were being stockpiled in corrals at Eltham on the Pamunkey River, having been offloaded there from towed schooners. The landing of the cattle was supervised by Captain John H. Woodward, the Civil War's equivalent of a trail boss. And trail these herds Woodward did, first taking some to Cumberland for distribution to the regiments there, and then on to White House where a huge corral had been built and where fresh stock originating from the cattle transports was held before being moved by road up to the consumer regiments. Once delivered to the troops, the cattle were butchered on the spot.[47]

Besides the Quartermaster and Commissary departments, the other significant user of vessels during the Peninsular Campaign was the Chief Surgeon and Medical Director for the Army of the Potomac, Charles J. Tripler. At the onset of the campaign, McClellan had ordered that steamers be made available as needed for transporting sick and wounded. In reality, at least in the opinion of many medical officers, "making available" did not always balance out with meeting needs. Tripler would complain of the inadequacy of the transports assigned to the care of the sick and wounded.

> ...many of them [the vessels] were unfit. Only two were fitted up, and I had not the means to fit more. I cannot afford the necessary details of medical officers for sick transports. Nurses, and particularly cooks, are not to be had. The bedding now on hand here is 2,524 blankets, 23 bed sacks, and 24 pillow ticks. I have this moment seen a bill of lading of 18 bales of blankets on board a transport in the river. The *ELM CITY* will be stationed here as a receiving ship for surgical cases and will receive four hundred. Another that will take two hundred will be ready at the end of the week.[48]

Conditions were not always so sparse on the vessels assigned to hospital duty. Some were more than adequately finished out for that service. In late May, the steamer *WILLIAM WHILDEN* arrived in front of Yorktown. Although on charter to the Quartermaster Department, she had been fitted out by the Sanitary Commission under the supervision of Dr. Henry H. Smith who, in more normal times, had served as the Surgeon General of the Commonwealth of Pennsylvania. A report on that vessel filed by Tripler described her equipment and the medical personnel she carried.

> [*WILLIAM WHILDEN* was] fitted up with bedding, stores, instruments, a corps of eighteen surgeons and dressers, and a full complement of Sisters of Charity for nurses. He [Doctor Smith] brought with him also the means of embalming the bodies of the dead....Soon after his arrival, the steamer *COMMODORE* was assigned to me by the Quartermaster Department. Doctor Smith took charge of her equipment and in a short time had her ready to receive nine hundred wounded. This vessel and the *WILLIAM WHILDEN* then became our receiving ships, one of which was to be constantly in position to receive the wounded.[49]

By April 20th, the transport *MASSACHUSETTS*, under the operation of the Quartermaster Department, was standing by at Fortress Monroe, ready to evacuate wounded. In early May, the *DANIEL WEBSTER NO. 1* was reported as being "somewhere" in the vicinity of the peninsula under the operation of the Sanitary Commission. At about this same time, the quartermasters assigned another vessel, the *OCEAN QUEEN*, to the Sanitary Commission. A fourth vessel, the *DONALDSON*, was scheduled to be utilized full time by the quartermasters for the transport of hospital supplies. It was authorized that whenever required, *DONALDSON* would assist in the transfer of wounded. At some point, probably either in late May or early June, the *KNICKERBOCKER* was placed under the army's charter to be utilized by the Sanitary Commission. A lack of military management authority over those ships which went under Sanitary Commission use could at times produce its share of problems. One such problem, both serious and ongoing in nature, was reported by Chief Medical Officer Tripler shortly after the campaign got into full stride.

The army being again in motion, more sick and a multitude of stragglers rushed in upon us. Our storeship and the hospital transports being up, I detailed the *DANIEL WEBSTER NO. 1* to convey a party of the worst cases to Boston. These men were ordered to be selected with great care from those in the hospital tents. Two hundred and sixty was the number to be received. Before one-half this number was sent from the hospital the ship was reported filled. Stragglers had rushed on board without authority and taken possession. I sent a brigade surgeon to expel them, but without avail. I then determined to send no more men from the peninsula on account of sickness if there were any means of avoiding it. Orders in relation to the selection of cases were useless. I am sure that hundreds of malingerers succeeded in deserting their colors on the hospital transports in spite of every effort of mine to prevent it. The regimental officers might have prevented it. I could not." [50]

In late June, the steamer *S. R. SPAULDING* was mentioned in dispatches as being regularly engaged in transporting wounded which she took aboard both at White House as well as at a hospital the army had established at Yorktown. Soon after this, the *LOUISIANA* was named as being in hospital use. Tripler had personally overseen her fitting out for that service.

While the aggregate number of wounded and sick evacuated by steamer from the peninsula is not accurately recorded, it most certainly was high. One battle alone, Fair Oaks, produced 3,580 Union wounded, most of whom were evacuated aboard steamers operating from White House.[51]

Charles S. Tripler was succeeded as the Army of the Potomac's Medical Director by Dr. Jonathan Letterman. In a report that Letterman would file regarding the movement of sick and wounded by transport, he made the claim that at one point in the campaign, ten transports had been assigned for the movement of wounded. He stated that during the transfer of operations from the York River over to the James River (when the hospital at White House was evacuated) 14,159 patients were shipped from White House by water. Some of these went to Fortress Monroe; others were transported directly to hospitals in the north. (In his report, Letterman neglected to mention the six hundred wounded who were left behind and taken captive by the Confederates.) Like Tripler before him, Letterman complained that the Medical Department's lack of control aboard the hospital ships had created great difficulty in separating out malingerers and deserters at the loading points. As proof of this, Letterman cited the case of three thousand patients who had arrived at Fortress Monroe from White House; many of them were found to be perfectly fit for duty and were ordered back to their regiments. Other reports which touched upon this form of malingering described how some men employed bloody bandages in an effort to gain entrance upon the hospital ships.

There was yet another use of shipping during the Peninsular Campaign, this one a bit unique. During 1861, under the instigation of the President, the War Department established the Department of Aeronautics under the leadership and direction of Professor Thaddeus S. C. Lowe. Lowe was a lighter than air balloon inventor whose balloons were to become the elevated eyes of the Union Army. Lowe was given the pay of a colonel but was never commissioned. The Department of Aeronautics was placed under the supervisory wing of the Topographic Engineers; but as the war progressed, it operated more or less autonomously, reporting directly to the commanding general of the particular field army to which Lowe and his observation balloons were assigned. During the Peninsular Campaign, that authority was, of course, George McClellan.

As gatherers of intelligence for McClellan, Lowe's balloons proved so effective that the general asked for and received special appropriations to equip the Department of Aeronautics with a total of seven balloons along with the winches and other apparatus needed for their operations. Although they were normally launched and controlled from land, the balloons were often transported by steamer to designated launching positions. One steamer so employed was the tug *ROTARY*. On at least one occasion, a balloon winch was fastened to the deck of the *ROTARY's* assigned barge. The balloon was raised, and the *ROTARY* towed it up and down the James River while observations were made from the balloon's gondola which floated aloft at an elevation of one thousand feet.[52]

Late Summer and Fall, 1862

With the conclusion of the Peninsular Campaign, the need for water transport diminished dramatically within the eastern theater of war. This curtailment was explained by Brigadier General Daniel H. Rucker who at the time was in charge of the Quartermaster Department's depot at Washington City.

> On the 4th of September 1862, Captain James M. Robinson, Assistant Quartermaster, USV, was ordered to report to me for duty, and was at once placed in charge of receiving and issuing forage, relieving Captain Dana, who remained in charge of the transportation department, which had by that date attained such a magnitude as to require the exclusive attention of the officer in charge. About the middle of September the work of unloading the vessels in which the supplies for the Army of the Potomac had been stored during the Peninsular Campaign was commenced. This was a long and laborious undertaking, as many of them contained assorted cargoes, articles of all kinds being mingled in the utmost confusion. The different classes of stores were carefully separated and turned over to their appropriate departments, additional buildings were erected for the protection and preservation of regimental and private property, and in a comparatively short time the fleet, which at one time was so large as almost to interdict the safe navigation of the river, entirely disappeared.[53]

The absence of shipping activity as described by Rucker related only to that which had been in support of McClellan. Movement of supply by water continued in support of the Federal army in the Washington perimeter. In any event, the lull turned out to be but a temporary respite. Rucker would later report that on the 14th of November the Army of the Potomac, then under the command of Major General Ambrose Burnside, was ordered to reoccupy Falmouth and vicinity on the western side of the Potomac. Arrangements were made to rebuild the wharves and storehouses at Aquia Creek which had been destroyed by fire on the occasion of their earlier abandonment. Barges were sent there to serve as temporary landings, and material was furnished with which to construct the necessary buildings. The subject of water transportation had again become one of importance. However, in utilizing Aquia Creek, which was a shallow estuary, it was necessary to employ only the lightest draft vessels. This limitation, did not enhance the efficiency of supply movement from there.[54]

Lee Invades the North

At the beginning of September 1862, the fifty-five thousand man Confederate Army of Northern Virginia under General Robert E. Lee marched northward toward the Potomac and crossed that river upstream from Harper's Ferry. Major General George B. McClellan, now in command of the defenses of Washington, moved northward through Frederick, Maryland, with the intent of blocking Lee.

At Turner's Gap and Crampton's Gap, two of Lee's divisions temporarily halted McClellan. This gave the part of Lee's army under Lieutenant General Thomas J. Jackson time to encircle Harper's Ferry with artillery emplaced on the heights along the Maryland side of the Potomac. That having been accomplished, the 12,000-man Union garrison there was forced to surrender. Jackson's main force then marched to join Lee who was by now in the vicinity of Sharpsburg, Maryland, on the Antietam Creek. When Jackson rejoined, Lee's total troop strength was about half that under McClellan -- hardly an optimistic outlook for the Southern side.

At Antietam, the two armies clashed. If McClellan had managed it differently, Antietam (or Sharpsburg) was a battle which could have ended the war. However, he committed his troops in a piecemeal manner rather than in a consolidated massive assault which in all probability would have succeeded. McClellan did win the battle -- but only at great cost. Casualties in dead and seriously wounded on both sides counted to 23,150. Another 3,043 were listed as missing and were never accounted for. In all, this was approximately 22% of those committed to battle, losses for each side being about equal. In light of the blood spilled, Antietam stands as the most tragic single day in American military history.[55] The day after the battle, Lee withdrew back across the Potomac. McClellan experienced some difficulty in moving up his resupply by rail following the Battle of Antietam. The difficulty became apparent on September 17 when the convergence of too many trains created a traffic jam. The time spent in sorting out the mess was perhaps the major reason why McClellan did not follow up his victory over Lee through pursuit of the Confederate Army across the Potomac on the day after the battle.[56]

McClellan's failure to pursue Lee resulted in his relief from command. His replacement would be Major General Ambrose E. Burnside.

~

As a result of Lee's eviction from Northern territory, together with Lincoln's conviction that the time had now come, the President issued an Executive Order which was preliminary to the Emancipation Proclamation. This Executive Order, dated September 22, 1862, stated that effective January 1, 1863, slaves in areas under a state of rebellion with the United States were to be declared forever free. The effect was electric in much of the North. From then on, at least in many circles, including much of the Union Army, the war became a crusade. As for the Negro: Whenever he had the opportunity, he flocked to the Union banner.

The South was now faced with the harsh reality that this war was to be a fight for survival if the Confederacy wished to remain politically independent from the United States.

---

[1]   Aboard the *USS CONGRESS* on temporary assignment at the time of that naval vessel's loss were two officers and eighty-seven men of Company D of the 99th New York Infantry Regiment. Appendix I contains a summarization of the history of the 99th New York. In that summary is a description of Company D's role as marines and gunners on the *USS CONGRESS*, starting in January 1862 to the date of that ship's destruction.

[2]   *Official Records of the Union and Confederate Navies in the War of the Rebellion,* (Washington, DC: Government Printing Office, 1894 - 1917), Series I, Volume 7, p 135.

[3]   *War of the Rebellion: Official Records of the Union and Confederate Armies,* (Washington, DC: Government Printing Office, 1880 - 1900). Facsimile Ed: (Harrisburg, PA: National Historical Society, 1971. Reprint. Historical Times, Inc., 1985), Series I, Volume 51, Part I, pp 548, 549.

[4]   *ORA*, I, 51, Part I, p 549. Although at the time the Union command did not know it, the Confederates had actually been considering an attack up the Potomac with the *CSS VIRGINIA*. In a letter sent from the Confederate Navy Dockyards at Gosport, Virginia, on February 28, Douglas F. Forrest wrote Jefferson Davis, President of the Confederate States, reporting on conferences with various Confederate naval officers who had suggested such an attack as being feasible. *ORN,* I, 7, pp 737-739.

[5]   Alexander C. Brown, *Juniper Waterway, A History of the Albemarle and Chesapeake Canal,* (Charlottesville, VA: University of Virginia Press, 1981). Also General Rush C. Hawkins, "Early Coast Operations in North Carolina, *Battles and Leaders*, I, p 657. The 1860s descriptions of the canal route can be geographically confusing in that the names of certain locations and water courses, especially those given by Hawkins, differ from those shown in *Atlas to Accompany the Official Records of the Union and Confederate Armies,* (Washington, DC: Government Printing Office, 1891-1895). For instance: Hawkins references as the "Currituck Canal" the southern portion of the Albemarle and Chesapeake Canal shown in *Atlas, ORA* which connects the Currituck Sound on the north to the North River on the canal's southern end. Additionally, Hawkins misnames the part of the Albemarle and Chesapeake Canal from where it proceeds from its southern point at Pungo Point to Great Bridge, Virginia, and thence from there into the southern branch of the Elizabeth River to Norfolk Harbor. Hawkins calls that portion the "Dismal Swamp Canal." In fact, the Dismal Swamp Canal was then and still is an entirely different water course being a canal which runs from Norfolk via Deep Creek to South Mills. Hawkins refers to the blocking of the "Currituck Canal" (meaning the southern branch of the Albemarle and Chesapeake Canal) as a Confederate enterprise when in fact that canal had been blocked in great part only the month before (April 1862) by the efforts of Lieutenant Flusser, USN. Obviously in his post-war writings of the circumstances involved, Hawkins had forgotten the Flusser Expedition of April 1862, an expedition which had caused a considerable delay in launching Hawkins's own reconnaissance that May. Flusser mentioned in his own report that some Confederate effort had been expended toward blocking the canal, but that had taken place prior to his more thorough effort.

[6]   When Confederate officers began sifting through the bags of mail carried aboard the *ARROW*, they discovered a letter dated May 12, 1863, marked "CONFIDENTIAL," and addressed to the Union military commander at New Berne. The letter was signed by one Augustus S. Montgomery who from our own research does not seem to have had any official connection to either the Union Army or to any established intelligence network of that army. In the communication, Montgomery spoke of a plan (apparently of his own invention) for a slave insurrection throughout the entirety of the southern states which he (Montgomery) was scheduling for the first of the coming August. Montgomery included elaborate instructions for the recipient officer to mark "approved" and then to pass the letter along to other Union officers for their approval and action. The Confederate officers who discovered Montgomery's correspondence passed it along to Governor Vance of North Carolina who in turn sent it to General Robert E. Lee who then passed the letter on to Confederate Secretary of War, James A. Seddon. Although stating that he, "attached no great importance to the matter," Seddon forwarded a copy of the letter to the governors of all the Confederate states to alert them of such a possibility. Beyond that

date, we could find no further reference to the Montgomery letter within *ORA*. In Lee's letter of transmittal to Secretary Seddon, Lee said that he had no idea as to who the writer was. It appears likely that Augustus Montgomery was an eccentric freelancer and that despite his efforts, the matter of a Negro insurrection was not taken seriously by anyone outside of Montgomery himself. *ORA*, I, 18, pp 1067-1069, 1072.

[7]   *ORA*, I, 46, Part II, pp 196, 197.

[8]   The railroad bridge at Harper's Ferry was destroyed in May of 1861. *ORA*, I, 2, p 32. Some confusion seems to exist with many writers of this period as to the condition of the railroad bridge -- extant or missing? -- in the late winter of 1861-1862. This confusion probably stems from undated photographs taken during that general time frame. We have based our own understanding of the condition of the bridges at Harper's Ferry immediately following the reoccupation by Union troops during March of 1862 on a sketch which accompanied a written description of the place and found within the essay by Warren Lee Goss, "Campaigning To No Purpose," *Battles and Leaders*, II, pp 153-159. A later Signal Corps photograph, allegedly dated August 1862, shows a reconstructed railroad bridge which was erected on the old bridge foundations.

[9]   *ORA*, I, 51, Part I, p 529. The Charleston mentioned by Banks was in the portion of western Virginia which had broken away to become the Union area of Kanawha. In 1863, Kanawha was approved for statehood, becoming West Virginia.

[10]   *ORA*, I, 5, pp 48, 49.

[11]   George Armroyd, *The Whole Internal Navigation of the United States*, (New York: Lenox Hill [Burt Franklin], 1830, reprint 1971).

[12]   Report No. 7, as reproduced within *ORA*, I, 11, Part I, p 157.

[13]   *ORA*, I, 51, Part I, p 514. See J. Russell Soley, "Early Operations on the Potomac River," *Battles and Leaders*, II, p 143 for a well written synopsis of the 1861-1862 Confederate gun blockade of the Potomac.

[14]   *ORA*, I, 5, p 50.

[15]   *ORA*, I, 11, Part I, p 157.

[16]   *ORA*, I, 5, p 46. Although one of the classifications within this report is for "schooners," it is apparent from the report of Captain Hodges that the "188 schooners" also encompassed a certain number of brigs and barks.

[17]   Although quartermaster reports allude to the transport of one hundred and ten thousand troops to the peninsula prior to the start of the actual campaign, McClellan's staff reported fifty-three thousand officers and men at hand there as of early April, with another thirty-two thousand still in transit -- totaling only eighty-five thousand in all. It is probable that the "one hundred ten thousand," which was the figure mentioned in the quartermaster reports, had included McDowell's men (thirty-five thousand) who were originally destined for the Peninsular Campaign but were never sent. *ORA*, I, 11, Part I, p 11.

[18]   Fortress Monroe was, and still is, nearly surrounded by water -- the Chesapeake to the east and south; Hampton Roads to the west. On its northern perimeter is an enclosed embayment known as Mill Creek, crossed in 1862 by a narrow causeway and bridge connecting the fortress area to the mainland. Immediately situated at the end of the causeway was the town of Hampton -- in 1862, a small port devoted to local use in normal times. It was at Hampton that the transports were unloaded.

[19]   *ORA*, I, 11, Part I, pp 6,7.

[20]   *ORA*, I, 11, Part I, pp 266-268.

[21]   *ORA*, I, 11, Part I, p 164.

[22]   *ORA*, I, 51, Part I, p 560. Assorted sources list widely varying casualty rates surrounding the action near Winchester. One estimate enumerating the dead and wounded claims that only twenty-three percent of Jackson's total strength was affected.

[23]   "*Wharfhead*" is an older term for the more modern term of "*pierhead*." Both terms mean essentially the same, being defined as that part of a pier or wharf which is farthest from the shore connected to the shore by bridging. During the Civil War, both terms were used in reports, but wharfhead was a more common usage.

[24]   *ORA*, I, 11, Part I, p 135. It is interesting that this innovative development in over-the-beach equipment, consisting of the barge/wharf landing units was first developed at a place called Cheeseman's Creek, a location which is less than four miles from the present day US Army Transportation Center at Fort Eustis, Virginia. It is at Fort Eustis that the US Army Transportation Corps presently conducts research and development of over-the-beach equipment for the transfer of troops and their equipment onto hostile shores. It is also worthy of note that Alexander's wharfhead idea was a predecessor to the "Whales" (floating steel roadways) developed for the "Mulberry Harbors" concept which was utilized at the Normandy beachhead during the Allied landings of June of 1944. It is intriguing to speculate as to whether the designers of the World War II "Mulberries" had been aware of the 1862 ideas of Lieutenant Colonel Alexander.

[25]   *ORA*, I, 11, Part I, p 136.

[26]   *ORA*, I, 11, Part I, p 137. *ORN*, I, 7 has a number of reports dealing with the Navy's support of Franklin's landing which makes interesting reading.

27   *ORA*, I, 11, Part I, p 139.

28   The depth of the Pamunkey was earlier the subject of a report of May 23 by Colonel Stewart Van Vliet to Quartermaster General Meigs. *ORA*, I, 11, Part I, p 163. The report concerning the movement to White House and the situation existing there is to be found the same volume of the *ORA*, but on p 159.

29   James A. Huston, *The Sinews of War: Army Logistics, 1775-1953*, (Washington, DC: Government Printing Office, 1966), pp 220-222.

30   *ORN*, I, 7, pp 236-238.

31   Richard Wheeler, *Sword Over Richmond*, (New York: Harper and Row, 1986), p 175. Wheeler states that the reporter was with the Baltimore *American*.

32   *ORN*, I, 7, p 788.

33   *ORA*, I, 11, Part I, p 1032.

34   *ORA*, I, 11, Part I, p 160.

35   *ORA*, I, 11 Part I, p 71.

36   *ORA*, I, 11, Part I, p 72.

37   *ORA*, I, 11, Part I, pp 80, 81.

38   *ORA*, I, 11, Part I, p 80.

39   *ORA*, I, 11, Part I, p 83. Major General John Pope had been transferred from the west and was given command of the Union Army of Virginia on July 26, 1862. McClellan retained command status over the Army of the Potomac until October of 1862.

40   *ORA*, I, 11, Part I, pp 84, 85.

41   The additional transports which Halleck had wrongly believed were assigned to the evacuation of McClellan's army from the peninsula were actually at the time assigned to the support of Major General Burnside.

42   *ORA*, I, 11, Part I, p 87.

43   Dispatch addressed to Major General H. W. Halleck from Major General George B. McClellan dated August 12, 1862, 12 noon, Headquarters, Army of the Potomac. See *ORA*, I, 11, Part I, p 89.

44   "Report of Chief Commissary," *ORA*, I, 11, Part I, p 176.

45   "Report of Brigadier General Stewart Van Vliet, Chief Quartermaster, Army of the Potomac," *ORA*, I, 11, Part I, p 158. Following the Peninsular Campaign of 1862, Colonel Van Vliet was promoted to brigadier general, but his promotion was not confirmed by the Senate.

46   *ORA*, I, 11, Part I, p 170.

47   A number of descriptions of cattle butchering yards are found within Medical Department and Sanitary Commission reports. These reports paint a revolting scene of poor sanitation which by its ill effects must have seriously added to the health problems of the army.

48   *ORA*, I, 11, Part I, pp 200, 201.

49   *ORA*, I, 11, Part I, p 181. The United States Sanitary Commission was established in June of 1861 as a charitable organization. Its president was Henry W. Bellows, the pastor of All Souls Unitarian Church in New York City. The Commission's major funding was derived through the efforts of seven thousand aid society branches scattered throughout the North. They held "Sanitary Fairs" and used as operating revenues proceeds obtained from fair admission fees as well as from the sale of donated goods. Throughout the war years, the Commission raised around seven million dollars and acted as the distribution agency for twice that amount in donated supplies. Assisting in the aid of the sick and wounded during the Civil War was another charitable organization known as the United States Christian Commission. Although not providing nursing or surgical care, as was the case with the Sanitary Commission, the Christian Commission maintained special diet kitchens and provided a great quantity of food stuffs for military patients.

50   *ORA*, I, 11, Part I, p 186.

51   *ORA*, I, 11, Part I, p 188.

52   *ORA*, III, 3, p 291. Lowe's report on his department as submitted for the period August 1861 through to May 1863 is contained in *ORA*, III, 3, pp 252-319.

53   *ORA*, I, 51, Part I, pp 1096, 1097.

54   *ORA*, I, 51, Part I, p 1097.

55   Counting together the Union and Confederate dead and wounded, the casualties at Antietam totaled slightly more than the aggregate of American casualties resulting from the Revolution, the War of 1812, and the Spanish-American War.

56   An account of the train jams of the B & O and on the Cumberland Valley railroads is to be found in Huston, pp 204-206.

PART IV

CAMPAIGNS IN
TENNESSEE AND KENTUCKY
AUGUST 1862-FEBRUARY 1863

The Summer and Fall

During late August of 1862, Braxton Bragg, the Confederate general in command of the Army of the Tennessee, launched an invasion northward from Chattanooga which was aimed at occupying the entirety of Tennessee and Kentucky. In conjunction with Bragg's move, another Confederate force under Brigadier General E. Kirby Smith marched out from Knoxville, Tennessee. Bragg and Smith were to converge their armies in a joint drive aimed against Louisville on the Ohio River. Together, both forces mustered about forty thousand men.

To combat this dual threat, Major General Don Carlos Buell, the Union commander on the Tennessee, rushed his troops north from Decatur and Bridgeport (both places on the Tennessee River). His aim was to cut Bragg and Smith off before they could do the harm intended which, if successful, would have split the Union longitudinally. Following weeks of maneuver and counter-maneuver, Buell finally clashed in strength with Bragg and Kirby Smith who by then had managed to come together at a town called Perryville in central Kentucky. That confrontation took place on October 8 and resulted in about equal punishment to both sides. The battle did, however, prove decisive in the Union's favor in that it forced Bragg, with a now-consolidated Confederate command, to abandon further offensive moves and withdraw into east Tennessee.

That Winter

In December, Bragg again moved north, this time to Murfreesborough where he established defensive positions. (Murfreesborough is on the Stone River, southeast of Nashville.)

Major General William S. Rosecrans, who had recently relieved Buell of command of the Union forces in Tennessee, had made his headquarters at Nashville. While there, he received orders to take the offensive against Bragg. The day following Christmas, Rosecrans started toward Murfreesborough. On December 31, he was poised in front of Bragg's defensive lines. A major battle began and lasted for three days. Bragg ended up with a slight edge; but his limited success was not sufficient to make him believe that he could hold if Rosecrans came at him a second time. Bragg's position possessed little in the way of terrain advantage, and his line of communication with Chattanooga was precarious. Acting wisely, Bragg chose to withdraw toward Chattanooga.

~

The supply apparatus which had maintained Rosecrans's force at Nashville, and which in fact was to maintain him for the entire time that he operated north of the Tennessee River, included both railroad and steamboats. In order to keep Rosecrans's army supplied, the Quartermaster Department had already placed a total of sixty-six steamboats into continuous service on the Cumberland River. Now that the Federals had fought a major battle, their need for replenishment had increased substantially. Bragg knew full well that if Rosecrans felt that his logistics were threatened at a point anywhere to his rear, the chances of him following after the retreating Confederate army would be lessened. To harass Rosecrans's rear, Bragg sent off Brigadier General Joseph Wheeler with two brigades of cavalry. Wheeler was ordered to damage as much as he could of the Federal lines of communication coming into Nashville from the north. Wheeler's efforts were vigorous; they continued past mid-January. Among those who suffered from Wheeler's cavalry were some who were normally considered immune from attack under the established rules of warfare.[1]

Following the battle on the Stone River, the Union wounded were first taken to Nashville. Those with wounds serious enough to warrant further evacuation were sent to Louisville, Kentucky, by steamer, via the Cumberland River and then the Ohio River.

The *HASTINGS*, *PARTHENIA*, and *TRIO* left Nashville on January 13, all of them carrying wounded. For purposes of identification, all were flying the hospital flag, a symbol which was intended to assure safe passage and which up to that time had been respected by the Confederates. In any event, Wheeler's brigade was not thought at that time to still be operating on either bank of the Cumberland. That was an optimistic prognosis which turned out to be wrong. One of Wheeler's regiments under the command of Colonel William B. Wade was in the vicinity of the Harpeth Shoals on the Cumberland, downriver from Nashville. Wade and his men had come into possession of substantial stocks of whiskey somewhere along the way, perhaps captured from the cargo of supply transports whose captains had jettisoned their cargoes in an attempt to outdistance the Confederate cavalry. The consumption of that whiskey by the troopers was to result in one of the more unforgivable episodes of what was beginning to become a conflict waged without charity.

Aboard the *HASTINGS*, in charge of 260 wounded officers and men, was Union Army Chaplain M. P. Gaddis. When the *HASTINGS* came into view, some of Wade's men, yelling from the shore, ordered that the vessel be brought over to the bank. Not sure of how to respond, the steamer's civilian pilot asked Gaddis to assume command, a request that Gaddis accepted. The chaplain shouted over to the enemy riders that the steamer was loaded with wounded, and that because of their critical conditions, the steamer could not stop. When he was answered with a volley of rifle fire, an alarmed Gaddis ordered the pilot to round into the current and go against the bank. The current in the river near the Harpeth Shoals was at the time unusually swift, and the steamer answered her rudder slowly, a dereliction which the rebels punished by letting go with two rounds from their horse-drawn cannon. This seriously injured one man and created a state of terror among the helpless wounded. No sooner had the *HASTINGS* come to rest against the bank than Wade (who by now was incoherently drunk) led a mob of men over the steamer's rail to begin a rampage of looting which included the taking of rations, personal possessions, and even the blankets off the wounded, and in not a few cases their outer clothing. Gaddis's pleas to desist were ignored. He found only one rebel officer sober enough and willing to try to bring some order into the situation. But it was a try only; the looting continued.

Prior to the capture of the *HASTINGS*, the *PARTHENIA* and *TRIO* had arrived in the vicinity and were now also ordered against the bank. Even though a heavy snow was falling, Wade's men ordered their cargo of wounded off for transfer to *HASTINGS*. Despite the rampage of the cavalrymen aboard *HASTINGS*, none of the rebels, least of all the drink-sodden Wade, had so far noticed that underlying the wounded were bales of cotton. Upon finally seeing it, Wade ordered that all the wounded be taken ashore so the cotton could be destroyed by burning it on the bank. Gaddis refused point blank to allow this; and on his urging, one of the rebel officers rode off to find Wheeler. After he was located, Wheeler told the messenger to get Gaddis to agree that if the cotton was left aboard that it would be burned under Gaddis's personal supervision when the steamer reached Louisville. Gaddis readily agreed, and finally *HASTINGS*, loaded down with its own miserable passengers as well as those from the other two hospital steamers, was given permission to proceed to Louisville.[2]

Simultaneous with the giving of permission for *HASTINGS* to depart, steaming down the river came the *W. H. SIDELL*, an Army gunboat under the command of infantry Lieutenant William Van Dorn. To all appearances, it seemed that Van Dorn intended to engage the rebels; but to the amazement of Gaddis and probably the Confederates as well, she was swung into the opposite bank without opening fire. Then, indicating an apparent willingness to surrender, Van Dorn crossed his gunboat over to the enemy's side where the Confederates threw *W. H. SIDELL's* guns into the river and made preparations to set the gunboat afire along with the now emptied *PARTHENIA* and *TRIO*.[3] As the *HASTINGS's* pilot turned his steamboat into the current, those aboard were witness to the sight of fires beginning to consume *PARTHENIA*, *TRIO*, and the *W. H. SIDELL*.

A considerable uproar arose over the surrender of *W. H. SIDELL*, one inquiry being directed to the commander of the Mississippi Squadron by the Secretary of the Navy who was under the false impression that the gunboat was at the time being operated by the Navy's Mississippi Squadron. Rear Admiral Porter was quick to set the record straight, at the same time getting in some digs against the Army.

U. .S. Mississippi Squadron
January 29, 1863

Honorable Gideon Welles, Secretary of the Navy, Washington
Sir:
    In answer to your communication, asking information about a gunboat burned on the Cumberland River, I have the honor to state that the vessel mentioned did not

belong to this squadron. She was called the *SIDELL**, and was, I believe, an old ferryboat, with a field piece on her.

The Army undertakes sometimes to get up an impromptu navy which generally ends by getting them into difficulty. There are five vessels of this squadron in the Cumberland and Tennessee rivers, which are detailed for convoy, and under the management of Lieutenant Commander LeRoy Fitch, who has until the late affair, kept the rivers open, and convoyed all vessels safely through.

I shall direct that no army vessels be allowed to ascend these rivers without a convoy, and I have detailed the *LEXINGTON*** and two more light-draft gunboats for the upper fleet. This will make forty guns on the Cumberland and Tennessee rivers. There are enough there now (twenty guns) to take care of these rivers, but the recklessness of the Army quartermasters is beyond anything I ever saw, and they employ persons who half the time are disloyal, and who throw these vessels purposely into the hands of the rebels. If the history of the Army quartermasters' proceedings out here were published, the world would not believe that there could be so much want of intelligence in the country.

I have the honor to be, very respectfully,

David D. Porter, Acting Rear Admiral
Commanding Mississippi Squadron[4]

*   *W. H. SIDELL*
** *USS*, commissioned Union naval vessel.

Despite the assurances to the Secretary that the Navy could keep both the Tennessee River and the Cumberland clear from enemy harassment, attacks continued by partisan units long after Wheeler's cavalry had withdrawn. A good deal of the security afforded steamers moving on the Cumberland was to be dependent on the Army's own efforts. One such effort was described as being in place in the area of the Harpeth Shoals during the following spring.

Brigadier General James A. Garfield, Chief of Staff:
I have barricaded the ferryboat *EXCELSIOR* with hay, and used it as a gunboat. Convoyed fleet above the Shoals with it; recovered the starboard gun from the wreck of the *SIDELL**; dispersed rebel band at the Shoals, who were waiting to fire on unprotected boats. Captured several of the men belonging to Woodward's command.

S. D. Bruce, Colonel, Commanding[5]

* *W. H. SIDELL*

In an attempt to provide a better measure of security on the upper Mississippi and on the Ohio, the Army armed a number of steamboats and temporarily classified them as "gunboats." They were:

	Armament
ALLEN COLLYER[1]	one 12-pounder
ARGYLE	one 32-pounder
BELFAST	one 12-pounder
COTTAGE	two 6-pounders
EMMA DUNCAN	one 12-pounder
G. A. GURLEY	two 12-pounders
GUNBOAT NO. 1	three 12-pounders
IZETTA	one 32-pounder
NEW ERA	one 12-pounder
NEW YORK	one 12-pounder
R. B. HAMILTON	one 12-pounder
W. A. HEALEY	one 12-pounder

[1] Correct spelling is *ALLEN COLLIER*

It is not clear from the record as to whether the Quartermaster Department or the regional army commands operated these gunboats. Crews were civilian in makeup, except for the gunners who would have been military personnel assigned to each vessel. The commercially operated mail boats *IDA MAY, FLORENCE, GLIDE,* and *SUNNYSIDE* were also equipped with cannon at this time.[6]

[1] Report No. 28, Washington City, October 15, 1865, which accompanied the Report of the Quartermaster General, submitted to the Secretary of War, as printed in Executive Documents, House of Representatives, 1st Session, 39th Congress.

[2] *War of the Rebellion: Official Records of the Union and Confederate Armies,* (Washington, DC: Government Printing Office, 1880 - 1900). Facsimile Ed: (Harrisburg, PA: National Historical Society, 1971. Reprint. Historical Times, Inc., 1985), Series I, Volume 20, Part I, pp 980, 981. In addition to his agreement to destroy the cotton after arrival in Louisville, Gaddis also had to pledge that the *HASTINGS* would not again be used as a military transport. Additionally, those wounded who were capable had to sign pledges that they would not return to duty unless exchanged.

[3] A crewman from the *W. H. SIDELL* was to later report that the reason its commander had surrendered without a shot being fired in the direction of the enemy was that the guns could not be raised high enough in elevation to reach the enemy on the opposite bank. Report of January 14, 1863, signed by R. B. Mitchell, to be found in *ORA,* I, 20, Part I, p 983. This same report stated that the civilian pilot had left the wheel which was why the gunboat had initially swung into the opposite bank.

[4] *Official Records of the Union and Confederate Navies in the War of the Rebellion.,* (Washington, DC: Government Printing Office, 1894 - 1917), Series I, Volume 24, p 19. With the exception of one or two suspect cases, we have found nothing to substantiate David D. Porter's charge of steamboat crews purposely giving their vessels into the hands of the enemy.

[5] *ORA,* I, 23, Part II, p 240.

[6] *ORA,* I, 52, Part I, pp 281, 282.

PART V

FURTHER EVENTS
ON THE WESTERN RIVERS

THE MISSISSIPPI MARINE BRIGADE

A Concept for an Amphibious Brigade

The month of October 1862 on the western rivers had marked the reorganization of the Ellet Ram Fleet which was incorporated as an integral part of a new amphibious organization to be known as the Mississippi Marine Brigade. The concept for such a brigade has been most often credited to Alfred W. Ellet. (In the late fall of 1862 Ellet was promoted from Lieutenant Colonel to Brigadier General of Volunteers.) Yet by way of hard evidence, Rear Admiral David D. Porter appears to have played the instigating role toward the brigade's establishment. Prior to his taking over command of the Western Gunboat Flotilla (renamed Upper Mississippi Squadron under the Navy), Porter was well aware of the interservice conflicts that the Ellets had created with the presence of their rams on the western rivers. Porter also seems to have been aware of the political influence of the Ellet family which, as it would turn out, reached as far as the White House. To a considerable extent, the future interrelationships between the Navy Department and the War Department in the western theater, if not elsewhere as well, would depend on how Porter resolved the conflicts of command. After having a talk with Alfred W. Ellet to gauge the full situation with the rams and to avail himself of Ellet's own opinions, Porter expressed his ideas for a resolution of the problem in a telegram he sent to Secretary of the Navy Gideon Welles, dated October 21, 1862.

> Sir:
>
> Before leaving Washington I suggested to the President and General McClernand the propriety of forming a naval brigade, consisting of one thousand infantry, one hundred cavalry, and a full battery of artillery, to be formed from regiments now in service, and to operate exclusively with this squadron.
>
> I have now to suggest a plan of organization which will at once ensure the highest degree of efficiency to the brigade proposed, and remove all difficulties in regard to the transfer of the Ram Fleet, by placing Colonel [Alfred] Ellet in command of this force.
>
> Colonel Ellet thinks he can promptly raise the men by enlistment, if authorized to do so, and this would be a far preferable way of procuring them, since there will be no difficulties arising from regimental officers already commissioned in the

appointment of just such officers in the brigade as the peculiar nature of the service demands.

This brigade will be invaluable, and will enable us to effectually operate against the numerous guerrilla bands and other scattered rebel forces along these rivers.

Without such a force constantly with the vessels cruising on the river we are unable to reach these bands, not having men enough in the crews of the vessels to land and follow them into the interior in their retreats out of the reach of the fire of the gunboats, nor can we march against them when informed of their camps near the streams and attempt those surprises which, with a ready force, would be so effective. It is now invariably found that in all attempts to procure a force from the Army posts nearest to the points where these bands are known to be, it arrives on the field only to find that the rebels are already many miles away and beyond pursuit.

The appointment of Colonel Ellet secures to the squadron the services of a gallant and highly meritorious officer in a field for which he is specially qualified, and does justice to him for his past services, while it secures greater efficiency in the Ram Fleet, as a more perfect organization in the hands of trained Navy officers and greater harmony will be experienced in all naval operations in consequence.[1]

It is somewhat unclear from that which Porter proposed to Welles as to whose direct operation the Ellet vessels might come under. If Porter was proposing that these rams (or armed transports) would be under the tactical command of naval officers, then he had badly misgauged Alfred W. Ellet's own ideas on the matter since Ellet wanted full operational control of all the vessels integral to the Brigade as well as tactical control while on operations. What Ellet actually ended up with was half the pie. Although the vessels of the old Ram Fleet were to remain with the Army, they would, to a much greater extent than before, come under the purview of the Navy. On November 7, 1862, Ellet received explicit orders as to the future relationship of his rams with the Navy's newly formed Upper Mississippi Squadron.

> Executive Mansion
> Ordered, that Brigadier General Ellet report to Rear Admiral Porter for instructions, and act under his direction until otherwise ordered by the War Department.
>
> Abraham Lincoln[2]

Discussions concerning the future for the Ellet rams had apparently gone well beyond the confines of mere military parameters. It was clear that neither the President nor the Secretary of the Navy wanted any redundancy of the problems which had arisen as a result of the independent attitude of the founder of the Ram Fleet, the now deceased Charles Ellet, Jr. The Lincoln order was the end result of what had been an interservice struggle. The essence of the difficulties encountered over the Ellet rams was detailed by Assistant Secretary of the Navy in a letter he sent on November 8, to Rear Admiral Porter.

> After long discussions, which culminated in arguments pro and con before the President yesterday in full Cabinet meeting, we beat our friend Edwin M. Stanton and the order signed by the President placing Brigadier General Ellet under your orders was signed by the President and a copy forwarded you by yesterday's mail. The proposition is yours, and I presume the War Department will fit it out and act in

good faith. I must confess to little confidence even in this arrangement, but as you proposed it we could do no better. If Ellet is the right kind of man all will go well, and if it goes wrong, Stanton will say it arose from placing him under a Navy officer. He says the western people have no confidence in them, [presumably meaning the Navy] and that they do not know how to get along with river men. Stanton lost his temper, so we beat him. The cool man always wins. Let me impress upon you to be incontrovertibly right in case of a difference with the Army. The President is just and sagacious. Give us success; nothing else wins. We have written to Stanton, asking him to pay off the indebtedness of the Western fleet to your paymasters, who can credit it to the men. We are making all the appointments you suggest -- chief engineers and all. The Secretary agrees to your making mortar boats if indispensable, but Stanton says the Army will have Vicksburg before Christmas. I believe we have attended to everything but the wharf boat, which I will try to get, but don't turn over anything you really wish to the Army if you ever wish it again....[3]

Authorization for the creation of the Mississippi Marine Brigade seems to have been issued in a somewhat piecemeal fashion. Ellet received authority to recruit as early as October 1862, but specific operational authority and funding does not seem to have been in his hands until December. The Brigade was to be recruited and trained at Saint Louis under Alfred W. Ellet's personal supervision. During this period, the rams operated more or less independently on various missions, most of them related to partisan suppression. These missions occurred both north and south of Memphis on the Mississippi River.

Recruiting the Brigade

The Mississippi Marine Brigade was to consist primarily of military personnel although the vessels' operating crews would mainly remain civilian in make up. The military personnel of the organization were recruited both from civilian life and from among soldiers recuperating from wounds or illnesses at Army hospitals. To some further extent, the Brigade was fleshed out by the inclusion of small infantry detachments which previously had been assigned temporarily to the Ram Fleet as riflemen and gunners.[4] The authority given Alfred W. Ellet to recruit convalescent soldiers would become a source of much ill feeling within the Army which was directed against Ellet and his brigade. Regimental commanders, who because of that recruiting policy had lost some of their men, felt -- and with a good deal of justification -- that they were being hijacked of men who otherwise would have been returned to their regiments. To fully appreciate the potential impact of Ellet's recruiting of hospitalized convalescents, one only has to examine the regimental roster of a typical unit which served on the Mississippi during the war. At any given time, as many as a quarter of a regiment might have been hospitalized. Imagine the outrage of a regimental commander who, on a given day, found that a substantial part of his regiment had been taken away from him. The authority for Ellet's unusual form of recruiting had come directly from the War Department. When that authority was questioned by other commanders, Ellet asked that the War Department put the authorization into an official dispatch.

War Department
December 21, 1862

To Brigadier General A. W. Ellet
    Saint Louis, Missouri: --
The Secretary of War authorizes you to recruit from convalescents in hospital. General Curtis will muster out such as enlist in your brigade. An officer will be sent immediately to pay bounty, etc.

H. W. Halleck, General in Chief[5]

One of the recruiting posters which Alfred W. Ellet distributed in the Saint Louis area must have characterized enlistment in the Brigade as a rather attractive alternative when balanced against the norm of military life.

THE MISSISSIPPI MARINE BRIGADE

Convalescent Soldiers -- Hurrah Boys!
    Brigadier General Ellet having obtained permission from the War Department to recruit convalescent soldiers from any hospital, is organizing a Mississippi Marine Brigade. A regiment is just organizing in Saint Louis, and promises to become the most renowned in the service.
    It is raised for and becomes a part of the above Brigade, commanded by Brigadier General A. W. Ellet, well known commander of the Mississippi Ram Fleet. The 'Ellet Scouts' will be furnished good quarters and transports fitted out expressly for them, where they will keep all their valuables, clothing, stores, etc., and with other parts of the Brigade, (consisting of infantry, cavalry, and artillery), on similar vessels, will keep company and act in concert with the Mississippi Ram Fleet. [The ram fleet became organizationally integrated as an element of the Brigade and was henceforth no longer a separate command.] No long, hard marches, camping without tents or food, or carrying heavy knapsacks, but good, comfortable quarters, and good facilities for cooking at all times.
    The 'Ellet Scouts' are expected to see plenty of active service on the Mississippi River and its tributaries in keeping it clear of rebel guerrillas, and securing to the public the free and safe navigation of the great highway. They are expected to act promptly and at short notice, in concert with some of the rams and gunboats at distant points, with secrecy and dispatch; and landing, to operate on shore in an attack, in the rear, or a sudden assault.
    This Brigade will become famous in the annals of the Mississippi river warfare, as the Ram Fleet has already done. Now is the time if ever you can serve your country and consult your own comfort at the same time. Every soldier re-enlisting in this Brigade is entitled to a final settlement, and all pay in arrears will be paid up promptly, besides two dollars premium, one month's pay in advance, and twenty-five dollars bounty for re-enlisting.
    Published by order of Brigadier General A. W. Ellet

Captain W. H. Wright, Recruiting Officer

The recruiting theme for the Brigade focused from the start upon the special advantages. It neglected, as recruiters so often do, the more unpleasant aspects of service life. One handbill which Ellet had distributed around Saint Louis was fairly typical of the technique used:

THE PROPOSED SERVICE IS ESPECIALLY ATTRACTIVE TO OLD SOLDIERS
IT HAS THE FOLLOWING ADVANTAGES:

1. There are no trenches to dig.
2. There are no rebel houses to guard.
3. There is no picket duty to perform.
4. There is no danger of camps in the mud, but always a chance to sleep under cover.
5. There is no chance of short rations.
6. Command will always be kept together.

Organization and Training of the Brigade

Some omissions and a general vagueness as to command structure within the history of the Ellet Ram Fleet and the succeeding Mississippi Marine Brigade is the unfortunate result of the disappearance of a great part of the unit's records which were lost while in transit to Washington after the Brigade was disbanded in January of 1865. (Warren D. Crandall, an officer who served in both the ram fleet and the Brigade, wrote a unit history, published in 1907, in which the loss of those records is discussed.) Luckily, copies of a number of Brigade orders were kept in the personal files of the organization's officers; these came to light in 1907 when Crandall put together the unit's operational history. George E. Currie was one such contributor. Currie, who served initially as a lieutenant on Ellet's staff, later rising to lieutenant colonel, described the organization and training of the Brigade within Crandall's history.

> During this period of organization, the new command was quartered at Benton Barracks, which comprised the Fair Grounds, in the northwestern outskirts of the city [Saint Louis]. There the men were collected, uniformed, and equipped, and, under the command of Lieutenant Colonel George E. Currie, a master of discipline and tactics, were daily exercised during the winter of 1862-1863 in company, regimental, and brigade drill.[6]

By December 1862, the Brigade had been brought to full strength.[7] It totaled 1,035 enlisted men, broken down into the following unit categories:

Number of companies	Number of men
Six infantry, organized	527 men
Four cavalry	168 men
One artillery	140 men and six guns, light artillery.
	200 hundred recruits just received

It appears that Ellet's strength, as he announced it to the Secretary of War, did not include the permanent guard units which had been previously assigned to the rams and which were still serving on the rams at the time of this report. Later, in February 1863, under Special Order 69, these guard units would become part of the Brigade.

Washington, DC
February 11, 1863

Special Order No. 69
        Extract XXII. The detachments from the 59th and 63rd Regiments Illinois Volunteers, now serving with the Mississippi Ram Fleet, are hereby permanently detached from their respective commands, and transferred to the Mississippi Marine Brigade....[8]

Ellet also did not enumerate the 6-month enrolled civilian employees who served as crews on the rams, the armed transports, and the support vessels. Ellet seems only to have addressed those personnel who were in Saint Louis in training at the time and who were to comprise the Brigade's assault landing forces.

The Brigade's *AUTOCRAT*, *BEN J. ADAMS*, *BALTIC*, *DIANA*, and *E. H. FAIRCHILD* had already undergone alterations specific to their new function as armed transports. The steamboat *WOODFORD*, which would serve as the Brigade's hospital boat, was in the refit stage at a Saint Louis shipyard.[9] By early March, the Brigade was being readied to leave Saint Louis for the Vicksburg area to join forces with Porter's squadron. A sixth transport, the *JOHN RAINE*, was scheduled to wait at Saint Louis for the two hundred additional recruits mentioned in Ellet's report but who were to finish their training stint. *SWITZERLAND*, *LANCASTER*, and *QUEEN OF THE WEST* were then on detached duty on the central Mississippi but would later rejoin. Smaller vessels which would serve the Brigade as tugs and towboats were being overhauled near Saint Louis and were expected to join the Brigade shortly. These were *LIONESS*, *T. D. HORNER*, *BELLE DARLINGTON*, *ALF CUTTING*, and *DICK FULTON*. All the vessels of the Brigade (except for the tugs) had already been fitted out with cannon.

The Brigade's six companies of infantry were organized as a regiment. Four separate cavalry companies were made part of that original regimental organization but would later become a separate battalion. The artillery battery is carried in most Union Army records under the designation "Walling's Battery".

As organizationally planned, each of the Brigade's transports was to have its own military commander who would hold authority over both the crew of the vessel and the assault troop unit which was to be regularly assigned. (As late as December 1862, some vessels still had civilians in command.) The actual working of the vessel was handled by its civilian crew as had been the usual case within the old Ram Fleet.[10]

According to the July 1864 Mississippi Marine Brigade's fleet roster entitled "Report of Persons of Mississippi Marine Brigade and Ram Fleet," civilian crewmembers were listed in the aggregate by job categories for the following vessels:

ALF CUTTING, tug
AUTOCRAT, transport
BEN J. ADAMS, transport
BALTIC, transport
BELLE DARLINGTON, tug
DIANA, transport
DICK FULTON, towboat

E. H. FAIRCHILD, commissary and QM boat
JOHN RAINE, transport
LIONESS, towboat
MONARCH, transport ram
SWITZERLAND, transport ram
T. D. HORNER, towboat

Job Categories

1 Chief Master	13 Second Engineers	1 Leadsman
12 First Masters	8 Third Engineers	1 Laundress
12 Second Masters	7 Fourth Engineers	251 Deck hands
10 Third Masters	10 Watchmen	76 Firemen
20 First Class Pilots	13 Cooks	10 "Lumpers"*
1 Second Class Pilot	13 Chambermaids	4 Clerks
2 Steersmen	7 Stewards	11 Carpenters
13 First Engineers	1 Greaser	12 Cabin Boys

* The job category "lumper" referred to the function of a carry-aboard longshoreman. In the case of the Brigade, these men were no doubt assigned to work on the attending coaling barges. In the United States today, the term "lumper" is most often heard around docks where fishing vessels are being unloaded; the term longshoreman today being more commonly associated with individuals who load or unload dry cargo.

The total number of civilians shown by this roster came to 509. If added to the military personnel as reported by Alfred W. Ellet during the same month, this would have brought the Brigade's total personnel to 1,851 persons. The civilian deck hands were predominantly Negro, although some operational reports seemed to infer that a few of them may have been Caucasian. The firemen were generally mixed in their racial makeup. The "lumpers" were almost certainly Negro, probably (as in the case of the Negro deck hands) contrabands who had volunteered for the jobs. The Brigade's attitude toward contraband labor seems to have been better than the general policy of the Union Army. (The pay records for the Brigade are extant only for the period 1863 and 1864.) A War Department order which was issued on New Years Day of 1864 spelled out the wage standard for contrabands attached to the military. The Brigade's wage policy, as it was set by Alfred W. Ellet during October of 1863, had paid more than double this rate. In January 1864, Ellet would be forced to reduce the scale for contraband civilian labor in order to be in fiscal step with the rest of the army. The pay reduction was a source of much controversy within the ranks of the Union Army's Negro regiments, and presumably it would have received the same reception on the part of the Negro civilians on the Brigade's vessels.

Headquarters, Mississippi Marine Brigade
January 1, 1864

Special Order No. 1

Special Order No. 87, October 14, 1863, issued from these headquarters granted to faithful male contrabands the rate of $25 per month wages after serving four months. That order is hereby modified by the following.

Four classes only of faithful Negro men shall be entitled to the benefits of that order: Deck hands; Firemen; First Cook, one to each vessel; Artificers (competent workmen). All the other male Negroes to be rated and paid at $10 per month.

The authorized female contrabands will be rated and paid $7 per month.

These orders will govern the rates and pay of all concerned now in or hereafter coming into the service from December 1, 1863.

Masters will be held responsible that men are rated and paid in a capacity in which they serve.

By command of Brigadier General A. W. Ellet

Captain W. D. Crandall, A.A.G.[11]

During the summer of 1864, the monthly wage scale for contraband crewmen would be increased for most job categories. The chambermaids, for instance, would begin receiving $20 monthly which was a considerable boost from the $7 they had received six months before. The mention of "female contrabands" clearly indicates that the "chambermaids" carried on the vessel rosters were Negroes. It is probably accurate to state that these women were the first of their sex to be formally attached to the United States military as part of a combatant force.

From one Brigade roster dated July 1864, we get a breakdown of Brigade military strength on that date and an idea as to how the assault units and gunners were distributed throughout the transports. There was a total of 1042 men on the eight listed vessels.[12]

Steamer *AUTOCRAT*	97 men
Steamer *DIANA*	244 men
Steamer *BEN J. ADAMS*	154 men
Steamer *E. H. FAIRCHILD*	128 men
Steamer *JOHN RAINE*	133 men
ex ram *BALTIC*	176 men
ex ram *SWITZERLAND*	64 men
ex ram *MONARCH*	46 men

According to Crandall, the Brigade carried on its roles seventeen officers as of the time of its activation. Crandall noted, though, that a number of the Brigade's officers never received their formal commissions, serving throughout the period of the Brigade activation in an acting capacity.

Those Brigade records which still exist do not give numbers on the quantity of mules and horses; however, the numbers of animals must have been substantial. Soon after the Brigade's organization, Brigadier General Ellet mounted most of his six infantry companies, some with horses, but most of them on mules. This gave the majority of the Brigade's infantry -- and not just its cavalry -- an extraordinary degree of mobility once they were landed ashore.

Detached Vessels of the Brigade

During Alfred W. Ellet's time at Saint Louis while he busied himself with readying his new organization for field service, Charles R. Ellet (originally a medical cadet who would soon be raised in rank to full colonel) had been given charge of those vessels of the old ram fleet which were then actively operating. Coordination of the operations of that detached part of the fleet during this time frame became a matter handled solely between Charles R. Ellet and Rear Admiral Porter.

An inventory which names the vessels which were operational as of the first week in December (1862) as well as their commanders is contained within a report that Charles R. Ellet submitted in answer to a request made of him by Porter. At the time, Charles R. Ellet was headquartered on the *MONARCH*.

Steam Ram *MONARCH*, Cairo, Illinois
December 4th, 1862.

Admiral:--

Your reply to my communication of December 4th has been received. The following is a list of the names of rams under my command, and of the names of their commanders:

1. *SWITZERLAND*, Major John W. Lawrence.
2. *QUEEN OF THE WEST*, Captain E. W. Sutherland.
3. *MONARCH*, Lieutenant E. W. Bartlett.
4. *LANCASTER*, Lieutenant W. F. Warren.
5. *LIONESS*, First Master Thomas O'Reilly [civilian].
6. *HORNER*,† First Master Robert Dalzell [civilian].
7. *FULTON*,‡ First Master S. Cadman [civilian].

The *HORNER*†, has been, for several months, up the Ohio River, and is now undergoing repairs. She is employed to carry stores for our Fleet, and is in the charge of Captain George Q. White, Assistant Quartermaster. I have sent the *LIONESS* up to Caseyville, to bring down two barges of Pittsburgh coal, which are waiting at that point. I expect her return in a few days. The company of soldiers which I am expecting has not yet arrived. I shall do all that is in my power to have the rams under my command, ready for service at the earliest possible date. The *MONARCH* and *LANCASTER* will take on coal today, if it can be obtained.[13]

† *T. D. HORNER*
‡ *DICK FULTON*

During the past summer, the volume of partisan activity had begun to increase along the river. Things had become so serious by the fall of 1862 that communications between points on the main river were at risk of being cut. A convoy system had been started by Porter to protect both military transportation as well as civilian traffic. The inauguration of the system was announced in public notices posted at all river ports and landings between Helena, Arkansas, and Cairo, Illinois. Convoying was scheduled to begin on October 28.

Gunboats will leave Cairo three times a week at least, and also leave Memphis for Cairo in the same way. All masters of steamers can have protection up and down river by applying to the commanding officers at Memphis, Cairo, and Helena.

The convoys will hoist a white flag with blue cross and fire a gun three hours before starting. Any masters with steamboats who wish to load with cotton on the way up will be protected by the convoy vessel while so doing by giving notice in time or before sailing to the naval officer in command of the convoy.

David D. Porter, Acting Rear Admiral
Commanding Mississippi Squadron[14]

Although it had not been scheduled on a regular basis, some convoying had already been taking place before this time, and Ellet's rams had been active as escorts whenever they could be spared from other duties. A good description of one such escort mission is contained within a report of Charles R. Ellet when he was still a medical cadet, prior to his promotion to colonel. Ellet had addressed his report of that mission to his uncle Alfred W. Ellet. At the time, Charles R. Ellet had command of *QUEEN OF THE WEST* following repairs from damage it had received in front of Vicksburg in the action against *CSS ARKANSAS*.[15]

US Ram *QUEEN OF THE WEST*
Off Helena, Arkansas

I have the honor to report to you that while returning yesterday with the *QUEEN OF THE WEST* from Eunice Landing in company with two transports, the *IATAN* and *ALHAMBRA* under the command of Lieutenant Colonel C. E. Lippincott, we were fired upon in the bend above Bolivar. The enemy had collected a force of seven hundred men and three field pieces, at this point, where the course of the channel renders it necessary for boats to run for several miles within a few yards of the bank. They intended to attack the fleet unexpectedly, as it passed through, but a fugitive Negro had brought us full information of their plans and position. The three boats, at the suggestion of Colonel Lippincott, were brought through the bend lashed together, the *QUEEN OF THE WEST* occupying the inside position. When within about forty yards of the bank, the enemy opened a heavy fire upon us of minié balls, canister and round shot, riddling the *QUEEN OF THE WEST* in every direction. Her guns, which were worked with great skill and bravery by Lieutenant Callahan and his detachment of artillerists, silenced one of the enemy's pieces, and threw shells which burst in the very midst of the guerrillas. The sharpshooters of the *QUEEN OF THE WEST* and the infantry of the transports kept up a constant fire on the riflemen of the enemy, whose loss must necessarily have been heavy. The fight lasted for twenty minutes, during which one man on the *QUEEN OF THE WEST* was killed, and another dangerously wounded. Both of the men were gunners belonging to Lieutenant Callahan's detachment. The *IATAN* lost two men killed. A few of the sharpshooters received slight injuries. The men all behaved very well. The enemy had intended to attack the fleet at two other points, but failed to do so; their losses having been probably much more severe than they had anticipated.

Very respectfully,

Charles Rivers Ellet, Medical Cadet, Commanding Division Ram Fleet[16]

Harassing of passing steamers took place both on the main river and on almost all of the Mississippi's tributaries south of Memphis. The enemy's efforts seem to have been well orchestrated in this regard. In his report at the end of the war to Quartermaster General Meigs, Lewis B. Parsons described the menace that the partisan actions created to the flow of military supply on the western rivers.

It could further be recollected that the rebel government had had an extended and effective organization under the direction of a cabinet officer for the sole purpose of the destruction of our transports, offering unparalleled rewards for the success of miscreants in this nefarious business,...[17]

Parsons was undoubtedly referring to a group of at least nineteen southern civilians who operated during 1863 under the sanction of Confederate Secretary of War James A. Seddon. Their given mission was to burn bridges on the Cumberland River in order to close off steamboat and railroad traffic to the Union Army depots located at Nashville and to destroy steamboats by sabotage when and wherever the opportunity presented itself. A report summarizing this activity was sent to Assistant Secretary of War Charles A. Dana by Colonel J. H. Baker, Provost Marshall General, Department of the Missouri in April of 1865. Baker listed ten steamers and stated there were also a number of wharfboats , all known to have been burned by this group. According to the confession of the first of the captured arsonists, the group was to have received

$400,000 once their work was accomplished. Of this, $34,800 in gold was paid in advance at the time their leaders left Richmond. The steamboats known to have been destroyed by this group were:

VESSEL	DATE, PLACE OF DESTRUCTION	STATUS AT TIME
CATAHOULA	September 1863 at Saint Louis	Under charter to Army
CHAMPION	August 1863 at Memphis	Under charter to Army
CHANCELLOR	Not given in report	In commercial service
CITY OF MADISON	August 1863 at Vicksburg	Under charter to Army
FOREST QUEEN	October 1863 at Saint Louis	In commercial service
HIAWATHA	September 1863 at Saint Louis	In commercial service
IMPERIAL	September 1863 at Saint Louis	In commercial service
JESSE K. BELL	September 1863 at Saint Louis	Under charter to Army
POST BOY	September 1863 at Saint Louis	In commercial service
ROBERT CAMPBELL[1]	September 1863 at Milliken's Bend	Under charter to Army

[1] This vessel was the *ROBERT CAMPBELL, JR.*

The Baker report speculated that of the "over seventy Saint Louis steamers lost by fire during the war, nine of which were fired by regular Confederate troops, the greater proportion of the balance were fired by those [persons] listed [Baker had listed the names of the saboteurs] or similar emissaries of the rebel government." By April of 1865, two of the saboteurs had confessed to their participation, one of them even admitting that he had had personal conversations in Richmond with President Jefferson Davis regarding the group's mission. The harm that these agents had done was summed up by Major General Grenville M. Dodge, Commander of the Department of the Missouri, who endorsed Baker's report for transmittal to Assistant Secretary Dana.

> Respectfully forwarded to the Assistant Secretary of War, Washington, DC.
> I consider it important that these parties be brought to justice, and would suggest that good detectives be sent to Richmond and Mobile to arrest the parties named as in the rebel service and obtain further evidence. There is no doubt of the guilt of the parties. They were in the habit of burning boats, storehouses, etc., taking to Richmond papers with full account of burning, there filing affidavits, and on that receiving their pay. They then came into our lines and squandered the money, which brought them to our notice, and on making arrests the entire *modus operandi* was divulged. We have a large amount of testimony in the case, but desire to obtain more proof before we go to trial, and, if possible, get all the parties.[18]

All sorts of ideas aimed at making life miserable for Union shipping were being proposed during this period to the Confederate high command. A southern civilian named James A. Crawford applied to the Confederate's acting secretary of war who at the time was J. P. Benjamin, for a letter of marque authorizing him to range the Ohio River to capture Northern steamboats. Since there was no possible way to take potential prizes past Union-held Cairo and thence down the Mississippi to Confederate territory, Crawford's scheme was to land captured cargo on the south bank of the Ohio from where it would be "wagoned south for adjudication at a Southern court." Benjamin replied to Crawford that since neither the laws of the [Confederate] Congress nor the laws of nations recognized privateering on anything but the high seas,

Crawford's request was denied.[19]   On the more practical side, the Confederacy encouraged any partisan activity aimed specifically against steamboats. The first full scale effort of this sort had taken place on the White River during the summer of 1862. Later, in 1863, special units to operate against river traffic were formed as part of the regular Confederate Army organization. One such unit consisted of a mounted infantry regiment; another, an infantry battalion with attached artillery and its own cavalry element.[20]

Writing during 1862 to a member of Grant's staff, Quartermaster Parsons had pleaded that something be done to put a stop to the constant firing into boats on the river. "It is moderately increasing the difficulties and expense of transportation, and I hope some plan can be adopted by which an end may be put to the infamous practice." Parsons's letter to Grant along with the complaints of others were the catalysts for putting into effect the system of convoying that was announced by Porter in October 1862. Although convoying did provide protection, the system tended to slow things down as steamers had to wait idle until the scheduled time of convoy departures.

A steamboat trip involved considerable hazard, with or without the harassment of an enemy. A typical trip on the river became the subject of a letter written by Colonel William Orme to his wife. At the time, Orme commanded the 94th Illinois Regiment. He wrote the letter while his regiment was on its way south from Saint Louis to join Sherman's army above Vicksburg. According to Orme, good progress was made for the first forty miles. At that point, they came upon a stretch of the river so shallow that the pilots dared go no farther during the hours of darkness. The vessel was then put up against the bank awaiting daylight. Nothing too eventful happened during the night except, "one of the men walked overboard, but it was fortunately while the boat was against the bank so he could swim to a place of safety and was saved." (Apparently there were no safety rails.) Early the next morning, the steamer proceeded downriver. At the end of the day, the pilot again tied to the bank. With the river so low, nighttime running was considered hazardous not only because of the danger of grounding but also for fear of hitting snags. Orme explained to his wife that captains of steamboats were extremely careful about snags since the government would not repay the owners for any damage or loss from marine casualty, the government only reimbursing if damage was caused by a direct action of the enemy. Orme wrote, probably quite correctly, that up to that time in the war, more boats had been sunk by hitting snags than from any other cause. On the third day of the trip and while still above Memphis, Orme was told by one of the pilots that he would normally expect to reach the city [Memphis] in about three hours from where they were, but as they were now part of a convoy, a considerable delay was anticipated since "the slowest boat keeps the pace." The pilots did not anticipate any danger from the enemy until they had passed Memphis. Beyond Memphis, he was told, partisans were in the regular habit of firing at passing steamboats from the western shore. Orme was told that in order to help counter partisan activity, a number of Union guard posts had been scattered along the river bank in this area, the purpose being to provide foray points for fast response once any enemy activity developed. For the 94th Illinois, the trip ended without incident after a voyage beginning at Saint Louis and lasting seven days.

Although Quartermaster Parsons had been one of the strongest advocates for convoy protection, he would complain that once a convoy system was put into place, there was a tendency to keep it in force even when the danger had seemingly passed. In a letter to Quartermaster General Meigs, he commented that it seemed "strange to insist on such stringent measures after the real danger was gone."[21] Besides giving protection to shipping, the Navy believed that convoying had a secondary advantage in that it was a way to help control elicit trade. A sizable proportion of the protection afforded steamboat travel on the Mississippi during the period of late 1862 and into mid-1863 came from those vessels of the Mississippi Marine Brigade which were acting independently of the parent brigade under the direct orders of Rear Admiral Porter.

Shortly after receiving his colonelcy, Charles R. Ellet received a rush appeal from Porter:

December 1, 1862

Colonel:

Can you send me a ram that carries a gun, without one moment's delay? Hickman [Kentucky], I believe, has been taken. Put on board every man you can raise. If you have no guns I will put howitzers on board. If you are all ready send me word by return of tug. The vessel will only be wanted for two days, so there need be no great preparation. Let the captain of her come and communicate with me.

Very respectfully, your obedient servant,

David D. Porter, Acting Rear Admiral
Commanding Mississippi Squadron[22]

The follow-up report of Colonel Ellet to his uncle Brigadier General Alfred W. Ellet, tells of his compliance with Porter's request and of related problems which were brought about by the mission.

Steam Ram *MONARCH*
Mound City, Illinois
December 2, 1862

Dear Uncle:

Just as I was about to retire last night a tug steamed up and brought me the dispatch I enclose from Admiral Porter. As luck would have, I was at that moment transferring coal from the *LANCASTER* to the *LIONESS*, in order to send the latter up to Caseyville. (Brooks had telegraphed to me to do so, as there were two barges there full of coal for me.)

I immediately stopped the transfer; woke up Bartlett and everyone whom I should need; had the ammunition of the *MONARCH* transferred to the *LANCASTER*; sent all our deck hands and firemen over -- all the well soldiers; put Captain Bouseman on as her first master, and appointed Bartlett her commander, with Warren for his second in command; sent Lindsy, my mate, over as a volunteer rifleman (I knew he would be efficient in case of a fight, either as sharpshooter, gunner, carpenter, or master), and last but not least woke up Doctor Robarts and sent him over. The doctor's ferocity at this movement was undisguised. He refused point blank at first, stating that he had all manner of promises from you to various effects, and that he wouldn't go. Finally he consented, and the boat steamed off at 3 a.m., carrying with her the flower of our little force at this point. I sent Bartlett down to receive further instructions, in the tug.

I hope you will approve of my doings and sayings in this matter. With the prospect of a fight before me I had to have medical assistance. I promised the doctor that the *LANCASTER* should return in two days, as Porter promised, if I could effect it. It would really be outrageous if Porter was to keep her there under the circumstances. He has plenty of gunboats to take her place. Still, if I find there is a real necessity for her presence there, or anywhere else, I shall be the last to make any objections. I am glad to see that with all their turtles and broken-backed rams they still have to depend, in every emergency, on the promptness and efficiency of the Ram Fleet. As long as I have a boat, a man, or a gun, it shall never be withheld when a friend or an enemy needs them. The good of the service is the main object, and I shall sacrifice everything to that.

I am, however, pretty near the end of my tether now; I must have more men and officers sent me.

The *LIONESS* will start for Caseyville tomorrow. I have sent her down to Cairo to coal. I have not yet heard from Lawrence. I will at once mail you any report I receive from him or Bartlett.

Last night, while in the very midst of preparation, a stoker, named Storey, who had been recently enlisted but not yet sworn in (I have no blanks), refused to go on the *LANCASTER*, saying he did not consider he belonged to the fleet yet. Anything else, he said, he would be glad to do, but he really could not go on the *LANCASTER*. I told him to pack his trunk and leave at once. He said he supposed, of course, I meant him to leave in the morning. I told him no, to leave now. So off he went in the middle of the night. It was harsh, but I thought it necessary.

I am determined to eradicate the idea that men in this fleet can shirk their duty in time of danger. The sooner that they come to know what is my intention on this point the better. I was glad to see that on this occasion Storey was the only man who offered any objections. All went with spirit and alacrity. I am confident of hearing a good account from the *LANCASTER* in case she gets into a fight.

Why do you never write to me, uncle? I have only had two short letters from you since you left.

Your affectionate nephew,

Charles Rivers Ellet[23]

The enemy occupation at Hickman turned out to be a false alarm. Following is the report of that mission as written up by Lieutenant E. W. Bartlett who was now the commander of *LANCASTER*.

On Board US Steam Ram *LANCASTER*
Off Mound City,   December 3, 1862

Sir:

Agreeable to your order of December 1, I took command of the *LANCASTER*, and on the morning of the 2d, at 2 o'clock, proceeded to Cairo and reported to Admiral D. D. Porter as ready for duty. From him, I received the following orders:

...Proceed to Columbus, where you will find the TYLER,* Lieutenant Commander Prichett. If she is not there, proceed to Hickman, where Lieutenant Commander Prichett will communicate my orders to you, and you will, if necessary, cooperate with him to carry them out.

D. D. Porter, Acting Rear Admiral, Commanding Mississippi Squadron

In accordance to the above orders, I proceeded to Hickman, where I found the *TYLER**, and communicated with Lieutenant [Commander] Prichett, and from him learned the following particulars: The captain in command of the post at Hickman, on the night of December 1, desired to send dispatches to Cairo, and signaled for a transport, which was passing up, to land; but as the boat passed on without stopping, he ordered his men to fire upon her, which they did with muskets. The captain of the boat supposing them to be the enemy, proceeded to Columbus and reported to General (Thomas A. Davies) that Hickman had been taken by the enemy, and that he was fired upon by them.

We lay at anchor off Hickman till 10 a.m., then took the *TYLER** in tow and proceeded to Cairo, arrived at that place at 7 p.m., then came to Mound City, where we arrived at 10 p.m.

I remain your most obedient servant,

E. W. Bartlett, Lieutenant[24]

* *A. O. TYLER*

Disciplinary Problems in the Brigade

On March 4, 1863, Brigadier General Alfred W. Ellet reported to Secretary of War Stanton that the Mississippi Marine Brigade would be ready for field duty within the week.

If the Brigade is to be viewed at that time in the light of its level of training and discipline, a lot was still lacking. Alfred W. Ellet had made the cardinal mistake of originally encouraging an over-familiarity between officers and enlisted men, a democratizing policy he had begun to put in place before the Brigade was even authorized. Back in September (1862), he had issued orders that on the rams, officers and enlisted men were to mess together. This order had not been well received by some of the officers who wisely saw the fallacy of it. Alfred W. Ellet remained adamant on the point, so much so that he issued a reprimand to the commander of the *MONARCH*.

> The commander of the fleet learns with regret that his order for the soldiers on all the boats to eat in the cabins of their respective boats, the same provisions, prepared in the same way, and at the same table with the officers, has been disregarded on board the *MONARCH*. He wishes it understood that this order is not a gratuity on his part, but is dictated from a sense of justice. The private soldier has without doubt a better legal right to whatever subsistence supplies are purchased for the fleet than any officer in the service upon it. Then, whatever he does not get he is wrongfully deprived of. The Lieutenant Colonel commanding therefore requires that his former order upon this subject be put into immediate effect upon the *MONARCH*.[25]

It would not be long before Alfred W. Ellet realized that his ideas of platonic democracy were not working. As a result of the fraternization and the accompanying over-familiarity it created, discipline began to suffer. The co-dining arrangements were soon abandoned, and things began to improve on the rams. Insubordination and disobedience were handled in the usual Army way, including confinement on bread and water. Minor infractions were sometimes handled with a touch of humor. For instance, there was the punishment for spitting on the deck: The offender had to mop up the spittle and then carry the mop until he caught someone else spitting. At that time, he passed the mop on to the next succeeding offender.

Although tightening of discipline did take place on those of the Brigade's vessels which were operating separate and apart throughout the winter of 1862-1863, the same tightening does not seem to have been put in place at the training barracks in

Saint Louis. It is easy to speculate that the reason for this was that Ellet and his officers were as busy recruiting as they were training. Any attempt to instill a more rigorous discipline, which could not have avoided public attention in a place as crowded as Saint Louis, would almost certainly have dampened enthusiasm for potential recruits who were then being led on to expect the easy life. The lack of firm control proved to be the cause of the organization's first problem and one which came to the forefront in but a matter of days after the Brigade left Saint Louis. While en route to Young's Point, mutiny broke out simultaneously on *BEN J. ADAMS*, *BALTIC*, *AUTOCRAT*, and *JOHN RAINE*. The fact that the trouble occurred on four separate vessels and almost at the exact same time seems to indicate that the revolt had been planned by its perpetrators. The cause of the trouble was the food -- or, more specifically -- the lack of food. Judging from a report filed at the time by Crandall who was then the Brigade's adjutant, there might have been a considerable justification for the trouble since he listed the rations then being issued as consisting of "two biscuits per man with rice and coffee." Whether Crandall was describing one meal, or one day's ration, is not clear; but either way, it could not have been a particularly attractive or plentiful diet. During the protests, the officer of the day on one of the rams was physically assaulted, being "violently struck in the face." Crandall, who was on the *BEN J. ADAMS*, claimed that the uprising was put down only when the officers present drew their revolvers and threatened to open fire on the men. Two of the more vocal mutineers were later sentenced to six months' hard labor with ball and chain. Others who had taken an active role, but who did not appear to be among the leaders, received lesser sentences.

The food shortage remained a problem for some time and was probably a cause for much of the unrest which continued well into 1863. In early April, the commissary sergeant aboard the *DIANA* noted in that transport's log that all the bread and meat rations were exhausted even though four days remained before it was time to draw new rations. Obviously, commissary management within the Mississippi Marine Brigade was at that time abysmally poor.

~

Later in this section, under the subtitle *Repercussions*, we will pick up again on the activities of detached units of the Mississippi Marine Brigade. These will include the loss of *LANCASTER* at Vicksburg and the assignment of *SWITZERLAND* to duty with Rear Admiral David Farragut's blockade of the Red River. In Part VII, we will again take up the operations of the Mississippi Marine Brigade following its arrival at Young's Point in the spring of 1863.

THE CENTRAL MISSISSIPPI: VICKSBURG AND RELATED OPERATIONS, JANUARY - JULY 1863

Vicksburg and Port Hudson had for some time been spared from a Union Navy blockade of the southern Mississippi. Movements of Confederate supplies had resumed as soon as Farragut moved back to New Orleans during the past summer (1862). For the defenders of Vicksburg, Farragut's retrograde had allowed a renewal of communications with the Red River country which was carried out mainly by small, shallow draft steamers which made their way up the Mississippi and into Vicksburg's back door by way of the Big Black River.

Major General Ulysses S. Grant, thoroughly fed up with Major General John A. McClernand's independent initiatives and distrustful of that citizen soldier's lack of military expertise, had enlisted Major General Henry W. Halleck's support in obtaining complete authority for himself in conjunction with all the facets which would become involved over the taking of Vicksburg. Halleck concurred in the need for one centralized authority, and he issued orders to that affect.

New Preparations Against Vicksburg

On January 15, 1863, Special Order No. 15 was cut by Grant's adjutant.[26] The order laid out the preliminary steps for a move against Vicksburg. It was Grant's intention to straighten out the wasteful confusion that had resulted from prior command overlaps. Who commanded what, and for what purpose, needed some very definitive clarification. The major effect of Special Order No. 15 was that it made clear that the taking of Vicksburg was now to become the sole concern of every commander operating in the Mississippi corridor. Major General McClernand was relegated to the command of XIII Corps which was to consist of those troops which McClernand had earlier taken with him on the Post on the Arkansas Expedition plus those troops then in garrison at Helena, Arkansas. Major General William T. Sherman and Major General James B. McPherson would each lead separate corps -- Sherman the XV Corps and McPherson the XVII Corps. The XVI Corps under Brigadier General Charles S. Hamilton was now to be made part of Grant's Mississippi command. XVI Corps would guard Grant's lines of communication including all river and rail corridors. No operational diversions were to be allowed on anyone's part without Grant's specific authorization.[27] Special Order No. 15 had stated in part the priorities which were to be set into place regarding certain categories dealing with logistics.

> III. It is regarded of primary importance [that] the [railroad] line east from Memphis to Corinth should be maintained; and so long as practicable, the line from Grand Junction to Corinth, via Jackson, Tennessee.

> IX. The Chief of Artillery and of Ordnance will immediately procure and ship ordnance stores for fifty thousand infantry, twenty-six batteries of artillery, and two thousand cavalry, at the rate of five hundred rounds per man for the infantry and cavalry, and refill caissons for the artillery twice. This supply is required in addition to the amount to be kept on hand by the troops at all times, but embracing all other stores for issue.

> XV. Division commanders will take thirty days' rations for future use.[28]

Grant ordered the quartermaster at Memphis to commandeer and place under charter to the Army all steamboats passing that place. Troops which were to take part in the operations against Vicksburg were to be loaded on these transports for shipment south to Young's Point. There, the troops were to be disembarked to go into encampment. As it would develop, Young's Point proved not to be the best of locations to bivouac troops. A no-let-up drizzle would contribute to a general misery, the situation made worse by occasional periods of heavy rain. Only the more fortunate troops, that is those regiments which were last to descend the river, remained dry, these last contingents being allowed to quarter aboard the steamers. Humanitarian in nature as this was for the troops involved, it also led to difficulty for the district quartermaster. Every time a steamboat was kept in such a static mode, it meant one less vessel available somewhere else for the movement of needed men and materiel.

Even though troops might remain dry, their quartering on board steamboats did not approach anything resembling comfort. Some who were quartered aboard the transports relate to having been crammed in along with horses, artillery, and the field equipment of their units. Few of the transports were supplied with any amenities, sanitary facilities and cooking arrangements being seldom present. An infantry colonel by the name of James Wright wrote to Quartermaster officer Lewis B. Parsons criticizing how his unit had been accommodated aboard one typical river boat.

> We have been quite well accommodated; however this last day and night, rain and snow making it disagreeable, and rendering the men liable to sickness from exposure.
> I suggest as a suitable and necessary provision for conveying so many men, there should be a small elevation from the floor on which the men could spread their beds and sleep. With us the water from the rain soaked all the blankets...There should also be a much more numerous provision of stoves on the upper and lower decks for drying the wet and warming the exposed.[29]

A letter written by a Sergeant Onley Andrus exhibited that sergeant's violent dislike for steamboat accommodations.

> This morning, they have taken the stock (mules and horses) off of the boat for the purpose of cleaning the deck, which is a good move, for of all the filthy holes I ever saw, this is the nastiest -- nasty enough to suit the most fastidious [sic].

The sergeant's viewpoint on the cuisine was equally critical.

> Perhaps when I tell you there is [sic] three regiments to cook over three stoves, and every man cooking for himself, you can form some idea of what sort of a time we have. We have hog and hard bread and coffee and tea. That is all we have to cook or eat. There is one more thing we will have, and that before long, too, that is the scurvy, unless we get potatoes before long.[30]

Colonel Charles Rivers Ellet and *QUEEN OF THE WEST*

During January 1863, a Confederate steamer of substantial size was reported to be lying alongside the Vicksburg wharf undergoing repairs there preparatory for her being placed into service. Appropriately, she had been named *CSS CITY OF VICKSBURG*. Speculation was afoot that this vessel was in the process of being converted into an armed ram. In light of that possibility, Rear Admiral Porter decided to end her career before it could begin. This would have to be accomplished in the same fashion as had been earlier attempted against the *CSS ARKANSAS*, that is while *CSS CITY OF VICKSBURG* lay at dockside -- this despite the fact that she would be under the protection of the city's guns. Porter turned to Charles R. Ellet who was now in charge of the detached vessels of the Mississippi Marine Brigade. Ellet assigned *QUEEN OF THE WEST* to the task and personally took command of her. Porter's instructions were to first destroy the *CSS CITY OF VICKSBURG*; and when that was done, proceed down the Mississippi and put a stop to the supply traffic flowing into Vicksburg from the Red River system. This double assignment that Charles R. Ellet had been given was a rather tall order for one lightly armed ram.

The attack by *QUEEN OF THE WEST* against *CSS CITY OF VICKSBURG* was temporarily delayed when her civilian pilot, one Isaiah Reeder, not only refused duty, but also created a considerable stir by attempting to talk other members of the crew into doing the same thing. Ellet neutralized Reeder by arresting him and placing him in confinement aboard one of Porter's gunboats. This action appeared to have a dampening effect on others in the crew who had been listening to the pilot's appeal for the others to also refuse duty.[31]

In practice, the way that civilians had been hired for service on the Ellet rams differed considerably from the method employed toward other civilians that the Army hired. When employed aboard the Ellet vessels, each crewmember was required to enter into a signed agreement which in certain respects might be likened to a military enlistment.[32] That agreement read:

> I _____ , Do Solemnly Swear. That I will bear true allegiance to the United States of America, and that I will serve them honestly and faithfully against all their enemies or opposers whatsoever and observe and obey the orders of the President of the United States, and the orders of the officers appointed over me, according to the rules and articles for the government of the forces of the United

States and all Government business entrusted to me shall be strictly and sacredly confidential, and I will use my influence to have good discipline in the service to which I belong, and continue well and truly to serve until I am discharged, provided the term of service shall not exceed six months from the date hereof. SO HELP ME GOD.

Signed _____

Dated and subscribed at _____

The Isaiah Reeder case became somewhat of a landmark in the Army's handling of its civilian employees during the Civil War, it being decided that the disciplinary jurisdiction of the military did apply to civilians serving on military vessels whether as direct employees or while under separate contract as was the case with most of the pilots.[33]

Somehow forewarned of Ellet's approaching attack against *CSS CITY OF VICKSBURG*, Vicksburg's cannoneers were ready and waiting. The bluffs overlooking the riverfront were packed with sharpshooters. Hundreds of the city's civilians, anxious to witness the action, had gathered at every available vantage point. They were not to be disappointed, as what followed turned into quite a show.

Ellet's own report of the attack relates an over-abundance of problems, problems which started at the onset.

US Steamer Ram QUEEN OF THE WEST
Below Vicksburg, Mississippi
February 2, 1863

Acting Rear Admiral David D. Porter
Commanding Mississippi Squadron;--
Admiral:

In compliance with your instructions, I started on the *QUEEN OF THE WEST* at 4:30 o'clock this morning, to pass the batteries at Vicksburg and sink the rebel steamer lying before that city. I discovered immediately on starting, that the change of the wheel, from its former position, to the narrow space behind the *QUEEN OF THE WEST's* bulwarks, did not permit the boat to be handled with sufficient accuracy. An hour or more was spent on rearranging the apparatus, and when we finally rounded the point, the sun had risen, and any advantage which would have resulted from the darkness was lost to us. The rebels opened a heavy fire upon us, as we neared the city, but we were only struck three times before reaching the steamer. She was lying in nearly the same position that the *ARKANSAS** occupied when General Ellet ran the *QUEEN OF THE WEST* into her on a former occasion. The same causes which prevented the destruction of the *ARKANSAS** then, saved the *CITY OF VICKSBURG** this morning. Her position was such that if we had run obliquely into her, as we came down, the bow of the *QUEEN OF THE WEST* would inevitably have glanced. We were compelled to partially round--o [sic] in order to strike. The consequence was that at the very moment of collision the current, very strong and rapid at this point, caught the stern of my boat and acting on her bow as a pivot, swung her round so rapidly that nearly all her momentum was lost.

I had anticipated this result, and therefore caused the starboard bow gun to be shotted [sic] with three of the incendiary projectiles recommended in your orders. As we swung around Sergeant J. H. Campbell, detailed for the purpose, fired this gun. A 64-pounder shell crashed through the barricade just before he reached the spot but he did not hesitate. The discharge took place at exactly the right moment, and set the rebel steamer in flames, which they subsequently succeeded in extinguishing. At this moment one of the enemy's shells set the cotton on fire near the starboard wheel, while the discharge of our own gun ignited that portion which was on the bow. The flames spread rapidly, and the dense smoke, rolling into the engine room, suffocated the engineers. I saw that, if I attempted to run into the *CITY OF VICKSBURG** again, my boat would certainly be burned. I ordered her to be headed down stream, and turned every man to extinguishing the flames. After much exertion we finally put out the fire, by cutting the burning bales loose. The enemy, of course, were not ideal. We were struck twelve times, but though the cabin was knocked to pieces, no material injury to the boat, or to any of those on her, was inflicted. About two regiments of rebel sharpshooters in rifle-pits kept up a continuous fire, but did no damage. The *QUEEN OF THE WEST* was struck twice in the hull, but above the water line. One of our guns was dismounted and ruined. I can only speak in the highest terms of the conduct of every man on board. All behaved with cool, determined courage.

I remain very respectfully,

Charles Rivers Ellet, Colonel Commanding Ram Fleet[34]

* *CSS*, commissioned Confederate naval vessel.

Following the action, Charles R. Ellet complied with Porter's instructions to continue south and attempt to stop the supply traffic which was coming from the Red River into Vicksburg. What transpired on that mission was addressed by Ellet on February 5, 1863, in his report to Porter. It tells not only of the successes gained but gives a good insight into Ellet's personality.

US Steam Ram *QUEEN OF THE WEST*

Admiral:

I have the honor to report to you that I left the landing below the Cut-off, about 1 o'clock p.m. on the 2d instant, and proceeded down the river. At Warrenton, a few miles below, the enemy had two batteries of four pieces each, of which four are 20-pounder rifled guns. They opened up on us as we passed, but only struck us twice, doing no injury.

On reaching the Big Black River I attempted to ascend it, but found it impossible from the narrowness of the stream. Passing it [the Big Black River], we reached Natchez just at midnight. I landed at Vidalia, on the opposite shore, threw out some pickets, and went into the village in the hope of picking up some rebel officers. There can be no telegraphic line between Vicksburg and this point, for not a word of our coming had reached the place, and the people scarcely knew who we were. One rebel, Colonel York, was halted, but made so rapid a retreat that he escaped the shots fired after him.

Leaving this point, I kept on down the river. We passed Ellis Cliffs at 3 o'clock a.m. There are no fortifications at that or at any other point between Warrenton and Port Hudson. We had got about fifteen miles below the mouth of Red River when we met a sidewheel steamer coming up. Her pilot blew the whistle for the *QUEEN OF THE WEST* to take the starboard side, supposing her to be a Southern boat. Receiving no answer, and not liking the *QUEEN OF THE WEST's* looks as she bore straight down upon him, he ran his boat ashore. As we neared her, numerous rebel officers sprang into the water and made their escape. She proved to be the *A. W. BAKER*; had just discharged her cargo at Port Hudson, and was returning for another. We captured on her five captains, two lieutenants, and a number of civilians, among them seven or eight ladies. I had just placed a guard on the boat, when another steamer was seen coming down the river. A shot across her bows, brought her to; she proved to be the *MORO*, laden with 110,000 pounds of pork, near five hundred hogs, and a large quantity of salt, destined for the rebel army at Port Hudson.

I placed Captain Asgill Conner in command of the captured boats, and as the *QUEEN OF THE WEST's* supply of coal was very limited, I thought it best to return. A short distance above our landing, I destroyed twenty-five thousand pounds of meal, awaiting transportation to Port Hudson.

On reaching Red River I stopped at a plantation to put ashore the ladies, who did not wish to go any farther. I also released the civilians. While doing so another steamboat, the *BERWICK BAY*, came out of Red River and was immediately seized. She was laden with supplies for the rebel forces at Port Hudson, consisting of two hundred barrels of molasses, ten hogsheads of sugar, and thirty thousand pounds of flour; she had also on board forty bales of cotton.

I ascended Red River fifteen miles in the hope of getting some more boats, but found nothing. Night came on as we again started on our return. I found at once that the progress of the three prizes was so slow that our short supply of coal would not permit us to wait for them. I accordingly ordered them to be set on fire; we had not time to transfer their cargoes.

We met with no interruption on our return until we reached Warrenton. Before arriving at this point, I landed and sent my prisoners around by land, under a strong guard, to avoid exposing them to the enemy's fire. On passing Warrenton we found another battery had been erected there, and the three combined opened a very heavy fire upon us; they struck us several times, but did no damage worth mentioning.

Very respectfully, your obedient servant,

Charles Rivers Ellet, Colonel, Commanding Ram Fleet[35]

Upon his return to the Vicksburg perimeter from downriver, Ellet found himself a celebrity in the eyes of both Rear Admiral Porter and Major General Sherman. Sherman had gone to the personal trouble of crossing over the De Soto Peninsula especially to congratulate Ellet. By way of response to Ellet's request for extra armament, Sherman dictated the following orders:

Headquarters, XV Corps Army Camp
Before Vicksburg; February 6, 1863

The officer in charge of the two 30-pounder rifle guns now in position at the mouth of the canal, will deliver them with their ammunition and implements to the order of Colonel Ellet, commanding the ram *QUEEN OF THE WEST*, now lying at the lower landing. The officer commanding the Infantry guard will assist, with all his men, in putting these guns and ammunition on board the *QUEEN OF THE WEST* in such manner as Colonel Ellet may request.

By order of Major General Sherman.

J. H. Hammond, A.A.G.[36]

The well-armed *QUEEN OF THE WEST*, her boilers and other vital points protected by cotton bales, was soon ready to steam southward again, this time to take up a blockading station near the mouth of the Red River. As consort, Ellet would take along the small ferryboat *DESOTO* towing a coal barge.[37] Ellet's instructions from Porter were to remain at or near the mouth of the Red River as long as coal could be sent down to him. Short forays up the Red River were authorized, but these were to be conditional on the understanding that Ellet's primary purpose was to blockade the Red

River against enemy goods being routed to Vicksburg. Raiding of shore installations was only to be of secondary importance. Ellet's interpretation of these limitations would turn out to be widely liberalized. His attitude from the onset of the mission seemed to indicate that he viewed his role to be more that of a riverine raider than a blockader. This attitude could have developed in his mind from the amphibious attack concept that had been established for the new Mississippi Marine Brigade which at that point was still in a training status at Saint Louis. All this aside, *QUEEN OF THE WEST* and its personnel had been placed on detached duty with the Navy, and Charles R. Ellet was directly under Porter's orders; therefore, any concept surrounding the mission of the Brigade should not have been relevant to his present assignment.

Traveling south aboard *QUEEN OF THE WEST* were three gentlemen of the press who were probably attracted by Ellet's adventurous reputation and who wanted to witness him in action. They were Finlay Anderson of the *New York Herald*; a Mr. Boardman of the *Chicago Tribune*; and a Mr. McCullough of the *Cincinnati Commercial*.[38] Anderson had a touch of tabloid flamboyance which he demonstrated by the lead line of his story sent to the *New York Herald* editor just before the ram left De Soto Landing. The piece started with -- "I don't know when you will hear again from your 'rampant' correspondent." He then went on to list the officers of the *QUEEN OF THE WEST*, a service most helpful to an historian since it provides valuable information about her manning. The arrangements on *QUEEN OF THE WEST* were probably fairly typical of the overall Ellet fleet up to that time. According to Anderson, there were, besides Colonel Charles R. Ellet, twelve ram fleet officers aboard the *QUEEN OF THE WEST*; only two of them were military officers. (Anderson placed the notation "civilian" before the names of the other ten.) In addition to listing all of these officers by name, the reporter stated that the ram carried as regular crew: an Army surgeon, two civilian carpenters, two civilian assistant steamboat masters, and two civilian "ordinary" crewmen. He made no mention of those others who were certainly aboard, namely Negro coal passers (probably at least ten in number) without whom the ram's boiler fires could not have functioned. The deletion of reference to these people followed the rather general habit at the time of ignoring the individualism of Negroes, especially contraband employees of the Army.[39]

QUEEN OF THE WEST's trip down the Mississippi proved uneventful; but such peaceful tranquillity was not to last. Ellet apparently had no intention of acting out his assigned role as passive guard at the mouth of the Red River. Instead, he immediately started up the Red River, bound for the point where the Red River met the Atchafalaya River (about six miles upstream from the point where the Red River emptied into the Mississippi). From its junction with the Red River, the Atchafalaya meandered southward, eventually merging with a network of bayous. Those bayous, in their due course, emptied into Grand Lake, part of the coastal saltwater zone of southwestern Louisiana. Grand Lake itself connected to the Gulf of Mexico through a network of tidal passes. It was through this meandering Atchafalaya system that some of the Confederate supply was finding its way northward into the Red River with the eventual destination of Vicksburg or Port Hudson. The Atchafalaya system was not, however, the only avenue for supplies feeding into the Red River. A large portion of supplies descended the Red River directly from Alexandria and Shreveport. Ellet would have best served the assigned mission given to him by Porter had he positioned himself at the junction of the Atchafalaya and the Red River since all Confederate shipping had to pass by that point. Instead, by entering the Atchafalaya, he left the Red River open for enemy traffic outbound for the Mississippi.

Ellet found that unlike much of the flatter Mississippi and Arkansas country to the north, the banks of the Atchafalaya were relatively steep, a factor which could severely increase the danger from enemy artillery. Whether or not this ever occurred to him at the time he entered the Atchafalaya is problematic. Along the Atchafalaya's eastern bank ran a wagon path which was discernible in large part from the river. The lookouts on *QUEEN OF THE WEST* soon spotted a train of wagons -- six in all -- proceeding north. On spotting the ram, the drivers jumped off their boxes and headed for the cover of the trees. Ellet put a landing force ashore to destroy the wagons. That accomplished, the *QUEEN OF THE WEST* continued steaming south until the hamlet of Simsport was reached. The locals there informed Ellet that shortly before the *QUEEN OF THE WEST* had come into sight, a scout had raced into town, warning of the ram's approach. Two steamers lying against the bank had gotten steam up and fled, but not before taking aboard a part of what had been the town's small garrison of troops. The rest of the garrison had hurried inland by wagon. This was the first time that a doctrine of search and destroy had been carried out by any detachment of the Mississippi Marine Brigade or, for that matter, its predecessor, the Ellet Ram Fleet, and the prospects must have been exciting to Ellet. So far, no resistance had materialized, but that was about to change. Near dusk, and on the way back to rejoin the unarmed *DESOTO* which had been left anchored at the junction of the Red River, the *QUEEN OF THE WEST* came under fire from riflemen concealed behind a levee. The *QUEEN OF THE WEST's* first master (a civilian) was wounded. It was by then too dark to put ashore a party to give chase, but the next morning, acting in retaliation for the attack of the preceding day, Ellet ordered that nearby buildings be burned. Later, rejoined with the *DESOTO*, Ellet proceeded up the Red River. By the following morning, Ellet was forty miles upstream from the Mississippi when he captured *ERA NO. 5*, a commercial steamboat loaded with corn consigned to the Confederate Army. Aboard were three very talkative Confederate Army officers who let Ellet know by way of idle conversation that about thirty miles farther upstream, three steamers were moored at a place called Gordon's Landing. This news encouraged Ellet to continue upriver, an impulsive decision in light of Porter's instructions to remain near the mouth of the Red River which by now was more than forty miles astern.

There remains considerable question as to whether Ellet, while proceeding toward Gordon's Landing, had received word by land courier that Porter was sending a gunboat to reinforce him. A gunboat was indeed on its way; and if Ellet knew of it, this news may have influenced him to go as far upriver as he did. It would seem, though, that he should have waited until it arrived before going any farther. In any event, the young colonel seems to have overlooked the reality that he had left behind, totally unguarded, the lower end of the Red River into which a number of ancillary water systems fed, most of them navigable. In addition to the Atchafalaya system, at least two bayous from the north discharged into the Red River close to its mouth.[40]

When *QUEEN OF THE WEST*, with *DESOTO* and now *ERA NO. 5* trailing, approached Gordon's Landing some hours later, Charles R. Ellet spotted smoke rising beyond the bend in the river. Assuming that it was from the steamers which the Confederates had told him were at the landing, but not exactly sure of what he might be faced with, Ellet ordered the *QUEEN OF THE WEST's* pilot to ease slowly around the bend. What first came into view were not steamers, but instead a rebel battery which immediately opened fire. Ellet shouted for the *QUEEN OF THE WEST's* pilot to back downstream. Then, whether as a result of a steering malfunction or panic on the pilot's part, the *QUEEN OF THE WEST* ran hard against the river's bank and grounded in full range of the enemy's guns. Shot after shot pounded the *QUEEN OF THE WEST*, one round severing her main steam trunk, eliminating any hope of further maneuver. Ellet ordered the crew to abandon, but not before kindling was put in place, preparatory to putting the *QUEEN OF THE WEST* to the torch. While this was taking place, Ellet instructed that the first master, who had been wounded on the Atchafalaya, be put into the ram's yawl. But it was found that the yawl had already been launched and was well downstream, loaded with escaping crewmembers. Unable now to set fire to the *QUEEN OF THE WEST* without the certainty of incinerating the wounded man, Ellet canceled his earlier order. The remaining crewmembers tossed over cotton bales and anything else that would float to act as life supports. Then they took to the water.[41]

After being picked out of the water by the crew of the *DESOTO*, Ellet ordered her pilot to comb the river for survivors before starting downstream to safety. Heavy fog had now set in. Unable to see more than six feet ahead, the pilot struck the river's bank with such an impact that the *DESOTO's* rudder was completely sheared off. Ellet now had to order that the *DESOTO* be set afire and abandoned. Fortunately, *ERA NO. 5* was still in proximity, so the survivors of both *DESOTO* and *QUEEN OF THE WEST* went aboard her. As *ERA NO. 5* turned downstream, her paddle wheels left in their wakes not only the wreckage of two of the Mississippi Marine Brigade's vessels, but much of Charles R. Ellet's reputation as well.

Being fearful of close pursuit, Ellet ordered full speed, a foolish act, considering the almost complete lack of visibility. As a result, *ERA NO. 5* ran hard aground on a shoal. No doubt by this point in a distraught condition, and possibly looking for a scapegoat for his own rashness, Ellet ordered the pilot placed under arrest for treachery.[42]

By jettisoning much of *ERA NO. 5's* cargo of corn, her crew, assisted by the survivors, managed to refloat the vessel. The remaining corn was then used as fuel since the supply of wood for the steamer's firebox was almost gone. There was just enough of that corn to get *ERA NO. 5* downriver and into the Mississippi where she met with the *USS INDIANOLA*. On being told of the recent disasters, the *USS INDIANOLA's* commander asked Ellet to guide him back up the Red River so that the gunboat could have a try at reducing the battery at Gordon's Landing. Ellet agreed. No sooner had the *USS INDIANOLA* and *ERA NO. 5* started back upriver, which was still masked in fog, when they came within a few feet of colliding with the rebel ram *WEBB*. *WEBB's* skipper, taken aback at the sight of *USS INDIANOLA*, turned tail, heading back upriver. Visibility was almost zero, and under such conditions, *USS INDIANOLA's* skipper decided that pursuit would be foolhardy. Both *USS INDIANOLA* and *ERA NO. 5* moved back to the Mississippi and anchored. Ellet then led a party of riflemen ashore to seize cotton from a nearby plantation. The cotton was brought aboard and stacked so as to provide protection against rifle fire for *ERA NO. 5's* deck house. Ellet then headed upriver toward De Soto Landing. The journey was enlivened on three occasions by enemy batteries which opened fire from the banks, but *ERA NO. 5* escaped without damage.

A few of the prisoners taken from *QUEEN OF THE WEST* were exchanged soon after capture. According to the surviving records kept by the Mississippi Marine Brigade's adjutant, others of them "were sent to distant places and finally to eastern prisons." One account written of the notorious Andersonville Prison in Georgia mentions a prisoner there "in the uniform of the Ram Fleet." Since only a few of the Ellet men were taken prisoner during the war, it is quite probable that this man was from the *QUEEN OF THE WEST*.[43]

The Confederates Score Some Telling Blows

Damage to the *QUEEN OF THE WEST* during the action at Gordon's Landing had been less extensive than Ellet and his crew had thought when they abandoned her. She was soon repaired, and under the enemy's flag, she proceeded out of the Red River to try and do battle against her former owners.

USS INDIANOLA had left the mouth of the Red River; and by the early evening of February 24, she had reached Grand Gulf where she was moored when four steamers were seen to be approaching from the south. Suspecting them to be of an enemy nature, *USS INDIANOLA* was immediately made ready for action. The vessels were indeed those of the enemy, the first in line being *QUEEN OF THE WEST* on a course set to ram. The *QUEEN OF THE WEST* struck before *USS INDIANOLA* could move out of her path. The ram's bow passed completely through a coal barge which was lashed alongside *USS INDIANOLA*. Before the Federal crew had time to cut the barge free, the ram *WEBB*, the second enemy vessel in line, struck *USS INDIANOLA*, bow to bow. The two remaining Confederate vessels had by then come up and were pouring in a heavy fire from their deck mounted field pieces. *USS INDIANOLA* lost most of her power from perforations to steam pipes. If that was not enough punishment, she received a third ramming -- this one probably by *QUEEN OF THE WEST*, although in the approaching darkness, and with the general disorientation which an action at short range can create, it was difficult to tell which of the enemy vessels had struck. Two more butting collisions followed, but neither of these last impacts did much damage. *WEBB* now came back to deliver another blow. That one put the *USS INDIANOLA's* starboard rudder out of order and caused a number of heavy leaks. A quick follow-up ramming by *WEBB* proved to be *USS INDIANOLA's* death blow. Just enough steam remained for her pilot to bring the boat against the river bank. She sank the instant her bow met the shore, coming to rest with the main deck just barely clear of the water. Her crew did not have time to set her afire before the Confederates were alongside. They immediately began salvage efforts.

It had not been a praiseworthy time for the Union on the western rivers. Within the span of a week, two fine combatant vessels of the Union had become the property of the Confederacy.

A Practical Joke Proves to be Expensive

The realization that the Mississippi, from Vicksburg south to Baton Rouge, was solidly in the hands of the Confederacy was an unexpected setback for Union fortunes. The situation as it stood did not bode well for a strategy aimed at starving out Vicksburg's defenders. Although most of the leaders in Federal uniform must have been in a low state of morale, at least one retained his sense of humor. On the orders of Rear Admiral Porter, an old coal barge, was made up to resemble a gunboat. This was done by constructing and installing imitation smoke stacks made of discarded ration barrels, their ends knocked out and stacked atop a fake superstructure. Smoke for the stacks was to come from jury-rigged clay furnaces. No one, least of all Porter, expected the fake to create anything more than a momentary alarm from those at Vicksburg and perhaps some wastage of shells until that point when the Confederates realized that they had been the victims of a joke. When all was in readiness, Porter's faux gunboat was set loose into the current to drift past the Vicksburg cannoneers. As the disguised barge came down the river, the Confederates, taking the bait, opened up with a full blown cannonade which continued until the barge was out of range. It still had not dawned on anyone in the city's defenses that they were victims of a hoax. Later, when the barge floated into view of the Confederate salvage party at Grand Gulf which had just refloated the *INDIANOLA*, smoke from the fake's clay furnaces was still belching through the barrels. What the enemy salvors saw coming their way had all the appearances of a Union gunboat about to do them harm. Choosing what they thought was their only option, the salvors rolled the *INDIANOLA's* cannon overboard, set the gunboat afire, and then high-tailed it ashore. Unattended, *INDIANOLA* burned down to the waterline. The crew of *QUEEN OF THE WEST*, having seen Porter's fake approaching, also fell victim to the ruse. Hell bent, they took the *QUEEN OF THE WEST* south into the Red River and then into the Atchafalaya, not stopping until they arrived at Grand Lake. (On April 14th, while still on Grand Lake, *QUEEN OF THE WEST* would be destroyed by Union gunboats which had moved up from the Gulf of Mexico.)[44] What had started out as nothing more than a diversionary bit of fun aimed at improving morale within the Union forces before Vicksburg, had turned into a tactical master stroke which helped to balance out the embarrassing naval defeats of the week before.

That part of the Mississippi between Vicksburg and Baton Rouge was now an area of the river where neither side was able to claim dominance.

Things Get Nastier on the River Above Vicksburg

This was a time of much ill feeling in the river war. Although the Mississippi River above Vicksburg was generally thought of as Union territory, control of that part of the river was being actively disputed. Things were becoming decidedly nasty with prisoners being put at risk of eye-for-an-eye retaliation. The problem had begun when the civilian tug *HERCULES* was captured by Confederate partisans in February (1863) and one of its crew was executed.[45] Confederate partisans seemed to have little regard as to who they were targeting. Even a well-marked hospital steamer belonging to the Upper Mississippi Squadron had been fired upon. During late February, Union officers posted warning notices at all river towns and landings above

Vicksburg. The idea behind the postings was to discourage partisan action against unarmed vessels by threatening to remove the attacker from the protections normally allowed to legitimate military personnel.

> Persons taken in the act of firing on unarmed vessels from the banks will be treated as highwaymen and assassins, and no quarter will be shown them.
> Persons strongly suspected of firing on unarmed vessels will not receive the usual treatment of prisoners of war, but will be kept in close confinement.
> If this savage and barbarous Confederate custom cannot be put a stop to, we will try what virtue there is in hanging.
> All persons, no matter who they are, who are caught in the act of pillaging the houses of the inhabitants along the river, levying contribution or burning cotton, will receive no quarter if caught in the act, or if proved upon them.[46]

This order was immediately challenged by Major General John C. Pemberton, the Confederate commander at Vicksburg. By way of answer, Pemberton issued his own notice, specifying that if Porter's orders to hang partisans were carried out, then prisoners which had recently been taken from *USS INDIANOLA* would suffer an identical fate. As far as can be determined, no hangings by either side took place as a direct result of this particular exchange of threatening correspondence. It can be said, though, that the ill feeling created by Porter's February 1863 order set the stage for the denial of quarter by both sides during some of the subsequent small unit actions. Bitterness was becoming widespread along the Mississippi, even before the *HERCULES* episode. During this same time frame, Captain E. W. Sutherland, the commander of the Brigade's ram *MONARCH*, on detached duty and operating upriver from Vicksburg, received a delegation of local ladies representing the "women of the town of Greenville." The ladies were requesting that the townspeople be allowed due notice should their town become an object of retaliation as threatened by Porter's notices. Sutherland tersely told the delegation that if Union vessels were ever fired upon from the vicinity of Greenville, that act, in and of itself, would be the town's only forewarning. The ladies later asked Sutherland if he would receive a party of Confederate officers to further discuss the matter of relationships with the local population. This was agreed to, and arrangements were made. Under a white flag, a rebel delegation headed by Colonel Samuel W. Ferguson met with Sutherland near Greenville. During that meeting, Ferguson showed some temper, accusing *MONARCH's* commander of firing upon the house of a harmless citizen -- no less a personage than Greenville's Methodist minister. While the minister lay sick with smallpox, his house had been struck by a shell. Although not actually harming anyone, the episode "had terrified the household generally." Ferguson blustered, "The time has come to run up the black flag, and if anything like this happens again, counter reprisals will swiftly follow." During his tirade, Ferguson repeated the prevailing Southern viewpoint that considered all Negroes or those of mixed color employed by the Union military -- be they free or ex-slave -- to be beyond the pale of being legitimate combatants. Ferguson was apparently aware that the vessels of the Mississippi Marine Brigade employed contrabands as stokers and deck hands since he announced to Sutherland that he would "hang every Negro that [he] could catch coming off the [Union] boats." [47] In the report of that meeting which Sutherland sent to Brigade headquarters, he put forth the information that Ferguson was not a partisan but rather was an officer of the regular Confederate Army. Sutherland based that belief on conversations with locals as well as from what a number of Confederate deserters had told him.[48] As far as is known, no Negro crewmen from the Mississippi Marine Brigade vessels were ever executed by the Confederate military; however, there were later cases of the enemy executing Negro troops who had surrendered to Confederate forces. One such episode occurred at Fort Pillow during April of 1864.

Farragut Runs the Port Hudson Batteries

Realizing that the section of the Mississippi between Baton Rouge and Vicksburg had become a military vacuum waiting to be filled, Rear Admiral Farragut decided that conditions were ripe to move his ships of the line from Baton Rouge north to the mouth of the Red River. The enemy batteries near Port Hudson would have to be dealt with before the Red River could be reached, but Farragut believed he could get by these without serious damage. Once he brought his ships to the mouth of the Red River, the river could be sealed by merely mooring ships at its junction with the Mississippi.

Getting past Port Hudson proved to be tougher than anticipated. Farragut only managed to get his flagship *USS HARTFORD* and one attending vessel above. The others were forced to turn back. In judging that event, Alfred Thayer Mahan placed a greater degree of significance on that limited accomplishment than was actually warranted when he wrote that the passage of the *USS HARTFORD* resulted in the Mississippi slipping finally from the control of the enemy.[49] It is difficult to agree with Mahan. Realistically, the only parts of the river between Baton Rouge and Vicksburg which had truly come under Union control were those immediate localities where the *USS HARTFORD* and her consort happened to be at any one point in time. Trans-Mississippi traffic continued to be carried on by the enemy even though it consisted mainly of short-haul ferrying from one bank to the other. Confederate land forces moved freely along both sides of the river, placing their harassing artillery batteries wherever they wished.

During the second half of March, Farragut steamed up the Mississippi to De Soto Landing from where he sent a message to Porter who was then across the De Soto Peninsula at Milliken's Bend. Farragut had come upriver to request from Porter the loan of either some of the Mississippi Marine Brigade's rams or a few of Porter's gunboats, to be utilized in setting up a tighter blockade at the entrance to the Red River and at other critical points south of Vicksburg. At the time, Porter was absent on an expedition into the Yazoo basin. He had taken with him most of his squadron, leaving only a small force to guard the mouth of the Yazoo and the Army supply dumps above Milliken's Bend.

Can Vicksburg Be Bypassed?

It was by now clear that Vicksburg could not be taken by frontal assault. For Grant to get his army directly past the guns of Vicksburg by way of the main river was thought to be so dangerous as to be impractical. On this Porter and Grant agreed. Consequently, alternatives would be tried during the winter months of 1862-1863. Two of these alternatives would involve a try at bypassing the city. The third alternative would be to starve out the defenders by cutting them off from all incoming supplies.

The first plan for bypass called for a continuation of the work which had been started in 1862 by Thomas Williams. This was the canal which would cut across the De Soto Peninsula. A change had since been made in Williams's original excavation plan. This change re-angled the upriver entrance so as to more perfectly align the canal with the river's flow. Although digging would continue well into the winter, it soon became obvious that fluctuating river levels would render such a canal unreliable. The optimism of the canal's proponents was destroyed for good when the enemy batteries at Vicksburg began to make the range of the diggers. The project was halted.

The second alternative was to dig a new canal, starting at a point about fifty miles above Vicksburg. This one would begin on the Mississippi's western bank and feed into a standing "deadwater" named Lake Providence. From Lake Providence, a cut would be made into Bayou Macon. Another cut would then feed from Bayou Macon into the Tensas- Washita river network which meandered southward to eventually meet with the Red River. If that route could be completed, it would have a two-fold advantage: it would allow transports to bypass Vicksburg well to the westward and completely out of range of Vicksburg's cannon; and it would allow Grant to physically join his army with the troops of Nathaniel Prentiss Banks which were located below Port Hudson. The joined forces would then attack Port Hudson from the south and east. Presumably, such an attack could not help but succeed. Then, the combined force would march north to encircle Vicksburg from its land side.

The disadvantage to this second alternative was the great distance of the water course which would have to be developed. From its beginning north of Vicksburg, the proposed route was over two hundred miles in length. From the standpoint of its construction, opening the route would not be an overly difficult endeavor. It depended in largest part upon completing the first opening from the Mississippi into Lake Providence together with a 6-mile channel leading from that lake through a deep flooded forest to Bayou Macon. The remainder of the proposed route southward to Bayou Macon was thought to be navigable in its natural state for shallow draft steamers. Success would then come to depend upon the ability of the quartermasters to assemble enough shallow draft steamers to handle the required troop lift and a reasonable follow up of supply vessels. The great distance from Lake Providence to the Red River precluded any multiple use of vessels by way of a shuttle system, at least until the initial troop lift could be completed. Finding sufficient numbers of watercraft which were narrow enough in beam and shallow enough in draft to navigate the backwaters would be difficult but not impossible, provided, of course, that the operation received full priority without competition from military endeavors elsewhere.

By the time the Lake Providence route had been cut out and made ready for steamer passage, it was March. By then, the vessels needed to traverse that route were being heavily allocated to an expedition for the control of the Coldwater- Sunflower- Yazoo basin. Grant had ordered a major amphibious operation into that basin, an operation aimed at pinching off Vicksburg's logistical arteries. This was to be Grant's third alternative, his siege concept. The Coldwater- Sunflower- Yazoo basin had been supplying the majority of foodstuffs and other materiel reaching into Vicksburg. According to Harry P. Owens in his work *Steamboats and the Cotton Economy*, forty Confederate steamers had been operating within the Coldwater- Sunflower- Yazoo basin during the winter months of 1862-1863, most of them being directly engaged in the supply of Vicksburg.[50] Taking control of the waterways in this basin would also effectively close down the railways which traversed it since in at least two locations that railway system crossed over the rivers of the basin by bridge. Now that the Red River supply route was reasonably well sealed, only the Coldwater- Sunflower- Yazoo system remained as an artery of logistical importance toward Pemberton's ability to hold Vicksburg. If that basin could also be denied to him, starvation might well decide the issue. Grant thought it was worth a hard try.

An expedition into the Coldwater- Sunflower- Yazoo basin was to be an amphibious strike conducted by shallow draft troop transports which would be supported by the Navy's gunboats. The transports would be selected on the basis of their size and draft. It was to prove difficult to find steamers with dimensions suitable for work in shallow, narrow streams and bayous. The shortage of such steamers precluded moving forward with Grant's other plan to bring an army south to the Red River via the Lake Providence route since the Lake Providence route required the same type of narrow beam, shallow draft vessel.

Yazoo Expedition, February - March

The name Yazoo Pass came from a stretch of water which had once been an open connection from the Mississippi into the Coldwater River. Blocked off by a levee, this old pass lay at a distance about one hundred and ninety miles upstream from Vicksburg and diagonally across from Helena, Arkansas. The eastern remnant of the old pass still connected with an open water area known as Moon Lake. That lake fed directly into the Coldwater River. The Coldwater River had its confluence with the Tallahatchie River which in turn connected with the Yazoo and the Yalobusha rivers. At the junction of the Tallahatchie and the Yalobusha, the Confederates had begun to erect a fortified strong point which they had christened Fort Pemberton. Reducing that strong point would be the key for control of the Coldwater- Sunflower- Yazoo basin. But before Fort Pemberton could be reached, the expedition would have to overcome an initial engineering challenge, i.e., a cut would have to be made through the blocked Yazoo Pass. The pass had been closed since 1856 by a flood control levee placed to protect the Yazoo basin from the spring flood waters of the Mississippi. In the years since that construction, blowdowns and other debris had choked off the pass with the heaviest of this occurring at the eastern end where the pass joined the Coldwater.

Within a communication to Rear Admiral Porter, Grant outlined the importance of the expedition.

...The Yalobusha is a navigable stream to Grenada. At this place the railroad branches, one going to Memphis, the other to Columbus, Kentucky. These roads cross the river on different bridges. The enemy are now repairing both these roads, and on the upper one, the one leading through the middle of west Tennessee, have made considerable progress. I am liable at all times to be compelled to divert from the Mississippi River Expedition [meaning the effort against Vicksburg] a large portion of my forces, on account of the existence of these roads. If their bridges can be destroyed, it would be a heavy blow to the enemy and of much service to us.

I have directed six hundred men, armed with rifles, to go up on transports to Delta, leaving here [Young's Point] tomorrow, to act as marines to the expedition. Have also ordered the regiment spoken of this morning to report at steamer *MAGNOLIA* at 10 a.m. tomorrow to join your service.

Respectfully,

U. S. Grant, Major General[51]

Porter's subsequent instructions to the naval officer commanding the expedition's gunboat contingent would outline the specifics of the Navy's responsibility. These instructions, along with Grant's communication to Porter, go a long way toward dispelling the all too common misconception that the intention of the Yazoo Pass Expedition was to create a backdoor approach to Vicksburg. The true goal, pure and simple, was to cut off supply communications to Vicksburg which emanated from the Coldwater- Sunflower- Yazoo basin.

US Mississippi Squadron
February 6, 1863

Lieutenant Commander Watson Smith
Commanding First Division Light Draft Vessels, Mississippi Squadron
Sir:

You will proceed with the *RATTLER** and *ROMEO** to Delta, near Helena, where you will find the *FOREST* ROSE* engaged in trying to enter the Yazoo Pass. You will order the *SIGNAL*,* now at White River, to accompany you; and if the *CRICKET** comes down while you are at Delta, detain her also, or the *LINDEN**.

Lieutenant Commander [James] Foster will also be ordered to accompany you.

You will obtain coal enough from Helena to enable you to carry on operations for some time. Your vessels had better all go to Helena and coal and start from there with as much coal in tow (say two barges) as will answer.

Do not enter the Yazoo Cut until the current is quite slack; and some small transport will have to go ahead, and the soldiers will cut away the trees and branches, so as not to endanger the smokestacks of the steamers.

Proceed carefully, and only in the daytime; six hundred or eight hundred soldiers will be detached to accompany you, and you will take one hundred on board of each light draft. See that the Army sends a very small steamer, with stores from Helena.

Get all the pilots you can who are acquainted with the different branches of the rivers. You may find them at Helena.

You will keep perfect order among the troops while on board your vessels or under your orders.

Subject them to strict military rules, and see that every order you give is promptly obeyed.

When you get to the Tallahatchie, proceed with all dispatch to ascend it as far as the railroad crossing, and completely destroy the railroad bridge at that point, after which you will, if possible, cut the telegraph wires and proceed down the river to the mouth of the Yalobusha.

You will fill up with coal and leave the coal barges at that place in charge of a light draft vessel and dash on to Grenada; destroy completely the railroad bridge, and retire at once down the river without any further damage, excepting to destroy means of transportation (which you will do in all cases) and you will destroy all small boats.

When you get to the [mouth of the] Yalobusha, you will proceed with all your force down the Yazoo River and endeavor to get into Sunflower River, where it is said all the large steamers are stowed away.

These you will not have time to capture; therefore you will destroy them, keeping an account, as near as you can, of the value of the property that falls into your hands.

Obtain all the information you can in relation to ironclads, and destroy them if you can while they are on the stocks.

If this duty is performed as I expect it to be, we will strike a terrible blow at the enemy, who do not anticipate an attack from such a quarter. But you must guard against surprise, and if overwhelmed run your vessels on the bank and set fire to them.

Be careful of your coal, and lay in wood where you can find it.

By going along only in the daytime, under low steam, you can cruise some time. But after doing the damage I have mentioned in my orders, ascend the river again to the Yazoo Cut-off, and report to me by a dispatch boat.

You will likely find Honey Island [Fort Pemberton] fortified. If it has guns on it, and you can take them, destroy them effectually and blow up the fort.

Do not risk anything by encumbering yourself with prisoners, except officers, whom you must not parole.

Do not engage batteries with the light vessels. The *CHILLICOTHE** will do the fighting. Let me hear from you as soon as possible, and give me full accounts of what you do.

Very respectfully, your obedient servant,

David D. Porter, Acting Rear Admiral
Commanding Mississippi Squadron[52]

* * *

* *USS*, commissioned Union naval vessel.

In the first week of February, work was started to clear the blowdowns immediately adjacent to the levee blocking Yazoo Pass. This chore took three days. The levee was then blown out by explosives. When the rush of the main river had sufficiently subsided, Watson Smith sent in the gunboat *USS FOREST ROSE* and the Army transport *CARL*, the latter having aboard a force of infantry.

That the levee into Yazoo Pass had been blown came as no surprise to the Confederates. Once again, the best possible intelligence had been provided to them, courtesy of Northern newspaper stories. When the enemy read of what was going to happen, they sent in a cavalry force to make matters difficult. The troopers felled trees along the full length of the old pass, thus augmenting the blowdowns still in place at the eastern end. Upon discovering what had been done, the infantry commander on the *CARL* departed by steamer for Helena, returning the next day with one hundred axmen who were set to work. The harder the Federals chopped to clear away the downed trees, the faster the Confederates chopped down new ones in the advance. Things began to take on the appearance of an impasse, as each side worked feverishly to undo the other's efforts. Meanwhile, the fallen trees served as a shielding barrier between the two groups of axmen. Only the most determined rifleman could squeeze himself through such a tangle. The riflemen with the most perseverance for getting through the tangles turned out to be the Federals; consequently, the Confederates withdrew.

Passage was cut into the Coldwater by the second week in February. At that time, Brigadier General Leonard F. Ross was instructed to load troops aboard fourteen Army transports which would carry his infantry into the Coldwater River. These were:[53]

CARL	LEBANON
CITIZEN	LEBANON NO. 2
J. W. CHEESEMAN	MAGNOLIA
JOHN BELL	MARINER
KEY WEST NO. 2	SAINT LOUIS
LAVINA LOGAN	SMALL
LAWYER	VOLUNTEER

Another transport, the STEPHEN BAYARD, had been badly damaged by an underwater obstruction while negotiating Yazoo Pass and was subsequently ordered back to the Mississippi.[54]

Lieutenant Commander Watson Smith's naval group consisted of two ironclads, five armed light draft gunboats, and a naval towboat. The infantry carried on the CARL and the MAGNOLIA would serve as marines for the naval group. They would be landed from the gunboats as flankers whenever they were needed to clear the banks of snipers. The CARL and MAGNOLIA would travel well in the van of the other transports, their troop passengers operating under Watson Smith's direct orders. The remaining transports were to be under Ross's command. The troops they carried would serve as an assault force once points of strong Confederate resistance were encountered. Two of the Mississippi Marine Brigade's vessels, the DICK FULTON and the LIONESS, along with the Navy's USS PETREL, were not part of the initial group but were to follow along in a day or two

On February 24, Watson Smith's and Leonard Ross's combined force steamed into the Coldwater. By the evening of February 25th, over twenty-four hours after they had started from Moon Lake, the advance gunboat element had progressed only about two miles. This slower than snail's pace was the result of floating debris which constantly fouled the stern wheels. Each time a forced stop was made, the vessels behind and ahead had to stop and hold position until the temporarily disabled vessel up ahead was ready to again proceed. The uncertainty as to what enemy forces might be in the area, when joined with the fact that the river was simply too narrow in most places to allow one vessel to pass another, mandated that the pace of each vessel was determined by the progress of the slowest one ahead of it. By March 3, the expedition was still in the Coldwater, the exhausted crews hacking their way forward. Watson Smith would report an average speed of only "1 1/2 miles per hour" -- and that was only when the column was underway, which was seldom.[55] Debris in the water was only one of the difficulties. The cover on the banks was so thick and the river so winding that the pilots had difficulty keeping visual contact with those vessels immediately ahead and behind. Each of the steamers was forced to keep two small boats in the water, one forward and one aft, in order to maintain proper contact. It was not until March 6 that Watson Smith's lead gunboat reached the Tallahatchie, a point only fifty miles from the place of beginning. An infantry patrol which Smith constantly kept ashore as forward scouts suddenly came upon a mobile artillery battery located so as to block movement into the Tallahatchie. The battery's infantry support proved insignificant, and the guns were soon overrun.

"Murphy's Law" now began to heckle Watson Smith and Ross. According to local inhabitants brought in for questioning, Fort Pemberton was being heavily fortified through the labor of three thousand slaves. A fast movement seemed imperative before the defenses became too strong to take. But then a further problem reared its head causing yet more delay. This was due to a shortage of coal for the steamers' fire boxes. Rations were also critically low. These deficiencies necessitated offloading troops from two of the rear most troop transports so that those two transports could return to the Mississippi for the needed replenishments. The troops which had been offloaded were distributed among the other transports, making the already crowded conditions aboard them quite impossible. As if things were not already bad enough, smallpox broke out among some of the Negroes who had not been vaccinated and who were serving as coal passers. And then to really top things off, Watson Smith came down with a "debilitating illness" (chronic dysentery). At that point, the expedition's command coordination began to disintegrate.

It was March 10 before the lead gunboat arrived within proximity of Fort Pemberton. Shortly before the fort came into view, a large raft-like structure was spotted. It was apparently rigged so that it could be drawn across the channel as a blocking device. Just below the raft, and anchored out in midstream, was the once proud *STAR OF THE WEST*, now renamed *CSS SAINT PHILIP*. Her location, along with the fact that no cannon were seen on her decks, led to the conclusion that she had been moored, ready for sinking as a blocking vessel. That conclusion proved to be correct.[56]

The enemy had chosen well for their site for a fort. Surrounded by flood water, it appeared impervious to any assault by infantry. Heavy bombardment seemed to be the only way to take the place; but when the lead gunboat opened fire, the rounds seemed to have little effect. The gunboats were the only medium from which to deliver a bombardment, and they were at a distinct disadvantage because they could not be brought into proper alignment due to the narrowness of the channel. The only gunboat able to fire was the one in the lead, and then only with its forward-facing gun.

Grant, operating without sufficient information, had developed the incorrect assumption that an infantry assault would be able to carry the fort. Accordingly, he had earlier ordered Brigadier General B. M. Prentiss, the commander of the Military District of Eastern Arkansas at Helena, to send more troops to assist Ross:

> General:
>   Direct the first division of troops coming from Memphis, probably the one commanded by Brigadier General John E. Smith, to pass into Moon Lake, and there await orders and transports from Major General McPherson. They will keep with

them all boats of less dimensions than 50 feet beam and 190 feet in length. All other transports they will send here.

There are also troops coming from Saint Louis. Direct them to land at Lake Providence, unless they receive other directions from these headquarters. They will retain all their large class boats, but release for the Yazoo [Expedition] their small ones. They will probably find at Lake Providence some of General McPherson's command awaiting transportation; but if they have gone, they will send these boats into Moon Lake to transport such troops as may be there.

Direct General C. C. Washburn to hold such a force of cavalry as you can spare -- not less than twelve hundred men -- in readiness to obey the summons of General McPherson. General McPherson, to avoid the delay of sending through these headquarters, is directed to call directly upon you for this cavalry as soon as he can use them and can send the transports. It would be well to send General Washburn to Moon Lake as soon as the weather and roads will permit of him doing service there, and have him that much nearer where he will be wanted.

I am, General, very respectfully, your obedient servant,

U. S. Grant[57]

Grant now decided on a secondary effort -- this one also involving an Army- Navy combined force -- to close against Fort Pemberton from the opposite direction. This force would enter, via Steele's Bayou, into a network of minor rivers and bayous which eventually led into the Yazoo downstream of Fort Pemberton. Steele's Bayou connected with the Mississippi near Vicksburg at a point slightly upstream from Milliken's Bend. Grant and Porter had personally reconnoitered the first part of this route, and from their examination, it looked to be practical.[58] A communication from Grant which was sent to Major General J. B. McPherson at the time of the Grant- Porter reconnaissance presents us with a synopsis of Grant's thinking, particularly as to the priority he was giving to the Yazoo expeditions as against putting the Lake Providence- Bayou Macon route back on the agenda for a bypass of Vicksburg. When Grant sent his dispatch to McPherson, he was anxiously awaiting some intelligence as to what was transpiring with the expeditions then on the Yazoo basin.

Before Vicksburg

Major General J. B. McPherson:

I returned this morning from a reconnaissance some thirty miles up Steele's Bayou. Admiral Porter and myself went in a large gunboat, preceded by four of the old 'turtles.' [A type of small Navy gunboat.]

These boats are pushing on with all dispatch to get into the Yazoo. It is important that a force should get in there with all dispatch. I have information direct from Vicksburg and the Yazoo River, both from persons who have been there and from late papers, that our gunboats had been down to Greenwood [Fort Pemberton] and exchanged a few shots with the fort at that place. The enemy have sent up reinforcements from Vicksburg, and some more guns. If we can get our boats in the rear of them in time, it will so confuse the enemy as to save Ross's force. If they do not, I shall feel restless for his fate, until I know that Quinby has reached him. Quinby will have the most abundant force for that route with his division and that of John E. Smith. I am now almost sorry that I directed the latter to join him.

It seems impossible to get steamers of the class we want. I sent long enough since for them to have received them from Pittsburgh, if necessary.

The route through Bayou Macon may prove a good thing for us yet in some operation. But this one, to get all our forces in one place, and that where it will be in striking distance of the enemy's lines of communication north, is the most important until firm foothold is secured on the side with the enemy. [Meaning control of the eastern side of the Mississippi River within the Yazoo-Sunflower river system and control of the railroads serving that general area.]

U. S. Grant[59]

There was no chance of releasing the transports once Quinby's force had joined Ross. The flooded conditions in the Yazoo basin prohibited putting troops into encampments ashore. Besides that, all retrograde movements which might have to be made would depend on the immediate availability of transports. Colonel Lewis B. Parsons, the quartermaster in charge of assembling steamers, tried desperately to meet Grant's requests for more vessels of the proper size; but Parsons's resources were already stretched thin, a fact he explained to Grant on March 16 in a lengthy telegram.

...It will be extremely difficult to replace any boats from the Ohio. Everybody is complaining of me here [Saint Louis] for want of boats. The forage quartermaster says we are interfering with his contracts upon the upper rivers and demands we do not take boats engaged bringing down forage, to which Colonel Allen, Chief Quartermaster, assents. The commissary wants his stores forwarded very promptly. General McNeil is said to be in a tight place, and we are required to send him three boats instanter [sic]. General [John] Pope demands that we send three more boats up the Missouri to chase up those poor devils, the Indians, etc.[60]

The fact is, General Rosecrans or General Wright have nearly all the small boats engaged on the Tennessee and Cumberland, and it seems they absolutely require them there, while we have already at or below Memphis the great bulk of our boats, and, consequently, it is extremely difficult doing our necessary business here. As you are aware, I sent you three small boats from the Ohio, and could only get permission to take eight more under any circumstances. We have sent you five more from here, and suppose several more have been sent from Cairo and Memphis. We have two or three more here repairing, which I hope to send in two or three days. I have also sent above the rapids for two or three I hear are running there, and will send them as soon as I can get them. There are also two on the Illinois, but Colonel Allen says they must not be taken unless I can supply their places with larger ones, which I cannot do. These are all the boats less than 200 feet long I can control, except such as we may seize at Cairo or when they come into port here.

There have gone to you, in addition, of large boats, since your order, as follows:

CHAMPION	capacity fifteen hundred men
CONTINENTAL	capacity two thousand men
ILLINOIS	capacity two thousand men.
JOHN J. ROE	capacity fifteen hundred men
*KENNETT**	capacity fifteen hundred men
MINNEHAHA	capacity twelve hundred men
PLANET	capacity fifteen hundred men
RUTH	capacity fifteen hundred men
VON PHUL	capacity fifteen hundred men

* *L. M. KENNETT*

Of small boats -- boats under 200 feet in length -- I have sent from here as follows:

ALONE	capacity five hundred men
BELLE CREOLE	capacity five hundred men
BLACK HAWK	capacity eight hundred men
GOLDEN ERA	capacity seven hundred men
*J. K. BELL**	capacity eight hundred men
LASALLE	capacity five hundred men
MACON	capacity five hundred men
NEVADA	capacity six hundred men
WHITE ROSE	capacity seven hundred men.

* JESSE K. BELL

From Cincinnati I sent

CITY BELLE	capacity six hundred men
DIADEM	capacity five hundred men
ELLA	capacity five hundred men
LADY FRANKLIN	capacity five hundred men
TYCOON	capacity eight hundred men.

The following boats leave here tonight or tomorrow:

CITY OF ALTON	capacity fifteen hundred men
SOUTHWESTERN	capacity one thousand men

...In all, a capacity for twenty-five thousand two hundred men. On these boats, however, I have sent about twenty-five hundred men, which leaves transportation for a little over the number of men required by you, though not by any means so many small boats as you desire. I think, in addition, there will be within a few days as many as six to ten more small boats. I regret my inability to comply with your orders almost as much as you can, but I have done my best.

Our wants for transportation here I have stated without exaggeration, and earnestly request, for the good of the whole service, that you will instruct the quartermaster of transportation to send back such boats as you can best spare as soon as can be safely done. I deeply regret that I cannot be permitted to accompany these boats, and share the labors and good fortune which, I trust, await you.

Very respectfully and sincerely, yours,

L. B. Parsons, Colonel and Assistant Quartermaster General
Superintendent Transportation[61]

In order to satisfy Grant's requirements for an adequate number of transports, a great deal of swapping around was obviously taking place everywhere on the western rivers. As Parsons's telegram had stated, Major General W. S. Rosecrans's Army of the Cumberland had its own problems of transport shortages. Rosecrans was willing to cooperate with Parsons but only to the extent that his own quartermasters did not end up on the short end.

Lieutenant Colonel John W. Taylor who was at Murfreesborough, Tennessee, and who was Rosecrans's quartermaster, had recently wired Parsons:

There are but four boats here that are under the exclusive control of this department; all of the others used for the transportation of supplies from the Ohio River. As soon as unloaded, General Rosecrans has no objection to the exchange of boats as [you] proposed, but if the short boats are taken, they must be replaced with larger boats. The success of the Army, indeed its very life, depends upon our having an increased supply of transportation now while we can make use of the river. The boats that were at Carthage have gone down the river.[62]

When a call for voluntary charterers failed to produce the necessary steamboats, the harried Parsons would put into force an order for the seizure of all river craft less than 200 feet long which were not already in the employ of either the Army or the Navy. The heavy call-up of steamers resulted in economic chaos not only within the steamboat industry per se, but within those industries which were directly and even indirectly dependent on river transport for their needs. Regular commerce was badly interrupted and in some places was actually brought to a halt. The hue and cry from those businessmen who were adversely affected was heard all the way to Washington. Pressures which were directed to the War Department from the White House resulted in the following communication sent by the War Department to Parsons's immediate superior at Saint Louis.

> Washington, DC
> March 19, 1863
>
> Colonel Robert Allen, Saint Louis:
> I cannot direct the seizures on the Ohio River unless in case of absolute necessity, and that necessity must be certified to by the Quartermaster's Department. Where boats can be procured for reasonable hire, violent measures should be avoided. General Grant's last dispatches to me do not indicate any necessity for violent seizures.
>
> H. W. Halleck[63]

This casual interpretation by those in Washington regarding Grant's need for vessels does not jibe with the tone of urgency contained in the requests which were going out to Parsons from Grant's headquarters. Nor does it seem to reflect a concern over the profiteering on the part of steamboat owners, a practice which Allen and his subordinate quartermasters were trying to control.

Altogether from the Ohio River system, Allen had gathered twenty-six boats, all under 200 feet, which he was sending south. In a report to Halleck, Allen bluntly stated that even this "fell short of the number required...This [Yazoo] expedition is so dependent upon its transportation that an insufficiency may prove fatal."[64]

For those on the Yazoo Expedition, the conditions aboard the transports were no doubt reaching intolerable levels. Although there are no surviving first hand accounts of those particular conditions, we did locate a related protest, written aboard a steamer then preparing to leave Helena to join up with Quinby for the move against Fort Pemberton. The writer, a brigadier general named Clinton B. Fisk, borrowed on past experience where troops had been held on board transports. Fisk had been appalled, not only by the living standards but by the dangerous condition of river steamers generally. For instance, one had sunk almost instantaneously after hitting a snag while on an earlier expedition into the White River.

...Nearly two hundred newly-made [graves] at Helena contain the bodies of my command who were murdered outright by crowding them into dirty, rotten transports, as closely as slaves in the 'middle passage.' It was a crime against humanity and heaven, the packing of our soldiers on the White River Expedition. You will, therefore, excuse me general, if I earnestly protest against any probable repetition of such an outrage upon the gallant men who confidently believe that I will do all that I can to insure their comfort and safety without prejudice to the good cause for which they will cheerfully fight.

The company from the 29th Iowa, on the *LUELLA*, lost all their arms and clothing by the sinking of that staunch vessel and one of my best officers, Lieutenant [Lucius B.] Nash will doubtless die from injuries received thereby.[65]

From what can be reconstructed from the reports of those involved in the operation, and from what was written in the years following, it appears that Ross was not made aware of the other plan to come against Fort Pemberton from the south via Steele's Bayou. This was an understandable communication gap, considering that at the time there was no telegraphic contact between Ross and Union command elements. The flooded condition and hostile state of the countryside within the Coldwater-Sunflower-Yazoo basin precluded the use of mounted couriers. Ross was thus operating without guidance from higher command and could only decide upon the situation he faced as he and his officers evaluated it. Ross's supplies were nearing depletion, despite the return of the two steamers which had come in from the Mississippi with replenishments. Tactically, the outlook for taking Fort Pemberton was becoming bleak. Watson Smith was now at the point of complete collapse from dysentery; his second in command, Lieutenant Commander James Foster, had to take over command of the gunboats. Foster concurred with Ross over the prognosis for success, and both agreed that to remain static in front of Fort Pemberton made little military sense. A retrograde movement back to Yazoo Pass was decided upon.

Before reaching the Coldwater, Foster's lead gunboat met a fleet of steamers bringing in the troops of John E. Smith and Quinby. They had with them enough supplies to handle their own needs and those of Ross's men for some time to come. Quinby was aware of Grant's plan to send another force via Steele's Bayou to cut Fort Pemberton off from its access to Vicksburg via the Yazoo. When Ross was informed of this, he agreed to accompany Smith and Quinby back to Fort Pemberton. Since it was imperative that the gunboats go with them, all three officers appealed to Foster who agreed; but in so doing, Foster stipulated that unless he was put under a direct order from Rear Admiral Porter to stay, he would leave for the Mississippi not later than the first of April. Quinby protested -- and probably quite rightly -- that if Foster's gunboats pulled out by April 1 (which was only a week off), there would not be time for the force entering the Yazoo via Steele's Bayou to arrive. Quinby would later put on record his protest regarding Foster's cutoff date. In a dispatch to Major General McPherson, Quinby would state, "It is one of the greatest evils of our service that the land and naval forces are left to a great measure independent of each other. The best concerted plans are liable to fail from the cause." But at the time, there was little choice on Quinby's part but to hope for the arrival by April 1 of Sherman and Porter, who each respectively commanded the Army and Navy elements of the force coming in by way of Steele's Bayou. The gunboats and Ross's transports led the way back to the junction of the Tallahatchie and the Yalobusha, there to take up their prior positions before Fort Pemberton and wait.

April 1 passed. Quinby had received no word as to Sherman's and Porter's progress, nor had he received instructions from Grant. He now had no choice but to withdraw since to remain before Fort Pemberton without the fire power offered by Foster's gunboats would have been foolhardy. On April 15, the last Army transport passed back into the Mississippi through the levee at Yazoo Pass. The Yazoo Pass phase of the attempt to take Fort Pemberton was over -- a complete failure.[66] If one attempts to assign reasons for the failure, the answers vary. It was probably a matter of getting to Fort Pemberton too late in the game. Had the gunboats arrived earlier at the fort, they might have pounded the place into submission before the Confederates had the opportunity to make the place as impregnable as it became. By the time the expedition finally did arrive, the fort had become impervious to assault by land because of the high flood waters which made the place unapproachable by infantry. Ironically, it was the breaching of the Yazoo Pass levee which had in largest part created this condition through the resultant flooding of the lower Tallahatchie and Yalobusha valleys. The slowness of getting to the scene of action was partially the result of lethargy on the part of Lieutenant Commander Watson Smith, the gunboat commander who accompanied Ross. An ill man moves slowly and with little enthusiasm, and Smith was very ill indeed. He died shortly after his evacuation back to the Mississippi. Not to be neglected in the equation for overall failure was the inadequacy of Union communications. Conversely, the Confederates at Fort Pemberton enjoyed a fast, open- river movement direct to Vicksburg via the Yazoo River. In addition, they had a direct rail route into that city.

The Steele's Bayou Expedition, coming at Fort Pemberton from the south, would be equally replete with difficulty.

Steele's Bayou

Grant's initial reconnaissance of Steele's Bayou, over which he and Porter had waxed enthusiastic, was only the first part of the complex route which would have to be followed before Fort Pemberton could be reached. The continuance of the route from Steele's Bayou was through a connection to another waterway which Porter would refer to in his post operation reports as [Big] "Black Bayou". Big Black Bayou led directly into Deer Creek; shortly thereafter, by way of a cutoff named Rolling Fork River, a connection was made into the Sunflower River. The Sunflower fed directly to the Yazoo River. It was upstream on the Yazoo that the expedition's destination, Fort Pemberton, was located.[67] Big Black Bayou's very narrowness and crookedness had at first glance seemed to preclude its use by steamboats; however, on a closer examination, it was determined that if fallen trees were pulled out of the way, vessels could be heaved (by windlasses or manpower) around the sharp bends. But it would be a tight squeeze.[68]

Porter would personally accompany the expedition's naval element which consisted of six gunboats and four mortar boats, the latter with their attendant tugs. Following along after the gunboats would be the transports, five in all. The gunboats and mortar boats would serve as the expedition's floating artillery. If Fort Pemberton could be reached, they were to batter the place from its southern side.

The gunboats and the transports were to enter Steele's Bayou where it emptied into the Yazoo (near that river's junction with the Mississippi). They were to proceed north on Steele's Bayou to a position which could be easily approached overland from Eagle Bend on the Mississippi. There they would embark Sherman's troops for the continuation of the passage up Steele's Bayou to the western entrance of Big Black Bayou. The steamer trip was broken for the troops once Big Black Bayou was reached. There they disembarked from the transports which turned back to the original embarkation point for a second load of troops. The trip through Big Black Bayou turned out to be a standing room only affair for which the troops took passage on the deck of an empty coal barge which, under the tow of a tug, performed a continuous shuttle service. The banks of Deer Creek, unlike the swampy edges of Steele's Bayou and Big Black Bayou, were high ground, so Sherman's regiments, after being landed from the coal barge, were put into marching column to proceed northward along the eastern bank of Deer Creek. If everything continued going as planned, they were to meet the transports on the Rolling Fork near where it joined the Sunflower River. Once the Sunflower was reached, it was anticipated that the transports would have relatively easy going from there to Fort Pemberton, so the troops were to reboard at that point for the remainder of the trip. Although the overland march along Deer Creek was only around twelve miles, the distance covered by the gunboats and the transports following the creek's winding, tree-choked course was over thirty miles. The nearer the fleet got to the Rolling Fork rendezvous, the more difficult things became. Enemy axmen had felled trees which were intertwined in such a way that getting through them became a momentous job even under the best of circumstances. The present circumstances were anything but the best. Snipers soon made life hazardous for Union axmen attempting to clear away the debris and for anyone appearing on the decks. When the gunboats and the transports were but a short way into the Rolling Fork, behind them the enemy began felling more trees. This effort was contested by landing parties sent to drive them off. Fortunately, the colonel of one of Sherman's regiments heard the firing and headed across country to investigate. On arriving at the blocked off fleet, and upon sizing up the situation, he deployed his men along the banks and drove off the enemy snipers and axmen. Porter would later describe the extremis of the situation at the time the rescuing regiment arrived.

> We might now have retraced our steps but we were all worn out. The officers
> and men had for six days and nights been constantly at work, or sleeping at the guns.
> We had lost our coal barge, and the provision vessel could not get through, being too
> high for such purpose.[69]

Notified by courier of what had occurred, Sherman came on the scene. Agreeing with Porter that they were at a no-win impasse, they jointly decided that their only option was to make a withdrawal. The troops were ordered to assist the exhausted sailors in clearing out the trees that were now down behind the fleet. No sooner had that work started than a Confederate force, estimated at three thousand in strength, suddenly appeared and attempted to deploy across the path of retreat; however, they were driven off.

On March 25, the expedition was back on the Mississippi. Casualties had been light, but everyone involved was much the worse for wear.

The Steele's Bayou Expedition had been a failure in the eyes of practically all concerned except perhaps Porter who would claim some good coming of it. In his report to the Secretary of the Navy, he boasted of the amount of cotton captured, "...enough to pay for the building of a good gunboat." Porter wrote, "The soldiers [Sherman's men] enjoyed themselves amazingly, the fine country through which we all traveled being quite different from the swamp where they have spent the winter." For those of all ranks who had been on the gunboats, the delights of the scenery were overshadowed because of what Porter admitted, in a separate and contradictory report, had been "mileage of the most severe labor officers and men ever went through." The same might well have been said for the crews of the transports and the infantry guards who had been assigned to the vessels.

The Army's transports employed in moving Sherman's troops on Steele's Bayou were: *DILIGENT, BLACK HAWK, EAGLE, SILVER WAVE, CHAMPION*. The Navy tug *FERN* was also used. Naval gunboats on the expedition were *USS LOUISVILLE*, *USS CINCINNATI*, *USS CARONDELET*, *USS MOUND CITY*, *USS PITTSBURG*, and *USS GENERAL STERLING PRICE*.

Repercussions

Brigadier General Alfred W. Ellet had arrived at Young's Point in mid-March of 1863, some days in advance of the bulk of the Mississippi Marine Brigade which was en route from its organizational training at Saint Louis. Just after his arrival, a crisis arose in his relationship with his nominal superior, Rear Admiral David D. Porter. While Porter was away from Young's Point accompanying the Steele's Bayou Expedition aimed against Fort Pemberton, the admiral had left Captain Henry Walke, in charge of all remaining naval craft which were at or near Milliken's Bend on the Mississippi. Walke's orders were to conduct a tight surveillance at the mouth of the Yazoo River during Porter's absence. The *SWITZERLAND* and *LANCASTER* had for some time been on detached service from the rest of the Brigade and had been directly subject to Walke's orders. At least that had been the case prior to the arrival of Ellet.

Practically simultaneous with Alfred W. Ellet's appearance on the scene at Young's Point had been the arrival to the south of Vicksburg of Rear Admiral Farragut on his flagship *USS HARTFORD* which was then moored at De Soto Landing at the southern side of the De Soto Peninsula. Assuming that Porter was still at Young's Point, Farragut sent an officer courier across the peninsula to request the loan of two or more of Porter's gunboats to go back downriver with him to assist in the blockade of the Red River. Walke messaged back to Farragut that in Porter's absence he had no authority to release any vessels to go below Vicksburg. Queried by Farragut about the

Mississippi Marine Brigade's *LANCASTER* and *SWITZERLAND*, Walke stated the same reservation but then annexed it by saying that the two rams could go with permission of Grant's headquarters. Farragut then approached Grant by courier and received authorization for both *LANCASTER* and *SWITZERLAND* to be assigned to Farragut's squadron. At this point, Colonel Charles R. Ellet was in company with his uncle while they both awaited the arrival of the Brigade from upriver. When it arrived, Charles Ellet was scheduled to take command of the Brigade's infantry regiment. He was still smarting over his loss of the *QUEEN OF THE WEST* on the Red River. Farragut's request presented an opportunity for the young colonel to repair his image by making a successful dash past Vicksburg. He received permission from his uncle the general to take personal charge of *SWITZERLAND* for the mission. His cousin Lieutenant Colonel John A. Ellet transferred to *LANCASTER* as its commander. Luck would not go with either of officer. In the attempt to get past Vicksburg, *LANCASTER* was holed and promptly sank. *SWITZERLAND* was hit but without overly serious damage. After Charles had pulled his cousin's crew from the water, he ran *SWITZERLAND* to safety at De Soto Landing. There, Charles turned over the command of *SWITZERLAND* to John while he himself returned overland to report to his uncle at Young's Point.

Rear Admiral Porter had meanwhile returned from his unsuccessful expedition through Steele's Bayou. Dead weary, and upon hearing the news of *LANCASTER's* loss, Porter flew into a rage, inaccurately accusing Alfred W. Ellet of usurping authority by granting permission for the vessel's to run past Vicksburg.

At the time, Porter had no knowledge of Grant's personal involvement in the decision to allow the *SWITZERLAND* and *LANCASTER* to attempt the run. It is clearly evident from reading Porter's correspondence that he feared he would be blamed for the failure to take Fort Pemberton. Porter was in his fifties and sick from some malady (probably dysentery). He was also becoming increasingly disgusted over anything and everything to do with Mississippi River operations, and the loss of *LANCASTER* was probably the last straw. Porter's state of mind was not helped by a telegraph received from Secretary of the Navy Gideon Welles. What Welles had to say to Porter included some acid remarks over the loss of the ram, an event which of course Porter had nothing to do with. The praise which Welles passed out to Farragut in that telegram, while mildly reproving Porter, did nothing to salvage Porter's low state of morale.

> Acting Rear Admiral D. D. Porter,
>   Commanding Mississippi Squadron, Cairo, IL
> Sir:
>   The Department is acquainted with your withdrawal from the Yazoo, by telegraph from General Grant, under date of the 25th ultimo [March]. Nothing definite or positive has been heard from the Yazoo Pass Expedition since it started. The Richmond papers announce that two of the rams attempted to pass the Vicksburg batteries in daylight and that one was sunk. It remains for your dispatches to inform the Department whether additional disgrace and disaster is to attach to the Navy from recklessness and disobedience of orders on the part of those not under the naval articles of war.
>   Rear Admiral Farragut is below Vicksburg, after a successful and gallant passage of the Port Hudson batteries. The occupation of the river between Vicksburg and Port Hudson is the severest blow that can be struck upon the enemy, is worth all the risk encountered by Rear Admiral Farragut, and, in the opinion of this

Department, is of far greater importance than the flanking expeditions which thus far have prevented the consummation of this most desirable object.

I desire that you will consult with Rear Admiral Farragut and decide how this object can best be obtained.

I am, respectfully, your obedient servant,

Gideon Welles, Secretary of the Navy.[70]

There are many gaps appearing in the correspondence dealing with the episode involving the loss of *LANCASTER*. It is evident, though, from surviving records that Porter had certainly developed a misunderstanding over the circumstances surrounding the dispatch of *SWITZERLAND* and *LANCASTER*. It would take some time before he would realize that Alfred W. Ellet had reacted correctly and had only dispatched the rams in direct response to Grant's permission.[71] Both Grant and Farragut, while stepping gingerly around Porter's sensitivities, backed the propriety of Alfred W. Ellet's action.

In a letter Grant addressed to Major General Halleck, dated March 27, Grant rationalized the affair.

...Since no casualties occurred, it was fortunate that she was lost; for had she not been at this time, she might have been at some other time, when more valuable vessels might have been risked, relying on this boat for assistance. It is almost certain that had she made a ram into another vessel she would have closed up like a spyglass, encompassing all aboard....[72]

Porter eventually grasped the facts as they had actually occurred, and he simmered down. The matter could have ended then and there had not a new factor reared its head, igniting Porter's quick fuse.

Lieutenant Colonel John A. Ellet, now south of Vicksburg with *SWITZERLAND* on his assignment to aid in the blocking of the Red River, had sent Alfred W. Ellet a copy of the orders he had received from Porter prior to *SWITZERLAND's* departure from De Soto Landing. Since the *SWITZERLAND* was an integral element of the Mississippi Marine Brigade, John naturally concluded that the Brigade's headquarters should be copied as to what was transpiring with its vessel -- this including any operational orders from naval commanders which directly involved that vessel, Porter's jurisdiction included. After sending a copy of Porter's orders to Alfred W. Ellet at Brigade headquarters, John A. Ellet informed Porter by courier that the admiral's orders were duly acknowledged and that they had been copied by way of information for the files of the Mississippi Marine Brigade. Porter's response to a process which had been nothing more than routine Army procedure was uncompromising fury. In the somewhat paranoid belief that his authority was being by-passed and that he had been slighted, Porter ordered John A. Ellet placed under arrest to await court-martial. This of course was completely unjustified. Further, it constituted an illegal action since Porter had no disciplinary authority over any Army officer, including one belonging to the Mississippi Marine Brigade. Alfred W. Ellet was then brusquely informed by Porter as to what had been done. This precipitated an angry exchange between the general and the admiral which ended with Porter next ordering that Alfred W. Ellet be relieved of his command -- an act for which Porter stood equally devoid of authority.

After he had a day or two to calm down, Porter must have realized that not only was the relief of the general beyond his powers, but by continuing with the matter, he was only making a fool of himself. By way of fence mending, Porter invited Alfred W. Ellet to meet with him. What transpired at that meeting is not of the record, but it can be presumed that it entailed some discussion on the correct transmission of orders, vis-à-vis Army procedures. At some point in that discussion, it must have come as a surprise to Porter to learn that the Army and Navy systems did not necessarily correspond. The court-martial order was dropped against John A. Ellet as was the capricious and unenforceable order relieving the general from command. It was perhaps provident that shortly after this, Porter and Alfred W. Ellet would find themselves geographically separated, the result of Porter ordering Ellet to proceed to the Tennessee River on a mission to be later described in this volume.

Grant's Plan That Finally Brought Success

The failure of the expeditions into the Coldwater- Sunflower- Yazoo basin narrowed Grant's options. The De Soto Canal idea had also proved itself unworkable. In a private note sent to Porter by one of his officers who had just inspected that canal, the prognosis for it was hopeless; the canal had in fact become more of a joke than anything else.

> I again visited the canal yesterday and am convinced it is not going to work. If you require the mortars, tugs, etc, [below Vicksburg], I shall have to run them past the batteries as I see no other way. I can't help feeling, though, that everything that goes down will stay there and won't [re]join this squadron. Well, till Vicksburg is taken, of course you are the best judge, and can see and know more about it than I, but I do hope you won't take anymore with you than you require, as I feel that they will all be wanted up this way. Of course this is only my opinion, based upon nothing but sad forebodings to the Army, all of which I did not mean to say, but kinder [sic] let it out accidentally. They tried to float some empty barges through the canal yesterday, but could not; they stuck and there they are; can't be got out, and won't go in; they only draw about 6 inches....[73]

The April rains then in progress marked the beginning of the Mississippi's malarial season. In most years one of the worst places for that scourge was the flooded land which lay north of Vicksburg. In 1863, the spring flooding had been more widespread than usual due in large part to the opening made in the levee at Yazoo Pass. Even to the most casual observer, it was clear that the Union Army could not remain operationally static within such an environment. Disease, worsening troop morale, and mounting political pressures were placing Grant into a position which was almost worse than the one held by Pemberton at Vicksburg. For Grant there were, however, a few bright spots. The enemy's disorganized military situation on the Louisiana (western) side of the Mississippi was creating a scenario which might allow a bypass of Vicksburg following along the internal waterways westward of the Mississippi. This was a more attractive proposition than had been the case in the past, provided the Federal supply line could be kept within workable limits. All that the enemy now possessed in strength adjacent to the western bank of the lower Mississippi were small units which launched lightning raids from which they made rapid withdrawals. Grant believed that sort of annoyance could be held in check with minimal effort. He could choose from two separate options for bypassing Vicksburg to the west of the river. First, there was the standing choice of the Lake Providence route with its southern termination near the mouth of the Red River. This route was over two hundred miles in length and would be long and cumbersome, particularly when viewed in light of the shortage of shallow draft steamers. Grant's second option was a shorter route which had recently come to light as the result of a cavalry reconnaissance. Grant's engineers evaluated the possibilities of this second route and reported that diagonally opposite the entrance to the Yazoo (above the river's big bend from Vicksburg and well out of sight and range of the city's guns) there was a narrow wagon trail which meandered inland from the hamlet of Duckport to the town of Richmond. From Richmond another wagon trail led back toward the Mississippi, emerging on the river at New Carthage. A cursory survey made of these trails disclosed them to be amenable to improvements which would give them good potential for troop movement. The end of the trail at New Carthage was eighteen miles south of Vicksburg and around twenty-five miles upstream from Grand Gulf. From New Carthage, Grant could conveniently move downriver and cross over to Grand Gulf. From there, he could come at Vicksburg from the south. After more completely surveying the route from Duckport, Grant's engineers determined that a bayou and canal network could be developed which would be complementary to a road system. A little less than three miles inland from Duckport was a fairly deep waterway called Walnut Bayou. This bayou connected directly to an extant canal which ran to the town of Richmond. From Richmond, the Roundaway River interconnected with the Bayou Vidal which itself meandered toward New Carthage. To open a through waterway route from Duckport to New Carthage which would be suitable for steamers meant dredging through only about three miles of flat land between Duckport and the Walnut Bayou. A survey of where that cut would have to be made showed the elevations to be the same at both Duckport and at Walnut Bayou, that is, if the cut was excavated in a due west direction. Since no gradient would be involved, construction of a canal would be relatively easy. Grant endorsed the project, and dredging machines were immediately brought in to do the work.[74] It is quite understandable that Grant's staff had not previously known of the wagon paths or of the possibility for a direct waterway route from Duckport to New Carthage. Prior to the war, mapping of that area had been perfunctory with only the most well developed features being shown.

Downstream at Grand Gulf, enemy batteries had been recently installed at the mouth of the Big Black River. This river was navigable during times of high water by small to medium-sized steamers. It was through this tributary to the main river that most of the supplies reaching Vicksburg from the Red River country had been getting into the city. Although Farragut had stopped the majority of that traffic, some of it had continued and was being carried on by short-haul ferries bringing supplies across the Mississippi from the Louisiana side. The Big Black meandered in a north-northeasterly direction until it reached a point ten miles east of Vicksburg at a place called Smith's

Ferry. At that location the river was crossed by the Vicksburg and Jackson Railroad. The Confederates had utilized that railroad for the short haul to the city of supplies offloaded from steamers at Smith's Ferry. Now, Grant intended using the Big Black River as a possible conduit for his own army's sustenance once he crossed the Mississippi to Grand Gulf. The supply route which Grant envisioned for his army, once it was across the Mississippi, would have its start at the Duckport Canal and would thence run through Richmond to New Carthage, either by wagon or by water, and thence down the Mississippi by steamer to the entrance of the Big Black. From there, supplies would be taken up the Big Black to the point of closest access to his advancing army.

The first order of business, in order to improve the wagon route for the expected heavy use by troops and supply wagons, was the construction of bridges. Grant anticipated marching the bulk of his army to New Carthage by road. Pole-propelled ferries were currently in place along the wagon route; however, such primitive ferries could not carry the high volume of supply needed by an army the size of Grant's. While bridge building was taking place, a number of large transports, along with Porter's gunboats, would have to come down the Mississippi past the Vicksburg batteries. The transports would be used to ferry Grant's army and its equipage from New Carthage across to Grand Gulf while the gunboats were to provide the artillery support for that river crossing. The inland waterway system to be opened from Duckport could be made navigable for the smallest class of steamers and barges but could not handle vessels with the draft of the gunboats or the large transports, thus the necessity for bringing the gunboats and transports down the main river past Vicksburg.

It was a foregone conclusion that the Confederates would launch some sort of counteraction once a crossing of the Mississippi had started. To keep that counteraction within limits, a series of troop diversions would be needed to tie up the enemy elsewhere. Providing one of those diversions became the job of Major General William T. Sherman who was to feint a landing at the mouth of the Yazoo opposite Milliken's Bend. This would be designed to fool the enemy into believing that an attack was to be made against Haines's Bluff which was the northern angle of Vicksburg's defensive perimeter. A second diversion was to be executed by Major General Nathaniel Banks who was already marshaling his forces to the south, preparatory to beginning an assault against Port Hudson. Once Banks launched his attack, he would tie up those Confederate forces near Port Hudson, preventing them from coming north to the aid of Pemberton at Vicksburg. A third diversion would be a cavalry raid launched from Memphis southward toward Grenada. This raid commanded by Colonel Benjamin H. Grierson would follow along a railroad line which longitudinally bisected the state of Mississippi. Grierson's cavalrymen would not ride back into Federal lines until they had reached the defensive perimeter of Baton Rouge. It was to be a ride of almost six hundred miles undertaken by a full brigade, an endeavor which up to that time in the war was unprecedented. Since Grant's move against Vicksburg's rear would depend largely for its success on the enemy's forces to the east of the city being preoccupied elsewhere, the cavalry raid was designed not only to tie up the enemy within the central and eastern sections of the state of Mississippi but also to cut off access to Vicksburg from the east by destroying rail lines.

The new bridges from Young's Point to New Carthage were constructed within a surprisingly short time. Their construction was a demonstration of the engineering skills which were practiced by the Union Army during the Civil War. The bridge which crossed Bayou Vidal was over 326 feet long, three-fourths of it built on trestles, the remainder on pontoons. Another of the bridges, the one crossing Negro Bayou, was 550 feet long, designed in such a way that its curvature (bending upstream) deflected the heavy current flow which otherwise could have undermined the bridge's foundations. A third bridge of 150 feet in length was built in the form of a trestle design running from a central pier.[75] At the same time, work was in progress on the bayous and canals. In anticipation of the completion of work on these waterways, quartermasters were scurrying around locating shallow draft barges and tugs capable of moving them.[76] So many old stumps were discovered in the bayou sections of the route that a saw barge had to be brought in to cut them out. (This was the same type of rig that had been utilized by General Pope's engineers at Island No. 10 during the spring of 1862.) When all the road bridging and the waterway preparations had been completed, Grant's engineers and quartermasters were in agreement that the combined routes would adequately handle Grant's initial troop movement to New Carthage plus the initial backup of supply which would be required after the army was in place prior to its crossing of the Mississippi.

Grant's personal staff as well as most of his general officers, including Sherman, had originally advised against crossing the Mississippi south of Vicksburg. They cited the difficulty of obtaining enough transportation to get across to the eastern side. Their concern was whether sufficient steamers could be brought down from Vicksburg for the troop lift. If judged by the previous attempt by *LANCASTER* and *SWITZERLAND* to pass Vicksburg's guns, the odds for getting transports down were deemed to be about 50-50. Grant responded to these criticisms by arguing that *LANCASTER* and *SWITZERLAND* had come down without any gunboat support. He believed that the transports could pass the batteries without too much risk provided Porter's gunboats came down with them and provided that the transports were manned "by courageous crews." The night of April 16 was selected for the trial run; three transports were to make the attempt. If it worked well, others were to follow in a day or so. The three transports -- all under charter to the Army -- were *SILVER WAVE*, *FOREST QUEEN*, and *HENRY CLAY*. They were to be manned by their regular civilian crews. None would carry troops for the trip down. Instead, all three, plus barges which were to be lashed alongside, would be loaded to capacity with rations. The secondary purpose for the barges was that they would help shield the boilers and steam pipes of the steamers from cannon fire. Gunboat accompaniment would be provided by the Navy's *USS BENTON*, *USS LAFAYETTE*, *USS GENERAL STERLING PRICE*, *USS PITTSBURG*, *USS CARONDELET*, *USS MOUND CITY*, and *USS TUSCUMBIA*. Rear Admiral Porter was to go along in overall command.

Just prior to midnight on April 16, the gunboats and the three transports got underway from Young's Point. Their run past Vicksburg did not turn out to be an easy one. Only one of the gunboats was damaged, and then only slightly, but the transports were not so lucky. *FOREST QUEEN* received one shot clear through her hull;

another shot took out a steam pipe which totally disabled her. Fortunately, one of the gunboats managed to get a line over, and *FOREST QUEEN* came through under tow. *HENRY CLAY* was hit repeatedly, set afire, and sunk. Many of her crew was plucked out of the river by the gunboats while others of them escaped to the western shore in the steamer's yawl boat. The official report which was filed on the operation discloses that the pilots of two of the transports (*SILVER WAVE* and *FOREST QUEEN*) attempted to turn back upstream when they first came under fire; but the alertness of one of the gunboat commanders thwarted that attempt. Porter's report also related that the crew of *HENRY CLAY* deserted the vessel even before she caught on fire. Her pilot showed more spunk, refusing to leave and imploring the others crew to see the thing through; but his pleadings had little effect. He was later picked up hanging to a plank. Two of the *HENRY CLAY* survivors, "a bartender and a chambermaid," were seen to reach the shore in a yawl boat. They must have had all they could stomach of river warfare and decided to depart for safer climes since neither one of them reported again for duty. The remainder of the *HENRY CLAY's* crew eventually reached the Union encampment at Milliken's Bend.[77] *SILVER WAVE* was the only one of the three which made it past on her own, but even she suffered minor damage.

The waterway network which was to complement the improved road system from Young's Point had recently gained special significance since during the two days just past, heavy rains had inundated them, particularly that part leading from Richmond to New Carthage. The rains had not, however, been of sufficient volume to make the canals and bayous navigable for large steamers. Grant's engineers who had done the development work on the canal and bayou section leading toward New Carthage from Richmond would now order that a break be made in the flood control levee at New Carthage. They hoped that by doing this they could back-flood the Bayou Vidal, thus deepening that waterway for medium draft steamers. To test its success, the transport *SILVER WAVE* started inland to try and reach Richmond, but her pilot encountered shallow spots which increased in frequency the farther inland he went. That attempt had to be given up. Apparently the route was going to be suitable only for small, shallow draft steamers and tugs with barges.

Thanks to what had literally been an around the clock effort by Grant's engineers and the crews of the dredging machines, the Duckport to Walnut Bayou canal was ready to accept traffic. Making that route's debut were two small, shallow draft steamers and a number of tugs with barges. The two steamers easily made it to Richmond, but a falling level in the Bayou Vidal stranded them at the waterway's southern terminus just short of New Carthage. The tugs with barges made it all the way through, and completed one more round trip before they too were dragging bottom. The drop that had been occurring in the water level was a relatively swift one, and within a matter of hours, the roads reappeared as muddy slicks. Log corduroying in the worst parts soon put the roads back into use, allowing the troop buildup at New Carthage to continue.

At the terminus of New Carthage, there had developed a scarcity of dry land suitable for bivouac areas, and the numbers of arriving regiments soon monopolized what space there was. Fortunately, another road had just been discovered which led about eight miles downriver to Perkins's Plantation, a more suitable place for bivouac. Upon inspecting the area, Grant decided to shift his entire assault force to that place.

Back at Young's Point, six more transports were being readied to run past Vicksburg. These were: *ANGLO-SAXON, EMPIRE CITY, HORIZON, J. W. CHEESEMAN, MODERATOR*, and *TIGRESS*. As before, none would risk carrying troops. Instead, each would have as freight one hundred thousand rations, along with a 40-day supply of coal for its own boilers. Cotton bales had been being piled along their decks to protect the boilers. The civilian crews, almost to the man, were showing signs of nervousness if not downright panic at the prospect before them. So apprehensive had they become over their chances for survival that at the last moment, most refused to make the trip. To replace them, an immediate call went out to troop commanders requesting volunteers who had any experience on steamboats. From the viewpoint of the average soldier, volunteering for this duty probably seemed preferable to marching to New Carthage. More than enough volunteers came forth, and the civilian pilots and a number of the steamboat engineers had chosen to stay aboard. It is unfortunate that in the writings of many historians of the Vicksburg Campaign, this particular episode of cowardice on the part of the civilian crews has outweighed the countless examples of steadfastness which were so evident among steamboat crews during the Civil War.[78]

All but one of the steamboats got through although they all suffered casualties and structural damage, one steamboat fatally but not sinking until safely past Vicksburg. A report of the passage was later filed by a member of Grant's staff for the information of the Secretary of War.

Young's Point, Louisiana, April 23, 1863
Via Memphis, Tennessee, April 25, -- 1:30 p.m.

Sir:

Last night six steamers and twelve barges [in tow] attempted to run the batteries at Vicksburg, about 11 p.m., when the moon went down. The first two steamers came within range, when heavy firing commenced. The *TIGRESS* received fifteen shots -- one in the stern carrying off two planks. She rounded to at Johnson's Plantation, three and a half miles below Vicksburg, grounded, and sank, breaking amidships. She is a total loss. Crew all safe. Colonel Lagow, on this steamer and in charge of all the boats, and the pilot, then went on the *CHEESEMAN**. The *ANGLO-SAXON* passed comparatively safe. The *MODERATOR* was badly cut up and had several wounded. She drifted by Warrenton batteries about 3 a.m. The *HORIZON* passed Warrenton at daylight. The *EMPIRE CITY* was totally disabled at Vicksburg, and was lashed, at Johnson's Plantation, to the *CHEESEMAN*,* both of which were seen to pass Warrenton, where the fire was heavy, shortly after daylight. The barges designed to carry troops are supposed to have all passed. One pilot was mortally wounded in the abdomen and another person in the thigh, both of whom must have died shortly after.

General Sherman took a position at Johnson's Plantation, with medical officers and six large boats, to render assistance. He hailed and boarded the steamers, and the surgeons did what they could. One wounded man was landed, but it was thought best not to remove the others. Some five hundred shots were fired, and discharge of musketry was kept up along the bank of the river to pick off the men, especially the pilots, some of whom, to avoid being injured by splinters, had their pilot houses taken down and stood exposed. The entire crews were taken from the troops, of whom about five hundred volunteered, when the crews of the boats objected. Large fires were made in Vicksburg and on the point opposite, to light up the river.

L. Thomas, Adjutant General[79]

* *J. W. CHEESEMAN*

With the arrival of these additional steamers at Perkins's Plantation, certain alterations were made in the planning for the crossing of the Mississippi. The departure point was changed for a second time, now to a place farther downriver called Hard Times. Hard Times had the advantage of being the eastern terminus of a wagon road which led directly overland from Richmond. The troops which had first been encamped at New Carthage and later at Perkins's Plantation would now be transferred to Hard Times. Two divisions still at Richmond were marched there directly.

While Grant's staff was arranging final preparations for the river crossing, Confederate forces throughout the Mississippi corridor were trying to counter the various diversionary threats which Grant had put into play. Sherman's concentration of troops on the north side of Vicksburg had kept Pemberton guessing. The cavalry raid, which was by now well underway in the interior of Mississippi, had already created the kind of consternation Grant had hoped it would. What was making the situation especially frustrating for Pemberton at Vicksburg was a lack of hard intelligence as to what was going on beyond his immediate scope of vision. For once, the Northern newspapers, usually the Confederate Army's best sources of information, had been gagged. Grant and Sherman, notorious in their distrust and dislike of the gentlemen of the press, had deliberately isolated reporters from the Army. A second reason for the lack of intelligence reaching the Confederates at Vicksburg was Pemberton's weakness in cavalry which otherwise would have been sent out as scouting units. Pemberton was not, however, completely oblivious to what Grant was about, and he had deduced that a river crossing was going to take place from some location near to Grand Gulf. He had already sent twenty-five hundred men from Vicksburg to reinforce what had initially been little more than a skeleton force assigned to guard the approaches to the Big Black River.

At eight in the morning on April 29th, Porter's gunboats opened fire against Confederate fortifications located on the bluffs at Grand Gulf. Grant was personally on hand to observe the effects. The troops which were to go over in the first wave of landings waited upstream, their transports moored to the western shore. Porter's gunboats kept up a steady cannonade all morning. By afternoon, although it was obvious that the Confederates must be suffering, their works still gave every sign of holding. During the bombardment, Porter's gunboats had suffered from counter bombardment. The gunboat *USS BENTON* had been hit forty-seven times; the *USS TUSCUMBIA*, eighty-one times -- damage which put her out of the action. Of the other five gunboats, all had suffered at least some minor damage. Considering the risk being incurred to the gunboats, Grant decided to select a landing place farther down the river where enemy artillery positions were not in evidence. To prevent the Confederates from moving their guns south of Grand Gulf, Porter kept up a desultory fire for the rest of that afternoon and into the night. Meanwhile, Grant ordered the transports to remain moored for the night to the levee diagonally across from Grand Gulf. At the first hint of dawn, the transports were to move to Bruinsburg about fifteen miles downstream. There, under the protective cover of the gunboats which were to accompany them, Grant's lead divisions were to be debarked onto the Mississippi's opposite shore.

By the end of the following morning, Grant had three full divisions across the river, totaling in all eighteen hundred men. There had been no opposition to the landings. As might be expected in such an undertaking, some confusion developed in matching up troops with their equipment, and for a time, this kept some of the regiments milling near the beachhead; but by four o'clock that afternoon, three full divisions were marching inland. It would be a little past midnight and a good ten miles from the landing site before an enemy force was encountered; but even then, the opposition was light and it was easily overcome.

On the north side of Vicksburg, Sherman, with his three divisions, was making the planned feint in front of Haines's Bluff. The threat worked. It would not be until late the next day that Pemberton realized that the main body of Federal troops was with Grant and that they were moving toward him from the south. Only then did Pemberton begin to move some of his troops out of his defensive perimeter in order to meet that threat.

The Duckport Canal- New Carthage waterway upon which so much depended had by now drained off to resemble nothing more than a series of shallow ditches. The reason was that the Mississippi's level had dropped to such an extent that the canal entrance at Duckport was above the water level of the river. Any further use of the Duckport- New Carthage waterway would depend on a rise of the Mississippi, a happening that was considered very unlikely this late into the year. The roadways from Milliken's Bend south to New Carthage were by now well dried; however, even if enough wagons had been available (which was not the case), the roads simply could not handle the required flow of supplies. The problem would only become exacerbated as the army distanced itself from the Bruinsburg landing site. Grant therefore decided to put his full reliance on moving quickly. Once Pemberton was pushed back into his Vicksburg entrenchments, the Yazoo River, as it ran in from the Mississippi up to Haines's Bluff, would be open to Union steamboats. Then, Grant would have full access to the quartermaster and commissary supplies stockpiled at Young's Point. But to make that happen, Pemberton first had to be forced into the city's entrenchments. In the meantime, the Union troops would depend on the limited rations which had been previously brought down on the transports from Vicksburg as well as on what they could forage from the enemy's countryside.

On May 1, upon receipt of new orders from Grant, Sherman moved his divisions back to the Mississippi's western bank at Milliken's Bend. There he left one division as a guard to the supply dumps at Young's Point while he marched his other two divisions by road to Hard Times where they were to be taken across the river. By May 8, Sherman's two divisions had caught up with Grant's advanced elements which by then had progressed to Hankinson's Ferry, a place located well upstream on the Big Black River. By the 15th, Sherman's two divisions and a full corps under McPherson (which was advancing on Grant's right flank) had reached Jackson, Mississippi. With Jackson now occupied, the railroad which previously had served Vicksburg from both the south and from the east was cut for good. On the 19th, Sherman's men pushed Pemberton into his inner fortifications. In Sherman's words:

> ...By 8 a.m. of May 19, we had composed the enemy to the north of Vicksburg, our right resting on the Mississippi River, [actually the right was on the Yazoo, not on the main river] with a plain view of our fleets at the mouth of the Yazoo and Young's Point, Vicksburg in plain sight, and nothing separated us from the enemy but a space of about four hundred yards of very difficult ground, cut up by almost impracticable ravines, and his line of entrenchments...By 4 p.m. the cavalry was on the high bluff behind, [Haines's Bluff] and Colonel Swan, being assured that the place had been evacuated, dispatched Captain Peters to go in and secure the place.[80]

Having secured Haines's Bluff and the adjacent section of the Yazoo River, Vicksburg's line of communication with the Coldwater- Sunflower- Yazoo basin was severed. Grant now possessed access to the Mississippi via the Yazoo, a situation which provided him with a direct route to Young's Point and its supplies. A constant shuttle of steamers soon started arriving at the landings in front of Haines's Bluff.

Grant had caught up with his logistics. The capitulation of Vicksburg remained but a matter of time. Most of the senior Union officers envisioned a fairly long siege. In an apparent deference to their opinions and simply as a precaution, Grant ordered that entrenchments be dug. As for Grant, he had a belly full of sieges. Circumstances, political and otherwise, cried out for a quick victory. On the 22nd of May, he ordered a general assault against Pemberton's entrenchments. Fighting continued throughout the day, but the assault was called off when it became obvious that Union casualties were reaching beyond acceptable limits. For the time being, Grant decided to wait things out. Confederate deserters soon began coming into the Union lines telling of skinned rats appearing on butcher counters in the Vicksburg markets. Already, the city's population of dogs and cats had disappeared. Starvation, Grant wisely concluded, would soon decide the issue.

On July 4, 1863, six weeks following Grant's decision to wait things out, Pemberton surrendered Vicksburg. Grant paroled Pemberton's entire army. His reasoning in granting this en masse parole was based in part on the difficulty he would have in handling so many prisoners and on the presumption that the beaten down Confederates would spread the germ of defeat throughout the South. It did seem to have that effect at Port Hudson. When rumors of the surrender reached the commander there, he realized the hopelessness of his own situation and also surrendered.

~

When Vicksburg was surrendered, the Confederate government in Richmond ordered that to deny their use to the Union, all steamers then still afloat in the Yazoo River and its tributaries were to be scuttled. These steamboats were in private ownership, and their owners were reimbursed for their losses. Shortly after this occurred, Joseph E. Montgomery purchased the future salvage rights from the Confederate government. Five months later, on January 23, Rear Admiral David D. Porter would execute a contract with a Memphis firm for raising the vessels. The contract was never carried out, and the vessels -- twenty-seven in all -- remained undisturbed until the end of the war when free-lance salvagers began trying to raise them. In June of 1865, following the capitulation of the Confederate States of America, Montgomery laid a claim before the United States. At the end of the war, the United States Navy awarded to the Missouri Wrecking Company a contract to raise the vessels. The claims court would deny to Montgomery the right of salvage, presumably because his "right" was based on a contract with a government which had been in rebellion against the United States and which was no longer in existence. What success the Missouri Wrecking Company had in salving the vessels is unknown.[81]

---

1   *Official Records of the Union and Confederate Navies in the War of the Rebellion, (Washington, DC: Government Printing Office, 1894 - 1917), Series* I, Volume 23, pp 428, 429.

2   *ORN,* I, 23, p 468.

3   *ORN,* I, 23, p 469.

4   Company K, 18th Illinois was one of the company-sized units transferred over to the Mississippi Marine Brigade as of December 11, 1862. A detachment of that company was aboard *QUEEN OF THE WEST* at the time of her loss on the Red River in February of 1863.

5   Warren D. Crandall, *History of the Ram Fleet and the Mississippi Marine Brigade in the War for the Union on the Mississippi and its Tributaries: The Story of the Ellets and Their Men,* (St. Louis: Privately published by the Society of Survivors, 1907), p 255.

6   Recruiting messages and correspondence containing descriptions of training during that period of the Brigade's history are from *Warfare Along the Mississippi: The Letters of Lieutenant Colonel George E. Currie,* Norman E. Clarke, Sr., editor. Clarke Historical Collection, (Ann Arbor: Edwards Brothers, 1961), pp 60-62.

7   Crandall, p 259.

8   Crandall, p 166.

9   By the time the Mississippi Marine Brigade left for Vicksburg in March of 1863, *WOODFORD* was ready.

10   The civilian crewmembers were enrolled through the same type of contractual agreement which had been previously applicable on the rams. Appendix E contains a discussion of the terms of the civilian crew contracts in use within the Ellet organization. These contracts had come into force as early as May of 1862.

11   The *Log of the DIANA* is held on microfilm at Clarke Historical Library, Central Michigan University, Mount Pleasant, MI.

12   Roster, Mississippi Marine Brigade, for July 1864. The hospital vessel *WOODFORD* was not listed in this July 1864 roster, since she had been lost that spring. An additional 300 military personnel were either absent on furlough or in hospital. This roster of July 1864 would indicate, if one counts the 300 in hospital and on furlough, that the Brigade had grown by 300 men since the year before. This additional 300 men may have accounted for troop guards who had been serving on the Brigade's vessels in 1863 but who were not counted in the original mustering of the Brigade at Saint Louis which Alfred W. Ellet had reported to the Secretary of War.

13   Crandall, p 142.

14   *ORN,* I, 23, pp 454, 455.

15   It appears that sometime during September of 1862, Medical Cadet Ellet received the command of a division of the Ram Fleet even though he still only held the rank of medical cadet. If measured against the norm in Army practice, this would have been a rather uncommon arrangement since Charles R. Ellet was outranked at the time by a number of commissioned officers then serving on the rams. But then, strange arrangements were rather commonplace, not only in the Ram Fleet but also in the successor Mississippi Marine Brigade.

16   Crandall, pp 130, 131.

17   *War of the Rebellion: Official Records of the Union and Confederate Armies, (Washington, DC: Government Printing Office, 1880 - 1900). Facsimile Ed: (Harrisburg, PA: National Historical Society, 1971. Reprint. Historical Times, Inc., 1985), Series* I, Volume 52, Part I, p 708.

18   *ORA,* I, 48, Part II, pp 194-197. Whether or not the saboteurs were tried could not be ascertained by us.

19   *ORA,* IV, 1, p 636, 669.

20   *ORA,* IV, 2, pp 639, 697.

21   Later in 1863, after Vicksburg had been taken, Parsons suggested that where partisan dangers were not overly concentrated and that perhaps eight or ten gunboats scattered along the river at various points between say, New Madrid and New Orleans, could accomplish acceptable security by offering immediate retaliatory response.

22   *ORN,* I, 23, p 523.

---

[23] ORN, I, 23, pp 525, 526. The "Brooks" to whom Ellet referred in his first paragraph was James Brooks, the quartermaster officer who was handling supply procurement for the Brigade's vessels.

[24] ORN, I, 23, pp 526, 527.

[25] Crandall, p 27.

[26] ORA, I, 17, Part II, pp 565, 566. This order should not be confused with "Sherman's Special Field Order No. 15" issued at Savannah, setting aside lands for freed slaves.

[27] ORA, I, 17, Part II, pp 576, 577, "Abstract of Returns, Department of the Tennessee."

[28] ORA, I, 17, Part II, pp 565.

[29] Schottenhamel cite: Wright to Parsons, Loose Letters, Parsons Collection.

[30] Fred L. Shannon, Ed., Civil War Letters of Sergeant Onley Andrus, (Urbana: Illinois Studies in the Social Sciences, 1947), p 47.

[31] For some unexplained reason -- call it lack of good communication in hiring policies -- Isaiah Reeder managed to get himself hired again as a pilot in Porter's Upper Mississippi Squadron during March 1863. While serving there as a civilian pilot on the USS BLACK HAWK near Island No. 10, he was arrested for expressing disloyal statements. ORN, I, 24, p 507.

[32] Crandall, pp 239, 240. Court-martial charges brought against Isaiah Reeder are discussed in ORN, I, 24, p 433. (In some reports Isaiah Reeder is incorrectly referred to as "Josiah Reeder.") Appendix E of this volume contains a detailed discussion of the Isaiah Reeder episode.

[33] Court-martial prosecution against Reeder was unsuccessful since by the time of the scheduled trial, most of the prosecution's witnesses had become prisoners of the Confederacy. ORN, I, 24, page 433 can be consulted to establish that "Isaiah" is the same person who was involved in the QUEEN OF THE WEST episode.

[34] Crandall, pp 156, 157.

[35] ORN, I, 24, pp 223, 224.

[36] Crandall, p 163.

[37] The DESOTO, a ferryboat which accompanied the QUEEN OF THE WEST south of Vicksburg during February of 1863 and which would be lost on that expedition, should not be confused with another vessel of the same name. The other vessel was the ex CSS DESOTO, once a Confederate gunboat captured by Federal forces in 1862 at Island No. 10 and which had been renamed USS GENERAL LYON.

[38] John S. C. Abbott, "Charles Ellet and His Naval Rams," Harper's New Monthly Magazine, XXXII, 1866, p 312.

[39] Crandall, p 165. Also not mentioned by the reporter was the detachment of Army enlisted men. They were assigned aboard as gunners and sharpshooters but were not considered as part of the operating crew. The detachment assigned to the QUEEN OF THE WEST had been on temporary loan to the ram fleet from an Illinois regiment. The day after Ellet left on this expedition, an order was received which permanently assigned the members of all such gunnery detachments to the Mississippi Marine Brigade.

[40] The various correspondence between Porter and Ellet which is contained within the ORA and ORN does not definitively establish, one way or the other, as to whether Ellet knew that Porter was sending a Navy gunboat. Porter's later critical comments of Ellet's actions infer that at some undefined point, Ellet had been made aware that a gunboat would join him. In The Gulf and Inland Waters, p 128, Alfred T. Mahan makes the claim that Ellet "knew the USS INDIANOLA was being sent down." Unfortunately, Mahan gives no source or any basis for having arrived at that conclusion. In Charles R. Ellet's own report of the expedition, he would write that it had been his intention to make a stab at capturing the three steamers, but should he come against a battery of enemy guns, as was earlier reported to him to be in place somewhere below Gordon's Landing, his advance decision was that he would turn back. Alfred Thayer Mahan, The Gulf and Inland Waters. (New York: Charles Scribner's Sons, 1883. Reprint, Campaigns of the Civil War Series. Wilmington, NC: Broadfoot Publishing Co., 1989).

[41] According to enemy sources, twenty-four were taken prisoner from the QUEEN OF THE WEST. Of these, ten were civilians and fourteen were military personnel. The military personnel were all enlisted men except for one officer, the ram's surgeon who had elected to remain to care for the wounded first master. According to Crandall's account of the events which he later put together from surviving records, two of the three reporters returned safely to the De Soto Landing. The third reporter, Finlay Anderson of the New York Herald, was captured. In contradiction to the Confederate accounts, Crandall's version claims that in addition to the QUEEN OF THE WEST's surgeon, another commissioned officer, Lieutenant George W. Bailey, was among those taken prisoner. Crandall, p 176. According to Crandall, there were "about thirty Negroes -- all missing from the ranks of the rescued" and assumed to have been taken prisoner. The discrepancies between the numbers given by the Confederates and those figures given by Crandall are not easily reconciled since the surviving rosters of the Brigade for this period in time do not include civilian employees. Crandall tells us that the civilian first master, J. D. Thompson, later died. A list of those taken prisoner, which was compiled at the time by the New York Tribune reporter who escaped, includes the surgeon as well as the names of six civilians and the reporter from the

New York Herald. That reporter also mentioned, without individually naming them, that "thirty Negroes" were also taken prisoner. The *Tribune* reporter datelined his story March 6, 1863.

[42]   Abbott, *Harper's,* p 312. Abbott stated that one of the reporters who had witnessed the grounding of the *ERA NO. 5* told him that Charles R. Ellet's charge of treachery laid against the *ERA NO. 5* pilot was totally without foundation, stating, "Those familiar with the treacherous and tortuous navigation of that stream, especially at that point, judge that the grounding was accidental." Abbott's article alleges that Charles R. Ellet was a user of morphine. If that was so, Ellet's nervous system must have been balanced on a fine wire as he would have been cut off from his drug supply which was on *QUEEN OF THE WEST.* Coupling the loss of both *QUEEN OF THE WEST* and *DESOTO* with the effects of drug withdrawal could well have put him over the emotional edge.

[43]   What was that special uniform mentioned as being seen at Andersonville Prison? In Currie, p 75, Currie describes the hat of the enlisted men of the Mississippi Marine Brigade (Ram Fleet) as being, "a cap of a semi-naval design." Within a letter, Major D. S. Talladay complains to Adjutant Crandall of a shortage of these special caps. See Records of the Mississippi Marine Brigade, Microfilm Identification No. 63-08-12-63, Order Book Correspondence for August 12, 1863, National Archives. A description of the cap is given in Crandall, p 258. "The Marine uniform was the same as that worn in the Army-at-large, save the caps, which were made with full round tops, broad, straight visors, and a wide green band with trimmings of gold lace. The arms issued were new, and wherever the command, or any part of it appeared, it was readily recognized and received many tokens of admiration." Photographs within the Crandall history depict caps of this configuration.

[44]   *Dictionary of American Naval Fighting Ships,* V, (Washington, DC: Government Printing Office, 1970), p 412.

[45]   The *HERCULES* had been engaged in transporting coal barges for the Army at the time of her loss. The attack against the tug took place on February 17, 1863. At the time, she was slightly north of Memphis. *ORN,* I, 24, pp 136, 366, 423.

[46]   *ORN,* I, 24, p 365.

[47]   *ORN,* I, 24, p 361.

[48]   Captain E. W. Sutherland, commander of the ram *MONARCH,* had married a local woman and therefore had a rather close liaison through his wife with the civilian population in the vicinity of Greenville. This relationship would later bring him under suspicion of being overly friendly with the enemy and force his resignation from the Army. Samuel W. Ferguson held a regular Confederate Army commission (artillery). At the time of his meeting with Sutherland, Ferguson was commanding about two hundred uniformed cavalry troops. Ferguson had told Sutherland that he was a graduate of West Point, a statement which was correct; Ferguson graduated from the United States Military Academy in 1857.

[49]   Mahan, p 139.

[50]   Harry P. Owens, *Steamboats and the Cotton Economy: River Trade in the Yazoo-Mississippi Delta,* (Jackson: University of Mississippi Press, 1990). Owens's book is highly recommended to those particularly interested in that part of the Confederate supply system which depended on the Coldwater- Sunflower- Yazoo rivers prior to the surrender of Vicksburg.

[51]   *ORN,* I, 24, pp 250.

[52]   *ORN,* I, 24, p 244. The "Honey Island" mentioned by Porter was also referenced by some as "Greenwood." This was the location for Fort Pemberton's construction.

[53]   *ORN,* I, 24, p 259.

[54]   *ORA,* I, 24, Part I, pp 310, 311.

[55]   *ORN,* I, 24, p 262, 263.

[56]   *STAR OF THE WEST,* was employed in January of 1861 in an attempt to reinforce Fort Sumter. After being fired on at that time, *STAR OF THE WEST* returned to New York with her troop passengers still aboard. This vessel was later used to evacuate Federal troops from Texas. She was captured by the Confederates and renamed *CSS SAINT PHILIP.* She sank in the Yazoo River in 1862.

[57]   *ORA,* I, 24, Part III, pp 93, 94. The difficulty in finding vessels of dimensions less than Grant's maximum specification, i.e.., vessels small enough to operate in the Yazoo system, was already being seen as a key impediment for the expedition's success. Even vessels with Grant's stated specification of "not over 190 feet long" proved to be too long. A follow-up communication sent to the quartermaster at Memphis stated that any vessel exceeding 180 feet could not negotiate the Yazoo Pass route. See communication of I. F. Quinby to C. S. Lyman, March 9, 1863, *ORA,* I, 24, Part III, p 96.

[58]   The original discovery of the Steele's Bayou route to the Yazoo should properly be attributed to Lieutenant McLeod Murphy, USN, who had made a preliminary reconnaissance preceding the one undertaken by Grant and Porter. Admiral David D. Porter, *The Naval History of the Civil War,* (Facsimile reprint, Secaucus, NJ: Castle, 1984), p 303.

---

59   *ORA*, I, 24, Part III, p 112.

60   The reference to General Pope was his need for transports for the campaign to be launched against the Sioux in the spring. The Indian campaign of 1863 is covered within Appendix G of this volume.

61   *ORA*, I, 24, Part III, pp 115, 116.

62   *ORA*, I, 24, Part III, p 116.

63   *ORA*, I, 24, Part III, p 121.

64   *ORA*, I, 24, Part III, p 122.

65   *ORN*, I, 24, pp 288, 289. Mention of the *LUELLA* and its sinking presents somewhat of a mystery since no exact account of the loss of a vessel of this name was found within either *ORA* or *ORN*. Way's volume of steamboat histories on the Mississippi describes a vessel of this name as having been lost "on the Yazoo Expedition," but Way gives no other details. Frederick Way, Jr., *Way's Packet Directory 1848 - 1983: Passenger Steamboats of the Mississippi River System Since the Advent of Photography in Mid-Continent America,* (Athens, OH: Ohio University Press, 1983). Way is probably wrong as to the location of the loss which, according to the Fisk correspondence, apparently took place somewhere on the White River. Ross endorsed Fisk's protest, noting his concurrence before sending the correspondence on to Brigadier General Quinby who passed it up to Grant. Whether Grant then endorsed it for transmission to Halleck is not of record. As part of his endorsement, Quinby commented that Brigadier General Fisk had, from the start, shown a lack of enthusiasm for the Yazoo Expedition then presently underway.

66   The numbers of transports which were utilized by the Union Army on the Yazoo Pass Expedition is not comprehensively recorded for all of the various movements. However, we do have a Confederate report by one Sam Henderson, a captain of Confederate scouts, who wrote that during the withdrawal of the expedition through the Coldwater toward Yazoo Pass, a total of "thirty-eight boats with lots of troops passed through Moon Lake and into the Mississippi River." *ORA*, I, 24, Part III, p 737. Henderson's tally was probably not inclusive of the Navy's gunboats or the tugs which did constant yeomen's service throughout by extracting both gunboats and transports which became entangled in the river's overhangs and by clearing logs and debris from the transports' paddle wheels.

67   Within *Atlas to Accompany the Official Records of the Union and Confederate Armies,* (Washington, DC: Government Printing Office, 1891-1895), Big Black Bayou, is shown as Indian Bayou. The best map of the Steele's Bayou route taken by Porter's gunboats during the aborted expedition toward the Yazoo can be found within *ORA*, I, 24, Part I, p 463. This map is reproduced in the Western Rivers photographic section.

68   For Rear Admiral Porter's account, see *ORN*, I, 24, p 474-478.

69   *ORN*, I, 24, p 477.

70   *ORN*, I, 24, p 522.

71   Crandall, p 196, letter dated March 24, 1863, Major General U. S. Grant to Brigadier General A. W. Ellet, commanding Mississippi Marine Brigade.

72   *ORA*, I, 24, pp 23, 24.

73   Letter to Rear Admiral Porter from Lieutenant Commander K. R. Breese, *ORN*, I, 24, p 580-582.

74   *ORN*, I, 24, p 596 contains a survey of the canal connecting Duckport and the Walnut Bayou. The survey entitled "Duckport Cut", which has been reproduced in this volume, discloses what apparently was a slough-like topography across which the canal would be dug. At the time the sketch was executed on April 28, 1863, dredging equipment was still at work in the cut. The area between Milliken's Bend and Grand Gulf which includes the road network as well as the waterway system running from Duckport to New Carthage via Richmond is shown on Plate XXXV, 4, *Atlas, ORA*.

75   *ORA*, I, 24, Part I, pp 126, 127.

76   *ORA*, I, 24, Part I, pp 25, 26.

77   *ORA*, I, 24, Part III, p 208.

78   It is significant to relate that the refusal of the crews of *TIGRESS, ANGLO-SAXON, J. W. CHEESEMAN, MODERATOR, HORIZON,* and *EMPIRE CITY* to make the run past Vicksburg did not involve any civilian crews under the direct hire of the Quartermaster Department. Rather, those involved were all employees of the steamboat owners. Unlike saltwater merchant seamen, privately employed civilian crews on the western rivers were not contractually obligated through their entry under ship's articles to serve for specific periods. The choice to quit, although far from heroic, was therefore theirs to make.

79   *ORA*, I, 24, Part I, pp 564, 565. The statement that "The entire crews were taken from the troops..." is not substantiated by various other accounts, wherein it has been mentioned that a number of the civilian engineers (and of course the pilots) had remained with their vessels.

80   *ORA*, I, 24, Part I, pp 775, 776.

81   *ORN*, I, 27, pp 269-271.

PART VI

UPDATE ON THE WAR SITUATION
ALL THEATERS, SUMMER OF 1863

THE SOUTH'S OFFENSIVE
(Summer of 1863)

In the eastern theater during the first three days of July 1863, a battle was fought at a place named Gettysburg. This had been Lee's second attempt to invade the North, and like the first, it failed. The cost to Lee -- through dead, wounded, and missing -- was over twenty-eight thousand men. Although victorious, the Union side suffered almost as severely, but the North still had the resources, both in men and materiel, necessary to wage a sustained war. The South did not.

By the middle of the summer, the Confederacy's gateways from the sea which had been so vital to its survival were beginning to close. Only two major ports remained open: Wilmington, North Carolina, and Charleston, South Carolina. A third, Mobile, Alabama, although still in Confederate hands, was relatively well blockaded resulting in few successful entries.

THE MISSISSIPPI CORRIDOR

All hope the Confederates had for aid coming from European powers -- moral or otherwise -- had evaporated with their defeats at Gettysburg and Vicksburg in July of 1863. After Vicksburg fell, the Confederacy was geographically divided -- east from west. It could be claimed at last that the Mississippi was again a Union thoroughfare; and as seeming proof of that, an unarmed steamboat, the *IMPERIAL*, made an unconvoyed voyage of eight days from Saint Louis to New Orleans later that month.

The fact that the *IMPERIAL* had made an unmolested run down the length of the Mississippi -- although highly symbolic -- did not prove that travel on the river would continue free of Confederate interference. Partisan action would soon resume and would continue in varied intensity through into 1865. This harassment would constitute everything from occasional attacks to temporary occupation of the western bank for entire stretches of the river.

To guard against attacks, steamers (both commercial and those controlled by the Quartermaster Department) would continue to mount defensive armament served by temporarily assigned Army gunners. On more than one occasion, naval convoying would have to be resumed.

In early August of 1863, Ulysses S. Grant removed his headquarters to New Orleans. While exercising his horse there one morning, he was thrown, suffering a concussion, broken ribs, and a leg injury. While bedridden, he turned over surrogate command to William Tecumseh Sherman.

In September, while still on crutches, Grant was asked to take command of the now consolidated Military Departments of the Tennessee, Cumberland, and Ohio. He departed for Louisville, Kentucky, to take over that command and left Sherman in charge of operations within the Mississippi arena. Sherman would continue to supervise those operations until March 1864 at which time he would leave the western theater and launch a major campaign which would take him from Atlanta, Georgia, to the sea.

THE CAROLINAS AND GEORGIA

Back in the fall of 1862, the leadership in the Navy Department had decided to occupy Charleston, South Carolina, but a firm date for when this was to occur was not set. The Confederates became convinced, probably by process of supposition joined with some hazy intelligence, that an attack was in the offing. Accordingly, they strengthened Charleston's defenses, emplacing heavy guns so as to provide interlocking fields of fire covering the harbor entrance. The lethal effect of these defenses was heightened by the addition of a moored buoyage system which gave the Confederates exact distances upon which to range their guns. The key point of Charleston's outer defenses was Battery Wagner which was located on Morris Island overlooking the approaches to the harbor's main channel (the southern channel). Battery Wagner's gunners had a clear field of fire for sweeping almost a mile of that channel's length. Rear Admiral Samuel F. DuPont, who in the late winter of 1863 was given the charge of taking Charleston, had strong reservations about the ability of his ironclads to slug it out against heavy guns in fixed positions. According to the information that DuPont had and which turned out to be an accurate appraisal, the enemy had all told seventy-six heavy cannon to bring to bear. DuPont counseled the Navy Department that any attempt to take Charleston by assault from the sea was an invitation to disaster. He was overruled; and on April 7, the Navy sent seven monitors, an armored gunboat, and an ironclad steamer which tried to work their way past the guns of Battery Wagner. Considerable damage resulted to those vessels. The admiral's *I told you so* attitude, as expressed in subsequent correspondence to Secretary of the Navy Gideon Welles and to Assistant Secretary of the Navy Gustavus V. Fox, resulted in DuPont being relieved. His successor was Rear Admiral John A. Dahlgren. Dahlgren had little seagoing experience. He was, though, a weapons specialist, being the inventor of the rifled cannon which bore his name. This ordinance background seemed appropriate to the task ahead since it now appeared -- at least from the Navy Department's viewpoint -- that taking Charleston was to be a contest of each side's heavy guns.

Taking Charleston became increasingly important in the minds of not only Welles and Fox, but President Lincoln as well. Confederate commerce raiders which had managed to evade the Union blockade had attained ominous results through the havoc they were causing to the Union merchant marine. As a direct result of the numbers of Northern ships being destroyed and captured by these raiders, insurance rates were skyrocketing to the point of being prohibitive. Ship owners began demanding that the Navy hunt down the raiders.[1] Hunting down the Confederate raiders would require the use of Navy ships not needed for blockade duty. However, the blockades of Charleston and Wilmington were so demanding of guard vessels that none could be spared for such a high seas hunt and still have a blockade worthy of the name. The obvious solution was to capture either Charleston or Wilmington, thereby freeing up the naval vessels employed in the blockade. At the time, Charleston was considered by far the easier place to take. There was also a certain political symbolism that it held as the birthplace of secession.

In July, Dahlgren began a naval bombardment in an attempt to soften up Battery Wagner's defenses prior to the Army making a land assault against it. On Folly Island to the south of Battery Wagner, the Army had already established a staging area for the assembly of troops. From there, the Army's artillery joined with Dahlgren's guns in pounding Battery Wagner and its subsidiary works located at the south end of Morris Island. Although the bombardment had little effect on the battlements of Battery Wagner, the Confederates at the subsidiary battery were driven out. They then joined the garrison at the main works.

Union troops moved from Folly Island onto Morris Island with the intent of establishing a forward departure zone from which the assault against Battery Wagner would be launched. On July 11, four companies of infantry supported by two backup regiments charged the works. Some of the lead elements managed to gain the enemy's parapets; but when the support regiments failed to come on, the attackers were driven back. Next followed a concentrated artillery and mortar bombardment which hammered at the Confederates for a full week. A second assault was attempted on July 19, this time with six thousand infantry. In the van was the 54th Massachusetts, a Negro regiment.[2] That assault also failed. All told, the attempt to take Battery Wagner had cost the Union attackers 1,515 casualties. Through to the first week in September, a constant bombardment was maintained while the Union infantry dug a series of snake-like trenches, moving them forward, ever closer to the enemy's battlements. When finally near enough to risk another assault, intelligence of what was about to happen leaked to the Confederates. They evacuated Battery Wagner the night before the planned attack was to take place.

Despite the cost in lives expended toward taking that fortification, Battery Wagner was but one part of the outer defenses for Charleston. The inner harbor defenses were covered by a separate system of interlocking artillery, making the harbor literally impregnable from an attack from seaward unless Dahlgren was willing to risk insupportable fleet casualties. On the positive side, the abandonment of Battery Wagner had narrowed the enemy's fields of fire covering the approaches to the harbor, thereby creating a much shorter front over which the blockading fleet had to patrol. As a consequence to this, at least some of the Union Navy's ships were freed up for other duties which paramountly included the hunt for the Confederate commerce raiders.

Charleston would remain in Confederate hands until February of 1865 when the Confederate garrison was forced to evacuate the city during Sherman's advance northward from Georgia.

~

During the year 1863, coastal South Carolina and Georgia was the scene of numerous raids conducted inland by Union troops operating in South Carolina from Hilton Head and Beaufort. Such raids were usually joint Army- Navy operations although some were exclusively Army in their makeup. Most of the troops employed in these raids were Negro regiments, locally recruited and composed of men who were familiar with the area being raided. Prominent among these regiments was the 1st South Carolina Infantry (colored) under the command of Colonel Thomas Wentworth Higginson.

In January of 1863, Higginson took his 1st South Carolina Infantry (colored) up the Saint Mary's River of Georgia aboard the transports *BEN DE FORD* and *PLANTER*, accompanied by the Army gunboat *JOHN ADAMS*. The primary purpose of that expedition, and many others like it, was to take away any slaves who wished to cross over into Union lines. The anticipation was that these people would include potential recruits for the Negro regiments then being organized. The secondary purpose of these raids was to harass the enemy, causing him to commit troops which otherwise would have been utilized elsewhere in more active theaters of war.[3]

Another 1863 raid in which the 1st South Carolina Infantry (colored) participated was a penetration up the South Edisto River in South Carolina. Transports involved were *ENOCH DEAN* and the tug *GOVERNOR MILTON*, the Army gunboat *JOHN ADAMS* accompanying. The purpose of that raid was to bring away Negroes and destroy a bridge thought to be vital to enemy communications with Charleston. The raid was successful insofar as bringing out the Negroes, but a Confederate battery and shallow water prevented a close approach to the bridge which was left intact. In the attempt to approach the bridge, the *GOVERNOR MILTON* grounded and had to be abandoned. Later that year, an Army gunboat, the *GEORGE WASHINGTON*, was sunk by a mobile enemy battery while attempting to move inland from the proximity of Port Royal Island.

These small scope operations were typical of the activity then taking place in Georgia and South Carolina. The Confederates were not passive in the coastal zone. They, too, conducted forays, and the Union garrisons and outposts along the Georgia and Carolina coasts were by no means considered secure.

Going beyond the pale of a mere raid was a joint Union Army- Navy expedition to capture Jacksonville, Florida. Jacksonville had first been occupied in March of 1862 by Federal troops which shortly withdrew. It was reoccupied in October of that same year. Because of the threat of what was reported to be an overwhelming enemy presence to the south of that city, the place was again evacuated, but Jacksonville was not to be ignored for long. During March of 1863, a sizable force left Hilton Head aboard the transports *BOSTON* and *GENERAL BURNSIDE*, escorted by the naval gunboats *USS NORWICH*, *USS UNCAS*, and the Army gunboat *JOHN ADAMS*. The intention was to take the city and remain in occupation. The city limits were entered without any opposition, and for all intents and purposes, the situation appeared secure. Within the month, however, the city was evacuated for a third time, this time, it seemed, because of sheer nervousness on the part of the department commander. There remained an ongoing uncertainty over Confederate strength in Florida, and the Federal department commander wanted a secure presence maintained at Beaufort, South Carolina, which he considered of much more importance than northern Florida. To accomplish his aim, he would require a reasonably heavy troop presence. Jacksonville was reoccupied for the fourth time in February 1864, an occupation resulting in the Battle of Olustee in which the Union forces were defeated, suffering in killed, missing, and wounded around 36% of the force committed.

The successful employment of Negro troops within the Department of the South would give rise by 1864 to a gradual replacement of white regiments which were then shipped north by sea, mainly as reinforcements to the Army of the Potomac. (The Department of the South -- as it was designated at that time -- included Florida, coastal South Carolina, and Georgia.)[4]

---

[1]   During 1862 and 1863, Confederate Navy commerce raiders sank or captured on the high seas 132 US flag merchant ships. Thomas J. Sharf, ed., *History of the Confederate States Navy from Its Organization to the Surrender of Its Last Vessel,* (New York: Rogers and Sherwood, 1887. Facsimile Reprint. New York: Crown Publishers, Fairfax Press, 1977), pp 814-818.

[2]   The 54th Massachusetts was the subject of the 1990s movie *Glory.*

[3]   One specific purpose for the January 1863 raid up the Saint Mary's River was to seize a supply of bricks to be used for the repair of Fort Clinch at Fernandina, Florida. Thomas Wentworth Higginson, *Army Life in a Black Regiment,* (Boston: Beacon Press, 1962 reprint of 1869 edition). *War of the Rebellion: Official Records of the Union and Confederate Armies, (Washington, DC: Government Printing Office, 1880 - 1900). Facsimile Ed: (Harrisburg, PA: National Historical Society, 1971. Reprint. Historical Times, Inc., 1985),* Series I, Volume 14, pp 195-198 contains Higginson's official report of that raid.

[4]   The returns of the Department of the South as dated April 30, 1864, list a total of 29 infantry and mounted regiments of which almost half were Negro regiments. *ORA,* I, 35, Part II, p 79.

PART VII

CONCLUDING THE WESTERN RIVERS AND THE GULF OF MEXICO

THE MISSISSIPPI MARINE BRIGADE OPERATIONS: APRIL 1863 TO ITS DISBANDMENT IN JANUARY 1865

With the Ellet Command North of Vicksburg, April-May 1863

On April 16, when Porter and part of his Mississippi Squadron passed south of Vicksburg in support of Grant's crossing of the Mississippi, Alfred W. Ellet, with his Mississippi Marine Brigade's vessels, had been left north of Vicksburg. (It will be remembered that at that time *SWITZERLAND* was remote from the rest of the newly formed Brigade, having been assigned to assist Rear Admiral Farragut in the blockade of the Red River. She would remain on that detached service for some months.) Keeping Ellet's brigade north of Vicksburg had probably been a good move on Porter's part, both for personal reasons and because it made tactical sense. Considerable partisan action involving attacks against the Army's supply vessels as well as commercial shipping had been taking place north of Vicksburg, and Ellet's new amphibious brigade was ideally suited to work against this menace.

Reports came in to Ellet that Confederate cavalry had established what was developing into a more or less static threat in the vicinity of Greenville, Mississippi, a river town halfway between Vicksburg and Memphis. But before Ellet had a chance to respond to this emergency, a dispatch arrived from Porter instructing him to move the Brigade to the Tennessee River. Once on the Tennessee, its mission would be to support a movement then being planned to help take the pressure off Major General William Starke Rosecrans's Army of the Cumberland which was again being threatened, this time by a large Confederate force moving north out of Alabama. Ellet's orders were to rendezvous as quickly as possible with Brigadier General Grenville M. Dodge at Hamburg Landing on the Tennessee River. A follow-up set of instructions from Porter caught up with Ellet while en route up the Mississippi. These orders instructed Ellet to convoy transports carrying a mounted infantry force under Colonel Abel D. Streight. Ellet was to rendezvous with the transports at Paducah and escort them to the big bend of the Tennessee at Eastport. Once at Eastport, Streight and Ellet were to join with Dodge in whatever program Dodge decided upon. The importance of the operation had been explained by Rosecrans in a dispatch he sent to Major General Hurlbut who was the commander of the southwestern section of Tennessee.

Murfreesborough, Tennessee
April 12, 1863

General S. A. Hurlbut
    Memphis, Tennessee--
Sir:

Colonel Streight with near two thousand picked men will probably reach Eastport by Thursday next. Dodge, with the Marine Brigade and the gunboats, can occupy or whip the Tuscumbia forces, and let my forces go directly to its main object -- the destruction of the railroads.

This great enterprise, fraught with great consequences, I beg you to commend to Dodge's care, enjoining on him to dispatch Streight, by every means, to his destination. Nothing, if possible, should for a moment arrest his progress.

W. S. Rosecrans[1]

Dodge's plan was that he, in company with Ellet's brigade, would attack any Confederate troops which were at Tuscumbia while Streight's command (which was to be completely mounted) would bypass Tuscumbia and head to Moulton, Alabama. From Moulton, Streight would ride eastward following along the mountain country of northern Alabama until he reached the rail line at Dalton, Georgia. (The rail line at Dalton interconnected with another rail system feeding to Chattanooga and to Atlanta.) By the time Streight had reached Dalton and rendered the rail there useless to the enemy, Dodge would hopefully have seized control of the railroad at Tuscumbia, this being part of the system which connected Corinth to Chattanooga. If that could be accomplished, then all rail communication north of the Tennessee would have been denied to the Confederates. With their primary transportation denied, they would be unable to maintain their presence in Tennessee. Braxton Bragg, the Confederate commander, would then have little choice but to retreat. With Bragg safely out of the way, Chattanooga, the key jump off location for any Union invasion of Georgia, would be ripe for the taking. The efforts about to be undertaken against Bragg were therefore considered by Rosecrans to be both defensive and offensive in nature. But by whatever measure, it was an important enterprise calling for decisive success on the part of Union arms.

Streight's command to be convoyed up the Tennessee River by Ellet consisted of a provisional brigade made up of four infantry regiments of Ohio and Illinois troops and two companies of Tennessee horse cavalry. For the campaign, the infantry regiments were to be mounted on mules, about half of which were to be assembled at Nashville, and the rest gathered together at Fort Henry.

The planning for the campaign began to unravel almost from the onset. The shipment of mules received at Nashville turned out to be young unbroken animals, a major portion of them suffering from equine distemper. That was only the first foul-up. Another concerned the orders received respectively by Streight and Ellet which were in discrepancy as to the place of the convoy rendezvous. Streight's orders were that he was to board the transports assigned to him and proceed down the Cumberland River to Palmyra where the troops were to be offloaded. Streight's command was then to cross the narrow land neck separating the Cumberland River from the Tennessee River and go into bivouac at Fort Henry. Meanwhile, his now empty transports were to descend the Cumberland into the Ohio River, then steam up the Tennessee to Fort Henry. At Fort Henry, Streight was supposed to meet with Ellet who was presumably in possession of a compatible set of orders. Ellet had not, however, received corresponding instructions, so while Streight was executing his movements, Ellet and the Mississippi Marine Brigade's vessels remained tied up at Paducah awaiting Streight's arrival.

At the point when one or both of the men deduced that plans had gone awry, telegraph lines began to buzz. The confusion was straightened out, and Ellet proceeded to Fort Henry. When he arrived there, Streight had riders out scouring the Tennessee countryside for enough healthy mules to mount his command. He had some success, but the number of mules remained far short of requirements. Unable to spend anymore time, Streight and Ellet steamed up the Tennessee to meet with Dodge. While Dodge was awaiting their arrival, he had managed to round up another two hundred mules which was almost sufficient to put the rest of Streight's force into the saddle. But that satisfactory state of affairs proved short-lived. The constant din of braying mules had attracted the attention of Confederate partisans who, sneaking past the Union pickets, opened a coral gate and stampeded about four hundred of the animals into the surrounding countryside. Once free, the mules proved elusive, and only about half of them were recovered. When Streight finally left Eastport to begin his ride toward Georgia, he had only enough mules to mount fifteen hundred men; he was forced to leave part of his command with Dodge.

Streight would never finish his ride. When well into the mountains of northern Alabama, he began experiencing harassing jabs at his flanks from enemy cavalry. The jabs soon turned into a continuous pummeling. After a fluid battle which lasted three days, Streight was forced to surrender his entire command.[2]

Back on the bend of the Tennessee, Dodge had set Ellet to the task of patrolling the river, the mission being to keep it open for supply movement from Fort Henry to the Muscle Shoals. It was a task that would prove difficult due to the rapidly falling river level. This drop of the Tennessee made it impossible to move the Brigade's deep draft vessels with any speed because of the risk of going aground. By the third week in April, river conditions were such that there was a serious potential for the Brigade's vessels to become stranded on the upper Tennessee for the remainder of the summer. This threat forced Ellet to work no farther upstream than Savannah Landing where he more or less headquartered his operations. From there, he sent mounted parties out with instructions to burn anything which might provide aid and comfort to the enemy. Large amounts of foodstuffs along with a number of lumber and grist mills were destroyed on these patrols.

On the morning of April 26th, the Mississippi Marine Brigade had its first real baptism of fire as a brigaded force. Near the mouth of the Duck River, an enemy infantry and cavalry unit -- later estimated by Alfred W. Ellet to have been seven hundred in strength -- opened fire on the lead transports. This occurred at a location where putting men ashore was difficult due to the steep bluffs. Once Ellet managed to get his infantry landed, the Confederates broke off.[3] The Brigade suffered two killed and one seriously wounded; the Confederates lost eleven, including, as it appeared, their commanding officer.

As the river level continued to drop, Ellet was forced farther downstream and finally all the way back to Fort Henry where he and his command were located by the end of April. Even that far down the river, the navigable depths were reaching a marginal state. By the end of the first week in May, it had become obvious that continued operations on the Tennessee could only end with the transports stranding fast on the bottom. Unable to make contact with Porter who was then somewhere south of Vicksburg at an unknown location, Alfred W. Ellet went to Paducah on the Ohio from where he telegraphed the Secretary of War.

May 7, 1863

E. M. Stanton, Secretary of War:
> I have returned from an attempt to ascend the Tennessee River a second time. The water is too low for me to get above the mouth of Duck River. I am now repairing damages that my boats sustained in the dangerous navigation. My orders from Admiral Porter confine me to the Tennessee River, making no provision for the present condition of the water. I cannot communicate with the admiral without great delay. Will you advise me what course to pursue?

Alfred W. Ellet, Brigadier General
Commanding Mississippi Marine Brigade[4]

Ellet rejoined his Brigade at Fort Henry while awaiting a reply from Stanton. When word had still not come from the Secretary after ten days, and with the river dropping still farther, Ellet moved his entire command out of the Tennessee. Allowing only a brief stopover at Cairo in order to take on coal and rations, he started back down the Mississippi. It seems apparent that at that juncture, Ellet still did not have an authorization to return south. Lieutenant Colonel George E. Currie's remembrances, as he would put them down some years later, give no clue as to what authority, if any, Ellet might have been acting under when going south of Cairo. It appears that the only order that came to Ellet was one dated May 20, three days after the Brigade had started back down the Mississippi from Cairo. That order was in partial conformity with the action Ellet had already undertaken.

> The Secretary of War thinks that such of your boats as may be available, and not required in the Tennessee and Cumberland, should proceed immediately to Vicksburg.

s/ H. W. Halleck.[5]

While en route south to Vicksburg, the Brigade's vessels touched at Memphis where Ellet discovered that security along the river had seriously deteriorated in his absence. Partisan activity had increased, both above and below Memphis. It had become so bad in fact that it was being assumed by the local Federal authorities that every male citizen native to the region possessed some form of Confederate affiliation. Commercial steamboat crews transiting the area were under suspicion of collaborating with the enemy -- or if not actually collaborating, then being at least engaged in the illegal cotton trade.

During Ellet's sojourn on the Tennessee, the ram *MONARCH* had been on detached duty from the Brigade and was operating from Memphis. This was on Alfred W. Ellet's own orders issued at the time he left for the Tennessee. *MONARCH's* availability to the district commander at Memphis gave rise to the following order issued shortly before the arrival there of the Brigade.

Headquarters, District of West Tennessee
Memphis, Tennessee, May 14, 1863

General Order No. 4.

The ram *MONARCH* will proceed tomorrow morning down the Mississippi River and arrest every trading boat found between Memphis and White River. All passengers on board who are women and children, or all persons not liable to conscription by the laws of the Confederate states, will be put ashore at the first landing together with any effects they may have; and parties liable to conscription are presumed to be in the rebel army, and will be brought as prisoners of war to this city.

The commander of the ram *MONARCH* will send each boat to this city under guard which will be furnished by Brigadier General Buckland, and no boat will be allowed to land except at Helena on the way up.

By order of Major General C. C. Washburn.

W. H. Morgan, A. A. G.[6]

During the time that Ellet's vessels were on their way down from Cairo, but before any of them reached Memphis, the Brigade's quartermaster, on the commissary boat *E. H. FAIRCHILD*, had fallen behind the rest. While anchored up for the night about one half mile above the town of Austin, *E. H. FAIRCHILD* was fired on from the bank. When Ellet received the report of the incident from *E. H. FAIRCHILD's* commander, he ordered an operation aimed at meting out retribution. The official report of what followed is a clear indication that Ellet had decided that it was time to remove his kid gloves insofar as relationships with the communities along the river.

Helena, Arkansas
May 25, 1863 Via Cairo, May 29

I have the honor to inform you that as my command was descending the river from Memphis on the evening of May 23, the commissary and quartermaster boat was fired into from the Mississippi side by a band of the enemy with two pieces of artillery, about six miles above Austin. I returned yesterday morning to Austin and landed my force. The enemy had, a few hours before my arrival, captured a small trading steamer, and burned her, taking her crew captive and appropriating her freight. I could obtain no intelligence from the inhabitants by which to guide my movements. My cavalry, under the command of Major Hubbard, two hundred strong, came up with the enemy one thousand strong, all mounted eight miles out. The fight lasted nearly two hours. The major was compelled to take shelter in a favorable bottom, where he succeeded in repulsing the enemy, and finally drove them off before the infantry could come to his relief. Our loss was two killed and nineteen wounded, mostly slight. The enemy left five dead upon the field and one lieutenant mortally wounded, and twenty-two stand of arms. We captured three prisoners. I burned the town of Austin, having first searched every building. As the fire progressed, the discharge of loaded fire arms was like volleys of musketry as the fire reached their hiding places, and two heavy explosions of powder also occurred. Of Major Hubbard and his battalion, I cannot speak too highly. They are deserving all praise. Every officer and man of the little force is reported to have acted with the most distinguished bravery and prompt obedience to orders.

Very respectfully, your obedient servant,

Alfred W. Ellet, Brigadier General[7]

The inference that the private homes which were ordered burned had caches of arms was seemingly Ellet's attempt at justifying the widespread destruction at Austin. In their own separately written versions of the raid, neither Crandall nor Currie (both officers serving under Ellet) corroborated Ellet as to the presence of arms, and each described only one explosion, that one having come from a single public building where gun powder had gone undiscovered in the search of the town which preceded the firing of the buildings. The burning of Austin did not enhance public relations between the locals and the Union's military. Ellet received mixed reviews on the affair in Northern newspapers and, to an extent, even from his own officers, some of whom had severe reservations over the need to burn the town.

Following the operation against Austin, Ellet and his command continued on to Young's Point, the encampment area and supply depot located on the Mississippi eight miles above Vicksburg. There, Ellet received orders to remain at Young's Point, serving as a guard force for the supply depot.

The Mississippi Marine Brigade's activities at Young's Point would take on a static character. The inactivity was not particularly suited to the adventurous nature of some of Ellet's officers. A group of them on the lookout for excitement hiked across the De Soto Peninsula to get a view of the Confederate gun emplacements on the Vicksburg side of the river. One of those officers was George E. Currie who spied what seemed to be sparks emanating from a factory-like building on Vicksburg's waterfront. According to some Confederate deserters who later in the day were questioned about this, the place was a foundry used to fabricate cannon balls. The raw material for the foundry was purported to be the cannon balls which the Confederates salvaged from the more or less constant barrage that was coming in from the Union artillery. Since most of the incoming rounds had to be melted down and remolded before they could be used in the Confederates' own guns, the foundry was in use almost continually. Requesting permission to establish a battery to go after the foundry, Currie and his friends got Ellet's go ahead. Porter, who was then at De Soto Landing on the southern side of the peninsula, agreed to loan two cannon for the enterprise. With the aid of a detachment of "one hundred enlisted men and fifty Negro boat hands" -- all from the roster of the Mississippi Marine Brigade -- the cannon were dragged ashore from one of the Navy's gunboats. They were then hauled across the peninsula to a location directly opposite from the foundry where a suitable gun emplacement was constructed. Currie was to christen that emplacement "*Fort Adams*" after the Brigade's transport to which he was at the time assigned. Work to complete the emplacement was performed in complete secrecy over a period of three nights. Prior to each break of day, so as to keep the Confederates from learning what was happening, all newly moved earth was camouflaged with cut grass and weeds.

When all was ready, the guns of "*Fort Adams*" opened fire. This immediately brought retaliatory fire from across the river. Later, in writing of the event, Currie claimed that on the first night, for every five cannon shots sent out from

"Fort Adams", the Vicksburg defenders sent "one hundred in return." Considering the acute shortage of ammunition in Vicksburg, which was the reason for the foundry's existence in the first instance, a ratio of one artillery round sent east to every twenty sent west toward *"Fort Adams"* appeared to be an excellent return on investment. During the second night of firing, Currie's gunners made a direct hit on the foundry, causing its furnace to explode.

The shelling of Vicksburg by the two guns which were mounted by the Mississippi Marine Brigade on the tip of the De Soto Peninsula should not give the reader the impression that this was an isolated instance of Union artillery fire directed against Vicksburg. On the contrary, Union mortars emplaced ashore on the banks of the Mississippi were keeping up a fire against the city almost around the clock. In addition, Grant's gunners were by this time firing into Vicksburg from the eastern side of the city.

A more suitable employment for the Mississippi Marine Brigade came about during the last days of the Vicksburg siege, the result of a request from Grant to Porter. Porter passed Grant's request along to Ellet with orders to move his vessels into the Yazoo and take up guard positions at Haines's Bluff.[8] These orders had just been just received by Ellet when fresh ones came in from Porter in response to a second request from Grant which read:

> Near Vicksburg, May 31, 1863
>
> Admiral:
>   Will you please direct the Marine Brigade to debark at Haines's Bluff, and send all their steamers, or as many of them as possible, to Memphis, to bring down reinforcements? I have ordered these troops, but it is a difficult matter to get transportation. I would especially request that any of these steamers that can be spared be got off at the earliest possible moment.
>
> U. S. Grant, Major General[9]

Ellet complied with the order, putting his men ashore and sending his vessels north to Memphis. Shortly after their return, Grant requested their loan again. This time, Grant wanted to lift a cavalry brigade down from Memphis. Porter endorsed the request and passed it along to Ellet who cheerfully acknowledged it, informing Grant's quartermaster that the boats would be on their way shortly. Grant then sent a wire to the involved cavalry commander at Memphis stating that "the boats of the Marine Brigade will be up tomorrow. They will be able to take five or six regiments..." However, just after that telegram had been sent, an amazed Grant discovered that the hurry-up cavalry lift that he had ordered could only be partially carried out. In contrast to the earlier dispatch of his vessels, Ellet had this time decided, on his own cognizance, that where his boats went, so would go the entire Mississippi Marine Brigade. None of Ellet's command were to be left behind at Haines's Bluff as, of course, Grant had assumed they would be. This action by Ellet left minimal space for additional personnel, much less the horses belonging to the cavalry brigade that Grant had requested be transported. On hearing what had happened, Grant fumed. A follow-up telegram to the cavalry commander made that evident.

All the marine boats will be up. General Ellet does not consent to leave his boats, but takes his whole command, horses and all; hence the limited number of men they can take. They [the Marine Brigade] are not subject to my orders, or it would be different. I will make inquiries about the *KENNETT* [a Quartermaster transport] and let you know as soon as possible.

U. S. Grant[10]

By alienating Grant over this troop lift issue, Alfred W. Ellet was slowly but steadily working himself into an untenable position. Grant's antagonism would permeate all the way to the Office of the Quartermaster General in Washington. The shortage of adequate troop lift on the western rivers was nothing new, especially to Grant who had in one way or another been bothered with the problem since 1861. Now, Ellet was adding to it. The question arising in many minds, including Grant's, was whether the tactical value of the Mississippi Marine Brigade was being countered by its tying up of so much valuable transport space. The episode, a prominent one between the principles at the time it incurred, appears to have blown over -- at least for the time being.

During June of 1863, open warfare between Ellet and Porter had not yet fully bloomed. It seems, in fact, that at times the two even enjoyed a degree of mutual admiration. That happy state of affairs is evidenced by a report of Porter's sent to Secretary Gideon Welles. Porter attached to it a report by Ellet concerning a tactical operation in which the Mississippi Marine Brigade had just participated. Porter praised Ellet for his accomplishment of that mission in which Ellet had targeted Confederate raiders who had attacked government leased plantations along the Mississippi's western bank. Taken over from their owners by the Union Army, the plantations were being worked either to grow cotton for the account of the Federal government's Treasury Department or to produce foodstuffs for the Army. During the attacks made against these plantations on the lower Mississippi, the Confederates had carried off an estimated twelve hundred former slaves who, working under Treasury Department and Union Army auspices, had been free salaried workers.[11] One of the plantations which was raided was at Milliken's Bend just six miles upriver from the Federal encampment at Young's Point. Ellet's report, which Porter had forwarded to the Secretary, told of the Brigade's vigorous response to those raids. While following up the trail of the attackers, Ellet's men came upon what appeared to be the charred bodies of what were thought to be Negroes who had apparently been deliberately burned to death. These bodies, or groups of bodies, were found at five separate locations. Whether they were the remains of workers or members of a Union Negro regiment which had been assigned as guard details on the plantation was impossible to tell with any certainty.[12] The raids against the plantations had taken place over a considerable area, so pursuit had to be carried out by separate units of the Mississippi Marine Brigade, the units being landed from the Brigade's transports at widely separated locations. The transport carrying one such unit was the *JOHN RAINE*. While passing near the entrance which led from the Mississippi into Lake Providence, *JOHN RAINE* was taken under fire from the bank by a mobile artillery battery. The cavalry commander aboard *JOHN RAINE*, Major Hubbard (the same officer who had distinguished himself at Austin) told the pilot to bring the steamer against the bank so he could land his force and silence the battery. But before Hubbard's horsemen reached the scene, the enemy fled, leaving behind "some hundreds of captured Negroes."

Another detachment of the Brigade came across a chilling find which at the time received considerable attention in the press. One of the officers, a Lieutenant S. K. Cole, told a reporter what he had seen, and the story later appeared in both the Memphis and the Saint Louis newspapers. The following is from the *Missouri Democrat.*

REBEL BARBARISM

How the Officers of the Negro Regiments and the Negroes Themselves Were Treated
The following is given us upon the authority of Lieutenant [S. K.] Cole, of the Mississippi Marine Brigade:
The day after the battle of Milliken's Bend, in June last, the Marine Brigade landed some ten miles below the Bend, and attacked and routed the guerrillas which had been repulsed by our troops and the gunboats the day previous. Major Hubbard's cavalry battalion, of the Marine Brigade, followed the retreating rebels to Tensas Bayou, and were horrified in the finding of skeletons of white officers commanding Negro regiments, who had been captured by the rebels at Milliken's Bend. In many cases these officers had been nailed to the trees and crucified; in this situation a fire was built around the tree, and they suffered a slow death from broiling. The charred and partially burned limbs were still fastened to the stakes. Other instances were noticed of charred skeletons of officers, which had been nailed to slabs, and the slabs placed against a house which was set on fire by the inhuman demons, the poor sufferers having been roasted alive until nothing was left but charred bones. Negro prisoners recaptured from the guerrillas confirmed these facts, which were amply corroborated by the bodies found as above described. The Negroes taken were to be resold into slavery, while the white officers were consumed by fire. Lieutenant Cole holds himself responsible for the truth of the statement.[13]

The authenticity of that happening will probably never be established. Major General Halleck, who was sent a copy of the story ordered Grant to investigate. Grant would later tell Halleck that the story was "...entirely sensational, I think...." The "I think," at best leaves one with the impression that Grant was himself unsure. We have seen nothing within *Official Records...Armies* or *Official Records...Navies* to either corroborate or cast doubt on Cole's account. A Lieutenant S. K. Cole was definitely an officer of the Brigade's cavalry, serving as first lieutenant of Company B, and both Crandall's history and Brigade roster confirm that Cole had been a participant in the subject operation. The reporter's telling of corpses burned, "...until nothing was left but charred bones," does, leaves one wondering how, in that case, the victim's race could have been determined, at least by those not trained in structural anatomy. The "proof" that officers were also victims was apparently based on the verbal testimony of the plantation Negroes who said they had seen it all happen. If remnants of uniforms indicating an officers' status were seen, it is not so indicated in any of the printed material alluding to the affair. However, when the alleged facts are coupled with a well proven case of the summary hanging of two captured Union prisoners of war who were the victims of the same Confederate troops supposedly involved in the burning incidents, it seems a reasonable probability that the burning atrocity had occurred.

Whether fact or fiction, the relationship between the two opposing armies was not made any better following the circulation of the Cole story.

By letter of July 2, 1863, Porter praised Ellet and his brigade for their performance in the pursuits of the raiders and asked Welles to intercede with the War Department to increase the size of the Mississippi Marine Brigade by one additional regiment of infantry and one of cavalry. Porter wrote: "I find the commanding officer, General Ellet, very prompt and zealous to carry out my orders, and he does not mind what duty he is performing as long as he can serve the cause." [14]

Porter's state of happiness with Ellet would soon become a memory when a difficulty arose between the two men over a series of letters which began appearing in newspapers both at Saint Louis and at Memphis. The letters had been written on the stationery of Mississippi Marine Brigade headquarters and signed by someone using the initials "J.J.B." (According to Crandall, these initials did not match any person on the muster role of the Mississippi Marine Brigade). "J.J.B.", whoever he was, used as his theme much in the way of praise for the dash and tactical skill of Alfred W. Ellet while claiming exactly the opposite for Porter. Porter hit the roof, suspecting Ellet as being directly involved. Ellet could do little but deny complicity. According to Crandall, Ellet attempted to find out who was doing the writing, but that investigation brought no results, and the perpetrator who initiated the correspondence was never discovered. Although it cannot be proven one way or the other, it seems doubtful that Ellet had an involvement over these letters. Crandall claimed that Porter eventually cooled off over the subject, but other evidence seems to contradict this. Correspondence found within *Official Records...Navies* clearly indicates that Porter's rancor over the matter continued during the remainder of the admiral's assignment to the Mississippi theater.[15]

Operations, Summer and Fall of 1863

The mercurial effect that Brigadier General Alfred W. Ellet and his brigade seemed to have had on Porter's temper took a real downturn following Porter's reading in the papers of the "J.J.B." letters. Although Porter had praised the Mississippi Marine Brigade's usefulness back in July, by August of 1863, Porter was launching a full blown campaign to get rid of Ellet and his brigade. In a letter to Secretary of the Navy Gideon Welles, Porter gave his fresh appraisal of the Ellet organization, one almost at opposite poles to his earlier opinion expressed when he wrote the Secretary on July 2 praising Ellet and his performance.

Mississippi Squadron, Flagship *BLACK HAWK**

Sir:
I have the honor to inform you of my arrival at this place, having left New Orleans on the 5th instant [August 5, 1863].

Admiral Farragut having withdrawn his vessels, I placed eleven gunboats at the most dangerous points below Vicksburg.

At present, the river all the way through is unusually quiet, but from information obtained along the route, the rebels are preparing for active guerrilla warfare along the river, making Simsport (in the Atchafalaya) [a point for headquartering]. As soon as General Grant can make arrangements, we will be after them again. At present, he is paralyzed for want of transportation.

I have ordered General Ellet to place the vessels of his brigade at his disposal, but the amount of troops transported is very small, as the brigade troops (about six hundred men) occupy a large portion of the vessels; hence I recommended placing the vessels and the old Ram Fleet under General Grant altogether. The latter are only fit for transports, and the brigade is of no use in its present state, as there are not men enough to operate anywhere along the river.

The vessels will carry nine thousand men for a short time, while now seven vessels are employed in carrying about six hundred men and three hundred horses. Now that General Grant is disposing his forces at different points on the river, for the purpose of protecting the whole country, I should feel a delicacy in ordering a party of soldiers to land within his jurisdiction, and interfere with his legitimate duties. There are other reasons which required that this transfer should be made: The people along this river are disposed to return to their allegiance, and a conciliatory course would go far toward strengthening that determination. That kind of spirit would not be so apt to be shown by an irregular body of men like those composing the brigade, who make raids into what they consider an enemy's country, as by troops stationed at certain points for the protection of the inhabitants, and who are acting under the immediate orders of the general commanding the department.[16]

* *USS*, commissioned Union naval vessel.

The Mississippi Marine Brigade was also beginning to gain a reputation, fairly or not, for acting the role of pillager against the local populations on the river. Through examining the facts that are available, some of that reputation was probably deserved, but in the main it was not. In a number of separate instances, it seems relatively certain that Ellet's men were scapegoats for the wrong doing of others. One report which contained an example of a legitimate accusation was sent to Porter by Lieutenant Commander Thomas O. Selfridge who at the time was the commanding officer of the *USS CONESTOGA*. Selfridge submitted no first-hand proof upon which to lay his charges.

> ...Whilst we were down at Red River, the Marine Brigade landed at Bolivar and committed numerous unnecessary depredations.[17]

Porter, in his new found enthusiasm for ridding himself of Ellet, was ready to believe the worst and more than willing to pass on anything defamatory -- proven or not -- which would serve the purpose of besmirching the Mississippi Marine Brigade's reputation. At about this time, Porter had dreamed up an idea for the creation of his own amphibious strike force, and he seems to have been counting on using that force to replace the function of Ellet's outfit. That ambition is brought to light within correspondence between Porter and Lieutenant Commander James A. Greer dated October 6, 1863. Greer's gunboat crew had recently captured a number of the enemy's horses and mules. Regarding the disposition of those animals, Porter had advised Greer:

> ...You will please therefore not send any more mules and horses, but you can land them at Jeff Davis's plantation and have them looked after. I want some good horses saved for I shall likely lose the Marine Brigade and shall set up a cavalry company made up of sailors. Whenever you capture saddles and bridles, take good care of them as I shall want them all for my cavalry company.[18]

Porter cautioned Greer against what he believed was a developing mercenary attitude over the taking of private property for purposes of prize money. The fact that Porter brought this up gives grounds to the speculation that some of Porter's own officers may have already slipped into such practices, practices for which Ellet and his men would soon be fallaciously blamed.[19]

Ellet's command had by now become the poor stepchild on the river, put there it seems by fate to become the scapegoats for just about anything to which blame could be attached. There is evidence, albeit circumstantial in nature, to suggest that Porter's attitude was the catalyst for the majority of the ill-will which was developing toward the Mississippi Marine Brigade. Once word of Porter's personal disfavor of Ellet got out, the animosity against the Brigade seems to have developed into a sort of contagion which spread throughout the Navy's Mississippi Squadron.[20] Events that had occurred back in the spring for which some blame might be attached to Ellet's men were now dredged up for general consumption. A perhaps not untypical example involved a deposition taken by one officer of the Mississippi Squadron which was forwarded to Porter. Instead of investigating the matter further, Porter merely fired it off to Major General McPherson in whose Army jurisdiction the alleged episode had taken place. The deposition, sworn to by a local citizen named V. T. Warren, stated that on May 23, at McGehee's Landing (a place south of Grand Gulf on the Mississippi River's western bank) a party of "soldiers" had gone ashore to loot, alighting from a steamer identified as being the *LADY PIKE*. (In the claim made against the government, the property pillaged had a value of $16,435.) The "soldiers," according to the deposition, were identified "by their uniforms" as belonging to the Mississippi Marine Brigade.[21] A follow-up investigation by McPherson's staff would disclose that the *LADY PIKE* was an Army transport but that it was not at that time, nor had it ever been attached to the Mississippi Marine Brigade. Porter would certainly have known this, but he had not made any qualification to that effect in his endorsement of the report when he passed it on to McPherson. Eight days after the *LADY PIKE* affair took place, it was alleged that some Mississippi Marine Brigade personnel had landed at nearby Kirk's Landing, doing considerable damage "to vegetable gardens and an orchard." The accusation over the ruined vegetable gardens was passed on to McPherson by Porter. Here, a Mississippi Marine Brigade association was indeed evident, and Ellet freely admitted this to McPherson. He stated that the matter was the result of foragers sent ashore from the Brigade's hospital steamer *WOODFORD*. There was, however, an extenuating circumstance which separated it from an act of criminal vandalism. The men from the *WOODFORD* had been ordered ashore for the explicit purpose of provisioning for the sick. A third complaint of illegal seizure alleged against the Brigade again went through Porter's hands and was again forwarded on to McPherson without comment. This time, though, things backfired against the Navy. An Army investigation showed the offenders to be a landing party from the gunboat *USS CONESTOGA*, a vessel which was part of Porter's own Mississippi Squadron.[22]

Yet another complaint made against the Brigade and which also passed through Porter's hands came from a plantation owner named John Routh. This one alleged that looting had taken place during July at Routh's plantation. This affair had so much notoriety attached to it that it ended up on the desk of Ulysses S. Grant. It was a significant example of some of the depredation which was taking place along the Mississippi and which could not be attached to the Union Army, or the Union Navy, or even to any Confederate armed force, regular or otherwise. According to the official account of the Routh affair, a mounted company of the Mississippi Marine Brigade operating off the *AUTOCRAT* had been sent ashore to reconnoiter at a place called Ashwood Landing. The lead scouts had come across five civilians walking along a cattle path. Upon being questioned, one of the men, namely John Routh, stated that he was the owner of the nearby plantation. Since all five were armed, and therefore suspicious, it was decided that Routh's residence should be searched. On arrival there, the company commander ordered his men to dismount while he himself entered the house, being accompanied by one or two of his officers. This left the enlisted men unsupervised in the yard. Once their officers were out of sight, the men took the opportunity to scatter among the plantation's outbuildings, probably on the lookout for anything to eat or drink that was loosely lying about. One of the officers coming out of the main house spotted some of his men entering an outbuilding. The officer called on the company commander to accompany him. The two entered the outbuilding and found, in addition to their own soldiers, a gang of the plantation's Negroes. In platonic good spirits, the troops and the Negroes were busily imbibing the contents of two broached whiskey barrels. The enlisted men were ordered back to their horses while the officers dumped the remaining whiskey onto the floor. In a subsequent search of Routh's outbuildings, lead shot and gun powder was found in amounts which were of sufficient quantity to allow labeling Routh as a suspected "partisan sympathizer." So far, the relatively minor damage which had occurred to Routh's property was justified under current military policy. The heavy damage occurred after the patrol left. Routh had apparently lost all disciplinary control over his former slaves who numbered between two and three hundred souls. The combination of freedom and now the whiskey caused them to go on a rampage. Without weapons, which the Brigade's patrol had confiscated, Routh and his friends were impotent to act. They had to stand by helplessly while everything Routh owned was either looted or destroyed. Since Routh had no possibility of recouping his losses from the ex-slaves, he cooked up a false claim charging that the damage to his property had been done by the soldiers. Alfred W. Ellet personally investigated the charges and discovered that most of the listed property which Routh said had been stolen by Ellet's men was in the hands of the former slaves. Some minor items of a very insignificant quantity were discovered by the Brigade's officers to be in the personal kits of some of their enlisted men, and these were immediately returned to Routh.[23]

Near the end of October 1863, Porter received the news that his efforts to rid himself of the jurisdictional command of the Mississippi Marine Brigade had in part born fruit. The Brigade was to be transferred to the jurisdiction of Major General William T. Sherman who now headed up the Army of the Tennessee, a geographical term which included jurisdiction of the Mississippi corridor. (Sherman, as earlier stated, had taken over from Grant who had been elevated to the overall command of the Military Departments of the Tennessee, the Cumberland, and the Ohio.) This transfer of the Mississippi Marine Brigade did not, however, rid Porter of Ellet's physical presence on the river. In a letter Porter sent to Sherman on other matters, the admiral added a postscript containing his unsolicited opinion concerning Ellet's brigade. As Porter quite obviously intended, this could not have helped Ellet's standing with Sherman.

> ...The general [Grant] and myself came to one conclusion long since that the brigade should be broken up, the vessels used as transports, and the officers and men put on shore. I cannot tell you of all the reports made to me against the brigade...Moreover, the Ellets have been guilty of some very dirty underhanded work toward myself in publishing contemptible articles in the papers...In these transactions, the Ellets were guilty of gross falsehoods in making malicious statements and lied deliberately in afterward denying them...The quartermasters can scarcely raise vessels to transport provisions, while these brigade vessels are idling away time at great expense. I hope you will break up the whole concern, as General Grant intended to do. The country will be served by so doing.[24]

Shortly after making these comments to Sherman, the admiral tried to blame Ellet for an occurrence that had transpired shortly before Grant had left for the Tennessee although Porter must surely have known that these particular depredations were caused by some of his own men. In the statements of the accusers they identified the culprits as "eastern officers," an identity based upon their manner of speech. Few of Ellet's officers were of eastern origins; however, that was one of the points which Porter chose to ignore. Within correspondence to Secretary Gideon Welles and which was made in answer to an inquiry over the subject, the admiral wrote:

> ...I am convinced that the whole of the report originated from the conduct of General Ellet's Fleet, which is still in existence, and has been passed to the Army with the Marine Brigade; or it is the Marine Brigade which commits depredations on friend and foes alike. I enclose [for] you copies of reports sent to me by parties who have suffered from these bands of plunderers, who have plundered, and claim to be attached to the Navy. The Marine Brigade has six rams accompanying it, which naturally gives use to the idea that they are tinclads [lightly armored naval river patrol craft]. They wear the naval uniform the same as we do, only trimmed in silver, instead of gold. While those persons were under my command, I controlled them, the same as naval vessels. These rams are frequently seen cruising about by our vessels, but courtesy to General Grant forbids my interfering with them. There will be no justice on this river to the inhabitants until the Ram Fleet is broken up and the Marine Brigade placed under strict Army control, which is not the case at present....
>
> David D. Porter, Rear Admiral[25]

Porter's description of the uniform as being the same as that of the Navy, "...only trimmed in silver instead of gold..." is the only reference we could locate in any wartime records or correspondence which stated that the uniform of the Mississippi Marine Brigade was similar to that of the Navy. Crandall (p 258) mentions the Brigade's uniform as being like the rest of the Army's except for a special hat. Other sources substantiate Crandall's statement. Enlisted men on the Navy's gunboats did not wear the same uniform as that worn by the Army's enlisted men on the Mississippi Marine Brigade's vessels. Porter's reference to the uniforms seems to be wide of the factual mark and may have been an effort to deliberately mislead the Navy Secretary. Porter's description of the uniforms "trimmed in silver" may possibly have been in reference to the civilian officers on the rams. These men would not, however, have been included in landing parties, so it would have been unlikely that an identification of the Brigade, once ashore, could have been made on the basis of the uniforms of its civilian officers.

The postscript which Porter had written to Sherman in late October had been forwarded to Grant who was then still at New Orleans. Grant decided that the time was ripe to rid the District of the Mississippi of the interservice discord being brought about by the existence of Ellet's force. It is not clear if Grant went about this solely to placate Porter, or if Grant and Sherman had similar viewpoints about Ellet. One of Grant's staff officers, acting for Grant, put the case for disbandment of the Mississippi Marine Brigade before Brigadier General Lorenzo Thomas, the Army's Adjutant General. Grant's staff member cited the various charges which had been made against Ellet's men, but he offered them with a qualification as to their authenticity.

> ...it is highly probable that these charges are exaggerated, yet on account of the great cost of maintaining the Brigade, and the slight service it renders, and the excellent use its boats could be put to, it is strongly recommended that the command be transferred to land service, and the boats turned over to the Quartermaster Department.[26]

The Adjutant General endorsed the request and passed it along with a cover letter to the Secretary of War, stating that the wish to see the Mississippi Marine Brigade and its fleet dispersed was held jointly by Grant and Porter. What had not been taken into account, either by Porter or by Grant, was the political protection that Ellet possessed. Ellet's brigade proved to be an entity that was not so easy to discard. In an August 24, 1863, communication, Halleck to Grant, Ellet's position was left at least partially secure for the time being.

> ...The Secretary of War does not approve the conversion of this marine or river brigade into a land brigade, but authorizes you to use any of General Ellet's brigade for temporary shore duty, and of his boats for temporary transports, whenever the exigencies of the service require their use.[27]

The rationale which was given by Halleck to Grant for the Secretary of War's overturn of what would ordinarily have been considered a routine reorganization request on the part of a theater commander, was that the Mississippi Marine Brigade's men had been enlisted specifically for the amphibious task they had been performing. To put the Brigade to another use could be considered a breach of enlistment contract. Some modification of the Secretary's protective attitude on the Ellet matter was made a few days later when Halleck wrote Grant that a covenant had been added to the Secretary's earlier instructions. Grant was now authorized, "...to take the proper measures to reduce it [the Brigade] to discipline, trying and punishing the guilty parties...." [28] Halleck offered a subtle way to get around the entire dilemma, one which would have the end effect of incorporating the Brigade into the shore-based army, not as a whole, but in bits and pieces.

> For reasons given in my letter of the 24th instant, it is not deemed advisable at present to break up this brigade, but you can detach and place on shore such portions of it as you may deem necessary for the good of the service.[29]

No affirmative steps seem to have followed Halleck's advice to detach units of the Brigade. For a while, it would remain whole. Whoever directly interceded with the Secretary to keep the Mississippi Marine Brigade in existence -- and it may even have been someone in Lincoln's cabinet -- had given the unit an extension of life which would last into the following year. But the relative autonomy which Alfred W. Ellet and his command had previously enjoyed had finally come to an end.

Throughout the late summer and into the early fall of 1863, there was a considerable shuffling and reshuffling of the Army's regiments along the Mississippi corridor. Sizable numbers of troops were being moved from Vicksburg to New Orleans for their subsequent transshipment to eastern commands. This meant an increase in the use of river transport, and Ellet found that his transports were being frequently called upon for detached troop lift service. By early winter, the shipping shortage on the river had eased somewhat, and only then did Ellet regain the full control of his vessels.

Internally, changes were taking place within the Brigade. One rather traumatic event was a falling out between Colonel Charles Rivers Ellet and his uncle, the general. This had culminated in the resignation of the younger man in August. Charles Rivers Ellet returned to his home where he died shortly thereafter. A reporter for *Harper's New Monthly Magazine*, writing of Charles Rivers Ellet's death, but seemingly unaware that he had resigned from the Army, claimed that a drug overdose may have been the direct cause of death.

> With the close of the hot summer, and also with the substantial close of his labors, which had for months tasked his mental and physical energies to the utmost, Charles Rivers Ellet applied for leave of absence, and in August retired to the home of his uncle, Doctor Ellet, at Bunker Hill, Illinois. A severe facial neuralgia had long troubled him, for which he was in the habit of taking some opiate. On the night of the 16th of October he complained of not feeling well, and said to his aunt before retiring that he would take something "for the pain in his face." Undoubtedly the ingredient was morphine, as he had frequently administered it before, preparing it himself. Whether from an overdose or from some weakness of the system, morning found him cold, and the soul gone from his earthly casket.[30]

Crandall, writing long after the war, put a more pleasant face on the circumstance of Charles Rivers Ellet's death by claiming it was the result of typhoid.

That summer (1863) the Brigade lost through transfer to other units a number of junior officers who had been solicited from within the Brigade's cavalry battalion. Nineteen of the Brigade's best non-commissioned officers in the infantry regiment left to become commissioned officers in the 4th Arkansas Volunteers (colored). A collapse in officer morale was becoming quite evident. An organization which had started out as a brave new concept had come to be looked upon as a pariah to be avoided if one wished to maintain a military reputation. A belief seems to have taken over that no matter what the Mississippi Marine Brigade did -- good or bad -- it was going to get a negative reaction from others. This was probably an accurate appraisal, particularly so when not only the Navy but even the senior Army commanders appeared poised to pounce upon the slightest suspicion of any irregularities. In reaction to those tendencies, great care began to be taken by the Brigade's officers when dealing out retribution against suspected partisans. One example of this careful approach was evident at Bayou Sara. Some locals from the community there, having taken on their fair share of whiskey at the neighborhood saloon, had fired upon some passing supply vessels. A landing force aboard one of the Brigade's transports was sent to Bayou Sara to investigate. The officer in charge of the detail lined up the entire male population of the town and asked for their explanation. Those present (some of whom showed signs of over indulgence) of course disavowed all responsibility. The landing officer then warned that further harassment of any kind against river traffic would bring serious consequences. He told them that this time the town, including all public and private property, would be spared -- except for the saloon which was to be burned. Leaving behind a sober town folk, the Mississippi Marine Brigade "passed on."[31]

During the fall of 1863, the Brigade's activity increased when it was given the responsibility for the security of the Mississippi between Vicksburg and Memphis. Following the taking of Vicksburg in July, considerable rhetoric in the way of political pronouncement had declared the Mississippi River an open pathway, but that turned out to be a misstatement of the realities. Parts of the river, particularly those sections along the Arkansas bank, remained uncontrolled vacuums, filled almost at will by roving enemy units. Some of these units had a legitimate status, but others had little if any formal affiliation with the Confederate military, operating more like banditry. The Confederate Army's presence could, however, become noticeable wherever a line of communication was put into place connecting regular enemy units located in Arkansas to other units operating in the Tennessee Valley. One such connection was discovered by a cavalry patrol of the Brigade searching a mile or so inland from the east bank of the Mississippi near the area of a former trouble spot, Greenville, Mississippi. This patrol captured a Confederate paymaster who was carrying $1,200,000 in Confederate bills and a draft payable at Alexandria, Louisiana, for $1,000,000. When captured, this paymaster was riding in an old fashioned stagecoach of prewar Army design (probably a wagon captured in Texas in 1861 when the Union garrisons in that state surrendered to Texas state troops). Upon vigorous questioning, the paymaster admitted that he was heading for Bolivar Court House Landing where arrangements had been made to cross the Mississippi River into Arkansas. According to documents accompanying the Confederate bills, some of the specie was consigned to the enemy's Trans-Mississippi Department; another part was earmarked for the purchase of various items such as copper, pig iron, and niter (the latter used in the manufacture of explosives). By now, Alfred W. Ellet had been in the Army long enough to realize the impropriety of a subordinate commander routing his reports directly to Washington; however, both Grant and Sherman were engaged elsewhere and had become difficult to reach. That circumstance provided to Ellet, or so he would later claim, a legitimate reason to bypass the regular chain of command when reporting the capture of the funds. Instead of following channels, he wrote directly to the Secretary of War, asking for instructions as to the disposition of the funds. If the truth be known, Ellet may have felt that the capture of such a large sum was a chance to bring his activities to the attention of the Secretary; therefore, it was an opportunity not to be missed. In any event, as judged in retrospect, it was an unwise move which cost Ellet more than a full measure in his standing with his superior officers.

Alfred W. Ellet had been frequently absenting himself from his command in order to journey to New Albany on the Ohio River. On the building ways at New Albany were two torpedo shaped wooden vessels, one of 180 feet in length and the other 210 feet; both were being constructed under order to the War Department. Each of them was of wooden hull construction, fitted with a metallic ram as an extension to their hulls. Additionally, each was to have a gun deck suitable in size and framing for the emplacement of cannon. As intended, they were to be armed transports for inclusion into the Mississippi Marine Brigade. Captain James Brooks, the quartermaster officer who had earlier been one of the Army's agents for the Western Gunboat Flotilla before it went over to the Navy, was supervising the work. The construction of the vessels had been approved by the Secretary of War who had taken a personal interest, even going so far as to change the specifications from the original design which called for iron sheeting over the wood. That change was made lest the Navy consider them gunboats and in consequence object to the Army's intrusion upon what the naval service had begun to consider its own exclusive domain. From what can be determined, it appears that considerable care was being taken at the time to keep the construction from the notice of Rear Admiral Porter. However, news traveled fast on the western river systems, and it was not long before Porter heard that something was being built for the Army near New Albany and that the Mississippi Marine Brigade was involved. Porter sent one of his officers upriver to investigate. Acting incognito, the officer dropped in at the builder's yard. As fortune (or misfortune) would have it, he arrived on a day when Captain Brooks was at the yard checking on progress. Not aware that the stranger he met was Porter's agent, Brooks quite innocently confirmed that the vessels were for Ellet. That afternoon, the agent wired to Porter the information, feeding Porter's worst apprehensions by concluding, "I think every effort will be made to keep up the ram fleet no matter what becomes of the Brigade." [32] Up to that time, Porter had felt confident that Ellet was nearing the end of his political tether and that the Navy would soon see the end of the Mississippi Marine Brigade and its vessels. Therefore, the news of what was occurring at New Albany came as a shock. Porter immediately fired off a priority message to Assistant Secretary of the Navy Fox, castigating Ellet for all of the wrongs ever committed -- true, alleged, or otherwise -- painting a picture of endless depredations as long as Ellet was allowed to continue in operation. Porter urged that Fox do everything in his power to prevent Ellet from getting the two new vessels and/or being allowed to operate a separate fleet if and when the Mississippi Marine Brigade was disbanded. Porter's basis for taking that position stressed the Act of July 16, 1862, the same act which had transferred to the Navy those Army owned gunboats within the western theater of operations. As a reminder, Porter copied Fox with the text of that act.

> *Be it enacted, etc.*, That the Western gunboat fleet, constructed by the War Department for operations on the western waters, shall be transferred to the Navy Department which will be hereafter charged with the expense of its repair, support, and maintenance: *Provided*, That all vessels now under construction or repair by authority of the War Department shall be completed and paid for under the authority of that Department, from appropriations made for that purpose.

In actuality, the Act of July 16, 1862, as it was written, contained no specific prohibition against future additions to the Mississippi Marine Brigade once vessels on the ways (as of July 16, 1862) had been transferred over to the Navy. In fact the act did not prohibit the supplying of vessels of a combatant class to any Army organization. Furthermore, funding for the constructions now taking place at New Albany had come from surplus funds that the Army had earmarked for the Brigade. It did not originate from funding designated for the now defunct Western Gunboat Flotilla. To Porter, however, such facts made little difference. The admiral was in the grips of an obsessive desire to rid himself of Ellet's operation, and any facts contrary to that purpose were no doubt considered by him as totally irrelevant.

One can only speculate as to the discussions which must have taken place in Washington between officials in the Navy Department and the War Department regarding these new rams. It was probably quite evident to all concerned that the matter went beyond just the two vessels under construction, being rather the result of Porter's desire to have the Brigade and its vessels disappear from the rivers. Secretary Stanton was probably aware that Ellet's men were not the villains they had been painted to be by Porter, but at the same time, he appreciated the necessity of keeping the lid on any interservice friction. At the time plans were being developed for a series of combined operations along the eastern seaboard and on the Virginia rivers. A cooperative spirit between the Army and the Navy was now more essential than it had ever been. Porter's obsession with Ellet aside, the Navy's sensitivity seems to have focused on the matter of gunboats in general. This is indicated by a message sent from Halleck to Major General Nathaniel P. Banks who was then operating in southwestern Texas. Banks had stated the need for armed vessels to assist in the surveillance of inland lagoons along the Texas coast. Somewhat incorrectly, Halleck informed Banks that the Navy had exclusive domain in such matters.

Washington, DC; December 7, 1863

General:

I have just received your letter of November 18, "off Aransas Pass."

In regard to the gunboats for your department, we must rely upon the Navy. Admiral Porter has been requested to give you all possible assistance in this matter. You may not be aware that by a law of last Congress, the building, purchasing, and commanding of gunboats are placed exclusively under the Navy Department. I will again ask that admirals commanding in the Gulf and in the Mississippi be directed to cooperate with you and render you all the aid in their power. You will also communicate with them, asking their assistance in any way you desire.

Very respectfully, your obedient servant,

H. W. Halleck, General-in-Chief[33]

Halleck's opinion on the matter of the Navy having exclusive domain over gunboats was incorrect; but if considered as a policy, it was one that was shortly superseded both on the Tennessee and Ohio rivers and within the sounds of the Carolinas and Georgia. In those areas, the Army maintained its own gunboat fleet throughout 1864 and into 1865, well past the surrender of Confederate forces. In fact, it had gunboats under construction at both New York and Philadelphia during both 1864 and 1865.

Nevertheless, Porter's efforts won out, and he received authorization to take over Ellet's two new vessels at New Albany. On December 7, Porter wired the Secretary of the Navy that he had formally taken possession.

Mississippi Squadron

Sir:

I have the honor to inform you that I have taken possession of the two rams at New Albany, and with your permission will name one of them the *AVENGER**, the other the *VINDICATOR**.

The contract having been made, they will be completed under the directions of Captain Brooks, US Army, who is superintending them, making such alterations as will render them efficient as vessels of war. Either of them will sink anything they may run into, no matter how strong; and no doubt they will be very serviceable vessels.

The contract is $85,000, paid from the money saved from the outfit of the Marine Brigade. Quartermaster General Meigs has given the necessary orders for their delivery and equipment.

I have the honor to be, very respectfully, your obedient servant,

David D. Porter, Rear Admiral[34]

* *USS*, commissioned Union naval vessel.

Ellet and His Command Move Downriver

Near the end of the year (1863), the river north of Vicksburg quieted down. The Mississippi Marine Brigade was then ordered south to be employed as a roving patrol force on that part of the Mississippi River lying between Grand Gulf and Natchez. This stretch of the river was then being threatened by hit and run penetrations of small enemy units, mainly cavalry accompanied by some light artillery. Most of the enemy units with which the Ellet force became engaged during this period were small in number and might just as well have been handled by landing parties of blue jackets which were by then actively working from Porter's gunboats.

During mid February, Colonel Charles A. Gilchrist of the 12th Louisiana Infantry (colored) was ordered to place himself and his regiment under the instructions of Ellet who at the time was located with most of the Brigade at or near Grand Gulf. Upon reporting at Grand Gulf, Gilchrist, in cooperation with Ellet was supposed to scour the surrounding area for abandoned enemy property, specifically corn, and establish a recruiting depot to which recruits would be brought from the countryside. What was to transpire instead was a rather large scale cotton seizing effort into which the troops of the 12th Louisiana were impressed as laborers. The cotton seizures, as alleged by Ellet in his conversations with Gilchrist, were to be for the account of the United States government. What instead seemed to have taken place were a series of complicated transactions in which Ellet, according to Gilchrist, appeared to orchestrate things for the benefit of a number of shady individuals who Gilchrist suspected as being private speculators. Upon returning from Grand Gulf, Gilchrist wrote his report of those events and submitted the report on March 15 to XVII Corps headquarters. The report was endorsed and forwarded to Sherman's departmental headquarters by Major General James B. McPherson who notated the need for "a thorough and searching investigation." [35]

Using the Mississippi Marine Brigade for what were essentially company-sized tasks was a practice which had come under question at the theater command level. Sherman expressed his views on the subject within a letter to McPherson, stating that the Mississippi Marine Brigade might be more suitably employed in movements elsewhere against major enemy units.[36] At the time of Sherman's letter to McPherson, Ellet's brigade was listed on returns as part of McPherson's XVII Corps. The XVII Corps was in turn being administered through the Army of the Tennessee. McPherson's corps was scheduled to become part of a planned expedition scheduled for early February which was to be staged for departure from Vicksburg and which had as its overall objective the broadening out of Union control of the eastern side of the Mississippi corridor. If a success, such an operation would restrict if not eliminate all enemy presence in the area of the corridor lying east of the Mississippi from Memphis south to Meridian, Mississippi. With the eastern side of the corridor cleared of enemy presence, Union Army movements in Tennessee would be safeguarded against harassment from the rear. Sherman and McPherson thought that Ellet's brigade could be a helpful reinforcement to those efforts. In making that assessment, both generals seemed to have overlooked the potential dangers from Confederate raids against the Federally leased plantations on the western banks of the Mississippi. These raids (which, as already stated, were then being conducted by small enemy units) were being launched out of western Louisiana and Arkansas with the raiders enjoying safe sanctuary once they moved back to their bases of operations. Although the enemy had not to date come in strength, this could conceivably change once the number of Union troops was decreased along the Mississippi. Complete control of the eastern side of the corridor, as could be accomplished by what Sherman was planning, would not necessarily benefit the security of the plantations located along the Mississippi's western banks. The threat against those plantations came almost entirely from the west, and it could come at many locations -- without warning, and with a strength not to date encountered. This could be a circumstance that was beyond the ability of Porter's blue jackets to handle. In Washington, Halleck appears to have appreciated this potential danger better than Sherman or McPherson.

Washington: February 16, 1864

It is deemed important by the Government that leased plantations on the Mississippi River receive due protection, and the Secretary of War desires that General Ellet's Marine Brigade be assigned to that service. It is understood that it has been so assigned temporarily by General Sherman.

H. W. Halleck[37]

What came to be called "The Meridian Campaign" was intended to produce "a swath of desolation fifty miles broad across the State of Mississippi which the present generation will not forget." In a March 1864 report filed at the end of that campaign, Sherman wrote, "the damage to the rail junction at Meridian will make it impossible for the enemy to operate with anything but light cavalry from the Pearl River westward to the Mississippi. Consequently I can [now] reduce the garrisons of Memphis, Vicksburg, and Natchez to mere guards..." [38] Confederate intentions were, though, that the Mississippi was to remain a distracting element against Union military ambitions conducted elsewhere. Thus, Sherman's plan to reduce garrison strengths along the river were to prove overly optimistic.

~

In the early spring of 1864, a major expedition would be launched into the Red River country of Louisiana. One of the units assigned to that effort would be the Mississippi Marine Brigade, together with its vessels. The departure of the Brigade for the Red River postponed an investigation over Ellet's cotton seizures at Grand Gulf. Something-- perhaps the attention given to the Red River Campaign-- seems to have waylaid any follow-up of Colonel Gilchrist's accusations.

~

In late March, just five days prior to when Alfred Ellet and his men were ordered to move from the Red River back to the Mississippi, Lieutenant General Leonidas Polk, commander of the Confederate Department of the Mississippi, would send a message to President Jefferson Davis at Richmond, suggesting a scheme aimed at retaking control of the Mississippi River all the way from Cairo south to the Gulf of Mexico. The plan went so far as to include the recapture of Vicksburg which was to be shortly followed by the taking back of Port Hudson and New Orleans. In what reads like an overblown fantasy, Polk theorized to Davis that by assigning each thirty miles of the banks of the river to a squadron of cavalry, river traffic as well as trans-Mississippi access could be completely denied to the Union. Polk's plan would begin to accomplish this through the purchase of one commercial steamboat which would be armed in secret. When readied, this one steamer would seize the first steamboat it came upon. This would then be followed by a string of seizures of other steamboats, capture by capture, in a sort of waterborne domino effect rolling downriver toward New Orleans. Polk counted on all of this happening with such quick and trouble-free efficiency that Federal forces would not know what was happening to them until it was all over. That such a concept could be made to work was predicated by Polk upon the knowledge that almost all of the Navy's Mississippi Squadron, as well as Ellet's brigade, were then absent, being participants in the Red River Campaign. It seemed almost certain at the time that all or part of the Union's fleet would soon be stranded by the Red River's drop in level. Polk was also counting on his knowledge that the Union Army Telegraph Service system did not directly connect many points along the Mississippi. He was aware that some gunboats still remained on the main river; but his plan included the capture of them as well, although he never did spell out the niceties of how those captures were going to be accomplished. In Polk's next sweep of the pen, he went on to state to Jefferson Davis that with the Mississippi Squadron's gunboats securely in his hands, the fall of Vicksburg, Helena, Memphis, and Port Hudson would "be an easy matter." When Polk's senior, Lieutenant General Braxton Bragg, was queried by Davis as to the plan's practicality, Bragg answered that it would not only fail, but that any troops committed to it would be destroyed in their entirety. Polk's grandiose scheme of reconquest was not given further consideration. This did not mean, however, that Confederate infantry and cavalry strikes along the river were discontinued; on the contrary, they continued to proliferate in both number and intensity.[39]

~

After Alfred W. Ellet and his Mississippi Marine Brigade had arrived back on the Mississippi from the Red River, elements of the Brigade were dispatched up the Yazoo and Sunflower river system to combat enemy activity reported to be heavy there. Two of Ellet's vessels (which had been recently fitted with heavier guns) were retained on standby at Vicksburg. Only the most minor contact with the enemy was made on the forays up the Yazoo and Sunflower.[40]

Following the sweeps up the Yazoo and Sunflower rivers, the Brigade's vessels would be scattered along the Mississippi, each of their commanders being assigned individual patrol sections. During this operational phase, Ellet put into practice a system for sending landing parties off each morning to probe inland from the banks on both the Arkansas and the Louisiana sides of the Mississippi.

In April 1864, an ominous factor entered the warfare along the river when enemy cavalry attacked Fort Pillow. (Fort Pillow was forty-five miles north of Memphis on the Mississippi's eastern bank.) The enemy cavalry under the command of Brigadier General James R. Chalmers was part of Nathan Bedford Forrest's corps. At the time, Fort Pillow was garrisoned by newly recruited Negro troops who were still in a state of training.[41] They simply were no match for the seasoned Confederates. After surrendering to the attackers, many of the Negro soldiers were shot down in cold blood.[42]

Constant activity attended the Brigade for the remainder of April and into May. The majority of the actions consisted of skirmishes with units of enemy cavalry which never exceeded more than a dozen men in number. These actions were usually preceded by vague reports of large numbers of enemy cavalry moving into an area. Upon responding, the Brigade's units (mainly landed in company strength) would most often come upon what had the appearance of a screening picket force which would then withdraw after a hasty exchange of fire. Sometimes it appeared to Ellet and his officers that the enemy had become a phantom.

During that spring, the Brigade never worked together as a complete unit. Instead, the transport commanders with their landing forces operated in their own assigned sectors. The idea was aimed at keeping the enemy from consolidating at any one point on the river. Despite the constant rumors coming into Brigade headquarters of the assembling of large enemy forces, suspicions grew that the enemy consisted only of locally based partisans. Some satisfaction was derived from the fact that the Brigade was making life miserable for the enemy, whoever he might be. This had even included the disruption of the enemy's sex life, a point that was related within the diary of Orderly Sergeant J. M. Fulkerson of the Brigade's Company B.

> We arrived early this forenoon at Egg Point, and a squad of our company went out with the mounted infantry on a scout. Lieutenant Benson took the advance guard, and I was also with the advance. We stopped when we got out about six miles, and the Lieutenant sent an advance guard a hundred yards or so ahead, while we stopped there to rest. Presently a rebel came riding down the road and came nearly up to our advance guard before he saw them, and then surrendered. We took from him a splendid revolver, and he said it was such a good joke on him getting captured, he thought he would like to have company, and told us of another rebel in the second house up the road, who was there, seeing his sweetheart. Lieutenant Benson took part of the advance and surrounded the first house, and I took the balance of the advance and surrounded the second house. A young lady begged me not to search the house, but we had it to do, and we found the rebel upstairs, covered up in bed.[43]

There is a significance to Fulkerson's account in its relevancy to the grade of loyalty shown toward one another on the part of at least some Confederate partisans. The lack of loyalty seems to have been especially common among those having origins in Kansas and Missouri. In general, the members of such partisan units walked a gray line between soldiery and banditry, with a leaning toward the latter.

The Mississippi Marine Brigade's adjutant, while writing of the activities on the Mississippi during 1864, relates the then current theory that some of William Clarke Quantrill's irregulars had moved into Arkansas from their usual operating areas in Missouri. Quantrill's status, or lack of status as a legal combatant was then and continues to be the subject of much controversy.[44]

Confederate activity along the river increased substantially in mid-May. John Sappington Marmaduke, a Confederate brigadier general, joined in the effort to harass Union commerce on the Mississippi. He did this through a program of deploying mobile artillery batteries, well supported by infantry units of regimental strength. The first contact between one of Marmaduke's units and a unit of the Mississippi Marine Brigade was at Greenville, Mississippi. Involved in this episode was an enemy battery of eight guns. The Brigade's transport *BALTIC* suffered extensively from that battery's fire, being hit nine times before the enemy commander moved his guns out of position.

Marmaduke's determination to deter if not halt Union traffic on the central Mississippi seemed to be nearing fruition. Independent river traffic between Memphis and Vicksburg nearly stopped. Any steamers that moved did so only under heavy convoy escort. In providing such escorts, Ellet's vessels began working in conjunction with those Navy tinclads which remained on the river.

From the Confederate correspondence which relates to this period, it appears that their activity along the banks of the Mississippi was primarily for the purpose of tying up Union forces, preventing them from being transferred to support the Red River Campaign. The attacks against shipping on the Mississippi were seen as the surest means for getting Union attention and accomplishing that goal.[45]

Running past the strong points which had been established by Marmaduke was anything but easy. The *BEN J. ADAMS* was struck by solid shot thirty-six times during one passage of a rebel battery position set up near Columbia, Mississippi (a little distance upriver from Greenville). *BEN J. ADAMS*'s commander, a Captain Newall, in a report made to the Mississippi Marine Brigade's adjutant, described some of the grizzly results of Confederate solid shot.

> As soon as we were out of range of the rebel guns, I walked aft, and a little way from where I had been standing, lay Dennis Murphy, a gallant Irishman belonging to Company K. While firing through a loophole in the barricade, a shell had torn off his lower jaw and his right shoulder. He was dead. Just beyond him lay Corporal Joseph Field, one of my own best men. He had been firing with his left side against the barricade, when a shell struck him in the abdomen, cutting away the outer covering and letting his bowels and liver out upon the deck. When I came to him, he was supporting his head on his hand, and his horrified comrades were about him. I stooped down and took his head in my hands, and turning his eyes upon my face with a look that has never been forgotten, he said, "Captain, can anything be done for me?" I replied, "No, Field, you will be dead in a few minutes. Have you any message for your friends?" "Tell them I die willingly for my country," said he. I ordered a mattress thrown from the nearest stateroom upon deck, scooped his warm, bloody entrails up in my hands, and laid them back upon him. We lifted and laid him upon the mattress, and he was dead.
>
> Passing through the midship gangway to the larboard side, I found another man, Charles H. Hallowell of Company G whose right arm a shell had taken off close to the shoulder. He lay with his head toward me, on the table, and as I approached, he reached back his left hand to me saying, "Captain, I was doing my duty when this was done."
>
> Upon the hurricane deck on the larboard side, we found another of my own men, James Mason. A shell had passed through his chest, tearing out his heart in its passage, and throwing it clear across the hurricane deck of the boat we were convoying past the battery.[46] [The other boat was lashed alongside the *BEN J. ADAMS*. An illustration within this volume depicts that action.]

The effect that Marmaduke's artillery was having on the vessels of the Mississippi Marine Brigade and on the morale of their crews was described by another of the Brigade's officer.

> They [the vessels] lacked the weight and reinforcement necessary to enable them to stand the recoil of the heavy guns placed upon them, and by which both the *DIANA* and the *BALTIC* were already badly strained. Besides, these vessels were occupied by men, willing indeed, and even eager to encounter danger, and capable, as any equal number of men with like equipment, to inflict punishment upon the enemy, but in their crowded condition upon the boats, they were like fowls shut up in a coop, destined for slaughter.[47]

The *BEN J. ADAMS* had been so badly riddled and the *BALTIC* and *DIANA* so badly strained as to necessitate their immediate repairs at shipyard.

The enemy's artillery which had been deployed along the banks of the Mississippi had taken a serious toll against shipping generally. Between May 26 and June 2, Marmaduke's artillery took under fire a total of twenty-one steamers. Of these, five had been sunk and five severely damaged.[48] Major General E. R. S. Canby, who was then commanding the Union's Military Division of West Mississippi, decided that Marmaduke's forces had to be eliminated. The only effective way to do that seemed to be a land operation which would drive Marmaduke from the banks of the Mississippi and decimate his command, thus destroying his ability to return.

Vicksburg, Mississippi, May 31, 1864

Major General A. J. Smith:

Attempts have been made by the rebels for several days past to interrupt the navigation of the Mississippi River at points on the Arkansas shore above and below Greenville, Mississippi. The force and character of the troops engaged is not definitely known, but I am informed by Major General Steele that a force of several thousand mounted men, supported by infantry, on the Saline, were below Pine Bluff with the presumed intention of interrupting his communications by the Arkansas and White rivers. It is believed that a considerable part of this force has been turned eastward to the Mississippi, and is now engaged in the attempt to interrupt the navigation of the river.

Your own command reinforced by a regiment of cavalry from the forces under Major General Slocum, and whatever force of the Marine Brigade may be within reach, will be employed by you for the purpose of destroying or capturing the rebel force, or at least giving them such a lesson as will deter them from a renewal of similar attempts. The most reliable information as to the character of the country in which you will operate and the routes by which the rebels reach and retreat, may be obtained from offices of the Marine Brigade, and [Lieutenant] Colonel Currie now on the *DIANA* is recommended to you as especially qualified for this purpose.

E. R. S. Canby, Commanding, Military Division, West Mississippi[49]

Expedition Against Marmaduke

On June 4, 1864, the Brigade's transports *DIANA*, *JOHN RAINE*, *BEN J. ADAMS*, and *E. H. FAIRCHILD* moved away from the Vicksburg wharf, followed by twenty-one troop transports carrying A. J. Smith's XVI Corps. (A. J. Smith and his corps had just returned to Vicksburg following participation in the Red River Campaign which had ingloriously terminated the month before.) Operational orders issued before the departure from Vicksburg are a clear indication that A. J. Smith anticipated coming up against a strong enemy force and that he expected he might land his men in the face of resistance. These orders illustrate A. J. Smith's special aptitude for the control of an amphibious expedition, much of that experience having been recently gained on the Red River.

Headquarters Detachment, XVI Army Corps
Vicksburg, Mississippi, June 3, 1864

Special Orders No. 47

    I. The transports carrying troops or stores belonging to this command, at the signal of one long whistle from the *HANNIBAL*, will immediately get up steam, and at the second long whistle, which will be one hour after the first, will swing out into the stream in the following order:

first	*HANNIBAL*	twelfth	*ADRIATIC*
second	*DES MOINES*	thirteenth	*MARMORA*
third	*MARS*	fourteenth	*WHITE CLOUD*
fourth	*HAZEL DELL*	fifteenth	*W. L. EWING*
fifth	*IDAHO*	sixteenth	*SHENANGO*
sixth	*EMMA BOYD*	seventeenth	*VENANGO*
seventh	*FREESTONE*	eighteenth	*DIADEM*
eighth	*CLARA BELL*	nineteenth	*LEVIATHAN*
ninth	*HAMILTON*	twentieth	*LIBERTY*
tenth	*JOHN J. ROE*	twenty-first	*EMERALD*
eleventh	*CHOUTEAU* *		

The boats will keep well closed up and will not leave the position assigned them in this order. The signals will only be repeated by the boats carrying division or brigade commanders. In case of landing, boats will still retain their places.

    The signals will be as follows: One long whistle, when tied up, to get under way (when under way one long whistle means to tie up or land); three whistles, close order; four whistles, open order; five whistles, want to communicate; six whistles, let me go ahead and reconnoiter; one gun, the enemy in sight; two short whistles and then a long one, I want assistance; three short whistles and then a long one, the enemy have a battery; four whistles and then a long one, the troops will land; one gun and a long whistle, all clear, you can pass.

    By order of Major General A. J. Smith:

J. Hough, Assistant Adjutant General[50]

* *HENRY CHOUTEAU*

    Marmaduke's force would not prove to be as powerful as had been expected. The units of Marmaduke's command which had been harassing traffic on the river north of Vicksburg were already running out of the tools with which to fight. In a report sent on May 30 to Marmaduke's adjutant, the colonel in charge of his artillery elements had written that his supply of ammunition was down to "twelve rifle shells, six solid shot smoothbore, and thirty shells for howitzers." This was hardly enough ammunition for targeting what A. J. Smith was bringing up the river. Confederate correspondence shows that Marmaduke was aware of A. J. Smith's expedition well before the transports even left Vicksburg. He had no intention of bringing on a battle against a full army corps while his own force in toto was under eleven hundred men.[51]

    On June 5, acting on information that a unit of the enemy was nearby, A. J. Smith, landed part of his command on the west bank of the Mississippi, close to the Arkansas-Louisiana border. Its forward elements soon made contact with the enemy picket line which immediately fell back. The Federals followed this up by some cautious probing. From what contact his own pickets were making, A. J. Smith realized that he was not dealing with a large force. He ordered his cavalry, including the mounted troops of Ellet's brigade, to assault across a bayou which was separating him from the enemy.[52] The advantage seemed to lay with the Confederates due to the bayou's considerable depth and its silty bottom which, as quickly discovered, made it impossible to ford. Unable to get across, the Federals maintained a hot exchange of fire along their entire line until the enemy, by now almost out of ammunition, withdrew. By the standards of 1864, casualties were very light with only about two hundred killed or severely wounded on the Federal side. Marmaduke's force suffered less than four killed and about thirty wounded.

After Marmaduke withdrew from the river, the Confederate command left operations there pretty much up to irregulars. The Mississippi Marine Brigade's adjutant would evaluate these irregulars, or partisans, as largely local in origin. He described a typical episode which took place during July and which illustrates that contention. A large patrol of the Brigade's cavalry was searching the Big Black River country to the south of Vicksburg when shortly after dawn, the patrol's forward scouts were charged by a company of uniformed cavalry. The charge was broken by the first volley, and the attackers retreated with only minor losses. It had been noticed during the action that the Confederates had not been carrying haversacks, nor did anyone recall seeing saddle bags. This gave rise to the suspicion that they had to be based in the immediate area. Later that day a house in the neighborhood was searched. Uniforms and other military equipage was discovered. A stakeout of the house was immediately set up. That evening three Confederate horsemen, all of which turned out to be sons of the house's owner, returned for the night and were captured. Interrogations of the local Negroes brought forth confirmation that most if not all of the enemy's presence remaining in the area consisted of persons native to the immediate region.

Joining with the Mississippi Marine Brigade in the type of search missions which preoccupied much of its activity throughout the remainder of that summer of 1864 were troops of the 1st Mississippi Cavalry (Colored) as well as units from various Negro infantry regiments. The Brigade's enlisted men seemed to have engendered a spirit of comradeship with these outfits, perhaps because of the Brigade's long association with contraband laborers who had been employed by the Ellets since the inception of the Ram Fleet. Comradeship with the Negro soldiers was displayed in a number of ways. At the end of one patrol action, "many a horse 'carried double' -- a Brigade trooper before, and a black infantryman behind." [53] To members of the Brigade it was evident that the Negro troops were ready to give as well as receive. On one operation, a unit of the Brigade had with it a regiment of Negro infantry which made, in Crandall's words, a most "gallant charge" crying out, "Fort Pillow -- No quarter! No quarter!" [54] Although at first the atrocities committed against the Negro troops at Fort Pillow may have triggered fear, that fear shortly turned to anger. Fort Pillow had become their rallying cry for revenge.

In July, Ellet lost the use of the Brigade's transports on two separate occasions when they were taken over by local quartermasters for troop lifts. During the intervals when it was without its vessels, the Brigade's mounted infantry elements operated as land-based troops, making rather long marches away from the river, an activity which was something quite alien to the men. Crandall's history is replete with accounts of the hardships encountered on these marches: Waking up "wet with dew." Bivouacs "without shade....It was noon before the men had their breakfast," etc. Such hardships would not have been noteworthy in the life of most Union soldiers to which that sort of hardship was commonplace. However, for the officers and men of the Brigade, the usual stringency of army life in the field had not been their experience, and it was not something they looked forward to repeating on a regular basis.

The Mississippi Marine Brigade is Disbanded

On August 4, 1864, the Mississippi Marine Brigade was in camp at a location a few miles to the south of Vicksburg when word was passed to company commanders to prepare for an inspection by Major General N. J. T. Dana, the commander of the Vicksburg District. This was one of the few times when the Brigade was subjected to an inspection carried out by an officer of such a high rank, and there was considerable speculation as to what had brought it on. During Dana's inspection, he said nothing to the Brigade's officers to indicate anything unusual. A day or so later, the Brigade's transports were returned from Quartermaster employment, and things again appeared to be perfectly normal. But this sense of the status quo evaporated the following week when company commanders were ordered to prepare up-to-date rosters of their men. On August 10, word went out that the Mississippi Marine Brigade was to be disbanded. Those enlisted men who still had to serve relatively lengthy terms of enlistment were to be sent back to the regiments from which they had originated while those with only short terms remaining were to be assigned temporary duty with the garrison at Vicksburg until they were due for discharge. All of the Brigade's officers would be mustered out of the service.[55]

Obviously, the decision to disband the Brigade had not taken into consideration the peculiar conditions under which the men had been enlisted, especially as it regarded those who had been signed up while convalescents in Army hospitals at Saint Louis and at Memphis. The last group constituted the majority. At the time of their enrollment, they were discharged from their old regiments before being reenlisted into the Mississippi Marine Brigade. Once this set of circumstances was explained to the Adjutant General's office in Washington, the previous instructions were canceled, and a successor organization was created into which the manpower of the infantry regiment of the Brigade, both officers and men, was transferred. As the remaining senior officer under Alfred W. Ellet, Lieutenant Colonel John A. Ellet was given the command.

Headquarters, Mississippi Marine Brigade

Special Orders No. 60

In compliance with orders received from Major General Dana commanding the District of Vicksburg, directing the disorganization of the Mississippi Marine Brigade, the First Infantry Regiment of the Mississippi Marine Brigade ceases to exist at this date. The following disposition will be made of the officers and enlisted men. The present organization of companies will continue subject to assignment of officers and men to complete them, when they will enter a new regimental organization, and each company will receive designation according to the rank of its commanding officer. The field and staff officers of the First Infantry Regiment, Mississippi Marine Brigade, are assigned to the new regimental organization. The officers of the Consolidated Marine Regiment, Lieutenant Colonel John A. Ellet commanding, will immediately enter upon the discharge of their several duties.

By command of Brigadier General A. W. Ellet

W. D. Crandall, Captain and Assistant Adjutant General[56]

According to Crandall's account of how the reorganization was received, the enlisted men, "were righteously indignant, and greatly excited when the orders were promulgated." The result was "a refusal of some of the men to leave the boats and go ashore." Finally, under the bayonets of provost troops called to the scene by Major General Dana, they were ordered off the boats. The men became less vocal upon seeing forty-eight of their fellows (the apparent ring leaders) marched off to military prison. After a short interval on a diet of bread and water and certain other refinements which accompanied prison life at Vicksburg, the forty-eight pledged their good behavior and were released to duty. Thus ended the second mutiny in the slightly less than 2-year life of the Mississippi Marine Brigade. (As the reader will recall, the first mutiny took place during early 1863 while the Brigade was en route to its first duty station at Young's Point from Saint Louis.)

Official Records...Armies as well as information on the reorganization within Record Group 92 and within Crandall's history are all silent regarding the disposition of the original cavalry squadron. The Mississippi Marine Brigade's vessels, including the supporting tugs, were transferred to the Quartermaster Department for regular transport service. The civilian crews were to remain aboard until the completion of their individual 6-month employment contracts.

During November, in response to an inquiry from the office of the Secretary of War, the locations of the Brigade's vessels were listed by a senior quartermaster.

Steamer *DIANA*, Morganza; steamer *BALTIC*, Morganza; steamer *AUTOCRAT*, Memphis; steamer *RAINE*,[1] Memphis; steamer *ADAMS*,[2] Vicksburg; steamer *FAIRCHILD*,[3] Vicksburg; ram *MONARCH*, New Orleans; ram *SWITZERLAND*, New Orleans; towboat *LIONESS*, New Orleans; towboat *HORNER*,[4] New Orleans; towboat *FULTON*,[5] Natchez; tug *BELLE DARLINGTON*, Vicksburg; tug *CLEVELAND*, New Orleans; tug *ALF CUTTING*, Morganza. These boats were nearly all in bad condition when received from Marine Brigade. Several of them are now at Saint Louis being overhauled and repaired. They are all required for reserve transportation and post service at different points on the river in this military division. It is thought that they can be taken care of and run by the Quartermaster's Department. They are and will be necessarily so much scattered that any person appointed to the general charge of them would hardly be able to manage them as well as the different quartermasters now in charge of and responsible for them.

C. G. Sawtelle[57]

[1] *JOHN RAINE* [2] *BEN J. ADAMS* [3] *E. H. FAIRCHILD* [4] *T. D. HORNER* [5] *DICK FULTON*

A month following the dissolution of the Mississippi Marine Brigade, Brigadier General Alfred W. Ellet resigned his commission and returned to civilian life.

~

The Consolidated Marine Regiment contained close to a thousand men as of its first muster.[58] Because Major General Dana distrusted the ability of the new command to perform well, the regiment was destined to remain inactive at Vicksburg, to not again take to the field during its remainder existence. The regiment's morale was at a low ebb from the very beginning. It remained that way with the enlisted men harboring their complaint that once the Mississippi Marine Brigade was dissolved, its members should have been made eligible for discharge. Practically all of the men considered the new organization to be nothing but a legal sham. Discontentment over the state of affairs was exhibited in a number of ways. First, there was a matter of morning reports upon which the company first sergeants, embellished the words, "Under protest!" Lieutenant Colonel John A. Ellet ordered a stop to this and all other visible signs of ill-discipline. This was generally complied with, and outwardly, the regiment settled into the normal routine of garrison duty, but the men's acceptance of their lot was but a thin veneer. They had quietly hired a Vicksburg attorney to represent them in a class action laid before the Administration in Washington. The attorney they hired was James H. Purdy with law offices in Vicksburg. Purdy had given his opinion that only a Presidential ruling could overcome the Army's reluctance to return the men to civilian life.[59] Purdy left for Washington, and after a wait of some weeks, he finally got in to see Lincoln. He laid out before the president a prepared rationale on behalf of his clients. Purdy based his argument on the promises made to the men by Alfred W. Ellet at the time of their enlistment either at Saint Louis or at Memphis. Essentially, that promise was that the service to be undertaken was to be performed aboard boats rather than under the land-based circumstances where the men now found themselves. After first requesting the advice of the War Department, Lincoln ruled that the men's present situation was not morally justified and instructed that they be discharged. This resulted in the following War Department order:

Washington, December 5, 1864

Special Order No. 431

The enlisted men of the organization formerly known as the Mississippi Marine Brigade, who enlisted for and were mustered into that organization, will upon receipt of this order, be mustered out of the service of the United States, and those detached from regiments in the field (without reenlisting) will be returned to their respective regiment to serve out their term of enlistment.

The Commanding Officer of the Military Division of the West Mississippi is charged with the execution of this order.

By order of the Secretary of War

E. D. Townsend, Assistant Adjutant General[60]

In early January of 1865, the men of the Consolidated Marine Regiment were lined up before pay tables to be mustered out of the Union Army. Lawyer Purdy was also there. Reportedly, Purdy received from each man the share of the legal fee he was owed; it was generally handed over with a smile.

A novel experiment in amphibious warfare had come to its end.

~

During its existence, the Mississippi Marine Brigade lost by deaths in combat two officers and twenty-six enlisted men. Two officers and 199 enlisted men died of disease.[61] Prior to the formation of the Brigade, the Ram Fleet had one death through combat, that being its founder Charles Ellet, Jr. There is no record as to deaths by disease within the original Ram Fleet. Neither is there a record of the numbers of persons taken prisoner of war from the Mississippi Marine Brigade although it is known that a number of men and at least one officer were captured in connection with the loss of the *QUEEN OF THE WEST* on the Red River during 1863, an event which occurred after the Brigade's establishment.

THE BROWNSVILLE CAMPAIGN
(October-December 1863)

Adjustments in Strategic Planning

The successes in taking Vicksburg and Port Hudson, together with the positive results of the Meridian Expedition, set the stage for yet another offensive, namely, an attempt to be made against Mobile, Alabama.

Once Mobile was taken, Major General Ulysses S. Grant's overall plan was to move against the South's underbelly using Mobile as his base. Once such a movement began, then those Confederate forces operating out of Alabama and which had threatened the Union presence in Tennessee would be caught between a great pincer, the upper jaw of that pincer moving down from the north, the lower jaw coming up from the south. With the enemy rendered impotent as a viable force in Alabama, all apprehension would be removed over invading Georgia. As the opening play for this strategy, everything hinged upon the taking of Mobile. But then a complication arose which would put the whole thing on hold.

In the early fall (1863), French troops had occupied central Mexico and were thought to be pushing in the direction of the Texas border. The occupation of any western hemisphere nation by a European power was a rank violation of the Monroe Doctrine and as such would normally have been contested by the United States through force of arms. But, the situation was now quite different from normal times; the United States could not fight both the Confederacy and the French. Solving the problem of ridding Mexico from a French occupation would have to wait. A point of immediate concern and one which called for immediate response, was the intelligence (considered reliable) that the Confederate governor of Texas had been approached by the French with a proposal that Texas secede from the Confederacy and reestablish itself as an independent republic, presumably allied to France. The specter of a foreign power holding influence, if not an actual presence in Texas, called for preemptive measures. Lincoln's reaction was to order a postponement of the attack on Mobile. He would now instruct that an expeditionary force be sent from New Orleans to occupy southwestern Texas in order to provide a barrier against French ambitions north of the Rio Grande River.

Departure for Texas

On October 26, 1863, a convoy of fourteen Army transports left the South West Pass of the Mississippi, outbound for Brazos Santiago in Texas. Under the overall command of Major General Nathaniel P. Banks, the transports carried the Second Division of the XIII Corps which was composed of Illinois and Iowa troops headed by Major General N. J. T. Dana. Also aboard, but organizationally separate from Dana's division, were two regiments of newly freed slaves (with a sprinkling of Negro freemen) who had been recruited at New Orleans. At the last moment prior to sailing, the expedition was reinforced by the addition of the 1st Texas Cavalry (Union).[62]

The fourteen transports which carried the Banks expedition from the Mississippi to Brazos Santiago were:

CLINTON	*NASSAU*
CONTINENTAL	*POCAHONTAS*
CORINTHIAN	*SAINT MARY'S*
CRESCENT	*THOMAS A. SCOTT*
EMPIRE CITY	*WARRIOR*
GENERAL BANKS	*WILLIAM BAGLEY*
MCCLELLAN	*ZEPHYR*

Naval escort to the transports was provided by *USS MONONGAHELA*, *USS OTSEGO*, and *USS VIRGINIA*. The Navy vessels were to provide fire support should the landings at Brazos Santiago be opposed. Accompanying the naval ships were a tug and two supply schooners, the schooners to serve as replenishment colliers for the naval ships once Texas was reached. The Army transports had not been provided with support colliers, a planning oversight to be later regretted. En route to Brazos Santiago, the convoy was subjected to wind and sea conditions which were serious enough to cause the loss of one of the Navy's colliers and the support tug.

When the expedition arrived off Brazos Santiago, a heavy surf was breaking the entire way across the entrance bar. It was inside that bar and within the protected waters of Laguna Madre that the troops were to be offloaded. The first attempt to get over the bar was made by the transport *NASSAU* which broached on her beam ends coming down hard on the bar. She stranded to become a total loss; fortunately, only five men drowned. Two or three of the smaller transports, drawing much less water, were able to get into the lagoon; however, after the experience of *NASSAU*, the masters of the larger transports prudently decided to lie off and await better weather conditions. Their troop passengers were then ferried through the surf to Brazos Island where they discovered that a small Confederate cavalry force had recently been encamped. Rather than face disproportionate odds, the enemy cavalry had fled over to the mainland well before the Union troops were landed. When later reporting on the lack of enemy resistance he had encountered at Brazos Santiago, Nathaniel Banks speculated that some Union incursions which at the time were penetrating into the bayou country of south central Louisiana, together with an earlier Union attempt to take Sabine Pass, Texas, had drawn most of the Confederate forces to the east.[63]

On November 3, following the successful landing of his expedition, Banks sent a victory dispatch off by fast courier vessel.

> The flag of the Union floated over Texas today at meridian precisely. Our enterprise has been a complete success. Making preparations for movements as directed. Details tomorrow.
>
> N. P. Banks, Major General, Commanding[64]

On November 6, Banks moved the entirety of his command from Brazos Island over the Laguna Madre to the mainland. Brownsville was shortly occupied with only a token resistance. Prior to that town's evacuation by its Confederate garrison, and in anticipation of losing their liquid refreshment to the approaching Federals, the Confederates had gone on a drunken spree which resulted in much looting and general destruction. The town's residents finally put a stop to it by armed interference. While putting together an organization aimed at stopping the looters, the town fathers accepted the leadership of a political refugee from Mexico by the name of Jose Maria Cobos. After the Confederates had gone from Brownsville, but before the Federal troops showed up, Cobos talked some of the armed citizens into crossing the Rio Grande into Mexican territory to occupy Matamoras. The French, although expected at any moment in Matamoras, had not yet appeared. The place was still in Mexican hands, and Don Manuel Ruiz, the governor of the providence, was still in residence there. Cobos would order the arrest of Ruiz.

Having been made aware of what had transpired at Matamoras, Banks found himself in a quandary as to how he would deal with the situation. He started out by making inquiries concerning Cobos. Who was the man? What were his ambitions? This brought forth a wide variety of opinions. One local school of thought had it that Cobos was anti-French, but another suggested that he was sympathetic to French interests and that he had taken over Matamoras with the idea of holding it, awaiting the arrival of French troops. Yet another appraisal suggested that he was merely an opportunist and that, as Banks himself would later opine, Cobos "was putting himself and friends in possession of power or property to treat with any party that can best subserve his and their interests." As it was with most facets of Mexican politics during that era, a variety of political factors was usually involved. Alliances have always been complex in Mexican society and often are vague in their structure. As it would develop in this case, there was Cobos's close relationship with a "General Cortina" then operating as a guerrilla leader in the surrounding countryside against what up to that time had been the established Mexican authority. Juan N. Cortina was recognized as having a long standing prejudice against the Anglo occupation of southwestern Texas. It was of special interest to Banks that Ruiz, the Mexican governor who Cobos had now imprisoned, was known to be an anti-Confederate and that he was thought to favor a border stability which only a Union occupation of the countryside lying north of the Rio Grande could give, both north and south of the river.[65] Although appreciating that Ruiz was the best man from the viewpoint of United States interests, Banks thought it wise to leave Mexican politics to the Mexicans and decided to let those at Matamoras settle their own messy affairs.

Banks's staff made preparations to move troops up the Rio Grande River as far as its navigational limit. At the same time, Banks issued orders to secure as much of the Texas coast as the size of his force would allow.

At Matamoras, the political scene kept realigning itself. Cortina now claimed to have evidence that Cobos was planning to turn Matamoras over to the French, and he ordered Cobos arrested. A trial followed which lasted all of a few minutes. The accused was sentenced to be shot, an act accomplished by a platoon of riflemen in full view of the town's population. To add a bit to this spectator sport, Cortina next ordered that one of Cobos's chief lieutenants run a gauntlet after which the bloodied victim in full flight was shot. Cortina then released Governor Ruiz, offering him the protection of a guard of Cortina's gunmen. Ruiz, not trusting Cortina's helpful nature, and sensing that the body guards could just as easily become his executioners, declined the offer and fled across the Rio Grande to sanctuary at Brownsville. With things getting beyond the point of any reasonable interpretation as to what might happen next, the American consul at Matamoras called on Banks for protection. Banks agreed to provide it, but only if the American Consulate actually came under attack. Fortunately for Banks's peace of mind, the Consulate remained sacrosanct, and a need for American troops to cross over into Mexican territory did not develop.

As an indication of his good will, Cortina put three shallow draft steamers at Banks's disposal for use on the Rio Grande. One of the steamers, the *MUSTANG*, was employed to carry seven companies of infantry up the river while three other companies marched parallel to the river. This upriver movement was three-fold in its purpose: First, to determine whether the Rio Grande could be utilized toward maintaining physical contact with Union forces then operating in New Mexico; second, and a more immediate requirement, to take possession of a steamer load of cotton reported as being stored at Rio Grande City; and third, to establish a garrison there. The Rio Grande proved barely passable, the poor navigating conditions being a result of the long dry summer just passed. Despite the fact that she carried an experienced pilot, the *MUSTANG*, ran aground continuously.; but she finally made it up to Rio Grande City where the cotton -- eighty-two bales of it -- was loaded on deck for the first stage of a journey to the mills of New England.

Toward the task of establishing a firm presence in southwestern Texas, Banks instructed Dana to move the brigade of Brigadier General Thomas E. Ransom up the inside passage of the Laguna Madre by shallow draft steamers and occupy Aransas Pass. Farther to the east, Matagorda Island (Fort Esperanza), was to be occupied by another brigade under Major General Washburn. The Washburn force was sent by way of the open Gulf aboard deeper draft transports. After he had secured Matagorda Island, Washburn was to follow up by occupying Corpus Christi. Meanwhile, Banks would lead a march inland from Brazos Santiago, roughly following the path of the Neuces River to San Patricio where, according to reports, a large Confederate column was being made up for duty in western Louisiana.

As the three separate operations were about to get underway, supply shortages began to surface which would plague the Banks expedition throughout its existence. From a supply standpoint, the Texas venture had been poorly planned, and it was now being poorly executed as well. Most of the steamers which had brought the expedition from New Orleans were stalled in place, unable to return to New Orleans, their coal bunkers having been almost depleted in the storm-hampered passage out. The expedition's resupply depended totally on those same steamers returning to New Orleans to reload for a return to Texas. Instead, they now lay idle awaiting coal before they could go anywhere. To add insult to injury, one of the few steamers able to make the return trip to New Orleans had left Texas before it had been completely offloaded. The expedition's entire reserve supply of small arms ammunition, a total of 180,000 rounds, was still aboard her when she left, having been stowed at the bottom of the ship's lower hold where it had been overlooked. It seemed that neither Banks's quartermasters or the ship's officers had taken the responsibility to check and see if the entire cargo had gone ashore. It was indeed fortunate that enemy opposition was as light as it had been.

To be sure, the weather had not been kind to Banks's shipping; but the weather's effects were being further magnified by acts of sheer incompetence. No one had thought to sound and buoy the Brazos Santiago bar after the landings. This had resulted in the loss of two more vessels, the supply schooners *A. H. PARTRIDGE* and *KATE*, both of which grounded on the bar and broke up. The steamer *WILLIAM BAGLEY* was lost at Aransas Pass for the same reason.

Thanks to the near total absence of Confederate resistance, all of Banks's military goals had been achieved by the second week in December -- this despite the lack of thought given to the supply end of things.

~

Unrelated to the Banks expedition, a combined assault force had been put together in September to occupy Sabine Pass, Texas. (Sabine Pass was a small coastal town located near the Texas-Louisiana border.) That attack was carried out by a force of naval vessels combined with a contingent of Army troops following on transports. The advance prognosis had been for an easy victory on the part of the attackers since Sabine Pass was known to be garrisoned by only a lone company of regular troops in command of a lieutenant, reinforced by a small force of local militia. Together, they put up such a spirited defense that the attack failed. Jefferson Davis would later call Sabine Pass the "Thermopylae of the Civil War."

~

On Christmas Day, 1863, Banks gave Major General F. J. Herron responsibility for holding that part of the Texas coast from Quintana to Brownsville. In passing command, Banks stipulated that the Union's intentions in Texas entailed seven objectives:

1. To defend the present holdings.
2. To maintain cordial relationships with those in power at Matamoras.
3. To recruit local citizens for service in the Union Army.
4. To maintain contact with the garrison that Banks had positioned at Rio Grande City. (The Rio Grande City garrison in turn was to establish regular patrol contact with Brigadier General James H. Carleton, the federal military governor of New Mexico.
5. To regularly employ scouts (or agents) in order to keep tabs on any and all foreign military forces which might be operating to the south in Mexico; and to determine the identity of suspected Confederate forces operating within the interior of Texas.
6. To link up with Union operations which might be later aimed at the capture of Galveston.
7. To prevent the eastward movement of Confederate supplies along the inland waterway of the Laguna Madre.[66]

Succeeding Operations in Southwestern Texas

In the summer of 1864, the French occupied the small settlement of Bagdad, a town which was located on the south side of the Rio Grande, downstream from Matamoras. In order to avoid confrontation with the French, the Union garrison evacuated Brownsville and moved to Brazos Santiago and Matagorda Island. No sooner had the Brownsville garrison pulled out than the place was reoccupied by Confederate troops.

~

Following the Confederate surrenders in Virginia and North Carolina during the spring of 1865, Texas would again become a focal point of attention requiring a strong Union military presence. An accounting of those 1865 events will be related later in this volume.

THE RED RIVER CAMPAIGN
(March-May 1864)

The Strategic Rationale

In a communication sent to Major General Henry W. Halleck, Major General Ulysses S. Grant wrote his analysis of the military situation for the western theater as it applied to the interrelationship of that theater with the war as a whole as he viewed it early in the winter of 1863-1864.

> From an early period in the rebellion, I had been impressed with the idea that active and continuous operations of all the troops that could be brought into the field, regardless of season and weather, were necessary to a speedy termination of the war. The resources of the enemy and his numerical strength were far inferior to ours; but as an offset to this, we had a vast territory with a population hostile to the Government to garrison, and long lines of river and railroad communications to protect, to enable us to supply the operating armies.
>
> The armies in the East and West acted independently and without concert like a balky team, no two ever pulling together, enabling the enemy to use to great advantage his interior lines of communication for transporting troops from east to west, reinforcing the army most vigorously pressed, and to furlough large numbers during seasons of inactivity on our part, to go to their homes and do the work of producing for the support of the armies.
>
> ...I therefore determined, first, to use the greatest number of troops practicable against the armed forces of the enemy, preventing him from using the same force at different seasons against first one and then another of our armies, and the possibility of repose for refitting and producing necessary supplies for carrying on resistance; second, to hammer continuously against the armed forces of the enemy and his resources, until by mere attrition, if in no other way, there should be nothing left to him but an equal submission with the loyal section of our common country to the constitution and laws of the land.[67]

What had been of top priority with Grant was the seizure of Mobile, Alabama. A distraction toward accomplishing that goal had been the recent French threat which had resulted in the Banks expedition to Texas. No sooner had Banks returned from Texas than a second delay came along. For some time, Lincoln had been receiving the counsel of those -- both political and military -- who advocated the conquest of western Louisiana as being essential to the conduct of the war. The political pressures the President was receiving came largely from the New England manufacturing states whose governors were alarmed over the shortage of cotton, a commodity needed to keep their textile mills operating. These economic factors were reinforced and abetted by the military's need for cloth and canvas goods with which to clothe and equip the troops. Salmon P. Chase, Lincoln's Secretary of the Treasury, but who was also a potential rival of Lincoln, was not above using his cabinet office to curry favor from the cotton manufacturers of New England and New York. Chase's idea for the resolution of the cotton shortage was a military occupation of eastern Texas in order to allow development of that area for cotton production. A military invasion deep into Louisiana, utilizing the Red River, seemed the best way to open Texas to Union occupation. Additionally, since the Red River country was itself a producer of cotton, the opportunity for capturing large amounts of that commodity could be an extra bonus to any invasion. The influence Chase had over the decision to undertake an expedition into the Red River country is somewhat problematic, but he most certainly was one of the most important factors in bringing Lincoln around toward making a favorable decision on the matter.

Over the years, certain historians have taken the position that the original military promoter for the Red River campaign was Nathaniel P. Banks. Perhaps Banks played a part, but any early-on enthusiasm for the idea was certainly not his alone.[68] A communication from Halleck sent to Banks on January 11, 1864, makes it fairly certain that at that early juncture, there was within the Army as a whole a considerable optimism for the idea, an optimism which apparently came from more than one general officer in the western theater.

> ...The best military opinions of the generals in the west seem to favor operations on the Red River, provided the stage of water will enable the gunboats to cooperate. I presume General Sherman will communicate with you on the subject. If the rebels could be driven south of that river, it would serve as a shorter and better line of defense for Arkansas and Missouri now occupied by General Steele; moreover, it would open to us the cotton and stores in northeastern Louisiana and southern Arkansas.
>
> I am inclined to think that this opens a better field of operations than any other for such troops as General Grant can spare during the winter. I have written to him and also to General Steele, on this subject..."[69]

Grant seemed to agree in principle that an expedition into western Louisiana via the Red River was militarily feasible. The reluctance he held concerning the concept was based along the lines of the relatively low priority it held in the overall military scheme of things and the fear that it could delay the progress of the war east of the Mississippi. His personal belief was that the western side of the Mississippi could be taken out of the war merely by maintaining static defensive forces along the Mississippi.

Having been pushed into agreement on a penetration of the Red River up to Shreveport, Louisiana, Grant set a time limit making it clear to those generals involved that beginning in early April, all military operations west of the Mississippi

River were to convert to defensive operations only. Mobile was not going to be allowed to go to the back burner. On March 31, 1864, Grant wrote Banks.

> Major General N. P. Banks:
>   First. If successful in your expedition against Shreveport, that you turn over the defense of the Red River to General Steele and the Navy.
>   Second. That you abandon Texas entirely, with the exception of your hold upon the Rio Grande. This can be held with four thousand men, if they will turn their attention immediately to fortifying their positions. At least one-half of the force required for this service might be taken from the colored troops.
>   Third. By properly fortifying on the Mississippi River, the force to guard it from Port Hudson to New Orleans can be reduced to ten thousand men, if not to a less number. Six thousand more would then hold all the rest of the territory necessary to hold until active operations can again be resumed west of the river. According to your last returns, this would give you a force of over thirty thousand effective men with which to move against Mobile. To this I expect to add five thousand men from Missouri. If, however, you think the force here stated too small to hold the territory regarded as necessary to hold possession of, I would say concentrate at least twenty-five thousand men of your present command for operations against Mobile. With these, and such additions as I can give you from elsewhere, lose no time in making a demonstration, to be followed by an attack upon Mobile. Two or more ironclads will be ordered to report to Admiral Farragut. This gives him a strong naval fleet with which to cooperate. You can make your own arrangements with the admiral for his cooperation, and select your own line of approach. My own idea of the matter is that Pascagoula should be your base; but, from your long service in the Gulf Department, you will know best about the matter. It is intended that your movements shall be cooperative with movements elsewhere, and you cannot now start too soon. All I would now add is that you commence the concentration of your forces at once. Preserve a profound secrecy of what you intend doing, and start at the earliest possible moment.
>   U. S. Grant, Lieutenant General[70]

Major General William T. Sherman, who was at the time Grant's immediate subordinate in the western theaters, and who as such was Banks's direct superior, had already written Banks that he was to assemble the twenty-five thousand men stipulated by Grant for the move on Mobile no later than April 15. If the Louisiana Expedition was to succeed, it would have to do so well before that close-off date.[71]

The Original Plan
          The penetration of the Red River to Shreveport via Alexandria, Louisiana, was to be based upon the thrust of three columns. The first column under Major General W. B. Franklin was to approach overland from Grand Lake to Alexandria. The second column under Brigadier General A. J. Smith was to proceed by way of steamers on the Red River. These two movements were to be reinforced by a third force consisting of a number of brigaded regiments moving by steamers from Atchafalaya Bay to the navigational limits of Bayou Teche at which point they were to march overland directly to Alexandria. There was to be a diversionary movement coming down from the north from Arkansas which was to consist of the VII Corps led by Major General Frederick Steele. Steele was to start from Little Rock aiming for

Shreveport. His objective was to divert any counter moves by Confederate forces coming out of Arkansas which might be initiated against the main Federal thrusts coming at Shreveport from the south and the east. When Franklin and A. J. Smith arrived at Alexandria, they were to report to Banks who would assume the overall command.

Alexandria was an intermediate port on the Red River, located about one-third of the way upriver between the river's juncture with the Mississippi and Shreveport. The supply for the combined armies would depend on the transports which would carry A. J. Smith's corps to Alexandria. From Alexandria, the transports would continue up the Red River under the guard of Rear Admiral David D. Porter's gunboats. The ability of the transports to navigate the Red River all the way to Shreveport would be a key element toward the expedition's success. Those familiar with the Red River knew that steamboat navigation could be carried up to Shreveport during the normal water levels of winter and spring; but in 1864, rainfall on the watershed which served the river was already far below what would normally have been expected for that time of year.

The Expedition Starts Out

Either as the result of blind optimism, or, as he would later claim, knowledge obtained from a "reliable expert of the river," Banks wired Halleck that the Red River customarily rose during the latter part of March.[72] On Banks's prognosis concerning the river level to be expected, a reinforced division under A. J. Smith assigned to thirty-four transports was making ready to leave Vicksburg, its line of advance and any subsequent withdrawal to be wholly dependent on a river which was getting shallower with every passing day. A substantial part of Ellet's Mississippi Marine Brigade would, with its vessels, accompany A. J. Smith. Rear Admiral David D. Porter would escort the transports with twenty of his Mississippi Squadron gunboats.[73]

The amphibious movement of the brigaded regiments which originated at Atchafalaya Bay would grind to a halt almost before it began when it was discovered that the waterway route via Bayou Teche could not handle the drafts of the transports.

Between early March of 1864 and the end of the Red River Expedition which came two months later, fifty-one steamers (not including the vessels of Ellet's Mississippi Marine Brigade) were to be employed as transports either to carry troops or cargo on the Red River. Besides the fifty-one, other transports were used for indirect support such as shuttling supplies to the mouth of the Red River for transshipment up the river. Of the fifty-one transports which were utilized in direct support on the Red River, twenty-four of them were assigned for the exclusive use of A. J. Smith's command. Those steamers assigned to the Red River Expedition had been selected because their light drafts and limited lengths and were thought to be particularly well suited for the conditions expected to be present on the river's shallow and narrow upper reaches. The biggest drawback for the quartermasters who were responsible for assembling these steamers was that similar light draft and restricted length vessels were also needed for operations elsewhere. The circumstance under which the Army quartermasters seemed to labor whenever dealing with vessel procurement on the western rivers was that there always seemed to be at least one or more major operations going on at any one time. March through May of 1864 would be no exception to that maxim. During that spring, the Cumberland River in Tennessee was the scene of much supply activity. Since the Cumberland was also shallow, the need there for light drafts was also on a priority call. Quartermaster Lewis B. Parsons, who had the overall authority to allocate shipping on the western rivers, rose to the challenge but not before voicing suspicions that the Red River Expedition's projected requirements seemed to exceed its actual needs. On February 17, Parsons wired directly to Banks: "...There must be some great error and many more boats taken than you expect to require." Parsons was perhaps under the impression that only A. J. Smith's corps would be involved when in reality the entirety of Banks's logistics would depend on the vessels being asked for once the point of troop rendezvous at Alexandria had been reached.

On March 10, the transports carrying A. J. Smith's troops moved away from the docks of Vicksburg. The following day, they arrived at the mouth of the Red River. (At this juncture of the expedition's deployment, Banks was himself still at New Orleans.) Before proceeding up the Red River, A. J. Smith met with Rear Admiral Porter to receive the first installment of what would become a long series of discouraging reports. He was told by Porter that Fort DeRussy-- which was at about the halfway point en route to Alexandria-- was garrisoned by the enemy. The fort's guns blocked the river, and they would have to be taken out before further progress could be made. Porter reported that the location of the enemy's guns in its relationship to the lay of the river was such that the gunboats would have great difficulty in directing an effective counter-fire. (That same advantage to the enemy had been discovered the year before by the unfortunate Charles Rivers Ellet and his *QUEEN OF THE WEST.*) It seemed obvious to A. J. Smith that the enemy emplacements would have to be approached from the land side and taken by infantry assault. A second piece of bad news came in to A. J. Smith via a courier dispatched to him from Franklin. The courier brought word that heavy rains had so delayed Franklin on his march up from Grand Lake that he did not expect to be able to rendezvous at Alexandria much before March 21. That would give the expedition only three weeks in which to finish its business and be back on the Mississippi in time for the move against Mobile. (Sherman, it will be remembered, had established April 15 as the deadline for the assemblage of troops for the movement against Mobile.)

A. J. Smith's transports and Porter's gunboats proceeded into the Red River for a seven mile distance at which point that river met the Atchafalaya. Turning into the Atchafalaya, the transports continued on to Simsport. At Simsport, A. J. Smith sent two of his regiments ashore to march overland along the road leading toward Fort DeRussy while he waited with the rest of his command in order to protect the transports until he could be sure that the country was free of any strong enemy force. When word came back that only light enemy resistance had been encountered,

Smith debarked his remaining troops to bring up the rear of the point regiments. The empty transports were then returned to the Red River with orders to follow upstream after the gunboats.

The area through which A. J. Smith and his men now traveled had not before felt a soldier's boot. Brigadier General T. Kilby Smith, one of A. J. Smith's brigade commanders, in describing the third day of that march, has left us a verbal picture of a countryside which must have been a tonic to men who had until recently been witness to the ruins of Vicksburg and its swampy environs.

> ...Now crossing the bayou and penetrating a swamp for a few miles, we suddenly emerged in one of the most beautiful prairies imaginable, high table land, gently undulating, watered by little lakes, with occasional groves, the landscape dotted with tasteful houses, gardens, and shrubbery. This prairie, called Avoyelles, is settled exclusively by French emigrants, many of whom, as our army passed, sought shelter under the tricolor of France.[74]

Little in the way of enemy presence was to be seen. An occasional rifle round from a withdrawing enemy scout would whistle overhead, but that was only an inconsequential annoyance. At a small town called Marksville, located two miles short of Fort DeRussy, local farmers told T. Kilby Smith's patrols that only about three hundred and fifty Confederates were garrisoned at the fort. This proved to be true; but the low numbers did not lessen the stiff resistance met when the assault against the fort first started. Resistance lasted, though, less than an hour at which point the garrison surrendered.

During the three days which A. J. Smith's force had spent advancing overland, Porter's gunboat crews had been extremely busy. The river up to Fort DeRussy was clogged by great windrows of uprooted trees, put there by the late winter's floods and added to by whatever the Confederates were able to drag down from the banks and push into the channel. All of this debris had to be cut away before the larger gunboats could continue. Performing the clearing task had taken up the three days which A. J. Smith's men had spent marching.

A. J. Smith ordered that the fort be leveled. Knowing that he would have to return the way he had come, he had no intention of leaving behind anything which could be reoccupied by the enemy. That which could not be leveled by man and horse labor was flattened by explosives. At A. J. Smith's invitation, Porter took aboard his gunboats whatever cannon the enemy had not spiked. While these cannon were being loaded onto the gunboats, another of Smith's brigade commanders, Brigadier General Joseph A. Mower, continued with his command toward Alexandria, marching along the river's bank under the protection of some gunboats assigned to him by Porter. When Mower arrived at Alexandria, he found the town empty except for a few civilians. All enemy troops that had previously been there had fled, apparently (from what the civilians told him) in the direction of Shreveport.

On March 19, an advance cavalry detachment from Franklin's corps rode into Alexandria. It was followed closely by the forward elements of Franklin's main infantry column. When Banks finally arrived at Alexandria on March 26, he ordered Franklin's force, along with about half of A. J. Smith's, to start an overland march toward Shreveport. A. J. Smith would accompany the overland movement. The remainder of his command under the charge of T. Kilby Smith was to stay with the transports while they continued steaming up the Red River. The quantity of wagons which Banks had with him was inadequate for carrying what his army would require during the time it would take to march to Shreveport. Since the transports were to be Banks's lifeline for supply, close contact would have to be maintained with them during much of the march. The orders T. Kilby Smith received from A. J. Smith as to procedure were specific.

Headquarters Red River Expedition
On Steamer *CLARA BELL*

Brigadier General T. K. Smith, Commanding Division, XVII Army Corps:

General:

    You will take charge of the river transportation belonging to the XVI and XVII Army Corps, and will conduct it to the mouth of Loggy Bayou, opposite Springfield, at the foot of Lake Cannisnia, and will then, after a careful reconnaissance toward Springfield, disembark one regiment and push it forward to Bayou Pierre, and hold the bridge at that point. On arriving at Mansfield, I will endeavor to communicate with you at Springfield, and it may be, send for supplies. From Mansfield you will receive further orders in regard to your movement toward Shreveport.

    I am, general, very respectfully, your obedient servant,

A. J. Smith, Brigadier General, Commanding[75]

To be able to move upriver from Alexandria, the transport fleet, together with Porter's gunboats, had first to surmount three separate, steep gradients in the river which was now experiencing a low water stage. These gradients formed noticeable rapids -- one set a little below Alexandria; another opposite the town; and a third set some miles farther up the river at Grand Ecore. They appeared, though, to be still passable. However, because rocks were showing in some places, none of the pilots on either the gunboats or on the transports professed any real confidence in getting over them. In the interest of prudence, T. Kilby Smith decided to offload his guard troops and march them up the river's bank to a small hamlet called Cotile (about thirteen miles upstream from Alexandria and above the Grand Ecore rapid.) At Cotile, the troops could then reboard, provided, of course, that the transports could make it up that far.

    The campaign was now quite clearly falling behind its allotted time schedule. Most of the general officers (excepting Banks himself) were developing pessimistic attitudes over the expedition being able to accomplish its goals in time to be back on the Mississippi when required. Rear Admiral Porter was among those who thought it could not be done. The lighter draft gunboats and the majority of the Quartermaster transports did manage to get over the two rapids at Alexandria, but the heavy gunboats could not negotiate them on that first try. Without the company of the Navy's heavier gunboats, the real punch of the fleet's firepower would be missing. Then, on April 3, a turn of luck brought about by a heavy rain resolved the problem. The river rose, and the heavier gunboats surmounted without mishap both the upper and the lower rapids. The Mississippi Marine Brigade's heavily armored transports were another story. Without much exception, the Brigade's vessels had been selected from the larger types of Mississippi steamboats. Their normal displacement had then been added to, first by the weight of their conversion into rams and even more so later when they were provided with cannon. Consequently, they drew more water than even the heaviest of Porter's gunboats. The first of Ellet's vessels which tried entering the lower rapids dragged bottom before getting halfway up and had to turn back. The Brigade's hospital ship *WOODFORD*, drawing somewhat less, almost made it; but with only a few yards left to go, she ran hard up on the remnants of an old wreck and punctured her hull. She quickly settled to the bottom, wedged between two large boulders. It looked like *WOODFORD* was going to stay there forever.[76]

While Alfred W. Ellet was pondering over what to do about the *WOODFORD*, he received an urgent dispatch from Major General James P. McPherson, the commander of the Vicksburg District. This was the military jurisdiction to which the Mississippi Marine Brigade was normally assigned. As we earlier related, the Vicksburg District and in fact most of the central Mississippi River was being plagued by partisan activity that was threatening to get worse, the partisans having been emboldened by the absence of Federal troops along the river and by the departure of the bulk of Porter's Mississippi Squadron. A mobile amphibious force to react to this enemy scourge on the Mississippi was no longer available once the Mississippi Marine Brigade had ascended the Red River. Now, traffic on the Mississippi, including much of the supply effort on that river for the support of the Red River Expedition, was in danger of coming to a standstill. Acknowledging the need, Banks released Ellet to McPherson's command, and the Brigade started back to the Mississippi, minus the grounded *WOODFORD* which became a total loss. Alfred W. Ellet also left behind the *LIONESS*, presumably at the request of Banks's quartermaster.

Ellet's journey back down the Red River would become a cause for complaint within a communication sent on to McPherson at Vicksburg by Brigadier General Charles P. Stone who was the chief of staff for Banks.

March 29, 1864

General:
I consider it my duty to inform you that the Marine Brigade is reported to these headquarters to have stopped at every landing thus far on its way out of Red River, solely for the purpose of pillaging and the destruction of private property.
Very respectfully, general, I am your most obedient servant,
Charles P. Stone, Brigadier General and Chief of Staff[77]

Stone did not give the source of his allegations, and none of the records which we have searched disclose that any subsequent investigation was made over the matter. When writing some forty years later in the Brigade's unit history, Crandall, who was with Ellet on the Red River, had a recollection of the men possessing "a plentiful supply of molasses and raw sugar which they obtained while on the Red River," but he makes no mention of any complaints arising because of those circumstances. One is left with the thought that the castigation directed by Stone against the Mississippi Marine Brigade may have had its origins with the officers of Porter's gunboats who, at the time of Ellet's passage back to the Mississippi, were conducting patrols on the Red River below Alexandria. Exaggerated charges may have grown out of some minor thefts of molasses, or the reports made to Stone may have been for the devious purpose of smoke-screening deeds perpetrated by the gunboat crews themselves.

With Banks on the Overland March Toward Shreveport

When Banks's advanced units arrived at a small country crossroads named Henderson's Hill, they met the first of the enemy's resistance, a few pot shots from an outpost guard detail which then withdrew. A short distance beyond the point where this took place was the hamlet of Natchitoches. There, the road diverted away from the river to run more or less directly to Shreveport. The road Banks had selected for his advance was, in places, as much as twenty miles distant from the river. With Natchitoches behind him, Banks had geographically divorced himself from the support of Porter's gunboats and from the resupply of food and ammunition that only the transports could provide. The country beyond Natchitoches was of sandy soil, the surroundings nothing but pine barrens almost totally lacking of water. It appears that neither Banks or any of his generals had any advance comprehension of how inhospitable this route would turn out to be. The pressure of the timetable under which the expedition was operating might have been the reason why Banks had not sent patrols out to reconnoiter. However, such an excuse, although perhaps acceptable on Banks's part, was certainly not excusable in the case of Franklin when you consider that he had spent a full week in comparative idleness while he waited at Alexandria for Banks to arrive from New Orleans. He should have utilized that time to evaluate all approach routes to Shreveport by sending out cavalry patrols prior to Banks's arrival. Such patrol activity would have disclosed another road which also led from Natchitoches to Shreveport but which for much of its path closely followed the river. Somewhat longer than the route Banks would travel, this second route would almost certainly have been the better choice since it would have meant that the transports would be close at hand throughout, thus negating the need for a wagon train. Such a selection would also have given the transports and the gunboats a security which they would lack once Banks left Natchitoches.

Before Banks headed away from the river, he ordered that the gunboats and transports be moved up past Grand Ecore. When Porter inspected the Grand Ecore rapids, he decided that he was again going to have a problem with his heavier gunboats. This time, there were no heavy rains to help things along as had been the case at the Alexandria rapids. Porter now had no choice but to send the heavier gunboats back to Alexandria to wait there for his return while he continued upriver with eleven of his lighter draft gunboats. T. Kilby Smith had better luck with his transports. Fourteen of them made it over the Grand Ecore rapids without incident.

As the fourteen transports were prepared for further movement toward Loggy Bayou, T. Kilby Smith issued instructions establishing the column placement and security arrangements for each transport.

Headquarters Division, XVII Army Corps
Steamer *HASTINGS*, Grand Ecore, Louisiana: April 7, 1864

Special Orders No. 21
I. The fleet will be prepared to sail at 11 a.m. in the following order:

1	*HASTINGS*	8	*THOMAS E. TUTT*
2	*CLARA BELL*	9	SIOUX CITY
3	*EMERALD*	10	*MARS*
4	*W. L. EWING*	11	*DES MOINES*
5	*LIBERTY*	12	*ADRIATIC*
6	*HAMILTON*	13	*SOUTH WESTER*
7	*J. H. LACY*	14	*DIADEM*

The same orders and signals as heretofore will be enforced and strictly followed.

Colonel J. B. Moore, commanding First Brigade, will furnish a company, properly officered, to each of the following boats as a guard: *CLARA BELL, LIBERTY, HAMILTON*, and *J. H. LACY*. Colonel L. M. Ward, commanding Second Brigade, will furnish a like guard to the steamers *MARS, DES MOINES, ADRIATIC, SOUTH WESTER*, and *DIADEM*.

The officers in command of the guard will be held strictly accountable for the conduct of their men. The guard [is] to be divided into proper reliefs, and must not take off their accouterments while on guard. None of the transports will land or troops debark, except by order of the commanding general or brigade commanders.

T. Kilby Smith, Brigadier General Commanding[78]

Transports which had encountered some initial difficulties in coming up over the rapids joined the following morning, making twenty-one transports now above Grand Ecore. T. Kilby Smith had been informed that they were coming, and he was waiting for them a mile or so upstream at the hamlet of Campti. While he waited, he drafted an operational annex which stands as an excellent example of the great care he took toward the matter of security. And well he should have, since for all he and Porter knew, they might soon be hemmed in by an enemy force, the numbers and quality of which was not known.

Headquarters Division, XVII Army Corps
Campti, Louisiana, April 7, 1864

Special Orders No. 21 [Annex]
I. Whenever the fleet lands for the night, Colonel J. B. Moore, commanding First Brigade, will throw out a strong picket on the bank, covering the fleet from the steamer *HASTINGS* to the steamer *THOMAS E. TUTT*. Colonel L. M. Ward, commanding Second Brigade, will establish a like picket, covering all the fleet in rear of the steamer *THOMAS E. TUTT*, his line joining that of Colonel Moore. The pickets will be posted under the direction of the brigade officer of the day. The pickets will be instructed to come in at the signal for starting -- one long whistle.

II. The order of march is modified as follows: *CLARA BELL* will move in the extreme rear of the fleet, under convoy of the gunboat *CHILLICOTHE**, and will report to the commanding officer of the same for orders.

III. The following boats that have not reported for orders will sail immediately in rear of the fleet in the following order: 1, *ROB ROY*; 2, *IBERVILLE*; 3, *JOHN WARNER*; 4, *UNIVERSE*; 5, *COLONEL COWLES*; 6, *METEOR*.

IV.   The *BLACK HAWK*, General Banks's headquarters boat, will move immediately in rear of the steamer *HASTINGS* and as consort. [Banks was not aboard, he was with the armies of Franklin and A. J. Smith on the road to Shreveport.] Lieutenant A. J. Boyington, 95th Illinois Volunteers, will report with his company on board steamer *BLACK HAWK* as guard till further orders.

V. Colonel J. B. Moore, commanding First Brigade, will furnish each of the following boats with a guard of at least twenty-five men, under command of a commissioned officer: *ROB ROY, IBERVILLE, JOHN WARNER*, and *UNIVERSE*. Colonel L. M. Ward, commanding Second Brigade, will furnish each of the following boats with a like guard: *COLONEL COWLES, METEOR*, and *SHREVEPORT*.[79]

* *USS*, commissioned Union naval vessel.

As a matter of well developed practice on the western rivers, discipline over both military and civilian steamboat personnel was enforced by the senior military officer aboard each transport. While the Army's *General Order No. 276* of 1863 went a long way in providing guidance for officers who held such responsibility, those regulations did not clarify the fine line which of necessity existed between the senior Army officer and a ship's civilian master. (Appendix H reproduces *General Order No. 276* of August 1863 which pertains to the duties of senior officers traveling aboard transports.) T. Kilby Smith seems to have been appreciative of that deficiency and knew that it could get to be a problem if not handled diplomatically. Accordingly, he issued orders to affect a better understanding. He was also mindful in that order of the need for signaling coordination between the transports and the Navy's gunboats.

Headquarters Division, XVII Army Corps
Steamer *HASTINGS*, Campti, Louisiana

General Orders No. 7
April 7, 1864

Each transport of the fleet will be governed by the signals ordered by the rear admiral commanding Mississippi Squadron, a copy of which will be posted in the pilot house. They will keep their position indicated in the order of march. If accident occurs to any boat, the fleet will stop till the necessary repairs are made. No boat will land for fuel or any purpose save by order, and transports will frequently communicate their condition and requirements to the commanding general on the headquarters boat *HASTINGS*. The most rigid discipline will be enforced by military commanders, not only upon the soldiers who guard the boats, but the crews and servants of the same, being careful, however, to treat steamboat officers with courtesy, and avoiding improper interference with the navigation of the boats. Pillaging will not be countenanced, and officers will be held personally and strictly accountable for their commands.

Attention is directed to Special Orders, No. 21, prohibiting the landing of soldiers without orders, and the same order will apply to the officers, crews, and servants of the boats.[80]

No sooner had the fleet gotten underway from Campti than movement was stalled when *IBERVILLE* went hard aground. To get her off, she had to be lightened of much of her cargo. About six in the evening, the fleet finally reached Coushatta Point which was three miles downriver from a narrow constriction in the river named the Coushatta Chute. Rather than approach the currents of the Coushatta Chute so late in the day, T. Kilby Smith ordered all the transports tied to the bank for the night. Mounted scouts who had been moving ahead of the fleet rode in shortly afterward to report that an enemy force had been seen in proximity to the Coushatta Chute. On hearing this, T. Kilby Smith landed a full brigade which moved to establish contact with the enemy. Their orders were to hold the Confederates in place so as to lessen the chances that the transports might be attacked during the night. In their present location, the transports were extremely vulnerable. The banks on each side of the river at the mooring site were steep bluffs, and the river there was so narrow that some of the larger vessels, if placed broadside to the current, could have touched the bank on both sides. The immediate threat of an enemy attack was laid to rest when a message came in from the senior officer ashore that the enemy had retreated.

By nine the next morning, the fleet was underway, and throughout that day, there were no incidents. That night the transports and gunboats moored at a place which the lead pilot referred to as Nine-Mile Bend. By the following afternoon (April 10) the mouth of Loggy Bayou had been reached; but further progress beyond that point was blocked by a sunken steamer whose top-hamper was barely showing above the water. Attached to that top-hamper was a large sign which teasingly invited the Yanks to a ball at Shreveport. Irrespective of the humor, the positioning of the wreck, which was obviously a deliberate sinking, was no joke; it blocked the entire width of the river. As long as the wreck was in place, the gunboats and transports were stymied from making further movement upstream. Fearing an ambush, T. Kilby Smith ordered flankers out on both banks. Meanwhile, Porter and some of his officers inspected the wreck to see what might be done. They determined that the removal of the wreck would take time.[81] Before reaching a course of action, a courier rode in with word that Banks's army had suffered serious reverses at a place called Mansfield. The messenger had no advice from either Banks or from A. J. Smith as to what T. Kilby Smith was to do, nor did the messenger know whether Banks was holding or retreating. T. Kilby Smith knew that if he stayed where he was and became cut off from return to Alexandria, the results might mean the loss of not only the transports but perhaps the entirety of Banks's army since the army's supply and its withdrawal from the Red River depended on the transports. In concurrence with a very worried David D. Porter, T. Kilby Smith decided the only course they had open to them was to move back to Alexandria.[82]

Banks's Defeat at Mansfield

What had happened to Banks at Mansfield was a self-imposed fiasco. It was described quite accurately in a dispatch sent by Porter a few days later to Secretary of the Navy Gideon Welles. It was written after the admiral had spoken to some members of Banks's staff who had been part of that action.

> ...The Army here has met with a great defeat, no matter what the generals try to make of it. With the defeat has come demoralization, and it will take some time to reorganize and make up the deficiencies in killed and prisoners. The whole affair has been seriously mismanaged. Finding the enemy retreating before them, with twenty-five thousand men yet unscattered, our troops moved on with a certainty of meeting with no serious opposition. It was known, however, at headquarters [presumably meaning Banks's headquarters] that the enemy were posted at Mansfield and talked of giving us battle, notwithstanding which six thousand raw cavalry were placed in advance with a large baggage train close after them, and only supported by

twenty-five hundred infantry under General Ransom, who protested strongly, but in vain, against the arrangement. The enemy, numbering fifteen thousand, took advantage of this state of things, attacked the head of the cavalry column with their whole force. Of course they were routed in a short time, fell back, running over the infantry, made a stampede among the wagons, and the whole mass was mixed up in inextricable confusion.

The action took place four miles this side of Mansfield and it was a disorderly rout as far as Pleasant Hill, fifteen miles, where a stand was made. The enemy followed, doubtless much surprised with their easy victory, until checked by the XIX Army Corps, under General Franklin, which opened its ranks and let the flying multitude pass to their rear. In their turn the XIX Corps attacked the enemy and repulsed them in a very short time, but not in time to save the cavalry train [supply wagons and ambulances], all of which fell into the hands of the rebels, and eighteen pieces of artillery. Had Franklin's corps been in front, a complete victory would have been ours. It was the worst managed affair that I ever heard of. I cannot ascertain where the fault was.

It was determined, I believe, to retreat that night or next morning, but the enemy attacked the next day (the 9th) and our army had to act on the defensive. The enemy came on with a boldness and desperation seldom met with during this war. Their canteens were found to be filled with Louisiana rum, which accounts for it. They were mowed down by our fire, and though at first they broke one of our wings, they had to stop when General A. J. Smith with eight thousand of the XVII Corps charging through the XIX Corps, met them with the bayonet, and the other troops rallying, poured in a destructive fire. The rebels fled in wild confusion, leaving their killed and wounded on the field and two of the guns captured from us the day before. General A. J. Smith chased them for two miles, when they disappeared, and did not stop until they had retreated six miles. This time we really gained the victory, though we came near losing it. Notwithstanding our success, it was decided to fall back to Grand Ecore, which was done. The rebels sent in a flag of truce, asking permission to bury their dead. They were, doubtless, much astonished to find no one there to receive it. [No one except, one would presume, some rear guard pickets.] This is one of those instances when two armies ran away from each other.[83]

Following the retreat from Mansfield, Banks seems not to have fully appreciated the reasons for his army's demoralization, the cause for which he himself stood in the greatest blame. One of the greatest sins any commander of troops can be guilty of in the eyes of his men is to leave his wounded to the enemy or to neglect to bury his dead. Banks had done both. The only excuse that a commander guilty of such things can give is that he was forced to leave the field by an overpowering enemy. In Banks's case, that had not been the circumstance.

While Banks was moving back in the direction of Alexandria, a messenger came in to him with a dispatch from Sherman ordering that A. J. Smith's command, as well as the transports which had been assigned to that command, be sent back to Vicksburg. Sherman reminded Banks of prior instructions which called for Banks's troops to be out of the Red River not later than mid-April.[84] With the enemy no doubt poised to strike at any time or at any place it chose, this was no time for Banks to release A. J. Smith. Sherman was not yet aware of the dire straits Banks was in, nor did he know that the bulk of the transports were by then well above Alexandria with a very good chance, because of the drop in the river levels, that they would remain there. When made aware of the situation, Sherman canceled the order.

Banks's logistics were about to take on a dangerous complexion. The senior quartermaster of the expedition made this amply clear in a dispatch he sent to the quartermaster at New Orleans.

Alexandria, Louisiana
April 12, 1864

Colonel:

We have met with a serious reverse at the front, and the Army has retreated to Grand Ecore, having lost a train of 165 wagons loaded with commissary stores and forage. I understand that we have lost three thousand men killed, wounded, and prisoners, and eighteen pieces of artillery; Nims lost four pieces; Colonel Benedict is killed and General Ransom wounded. I have received urgent orders from General Stone to send up all the commissary and quartermaster stores possible, but have no means of doing it. I have been obliged to send up the *MITTIE STEVENS* with commissary stores. The river is falling rapidly, so that boats drawing more than five feet six inches are unable to cross [the rapids], and by tomorrow night boats drawing over five feet will not be able to cross. The river is falling four inches per day steadily. I most urgently request that all boats not drawing over four feet loaded may be seized at once and sent up here loaded light, and at the same time well coaled. I think the coast packets might be used in this emergency, and probably three or four sternwheel boats could be procured at Vicksburg.

I am hauling wood from Governor Moore's plantation, eight miles from this place, and will soon be out of fuel. I have to request that coal may be sent up as soon as possible....[85]

With T. Kilby Smith and Porter at Loggy Bayou

When on April 10, T. Kilby Smith and Porter found their upstream passage blocked at Loggy Bayou, they decided to reverse direction and move back to Grand Ecore.

The task of turning the transports and the gunboats was to be a challenge unto itself. Both sides of the river were covered by a natural accumulation of debris consisting of trees and huge root masses which had intertwined and lodged tightly against the shore. Approaching darkness would make a turning maneuver extremely difficult; however, to remain where they were for the night would be even more dangerous should the enemy decided to attack. The only feasible solution was to back the boats down the river until an area was reached where the river was wide enough to allow for turning. Such an area was not available for at last six miles, and backing that distance would not prove to be an easy matter for steamers with stern wheels. By the time dawn broke the next morning, almost all of the transports were in a crippled condition; the rudders of many were unshipped, and a number had broken paddle wheels. Despite the damage, all did manage to turn around once the wide place in the river had been reached. Hasty repairs were then made, and the transports proceeded.[86] Because the repairs were far from adequate, it became necessary to keep each vessel well separated as the fleet made its way downstream. While this separation lessened the risks of collision, at the same time, it severely limited the ability of the shepherding gunboats to provide protection.

Close to the noon hour on the next day (April 12), scattered enemy infantry units began to make their appearance along the river bank. The situation, as it had developed by that afternoon, was described by T. Kilby Smith in his report which followed the action.

> ...The *HASTINGS* [T. Kilby Smith was on board her] went under the bank on the south side of the river, near Pleasant Hill Landing, to repair wheel, which had become unserviceable; the *ALICE VIVIAN*, a boat that had reported the day before, lying midway in the stream, fast aground. THE *BLACK HAWK* towing the gunboat *OSAGE**. The *VIVIAN*** signaled for help. I ordered the *CLARA BELL* to report to her. *CLARA BELL* failing to move her, the *EMERALD* was ordered to her. About this time, the *ROB ROY* ran astern of the *BLACK HAWK*, and the enemy, a brigade about twelve hundred strong with four field pieces, commanded by General [Thomas] Green, of Texas, formed upon the bank, putting their pieces in battery within point-blank range of the *HASTINGS*, the nearest boat....[87]

* *USS*, commissioned Union naval vessel.
** *ALICE VIVIAN*

As desperate as things had become, the contest was far from one-sided. Most of the transports had been equipped with one or more artillery pieces, and these, along with the cannon which were integral to the equipment of the troops, provided a respectable answer to the enemy's fire. The transport *ROB ROY* was practically a gunboat as she had been equipped with four Parrott guns, giving her a 30-pound battery. Smith's report continued.

> [The *HASTINGS*] opened up with a section of Lieutenant Tiemeyer's battery; one gun of which was mounted upon the forecastle of the *EMERALD*; the siege guns, which were upon the hurricane deck of the *BLACK HAWK*, the latter admirably handled by Colonel Albert of General Banks's staff...My soldiers were all upon the hurricane decks, protected by cotton bales, bales of hay, and sacks of oats, sufficient barricades to rifle-balls, enabling them to mark the enemy with deadly aim.[88]

Those transports still able to make way continued downstream, but *ALICE VIVIAN* remained hard aground. Because of her position in the channel, she blocked *CLARA BELL*, *BLACK HAWK*, *EMERALD*, and *ROB ROY*. The Navy gunboats *USS LEXINGTON*, *USS NEOSHO*, *USS GUNBOAT NO. 13*, and *USS FORT HINDMAN* remained to protect them. The Navy gunners added their grape shot and canister to that which the gunners on the stranded transports were dishing out. Altogether, this combined counter-fire was enough to cause the Confederates to withdraw. From the confusing reports which later ensued, it is difficult to establish the damage which had been done to the Confederates. T. Kilby Smith stated that there were "many casualties." Porter had not been there, being instead with the gunboats and transports which had been able to move downriver. From his secondhand knowledge of the action, he would claim "about seven hundred" enemy casualties. Lieutenant Commander Selfridge, the senior naval officer who was there, reported an estimate of "two hundred" enemy dead. One point which was universally agreed upon was that the enemy commander, Thomas Green, had quite literally lost his head, a cannon ball having cleanly removed it from his neck. One witness stated that the gory scene had a "demoralizing" effect on the enemy and had seemed to be the immediate cause for their withdrawal.[89]

After dark, concentrated effort finally managed to free the *ALICE VIVIAN*. Able to move again, the contingent of previous stalled vessels started downstream. T. Kilby Smith led out well in advance on *HASTINGS*. After about a mile of clear steaming, he sent a dispatch boat back to report "all clear" so the others could then follow. Around midnight, the entire group tied to the river bank to wait out the rest of the night. With the first streaks of dawn, they were again underway. Soon they were back up with Porter and the rest of the fleet, all pleasantly steaming along toward Grand Ecore. But that state of affairs was not to last. The transport *JOHN WARNER*, which was traveling closely behind Porter's lead gunboat, hung up on an obstruction which blocked the transports behind her. The delay gave the Confederates time to move up a battery of guns which began to shell the fleet.

Shortly before the *JOHN WARNER* grounded, Porter had gone ahead to Grand Ecore. If he could find any of Banks's troops there, he intended to ask that they be sent upriver to secure the bank in advance of the descending fleet. Before he left, Porter had put Selfridge in charge of the gunboats. At the time that the Confederate battery had opened fire. T. Kilby Smith went over by launch to Selfridge's gunboat to get the naval officer's opinion as to what to do next. As the two officers sized things up, it appeared that the terrain separating the fleet from the enemy battery made it impractical to silence the guns by a frontal infantry attack -- that is without undertaking a 6-mile round-about march to avoid an intervening lake. If to make such an attack the transports were divested of their troops, the fleet would be left completely vulnerable. Remembering the layout of the river from when they had come up it a few days before, Selfridge believed that the gunboats -- if they were moved some distance downriver -- could be aligned so as to enfilade the enemy's guns. Selfridge's memory on this proved to be correct. Once the gunboats were in the new position and commenced fire, the Confederates were driven off.

The remainder of that day was spent hauling away at the hard-aground *JOHN WARNER* which was finally pushed over to the edge of the channel, just enough to let the others pass by. During the attempt to push the *JOHN WARNER* clear, the *IBERVILLE* went aground as well. One of the gunboats would remain behind as guard over the two marooned transports.

Just as the fleet passed Campti, it met up with troops marching upstream in response to Porter's request. Bolstered in his defenses by flanking protection along the river bank, T. Kilby Smith was able to turn back to the aid of the two stranded transports. Eventually, through a combination of rocking and hauling, both of the grounded vessels broke loose of the mud.

By the evening of April 16, T. Kilby Smith's transports and Porter's gunboats were safely moored to the bank at Grand Ecore. Most of Banks's army had arrived there, a circumstance which confirmed the wisdom of T. Kilby Smith's decision to move the transport fleet downriver, as now the army was rejoined to its supply element as well as to the fire support afforded by the gunboats. The situation had certainly improved over what it had been a few days past; but no one on a command level, either on the Army's or the Navy's side, really felt secure. The danger of a Confederate attack still existed, a situation made worse by the fact that the size and location of Confederate units were largely unknown. A second and more significant worry concerned the condition of the river at the Grande Ecore and Alexandria rapids. The water level had fallen even more over the past day or so, and it was continuing to fall. If Porter's gunboats became stranded above Alexandria, they would be ripe for destruction or capture, and that could create a serious regression toward the Union's control of the entire western theater.

Porter was betting that freshets -- if they came -- would raise the river level enough to allow passage over the Grand Ecore and Alexandria rapids. Not wishing to leave the matter entirely up to nature, A. J. Smith's quartermaster, one D. N. Welch, was doing all he could toward preparing the transports for the passage down. Welch ordered off all cargo and ships stores and whatever else could come ashore in order to lighten the transports' drafts. A shuttle of wagons would take care of transporting these items to a point below the Alexandria rapids where they could be loaded back aboard the transports. Welch's efforts proved so successful that by the end of the day on April 23rd, he could report that twelve of the lighter draft transports had made it over all three sets of rapids. The rest had passed over the rapids at Grande Ecore but still remained upstream of Alexandria with the sets of rapids abreast of the town still remaining as obstacles. These larger steamers and Porter's larger gunboats simply carried too much draft to risk a try over the Alexandria rapids until such time that the river's level again rose. The twelve transports which Welch had been able to get down had joined fourteen other Quartermaster steamers which were tied up at Alexandria, these having come up from the Mississippi with supplies. All of those transports were to stand by to await Banks's movement back to the Mississippi which was not to begin until Porter's gunboats were all safely below Alexandria. As things stood, the situation was at an impasse. The army could not move back to the Mississippi and leave the gunboats; meanwhile the gunboats remained virtually immobile above the rapids.

The reason for the low water on the Red River had now become the prime topic of discussion. In a dispatch Porter sent to the Secretary of the Navy, the admiral expressed his own personal theory.

> ...All the [other] rivers are full and rising, but the Red River is falling at the rate of two inches a day, a most unusual occurrence since the river is usually full until the middle of June...When the rebels heard we had first arrived at Grande Ecore, they commenced turning the source of water supply off into the lakes, which would have been remedied had the Army succeeded in getting to Shreveport. I cannot blame myself for coming up at the only season when the water rises...[90]

Wellington W. Withenbury, a civilian pilot hired by Porter, would later testify before the Congressional Committee on the Conduct of the War that the low state of the river was the worst he had seen since 1855. In all other years, according to Withenbury, the river continued high until the "last of July." Porter's theory that the rebels had dammed the river's source seems to have been just that -- a theory -- and one perhaps resting with Porter alone. Porter's comments made to the Secretary had all the earmarks of someone attempting to invent a platform on which to stand in the event the gunboats became a permanent fixture on the Red River. None of the myriad of reports, Union or Confederate, which are to be found in *Official Records...Armies* or *Official Records...Navies* or in the various memoirs and correspondence which we have examined contend that the Confederates had dammed the river. The more accurate assessment is that the river was unusually low that year because of a lack of rainfall, a weather condition that was seemingly localized to that drainage system.[91]

~

What had but a month before promised to be the Union's complete control over the Mississippi corridor, as well as the region of northwestern Louisiana, was now in serious doubt.

In mid-March, Ulysses S. Grant, who had been named General-in-Chief of the Union Army with the rank of lieutenant general, had left the west for Washington. After his arrival in that city and following his meeting with Lincoln, Grant elected to take the field with the Army of the Potomac. Major General Henry W. Halleck, who had previously been Grant's superior, would now become his deputy. Halleck would act as the Army's Chief of Staff with headquarters at the War Department. Essentially, Grant delegated to Halleck the task of chief administrator to handle the everyday matters of running the Army's business and to transmit Grant's orders to the theater commanders. (Major General George Gordon Meade, the nominal commander of the Army of the Potomac, would retain that function even though Grant was physically present with that army in Virginia.)

As General-in-Chief, Grant held the ultimate determination over matters in all theaters. He would be apprised, via Halleck's office at the War Department, of what was transpiring in the west and along the southern coastlines. The muddle which Banks had gotten himself into on the Red River was, therefore, a matter over which Grant exercised all final decisions. Grant laid the blame for what had happened squarely on Banks. In a telegram sent to Halleck, Grant made it absolutely clear that the gunboats were not to be abandoned.

> Culpeper Court House, Virginia
> April 25, 1864-8 p.m.
> A. J. Smith will have to stay with General Banks until the gunboats are out of their difficulty. General Banks ought to be ordered to New Orleans and leave all further execution on Red River in other hands. I have just received two private letters, one from New Orleans, and one (anonymous) from the XIII Corps, giving deplorable accounts of General Banks's mismanagement. His own report and these letters clearly show all his disasters to be attributable to his incompetence. Send troops for General Sherman where he wants them.
> U. S. Grant, Lieutenant General[92]

In a second telegram sent later that same day to Halleck, Grant drew the curtain down on any further offensive operations in the Red River country.

> Headquarters, Culpeper, Virginia
> April 25, 1864
> I would send orders to General Steele to return to Little Rock; to General Banks to return himself immediately to New Orleans and make preparations to carry out his previous instructions the moment his troops returned; to place the senior officer under himself in command of the troops in the field, with instructions to see the gunboats safely out of Red River as soon as possible, and then return all the troops rapidly to where they belong. If before receiving these instructions he has

taken Shreveport, then to leave General Steele and the Navy in charge of the river, giving General Steele, if necessary, all of [A. J.] Smith's troops.

U. S. Grant, Lieutenant General[93]

As a result of Grant's orders of April 25, Steele's movement toward Shreveport was aborted. When Steele had left central Arkansas to move in support of Banks, the power vacuum left in his rear was quickly filled by the Confederates. The enemy was now in a position to block Steele's return. What had before been a stabilized situation in Arkansas was now open for grabs. If Steele could not regain his prior superiority in the area, then that portion of the Mississippi River's western bank located in Arkansas would almost certainly turn into a Confederate controlled shooting gallery with Union shipping the target. There were indications that this had already taken place which is why McPherson had earlier ordered Ellet and his brigade out of the Red River and back onto the Mississippi.

The Dams at Alexandria

Any rescue of the gunboats and the heavier transports still above the Alexandria rapids was going to depend on the skills of civil engineers attached to Major General William B. Franklin's command. These engineers would end up constructing a system of dams for the purpose of creating sluiceways or flumes through which the gunboats and transports could be floated to the deeper water below the rapids. While it is sometimes claimed that the idea for creating the dams at Alexandria was conceived after the fleet arrived above that town following the retrograde movement from Loggy Bayou, the concept was actually first proposed on April 9 by Lieutenant Colonel Joseph Bailey, the XIX Corps senior engineering officer. That was well before T. Kilby Smith and Porter had started back down the river.[94] Franklin, himself a civil engineer, gave his conceptual approval; but no further action would be taken for the next three weeks. There was nothing particularly novel about the concept of floating heavy objects over rapids through the use of sluiceways. Brigadier General James Clinton had put into execution the same kind of scheme for floating bateaux down the Susquehanna River during an expedition against the Iroquois Indians in 1779.[95]

On April 17, Franklin sent Bailey to confer with Rear Admiral Porter about salvaging the gunboat *USS EASTPORT* which had earlier run on a moored torpedo (mine) above Alexandria and was now resting solidly, hull down, on the bottom of the river.[96] None of the series of ideas suggested by engineer Bailey seemed to work; *USS EASTPORT* was finally ordered abandoned. On direct orders issued by Porter on April 26, she was blown up to keep her from the enemy. During the conferences over the *USS EASTPORT*, Bailey took the opportunity to describe to Porter how a constructed sluiceway might be utilized to get the fleet down over the rapids. Porter was willing to listen to anything which would get his fleet back to the Mississippi; but as the admiral's own correspondence at the time suggests, he was initially skeptical over the idea. Nevertheless, when he considered the slim chance of having a rainfall sufficient to raise the river's level, Bailey's plan seemed to be worth a try. Banks's adjutant issued orders to commence the work. A vast amount of labor was going to be required, and Bailey at first had a difficult time locating troop commanders who were willing to offer their units as work details. Most of those officers, one can reasonably suppose, recalled the various canal digging projects which preceded the taking of Vicksburg, all of which had proven disappointments. To those officers, the building of Bailey's dam fell into the same "wild scheme" category. Nevertheless, the obvious need to do something which could save the fleet outweighed the skepticism. Bailey soon got his laborers.

The original plan as conceived by Bailey was for one dam, to be located slightly downstream of the lower rapids. Lieutenant Colonel Uri B. Pearsall and Colonel George D. Robinson, both civil engineers, had disagreed with Bailey at the time, arguing that the relatively steep gradient of the river called for two dams, one at each of the Alexandria rapids. Bailey's idea for one dam won the argument.

Troops assigned from the 97th and 99th US Infantry Regiments (Colored) worked from one side of the river. The 29th Maine Infantry, together with the 110th and 61st New York Infantry, and the Pioneers of the XIII Corps worked from the other side. Porter's gunboat sailors began the dam project as idle observers, a status which was not looked upon with much favor by the army men working up to their necks in the water. One of the supervising engineers lodged a complaint over this with Porter. Following that, the sailors went to work with the rest.

Bailey described the dam in some side notes which accompanied drawings he later made and which the War Department later published in the *Atlas to Accompany the Official Records of the Union and Confederate Armies.*

At this point where the main dam was constructed, the river is 758 feet wide, with from four to six feet of water running at about ten miles per hour.

Two coal barges, 24 x 170 feet were sunk in the channel, having been filled with stone, brick, and iron taken from foundries and sugar mills in the vicinity. Between them was a chute of 66 feet in breadth. From the barges to the right hand bank, the dam was built of cribs of stone; that to the left bank was constructed of trees with their branches entire.

The increase of water caused by the main dam was 5 feet 4 inches...[97]

This brief description by Bailey disguises the magnitude of the effort. According to Porter's account, three thousand men working in relays were assigned to the project.

By the time the dam was completed on May 8, the velocity of the flow through the sluiceway had become so great that the sunken barges had to be held in place by means of hawsers secured to upstream braces. But this tethering proved insufficient. The same day following completion of the work, but before any of the stranded vessels were made ready for passage, one of the barges broke its mooring and began to drag the other barge downstream with it. Both of them swung sideways and came to rest against the cribs of stone running out from the right bank. This at first caused considerable alarm, but it turned out to be a provident accident since the effect was to lengthen and deepen the sluiceway.[98]

The first vessels to attempt the run through the sluiceway were the light draft gunboats *USS LEXINGTON*, *USS FORT HINDMAN*, *USS NEOSHO*, and *USS OSAGE*. Because of the gradient of the river, the upper rapids naturally had the least water backed up over them; therefore, the chances of going aground in that stretch was the greatest. While going down, two of the four gunboats scraped hard on the rocks. That proved that the deeper draft gunboats and most, if not all of the transports, would not be able to make it under the present conditions. Pearsall and Robinson had been right about the need for two dams. However, Bailey, still sticking to his plan for one dam, decided that he could resolve the problem by raising the wings of the dam. He calculated that this would bring the river level up another fourteen inches which was considered by Porter's officers to be enough to get the deeper draft gunboats through. When the improvement work on the dam's wings was completed, *USS CHILLICOTHE* and *USS CARONDELET* were selected to make the try. *USS CHILLICOTHE* made it through; however, *USS CARONDELET* struck bottom, swung sideways, and came to rest hard against the dam's wing on the left bank. She lay there with her stern jutting diagonally into the lower end of the sluiceway, partially blocking it. Herculean efforts could not pull her clear. Even though everyone seemed to agree that there was hardly enough room to get another vessel past, *USS MOUND CITY* was ordered to try anyway. This proved to be a mistake. *USS MOUND CITY* grounded out, dead abeam of the *USS CARONDELET*, completely blocking the sluiceway.

Five gunboats and twelve transports still remained above the rapids. Belatedly, it would seem, Bailey accepted as necessary the suggestion of Pearsall and Robinson for a second dam at the upper rapids. Although it took less time to construct, the second dam was as involved a piece of construction as the first one had been.[99]

When the second dam was finished, it elevated the river's level by six and a half feet and turned the project into a success. The two gunboats which had grounded on the upper rapid and which blocked the channel were floated off. Orders were then issued to the commanders of the gunboats and to those masters of transports still above the rapids to make ready to bring their vessels through. All but the *HASTINGS* (which hit a snag and sank) came down without injury.

Although the last major obstacle which had held up a withdrawal from Alexandria had now been overcome, one problem still remained. Was the river below Alexandria clear of enemy gun positions? There were several indications that it was not. At the end of the first week in May, news had come upriver that a Confederate battery was being dug in at Marksville, a place about halfway between Alexandria and the junction of the Red River with the Mississippi. One supply steamer on its way up to Alexandria had already been sunk trying to run past these enemy guns. Until such emplacements were neutralized, movement either way on the river would have to be halted. A. J. Smith's transports would soon be moving downriver, and he agreed with Porter that the best way to handle the matter would be to take out the enemy's guns at the time they were encountered. This could best be accomplished by sweeping the banks with infantry working just in advance of the lead gunboats. In cases where the enemy was too well dug in, he would be blasted out with cannon fire from the gunboats.

The Cotton Capers

As the time of departure neared, the scene at Alexandria can only be described as chaotic. There is little evidence that any central authority was being exercised by Major General Banks. For his part, Rear Admiral Porter had taken on a completely independent attitude, absent of any willingness to cooperate with Banks's policies, at least if those policies conflicted with Porter's own ideas as to how matters should be conducted. This especially concerned seizures of cotton.

While waiting to leave for the Mississippi, the transports remained moored against the docks at Alexandria. Most had already been loaded to capacity with cotton. According to one observer, the total amount of cotton which went aboard the Army transports amounted to "twenty thousand bales." Banks, in his excuse-ridden report of the Red River Campaign, gives no direct indication as to who ordered that the cotton be loaded. However, in a glancing mention, he wrote that where cotton or other property interfered with the evacuation of materiel or personnel (including fleeing Negroes), the cotton was unloaded from the transports and left on the docks. The truth may be that at some point Banks began to develop second thoughts on the propriety of allocating space for cotton above the needs of humanity. Porter, as will be seen, did not share in that same compassion.

In conformity with policies that had been established by the Administration in Washington, Banks issued orders that private property was not to be seized; however, any property (including cotton) which could legitimately be considered as belonging to the Confederate government, established either by direct or circumstantial evidence, was open to confiscation. There is nothing in the record as to whether Banks tried to circumvent these instructions. Almost certainly, Banks was not in collusion with civilian cotton brokers as some have alleged he was. As Ludwell Johnson painstakingly brings out in *Red River Campaign: Politics and Cotton in the Civil War*, Banks forbid dealings on the part of cotton brokers from the north who followed along after the Army. The only record of Banks having authorized civilians to purchase cotton during the Red River operation was in the case of two entrepreneurs who held Federal passes to carry on this business, those passes having been signed by President Lincoln.[100]

When dealing with contraband, especially cotton, a special circumstance attached itself to Porter and his subordinate naval officers, a circumstance not shared by the Army. If a confiscation was carried out under the orders of a commander of a naval vessel, and if that confiscation was later deemed to be legal, prize money would ensue. In the case of cotton seizures on the western rivers, the cotton was supposed to be turned over by the involved senior naval officer to authorized Treasury agents who were located both at Cairo and at Mound City. These agents received and then stored the cotton before it was sold into the commercial market place. The money resulting from these sales was then in large part allocated as prize money to the commodity's Navy captors.

The methods used by the Navy in the seizure of cotton on the Red River went well beyond the pale of legitimacy. The evidence is certain that the officers of Porter's command perpetuated case after case of outright fraud, and there is little doubt but that Porter was aware of these frauds. In fact, Porter's own officers alleged that Porter himself instructed some of the gunboat commanders to stamp previously unmarked cotton bales on one end with the symbol *"CS"* (Confederate States), the other end to be marked with the symbol *"USN"* (United States Navy). These bales were then loaded on the gunboats for transshipment to the Treasury agents at Cairo and/or Mound City.

For Porter, the effort to garner as much cotton as possible had with it a considerable personal incentive. Under the naval prize law then in effect, fifty percent of the Navy's proceeds of all captured enemy property went into a fund for disabled seamen. The remaining fifty percent went to the naval personnel who were immediately involved with the captures. As commanding officer of naval forces on the western rivers, Porter received five percent off the top of that last fifty percent.

Seizures of cotton or anything else from private owners was illegal if the owner could first prove that he was a Unionist. Banks had put into a practice a method by which the local citizens could legally establish their loyalty. He did this by ordering that civil elective procedures take place both at Grande Ecore and at Alexandria. These elections offered to the local cotton growers the opportunity to declare in writing their loyalty to the Union. Those planters declaring affirmatively were to be given private property protection which included the safeguard of their cotton. Such individuals were thereafter free to sell into the open market. On the other hand, those who voted their loyalty to the Confederacy (or who declined to vote at all) automatically opened the way for the confiscation of their property. Once in place, Banks's election system put some unwelcome obstacles in the way of the Navy's cotton seizures. This fueled a growing animosity between Banks and Porter. The election system did not, however, prevent Porter's men from seizing cotton, no matter the ownership. Porter's *"CS"* stamps saw to that. It even seems that Porter personally participated in these acts of illegal confiscation. According to sworn testimony taken by a Confederate commissioner canvassing Alexandria's citizens following the Federal evacuation, "Rear Admiral Porter was present, witnessed the fraud [the stamping of the privately owned bales], and seemed in high glee at the adroitness with which his rascally ingenuity could outwit Banks and appropriate the spoils of the expedition." [101] That the gunboat crews seized huge amounts of cotton from far and wide is well documented within hearing records of the US Congress which later investigated the affair.[102] In testimony given to the Congressional Committee on the Conduct of the War, Brigadier General William Dwight stated that Porter's officers commandeered wagons and manned them with bluejackets which he sent out to scour the countryside. These cotton hunting forays extended up to seven or eight miles away from the river. During the Congressional hearings, Wellington W. Withenbury, a civilian river pilot employed by Porter, substantiated reports that Porter's men had stamped private cotton with *"CS"*, a mark, Withenbury explained, which was supposed to indicate that the cotton had been the property of the Confederate States of America. This stamping, according to Withenbury, was done prior to the point when the bales were loaded onto the wagons for transport to the gunboats.[103] The Navy's cotton capers went so far as the actual takeover of farmers' cotton presses which were then worked by crews off the gunboats. The gunboat crews pressed all the loose cotton they could find into transportable bales which were then stenciled with the bogus stampings. Lieutenant Commander Thomas O. Selfridge wrote later that he had witnessed this taking place, stating that although he had not personally authorized such behavior, he had "winked" at what was going on.[104] Correspondence from naval gunboat commanders addressed to Porter regarding the cotton seizures on the Red River is replete with largely unprovable statements as to the supposed affiliations of cotton owners with the Confederate cause. One such report written by Lieutenant Commander James A. Greer of the USS BENTON lists 169 bales of cotton of largely disputable ownership which were seized by Greer's crew.[105] Porter later denied any illegal seizures, blaming, as was his all too common practice, the "Marine Brigade" (meaning the Mississippi Marine Brigade), elaborating that the members of the "Marine Brigade" had represented themselves as being from the Navy's gunboats.[106]

That Porter was a prevaricator and not at all adverse to implicating others in order to protect himself or better his own position is, we believe, indisputable. This would be brought out with specific clarity by no less a personage than Secretary of the Navy Gideon Welles. His diary entry for October 1, 1862, stated:

> ...[Porter] has great energy, excessive and sometimes not over-scrupulous ambition, is impressed with and boastful of his own powers, given to exaggeration in relation to himself -- a Porter infirmity -- is not generous to older and superior living officers whom he is too ready to traduce...[107]

In the 1870s, Gideon Welles revised his original wartime diary entries, and in 1911, the revised diary was published in three volumes. The revision which he had made to his October 1, 1862, entry would then read:

> ...David [Porter] was not always reliable on unimportant matters, but amplified and colored transactions, where he was personally interested especially... I did not always consider David to be depended upon if he had an end to obtain and he had no hesitation in trampling down a brother officer if it would benefit himself.[108]

Welles's revisions from his original wartime entries were made in light of his subsequent evaluations of the personalities involved and of the events. In the case of David D. Porter, Welles's opinions held in the 1870s and which were expressed in the 1911 publication, were no doubt Welles's reaction to Porter's post war writings which in substantial part Welles had found to be inaccurate. Charles L. Dufour, in his published work on the taking of New Orleans, has discussed in considerable depth the tendency of Porter to not only lie but to take credit for events where the credit more properly belonged to others. Dufour quotes a letter written to Welles in 1871 by Gustavus V. Fox who had been Assistant Secretary of the Navy under Welles. In discussing events surrounding the earlier conquest of New Orleans, Fox stated his own denunciation of Porter:

> ...[he] has attained the heights of his ambition by means which have brought him in general contempt, and he has lost the happiness he had when we took him by the hand... Finally Porter, so soon as we leave Washington and to his young officers,

claims to have conceived the plan of a naval ascent of the Missi[sic]. Well may we explain with Pilate, 'What is truth?'[109]

There was usually a problem connected with the Navy's prize money system whenever the Army and the Navy were engaged in joint operations such as those on the Red River. This was discussed by witnesses at the Congressional hearings held during 1863 which involved the Red River campaign. One witness related the ill effect it had upon the interrelationship between Army and Navy personnel. "It was rather demoralizing to the soldiers to see the Navy seizing the cotton for the prize [money] on land while they [the Army] did not get any [prize money].[110]

Alexandria Is Left Burning

Under the orders that were issued for the combined fleet to move out from Alexandria, the Army transports, for their protection, were to be intermixed with the Navy's gunboats. Most of A. J. Smith's command would accompany the transports while Franklin's force would march out by land to Simsport.

An order relating to incendiary behavior had been issued from Franklin's headquarters on April 27, well in advance of the withdrawal. That order was in reaction to destructive behavior inherent to some of the regiments.

> Headquarters, XIX Army Corps and US Forces in West Louisiana
> Alexandria, Louisiana, April 27, 1864
> The advance of this Army in its march from Grande Ecore to this place having been accompanied by indiscriminate marauding and incendiarism, disgraceful to the army of a civilized nation, and no clue having hitherto been found by which the guilty parties can be detected, a reward of $500 is hereby offered for such evidence as will convict the accused of incendiarism before a general court martial to be paid to the person furnishing the evidence upon the conviction of the accused.
> By order of Major General Franklin:
> /s/ William Hoffman, Assistant Adjutant General[111]

Judging by what was to now occur, Franklin's earlier order seems to have made little impression. Fire-bug tendencies seemed to be also peculiar to A. J. Smith's corps. As the troop transports and Porter's gunboats made ready for departure, fires began breaking out at diverse locations throughout the town. A curious vagueness as to the source of those fires is evident within the reports later submitted by both naval and army officers. The reports were written as if the entire topic was best left up in the air with the blame unresolved. There is but little doubt that the fires which were to break out at Alexandria were deliberately set. The torching was probably the result of a general lack of discipline prevalent among many of the western regiments, but there also may have been a deliberateness attached to the setting of the fires which emanated from troop commanders. T. C. Manning, a commissioner who was appointed by Louisiana's Confederate governor after the Union evacuation, took testimony from local citizens about what happened. These witnesses claimed that after the fires started, A. J. Smith was seen riding up and down the streets, sword in hand, exclaiming, "Hurrah, boys, this looks like war."[112] The "Atilla the Hun" type of performance on the part of A. J. Smith may have become ingrained into the man during his earlier service with Sherman on the Meridian Expedition. On that expedition, Sherman had imbued his subordinate commanders with the philosophy of leaving the enemy country desolate and in ruins. However, not all Union soldiers shared that philosophy. Some, in fact, condemned it. The historian of the 114th New York was one such individual. He would write, "The wanton useless destruction of property has well earned A. J. Smith's command a lasting disgrace." [113] In contrast to the alleged behavior of A. J. Smith, the same witness stated that he saw Banks supervising details of men trying to put out the fires but that their efforts proved unsuccessful. There were simply too many arsonists at work over too large an area. One report states that nine-tenths of the overall town was consumed, but that may have been an overestimate. Beyond dispute, though, the entire business section as well as all public buildings, hotels, and downtown residences did go up in smoke.

As the gunboats and transports pulled away from Alexandria, the last thing their crews and passengers saw were pitiful clusters of civilians crowding up against the river bank trying to escape the flames. Among these pathetic people were the families of citizens of Louisiana who had been sworn into Union Army regiments over the two months just passed. Numbering in the many scores, the wives of these men begged to be evacuated with their children; but because of the overcrowded conditions on the transports, the quartermasters had to refuse. Space had already been taken up by many of the local Negroes wishing transportation to the Union lines at Vicksburg or at New Orleans, but not even all of them could be accommodated. Porter, of course, could not oblige either of these groups since his gunboats were by now piled with the revenue producing cotton upon which his squadron's prize money would depend. Much later, Porter would hypocritically write of the civilians left behind, placing special emphasis on the case of the unfortunate Negroes.

> Out of the hundreds of Negroes who had been promised transportation for themselves, their families and their effects, very few got away, and the last that was seen of these poor wretches, they sat down in despair upon the river bank, where they had conveyed their little all to try and escape the conflagration.[114]

When measured by its scope, the withdrawal from Alexandria was a more consolidated movement than had been the comparatively piecemeal arrival of troops at the campaign's beginning. The number of troops going out totaled close to thirty-one thousand. Although a considerable amount of equipment, i.e., wagons and ambulances, had been lost during the retreat from Mansfield, replacements for those losses had since been sent up the river. All of that rolling equipment was now going back out with Franklin. Leaving Alexandria would go 976 wagons and 105 ambulances along with the teams to pull them. There were also twelve thousand horses and mules belonging to the cavalry and the artillery.

Soon after leaving Alexandria, the transport fleet began experiencing personnel casualties from sporadic sniping. This was followed by artillery shelling which was far more serious. The transports *JOHN WARNER*, *CITY BELLE*, and *EMMA* were sunk before the responsible enemy gun emplacements could be overrun.

Franklin's force met no opposition on its overland march to Simsport. Prior to Franklin leaving Alexandria, an order had gone out to all quartermasters, as well as naval gunboat commanders on the lower Mississippi, to intercept any shipping moving on the Mississippi River north of Morganza. Steamboat captains were to be notified that until the army was safely evacuated from the Red River country, their vessels would be subject to the orders of the Army Quartermaster Department. Since most steamboats drew too much water to make it up the Atchafalaya River to Simsport, it was decided that Franklin's troops would rendezvous with the boats either at Morganza or at the Red River Landing, both places being located just off the main channel of the Mississippi.[115] To reach either place, Franklin had first to cross over the Atchafalaya which was not bridged. Once again, the ingenuity of the Army engineers would rise to the challenge. The transports coming down the Red River from Alexandria with A. J. Smith's command were intercepted as they passed Fort DeRussy. Their captains were ordered to divert up the Atchafalaya to Simsport. On their arrival at Simsport, the army engineers supervised the mooring of the transports into a chain-like arrangement, side against side, until they formed a troop walkover from one bank of the Atchafalaya to the other. Once Franklin's men passed over this improvised bridge of steamboats, they were directed to one of two preselected roads. One led to the Red River Landing; the other went through to Morganza. After all of Franklin's men had crossed the Atchafalaya, A. J. Smith repossessed his transports; and he and his corps continued on to Vicksburg.[116]

Postmortem of the Red River Expedition

By May 22, 1864, operations in the Red River country had come to an inglorious end. Although the campaign had been a military adventure of considerable magnitude, it was one totally devoid of worthwhile results. If anything, the Red River Campaign had been a deterrent to the Union's progress on more important fronts and may well have lengthened the Civil War by some months. Much of the blame for the campaign's failure rested with Banks, particularly his overland deployment from Natchitoches toward Shreveport, which resulted in the repulse at Mansfield.

Had the gunboats not been able to get below the rapids of Alexandria, the expedition would have turned into a very serious disaster for Union arms.

In terms of the human cost, the overall loss of life to both the Union Army and the Union Navy was 5,412 officers and men, not counting the 2,750 from Steele's army who were lost in the Arkansas phase of the campaign.[117]

For the harm the campaign caused in tarnishing the image of the Federal government in the eyes of the people of Louisiana, the burning of Alexandria leads the list of wrongs. Equally harmful to the Federal government's image was the "liberation" of the cotton by Porter. In that endeavor, Porter's men had acted more like buccaneers than sailors of the United States Navy. In the eyes of those Louisiana citizens who were victimized, the guilt rested not just with Porter's sailors but with the United States as a whole. The ill-feeling survived long after the war and probably exists even today in some sections of the Red River country.

ARMY TRANSPORTS KNOWN TO HAVE BEEN PART OF
RED RIVER EXPEDITION, March-May of 1864

Note: See Appendix N for a list of naval gunboats and naval auxiliaries which were with Porter on the Red River Campaign of 1864.[118]

*ADRIATIC**	*EMMA* e	*METEOR**
ALFRED CUTTING ‡ f k	*GILLUM*	*MITTIE STEVENS*
ALICE VIVIAN#	*HAMILTON**	*PAULINE*
ANYONE	*HASTINGS** b	*POLAR STAR*
ARIZONA	*IBERVILLE**	*RED CHIEF*
AUTOCRAT f	*ILLINOIS*	*ROB ROY**
BALTIC f	*J. C. LACY**	*SALLIE ROBINSON*
BELLA DONNA	*JAMES BATTLE*	*SHREVEPORT**
BELLE CREOLE	*JENNIE ROGERS*	*SILVER WAVE*
BELLE DARLINGTON ‡ f	*JOHN H. GROESBECK*	*SIOUX CITY**
BLACK HAWK * a	*JOHN RAINE* f	*SOUTH WESTER**
CHOUTEAU m	*JOHN WARNER** c i	*STARLIGHT*
CITY BELLE c h	*KATE DALE*	*SUPERIOR*
*CLARA BELL**	*LA CROSSE* d	*T. D. HORNER* f
CLEVELAND ‡ f	*LAUREL HILL*	*TEXAS*
*COLONEL COWLES**	*LIBERTY**	*THOMAS E. TUTT**
*DES MOINES**	*LIONESS* f	*UNIVERSE**
*DIADEM**	*LOUISIANA BELLE*	*W. L. EWING**
DIANA f	*LUMINARY*	*WOODFORD* f g
*EMERALD**	*MARS**	

* Vessel is known to have passed upriver of Grand Ecore as of April 7, 1864, in the attempt to reach Shreveport by river.

‡ Tug

Vessel went above Grande Ecore after the rest of the fleet had passed upriver and following April 8.

a Not to be confused with Navy gunboat of same name. As an odd coincidence, this transport was Major General Banks's flagship; the Navy's gunboat of the same name was Rear Admiral Porter's flagship. The duplication of this name can create confusion when one reads the official reports of the Red River Expedition.

b Was Brigadier General T. Kilby Smith's flagship. Sunk by snag, April 23.

c Captured by enemy after being partially destroyed by enemy battery fire during the evacuation from Alexandria.

d Burned by enemy after being shelled by enemy at Marksville when coming downriver from Alexandria during the week of 1 May.

e Captured from Confederates. Put into Quartermaster Department service. Destroyed by enemy battery during the evacuation from Alexandria on the week of May 1.

f Mississippi Marine Brigade

g Hospital vessel. Grounded at Alexandria rapids. Was later scuttled there to avoid capture by enemy.

h Lost with over 350 casualties; a number of men taken prisoner.

i Lost with around 150 casualties.

k Appears variously in reports as *ALF CUTTING*, *A. CUTTING*, and *ALPH CUTTING*. *ALF CUTTING* seems to be correct

m *HENRY CHOUTEAU*

THE STRUGGLE FOR CHATTANOOGA AND NASHVILLE
(1863-1864)

On the Banks of the Tennessee with Rosecrans

During the late summer of 1863, Major General William S. Rosecrans moved the Army of the Cumberland into what had previously been Confederate-held territory. He aligned his army along the banks of the upper Tennessee River, spreading it over a wide front which had its beginnings at the junction of the Elk and the Tennessee rivers and then ran eastward to Bridgeport, a small hamlet on the Tennessee River a few miles downstream from the city of Chattanooga. Rosecrans's support depended on a tenuous umbilical comprised of rail and, to an extent, steamboats. The most essential link in this transport was a single rail track which ran south from Nashville to Stevenson, a hamlet located on the northern bank of the Tennessee River not far above Muscle Shoals. For all practical purposes, Muscle Shoals represented the head of steamboat navigation for vessels moving up the Tennessee River from the Ohio. From Stevenson, a spur railroad line ran eastward along the northern bank of the Tennessee to Bridgeport. A second rail line owned by the Central Alabama ran westward and terminated at Decatur. In the past, that line had connected from Decatur to Nashville; but by the time Rosecrans had advanced his front to the Tennessee River, large portions of its track had been destroyed by enemy partisans. It was now virtually beyond any timely repair. Another railroad line known as the Memphis and Charleston ran from Stevenson westward toward Memphis. This line crossed the Tennessee River at Decatur, having at one time come together there with the now ruined Central Alabama track.

For Rosecrans's immediate purpose, it was the Nashville to Stevenson track that constituted the major means of moving in most of his supplies. A minor share of supply came up the Tennessee River by steamboat from the Ohio River. The steamboats off-loaded their cargoes to rail cars on the downstream side of Muscle Shoals for transshipment east on the Memphis and Charleston to the temporary supply depots which had been established at Stevenson and at Bridgeport. (For a pictorial presentation of the rail system serving the Tennessee theater of operations, the reader is advised to consult the map entitled "Theater of Operations, Valley of the Tennessee" on page 167.) To the constant worry of Rosecrans's quartermaster and his commissary officers, the Nashville to Stevenson track suffered from frequent disruptions of service, the result of partisan activity. Whenever the partisans destroyed a bridge, rail service could be delayed for days at a time.

The security of Rosecrans's eastern flank depended on Major General Ambrose Burnside and his small Army of the Ohio. In early September 1863, Burnside had occupied the vital railroad town of Knoxville. When Burnside came into possession of Knoxville, he effectively blocked communication between those Confederate forces under General Braxton Bragg which were then at Chattanooga and those of General Robert E. Lee in northern Virginia.[119]

When Rosecrans reached the banks of the Tennessee River at Bridgeport, he discovered that the railroad bridge which crossed there over the Tennessee to the river's southern bank had been destroyed by the enemy. To again span the river, Rosecrans's engineers erected pontoon bridges at Bridgeport, at Caperton's Ferry, and at Shellmound, and a fourth one adjacent to the mouth of Battle Creek. Using these bridges, Rosecrans's men crossed the Tennessee and seized Lookout Mountain, the highest point overlooking the city of Chattanooga. Command of this high ground by Rosecrans forced the enemy to evacuate the city. After Major General Henry W. Halleck, the Army's General-in-Chief at the War Department, received the news that Chattanooga had been taken, he told Rosecrans to press on toward Dalton, Georgia. (Ulysses S. Grant would not replace Halleck as General-in-Chief until March of 1864.)

With Chattanooga occupied, Burnside's location on Rosecrans's eastern flank took on added significance. Halleck would write Burnside at Knoxville on September 13, explaining the roll Burnside was expected to play in providing support to Rosecrans.

> It is important that all the available forces of your command be pushed forward in east Tennessee. All your scattered forces should be concentrated there. So long as you hold Tennessee, Kentucky is perfectly safe. Move your infantry as rapidly as possible toward Chattanooga to connect with Rosecrans. Bragg may merely hold the passes of the mountains to cover Atlanta and move his main army through northern Alabama to reach the Tennessee River and turn Rosecrans right and cut off his supplies. In this case, he [Rosecrans] will turn Chattanooga over to you and move to intercept Bragg.
>
> H. W. Halleck, General-in-Chief[120]

For Burnside to diminish his force at Knoxville had a certain danger attached to it. The major importance of that place had all along been to deny the movement of Confederate troops from Virginia to Chattanooga. Intelligence reports had indicated that Robert E. Lee was making preparations for an offensive against the Army of the Potomac. If that proved correct, it would reduce the possibility of Lee moving reinforcements toward Knoxville from the east. However, Burnside believed that second guessing what the enemy might or might not do was a dangerous game to play, and within a return communication to Halleck, he argued that to deplete his force by moving most of it toward Chattanooga would be risky. Halleck seems to have accepted this advice since he turned to other western commanders for the support

Rosecrans needed at Chattanooga. Messages were sent simultaneously to Ulysses S. Grant, William T. Sherman, and Stephen Hurlbut. Although each of these major generals was told to guard against any enemy movements in their regions, they were to send to Rosecrans those of their troops which could be spared. Halleck believed that a drawdown of troop strength elsewhere in the western theater was probably safe since the Confederate high command would almost certainly place its priorities on stopping any further Federal advance toward Georgia.[121] To isolate Bragg from any assistance which Lee might send to him, Halleck ordered Major General George G. Meade to gain Robert E. Lee's full attention by moving against Lee's lines in Virginia.

Halleck was nervous over Rosecrans's ability as a commander. He wanted Grant to take the command reins of the entire western theater and relocate so as to directly oversee Rosecrans's operations. Grant was at the time still immobilized from his riding accident at New Orleans and would be in no shape to take the field for at least another few weeks.

Halleck's concern over Rosecrans's situation had not been misplaced. That officer's front, spread over a 40-mile wide stretch, allowed a number of weak spots that could easily be exploited by an observant enemy. Well aware of his danger, Rosecrans ordered a shrinking in of his lines; but that was a decision made a little too late. On September 19, before Rosecrans's orders could be fully executed, Bragg struck the Federal lines at Chickamauga Creek in a battle which lasted two days and which resulted in a loss to Rosecrans totaling over sixteen thousand men, counting his dead, wounded, and missing. Forced back, Rosecrans took the unwise step of ordering into a tight defense perimeter around Chattanooga those troops which might otherwise have been more advantageously deployed. This left the routes into the city from every direction but the north open for the enemy's taking. Realizing his opportunity, Bragg moved to occupy these approaches. The enemy's guns now commanded all of the Tennessee River from just downstream of the city to well past Kelly's Landing. The only remaining access left open to the city was a cable ferry called the "Flying Bridge" which connected directly with a road on the northern shore of the river. The road was a poor one, being a morass of mud, its condition worsening with each rain.

The situation at Chattanooga was serious enough, but it became more so on September 30 when Major General Joseph Wheeler led a division of Confederate cavalry northward across the upper Tennessee River to strike at Rosecrans's lines of communications leading to Nashville. Wheeler's troopers attacked two quartermaster wagon train columns, burning an estimated eight hundred wagons along with their contents. On October 17, Wheeler returned over the Tennessee at Muscle Shoals near to which he destroyed a considerable amount of rail track and bridging.

On the same day that the battle at Chickamauga took place, Grant had arrived at Louisville, Kentucky, where he took over what now were to be his subordinate commands of the Departments of the Cumberland and the Ohio. Still on crutches, it would be days before Grant could travel south to Rosecrans's headquarters. Knowing of Grant's disability, Secretary of War Stanton had recently sent Charles A. Dana west. Dana, a civilian, was by profession a journalist. Although he had been appointed to fill the role of an undersecretary in the War Department, his true function was as a trouble-shooter at large. Dana was to remain at Rosecrans's headquarters at least until Grant was fit to take the field. The more Dana saw of the situation, the more derogatory his reports to the Secretary of War became over Rosecrans's inability to handle the situation at Chattanooga. As Dana saw it, the major danger had become the matter of supply which had already reached a level of severity by the third week of October when only a tiny fraction of what was needed by the army was making its way into the city. The little amount that did arrive had to come in by wagon from the north over a 60-mile road which meandered through what was known as the Sequatchie Valley. Dana described to Stanton the dire straits in which Rosecrans now found himself.

> ...Meanwhile, our condition and prospects grow worse and worse. The roads are in such a state that wagons are eight days making the journey from Stevenson to Chattanooga, and some which left on the 10th [October] have not yet arrived. Though subsistence stores are so nearly exhausted here, the wagons are compelled to throw overboard portions of their precious cargo in order to get through at all. The returning trains [wagon trains] have now for some days been stopped on the side of the Sequatchie [River], and a civilian who reached here last night states that he saw fully five hundred teams halted between the mountains and the river, without forage for the animals and unable to move in any direction...[122]

Dana went on to report the lowering of troop morale at Chattanooga, relating that one brigade commander, upon passing an infantry company busy at building defensive works, was greeted with the chant of "crackers," a protest over the dwindling rations of hardtack.

In the midst of this deprivation, two army corps, the XI Corps and the XII Corps, both from the Army of the Potomac and numbering in all twenty thousand men, had arrived as reinforcements. Under the command of Major General Joseph Hooker, these reinforcements had been sent from the east by rail, routing through Nashville and then on to Stevenson. They were now in bivouac in the hill country surrounding Bridgeport, as to move them into Chattanooga, only to see them starve alongside the hungry troops already in the city, would have been an act of insanity.

The advanced elements under Sherman were starting to come in from the Mississippi corridor over the Memphis and Charleston line. Sherman's progress was subjected to repeated delays as a result of his engineers having to repair lengthy sections of the track and bridges destroyed by the cavalry under Joseph Wheeler. This type of destruction was an ongoing event even after Wheeler's main force withdrew since small hit-and-run detachments remained behind and continued to harass the right of way. The rail line going south from Nashville to Stevenson was also receiving its share of enemy attention. To prevent this damage, Hooker kept beefing up his guard detachments along the right of way until such time that an entire division had been dedicated to the task.

Grant Takes Over At Chattanooga

Finally off his crutches and worried by the reports going from Dana to the Secretary of War, with which he was being copied, Grant traveled south by rail from

Louisville. He was equipped with fresh instructions from Halleck to relieve Rosecrans if he felt it necessary. On the way from Louisville, Grant narrowly missed disaster when the engineer of the train on which he was riding applied the brakes just in time to avoid plunging over a bridge embankment. The bridge had been blown up the night before by Confederate partisans.

It was immediately clear to Grant that a new broom was required at Chattanooga. He relieved Rosecrans of his command, putting Major General George H. Thomas in his place. The immediate problem Grant and Thomas faced was the question of quickly getting supplies into Chattanooga. The first substantive idea for accomplishing this had its origins with Brigadier General William F. Smith who was then the senior engineering officer for the Army of the Cumberland. On a recent reconnaissance of the Tennessee River above Bridgeport, William F. Smith had observed that the river was easily navigable as far upstream as Kelly's Landing. Beyond that point, the river took a bend northward before taking a heading more directly toward Chattanooga. At the northerly apex of that bend, the river was bound in by high rocky bluffs, a constriction which created a current that the locals referred to as "The Suck." [123] The currents at The Suck were strong enough to immobilize further upstream movement unless vessels were aided by a steam driven apparatus, consisting of blocks and tackles, which had been long ago installed upon the banks there by commercial steamboat interests. W. F. Smith had concluded that the most efficient way to utilize the river as an avenue of supply to Chattanooga was to avoid The Suck entirely by having steamers go only as far as Kelly's Landing. There they could off-load to wagons which would take their cargoes overland by road to Brown's Landing which was on the upstream side of The Suck. [124] If a pontoon bridge could be put into place from Brown's Landing directly over to the Tennessee's northern bank, there would be only a short wagon haul by an existing road leading from there to the Flying Bridge (an extant cable ferry) which allowed a crossing of the Tennessee from its northern bank directly into Chattanooga. The road leading to the Flying Bridge from the area of the proposed pontoon bridge at Brown's Landing was entirely shielded from enemy gun emplacements which were located on Lookout Mountain on the Tennessee's southern side. This road was in close proximity to standing timber which would allow for an easy corduroying with logs to give it an all-weather capability. The same corduroy treatment could be given the road running between Kelly's Landing and Brown's Landing. Among the advantages William F. Smith saw for his proposed route was that steamboats could be utilized for most of the distance, a virtual necessity since the supply of animals to haul wagons was by then critical due to the high loss of horses and mules which had been occurring on the Sequatchie Valley road, and because of the difficulty of obtaining forage for those few animals remaining. With W. F. Smith's plan, draft animals would only be required to handle the short overland haul from Kelly's Landing to the Flying Bridge (via the proposed pontoon bridge at Brown's Landing). The problem was that at present, both Brown's Landing and Kelly's Landing and the road between them were in the line of enemy fire. W. F. Smith had rationalized that in order to make use of his route, the southern bank of the Tennessee, from a point just above Brown's Landing all the way downriver to Bridgeport would first have to be occupied by Union forces. The reader is referred to the sketch map in this volume which is entitled *Chattanooga in Relationship to Supply* which shows the route's relationship to the surrounding terrain features extant in 1863.[125]   It was readily apparent that neither Brown's Landing nor Kelly's Landing could be seen by the enemy from Lookout Mountain. But what did command these two landings as well as much of the roadway connecting them was the northeast section of a high ground feature called Raccoon Mountain. William F. Smith did not think that Raccoon Mountain was heavily defended, and he maintained that it could be taken without serious losses. He felt certain that once it was taken, it could be held. To gain a perspective of the overall terrain, Grant and Thomas rode out with W. F. Smith along the Tennessee's northern shore. Viewing the south bank of the river through their field glasses, both senior generals agreed with W. F. Smith that the ground which overlooked Brown's and Kelly's landings did not appear to be overly difficult to take by assault. W. F. Smith next outlined what he had in mind for that phase of the operation. He suggested marching a strong infantry force, accompanied by field guns, over the pontoon bridge at Bridgeport to the Tennessee's southern bank, its mission being to move eastward and seize Raccoon Mountain to its summit. Once in position on Raccoon Mountain, these troops would be joined by a second body of troops which would seal off the approaches to the landing sites from the east. This second deployment would necessitate the use of fifty pontoon boats which were presently available at Chattanooga. With one thousand infantry loaded aboard these boats, they could be floated down the river from Chattanooga to Brown's Landing. The most difficult part in all this was that during a part of that float, they would be virtually under the noses of Confederate gunners located on Lookout Mountain. This exposure could result in the destruction of the boats as well as their occupants. W. F. Smith stressed the point that if the operation was kept secret and if the movement down the river was conducted during the hours of complete darkness, it could be carried out without discovery. Once the pontoon boats reached Brown's Landing, their oarsmen would swing into the south bank and land the troops which could be expected to quickly overpower any small Confederate force that was nearby. While these troops were establishing their initial beachhead, the oarsmen in the pontoon boats would row across the river to the northern landing and reload with fresh troops previously marched down to that point over the 2-mile road from the Flying Bridge. These troops would be ferried across to the southern bank to join the initial assault force in setting up a perimeter defense on high ground covering Brown's Landing, with special attention being given to the eastern slope of Raccoon Mountain which faced in the direction of Lookout Mountain and from where a counterattacking force could be expected to come. Meanwhile, over the 2-mile road leading from the Flying Bridge would come a train of wagons loaded with planking. The planking would become the bridge floor to overlay the pontoon boats which had carried the troops downriver from Chattanooga and which, once emptied of their troop passengers, would be moored in such a way so as to connect to the northern shore from Brown's Landing. Once the high ground of Raccoon Mountain was secured and the pontoon bridge was in place at Brown's Landing, the supply steamers could begin their cargo shuttles from Bridgeport to Kelly's Landing. From Kelly's Landing, wagons would take the cargo by road into Chattanooga via this pontoon bridge. To Grant, W. F. Smith's plan seemed well thought out, and he quickly approved it. Joined to that approval were orders that all preparations, including the corduroying of the road between Brown's Landing and the Flying Bridge, were to go forward on an immediate priority basis. The corduroying of the road between Kelly's and Brown's landings would, of course, have to wait until Raccoon Mountain was secured.

The *Cracker Line* Is Created

The group of steamers which would provide the waterborne element of William F. Smith's plan had their beginning with the rather pathetic form of one flat-bottomed scow which the Army's quartermasters had discovered at Bridgeport. Before long, this scow would be converted into a steamboat christened *CHATTANOOGA*. In reality, *CHATTANOOGA* was really nothing but a cargo lighter which was to be refitted with steam power and a covered deck. Her steam plant was to be powerful enough for her pilot to handle a barge on each side while running upstream against the river's current. With two barges in tow alongside, *CHATTANOOGA* would have a unit load capacity of around forty thousand rations plus twenty tons of animal forage. (The animal forage was needed to feed the draft animals which would haul the supply wagons carrying cargo from Kelly's Landing into Chattanooga.) Considering that the number of troops bottled up in Chattanooga numbered around forty thousand men, one trip upriver by the *CHATTANOOGA*, if made on a daily basis, could theoretically ward off their starvation. Of course this would be cutting things very close, providing nothing more than bare subsistence. If Thomas was going to be reinforced at Chattanooga by Hooker's and Sherman's separate corps, and if the resultant consolidated army was to be provided with enough logistical buildup to enable it to move out of Chattanooga and into Georgia, a much larger supply lift would be required. *CHATTANOOGA* was the first of a fleet of several vessels which would come to be known as *"The Cracker Line"*.

The completion of the *CHATTANOOGA* was of such priority that it became a matter of top attention for Hooker's quartermaster Colonel William G. LeDuc who surveyed the progress on her at least once daily. LeDuc delegated the on-the-spot construction to Captain Arthur Edwards. He in turn employed a builder named Turner who had some prewar shipbuilding experience on the Great Lakes. Together, Edwards and Turner rounded up whatever building talent they could find. This consisted of house carpenters from the local labor market, augmented by as many soldiers with carpentry backgrounds as could fit on the scow's deck.

Shortly after construction began, the Tennessee River started to rise, a result of heavy rains. The building ways upon which *CHATTANOOGA* rested had been located so that the scow was five or six feet higher than the river's normal level. Now, with the rise of water, the ways were almost awash, and *CHATTANOOGA* was about ready to float off her blocks. This was the situation Edwards and LeDuc found on October 16, when they made their morning inspection. When they arrived, Turner was busy supervising the loading of pig iron onto the scow's deck, his theory being to weigh down the scow on the ways until such time that the river receded. LeDuc and Edwards looked upon this scheme as self-defeating. Once the river water flooded the work site, all work would have to stop until the water level went down. This would probably take days, and after that, more time would be wasted while the water logged planking dried enough to accept caulking and pitch. In the meantime, the situation at Chattanooga would have become so acute that the garrison would have been starved out. There had to be a better way, and LeDuc soon found it when he spotted a number of low-sided pontoon boats laying up against the river bank. LeDuc determined that by flooding the pontoons, he could sink them and then push them in under the scow's hull. The building blocks would be progressively knocked clear at the same time that the pontoons were shoved in to take their place. Once the hull was resting entirely on the pontoons, the pontoons would be pumped out so they would again float once the river level rose. The scow's hull would thus ride above the water on the pontoons. The integral unit could be moored to the bank while work continued uninterrupted under canvas. The whole idea came off without a hitch, and by two o'clock the next morning, the CHATTANOOGA was afloat on the pontoons. A week later (October 24), she was ready for launching, a feat accomplished through the simple expedient of flooding the pontoons. Once sunk, they were then pulled clear. By the end of that day, CHATTANOOGA's steam plant was fully installed, and she was ready for service.

While work was taking place on the CHATTANOOGA, another hull (this one an old flat bed cable ferry) was being converted into a covered steam lighter which would be christened CHICKAMAUGA. She was launched two days after the CHATTANOOGA.

Upriver, things were reaching a state of crisis. The wagon route into Chattanooga from the Sequatchie Valley was by now almost impassable. That bane of mobility -- deep mud -- had finally won out. The scene along the Sequatchie Valley road and within Chattanooga itself was described by one eye witness, Joseph S. Fullerton, the then assistant adjutant general of IV Corps.

> ...Ten thousand dead mules walled the sides of the road from Bridgeport to Chattanooga. In Chattanooga, the men were on less than half rations. Guards stood at the troughs of artillery horses to keep the soldiers from taking the scant supply of corn allowed these starving animals. Many horses died of starvation, and most of those that survived grew too weak for use in pulling the lightest guns. Men followed the wagons as they came over the river, picking up the grains of corn and bits of cracker that fell to the ground." [126]

Grant had ordered that five river craft (then lying partially submerged in front of Chattanooga) be raised, quickly patched, and floated down to Bridgeport where they would be modified for Cracker Line service which he hoped would be inaugurated in time to save the city. These submerged wrecks carried the names: DUNBAR, JAMES GLOVER, HOLSTON, PAINT ROCK, and TENNESSEE. [127] While these steamers were being made ready, plans were put into force for the deployments which were to secure the all important Kelly's and Brown's landings.

Rail Communication and Its Inter-relationship to the Steamship Routes of the Tennessee and Cumberland Rivers

Whether or not William F. Smith's plan to relieve Chattanooga by use of steamers proved successful, a major problem would still remain toward supplying the Union's army located along the Tennessee River. As already related, the majority of what that army required came from the huge quartermaster, commissary, and ordnance depots which had been established at Nashville. Rail shipments coming down from Nashville were routed through Stevenson where they were then switched over to the Bridgeport spur. The supplies had been carried by wagon from Bridgeport into Chattanooga over the Sequatchie Road until that road became impassable. Provided that W. F. Smith's idea of supplying the city of Chattanooga by steamer became a functional reality, supplies could then be sent by steamer from the railhead at Bridgeport to Kelly's Landing and from there by wagon into Chattanooga. Regardless of how well the steamer plan worked, it would depend for its cargo on the rail route from Nashville to Bridgeport which could be disrupted at any time, and any disruption would stall the entire flow. Hooker's infantrymen who were assigned to guard the right of way could not guarantee its total protection since the terrain between Nashville and Bridgeport was rugged and heavily wooded, making it ideal for concealed approach by enemy raiders. One all too common example of that enemy destruction was reported to Major General Thomas's chief of staff.

> I have the honor to report another accident upon the road last night. The rebels placed a torpedo upon the track just south of the tunnel, and as soon as the engine struck it, it blew her up, throwing her across the track and making a complete wreck of her. I have a large force at work getting things righted again.
> W. P. Innes, Colonel and Military Superintendent[128]

Even if the railway from Nashville had not been subject to the enemy's unwelcome attention, the very fact that the entire right of way from Nashville was only a single track was creating unacceptable bottlenecks. To make the rail portion an efficient supply route, empty trains would have to be able to return nonstop to Nashville, something that was rarely, if ever, the case at present. The way the system now worked, every return train had to be carefully scheduled so as to avoid interference with southbound traffic. There were some sidings available along the way, but these were few and far between; and even then, every time a train crew had to use a siding, a great deal of time was wasted in the switching process. Rather than construct an entirely new parallel track, it was decided to undertake the repair of the badly damaged Central Alabama Railroad. (The reader will remember that this was the line which led from its southern terminus at Decatur northward to Nashville.) The job of putting the Central Alabama back into working order would not be easy since the damage it had sustained from the enemy was extensive. Lengthy sections of track had been bent beyond use, and almost all of its bridges had been burned. Still, it was clear that Grant's requirements for supplies could never be satisfactorily fulfilled until a 2-way rail system was put in place to Nashville. On the basis of that reasoning, Grant ordered that full resources be dedicated to the task of reconstructing the Central Alabama.

Not to be overlooked, insofar as what made up the supply arteries for the Union's army operating on the Tennessee, were the Tennessee and Cumberland rivers. Even though the upper Tennessee Valley was much better served by rail than was the Mississippi corridor, river transportation still took on an important role although steamboat usage fluctuated depending on the navigable stages of the two rivers. Colonel Lewis Parsons, who had now been given overall charge of transportation functions within the western theater, continually emphasized to his subordinate quartermasters the relevance of river transportation in the movement of military materiel. One of Parsons's memoranda on the subject explained that a typical steamboat with a tonnage capacity of between one thousand and eighteen hundred tons would require the equivalent in rail capacity of at least two hundred cars, or ten full trains. The quartermasters were instructed to make maximum use of steamboats so as to shorten rail distances where possible. In line with this, Parsons instructed that rail and river movements be coordinated to their fullest extent. Quartermasters were to arrange freight movement so that trains would be at loading quays at the proper time to meet the steamboats. Such arrangements were to apply at Nashville and at Johnsonville. (Steamers connected at Johnsonville with the short rail spur which led to Nashville.) It was also to apply at Muscle Shoals where steamers unloaded onto cars for the rail haul eastward to Bridgeport.

Acting Upon William F. Smith's Plan

On the night of October 25, three divisions of Major General Joseph Hooker's corps crossed over the pontoon bridge at Bridgeport on their way to secure those commanding approaches on Raccoon Mountain which overlooked the roadway between Kelly's and Brown's landings. Hooker's route of march would take him by way of the town of Whiteside and then through the crossroads at Wauhatchie.

At three o'clock in the morning on October 27, a brigade of twelve hundred and fifty men under the command of Brigadier General William B. Hazen boarded pontoon boats for the downriver float from the city of Chattanooga to Brown's Landing. The river distance to be covered would be nine miles, an uncomfortable part of it open to possible observation by the enemy. To lessen the chance of being discovered, Hazen's departure had been planned to coincide with the setting of the moon. Luck was with him. About the time of moon set, a light fog settled in and hung close to the surface of the river, diffusing the reflection from enemy picket fires located along the southern bank. Hazen and his brigade made it downriver without being spotted despite the fact that enemy pickets were seen clearly by the men in the boats. Even the enemy's conversation was heard at one point. As had been pre-arranged, a detail of W. F. Smith's engineers had set up range lights on the northern bank of the river opposite Brown's Landing. Once the boats came into line of this range, Hazen's oarsmen ran the reverse of the range so as to put the troops ashore on the southern bank. Some light resistance from scattered enemy pickets was encountered, but this hardly hampered Hazen's establishment of a beachhead. Meanwhile, the crews of the now emptied pontoon boats rowed to the northern shore to return with full loads of reinforcements which had been brought by road from Chattanooga. As soon as these troops had joined him, Hazen moved up to higher ground on the side of Raccoon Mountain. There he encountered some stiffer enemy opposition, but it proved to be more noisy than lethal. By the time daylight illuminated the scene, a close perimeter defense commanding the approaches to Brown's Landing had been set into place. By late that afternoon, the forward elements of Hooker's force had joined and had gone into forward positions over a wide arc protecting the approaches to both landings and the roadway running between them.

The southern bank of the Tennessee River, ranging from about a half mile above Brown's Landing downstream all the way to Bridgeport, was now well guarded by the steel of twenty thousand Union bayonets. Details were at work log corduroying the roads between the landings. Other details on the river's opposite shore were finishing up the job of corduroying the road leading from the Brown's Landing pontoon bridge to the Flying Bridge at Chattanooga. The pontoon boats had been planked over, and the pontoon bridge was ready to accept wagon traffic. Except for an unsuccessful attack against one of Hooker's regiments covering the crossroads at Wauhatchie, the Confederates appeared resigned toward accepting the fact that Hooker's and Hazen's troops were too well organized in their positions to be dislodged. Grant would wire Halleck his triumphant report of the day's happenings.

> General Thomas's plan [really the plan of Brigadier General William F. Smith] for securing the river and south side road hence to Bridgeport has proven eminently successful. The question of supplies may now be regarded as settled. If the rebels give us one week more time, I think all danger of losing territory now held by us will have passed away, and preparations may commence for offensive operations.[129]

Grant took a personal interest in seeing that the movement of supplies into Chattanooga was expedited.

> It seems the steamer *PAINT ROCK* should by all means be got down to Brown's Ferry [Brown's Landing] before morning, even if a house has to be torn down to provide the necessary fuel. There is every probability before tomorrow night to prevent our accomplishing this.[130]

What Grant had meant by his phrase "...before tomorrow night to prevent our accomplishing this," concerned a report he had just received that the enemy was going to beef up its artillery on Lookout Mountain, upriver from Brown's Landing. In that event, the *PAINT ROCK* might find it difficult to make the downriver passage from Chattanooga. By morning, Lieutenant Colonel Henry C. Hodges, the resident quartermaster at Bridgeport, was able to tell Grant's headquarters that *PAINT ROCK* had safely passed down, in the process only being holed once and that damage merely to one of her steam pipes. The damage was quickly repaired at the safe location of Brown's Landing before she moved through an opening made for her at the pontoon bridge. Once at Bridgeport, she was assigned two loaded barges which were lashed alongside. She then proceeded back upriver in the wakes of *CHATTANOOGA* and *CHICKAMAUGA*, bound for Kelly's Landing.[131]

Upon *CHATTANOOGA's* arrival at Kelly's Landing, willing hands were waiting to unload the cargo of rations and animal forage. Only a small part of that first cargo reached Chattanooga. Elements of Hooker's corps, as well as Hazen's brigade which was encamped nearby to the landing, were themselves practically deplete of rations, and they helped themselves, thus entirely consuming *CHATTANOOGA's* cargo. The loads which followed on the *CHICKAMAUGA* and the *PAINT ROCK* did make it into Chattanooga. By the time the wagons carrying that first cargo crossed over into the city, the commissary's inventory there was down to a mere four boxes of hard tack.

The so-called *Cracker Line* would eventually consist of fifteen steamers, ten of them built from the ground up by Captain Edwards at Bridgeport. Those built at Bridgeport were:

ATLANTA	*LOOKOUT*
BRIDGEPORT	*MISSIONARY*
GENERAL SHERMAN	*RESACA*
GENERAL THOMAS	*STONE RIVER*
KINGSTON	*WAUHATCHIE*

Five others, *DUNBAR*, *JAMES GLOVER*, *HOLSTON*, *TENNESSEE*, and *PAINT ROCK*, were modified from the wrecks salvaged at Chattanooga. Very few of the materials and equipment used by Edwards in his shipbuilding program at Bridgeport (including the steam power plants) were available to him locally. Most of it had to be shipped in from the Ohio Valley by rail via Nashville.[132]

Events Which Followed the Relief of Chattanooga

At the time that the supply crisis at Chattanooga was being rectified through the use of the *Cracker Line*, Sherman's corps were still struggling to maintain security for that part of his communications in the area between Corinth and Memphis. The Confederates were determined to see to it that those communications were severed. On October 11, Sherman had left Memphis by special train, en route to Corinth. On that trip Sherman would receive a first-hand insight into the type of harassment being brought against the Memphis and Charleston Railroad. When passing through Colliersville, Sherman's train was stopped because of an enemy raid then in progress against the town. It turned out to be a close call for Sherman, so close in fact that the attackers for a while had possession of the rear end of the train from which they actually captured Sherman's horse. Throughout the winter of 1863-1864, the Memphis and Charleston remained under continual pressure from the enemy. Its vulnerability was appreciated by Halleck who on October 14 wrote Sherman on the subject.

> Yours of the 10th is received. The important matter to be attended to is that of supplies. When Eastport can be reached by boats, the use of the railroad can be dispensed with; but until that time, it must be guarded as far as used...[133]

On October 19, Sherman, who was then at Luka (ten miles west of the bend of the Tennessee), received word that the level of the river had begun to rise and that two of the Navy's gunboats had made it up as far as Eastport below Muscle Shoals. With the Tennessee River finally open to traffic, Sherman ordered his Fourth Division to cross over to the Tennessee's northern bank and march upriver to Florence. Eight days later, and fairly well assured that navigation on the Tennessee could be depended upon, at least for a while, Sherman received an affirmation from Grant that the part of the track of the Memphis and Charleston running westward from Eastport could be considered as no longer necessary to military operations.

By November 1, Sherman, with the aid of two Army transports and the two naval gunboats earlier mentioned as being at Eastport, had crossed his troops over the Tennessee River to its northern side. By November 13, Sherman's entire command had reached Bridgeport and was preparing to move on to Chattanooga. Sherman went on ahead to Chattanooga for a conference with Grant, catching a ride to Kelly's Landing on one of the steamboats of the *Cracker Line*. A mount was waiting there for him for the ride into Chattanooga. The following morning, in company with Grant and Thomas, Sherman surveyed the enemy's defensive positions on Lookout Mountain.

Reforms And Demands On the Transportation System

On the 25th of November, a battle was fought at a location which came to be known as Missionary Ridge. The result was that the entirety of Lookout Mountain came into the possession of Federal troops. The way to Atlanta was now open, but before Grant's combined armies could move out from Chattanooga, provisions would have to be made toward the safeguarding of the army's logistical tail. Besides the security problems which were inherent to the rail communication leading south from Nashville, there was inefficiency with the entire rail network which connected to Nashville from the north and from the east. In the 1860s, the railroad industry was plagued by a multitude of separate ownerships. The industry had never cooperated in developing a method to enable rolling stock to be interchanged from one line's jurisdiction to another. Instead, the system called for the transfer of freight from the cars of one line to those of another once the limits of a particular railroad's jurisdictional ownership had been reached. This meant that an inordinate amount of time was wasted in the off-loading and reloading of cargoes. The Army's quartermasters would temporarily resolve this problem, starting in 1863, by arbitrarily routing cars directly onto the tracks of interconnecting railroads. The positive side of this practice was that considerable time was saved and much less freight was lost or damaged, all of course to the Army's benefit. From the viewpoint of the railroad executives, this system was a fiscal and operational disaster. Rolling stock belonging to companies as far away as New York, Pennsylvania, and Maryland might end up say at Stevenson or Bridgeport on the Tennessee, and in such cases, retrieval of the cars proved extremely difficult. More often than not, the empties were not shunted back to their place of origin but instead were reused over and over again to move stockpiled supplies from storage depots within the Army's immediate operational area. In a few instances, quartermasters in the west ferried locomotives across the Ohio River and sent them south to Nashville to relieve the shortages of railroad equipment operating from that depot.[134] Complaints on this and other matters emanated from railroad executives, and some of these complaints reached as far as the White House. This resulted in inquiries being directed by the President to the office of Quartermaster General Meigs. Eventually, a method was developed which allowed for more timely retrieval of rolling stock; but from the railroad companies' standpoint, the retrieval time continued to be imperfect as long as the war lasted.

~

The steamboat remained an essential part of the transportation of supplies within the Tennessee Valley up through to the taking of Atlanta. During the fall of 1863, new demands arose for steamboat employment. One need, unrelated to supply, came from the circumstance surrounding terms of enlistment which were beginning to run out for those men who had joined the Army during the war's opening months. The Army's hope was to retain as many of these battle conditioned veterans as it could. As an incentive to those willing to stay in the Army, a 30-day furlough was promised, the furlough to begin immediately upon reenlisting. The recruiters were to quickly discover that the success of the program hinged upon a quick delivery of the furlough promise, a promise which translated into a need for immediate transportation to carry the furloughed men to their homes. Requests for steamers to handle the furlough traffic in the western theater came from as far south as New Orleans and from as far north as Saint Louis.

~

Furlough requirements were but one call made on river transportation with which the harried quartermasters had to deal. In the spring of 1863, a large force of Sioux Indians had been reported to be assembling on the central Missouri, preparatory to going on the warpath. If the Indian threat was to go unchallenged in deference to the bigger war in the east, the Indians could have virtually driven white settlement from the entire Missouri country and subsequently, perhaps, from the state of Minnesota as well. That price would have been too high to accept, both politically and economically. The Army was, therefore, forced to take on the Indians despite its far ranging commitments elsewhere. Operations against the Sioux Indians were conducted during the summer of 1863 and again in the summer of 1864.

Steamboats which could ascend the Missouri River would provide the supplies needed for the campaigns against the Indians. (Appendix G is a summary of the Indian campaigns of 1863 and 1864 and the role that the steamboat played in those campaigns.)

PREPARING FOR DISMEMBERMENT OF THE CONFEDERACY

It had been believed that Burnside was secure from counterattack at Knoxville, but this proved to be an incorrect assumption. In November of 1863, Burnside had found himself under siege by a strong enemy force under Lieutenant General James Longstreet. Grant ordered Sherman to Burnside's relief.

> Headquarters Military Division of the Mississippi
> Chattanooga, Tennessee, November 25, 1863

> Major General Sherman
> No doubt you witnessed the handsome manner in which Thomas's troops carried Missionary Ridge this afternoon, and can feel a just pride, too, in the part taken by the forces under your command in taking first so much of the same range of hills, and then in attracting the attention of so many of the enemy as to make Thomas's part certain of success. The next thing now will be to relieve Burnside. I have heard from him to the evening of the 23rd. At that time he had from ten to twelve days' supplies, and spoke hopefully of being able to hold out that length of time.

> My plan is to move your forces out gradually until they reach the railroad between Cleveland and Dalton. [General] Granger will move up the south side of the Tennessee with a column of twenty thousand men, taking no wagons, or but few, with him. His men will carry four days' rations, and the steamer *CHATTANOOGA*, loaded with rations, will accompany the expedition.

> I take it for granted that Bragg's entire force has left. If not, of course, the first thing is to dispose of him. If he has gone, the only thing necessary to do tomorrow will be to send out a reconnaissance to ascertain the whereabouts of the enemy.
> Yours truly,

> U. S. Grant, Major General[135]

Sherman's move toward Knoxville resulted in Longstreet's withdrawal. Before returning to Chattanooga, Sherman distributed part of his command to secure eastern Tennessee. This gave Burnside a free hand to press the retreat of Longstreet.

Despite the success of the *Cracker Line* in alleviating the supply crisis at Chattanooga, the break in supply flow created by the off-loading from rail to river transport and then back again to rail once Chattanooga was reached, created delays which could hamper the supply of a large scale offensive such as that which was contemplated for the coming spring. That campaign would take a large part of the western army well into central Georgia. It was estimated that once the army left Chattanooga, filling the needs for its one hundred thousand men and thirty-five thousand horses would require the contents of one hundred thirty rail cars, to be delivered on a daily basis. Only an unbroken rail link from Nashville could move this amount of materiel; but in the late fall of 1863, all rail service was broken at Bridgeport. To provide through service beyond that point into Chattanooga, Grant ordered the rebuilding of the railroad bridge at Bridgeport. From a junction at Chattanooga, tracks led to Dalton, Georgia. From Dalton, Sherman hoped to utilize an extant rail line which continued to Atlanta. The use of those lines would, of course, depend upon whether or not the Confederates decided to destroy them.

After the railroad bridge was rebuilt at Bridgeport, the *Cracker Line* continued to operate; but its significance diminished, and the steamboats of the *Cracker Line* were utilized only as supplementary transport.

~

During December 1863, Sherman met with Grant for the purpose of discussing a major expedition to be conducted from Vicksburg toward Meridian, Mississippi. (That expedition was briefly discussed earlier insofar as its relationship to the operations on the Mississippi.) The Meridian raid, it will be remembered, had as its major purpose the broadening out of Union domination of the eastern side of the Mississippi corridor. Both Grant and Sherman appreciated that any major movement into the heart of Georgia, as was now being planned to take place from Chattanooga, could only be safely executed if the enemy was sufficiently weakened in the western theater. The Meridian raid was designed to do just that. In order to provide the necessary force for such a raid, Sherman had sent part of his command back from the Tennessee to Vicksburg from where, in February, he launched two heavy columns toward Meridian. By the end of February, Sherman had accomplished his intentions of putting a substantial part of eastern Mississippi to the torch, and he was back at Vicksburg. The Meridian Expedition, insofar as the destruction it had caused to the enemy countryside, was merely a dress rehearsal for what was soon to be the fate of Georgia.

When Sherman reached Vicksburg, awaiting him there was an urgent request from Grant asking that he return to Chattanooga to begin preparations for the spring campaign into Georgia.

Grant Goes East and Sherman Takes Over in the West
When Grant, now a lieutenant general, left for the east, he placed Sherman in supreme command of the Army of the West, a theater command which included the subordinate armies of the Cumberland, the Tennessee, and the Ohio. Sherman was to be his own boss except that any major strategic planning was to be subject to Grant's final approval.

For Henry W. Halleck, Grant's elevation was in effect a demotion; but in deference to Halleck's ability as an administrator, Halleck was given the newly titled position of Chief of Staff of the Army, a job which, as a practical matter, he had been performing all along.

During the coming summer, Sherman outfought Confederate efforts to block his way to Atlanta, and on September 2, he occupied that city. Lieutenant General John B. Hood was the Confederate commander charged with trying to hold Sherman in check. As Sherman's men were marching into Atlanta, Hood had swung to the northeast of the city with the intent of pulling Sherman off in pursuit while at the same time positioning his own forces to block off the rail line through Dalton which connected Sherman to his supply depot at Chattanooga. This attempt would fail, and Hood was forced to withdraw toward the southwest.

Thomas and his Army of the Cumberland was assigned the job of protecting the Union rear while Sherman returned to Atlanta to prepare for the march that would take him to Savannah and the Atlantic coast. Effectively prevented by Thomas from moving against Sherman, Hood retreated into the heartland of Alabama where he set about reorganizing and replenishing his badly battered force.

Hood Moves Against Sherman's Communications

In late September (1864), Hood moved north and established an advanced supply depot at the hamlet of Cherokee, a station stop on the Memphis and Charleston Railroad. This station stop was a mile or so west of Tuscumbia, near the great bend of the Tennessee River.

The reader will remember that the Memphis and Charleston Railroad ran east from Memphis via Decatur, to continue on to Stevenson. From there, it connected by spur line·to Bridgeport. This was the same railroad originating from Memphis which Sherman's troops had so painfully tried to protect during the fall months of 1863. Following that time, and when Grant instructed Sherman that the track to the west of Eastport could be neglected, little attention had been given to either that track or to the country through which it passed. Accordingly, the area had been more or less left open for grabs. During the next summer (1864), low water conditions had curtailed steamboat travel on the Tennessee. Once the navigation of the river was halted to the beginning of the great bend at Eastport, the Navy's interest in that part of the river virtually ended. This overall lack of attention became an open invitation for the enemy to reoccupy the area.

When Hood's location became known to Union authorities, an amphibious force was sent up the Tennessee to deal with it. The force consisted of two of the Navy's tinclad gunboats escorting three Army transports, *CITY OF PEKIN*, *KENTON*, and *AURORA*. When the Navy tinclads arrived at Eastport in convoy to the three transports, they were to discover that two of Forrest's cavalry regiments were comfortably in residence and well supported by a detachment of field artillery. A cannon duel commenced, forcing the tinclads to retire, but not before two of the accompanying transports, *AURORA* and *KENTON*, were hit and set afire. Their crews managed to control the flames, and neither vessel had to be abandoned.[136] The repulse of the Federal force came as a surprise to the Union command which at the time was apparently not cognizant that the Confederates were back in such strength along the mid-section of the Tennessee River. On October 17, Sherman instructed that steps be taken toward unseating the enemy and bringing the area back under control.

> Order in my name the renewal of the attempt to get Eastport, and ask Admiral Porter, if necessary, to send up an ironclad. We should command the Tennessee River up to the Muscle Shoals perfectly.[137]

When addressing the above order Sherman was apparently unaware that Rear Admiral David D. Porter had left the western theater, having been ordered east. Captain Samuel P. Lee had taken over Porter's responsibilities on the western rivers, and it was he who reacted to Sherman's request by establishing a system of gunboat patrols as far upstream on the Tennessee as Eastport. These patrols were made by tinclads since the heavier and deeper draft ironclads could not be put into that service due to the shallowness of the river. Tinclads would have to suffice until the winter rains brought the water level back up. Beyond Eastport, that is above Muscle Shoals and upstream in the direction of Chattanooga, the Army's gunboats *GENERAL GRANT* and *GENERAL THOMAS* were already cruising; but their efforts were of dubious effectiveness because of the large distances which were involved.[138] The need for other gunboats to patrol above Muscle Shoals was met by the addition of *STONE RIVER*, *GENERAL SHERMAN* and *GENERAL BURNSIDE*. These last three were originally built as freight carriers for the *Cracker Line*, but since then, they had been lightly armored and equipped with cannon. *GENERAL BURNSIDE*, *GENERAL SHERMAN*, *GENERAL THOMAS* and *GENERAL GRANT*, having been chartered to the Navy, were officered and crewed by naval personnel. *STONE RIVER* carried an Army-hired civilian crew and Army gunners.

From the late spring into the early fall, the primary transportation for incoming military cargo to the depots at Nashville had been rail with the cars routed through a major junction located at Louisville, Kentucky. Rains during that fall and into the winter had raised the levels of the Tennessee and Cumberland rivers making them again navigable for deep draft steamers. Once the rivers came back into use, the tonnage shipped into the depots at Nashville substantially increased through the use of steamers. Although the Tennessee River did not serve Nashville directly, a direct rail spur connection from Johnsonville connected the Tennessee to the Nashville depots. Johnsonville was located on the Tennessee, a short distance upstream from Reynoldsburg, or about half way between the Tennessee River's meeting point with the Ohio and the upstream great bend at Eastport.[139] Of the two rivers providing service to the Nashville depots, the first which could be utilized following the end of the summer period of drought was the Tennessee as its channels were deeper than those of the Cumberland. When water levels allowed a choice in the matter, the Cumberland was preferred since it served Nashville directly. During the navigation season of 1864, when an extraordinarily heavy volume of cargo was being sent to Nashville, there was not sufficient wharfage available there; thus both rivers continued to be used to the fullest extent of their cargo handling capacity.

In late October, the enemy began to interfere in what up to that point had been a smoothly run operation on the Tennessee River. There had been some light partisan activity along the river's banks, but to date, it had been relatively minor. On the morning of October 30, the light gunboat *USS UNDINE* (*GUNBOAT NO. 55*) was at anchor on station below Reynoldsburg from where her commander answered the request of the pilot of the transport *ANNA* to provide convoy protection downriver to the railroad bridge at Sandy Island.[140] When *USS UNDINE* and *ANNA* came in sight of the railroad bridge, the gunboat left *ANNA* and returned back upriver. She was no sooner out of sight than firing was heard coming from the direction of the bridge. *USS UNDINE* immediately returned to the aid of *ANNA*, only to come under fire herself. A 55-minute exchange of fire commenced between the gunboat and a horse-drawn rebel battery. The *USS UNDINE*, in a badly damaged condition, was finally forced to withdraw. *ANNA* had, meanwhile, been holed so badly that those who later examined the damage likened her condition to that of Swiss cheese. In fact, she was so badly damaged that both the Confederate gunners and the skipper of *USS UNDINE* reported that she had been "destroyed." [141]

After withdrawing from the scene of the action, the *USS UNDINE* came to anchor a short distance upstream. Those aboard who were still able attended to the care of the wounded. Suddenly the transport *VENUS* came into view. Ignoring the *USS UNDINE's* frantic signals to turn back, the *VENUS's* pilot ordered the anchor dropped near to what her pilot must have believed was the protection of *USS UNDINE's* guns. Instead he had placed his vessel in full line of sight and range of the downstream Confederate battery. A few minutes after the *VENUS* put in its appearance, the transport *J. W. CHEESEMAN* with a barge in tow came downriver. She, too, ignored the gunboat's signals to stop, continuing straight into range of the Confederates' cannon which promptly blew away *J. W. CHEESEMAN's* steam pipes, causing her to lose all power. Unable to maneuver, *J. W. CHEESEMAN* drifted in against the west bank, well within reach of the enemy. While *J. W. CHEESEMAN's* crew was being gathered up as prisoners, the Confederate artillerymen went about the job of shifting the location of their field pieces so as to again bear against *USS UNDINE*. The crew of the gunboat stood up under this fire for almost an hour before being forced to abandon ship. Most of the Navy men managed to escape into the countryside; but the civilian crewmembers from *VENUS* were not so lucky. All of them were captured. The Confederates then took *VENUS* upriver, but before long, they were spotted by another Federal gunboat which recaptured *VENUS* and took her in tow to the wharf at Johnsonville. In the meantime, a third Federal gunboat, the *USS KEY WEST*, surprised the Confederates who had boarded *USS UNDINE* and who were attempting to get her underway. She could not be defended since her guns had been spiked by her Federal crew at the time she had been abandoned. Before leaving, the Confederates set *USS UNDINE* afire, rendering her a total loss.

The quartermaster at Johnsonville telegraphed his superior, telling him of the trouble which was developing on the river, including the action at the Sandy Island bridge which had been but one part of the developing emergency.

The new boat *MAZEPPA*, with seven hundred tons of freight from Cincinnati, was captured and burned at Fort Heiman, two miles this way from Fort Henry, on opposite side of the river, on Friday. The *NAUGATUCK* and *ALICE* were captured at Widow Reynolds Bar, forty miles this way from Paducah, on Saturday. *GUNBOAT NO. 55* [*USS UNDINE*] with transports *VENUS* and [*J. W.*] *CHEESEMAN** were captured yesterday without being disabled near Paris Landing, forty miles below here and four miles this way from Fort Heiman. our information is reliable that Forrest intends to attack this place, with from eight thousand to ten thousand men, within next three or four days. Our employees will be ready and do good service.

Henry Howland, Captain and Assistant Quartermaster[142]

* *J. W. CHEESEMAN*

The "Forrest," who Henry Howland referred to in his telegram, was Confederate cavalryman Nathan Bedford Forrest whose force comprised the early phase of an offensive being launched into Tennessee by Hood. The situation at Johnsonville had already become precarious. Despite Howland's claim of reliable information as to the enemy's intent, no one really knew what Forrest was up to nor did they know the size of his force.

Word that Forrest's men were active on the Tennessee reached Lieutenant Commander LeRoy Fitch, the senior naval officer on the Ohio, whose jurisdiction included the entirety of the Cumberland River and the Tennessee River as far upstream as Muscle Shoals. To defend his entire area of responsibility, Fitch possessed only tinclads. The light armor of these tinclads put Fitch at a distinct disadvantage when trying to match blows against artillery directed from the shore. Undaunted at first by his handicap, Fitch started up the Tennessee with six of the tinclads, determined to drive the rebels from the river's banks. When they arrived in the general neighborhood where the attack against *USS UNDINE* had taken place, no sign of the enemy could be found. Things remained that way until around dusk by which time Fitch had steamed to within six miles of Johnsonville. At that point, a large group of men was sighted on the west bank in what appeared to be some kind of encampment. Fitch opened fire from his lead boat, but his cannon seemed to do little more than extinguish a few campfires. Remaining in place, the tinclad crews were on full alert throughout the night. The following morning, Fitch proceeded up the river toward Johnsonville. Just downriver of that place, the channel was constricted by a long, narrow island which crowded traffic against the western shore. As Fitch was about to pass close between this island and the river's western bank, enemy artillery was spotted. Although three of the gunboats were already in the full line of fire of these guns, they did not open fire. Instead, the enemy gunners shifted their pieces behind the cover of an embankment.

At Johnsonville, the gunboat *USS KEY WEST* was tied against the wharf. Upon seeing what was taking place, her commander cast off his lines and started downstream to assist Fitch's group. It was then that a second enemy battery, to date unseen and some distance upriver from the first battery, opened fire on *USS KEY WEST*, forcing her back upriver. Fitch could see that in order to get upstream as far as Johnsonville, he would have to pass both enemy batteries at a distance off not much farther than fifty yards. Even if he could get by the guns without incurring serious damage to his tinclads, once past, he would then be exposed to a stern-on fire to which the tinclads were the most vulnerable. While Fitch was mind-searching on how to circumvent this dilemma, a mounted messenger who had earlier been scouting downriver, and who was now returning to report, shouted from the bank that the enemy was in the act of moving into position below Fitch a third section of what appeared to be heavy guns. Certain that the light tinclads could not stand up under the fire of any well directed artillery, and not wanting his return to the Ohio to be blocked, Fitch ordered an immediate withdrawal. Those at Johnsonville would have to be left to handle things on their own.[143]

Major General George H. Thomas, to whom Sherman had given the responsibility for safeguarding Tennessee and keeping Hood in check, was now headquartered at Nashville. As soon as he became aware of what was occurring on the Tennessee River and the danger this activity posed for the sub-depot at Johnsonville, Thomas instructed Colonel C. R. Thompson, the troop commander at Johnsonville, that the sub-depot, with its mountain of supplies awaiting shipment by the rail spur to Nashville, was too important to sacrifice. It was not to be abandoned under any circumstances. Thompson had reported his strength to Thomas at not more than eight hundred officers and men supported by six 10-pounder artillery pieces.[144] Thompson immediately began bolstering his strength by calling in infantry detachments from the guard posts along the rail spur which led to Nashville. This added perhaps another five hundred men to his troop complement. Utilizing ordnance stores awaiting shipment, Thompson armed the five hundred or so civilian Quartermaster employees, thus further increasing the number of defenders.[145] Supporting the defenses were the Navy's tinclad gunboats *USS KEY WEST*, *USS ELFIN*, and *USS TAWAH*. Two 20-pound Parrott guns had been salvaged from the cargo of the *VENUS*, and these were added to Thompson's complement of field guns.

The enemy's strength remained an unknown factor, not only to those at Johnsonville but to Thomas's headquarters at Nashville as well. Believing that Forrest's presence on the Tennessee River was his most immediate danger, Thomas dispatched four trains to move as much materiel from the sub-depot to Nashville as time would allow.

On November 3, Lieutenant E. M. King, the commander of the Navy's three tinclads moored at Johnsonville, drafted a memo to the senior quartermaster at the sub-depot relevant to suggested actions to be taken if the enemy should attack in strength.

> Sir:
> In the event of the gunboats being attacked tonight and disabled, I think it will be well for you to make preparation for destroying by fire all the transports now here so that they may not fall into the enemy's hands. I think it will be well for you to be prepared beforehand. The gunboats will do everything possible to prevent any surprise, but be prepared.[146]

Upon receipt of King's advice, Howland penned an order to an assistant quartermaster, instructing him to prepare to set fire to the transports lying at the wharves, but with the proviso that this was not to be done unless the appearance of the enemy appeared imminent. Who was to make the determination as to what "imminent" meant was not disclosed by Howland, and apparently the junior quartermaster did not ask.

Henry Howland seems to have considered his own decisions regarding the defense of Johnsonville to be independent of Colonel Thompson's role as troop commander. There is no evidence to suggest that Howland ever consulted with Thompson. Lieutenant King appears to have ignored Thompson as well.

On November 4 the Confederates opened artillery fire against Johnsonville from across the river. King's tinclads returned the fire in a duel which lasted only twenty minutes. During that time, all three of the tinclads became disabled. On the orders of King, their seacocks were opened, and they were then set afire.

An hour or so before the enemy bombardment had begun, word was received from a mounted scout that the Confederates were crossing the river somewhere upstream of Johnsonville, using for that purpose a cutter and a small gig which had belonged to the *USS UNDINE* and which the enemy had presumably transported up along the river bank by wagon. This latest news added to the sense of panic which seems to have been prevalent from the onset among many of the officers at the sub-depot.[147] The assistant quartermaster to whom Howland had addressed his instructions the day prior now assumed that since the enemy was crossing the river and the gunboats had been set afire, the time had arrived for him to fire the transports. This he did. Once ignited, the transports burned so furiously that the flames spread to a warehouse. Before the hour was out, all the warehouses along with the stores they contained had gone up in smoke. The transports which burned that day were *MOUNTAINEER*, *DOANE NO. 2*, *ARCOLA*, *AURORA*, *DUKE*, *GOODY FRIENDS*, *J. B. FORD*, and the recaptured *VENUS*. Ten barges were also burned. At the time the fires were set, at least half of the transports and all of the barges had been loaded to capacity with Army cargo.

The burning of Johnsonville at the hands of its own defenders was a disaster that certainly need not have happened. Any thinking officer should have realized that the cutter and the gig from the *USS UNDINE* were far too small to ferry across the river -- at least within a reasonable period of time -- a force large enough to have seriously threatened the sub-depot, especially in light of the number of troops in its defense force. Howland's report on the affair stands absent of any logical excuse for his having set into motion the instructions which resulted in the transports being burned. His guilt on that score was heightened by the orders he received some days earlier from Thomas who at the time had answered an inquiry from Howland as to whether he should destroy the stores and the buildings at Johnsonville in the event of an attack by enemy forces. Thomas's answer to that inquiry should have left little doubt as to what Howland's instructions had been were.

> ...If the place must be evacuated, there will be no destruction of public property,
> whatever, but the place will be left just as it now is.[148]

The excuse Howland would attempt when he appeared before a convened board of inquiry was that the transports (and barges) were not the same as "public property" and that the firing of the warehouses was the result of accident. The first part was, of course, ridiculous since the transports had all been on charter to the Army.

Under the terms of the Army's charter agreements, a vessel's loss while in service was compensable to the owners by the government unless the loss was a result of marine casualty not related to an act of the enemy. Destruction at the hand of an officer of the United States government could not -- even by any wild stretch of the imagination -- be attributable to marine casualty, nor could it be laid to the acts of an enemy. As an officer in the Quartermaster Department, Howland must have been well aware of the Army's charter terms. There was also the matter of the cargoes on the transports, all of it clearly being Army property. Lieutenant Colonel William Sinclair who was assigned by the Inspector General to investigate the affair was harsh in his criticism of what had happened. Not only did Sinclair believe that the firing of the vessels had been at best unnecessary and certainly contrary to orders, but he also brought out that there was little excuse for Howland not having ordered the unloading of the barges and the transports at some point in time before the attack. Sinclair also criticized the Navy for its part in the Johnsonville disaster, charging that naval officers off the tinclads had been guilty of looting Army property and had encouraged their men to do likewise. He leveled that same accusation against Howland's quartermaster personnel.[149]

Forrest's raid along the Tennessee had a serious impact. By the time he was through creating havoc not only along the Tennessee but along the Cumberland as well, Forrest could accurately claim (counting the Federals' self-inflicted losses at Johnsonville) that he had been the cause of the destruction of "four gunboats; fourteen transports; and seventeen barges." Besides the vessels that were destroyed, Forrest's troopers caused considerable damage to rail lines and to the vital bridges that served them. All told, the damage to Federal property from Forrest's raid was estimated at the time to be in the neighborhood of six and a half million dollars, a huge sum for that day and age.[150]

Hood Strikes North of the Tennessee

On November 15, 1864, Confederate General John B. Hood crossed over the Tennessee River at Tuscumbia and headed north with two widely separated columns. It was clear to Thomas that Hood had in mind the Union Army depots at Nashville. Reacting, Thomas sent a reinforced corps under Major General John Schofield to cut Hood off at Columbia (a town midway between Tuscumbia and Nashville). Thomas placed the remainder of his command into defensive positions in front of Nashville.

In a sharp action at Columbia, Schofield was forced back when Hood threatened to outflank him. Schofield regrouped and dug in at Franklin where he was reinforced by fresh troops sent to him by Thomas. Schofield then checked two strong assaults by Hood, badly punishing the Southerners in the process. So far since leaving Tuscumbia, Hood had lost almost six thousand men.

While Schofield had been preparing to blunt Hood's strength, Major General A. J. Smith arrived at Saint Louis following his chase after a Confederate army west of the Mississippi (a campaign to be discussed in the following chapter). Awaiting him at Saint Louis were fresh orders to support Thomas at Nashville. To reach

Nashville, Smith's XVI Corps was transported aboard twenty-seven steamers. He arrived on November 30.

Following the action at Franklin, Schofield had moved his corps back to the defensive perimeter Thomas had established in front of Nashville. Because of the damage Hood had sustained at Columbia and at Franklin, he felt he no longer had enough strength to attempt another frontal attack. Instead, he decided to remain static, believing that as long as his army could stay in Tennessee, he would be a decisive impediment to whatever Sherman might have in mind for Georgia. Hood's effective strength had dropped by now to twenty-three thousand men. Thomas had close to seventy thousand men opposing him once A. J. Smith's corps had joined. Considering the outnumbered situation in which Hood now found himself, any optimism that he had toward holding his position rested on the remote possibility that he would be reinforced by fresh troops coming out of Texas. That hope was unrealistic, and it would never materialize.[151]

On December 15, one month to the day from when Hood's army had first crossed over the Tennessee, Thomas marched out of his Nashville defenses and assaulted Hood's lines. The battle went badly for the Confederates. On the following day, Hood began a retreat back toward Tuscumbia. The day after Christmas, he crossed back over the Tennessee into Alabama. Hood would take his command deep into that state where it was joined to the defense force holding at Mobile. His army would no longer be able to take the offensive, either in terms of troop strength or in equipment. Tennessee did not, however, become a secure area because of Hood's withdrawal. Harassment by medium and small sized cavalry units made against Union transportation -- both river and rail -- continued throughout most of the winter of 1864-1865; but things never again reached the point of seriously jeopardizing Union communications within Tennessee.

Sherman's Rear Echelon

Prior to the taking of Atlanta, the bulk of quartermaster, commissary, and ordnance supplies had reached Sherman from the huge depots at Nashville. In turn, the Nashville depots built their stocks from shipments coming to them by rail and by river from the states north of the Ohio and from the Middle Atlantic. That which came to Nashville by water traveled by one of two routes. The first route utilized the Ohio River and then fed into the Tennessee River and up that river to the quartermaster sub-depot at Johnsonville; from Johnsonville, the cargoes were transshipped overland by rail spur to Nashville. The second river route began on the Ohio and followed up the Cumberland River directly to the docks at Nashville. Between February 1 and May 27 of 1864, the quartermaster officer at Nashville reported that 614 steamboats and barges had discharged their cargoes at the Nashville wharves. In the aggregate, the cargoes amounted to 158,016 tons. (Presumably, these tonnage figures represented only that waterborne cargo which arrived at Nashville by way of the Cumberland River and did not include that which was landed at Johnsonville on the Tennessee and transshipped to Nashville by the rail spur.)[152] Once at the Nashville depots, supplies were moved south by rail to Chattanooga via the newly constructed railroad bridge which crossed the Tennessee at Bridgeport. From Chattanooga, the trains were switched over to the tracks which ran to Dalton, Georgia. At Dalton, the goods were transferred from the cars onto wagons and sent forward to the troop consumers in the field. Any delay or break in these routing links became critical. Sherman made his position regarding his logistics simplistically emphatic to Lieutenant Colonel James L. Donaldson, the quartermaster officer in charge of the movement of supplies from Nashville. He wired Donaldson that he had no specific orders to give, "...only supply my army or I will eat your mules." The mules to which Sherman referred were those draft animals employed in the movement of supplies to the field from the rail line at Dalton. Fortunately for Donaldson's mules, the situation never reached a point where Sherman had to exercise his threat although at times the transportation network was severely stressed. One particular crisis occurred during mid-summer when drought conditions caused the level of the Cumberland River to drop to below twelve inches over the Harpeth Shoals. Donaldson overcame that handicap by selecting out from the supply fleet those steamers possessing a shallow enough draft to transcend the shoals, provided they were given some ancillary power from the bank. He provided this power from a pool of oxen, consisting in all of one hundred yoke. Using the oxen, the steamers were hauled over the shallows to the deeper water above. That solution was but one of a score of improvisations that were dreamed up to solve supply problems, both major and minor, as they developed. Donaldson would later estimate that from the time Sherman left Chattanooga until he marched into Atlanta, close to 165,000 men had been employed in the handling and transportation of supplies.[153]

On November 16, the date when Sherman set out from Atlanta on his march to the sea, he would deliberately terminate his supply umbilical to Nashville. This decision to cut his communications with the rear was well based. First, there was the distance which would be involved and which by itself would make the movement of supplies from the west increasingly difficult if not impossible. Second, the enemy could be expected to become increasingly disruptive as the supply lines lengthened. The only counteraction to such disruptions would have to come from a large commitment of guard troops, and Sherman could ill afford that sort of manpower commitment.

The Georgia countryside through which Sherman's army was to march was reported to be free of the kind of enemy presence which might materially slow its progress. Most importantly, the country between Atlanta and Savannah was considered to be bountiful in agricultural products. Provided the march was made in three or more parallel columns, foragers (or "bummers" as they came to be called) could productively work out to the sides of each of the march routes. As experience was to prove, the estimates of what Georgia could offer Sherman by way of subsistence did not do justice to the actual largess which Sherman's foragers gathered. Most of the men who marched east with Sherman from Atlanta would remember into their dotage that they were better fed on that march than at any time during the war. On the other hand, for the Georgians, it was to be a time of destruction of all they had known and cherished. Sherman would leave behind him a country destitute and in flames.

MOBILE BAY
(August 1864)

It had long been the intention of Lieutenant General Ulysses S. Grant to attack and occupy Mobile, Alabama, a plan first made in the fall of 1863 but which had been delayed because of the Red River Expedition. By the time Grant's plan was finally acted upon, Mobile had become lowered on the scale of military priorities. When the attack came, it was not in the form of an envelopment from both the land and sea sides as first envisioned. Instead, it was launched from the sea alone.

The heaviest Confederate opposition was forecast to be from the cannon of the three forts located on the barrier islands protecting the outer bay. The once substantial troop presence had been recently drawn upon by large troop drafts sent to reinforce the enemy's army in northern Alabama.

A fleet under Rear Admiral David G. Farragut reached Mobile's outer bay in August of 1864. Transports shielded by the Navy's ships landed troops from XIII Corps as soon as the Navy's guns had reduced the forts. The three forts were occupied with minimal casualties on the part of the attacking Federals. A bold advance by Farragut's fleet *("Damn the Torpedoes...!")* soon rendered impotent those Confederate vessels which were present.

Federal forces garrisoned the outer islands of Mobile Bay throughout the remainder of the war. As a port, Mobile was thereafter denied to blockade runners, but the city itself remained in possession of the Confederacy until April of 1865. Its garrison surrendered three days after Lee's capitulation at Appomattox.

Transports known to have been employed in carrying troops to Mobile Bay from New Orleans were:[154]

AMERICA	*JAMES BATTLE*	*OCTORARA*
BALTIC	*JOSEPHINE*	*PATROON*
BROWN †	*KATE DALE*	*SAINT CHARLES*
CLYDE ‡	*LAURA*	*SAINT MARY'S*
CONEMAUGH	*MARINE*	*SUWANEE*
EVENING STAR		*TAMAULIPAS*

† Impossible to determine which *BROWN*
‡ May have been *REBECCA CLYDE*

THE DEFEAT OF PRICE
(Fall of 1864)

A Union troop movement of major proportions was carried out by steamboat during the early fall of 1864. The purpose behind this lift was a counteraction against Major General Sterling Price who had assembled a rag-tag bunch of Confederates in Arkansas with the intent of marching them on Saint Louis. From there, Price had planned an invasion of Illinois. When it became clear that Price was advancing on Saint Louis, it was decided to intercept him before he could get out of central Missouri. Two separate Union forces-- one under Brigadier General Joseph A. Mower, the other under Major General A. J. Smith-- would be sent up the Missouri River against Price.

Seven thousand Union cavalry with some accompanying artillery, all under the leadership of Mower, were loaded onto forty steamers which had been hastily gathered at Cape Girardeau. Mower moved up the Mississippi and into the Missouri River on a total voyage of 350 miles which terminated at Jefferson City, Missouri. The trip up the river had not been a comfortable one. The Missouri was near low water, and only small steamers of light drafts could be used to make the trip. Conditions on the steamers were badly cramped, and frequent grounding slowed progress. Despite the problems, Jefferson City was reached, and Mower moved to put his troopers astride of Price's advance.

At the time A. J. Smith received orders to move against Price, his corps was at Saint Louis preparing to board transports which would carry them east. That move was shelved. Smith's corps would instead board steamers for a ride up the Missouri and a subsequent overland march to intercept Price.

Because of the fast reaction time in putting together the river transportation for both Mower and A. J. Smith, Price's advance was thwarted, and he was forced to retreat. By the time he had reached the relative safety of Central Arkansas, Price had lost almost half of his command, the result of forty-three delaying actions fought against him by Mower and A. J. Smith as well as harassment against his flanks by hastily mobilized militia. As a result of those defeats and the demoralization they created among those with Southern sympathies, Confederate activity of any notable significance in Arkansas and southern Missouri was curtailed for the remainder of the war. Small unit raids, mostly of partisan origin, would continue to tie down some Federal forces in the region, but the number of troops needed to contain those annoyances was no where near as large as it had been.

~

Because of the elimination of Price as a substantive threat, starting with the new year of 1865, Grant had a freer hand in his options to transfer troop strength from the west to the eastern theater of war. Troops which were transferred from that part of the Mississippi River corridor lying to the south of Vicksburg traveled east by ocean steamer from New Orleans. Those troops which were transferred from the regions generally north of Vicksburg (inclusive of those which were sent from the Tennessee Valley) went east by rail.

---

[1]   Warren D. Crandall, *History of the Ram Fleet and the Mississippi Marine Brigade in the War for the Union on the Mississippi and its Tributaries: The Story of the Ellets and Their Men,* (St. Louis: Privately published by the Society of Survivors, 1907), p 274.

[2]   Streight, along with some of his officers and a few of his men, was later exchanged; however, the majority of his enlisted men ended up in the Confederate prison pen at Andersonville, Georgia.

[3]   Crandall, pp 277, 278, contradicts Alfred W. Ellet's estimate of "a seven hundred enemy force." Crandall claims that only about five hundred of the enemy made the April 26 attack against the Brigade.

[4]   *ORA,* I, 23, Part II, p 314.

[5]   Crandall, p 284.

[6]   Crandall, p 284.

[7]   *War of the Rebellion: Official Records of the Union and Confederate Armies*, (Washington, DC: Government Printing Office, 1880 - 1900). Facsimile Ed: (Harrisburg, PA: National Historical Society, 1971. Reprint. Historical Times, Inc., 1985), Series I, Volume 24, Part II, p 431.

[8]   *Personal Memoirs of U. S. Grant,* (New York: C. L. Webster and Co., 1886), I, p 544.

[9]   Crandall, p 296.

[10]   *Official Records of the Union and Confederate Navies in the War of the Rebellion,* (Washington, DC: Government Printing Office, 1894 - 1917), Series I, 25, pp 319, 320.

[11]   A most informative discussion on the Treasury Department's management of plantations along the lower Mississippi is found within Gates, pp 365-369.

[12]   *ORN,* I, 25, pp 215, 216.

[13]   *ORA,* I, 24, Part III, pp 589, 590.

[14]   *ORN,* I, 25, pp 212-214.

[15]   In his memoirs published some years after the war, Admiral David D. Porter wrote extensively of the events on the western rivers. Yet he never mentioned the matter of the "*J.J.B.*" letters. It is surprising that Porter's only comments referencing either Alfred W. Ellet or the Mississippi Marine Brigade are contained in one sentence. "The organization consisted of two thousand men, well equipped and fairly disciplined." Admiral David D. Porter, *The Naval History of the Civil War,* (Facsimile reprint, Secaucus, NJ: Castle, 1984), p 325. The lack of interest on Porter's part, as shown in his memoirs, was directly converse to the admiral's substantial correspondence just following the "*J.J.B.*" incident wherein Porter took it upon himself to lambaste Ellet and his brigade.

[16]   *ORN,* I, 25, p 370.

[17]   *ORN,* I, 25, p 429.

[18]   "Jeff Davis's plantation" which Porter's correspondence refers to was described by a reporter writing in the *New York Tribune,* March 6, 1863, as actually being owned in the 1860s by a "Dr. New." It had originally been the plantation of President Zachary Taylor who left it to his heirs, one of whom was Jefferson Davis. Taylor's heirs sold it to Dr. New who then planted cotton on most of its two thousand acres. The plantation was located

on the Mississippi's eastern shore on the next bend in the river below New Carthage. It is shown by name upon *Atlas to Accompany the Official Records of the Union and Confederate Armies,* (Washington, DC: Government Printing Office, 1891-1895), Plate XXXV, (4).

[19]   *ORN,* I, 25, pp 449, 450.

[20]   Following the withdrawal of Farragut from the Mississippi River, the Navy's upper and lower gunboat squadrons were merged under one command known as the Mississippi Squadron. As of May 20, 1863, the Mississippi River was divided into divisions under the overall command of the Mississippi Squadron commander. *ORN,* I, 25, pp 124, 125, 377, 379, 642.

[21]   *ORN,* I, 25, pp 726, 727.

[22]   *ORN,* I, 25, pp 727, 728.

[23]   *ORN,* I, 25, pp 727-730.

[24]   *ORN,* I, 25, p 524.

[25]   *ORN,* I, 25, pp 293, 294.

[26]   Crandall, p 315.

[27]   Crandall, pp 316, 317.

[28]   Crandall, pp 316, 317.

[29]   Crandall, p 317.

[30]   John S. C. Abbott, "Charles Ellet and his Naval Rams," *Harper's New Monthly Magazine,* XXXII, 1866, p 312.

[31]   Crandall, p 320.

[32]   *ORN,* I, 25, p 559.

[33]   *ORN,* I, 25, p 624.

[34]   *ORN,* I, 25, p 623.

[35]   *ORA,* I, 32, Part I, pp 395-401.

[36]   Crandall, p 363.

[37]   *ORA,* I, 32, Part II, p 407.

[38]   *ORA,* I, 32, Part II, p 498.

[39]   *ORA,* I, 34 Part II, pp 1064-1067.

[40]   Not so lucky was a naval patrol which was accompanied by troops carried aboard the transport *FREESTONE.* This expedition had been sent up the Yazoo during the third week in April. The crew of the Navy gunboat *USS PETREL,* which was in escort to *FREESTONE,* would be captured. *ORN,* I, 26, pp 249-259.

[41]   Accounts of what took place at Fort Pillow are confusing. We believe that the most accurate one is to be found within the R*eport of the Joint Committee on the Conduct and Expenditures of the War;* "Fort Pillow Massacre and Returned Prisoners," 38th Congress, 1st Session, Senate, Rep. Com. No. 63, May 5, 1864.

[42]   Through the survivors, word on what had happened spread along the river. It was at first feared that this information would adversely affect the numerous Negro units scattered in small garrisons along the Mississippi. In part this proved to be correct. However, in other cases, the resolve of the Negroes was strengthened, and their eagerness to fight the enemy increased.

[43]   Crandall, pp 393, 394.

[44]   It is relatively clear that early in the war, William Clarke Quantrill was commissioned a captain in the Confederate Army. He claimed to have been elevated to colonel, but those who have researched this claim, allege that there is no record that such a commission, if ever given, was confirmed by the Confederate government. Quantrill's bands always consisted of irregulars. As a force, his units were constantly fluctuating in strength, depending on the promised opportunity for loot and the amount of personal risk that such irregular service held at any given time. Quantrill counted among his lieutenants such people as William "Bloody Bill" Anderson, the Younger Brothers, and the James Brothers. After the war, these men would gain notoriety as criminals. During the war, Quantrill's most infamous exploit was the (1863) sacking of Lawrence, Kansas. Source: Michael Freeman, *Inside War,* (New York: Oxford University Press, 1989).

[45]   *ORA,* I, 41, Part I, p 123.

[46]   Crandall, pp 403, 404.

[47]   Crandall, p 405.

[48]   *ORA,* I, 34, Part I, p 952.

[49]   *ORA,* I, 34, Part IV, p 137,138.

[50]   *ORA,* I, 34, Part IV, p 186.

[51]   *ORA,* I, 34, Part I, pp 949, 950.

[52]   The bayou was identified by some of the participating Union commanders as "Fish Bayou"; other commanders called it by the name "Ditch Bayou". However, neither of these names is shown in the Index, *Atlas,*

ORA. From the geographic description, we believe it to have been the bayou shown in *Atlas, ORA* which led north out of Old River Lake and which terminated at the entrance to Bayou Macon.

[53]   Crandall, p 428.

[54]   Crandall, p 427.

[55]   Special Orders No. 86 cut at New Orleans, August 3, 1864, from Crandall.

[56]   Crandall, p 441.

[57]   *ORA,* I, 41, Part IV, p 609.

[58]   The detailed organization of the Consolidated Marine Regiment is outlined within Crandall, pp 445, 446.

[59]   Attorney James H. Purdy was formerly a major in the 59th New York Infantry and had been wounded at Antietam. At the time that he was hired by the enlisted men, Purdy was in partnership with another retired Union officer; together, they had set up a law practice in Vicksburg.

[60]   Crandall, p 454. The reference within the Townsend order of December 5, 1864, to those "detached from regiments in the field (without reenlisting)" was to those units which on February 11, 1863, had been permanently detached from their prior commands and transferred to the Mississippi Marine Brigade. These units were from the 59th and 63rd Illinois Infantry Regiments.

[61]   Frederick H. Dyer, *A Compendium of the War of the Rebellion,* (Reprint. Dayton, OH: The Press of Morningside Bookshop, 1978), pp 1302, 1303, 1319-1321.

[62]   The Texans who were with Banks on the Brownsville Expedition of October-December 1863 were Unionists who had been enlisted into the 1st Texas Cavalry (Union) at New Orleans back in November of 1862. These men were not the only Texans who would flock to the Union banner. After Brownsville, Texas, was occupied by Banks in November of 1863, a substantial number of Texans traveled both to Brownsville and to Brazos Santiago to enlist in the Union Army. Two organizations, the first designated the 2nd Texas Cavalry (Union) and the second, the Independent Company of Partisan Texas Rangers (Union), were formed from these volunteers. During the last months of the Civil War, a cavalry battalion given the designation 2nd Texas Cavalry (Union), was organized at Brazos Santiago. Sources: *Compendium;* also *ORA,* I, 26, Part I, p 398.

[63]   *ORA,* I, 26, Part I, pp 397, 398.

[64]   *ORA,* I, 26, Part I, p 396.

[65]   *ORA,* I, 26, Part I, pp 399, 401.

[66]   ORA, I, 26, Part I, pp 880, 881.

[67]   ORA, I, 34, Part I, pp 8, 9.

[68]   *ORA,* I, 32, Part III, p 242, 243.

[69]   ORA, I, 34, Part II, pp 55, 56. At the time of Halleck's communication to Banks, the area in Arkansas and Missouri "occupied by General Steele" was a tenuous holding at best.

[70]   ORA, I, 34, Part I, p 11.

[71]   *ORA,* I, 34, Part II, p 494.

[72]   The "reliable expert" was never named; however, it may well have been Sherman who wrote to Banks on January 31 telling him that based on his (Sherman's) personal knowledge, twelve feet of water could be expected over the rapids between the end of March and June during a normal year. William Tecumseh Sherman, *Memoirs of General W. T. Sherman,* (New York: The Library of America, 1990), pp 421, 422.

[73]   Troop strength is from the report of Banks; *ORA,* I, 34, Part I, pp 203, 204.

[74]   ORA, I, 34, Part I, p 377.

[75]   ORA, I, 34, Part I, p 379.

[76]   According to Wellington W. Withenbury, a pilot with long experience on the Red River, the stranding of *WOODFORD* was a result of her pilot's lack of knowledge of the river. He testified to that effect before the Congressional Committee on the Conduct of the War, 38th Congress, Second Session, 1865. See "The Red River Expedition," *Report of the Congressional Committee on the Conduct of the War,* (Washington: Government Printing Office, 1865), Volume 2, p 286.

[77]   *ORA,* I, 34, Part II, p 768.

[78]   *ORA,* I, 34, Part I, p 379.

[79]   *ORA,* I, 34, Part I, pp 379, 380. T. Kilby Smith's orders of April 7 (Special Order No. 21 and its Annex) designated fourteen transports in the van column with six to follow. He did not include *BLACK HAWK* in either the Order or the Annex and which brought the number of transports above Grande Ecore to twenty-one.

[80]   *ORA,* I, 34, Part I, p 380. T. Kilby Smith's orders named a total of twenty-one transports which went above Grande Ecore. (The *ALICE VIVIAN* would report to Smith four days later, having come upriver without escort. This would bring the total to twenty-two.) There had been, up to that time, (April 7) a total of forty Army transports, not counting the vessels of the Mississippi Marine Brigade, which had ascended the Red River as far as Alexandria. Those transports which could not get up over the rapids because of their draft either remained at Alexandria or were assigned to shuttle service between the Mississippi and Alexandria.

[81]   *ORN*, I, 26, p 60. According to the name board, the hulk was the *NEW FALLS CITY*. Examination disclosed that the Confederates had loaded her down with bank soil before scuttling.

[82]   *ORA*, I, 34, Part I, pp 380, 381. Also, see Rear Admiral Porter to Major General W. T. Sherman of April 16, 1864, in *ORN*, I, 26, pp 57-63.

[83]   *ORN*, I, 26, pp 45-48.

[84]   *ORA*, I, 32, Part III, pp 242, 243. Also *ORA*, I, 34, Part III, p 24.

[85]   *ORA*, I, 34, Part III, p 140. The mention of "coast packets" is interesting since it provides proof that under some circumstances, steamers used normally in the Gulf of Mexico were employed on at least the lower Mississippi system during the war.

[86]   See T. Kilby Smith's report, *ORA*, I, 34, Part I, p 381.

[87]   *ORA*, I, 34, Part I, p 381. It is curious to compare T. K. Smith's estimate of the enemy force (twelve hundred men) as against Rear Admiral Porter's of twenty-five hundred men. See *ORN*, I, 26, p 54.

[88]   *ORA*, I, 34, Part I, p 381.

[89]   Some very volatile differences in opinion soon took root as to who on the Union side deserved the most credit that day. Brigadier General T. Kilby Smith's account differs so widely from that of Lieutenant Commander Selfridge that they seem to have related entirely different events. For instance, Selfridge completely ignored the part the Army transports played, as if they had not been there, instead giving all the credit to the Navy gunboats. It was Selfridge's account which Porter would use exclusively when years later he recounted the action in his memoir. See Porter, pp 513, 514.

[90]   *ORN*, I, 26, pp 68-70.

[91]   Report of the Confederate General commanding, to the President of the Confederate States, August 21, 1864. *ORA*, I, 41, Part I, p 115-117. This report helps confirm that Confederate forces made no attempt to dam the Red River or its tributaries during the winter of 1863-1864.

[92]   *ORA*, I, 34, Part III, p 279.

[93]   *ORA*, I, 34, Part III, p 279. Grant's mention of "previous instructions" held by Banks may refer to operations to be conducted against Mobile, but this is only our conjecture.

[94]   *ORA*, I, 34, Part I, pp 402, 403. Lieutenant Colonel Uri B. Pearsall, commander of the 99th US Infantry (colored) troops (formerly the 5th Engineers Corps de Afrique), later claimed to be the originator of the plan. See *ORA*, I, Part I, pp 253-256. Pearsall's report was probably the origin of the incorrect impression. When Pearsall took credit for proposing the dams, he did not appear to be cognizant of Bailey's original proposal which had been made on April 9.

[95]   Charles Dana Gibson with E. Kay Gibson, *Marine Transportation in War, The U. S. Army Experience, 1775-1860*, (Camden, ME: Ensign Press, 1992), p 32. The use of dams to create either flumes or some similar rushes of water had become a common practice by the 1800s, particularly for lumbering operations where logs had to be floated downstream over what were normally shallow river beds. Most civil engineers who possessed prewar experience in areas where there was a lumbering industry would have been quite familiar with the construction and use of such dams. To create a sluiceway, one had only to raise the level of a river by partially damming the flow at a point somewhat downstream of the shallow area over which a deeper passage was desired. The dam builders would leave a "chute" through which the now elevated water was allowed to flow. If the area to pass over was an especially shallow one, the sluiceway could be temporarily blocked by a secondary dam laid across the face of the sluiceway. Once the desired head of water was reached, the temporary dam would be knocked out, and the objects to be floated over, would be released into the flow of the current. Gunboats and transports were, of course, somewhat different than logs, but the principle was identical.
    The technique for overcoming rapids by utilizing sluiceways seems to have had its origins with the American Indian. In 1761, Lieutenant John Montressor of the British Army wrote of the technique as he witnessed it during a scouting expedition over the old Indian trade route from Quebec to Moosehead Lake in the now state of Maine. Montressor related that the Indians would break open beaver dams to provide a head of water to carry their canoes over shallow areas lying downstream of the beaver dams. According to Montressor, the value of beaver dams for this purpose was so well recognized that the Governor of Canada had ordered that on regular travel routes, no beaver were to be hunted or otherwise killed. Montressor's journal is to be found within Kenneth Roberts's, *March to Quebec*, (Rockport, ME: Down East Books, 1980). George Armroyd's *Internal Navigation of the United States*, (New York: Burt Franklin, 1830, reprint by Lenox Hill, 1971) contains a 5-page treatise on "sluice navigation" (pp 292-296) which, as Armroyd presents it, was suitable for fairly small vessels with crews of three or four men, carrying no more than a few tons of freight. Armroyd maintains that for larger vessels, the results can be dangerous. He advocated sluiceways whenever the construction of canals would be cost prohibitive. He describes a sluiceway system then in use (1830) on the Kantaway River (a tributary to the Ohio River). It seems quite probable that most civil engineers of the mid-19th century would have been familiar with Armroyd's text.

[96]   The *USS EASTPORT* had hit a mine on April 15 while nine miles above Grand Ecore. The Navy's pump boats *CHAMPION NO. 3* and *CHAMPION NO. 5* had been sent up from Alexandria to effect her rescue. The floating was accomplished on or around April 21 which was also the time when Grand Ecore was being evacuated. After *USS EASTPORT* was floated, she was taken under tow; however, the *USS EASTPORT*'s greater than average draft (she was now even deeper in the water than normal because of her damaged condition) caused her to continually drag along the bottom until she finally grounded. Attempts to move her farther had to be halted.

[97]   Description of main dam on the Red River constructed under supervision of Lieutenant Colonel Joseph Bailey is taken from notes attached to section map of "Falls and Dam in Red River", Plate LIII, *Atlas, ORA*.

[98]   Report of Lieutenant Colonel U. B. Pearsall as found in *ORA*, I, 34, Part I, pp 253-256.

[99]   Banks was a more than interested observer during these efforts which he referred to as the construction of "the second series of dams." See *ORA*, I, 34, Part I, p 210. Lieutenant Colonel Joseph Bailey, the senior engineer in charge of the dam construction and the man who perhaps wrongly has ended up with the major credit for its eventual success, neglected in his official report to make any mention of the stranding of either the *USS CARONDELET* or the *USS MOUND CITY*. Reports by other Army officers and by Rear Admiral Porter specifically reference both strandings in their proper sequence of events. By not mentioning the early strandings, Bailey had placed himself, probably deliberately, in a much better light. It appears that this part of his report was an attempt to vindicate his own lack of foresight for not initially adopting the recommendation of Colonel Robinson and Lieutenant Colonel Pearsall to build the second dam. A donnybrook developed later over the question of who was owed the major credit for the eventual success in getting the fleet out of the Red River. Colonel Robinson states in his own version of the affair that two dams were originally recommended by Pearsall but that Bailey at the time had rejected the idea outright. Robinson's report is in *ORA*, I, 34, Part I, pp 248-253. Bailey does give some credit, it is true, to almost everyone involved, including Pearsall, but he totally glossed over the essential contribution of the second dam. There are other confusing elements within the official reports which discuss the project. For instance, Pearsall's report, filed on August 1, claimed that the work on the second dam took two full work days while Robinson's report, which was filed on June 13 (much closer to the actual happenings), claimed three days. The reports filed by Porter and Banks also state three days. Of engineering relevance concerning the second dam is the possibility that the "cribs of stone" shown on the sketch plans accompanying Bailey's report, and which appear as Plate LIII in *Atlas, ORA*, were extant structures in place prior to the expedition of March-May 1864. Considering how quickly the second dam was constructed, it may have been an addition to that existing structure.

[100]   Ludwell H. Johnson, *Red River Campaign: Politics and Cotton in the Civil War*. (Baltimore, MD: Johns Hopkins University Press, 1958), p 105. Also "Red River Expedition," *Report of the Joint Committee on the Conduct of the War*, 38th Congress, Second Session, (Washington: Government Printing Office, 1865), pp 71-73, 90.

[101]   David C. Edmonds, editor, *The Conduct of Federal Troops In Louisiana During the Invasions of 1863 and 1864: Official Report*. Compiled from sworn testimony, under direction of Governor Henry W. Allen, Shreveport, April 1865. (Lafayette, LA: Acadiana Press, 1988), p 141, fn 5.

[102]   "Red River Expedition," *Report of the Joint Committee*, pp xiv, xv, 74, 81-83, 87.

[103]   *ORA*, I, 34, Part I, pp 213, 214. Also "Red River Expedition," *Report of the Joint Committee*, pp 54, 66, 72-74, 80, 81, 176, 177, 197, 198, 208, 209, 223-225, 283-285, 302.

[104]   *Memoirs of Thomas O. Selfridge*, (New York and London: G. P. Putnam's Sons, 1924), pp 96, 97.

[105]   *ORN*, I, 26, pp 306, 307.

[106]   *ORN*, I, 26, p 363.

[107]   Original diary entry from *Diary of Gideon Welles*, edited by Howard K. Beale, (New York: W. W. Norton and Company, Inc., 1960) I, p. 157.

[108]   *Diary of Gideon Welles, Secretary of the Navy under Lincoln and Johnson*, (Boston: Houghton, Mifflin Company, 1911), I, p 157.

[109]   Charles L. Dufour, *The Night the War Was Lost*, (Lincoln, NE: University of Nebraska Press, 1990), pp 135-148.

[110]   "Red River Expedition," *Report of the Joint Committee*, pp 18, 78. Although not a subject raised during these Congressional hearings, it is of interest that the crews of the Army's vessels were also allowed prize money, a privilege awarded under the authority of the federal statutes of 1862. It is unclear, though, as to whether this privilege was commonly applied on the western rivers. Only one case could be located by us which involved the award of prize money to crewmen of a non naval vessel on the western rivers. That case related to the Ellets and the original ram fleet and dealt with captures made at the battle of Memphis back in 1862. A discussion on prize law pertinent to the crews of Army vessels is found within Appendix E. Appendix M discusses a federal court

case concerning a prize claim involving the seizure of cotton on the Mississippi by an Army cavalry force operating from Army transports.

[111] *ORA*, I, 34, Part III, p 307.

[112] Edmonds, p 152.

[113] Johnson, p 224.

[114] Porter, p 533.

[115] One vessel whose draft had not allowed it to reach Simsport was the *USS AVENGER*, one of the two newly constructed rams which Alfred W. Ellet had hoped to add to his Mississippi Marine Brigade fleet back in December 1863 but which had been taken over by Porter. At the Red River Landing, the *USS AVENGER* took Major General Nathaniel P. Banks on board and headed for New Orleans. Shortly after Banks arrived at New Orleans, he resigned from the Army in virtual disgrace. For more on *USS AVENGER* see *Dictionary of American Naval Fighting Ships*, Volume I-A, 1991 edition.

[116] *ORA*, I, 34, Part III, p 665. Also "Red River Expedition," *Report of the Joint Committee*, p 335. Also see *ORN*, I, 26, pp 149, 153-155, 793 as well as Porter, p 533.

[117] The campaign had also been costly in terms of vessels. The Navy lost three of its gunboats and two auxiliaries. The Army lost four transport as well as the hospital steamer *WOODFORD*.

[118] Names of vessels which were part of the Red River Expedition are from *ORA*, I, 34, Part I, pp 379, 380, 474-475, and 621; Part III, pp 36, 60, 71, 268-9, 715 and from *ORN*, I, 26, pp 25, 105-107, 130. See Crandall for Mississippi Marine Brigade vessels which were on the Red River Expedition during March and April, 1864.

[119] Both Robert E. Lee and Braxton Bragg were full generals in the Confederate Army. At this time (September 1863), the highest rank in the Union Army was major general.

[120] *ORA*, I, 30, Part I, p 35.

[121] *ORA*, I, 30, Part I, pp 35, 36.

[122] *ORA*, I, 30, Part I, pp 220, 221.

[123] The Suck is shown on Plate CXLIX of *Atlas, ORA* as well as upon the sketch map we have provided which is entitled "The *Cracker Line* Route Into Chattanooga.".

[124] Within some official reports and within the *Atlas, ORA*, Brown's Landing is referred to as "Brown's Ferry".

[125] Major General Joseph Hooker's quartermaster, Colonel William G. LeDuc, executed a survey report of the river between Chattanooga and Bridgeport on October 2, 1863. LeDuc's report contains an excellent description of the area at that time. See General William G. LeDuc, "The Little Steamboat That Opened the *Cracker Line*," *Battles and Leaders*, III, pp 676-678.

[126] General Joseph S. Fullerton, "The Army of the Cumberland," *Battles and Leaders*, III, p 719.

[127] Reports in *ORA* which mention the five salvaged wrecks at Chattanooga are conflicting as to whether they were scuttled by the Confederates when they evacuated Chattanooga, or sunk by Union artillery fire prior to the occupation of that city by Rosecrans's force.

[128] *ORA*, I, 31, Part I, p 755.

[129] *ORA*, I, 31, Part I, p 56.

[130] *ORA*, I, 31, Part I, p 60.

[131] Hodges's report makes mention of having to get the *PAINT ROCK* up through the Suck before her cargo could be unloaded. If the report was factually correct, that circumstance was probably the fault of overtaxed wagon teams working overland from Kelly's Landing. The shortage of draft animals could have made it necessary on occasion for the supply steamers to pass by Kelly's Landing and be routed around the great bend through the Suck to off-load to wagons at the northern end of the Brown's Landing pontoon bridge. See *ORA*, I, 31, Part I, p 67. The Pictorial Division of the National Archives possesses two photographs taken around the end of 1863 which show steamers being mechanically assisted through a difficult area of the Tennessee River below Chattanooga. The captions of those two photographs state that the area was the Suck; however, the terrain features seem more typical of the Narrows which was further downriver. One of these photographs is reproduced in this volume. We have been told by personnel at the Chickamauga Battlefield facility that the river banks between Chattanooga and Bridgeport underwent extensive change after the turn of the century making present-day visual comparisons quite difficult.

[132] Edwards later built two gunboats at Bridgeport to the Quartermaster Department's account. These two vessels, *GENERAL GRANT* and *GENERAL BURNSIDE*, were chartered to the Navy and were operated by the Navy as guard boats on the upper Tennessee. They were returned to the Army following the end of the war. The Navy also operated the *GENERAL SHERMAN* and *GENERAL THOMAS* which would be converted into gunboats from their former freight carrying roles. A Quartermaster Department listing prepared during the first months following the war listed *GENERAL BURNSIDE* and *GENERAL GRANT* and two other vessels, "*GUNBOAT A*" and a "*GUNBOAT B*", as being built at Bridgeport. However, the Quartermaster clerk who prepared that list was apparently not aware that the "A" and "B" designations had been dropped in favor of the assigned names,

GENERAL BURNSIDE and *GENERAL GRANT.* Identification of ten of the vessels built by Captain Edwards at Bridgeport has been gleaned from *Executive Document No. 337,* House of Representatives, 40th Congress, 2nd Session and from the Quartermaster General's Report as incorporated within the Report of the Secretary of War to the Congress, incorporated to which were field reports dated during 1866. The information on the *CHATTANOOGA* and the *CHICKAMAUGA* which were converted at Bridgeport, and the five hulks which were salvaged at Chattanooga, was derived from assorted Quartermaster Department lists located within *Executive Document No. 337*, House of Representatives, 40th Congress, Second Session. The vessels turned over to the Navy are listed in *ORN,* I, 26, p 556.

[133]   Sherman, p 379.

[134]   In one recorded case, the Army commandeered at a Philadelphia foundry three locomotives being constructed there for the New York and Harlem Valley Railroad of New York State. These three locomotives were then moved to the west to help alleviate the shortage of railroad equipment in that theater. *ORA,* III, 3, p 1083.

[135]   Sherman, p 390.

[136]   Full reports on this action are to be found in *ORN,* I, 26, pp 582-586.

[137]   *ORN,* I, 26, p 589.

[138]   *ORN,* I, 26, pp 590, 591.

[139]   Johnsonville is sometimes difficult to find on maps of the Civil War era. Within the *Atlas, ORA,* it is shown on some of the maps but not on others. The town is indicated on Plate XXIV where the railroad spur connection to Nashville also appears. Plate CXV depicts a detailed plan of Johnsonville. The map opposite page 30 of *ORN,* I, 26, also shows the town. Johnsonville is also depicted on our map, page 167 this volume. On present day maps, the geographic area known in the 1860s as the town of Johnsonville is now under water. Close to the location of the original town, is the present-day town New Johnsonville, a relocation made necessary when the Tennessee River was dammed in the 1930s under the program of the Tennessee Valley Authority.

[140]   The railroad bridge referred to by the pilot of the *USS UNDINE* crossed the Tennessee River at Sandy Island near the narrow land constriction separating the Tennessee and the Cumberland rivers.

[141]   Despite the reports of *ANNA's* destruction, her crew managed to get her to the safety of the Ohio River and then into a repair yard.

[142]   *ORN,* I, 26, p 604.

[143]   *ORN,* I, 26, pp 611-614.

[144]   In a telegram to Washington dated p.m., November 4, which dealt with the Johnsonville emergency, Major General George H. Thomas indicated his belief that at that time the troop strength at Johnsonville "was nearly four thousand men." If Colonel C. R. Thompson's estimate of "less than eight hundred officers and men" was correct, then Thomas obviously overstated the situation. *ORN,* I, 26, pp 619, 620.

[145]   Most of these employees were Negroes, many of them contrabands who most probably were totally unfamiliar with the use of firearms. The defense of Johnsonville and Nashville in the fall of 1864 appears to have been one of the few isolated instances during the Civil War when a body of shore-based civilian employees of the War Department were ordered to take up arms.

[146]   *ORN,* I, 26, p 623.

[147]   Thompson to Thomas within *ORA,* I, 39, Part III, p 654.

[148]   *ORA,* I, 45, Part I, p 1001.

[149]   *ORA,* I, 39, Part I, pp 860-863.

[150]   *ORA,* I, 52, Part II, p 777.

[151]   General J. B. Hood, "The Invasion of Tennessee," *Battles and Leaders*, IV, p 435.

[152]   Report of Brigadier General Lewis B. Parsons to Major General M. C. Meigs, October 15, 1865, as found in *ORA,* I, 52, Part I, p 706.

[153]   Erna Risch, *Quartermaster Support of the Army: A History of the Corps 1775 - 1939,* (Washington, DC: Office of the Quartermaster General, 1962), pp 433, 434.

[154]   Reports concerning the attack against Mobile Bay and which mention the transports involved are scattered throughout *ORA,* I, 39, Part I; *ORA,* I, 49, and *ORA,* I, 52.

PART VIII

THE EASTERN THEATER
1864 - 1865

THE GENERAL SITUATION
(Spring 1864)

Territorial Control

As of April 1864, the coastal fringes of South Carolina and Georgia were firmly in Union hands. Union strong points were maintained in South Carolina at Beaufort, Folly Island near Charleston, Morris Island near Charleston, and farther south at Hilton Head and at Port Royal. In Georgia, a garrison was maintained at Fort Pulaski on the lower Savannah River. In Florida, Fernandina, Mayport, Saint Augustine, and Key West had Union garrisons. Jacksonville was occupied, but only on an on-again, off-again basis.

The open sounds of North Carolina were by now completely dominated by the Union Navy, but that absolute control did not include the navigable portions of the rivers leading into those sounds. There were moderate-sized garrisons of Federal troops in North Carolina in the communities of New Berne, Plymouth, and Washington; but these were under constant threat of attack and dislodgement by the enemy, a circumstance that had existed since 1862 when those posts had first been established. The uncertain tenure of the Union presence was demonstrated on April 20 when Confederate troops (with the aid of the ironclad *CSS ALBEMARLE*) defeated the garrison at Plymouth, an attack which resulted in heavy losses to the defenders.

Those land areas lying south of Norfolk which were adjacent to the Albemarle and Chesapeake Canal and the Dismal Swamp Canal were in Union hands, but these were rather tenuous holdings since that part of the countryside continued to be subjected to small unit enemy raids.

In the Chesapeake Bay region, the lower reaches of the James and the York rivers were firmly occupied by Union forces, but the upper tidal sections of both of those rivers were within Confederate lines. Farther to the north on the Chesapeake, the western shore was at times a sort of no-man's land. North of the York River, the mouths of most rivers entering the Chesapeake on the Virginia side were under what could be termed Union Navy containment; however, under the cover of darkness, considerable smuggling went on. On the Virginia side, this was carried out by Confederates, and across the bay on the Maryland side by Southern sympathizers or just plain entrepreneurs.

The Army of the Potomac had spent the winter of 1863-1864 in cantonment while holding a static line along the northern bank of the Rapidan River. The land area which lay between the army on the Rapidan and the capital at Washington was relatively secure, being maintained through a system of strong outposts situated along the main line of communication and through roving cavalry patrols. Supplies were transported over the Orange and Alexandria Railroad as well as by wagon trains from the depots at Washington and at Alexandria.

Lee's Army of Northern Virginia had occupied opposing entrenchments along the southern banks of the Rapidan during the winter of 1863-1864. Lee's main commissary source was the Shenandoah Valley. Richmond and all it stood for, both from a political sense and for its value as a transportation center, as well as a manufacturing center for war materiel, could not be held without the succor of the Shenandoah; therefore, it would be Confederate policy to defend the Shenandoah at all costs.

Strategic Planning

Despite occasional setbacks, the military situation overwhelmingly favored the Union. The political scenario as it might affect the outcome of the war was nowhere near as promising. Only six months remained until the next presidential election, and the outlook for Lincoln to remain in office was uncertain. In the north, the public-at-large was beginning to weary of what appeared to be a war without end, one which was draining off the North's best manhood along with an inordinate amount of its wealth. Viewed by a public which had yet to witness any sustained progress within the Eastern Theater of the war, the deadlock between the Army of the Potomac and Lee's Army of Northern Virginia appeared to be almost a permanent thing. True, Gettysburg in July of 1863 had been a point of serious downturn for Southern fortunes; but once Lee was back on Virginia's soil, he appeared to be as invincible as ever. The successes which would later be obtained by Sherman's army in Georgia were well into the future. Sherman would not leave Chattanooga for his advance on Atlanta until May, and he would not leave Atlanta for his march to the sea until the fall.

For those charged with developing Union strategy in the early spring of 1864, it was amply clear that if the war was going to be carried to a victorious conclusion, one in favor of the Union, then some clear path of success had to become evident before the November elections. Lincoln appreciated the reality of this, and so did the Army's new general-in-chief, Lieutenant General Ulysses S. Grant. Grant's plan for a spring offensive was, therefore, to be geared toward a campaign of absolute conquest. In order to succeed, he would have to force the Confederates to stretch their limited manpower and logistical resources to the breaking point. This meant that Federal armies would have to attack simultaneously on a number of fronts. To a large extent, Grant's forthcoming campaign was to be a war of attrition. Such a strategy was in Grant's favor. The South's manpower barrel was rapidly emptying. Already, men well into their fifties were being called to the colors. For the Northern armies, the amount of manpower available to be fed to the cannons was still adequate in numbers even though the quality of that resource was noticeably deteriorating.

The Draft Act of 1863

Back in March 1863, President Lincoln had signed the nation's first draft act, the major means remaining to the federal government by which enough men could be obtained to fill the Army's ranks. The patriotic enthusiasm which had caused men to voluntarily flock to the colors during the first two years of the war was something in the past. The original ranks of 1861 had been seriously depleted through a combination of battle casualties, desertion, disease, and the ending of terms of enlistment. The shortage in the army's troop strength caused by these factors, and which together gave rise to the need for a draft, would have various side effects. One effect would be shortages developing among the civilian crews on vessels employed in the service of the Quartermaster Department. Prior to the draft act of 1863, state militias had been subject to draft call-up by units as authorized by the Act of August 9, 1862. Under that act, militia units were mobilized into the federal service, usually for periods of up to ninety days. Certain civilian occupations were, however, automatically deferred from militia call-ups. These deferments were for telegraph operators; railroad engineers; those employed in any public arsenal; political officers of the United States; Customs officers and clerks; postal personnel including stage drivers involved with the mails; ferryboat workers; all mariners actually employed in the sea service of any citizen or merchant within the United States, and all engineers and pilots of registered or licensed steamboats and steam ships. The later citizen's Draft Act of March 3, 1863, in its Section 7, specifically referenced certain occupations no longer being exempt, among which were mariners.[1] As more and more merchant seamen were called up by the citizen's draft, crew quality on the Quartermaster's transports suffered accordingly.

Besides the draft, a bounty system had been inaugurated which was designed to entice men to enlist. When lumped together, the draft and the bounty system, had an adverse effect in that they resulted in high desertion rates before men even reached the army. Men would sign up for the bounty, then desert, sign up again under another name, and then desert again. In the majority of cases, the deserters managed to escape detection.

Chaos at Sea for an Army Recruit

In an attempt to stop the desertion of draftees and bounty men, the army began incarcerating them within containment facilities until such time that they could be shipped to training camps. Some of the men involved were from the lower elements of society, and since a goodly number of them had already experienced time in jail, such incarceration by the military was probably not overly stressful. to them. But to those whose motives for joining the colors were honest and sincere, it must have had a traumatic effect. One such unfortunate was 16-year-old Frank Wilkeson. Wilkeson was a farmer's son from upstate New York who, after enlisting soon found himself housed under guard outside of Albany, New York. This housing was in a facility which before the war had been a county prison. After two miserable weeks in this lock-up, Wilkeson and his fellow novice soldiers were shipped by Hudson River steamer to New

York City. They were then marched, still under guard, through that city's streets to an ocean transport scheduled to depart the next day for Alexandria, Virginia. (At the time, Alexandria was the main recruit depot for men assigned to the Army of the Potomac.) It was still daylight when Wilkeson and his companions filed up the transport's gangway. What happened that night is contained in memoirs which Wilkeson wrote and published some years after the war.

> The light grew dimmer and dimmer, and then the interior of the hold was dark, except such portions as were dimly lighted by the bars of light that shot through the ports and that which was reflected down the hatches in square columns. We fought and howled and swore with rage and pain. Through it all the smell was overpowering. The deadly, penetrating odors of ulcerous men, who suffered from unnameable diseases, of stale tobacco smoke, the sickening fumes of dead whiskey, and the smell of many unclean ruffians made the air heavy with a horrible stench. Many recruits lost their bounty money. They were robbed and beaten almost to death. Exhaustion quieted the devils down during the night, and then we slept on the filthy floor. There was not a bunk in the entire hold. The next morning we awoke with sore heads and faint stomachs, and, under orders, washed out the vast room as well as we could. We remained in New York harbor for two days, waiting for the officer who had killed the runaway to be tried and acquitted. During the delay the guards refused to allow a row boat to come near us. Then we started for Alexandria, in Virginia.
>
> Shortly after we had begun to steam for the sea I saw the two alert-eyed recruits, who had attracted my attention when we were on the Hudson River steamboat, in the hold with us. I am positive that they were not with us while we lay in New York harbor. They walked among us for a couple of hours, talking pleasantly. The younger of the twain inquired kindly as to how I got my face pounded, and he got me a bowl of clean water to bathe it in. Toward noon they produced chuck-luck cloths and dice boxes, and furious gambling began. I was the only man on board who was not bounty paid or laden. I had but $10, which my father had given to me when I was in the [Albany,] New York barracks, so I could not join in the sport. I have seen gambling -- and wild, reckless gambling too -- in many mining camps, and in towns where Texas cattle were sold, and in new railroad towns beyond the Missouri; but never since the war closed have I seen such reckless gambling as went on day and night in this vessel. Men crowded around the brace games, and speedily lost their bounties. Then the losers would boldly, in broad daylight, rob their comrades. I saw gangs of robbers knock men down and go through their pockets, and unbuckle money belts from their waists; and if they protested, their cries were silenced with boot heels stamped into their faces.
>
> By the time this floating hell and its cargo of cowardly devils had got into Chesapeake Bay, the two alert-eyed gamblers possessed about all the money the six hundred recruits had. Then they grew fearful of the men they had robbed, and hired some of the soldiers to guard them. I saw two soldiers paid $100 each for guarding them while they slept. Unguarded, they would have been killed and torn limb from limb. At Alexandria we, dirty and smelling so vilely that the street dogs refused to approach us, were marched to clean barracks and well fed. That evening I paid a soldier $5 to stand over a bathtub and watch me while I bathed. I had to go outside of the barracks to bathe. The next morning the two alert-eyed gamblers were missing. I never saw them again. I knew that they were not recruits, but gamblers in league with high officials -- gamblers carefully selected for their professional skill and pleasing address, and that they had been sent on the sea voyage to rob the bounty laden recruits. The trip had been exceedingly profitable. At the lowest calculation

there had been $240,000 in the recruits' pockets when they left New York. I do not believe the same pockets contained $70,000 when we arrived at Alexandria.[2]

The killing to which Wilkeson referred involved a man who attempted to break ranks while the recruits were being marched from the Hudson River steamer to the ocean transport at New York. The officer in charge of the armed escort chased the man down and shot him through the back of the head. During the trip down the Hudson from Albany to New York, guards had shot two other men who had jumped overboard in an attempt to escape.

Certainly not all of the transports carrying recruits were as unregulated and riotous as the one on which Wilkeson traveled to Virginia. It may be that he exaggerated the conditions he witnessed. Exaggeration is certainly not uncommon whenever veterans relate their experiences twenty years or more after the event, yet in most such cases there is usually a strong vein of accuracy woven into the telling. Riotous conduct on the part of Union Army recruits, who in all too many cases after 1863 were the sweepings of northern cities, did take place on several occasions, and Wilkeson's experiences would have been but one such episode.

The transition which saw recruits turned into soldiers started once they arrived at a training depot or, as happened to some, when they were assigned directly to a line regiment. Discipline was the first hard lesson to be learned. The teaching methods were often draconian, but brutality had become a necessary factor that was applied to those who could not be reached by less persuasive means. The draftees and the bounty men of post 1863 were by no means an improvement over what once had been an enthusiastic all-volunteer army. Nevertheless, most of these men soon became conditioned to the life of soldiering, and they blended into the Union juggernaut that by April 1865 would beat the Confederacy to its knees.

THE ARMY'S GUNBOATS AND AMPHIBIOUS UNITS
IN THE EASTERN THEATER

Beginning in 1861, Army personnel had been attached as part of the crews aboard some of the Army's vessels operating within the Eastern Theater. The idea for such employment seems to have originated with Major General Benjamin Butler during the planning which resulted in the expedition to Hatteras Inlet in August of 1861. Brigadier General John G. Foster carried on the concept. (Foster had been part of the second expedition to the North Carolina sounds under Burnside which in 1862 had taken Roanoke Island and New Berne.)[3]

During the spring of 1863, Foster had met in conference with the commander of the North Atlantic Blockading Squadron, Rear Admiral S. P. Lee. Lee was then the senior naval officer of a region which included the coastal belt of North Carolina, the same area over which Foster held military responsibility. Lee's primary job was to bottle up those ports through which blockade runners attempted ingress and egress. Although blockading responsibility was essentially a matter of ocean surveillance, the Navy was also tasked with supporting the Army's presence within the inland sounds and rivers of the Carolinas. During their meeting, Lee emphasized to Foster that the Navy did not possess enough shallow draft gunboats to patrol the outer sounds and all of the tidal river mouths leading off from those sounds. It was on the banks of many of those tidal rivers that the Army had established its garrisons. Lee explained that the situation would soon worsen since a number of the Navy's gunboats now on station within the inland sounds were scheduled to be withdrawn for service elsewhere. Lee told Foster that the Navy was already stretched far too thinly throughout the Carolina tidal zone, and he believed this would invite a takeover by the Confederates. Foster could only bow to the reality of what Lee had said, and he told the admiral that he would undertake to reduce the number of garrisons by consolidating them into a more manageable arrangement. Not long after this meeting, it became apparent to Foster that despite reductions in the number of garrisons, the support afforded by the Navy's gunboats had become so limited as to present an imminent danger.

At about this time, there were rumors afoot that the enemy was building at least one heavy ironclad to challenge Union supremacy on the Carolina sounds. Foster came to the realization that the Army would have to handle its own security on the sounds, but to do this, it would need a fleet of its own heavy gunboats.

The Army's Gunboats and Attack Transports

In the fall (1863), Foster arranged for the purchase of four ferryboat type hulls which were then either undergoing construction, or were about to undergo construction, at the shipyard of Norman Wiard in New York City. No plans or photographs seem to be in existence which show the four vessels which Foster ordered from the Wiard yard. One report written at the time describes them as having a length overall of "upwards of 140 feet and drawing 3 1/2 feet." Their freeboard was extraordinarily low, one comment made at that time stating that they were suitable only for river and sound navigation, and then only in fine weather. Foster had specifications drawn for their completion, these calling for the vessels to be sheathed with armor. The decks would be reinforced so they could carry either four 3.67 caliber cannon or four 12-pound howitzers. When completed, they were to be named *GENERAL BURNSIDE*, *RENO*, *PARKE*, and *GENERAL FOSTER*.

The *RENO* appears in the records as having been operational near New Berne, North Carolina, in January of 1864. The *GENERAL BURNSIDE* is not mentioned in records until that February, and the *PARKE* not until some weeks later. The last of this group to be completed was probably the *GENERAL FOSTER* which appears to have been operational in October when she was reported as landing a reconnaissance force on the Wicomico River in Virginia.[4]

During the summer of 1864, two more gunboats are known to have been under construction in New York, being scheduled for assignment to an organization which would come to be known as Graham's Naval Brigade, an organization which is described later in this chapter. These two gunboats would be named *SAVANNAH* and *AUGUSTA*. Although their plans were never located by the War Department editors who compiled the *Official Records...Armies*, it is probable that they were of similar design and armament to the preceding four that had been ordered by Foster. Both were delivered in early 1865 and became operational soon after.[5]

For some time, the Army's regional commands within the Department of Virginia and North Carolina (which following November of 1863 had become incorporated under the jurisdiction of Butler's Army of the James) had a number of shallow draft vessels fitted out as gunboats. Some were tinclads while others were only of reinforced wooden construction. They were named

BOMBSHELL	*SAMUEL RUATAN*
C. P. SMITH	*SEYMOUR*
CURRITUCK	*SHRAPNEL*
FLORA TEMPLE	*SMITH BRIGGS*
GENERAL JESUP	*WEST END*
GRENADE	*YOUNG ROVER*

Another Army gunboat, *ALLISON*, was operating in the Carolina sounds up until the spring of 1863; but following that time, nothing is known of her in a gunboat capacity. There may have been another gunboat, that one named *VIDETTE* (sometimes in the records spelled *"VEDETTE"*), which is mentioned in an 1864 report as having been on the North Carolina sounds during that time.[6]

The twelve known to be operating by late 1863 were only lightly armored, and they were too few and too widely distributed to have substantially aided in the security of the North Carolina garrisons. In fact, the evidence is fairly certain that eight of the twelve had operated for most of their time in the Chesapeake area rather than in the sounds of the Carolinas -- *C. P. SMITH*, *FLORA TEMPLE*, *SAMUEL RUATAN*, *SMITH BRIGGS*, *WEST END*, and *YOUNG ROVER* seem to have been employed on routine patrols and, on occasion, amphibious landing operations along the Virginia side of the Chesapeake Bay. This activity began for them shortly following the New Year in 1863. In August of 1863, *CURRITUCK* and *GENERAL JESUP* are known to have been assigned to inland blockade duty, starting from the Elizabeth River at Norfolk, south through the Dismal Swamp Canal, to the Pasquotank River below Elizabeth City. As to the remaining three: *BOMBSHELL* was lost at Plymouth, North Carolina, the victim of a Confederate attack on that place in April of 1864.[7] *SHRAPNEL, GRENADE*, and *SEYMOUR* appear to have been the only two Army gunboats which were operating on the North Carolina sounds in early 1864.[8] (Two years earlier, the Army gunboat *PICKET* and nineteen of her crew were lost during an attack on Washington, North Carolina.) Two more vessels that the Army began utilizing as gunboats during 1864 were the *SAMUEL L. BREWSTER* and the *CHARLES CHAMBERLAIN*; both are known to have spent most if not all of their operational time on the Virginia estuaries off-lying Chesapeake Bay.

Besides operating its own gunboats, the Army maintained, both on the sounds of North Carolina as well as on the estuaries off the Chesapeake estuaries, a number of armed transports which were regularly assigned to amphibious attack missions. Some of these vessels were owned by the Quartermaster Department, and some were chartered to the Quartermaster through various formats. One such transport was the *S. R. SPAULDING* which worked in close conjunction with the gunboat *SAMUEL L. BREWSTER* until the latter vessel was lost, a result of enemy action in May of 1864.

A staff member of the Quartermaster General's office addressed a memo to the Secretary of War on November 1864 at a time when the Union was at last gaining a full operational ascendancy over the coastal zones of the Carolinas and Georgia. The memorandum spoke to the Army's changing need for combatant vessels. It also mentions the development at that time of what appears to have been "down-ramp" assault craft which were under construction "at Philadelphia" and which had been designed especially for the Army for its use in amphibious attack operations.

> Commanding generals of all maritime departments desire to have, subject to their immediate orders, a few armed light-draft gunboats or transports, to be used in movements of troops upon the bays and inland channels of navigation, in which they find it difficult always to command the services of the naval flotilla.

At a time when the naval fleets were imperfectly organized this aid from the Quartermaster's Department was no doubt necessary. Now the policy of continuing the employment of these vessels, except as transports, is doubtful. Quite a number of these vessels still remain in service upon the James and the waters of North and South Carolina.

The department is constructing at Philadelphia four light-draft steam ferry transports, capable of carrying a battery of artillery, with its horses, a train of wagons, or a regiment of infantry, crossing the widest estuaries, or even making short sea voyages, and still of such light draft as to run inshore and make landings without the construction of wharves or docks. They are of about 350 tons burden, strongly built, and will be very useful in operations along the South Atlantic and Gulf coasts, and in ascending the navigable rivers which empty into the Gulf of Mexico...[9]

The actual date of operational availability for the four assault craft being built in Philadelphia is not clear. It is known, though, that they went into service at some point during the early spring of 1865. Correspondence from the Office of the Quartermaster General dated in June mentions all four, describing them as being "twin-screw" and named *FOOTE, STANTON, WELLES*, and *PORTER*. At that time, the four were located along the "South Atlantic Coast" (probably North Carolina) where they were later adapted so they could make an open ocean passage to Texas. After arrival in Texas, they were to operate within the coastal lagoons in support of Major General Philip H. Sheridan's expeditionary force.[10]

Graham's Naval Brigade

The concept for an Army "naval brigade" to be used within the eastern theater originated with Colonel William A. Howard during 1863. Howard had been the commander of an earlier unit, the 1st New York Marine Artillery "Naval Brigade" (also sometimes loosely referred to only as the "naval brigade"). That unit was disbanded in March of 1863, and its men distributed at that time to other organizations.[11] Following the 1st New York Marine Artillery "Naval Brigade's" disbandment, Howard was sent to New York with authorization to recruit a regiment to be designated as the 13th New York Heavy Artillery.[12] Company A of the 13th New York Heavy Artillery was sworn in during August of 1863 at Elmira, New York. That fall the regiment began moving by increments to its first assigned duty station which was Norfolk, Virginia. Following their recruitment, some companies were immediately forwarded on to New Berne, North Carolina, where they became part of that town's garrison. Companies I, K, L, and, for a time, Company M would be assigned as part of the permanent crews of the four vessels which Major General J. G. Foster had ordered converted at the Wiard yard in New York during October 1863 and which appear to have become readied for operational duty beginning in early 1864. The Army gunboats *SAVANNAH* and *AUGUSTA* were also manned by men from these companies.[13]

Despite the fact that the concept for a naval brigade had originated with William A. Howard, its command would go instead to a former naval midshipman, Charles K. Graham. Graham had joined the Army from civilian life at the outbreak of the war, and by 1864, he had risen to the rank of brigadier general. On February 9, 1864, the following order was issued under the signature of Butler's adjutant.

Fortress Monroe, Virginia
February 9, 1864

General Orders No. 18.
    Brigadier General Charles K. Graham, USV, is hereby placed in command of all Army gunboats in this department, and will be obeyed and respected accordingly.
    By command of Major General B. F. Butler:
        R. S. Davis, Major and Assistant Adjutant General[14]

    From the start, Graham was given a relatively free hand with the employment of his command. Organizationally, it was carried on the roster of the Army of the James as "Graham's Naval Brigade." Graham reported directly to General Headquarters, Department of Virginia and North Carolina, the department which had become part of Benjamin Butler's Army of the James. This chain of command arrangement seems to have pertained to all circumstances in which Graham's Naval Brigade was involved, whether within the jurisdiction of the Army of the James or on detached duty to any other military jurisdiction.[15] By the summer of 1864, Graham's Naval Brigade was composed of the detached Companies A, B, F, G of the 3rd Pennsylvania Heavy Artillery and the detached Companies I, K, L of the 13th New York Heavy Artillery. There were also a few assignments of individuals and detachments from other regiments, e.g., the 99th New York Infantry.[16] As of mid-year 1864, the troop strength assigned to Graham's Naval Brigade had reached 845 officers and men.[17] The Brigade was bereft of any regimental structure, being organized solely of infantry companies detached from established regiments. Each company was commanded by either a captain or a lieutenant reporting directly to the brigade's adjutant regarding the particular company's activity and location, including any information on vessels for which that company commander held responsibility.
    In the summer of 1864, Graham had his eye on six extant Army gunboats. Major General J. G. Foster suggested to Major General Halleck that these be assigned to the duties of a roving amphibious assault force.

Headquarters Department of the South, Hilton Head, South Carolina
June 22, 1864

Major General H. W. Halleck, Chief of Staff
Armies of the United States; Washington, DC
General:
    I beg leave again to refer to the want of light draught vessels for the operations that I contemplate in this department. With several light draught steamers, such as we had at Fortress Monroe and in North Carolina, I could at any time make incursions through the creeks and inland waters of this department that would result in the destruction of much rebel property, bridges, trestle-work, cotton, etc. If I could have the four light draught steamers *BURNSIDE*,[1] *RENO, PARKE,* and *FOSTER*,[2] with the two new ones now built in New York, the *SAVANNAH* and *AUGUSTA*, with the 13th New York Volunteers (heavy artillery), Colonel Howard, to man them, I could keep up a small force in constant motion harassing the enemy. For this advantage I would be willing to exchange two or three regiments of the best infantry.

I enclose you [sic] a drawing of these boats.* Each of them has six launches, and is armed with six boat howitzers.

I have the honor to be, very respectfully, your obedient servant.

J. G. Foster, Major General, Commanding[18]

[1] *GENERAL BURNSIDE*

[2] *GENERAL FOSTER*

* The editors of *Official Records...Armies* were not able to locate the drawing.

Although this particular request was objected to by the Quartermaster Department on the apparent grounds that the vessels were instead needed as local use transports, all indications are that the request was approved and acted on. Subsequently, all six named vessels were operational in a gunboat/attack transport role as part of Graham's organization.[19]

Most of the operations of Graham's Naval Brigade were conducted by one or two gunboats in concert with transports which carried aboard one or more companies of that brigade to serve as landing forces either for reconnaissance or for assault against suspected enemy trouble spots. More often than not, the companies as well as the vessels of the brigade were separated over a wide geographic area. During the first attack against Fort Fisher in North Carolina, which took place during December of 1864, details from Graham's Naval Brigade accompanied the expedition to man twenty surf boats which were employed in taking the assault troops into the beach.[20]

The evidence is quite clear that some if not all of the Army gunboats in the eastern theater had mixed crews consisting of both enlisted men and civilian employees of the Quartermaster Department.[21] By 1864, the vessel commanders were probably all military officers. Two of the gunboats seem to have had naval officers in command who had been loaned by the Navy for that particular purpose but who while on that assignment reported directly to the adjutant of Graham's Naval Brigade. *SAMUEL L. BREWSTER*, was commented upon by some of the Navy people on the James River during 1864 as having considerable firepower and being crewed by "fifty-two souls, all belonging to the Army with the exception of her master (a loaned Navy ensign) and two engineers. "[22]

At least as late as January of 1865, Graham's Naval Brigade supplied gun crews for quartermaster transports which operated in areas where enemy attacks could be expected. The Albemarle and Chesapeake Canal was one such area upon which the transports *GAZELLE* and *CLINTON* each carried gun crews assigned by Graham's adjutant. These gun crews, consisted of a sergeant and ten men, commonly manning a 6-pounder field howitzer.[23]

Recruitment policies within the eastern commands during the period from 1863 through to the end of the war did not allow specific terms of military enlistment for the filling of crew positions on gunboat or attack transports, e.g., pilots, mates or engineers. Once in the Army, though, officers and men could be assigned to fill such crew vacancies. There existed a rather large pay differential between the civilian elements and the military elements on Army combatant craft (often assigned upon the same vessel), but this does not seem to have provoked any serious morale problems.

One particular concern arose from within the civilian element of the gunboat crews over an apprehension of their status should they become prisoners of the enemy. This came into focus when the gunboat *SMITH BRIGGS* was lost to enemy action on February 1, 1864, while on a mission up the James River. The entire crew, both military and civilian, was made captive. At that time, Graham's headquarters urged that the Prisoner Exchange Agent for the Union side take a bargaining position with the Confederates making a point that those civilians holding jobs on the Army's gunboats or attack transports -- while engaged in the senior capacities of pilots, masters, or engineers -- be considered the equivalent of commissioned officers for purposes both of incarceration and for status during prisoner exchanges.[24] Graham's proposal for officer status for certain civilian categories may not have been necessary since the "Dix-Hill Cartel Agreement for the General Exchange of Prisoners of War," as it was entered into between the Union and the Confederate governments during 1862, had made it clear that civilian employees of the Army were to be handled in the same fashion as military and naval personnel holding equivalent job assignments. It is not known if Graham's proposal was ever commented upon by the War Department or if it was endorsed on to the Prisoner Exchange Agent who would have been directly responsible for negotiations.[25]

Although Graham's Naval Brigade was small in size, it was an active and important factor in operations conducted against Confederate forces in northern Virginia and within the estuaries of the sounds of North Carolina.

THE VIRGINIA CAMPAIGN OF 1864

On April 9, 1864, Lieutenant General Ulysses S. Grant issued orders for a general offensive. This was to be a campaign which would not be isolated to just one theater; rather it was to involve widely separated commands. To the south and west, Major General William T. Sherman was to push as far as he could into Georgia, doing so without giving respite to the enemy. Major General Franz Sigel was to strike southward down the Shenandoah Valley. When Sigel reached the rail line of the Tennessee and Virginia, he was to destroy the rails and bridging. After that, he was to swing eastward toward Lynchburg. If Sigel was successful in reaching Lynchburg, he would cut Robert E. Lee's army off from the bounty of the Shenandoah. Major General George G. Meade's Army of the Potomac, was to drive directly over the Rapidan, forcing Lee back in the direction of Richmond. As a diversion calculated to divide the enemy's strength, Major General Benjamin Butler with his Army of the James was to make a thrust at Richmond's back door by way of the James River.

Meade, as it had been well established for some time, was to handle the localized deployment of the Army of the Potomac; but Grant would stay with him to call the major shots as the developing situation would dictate. Communication with the other players -- Sherman, Sigel, and Butler -- would be directed by Grant via the Army's Chief of Staff, Major General Henry W. Halleck, who would remain headquartered at the War Department in Washington. The telegraph would play a major role in joining all the many parts to Grant. (For a description of the role of telegraphy in the Virginia Campaign of 1864-1865, see Appendix J.)

Grant's standing orders to Meade were concise and directly to the point.

> ...Wherever Lee goes, there you will go also. The only point upon which I am now in doubt is whether it will be better to cross the Rapidan above or below him...By crossing above, Lee is cut off from all chances of ignoring Richmond and going north on a raid; but if we take this route, all we do must be done while the rations we start with hold out; we separate from Butler, so that he cannot be directed how to cooperate. By the other route, [meaning around Lee's eastern flank] Brandy Station can be used as a base of supplies until another is secured on the York or James River.
>
> ...There will be naval cooperation on the James River, and transports and ferries will be provided, so that should Lee fall back into his entrenchments at Richmond, Butler's force and yours will be a unit, or at least can be made to act as such.[26]

Butler From Fortress Monroe

That part of the campaign for which Benjamin Butler was given direct responsibility was, from its onset, to be largely an amphibious undertaking. Butler's initial advance on the James River would be made aboard transports under the escort of naval gunboats. In his orders to Butler which were issued on April 2, Grant laid out the ground rules that Butler was to follow.

> ...In the spring campaign, which it is desirable shall commence at as early a day as practicable, it is proposed to have cooperative action of all the armies in the field, as far as this object can be accomplished.
>
> ...The necessity of covering Washington with the Army of the Potomac, and of covering your department with your army, makes it impossible to unite these forces at the beginning of any move...You will collect all the forces from your command that can be spared from garrison duty -- I should say not less than twenty thousand effective men -- to operate on the south side of James River, Richmond being your objective point. To the force you already have will be added ten thousand men from South Carolina. [This was the X Corps, whose regiments were to be joined to the XXIV Corps.]
>
> ...When you are notified to move, take City Point [at the junction of the James River with the Appomattox River] with as much force as possible. Fortify or rather entrench, at once, and concentrate all your troops for the field there as rapidly as you can.
>
> ...cooperation between your force and the Army of the Potomac -- must be your guide. This indicates the necessity of your holding close to the south bank of the James as you advance. Then should the enemy be forced into his entrenchments in Richmond, the Army of the Potomac would follow and by means of transports the two armies would become a unit...[27]

Following receipt of Grant's orders, Butler's staff began putting into place those steps necessary for the launching of Butler's part of the campaign. This paramountly involved a request to the Quartermaster Department for vessels for troop lift and the follow-up supply. Upon receipt of that request, Quartermaster General Meigs wired Captain George D. Wise, the officer most often called upon in the past when there was a need for an extraordinary amount of shipping. Together with the quartermasters stationed at a number of northern ports, Wise would coordinate the gathering together of the necessary vessels. The instructions given to the quartermasters were that they were to assemble all the light draft steamers that could be found in their respective ports, together with a considerable number of schooners and barges. Meigs had already told Wise to hold over any steamers presently employed in the quartermaster's regular shuttle service between Fortress Monroe and northern ports. These vessels were to be diverted up Chesapeake Bay and into the Potomac to Alexandria or Washington, to pick up troops being assembled as reinforcements for Butler and were then to sail for Fortress Monroe.[28] Three days following his initial instructions from Meigs, Wise was able to report back that enough vessels had been gathered to perform the troop lift up the James River from Fortress Monroe.

Philadelphia, PA
April 19, 1864

Brigadier General M. C. Meigs
    Quartermaster General:

Sidewheel boats:
CHAMPION (309 tons), 600 men
FAVORITE (350 tons), 300 men
GEORGE WEEMS (440 tons), 800 men
HIGHLAND LIGHT (291 tons), 600 men
JEFFERSON (400 tons), 500 men
JOHN A. WARNER (600 tons), 1200 men
KENT (281 tons), 400 men
KEYPORT (350 tons), 350 men
KINGSTON (400 tons), 500 men.

MATILDA (700 tons, 1500 men
PIONEER (256 tons), 500 men
PLANTER (400 tons), 800 men
PORTSMOUTH (400 tons), 500 men
ROCKLAND (300 tons), 350 men
TALLACA (400 tons), 600 men
WINONAH (600 tons), 1000 men
WYOMING (400 tons), 500 men

Propellers:
BEVERLY (190 tons), 200 men
BRAYERLY (170 tons), 200 men
EMMA (185 tons), 200 men.
LEADER (200 tons), 200 men
MAYFLOWER (200 tons), 300 men

MAYFLOWER (220 tons), 350 men
REBECCA BARTON (350 tons),
    400 men
WALLACE (190 tons), 200 men
a sea steamer [unnamed] of (140 tons),
    200 men

Steam tugs:
AJAX
BISHOP
DELANEY
[EDWARD] PALMER

HUTCHINS
MARY FREEMAN
TEMPEST
VATTERLIN

50 canal barges, average capacity, 150 men.

    Should judge I had comfortable transportation for twenty thousand men, and steam tugs sufficient for towing barges. If required I can obtain more propellers and barges. From this date [on] all ordered to Fortress Monroe. Unless otherwise ordered, [I] will leave early tomorrow for New York.
        George D. Wise, Captain and Assistant Quartermaster[29]

Congestion on the Waterways

    The abundance of shipping activity on the Chesapeake and its tributaries, as well as at other points of concentration, had given rise to a number of collisions to which the Navy had apparently been party. During the mid-nineteenth century, there was no standardized, much less legislated system in place for vessels passing or overtaking each other. There were informal local practices, but these varied from place to place. To bring some order out of the wartime traffic chaos, the Navy decided upon establishing its own system based, one might suspect, upon the practices prevailing generally along the coasts and in the rivers. On May 4, 1864, the Navy Department issued its General Order No. 34. This order specified meeting and overtaking rules for both steam and sail vessels of the Navy, addended to which were instructions laying out procedures for commanding offices to follow should a collision occur.

On August 13, the War Department issued General Order 246, reiterating the Navy Department's order which was to be "immediately adopted on all vessels owned or chartered by the Quartermaster Department of the Army." Although nothing was done by the Congress regarding collision rules applicable to commercial vessels until well after the Civil War had ended, these 1864 Navy rules -- once they became familiar to government mariners -- must have helped settle a number of litigious confrontations.[30]

The Army of the Potomac Crosses the Rapidan

On May 4, Meade vacated the Army of the Potomac's winter quarters on the east bank of the Rapidan. He crossed the army over the river at Germanna Ford and at Ely's Ford. In close trail behind the infantry and the artillery regiments was a wagon train consisting of over four thousand wagons which contained the army's sustenance including its reserve ordnance.

Other than light picket actions, there was little enemy resistance to the Rapidan River crossing. It was not until the next day at Wilderness Tavern that serious opposition was encountered. This was at the same place where a year earlier, in an action which has come to be known by some as the First Battle of the Wilderness, Robert E. Lee had held back Union forces under Hooker with terrible losses suffered by both sides. A similar slaughter would now take place. This time, though, the Army of the Potomac would not be stopped but instead would continue battering its way toward Richmond.

Grant had initially announced that once the Army of the Potomac crossed the Rapidan, it would have to depend on the rations with which it started out; but such self-reliance had a limitation of time and distance attached to it, a circumstance of which Grant and Meade, and especially the quartermasters, were certainly aware from the onset. After the army had crossed the Rapidan, its rate of advance became in largest part factored on the security of its line of communication which stretched northward to Alexandria on the Potomac. As the Army of the Potomac moved south, the quartermasters would find it increasingly difficult to transport supplies from the depots at Alexandria. All such overland movements needed the accompaniment of inordinately strong escorts to guard against the attacks of enemy cavalry, but strong escorts were something Meade could no longer spare without depriving his cavalry arm of its integral strength which was needed for other vital chores. As the army advanced, the Virginia rivers, penetrating as they did into the countryside, would begin to take on special consideration for use as supply routes. The first to be used for that purpose was the Rappahannock. Port Royal, located on the south bank of that river, was selected for an advance supply depot since its location marked the navigable limit for deep draft vessels. From Port Royal, the majority of the supplies would be taken by wagon to the right of way of the Richmond, Fredericksburg, and Potomac Railroad, to be loaded onto cars for movement south to the advancing army.

Butler Prepares to Move

Prior to the start of the Virginia Campaign of 1864, the holdings by Union forces on the James River had been restricted to Fortress Monroe and Williamsburg. The stretch of the James River above Williamsburg was not permanently occupied by either side, so both Union and Confederate cavalry patrols circulated through the surrounding countryside more or less at will. Upstream on the James River, the Confederates had established fortifications at Drewry's Bluff. They also had placed gun emplacements about four miles above the mouth of the Appomattox, overlooking Point of Rocks.

Where the James met with the Appomattox, the two rivers were separated by a peninsula which is shown on maps of that day as the Chesterfield Peninsula. Butler and his staff had selected this land feature as a forward base from which to launch the Army of the James against Richmond. The end of the Chesterfield Peninsula provided a broad front of shoreline, part of a plantation of colonial vintage called Bermuda Hundred. It was on this shore that Butler would make his landings. Some wharfage was known to serve the old plantation, but the condition of those wharves was unknown. Once Butler's troops were ashore, the plan called for an advance up the Chesterfield Peninsula to a preselected point where a defensive line was to be established. Its northern end would anchor on the James River at Trent's Reach; its southern end at Cobb's Plantation on the Appomattox River. The distance between these points was a little less than four miles over terrain considered by Butler's staff officers to be easily defended once adequate firing positions could be dug into place. The location for the defensive line had been chosen because it was out of artillery range of the wharves at Bermuda Hundred, a point of serious consideration should the enemy bring up field guns to shell the wharves at Bermuda Hundred over which Butler's supplies would have to come. Once the defensive line was established, Butler's next move was to be against a railroad spur which connected Petersburg with Richmond.

The enemy's fixed fortifications at Drewry's Bluff were on the southern bank of the James River, about five miles above Trent's Reach. At Chaffin's Bluff which was directly across the James River from Drewry's Bluff, there were secondary gun positions. These two emplacements provided interlocking fire and were deemed to be difficult to take by frontal assault. From Drewry's Bluff, the Confederate defense line extended about three miles in a southwest direction. The end of that line was situated so as to offer a clear field of protective fire covering the rail spur which served Richmond from Petersburg. This was the rail line that Butler planned to cut.

Reports concerning the quality and quantity of enemy troops that might be expected to oppose the landings were so diverse in their estimates as to be virtually worthless. Generally, though, it was expected that strong opposition would not be made as it was thought unlikely that the Confederates would risk leaving well dug-in positions. Nevertheless, Butler decided to play it safe by ordering a diversionary movement up the York River, hoping by this to draw off any enemy force which could be moved onto the Chesterfield Peninsula to give him trouble. The diversion was in the form of two troop transports well loaded with infantry and under the escort of gunboats. This force departed from Yorktown bound up the York River toward White House (a small landing place situated on the Pamunkey River which was a tributary to the York.) Butler would order yet a second diversionary movement which he hoped would prevent Confederate reinforcements from coming up from the south. Brigadier General August V. Kautz and a full division of cavalry were to ride out from Suffolk, Virginia (a town located just south of Norfolk). Kautz's orders were to destroy sections of the Petersburg- Weldon Railroad which connected Petersburg with the port of Wilmington, North Carolina. The disruption of rail communication from Wilmington to Petersburg would not only seriously hamper any Confederate attempts to rush reinforcements up from the south, but it would also cut off one of the major sources of supply for the Richmond defenders. Kautz's troopers would manage to mangle a mile or two of track along with two major railroad bridges, but the enemy's engineers repaired the damage within a few days so Kautz's efforts, insofar as the rail line was concerned, would prove negligible. His main goal, to create a distraction, would be a success as judged by the alarm that it created in Confederate command circles.

The cavalry raid ordered by Grant and commanded by Sigel was well underway. This force was to go south through the Shenandoah Valley in an attempt to sweep the valley of enemy presence and would then cross over the Blue Ridge Mountains and cut the rail link running from Lynchburg into Richmond. Sigel's raid started well, but he never got close to accomplishing his goals. At New Market, a town roughly midway down the length of the Shenandoah Valley, Sigel was halted by a determined Confederate force which forced him to withdraw. The rail link between Lynchburg and Richmond remained inviolate.

Rear Admiral Lee, the Navy's senior officer on the lower Chesapeake, had been instructed by the Secretary of the Navy to cooperate with Butler. He did so by commencing a mine sweeping operation before Butler's transports started for Bermuda Hundred. The sweeping took the better part of a day. When complete, Lee sent a courier vessel to Butler's headquarters on the transport *GREYHOUND* to inform that the way was clear.[31] Although Rear Admiral Lee felt safe at the time in reporting to Butler that the river up to City Point was free of mines, what most worried both Butler and Lee was the threat of a naval attack which the enemy might launch against the troop transports. Allegedly moored to the Richmond docks were three heavy ironclads together with a number of wooden vessels rigged out as gunboats, the exact number of which varied, depending on the person bringing in the information[32]. As postwar research of Confederate records would later disclose, the reports as of the end of April concerning Confederate naval strength at Richmond had been widely inflated; but at the time they were received, the information was taken at face value, and it was not at all reassuring.[33] In the spring of 1864, the Union Navy had found itself heavily committed on other fronts, and little in the way of gunboat reinforcement could be spared to assist with the situation then developing on the James River. By early May, Rear Admiral Lee received two additional gunboats, but there was no hope of his getting any more, at least over the short range. Although Lee knew that what he had to work with was inadequate to meet any strong threat coming at him from upriver, his flotilla on the lower Chesapeake would have to do the best it could with what it had on hand, together with any assistance that might be forthcoming from Graham's small fleet of Army gunboats.

The group of transports which was to move Butler upriver was by now rendezvoused at Fortress Monroe preparatory to taking on troops. The quartermasters had assembled vessels of all sizes and conceivable designs ranging from deep-water transports to shallow draft bay steamers. The guns and horses of the artillery, along with supply wagons and ambulances, were to make the upriver trip aboard barges under tow of tugs. To avoid the arrival of the entire assemblage off Bermuda Hundred at the same time, each vessel waiting in turn to off-load, the transport fleet had been organized into two separate sections which were further divided into subsections. The advanced section was named the "First Fleet"; the following section, the "Second Fleet." Army gunboats would take the van of the First Fleet, to be closely followed by transports carrying two regiments of infantry (colored). These two regiments were to secure the immediate beachhead, being backed up for that job by two batteries of light artillery. The assault force consisting of the First Fleet was scheduled to sail from Fortress Monroe at seven o'clock on the evening of May 5, to be followed by the Second Fleet under the escort of Lee's gunboats.[34] All told, there were fifty-nine transports plus the tug assisted barges which were along to carry the artillery, the ambulances, and the supply wagons.[35]

Two regiments of US cavalry (colored) were to pace the progress of the fleet along the banks, their assignment being to neutralize any enemy artillery which might have been set into position on the bank. On the river's south bank, eleven miles below Bermuda Hundred, there was an old masonry structure known as Fort Powhatan. Patrols reported that the place had been vacated of enemy presence, but it posed a potential problem should the Confederates reoccupy it after the fleet had passed. Wanting to ensure against that happening, Butler ordered that a troop element from the Second Fleet land and occupy it. Then, when the Second Fleet reached City Point, another regiment was to go ashore and establish a presence there as well. Both Fort Powhatan and City Point would be occupied without opposition. At the time, City Point (a small town at the entrance to the Appomattox River) "...consisted only of 'a few shabby houses ranged along two or three short lanes or streets; and the spacious grounds and dilapidated house of one Dr. Eppes.' "[36] A river port once active in the cotton and tobacco trade, City Point was served by a railroad spur which joined to the main rail system connecting Petersburg and Richmond.

When the transports arrived off Bermuda Hundred, there was not even a stray musket shot sent their way. It had been hoped that the wharves there would be adequate for bringing the steamers alongside; but when the first transport tried it, the pilot discovered that shoals had built up against the dock face. An alternative plan had to be quickly developed for off-loading the vessels. At first, small boats ferried the troops in from the transports, but this was found to be too slow. The solution was to moor barges alongside the wharves so they would span out over the shoals. This created a sort of causeway against which the transports could dock and onto which the troops were rapidly disembarked. By the end of the day, Butler had all of his infantry ashore. As each regiment was landed, its colonel was ordered to take up a temporary position near the shoreline and wait there until daylight when an advance along a wide front would start toward the preselected location for the defense line. When daylight broke, the advance began. Only once during that deployment were enemy patrols encountered, but these were quickly brushed aside. The northern half of the defense line was found to be an excellent choice with a number of advantageous positions for the emplacement of artillery. The planned location of the southern end of the line required some slight change near to where it reached the Appomattox at Cobb's Plantation; but that was soon adjusted with good fields of fire established to cover all the approaches.

While the deployment of troops and guns was being made along the defense line, Butler called a meeting of his two corps commanders, Major Generals W. F. Smith and Quincy Gillmore. Butler told them that he was greatly encouraged by the absence of resistance and by the patrol reports which were coming in that the enemy's works at Drewry's Bluff were weakly manned. Proposing an immediate frontal assault against these works, Butler argued that the opportune time was the present. The longer they waited, he maintained, the more time the enemy would have to bring up additional troops. Both W. F. Smith and Gillmore had strong negative reactions to the idea, so Butler dropped the matter. Not two hours had passed after that meeting when an officer courier brought Butler the news that both corps commanders had reversed their earlier opinions; they now believed an assault to be a viable option. This vacillating of opinions so angered Butler that he deferred the whole idea, postponing any discussion on it to a later time.

Did Butler miss his golden opportunity by not attacking on the morning following the landings when the enemy's strength was at the lowest ebb? That question has long been argued, but the probable answer is that he did. Nevertheless, the instructions he had received from Grant had given him the primary objective of securing the lower Chesterfield Peninsula and by so doing, controlling the approaches to City Point. This Butler had already accomplished. To now risk a setback by assaulting the fortification at Drewry's Bluff with the possibility of weakening his ability to remain on the Chesterfield Peninsula could have had a most adverse effect on the overall campaign.

With Grant and the Army of the Potomac

By May 10, Meade's Army of the Potomac had fought its way through the Wilderness and had advanced upon a place named Spotsylvania where they were to find Robert E. Lee well dug in. An assault against Lee failed, resulting in heavy losses to the attackers. Two days later, a second attempt to overrun Lee was tried, but that resulted in even more horrific losses. Lee was putting an ever-increasing reliance on going to ground, and the closer he was pushed in the direction of Richmond, the more dogged he seemed to be getting. On May 18, Grant told Meade to send two full corps against Lee's lines; but this assault failed as well. A third attack, this time against the Confederate's flank, was also repulsed. The whole effort was beginning to look like a slaughter without hope of achieving any satisfactory results. Grant had to consider the morale of the troops as well as the political implications of a casualty rate which was mounting by multiples every time Robert E. Lee chose to hold his ground. Grant was not the heartless soldier that he is often depicted to be, and such losses, unless they could clearly be shown to produce a sound benefit, were an antithesis to Grant's theory of waging war. He now ordered Meade to begin preparations to swing clear of Lee's front and try to move around the enemy's flank. The aim was to do this without making contact, but the maneuver was discovered. Lee tried to stop it but could not, and the Army of the Potomac was again on the move, heading east and south, with Richmond its obvious destination.

With the aim of blocking the Yankee army, Lee would now march toward the North Anna River, there to entrench on that river's southern bank. Grant would again order Meade to move around Lee on an evasive line of march aimed at taking the Army of the Potomac across the James River to join with Butler. But now, Lee would successfully maneuver into the Union path of advance. A bloody confrontation was about to take place at a spot in the road called Cold Harbor.

The Supply Lines Readjusted

Once the Union Army reached the Pamunkey River, Meade's quartermasters would be in the position to avail themselves of supplies directly off-loaded from steamer and tug-barge units routed in from Chesapeake Bay. Once that happened, the Army of the Potomac's logistics would be greatly simplified.

The day after the Army of the Potomac reached the North Anna, Grant felt confident that he could surmount Lee's efforts to hold him. He was so confident that he dispatched instructions to Halleck to prepare to switch the advance supply depots to White House on the Pamunkey. Halleck was less than enthusiastic over the idea and argued against it in a telegraphed reply he sent to Grant, contending that the overland supply routing from the Rappahannock should be retained. Grant responded, explaining to Halleck, among other things, his reasons for abandoning what had become an increasingly difficult situation when dealing with the overland supply route. He also described a new concept for the campaign which, to a marked degree, departed from the strategy which had been originally planned.

June 5, 1864

Major General Halleck,
Chief of Staff of the Army, Washington, DC:
General:

A full survey of all the ground satisfies me that it would not be practicable to hold a line northeast of Richmond that would protect the Fredericksburg railroad, to enable us to use it for supplying the Army. To do so would give us a long vulnerable line of road to protect, exhausting much of our strength in guarding it, and would leave open to the enemy all of his lines of communication on the south side of the James. My idea from the start has been to beat Lee's army, if possible, north of Richmond, then, after destroying his lines of communication north of the James River, to transfer the Army to the south side and besiege Lee in Richmond, or follow him south if he should retreat.

I now find, after more than thirty days of trial, that the enemy deems it of the first importance to run no risks with the armies they now have. They act purely on the defensive, behind breast works, or feebly on the offensive immediately in front of them, and where in case of repulse they can instantly retire behind them. Without a greater sacrifice of human life than I am willing to make, all cannot be accomplished that I had designed outside of the city. I have, therefore, resolved upon the following plan: I will continue to hold substantially the ground now occupied by the Army of the Potomac, taking advantage of any favorable circumstance that may present itself, until the cavalry can be sent west to destroy the Virginia Central Railroad from about Beaver Dam for some twenty-five or thirty miles west. When this is effected, I will move the Army to the south side of James River, either by crossing the Chickahominy and marching near to City Point, or by going to the mouth of the Chickahominy on the north side and crossing there. To provide for this last and most probable contingency six or more ferryboats of the largest class ought to be immediately provided.

Once on the south side of the James River, I can cut off all sources of supply to the enemy, except what is furnished by the canal. If [Major General David] Hunter succeeds in reaching Lynchburg that will be lost to him also. Should Hunter not succeed, I will still make the effort to destroy the canal by sending cavalry up the south side of the river with a pontoon train to cross wherever they can. The feeling of the two armies now seems to be that the rebels can protect themselves only by strong entrenchments, while our Army is not only confident of protecting itself without entrenchments, but that it can beat and drive the enemy wherever and whenever he can be found without this protection.

Very respectfully,

U. S. Grant, Lieutenant General[37]

Whether moved to Grant's point of view or not, Grant was the boss. Halleck put the changeover of supply bases into motion, notifying all concerned quartermaster, ordnance, and commissary officers to that effect.

No further shipments of troops or supplies will be made to Port Royal, Virginia. General Abercrombie has been directed to send forward to General Grant's army everything now on the way, and to have everything away and the depot broken up by the first of June. The depot will be transferred to the Pamunkey River, and everything hereafter for the Army of the Potomac will be sent to White House.

H. W. Halleck, Major General and Chief of Staff

(Copies sent to Surgeon General, Commissary General, and the commanding officer, Department of Washington.)[38]

Military success against Lee would depend in large part on Grant's ability to cut the Southern army's communications off from its supply routing through Richmond. This meant blocking off the James River and Kanawha Canal serving that city from the upper James River Valley. It also meant severing the rail connections coming into that city from the Carolinas to the south and from the Shenandoah Valley to the west. The canal which Grant had mentioned in his to Halleck of June 5, 1864, was the James River and Kanawha Canal, built in the 1840s, which paralleled the James River, bypassing its many rapids. Using the canal, which was 196 miles in length, goods originating from the upper James River Valley could be brought directly into Richmond on canal boats.

Earlier cavalry raids against the rail lines leading into Richmond had been far from satisfactory, the enemy usually repairing the damage in a matter of days. Grant would now instruct his commanders that whenever rail lines were ordered destroyed, the rails should be so bent or twisted as to make repair of the right of way impossible without a supply of new rails, an item now almost impossible to procure anywhere in the Confederacy.

One of the officers Grant was counting on to destroy the enemy's communications was Major General David Hunter. Hunter, with a strong cavalry force, was to make a sweep through the Shenandoah Valley and then across the Blue Ridge Mountains to the railroad junction town of Lynchburg. Like Sigel before him, Hunter would be stopped and sent into retreat; however, unlike Sigel, Hunter's path of retreat would not be left open for him to return the way he had come. Instead, he was forced over the Appalachian Ridge into West Virginia. Hunter's inability to return north dislocated him from the eastern theater and made him of no further use to Grant. With the resources of the Shenandoah Valley and the railroad leading from it still available to the Confederates, it began to look like Robert E. Lee had the cards to remain in the game for much longer than Grant had planned.

Butler Probes the Confederate Positions

On May 7, Butler moved out of his well-entrenched defense line on the Chesterfield Peninsula with the intent of striking at the Petersburg- Richmond rail spur. It was on that rail line that the materiel coming up from the Carolinas was routing to Richmond through Petersburg. Butler's first attempt to reach the rail line was inconclusive. On May 9 he tried again, this time succeeding in the destruction of a considerable amount of track. Rather than move back to his defense lines, he remained on the ground he was occupying, intending to hold a permanent position there. During the same time frame when this was taking place, Graham's gunboats, supported by two of Rear Admiral Lee's ironclads, conducted an exchange of fire with Fort Clifton, an enemy strong point located on the Appomattox a mile or so upstream from Cobb's Plantation. The Confederates came off best in the exchange, so badly damaging the Army gunboat *SAMUEL L. BREWSTER* that she had to be abandoned.[39]

On May 12, Butler tried an attack against the Confederate's forward line of trenches protecting the approaches to the fortifications at Drewry's Bluff. He drove the enemy back to the main line of their defenses at which point he was close enough to see that the emplacements would be a tough nut to crack. Butler would request support from Rear Admiral Lee whose ironclads and monitors had the firepower needed to soften the enemy's positions preliminary to an infantry assault. The response from Lee was disappointing.

> Flagship, North Atlantic Blockading Squadron
> James River, May 13, 1864 -- 12:10 p.m.
>
> General:
>
> Your dispatch dated near Drewry's Bluff, May 13, 9 a.m., is just delivered by Major Ludlow. Owing to the shoal water in Trent's Reach, as shown by the Coast Survey chart, the draft of the monitors, the torpedoes in the river, and the occupation by the enemy of the high left bank, it will be very difficult if not impracticable, at present, to get the gunboats and monitors up to the point you indicate, opposite Doctor Howlett's above Trent's Reach.
>
> To remove the torpedoes we must drag the river and search the banks for wires -- lines by which they are exploded. This requires that we should occupy or

control the left bank of the river. The number and kind of gunboats are barely sufficient to cover your communications at Wilson's Wharf, Powhatan Reach, City Point, in the Appomattox, and at Bermuda Hundred, and our communications to this point.

The enemy are now occupying in considerable force the high bank on the left side of the river, over the narrow channels around Jones's Neck, and protecting their torpedoes there, and the same difficulties will be found in the reach under the high left bank at and below the lower side of Dutch Gap. It requires many more than the small number of gunboats I have above Turkey Bend to clear and control the left bank in the absence of military occupation of controlling points in the reaches, so as to keep open our communications and get our supplies, especially of coal, of which the monitors carry but ten days' supply, and without which they cannot breathe nor turn their turrets.

The explosion of the gunboat *COMMODORE JONES* by a torpedo shows that the river must be cleared of them before we can ascend, and the quick destruction of the gunboat *SHAWSHEEN** just in our rear in Turkey Bend by a rebel battery shows that considerable naval force will be necessary to keep open our communication even if we can clear out the torpedoes, and by lightening the monitors, with the aid of transports, reach the point indicated in the absence of military occupation of certain points on the left bank. I greatly need the military forces on the left bank, for which I have heretofore applied. Our crews are barely sufficient to man the guns. When more gunboats arrive, I have to protect my communications, and I shall meanwhile endeavor, though greatly needing Army aid, to clear the high banks and to open the channel in Jones's Reach. I ought to have a cooperating Army force to occupy such points in the reaches, on this narrow river with overhanging banks, as Wilson's Wharf and Powhatan Reach, to aid us to clear out the river, open and keep it open.

Cannot you cooperate? In the meantime I will protect you from rebel operations in the river.

Very respectfully yours,

S. P. Lee, Rear Admiral, Commanding
North Atlantic Blockading Squadron[40]

* *USS*, commissioned Union naval vessel.

Confederate troop strength in front of Butler's positions had by now increased substantially. The Confederates launched attacks on May 15 and 16 -- their intention being to cut Butler off from the landing facilities at Bermuda Hundred. Although they did not succeed, they did drive the Federals back to their original defense line stretching across the Chesterfield Peninsula.

Any thought on Butler's part beyond just holding his line and the enclave that he had established at City Point were now out of the question. Taking Richmond would have to await the arrival of Grant and the Army of the Potomac. All told, Butler's ambition to go beyond his originally established defense line had cost him three thousand casualties. The end result of that effort was a stalemate with each side now restricted to its trenches.[41]

The stalemate along Butler's immediate front did not mean that all activity between the opposing parties had ceased. On May 24, a Union garrison of eleven hundred Negro troops, which Butler had positioned to guard a section of the river some miles downstream from Bermuda Hundred, was attacked by a force of Confederate cavalry which soon gained the upper hand. Fortunately, a troop commander riding aboard a transport which was passing up the river saw what was taking place and landed his men to assist. The enemy cavalry withdrew. Had the Confederates been triumphant, the outcome might have been serious since possession by the enemy could have blocked the James River in Butler's rear. Just before this incident, Butler had received a request from Meade for the loan of a corps, but the downriver attack gave pause as to the wisdom of allowing any decrease of troop strength on the James. Accordingly, Butler begged off from complying. However, when Meade again asked for a corps, this time with Grant's endorsement, Butler had little choice but to obey. On May 26, XVIII Corps under W. F. Smith was detached from the Army of the James and organizationally joined to the Army of the Potomac.

Worried over the security of City Point, Butler ordered the construction of a pontoon bridge from the Chesterfield Peninsula over the Appomattox River to City Point. When completed, Butler moved some of his troops over the Appomattox to bolster City Point's perimeter defenses.

The James River Is Crossed By Grant

Three days into the month of June, the Army of the Potomac (now reinforced by W. F. Smith's XVIII Corps), was facing a very determined Robert E. Lee and his Army of Northern Virginia at the place called Cold Harbor. The battle which followed lasted for two terrible days. Of all the fights the Army of the Potomac had waged since crossing the Rapidan the month before, Cold Harbor was the most bitter and costly. Charging Lee's dug-in positions, Federal losses within the space of one hour came to almost seven thousand men, this on top of a casualty return of five thousand just two days earlier. Realizing that Lee's defenses at Cold Harbor could not be breached, Grant instructed Meade to work around the Confederate wing and move toward the James River. This time, Lee did not block the move.

Earlier, Grant had asked for ferryboats to handle a possible crossing of the James River. Halleck took steps to see that they would be ready when needed and reported this to Grant.

> Lieutenant General Grant, In the field:
> General:
> Your letter of the 5th, by Lieutenant Colonel Babcock, was received last evening. General Meigs has been advised of your wishes in regard to ferryboats. He will keep all he has or can procure in the vicinity of Fortress Monroe subject to your orders. Many of the sidewheel boats in the Quartermaster Department will also answer all the purposes of ferryboats. The barges will also be excellent for teams and stores, and can be towed by the tugs. Everything will be sent forward as soon as you direct. They are now mostly engaged as transports to White House. Nothing has recently been heard of Generals Hunter and Crook. Sherman is still doing well, but some apprehension has been felt about Forrest's movements to cut off his communications..."
> Very respectfully, your obedient servant,
> H. W. Halleck, Major General and Chief of Staff[42]

Not wanting to be totally dependent on what the quartermasters could provide in the way of vessels, Grant would now order the construction of a pontoon bridge.

Cold Harbor, Virginia, June 12, 1864

Colonel Biggs, Chief Quartermaster, XVIII Corps:

Lieutenant Colonel Dent, of my staff, has gone to Fortress Monroe and Bermuda Hundred to make, or rather communicate, the necessary orders for securing the crossing of the Army over James River at Fort Powhatan. Special instructions were not given, however, to send ferryboats, pontoons, etc, that may yet be at Fortress Monroe. This will be understood, no doubt, by General Butler from the instructions that have gone to him; but to expedite, I now direct that you forward up the James River all things within your charge, and request the engineer officer at Fortress Monroe, for me, to send all the pontoon bridge material he may have on hand. Send also all the lumber you can, particularly the 2-inch plank. This will not be construed to interfere with sending the amount of transportation to the White House heretofore called for.

U. S. Grant, Lieutenant General[43]

The original location at Fort Powhatan which had been selected for assembling the pontoon bridge was soon changed. The new location was from the north bank of the river at Douthat's Wharf to the southern bank at Wilcox's Landing, that landing being at the end of the Fleur de Hundred Road. The construction of the pontoon bridge was a monumental undertaking since the river at this point was 2,100 feet wide, making this the longest pontoon span to date put in place by the Union Army. The bridge, which employed 101 pontoons and was anchored by three schooners, was constructed in eight hours by 450 men.

By the morning of June 14, some of the lead elements of the Army of the Potomac had already crossed the river on ferryboats as the pontoon bridge had not yet been completed. Grant's specific requests for ferryboats had not been made without sound reason. Ferries, equipped as they usually were with ramps, could land artillery and cavalry onto any handy bank where the approach was of sufficient depth and the bank of relatively firm consistency and not overly steep. A problem, though, was that not enough ferries had been provided, despite the fact that there seemed to have been plenty of them in the area and in quartermaster service at the time. The situation brought a howl of complaint from one of Meade's corps commanders.

Headquarters, II Army Corps, Wilcox's Landing
June 14, 1864 -- 7:55 p.m.

Major General [Andrew A.] Humphreys
Chief of Staff, Army of the Potomac:
General:

I have embarked one battery, but there is considerable difficulty about landing it on the other side. If we had some ferryboats here, such as I have seen passing up the river, they could be used to great advantage.

I am, sir, very respectfully, your obedient servant,

Winfield S. Hancock, Major General[44]

When the draft of the vessels being employed permitted it, those parts of the Army of the Potomac which reached the James River prior to the completion of the pontoon bridge were taken directly to City Point. Those vessels which drew too much water to enter the Appomattox were unloaded of their troops at Bermuda Hundred, and the men were marched from there to City Point using the pontoon bridge which Butler had earlier ordered built across the Appomattox River.

Once the engineers had completed the pontoon bridge over the James River, the river's crossing was greatly accelerated. The defense line earlier established to protect City Point and which had been put in place by Butler's orders was now becoming too restrictive to accommodate the influx of arriving troops, so it was enlarged. After the new perimeter was established, probing attacks were started against enemy positions located between City Point and Petersburg. On June 17, Grant would wire Halleck, informing him of the progress which had been made.

> Major General H. W. Halleck, Chief of Staff:
> The IX Corps this morning carried two more redoubts, forming part of the defenses of Petersburg, capturing 450 prisoners and four guns. Our successes are being followed up.
> Our forces drew out from within fifty yards of the enemy's entrenchments at Cold Harbor, made a flank movement of an average of about fifty miles' march, crossing the Chickahominy and James Rivers, the latter 2,000 feet wide and 84 feet deep at point of crossing, and surprised the enemy's rear at Petersburg. This was done without the loss of wagon or piece of artillery and with the loss of only about 150 stragglers, picked up by the enemy. In covering this move Warren's corps and Wilson's cavalry had frequent skirmishes with the enemy, each losing from fifty to sixty killed and wounded, but inflicting an equal, if not greater, loss upon the enemy.
> The XVIII Corps (Smith's) was transported from White House to Bermuda Hundred by water, moved out near to Petersburg the night of its arrival, and surprised or rather captured the very strong works northeast of Petersburg before sufficient force could be got in there by the enemy to hold them. He was joined the night following this capture by the II Corps which in turn captured more of the enemy's redoubts farther south, and this corps was followed by the IX, with the result above stated. All the troops are now up except two divisions covering the wagon trains, and they will be up tonight. The enemy in their endeavor to reinforce Petersburg abandoned their entrenchments in front of Bermuda Hundred. They no doubt expected troops from north of the James River to take their place before we discovered it. General Butler took advantage of this and moved a force at once upon the railroad and plank road between Richmond and Petersburg, which I hope to retain possession of. Too much credit cannot be given the troops and their commanders for the energy and fortitude displayed during the last five days. Day and night have been all the same, no delays being allowed on any account.
> U. S. Grant, Lieutenant General[45]

As of noon on June 17, some elements of the Army of the Potomac had still not crossed over the James to its southern bank. The part of the army left to cross included the all important beef cattle herd and the Army's wagon train. These were being protected by the two infantry divisions which Grant had mentioned in his wire to Halleck. Those elements still left on the northern bank had become increasingly vulnerable to attack by the enemy's cavalry. The time required to load the beef animals onto steamers and then unload them somewhere on the south bank would be excessive and would endanger the overall operation. To cross the cattle over the river via the pontoon bridge was considered hazardous because of the heavy vibrations which would develop from the rhythm of the cattle's hooves. A better way was decided upon by Meade's adjutant general who informed the commissary officer in charge of the cattle herd as to the procedure which was to be used.

Headquarters, Engineer Brigade
June 17, 1864

Captain Woodward, Commissary of Subsistence
Dear Sir:

     I understand that you have some one thousand of beef cattle to cross this river. I am satisfied that they can be safely crossed by swimming them, as was done at Edwards Ferry last June, a boat leading the front animals, with perhaps a boat on each side, as the crossing of them by squads of four or five, with intervals and men between, would take many hours of time, or otherwise they would be sure to ruin the bridge by their grouping. Under these circumstances, with the danger of loss of the bridge by capture from the delay or the great injury by the cattle if we attempt to cross them rapidly or in a body, I shall fear, without General Meade's direct order, to allow them to cross the bridge, and deem it my duty to take it up at once as soon as General Ferrero advises me that he can dispense with it. Trusting that you will be able to make the arrangements to swim these cattle over,

H. W. Benham[46]

     Once the rear guard of the last division had crossed over the James River, the pontoon bridge was dismantled, totally severing all land connection from the north. The bridge was broken into three sections and was towed to City Point where it appears to have been used as piers for offloading supply vessels.

     Once the Army of the Potomac crossed to the south side of the James River, its reinforcements, its supplies, and the evacuation of its wounded became entirely dependent on waterborne transportation which would be routed in from Chesapeake Bay.

In Front of Petersburg and Richmond

     A stand-off lasting for the next eight and a half months would now commence. During that time, Grant's army (consisting of the combined Army of the Potomac and the Army of the James) would remain static in its trenches in front of Petersburg and on the Chesterfield Peninsula. A dramatic attempt would be made to breach the Confederate lines by using a colossal mine which was exploded beneath the enemy's entrenchments. However, a lack of advance planning aimed toward taking advantage of a breach in the enemy's line created by the explosion, caused the scheme to fail.

     Another idea that failed to work came to be known as "The Dutch Gap Canal." It seems that most of the long sieges conducted during the American Civil War -- that is, those involving a river scenario -- had some sort of canal idea connected to it, the plans being to create bypasses of enemy strong points. Island No. 10 and Vicksburg were examples. The 1864-1865 siege of Richmond is another. In the case of the siege of Richmond, the idea for a canal came from Benjamin Butler who theorized that if the Navy was ever to get its gunboats past the rapids of Trent's Reach on the

James River in order to shell Drewry's Bluff, a bypass of those rapids would be required. Downriver some distance from Trent's Reach, the James River looped almost back on itself, and the intervening land separating the river's course at that point was only about 60 yards in width. The terrain at that point was composed of high bluffs of heavy clay material. To cut through the bluffs, Butler set hundreds of his men to work, hacking into the clay. It was to be no easy job. The digging itself was inordinately difficult, and Confederate sniper fire made life miserable and dangerous for those who labored. The canal project started in August 1864 and extended through that December. On New Year's Day of 1865 Butler ordered a mammoth powder charge ignited which was intended to break through the remnant clay at the canal's northern end, but this resulted only in the collapse of much of the work already done. The Dutch Gap Canal was finally completed in April of 1865, but this was too late to aid in the campaign.

For the Union besiegers of Petersburg, City Point would become the receiving point for all supply. The depot which was developed there was unparalleled in scope. The chief quartermaster who became the coordinator of all incoming and outgoing shipping at City Point was Brigadier General Rufus Ingalls.[47] Over 110,000 officers and men were to be supplied and otherwise provided for by what came upriver on the James.[48] At first most of the materiel that came in to City Point originated from the quartermaster, commissary, and ordinance depots located at Alexandria and Washington; but when the reserves from those places were depleted, most shipments came directly from ports to the north, mainly from New York.

Initially when cargoes were unloaded at City Point, they were forwarded by wagon to the front line troops. In a July 1 report to Quartermaster General Meigs, Ingalls noted that the movement of supplies from the docks required 4,440 standard Army wagons, 140 two-horse light wagons, and 907 ambulances. To pull them, Ingalls employed at that time a total of 41,329 horses and 23,961 mules. Besides the number of draft animals, there were upwards of 14,000 cavalry mounts, a number which would vary depending on the mounted missions taking place at the time. Feeding such a huge number of horses and mules, along with the hundreds of beef cattle awaiting slaughter in the commissary pens, required prodigious quantities of grain and hay.[49] Forage (hay) was perhaps the most critical commodity with which the Union Army's quartermasters in Virginia had to deal. So important was forage that a special division of the Quartermaster Department was established to handle its procurement. Except for the period of freeze-up which for a time blocked all shipments to City Point, the average daily hay shipment arriving there during the winter of 1864-1865 was six hundred tons.[50] Schooners were commonly involved in the transportation of forage but also used for that purpose were barges which arrived under the tow of steam tugs. It is reasonably safe to assume that all of the hay coming in to City Point was shipped there in a compressed or packaged form. (Within this volume there are photographs showing baled hay at City Point. Appendix L provides a detailed discussion of the hay industry in the northern states during the 1860s and examines the methods of production as well as that commodity's importance to the Union Army during the Civil War.) The very bulkiness of hay (even though shipped in baled form) taken together with the fact that the hay harvest season of 1864 was well below average, created a situation whereby little stockpiling had taken place either by the Army or on the producing farms. The absence of forage reserves would create a severe problem for Grant's army during the coming winter after freezing weather had closed down most of the northern ports.[51]

The City Point depot became not only a huge depository for the reception and storage of quartermaster, commissary, and ordnance materiel, but the place developed into a sizable industrial complex as well. Repair installations employing wheelwrights, carpenters, blacksmiths, saddlers, laborers, and clerks to the aggregate of sixteen hundred men became established there.[52] Bakeries were built to handle the daily consumption of the Army's biscuit ration. There was also a complex of corrals, with drovers permanently assigned to receive beef animals as well as replacement horses and mules, all coming in by sea aboard the transports. The amount of incoming shipping to City Point was probably at its highest in the weeks immediately following Grant's arrival since the first order of business after replenishing the army was to stockpile supplies to be held for emergencies. We have no accurate accounting of ship arrivals during this peak period, but it may have closely equaled the volume represented later during the spring of 1865, a period which followed a time of severe deprivation for the army. In the 1864-1865 winter, ice blockages halted shipments from the north, and this created an almost complete pull-down of stockpiles. Captain George D. Wise, reporting to Quartermaster General Meigs on vessels dedicated to the support of Grant before Richmond in the spring, enumerated 390 bottoms which he broke down into categories of: 190 steamers; 60 steam tugs; 40 sail vessels and 100 barges.[53]

The original wharfage at City Point, which had been built by commercial interests before the war, was inadequate for the high volume of shipping which began arriving. To rectify the problem, the Military Railroad Construction Corps set to work and built the necessary wharves. One of them was equipped with an A-frame beam and lifting mechanism for transferring fully loaded rail cars from the decks of barges onto rail tracks which ran out to the wharf head. Through this means, the rail cars could be switched directly to the reconstructed tracks of the City Point Railroad. At its opposite terminus were located the Union entrenchments at Petersburg. Once the City Point Railroad was made fully operational, Ingalls was able to substantially reduce his dependence on wagons. This had the attendant advantage of reducing the number of dray animals he had to maintain.

Eventually, the complex at City Point covered several hundred acres. In addition to the supply and repair facilities, the depot included five major Medical Department hospitals. (One of these hospitals handled only Negro troops.) During the summer of 1864, field tents were used for the wounded and the sick; but once the chill of fall arrived, these were replaced by floored pavilions and full log structures. Taken together, the occupancy for all five hospitals had been planned at around six thousand patients. The medical director at City Point set into place a system for the severely wounded whereby once their condition was stabilized, they were to be placed on hospital ships and sent north. Patients who were expected to recover sufficiently so as to return to duty within a reasonable period of time spent their entire time of treatment at the City Point facilities. Disease was an even more serious problem and one which started in earnest during June. This was in large part due to the swampy nature of the country which encouraged mosquitoes bearing the malaria parasite. Intestinal sicknesses, such as chronic diarrhea and dysentery, were aggravated by the congestion of so many thousands of men. Poor sanitation discipline, which was especially lacking among the newer recruits and draftees, caused these ailments to reach rampant proportions. According to Mary C. Gillett, writing in her book *The Army Medical Department, 1818-1865,* by July, the overall disease rate for the combined Union armies entrenched before Petersburg and Richmond had risen to 4.6% which was twice the average for the Union Army on campaign.[54]

Availability of Shipping and the Demands Put Upon It

Once the Army of the Potomac was across the James River and in entrenched positions before Petersburg, Grant had a breathing spell which gave the opportunity to reshuffle some troop strength from the western theater. On June 25 and upon Grant's request, Quartermaster General Meigs ordered Ingalls to dispatch as many transports as could be spared from the Army's current needs to proceed to New Orleans and load troops to bring to Virginia. In reply, Ingalls reported to Meigs the status of shipping then serving City Point, naming those vessels which were available and which could be spared for transporting troops north from New Orleans.

> City Point, Virginia, June 26, 1864 -- 9 a.m.
> (Received 10:15 a.m. 26th.)
>
> Brigadier General M. C. Meigs, Quartermaster General:
>
> Your dispatch of 11:30 a.m. yesterday was received by me at 9:30 p.m. The only ocean steamers in this river are the *C. THOMAS,*† *SUWANEE, REBECCA BARTON,* and *ELLEN S. TERRY.* I have given them the order you directed. They [each] can carry an average of six hundred men. I have directed Colonel Biggs, at Fortress Monroe to order the *CITY OF BALTIMORE, CASSANDRA, KENT, EASTERN CITY, BLACKSTONE, CONSTITUTION,* and *TILLIE.* To this list will probably be added the *SPAULDING*‡. He will report direct to you what they will carry. I do not know. I think that some of them are still laden with forage and subsistence.
>
> Rufus Ingalls, Chief Quartermaster[55]
>
> † *CHARLES THOMAS*
> ‡ *S. R. SPAULDING*

The overall demands on shipping had increased noticeably by late June, and availability was falling short of the demand. In addition to the normal needs, there were special requests. One such was sent to the Surgeon General's Office in Washington by the medical director at City Point. Hospitals had become dangerously overcrowded, and there was a need to send north almost six thousand patients considered qualified for transfer to rear echelon hospitals. This request, and others like it, came at the same time that the quartermasters were being called upon to bring troop reinforcements to Grant from New Orleans.[56]

During the first week of July reports began flooding into the War Department that a strong enemy force under Jubal Early was moving north up the Shenandoah Valley. Some of Early's advance elements had already reached the shores of the Potomac. Fearful that an attack against Washington was in the offing, and apprehensive of the political repercussions which could result if the city was even temporarily occupied by the enemy, Grant queried Halleck by telegram on the advisability of sending some of the troops from in front of Petersburg to assist in Washington's defense. Halleck's reply to Grant did not indicate a high degree of alarm at that time.

> Washington
> July 5, 1864 -- 10:30 p.m.
>
> Lieutenant General Grant, City Point, Virginia
>
> All available water transportation is now at Fortress Monroe and in James River. General Meigs recommends that it all be placed under General Ingalls, as, by a divided command, there is conflict of orders. As Hunter's force is now coming within reach, I think your operations should not be interfered with by sending troops here. [Hunter was the Federal cavalry commander who had been previously forced to retreat from the Shenandoah into West Virginia but who was now nearing Washington to assist in its defense. Ed.] If Washington and Baltimore should be so seriously threatened as to require your aid, I will inform you in time. Although most of our forces are not of a character suitable for the field (invalids and militia), yet I have no apprehensions at present about the safety of Washington, Baltimore, Harper's Ferry, or Cumberland. These points cover our supplies, and raids between cannot effect any damage that cannot soon be repaired. If, however, you can send us your dismounted cavalry, we can use it to advantage, and, perhaps, soon return it remounted.
>
> H. W. Halleck, Major General and Chief of Staff[57]

Grant wired back to Halleck that the dismounted cavalry was on its way; he was also sending along a division of infantry.

By July 6, Early was in force north of the Potomac. He dispatched a brigade of cavalry in the direction of Baltimore, intending to cut communications between that city and Washington and then free Confederate prisoners of war held at Point Lookout, Maryland. On July 8, it began to look like Washington would be next on Early's agenda. Grant was not about to let that happen. Despite Halleck's optimism over the city's safety, Grant now ordered one full corps plus part of another to embark by steamer from City Point. Orders were concurrently issued which stopped all scheduled dispatch of transports to New Orleans.[58] Shortly after receiving his order to leave for the defense of Washington, the commander of VI Corps sent one of his staff officers with a message for Rufus Ingalls, the officer in charge at the City Point docks, alerting him that VI Corps would soon arrive on the docks.

> Headquarters, VI Corps
> July 9, 1864 -- 9 p.m.
>
> Brigadier General R. Ingalls, Chief Quartermaster, etc.:
>
> I am ordered to march my corps to City Point. There will be about eleven thousand men and they will start within an hour. Can't you furnish me with a small boat for my headquarters, horses, orderlies, etc? Please acknowledge.
>
> H. G. Wright, Major General[59]

Ingalls was already well into his preparations. He scratched off a reply to be taken back to Wright.

> Headquarters, Armies of the United States
> July 9, 1864
>
> Major General H. G. Wright, Commanding VI Corps:
>
> Transportation is now ready for five thousand men. Boats will be here in time for the balance. A small steamer can be furnished for your headquarters, etc. Will you please inform me when the head of your column will reach here?
>
> Rufus Ingalls, Brigadier General[60]

Over the next two days, VI Corps and some of the regiments of XIX Corps were loaded aboard transports outbound for Alexandria where, upon arrival, they marched over the bridge spanning the Potomac River bridge and through the streets of Washington on their way to man the capital's northern defense perimeter.

By the time Early reached the outskirts of Washington on July 11, his opportunity had passed. Thanks in the main to the efforts of Ingalls who had promptly provided shipping when and to where it was needed, Washington's defenses were too heavily manned for Early to even consider an attack. The Southerner backed away and began a retreat into Virginia, his columns burdened with loot, not the least of which was $200,000 in cash which had been extracted as ransom from the people of Frederick, Maryland. The Confederates were pursued, but the chase, plagued by confusion and much inefficiency on the part of the pursuers, allowed Early to escape unscathed.

A Standby Fleet Complicates Grant's Logistics

The underlying strategy of Grant's offensive against Lee's Army of Northern Virginia during the spring and summer months of 1864 had initially adhered to the Administration's policy that the Army of the Potomac should always keep Washington at its back. After the Battle of Cold Harbor, when Grant decided to move south of the James River, land communication with Washington became a thing of the past. From the standpoint of protecting Washington, the Army of the Potomac was no longer to be a physical barrier in place against Lee's Army of Northern Virginia. From the viewpoint of some, this posed a potential danger; but there was an extenuating circumstance which removed much of the concern. The Chesapeake Bay had become a Federal lake in the most complete sense of control and security, and as such, it provided an unhampered line of communication between the Army of the Potomac and Washington. As a practical matter, the supply route by water would turn out to be far superior to the overland one through the Virginia countryside. The proof of this had already been demonstrated when the full VI Corps and part of the XIX Corps had been rushed by steamer to the capital's defense. By water, City Point was only 230 miles from Washington, a voyage of less than thirty hours for even the slowest class of steamer. Furthermore, Chesapeake Bay was a comparatively protected body of water, meaning that only the most severe weather fronts would normally delay transit. From a troop movement standpoint, both in terms of speed and efficiency, the water route clearly held the edge over the land route. The only thing which marred this state of affairs was the recently instituted requirement, as instigated by the Lincoln cabinet, that a reserve of shipping be maintained in case Washington was again threatened by a Confederate raid. This meant that a fairly large tonnage of shipping had to remain virtually idle. This soon created an adverse impact on the supply lift which was at a peak demand due to the necessity for building up quartermaster and commissary reserves at City Point for use over the coming winter. Maintaining an idle fleet on standby was also expensive, and the pinch against the government's pocketbook was being felt with considerable discomfiture -- serious enough to warrant a cautionary comment by the Quartermaster General as addressed to the Secretary of War and then sent on to Grant.

> Quartermaster General's Office
> September 27, 1864

> Honorable Edwin M. Stanton, Secretary of War:
> Sir:
>
> A large quantity of steam and other water transportation has been collected in the waters of the Chesapeake in order to be ready for any sudden general movement of troops. The expense is great, and I have therefore to ask whether, in view of the late successes in the Shenandoah Valley, it will be prudent to reduce this transportation to what may be necessary for current wants and supplies of the troops operating on the James River.
>
> I am, etc.
>
> M. C. Meigs, Quartermaster General[61]

There is nothing evident within either correspondence or published orders which relates to Grant's advice to the Secretary or to any decision -- if there was a decision -- insofar as a time frame for maintaining the standby fleet. The whole discussion soon became a moot issue because of heavy shipping requirements during the late fall which arose following Sherman's arrival at Savannah and which mandated the use of every vessel capable of carrying cargo.

OPERATIONS ALONG THE CAROLINA AND GEORGIA COASTS

Of special importance to the Confederate defense of the eastern Carolinas and Georgia was the Savannah and Charleston Railroad. This line interconnected from Savannah through Charleston to Wilmington, North Carolina, where it met with the Petersburg- Weldon rail system which continued through to Richmond. This rail network provided the Confederates with their only practical means for quickly moving troops along the eastern seaboard. When in the mid fall of 1864 it became certain that Sherman would soon reach the sea somewhere near Savannah, the existence of the Savannah and Charleston posed an imminent threat to Union planners since the enemy could use this railroad to rush reinforcements to Savannah's defense. It also provided the means by which the Confederate garrison at Savannah could evacuate if their capitulation became necessary. Looked at from all eventualities, it was imperative that the Confederates be denied the use of the Savannah and Charleston. Major General John G. Foster, who then commanded the Federal Department of the South, and Rear Admiral John A. B. Dahlgren, who commanded the South Atlantic Blockading Squadron, jointly suggested an expedition to cut the railroad. They proposed to accomplish this by ascending Port Royal Sound and entering into the Broad River from where a strong landing force would march overland to destroy a substantial section of the railroad, inclusive of three of its bridges. Once that was carried out, the combined Army- Navy force would march westward and link up with Sherman.

The naval element of the combined land force that was to ascend the Broad River was a product of orders that Dahlgren had issued to the commanders of his squadron during the past summer. These orders stated that each of the squadron's ships was to assign a detail of sailors and marines for operations ashore.[62] Dahlgren's original purpose for doing this had been to create a force to carry out raids up the rivers of South Carolina and Georgia which would be conducted under naval command. Another reason for Dahlgren's creation of naval landing parties was the prospect of a renewed assault against the port of Charleston in which naval landing forces were to participate. In early 1864, a study had been undertaken jointly by both the Army and Navy for an attack against Charleston, but the idea for such an attack would later be canceled following the taking of Wilmington, North Carolina.

Raids utilizing some of Dahlgren's landing parties had already taken place from Saint Simon's Sound, Georgia, during September 1864. Although rather small in their scope, raids such as these provided experience in land warfare for the naval personnel taking part.[63] In November, Dahlgren inaugurated steps toward consolidation of the individual vessel landing forces into a "naval brigade" under the command of Commander George H. Preble. Dahlgren suggested joining this brigade to a provisional division to be known as the Coastal Division which Major General Foster had ordered to be organized under the command of Brigadier General John P. Hatch. Once organized, the Coastal Division's strength in Army personnel was around five thousand officers and men. When the naval brigade was assigned to it, another five hundred officers and men were added.[64] As it was first organized in November, Hatch's Coastal Division consisted of two infantry brigades with artillery and cavalry units attached in support. The regiments which made up the two brigades were generally under strength, but at this late date in the war, few regiments possessed anywhere near their authorized complements.[65]

HATCH'S COASTAL DIVISION[66]

FIRST BRIGADE
56th New York Infantry
127th New York Infantry
144th New York Infantry
157th New York Infantry
25th Ohio Infantry
32nd US Infantry (colored)
34th US Infantry (colored)
75th Ohio Infantry
107th Ohio Infantry

SECOND BRIGADE
54th Massachusetts Infantry (colored)[67]
55th Massachusetts Infantry (colored)
32nd US Infantry (colored)
35th US Infantry (colored)

ARTILLERY
3rd Rhode Island Artillery, Battery A,
3rd New York Artillery, Batteries B and F

CAVALRY
4th Massachusetts Cavalry, 2nd Battalion

PREBLE'S NAVAL BRIGADE became attached only for the expedition up the Broad River. It consisted of both bluejackets and marines from the vessels of the South Atlantic Blockading Squadron, totaling in all 30 officers and 463 men.

On the early morning of November 28, the Army elements of Hatch's Coastal Division embarked onto their assigned transports at Hilton Head. Leading the transports up the Port Royal Sound were a number of Dahlgren's gunboats. The units of Preble's Naval Brigade were distributed aboard the gunboats. It was still dark when the expedition left Hilton Head. As daylight came on, fog settled in, worsening the visibility. Some of the pilots became disoriented and found themselves detached from the rest of the fleet; others ran their vessel's aground. One pilot who lost his way was assigned aboard the *CANONICUS*, a transport which carried Army engineers and equipment which was to be used to build wharfage on which to land the division's artillery. *CANONICUS* would not arrive at its assigned landing site until very late in the day -- too late to support the landings. The landings were made without encountering opposition, a fortunate circumstance considering the scattering of the transports and the lack of artillery support.

The terrain between the Broad River and the railroad was unknown to Hatch and his officers. Local guides had been brought along; but their knowledge proved less than adequate. They lost their way twice before finding the narrow road that the maps had shown leading toward the railroad. As a combined result of the fog and the confusion of the guides, the enemy had time to move in a reactionary force which was closely equal to Hatch's strength. The Confederates' arrival stopped the Federals solidly in their tracks. Hatch ordered his regimental commanders to dig in on a ridge which was close enough to the river that they would not be cut off if the enemy tried to outflank them.

Shortly after Hatch had consolidated his defenses, Major General Foster arrived from his headquarters at Hilton Head. He immediately ordered a series of probes made in regimental strength. One of the probes succeeded in getting to within three-fourths of a mile of the railroad before being forced back. Deserters who had crossed over into the Federal lines reported that Confederate reinforcements were coming in by rail, a piece of news which diminished Foster and Hatch's hopes for any immediate success.[68]

On December 9, a try was made to break through the enemy's lines, an effort in which all of Hatch's regiments participated; but this attempt failed. The prospects for doing any better in the future seemed dim as the enemy's strength was by now estimated to have increased at least four-fold since the landings.[69] It was becoming evident that Hatch's men were not going to progress beyond their present positions which were stretched across the Gregory Peninsula (Boyd's Neck on some maps), a narrow neck of land which jutted into the Broad River. Hatch's entrenchments were improved daily, and with the Broad River solidly under the protection of the Navy's gunboats, there was no way that the Federal force or its supply could be cut off from the rear. Foster decided to leave Hatch holding in place, rationalizing that the Gregory Peninsula was a perfect base from which to launch future operations.

By agreement with Foster, Dahlgren ordered Commander Preble to return to Hilton Head and disband his brigade of naval personnel, its various detachments to be reassigned back to their respective ships.

First Expedition to Fort Fisher

Early in 1863, discussions had taken place within the Union high command suggesting that the final drive against Lee's army should be launched from a coastal enclave in the Carolinas. The idea was rejected at the time, primarily because if any part of such an expedition had to be recalled for the defense of Washington, the distance it would have to travel by sea around storm-wracked Cape Hatteras could take days to accomplish.[70] The situation was quite different by 1864. A final thrust against Lee's army was a thing now in being, and even though the opposing armies found themselves deadlocked in front of Petersburg and Richmond, Lee could not maneuver without giving up both places which clearly was something he could not afford to do.

What enabled Lee to withstand the siege laid against him was his access to resupply for both his army and the civilian population of Richmond and Petersburg. His supply access was by way of a rail line (and to an extent by canal) connecting to the Shenandoah Valley through Lynchburg and by another rail link coming to him from the east which gave him supply from overseas via Wilmington, North Carolina. The Lynchburg rail connection could be damaged and even destroyed through cavalry raids; however, the ground itself could not be held afterward. This would still leave access by wagons and by canal boat. The link to the sea was another matter since it could be cut with finality once the ports were taken.

As a port of entry, Charleston, South Carolina, was no longer the problem it once had been. From January through to June 1864, only seven enemy blockade runners had made it safely into Charleston, and only four of them had been able to make it out again. Wilmington, North Carolina, was much more of a success story for the Confederates. During that same period of time, eighty-eight blockade runners had broken through into the Cape Fear River and had made it upriver to Wilmington. Eighty-five of them had broken out again.[71] Contrary to a common impression which surrounds the history of the blockade of the Confederacy, civilian consigned cargoes played a decreasing part in entries as the war went on while cargoes destined for the military substantially increased. A factor which is often overlooked when examining the importance of Wilmington for the maintenance of Lee's army in 1864 is that starting the year before, the Confederate Army had itself begun operating vessels which were totally dedicated to the carriage of military materiel.[72] Military goods which came ashore at Wilmington during the initial stage of the siege of Richmond and Petersburg were routed directly onto rail cars and sent to Lee's army via the Petersburg-Weldon Railroad. Damage which had been caused by Union cavalry raids conducted against that railroad's right of way in the late spring and early summer of 1864 was repaired shortly following the raids. That line had continued in use until late August when the tracks became cut off by Grant's envelopment of that railroad's approaches to Petersburg. Following that time, another railroad, the South Side Line, which led from Wilmington directly to Richmond via Greensboro and Raleigh became Lee's new rail link. Though it offered a less direct route from Wilmington than had the Petersburg-Weldon Railroad, the South Side Line did provide an all-important logistical link which was enabling Lee to hold on to both cities. It was apparent to Grant that the most effective ways to deprive Lee would be to eliminate Wilmington from the Confederate supply matrix. Although it was perhaps feasible to isolate Wilmington through attack by land, that was something that would have to wait until Sherman's army reached the coast, and as of mid-summer (1864), Sherman had yet to leave Atlanta. The only realistic option available to Grant at the present time was to seal Wilmington off from the sea. To do that, the blockade of Wilmington would have to be much more effective; but three years of effort had proven this a most difficult, if not impossible undertaking. The features of the coastline and sea bottom adjacent to the Cape Fear River entrances, when compounded by the Confederate fortifications guarding the inlet, prevented a close-in surveillance by the Union blockade fleet.

The defenses commanding the Cape Fear River were in the form of fortifications which had their origins beginning in 1861 when the state of North Carolina established an isolated battery of heavy guns at Federal Point. From that embryonic beginning had grown a huge fortification named Fort Fisher and its subsidiary works. Fort Fisher was studded from end to end with heavy guns -- forty-four of them -- the most modern cannon. The main fortification was constructed in the shape of a huge inverted "L", the short face running in an east-west direction and stretching across a narrow peninsula which separated the open sea from the Cape Fear River.[73] The distance of that short face was 682 yards. A log palisade had been built a short distance to the north of this face and had been reinforced by a network of mines set to be triggered by wires running from galvanic batteries located within the fort. Beginning on the eastern side of the short face and running in a southerly direction was the long leg of the "L" which was 1,898 yards in length. This long leg ran parallel to the ocean beach. Along this front facing the sea were a series of bastions laid out so that defensive fire could be directed anywhere down the front of the face. The southern tip of the longer leg was capped by heavy guns emplaced in what was called the "Mound Battery." One mile to the west-southwest of Mound Battery, and separated from the Fort Fisher complex, was an emplacement named Fort Buchanan which directly commanded New Inlet, one of two entrances by which blockade runners could come into the Cape Fear River from the sea. In addition to covering New Inlet, the guns at Fort Buchanan could also be directed to the west should Union warships manage to get into the river by running either one of the two inlets.[74] In 1865, the south side of New Inlet was bounded by a narrow land spit projecting northward from Smith's Island. The second inlet from the sea into the Cape Fear River was located on the south end of Smith's Island, the opposite shore of that inlet being at Southport. The channel of this inlet ran almost parallel with Smith Island's southern shoreline and was known as the Main Ship Channel. This inlet was the more used entrance into the Cape Fear River, being the route preferred by most of the blockade runners. A battery of heavy guns located at the south end of Smith's Island had a field of fire which covered most of the length of the channel.

The difficulty which the Navy faced in blockading the entrances to the Cape Fear River was that there was an intervening distance of ten miles between the two inlets. To make matters more difficult for the Navy, the Cape Fear Shoals which separated the two inlets jutted out some twenty miles eastward into the Atlantic. To adequately cover the approaches to both inlets with even a modicum of surveillance, required a naval patrol arc which covered a distance of over fifty sea miles. Close-in coverage of the inlets themselves was considered overly dangerous due to the heavy guns covering their approaches.

If there was any doubt held by those either at the War Department or at the Navy Department over the necessity for closing off the Cape Fear River to Confederate shipping, it was quickly dispelled on August 6 when the commerce raider *CSS TALLAHASSEE* cleared out of Wilmington for the high seas. Once she had run past the Union blockading fleet, her commander set a course for the offings of New York where he commenced to create havoc with the property of northern ship owners. *CSS TALLAHASSEE* captured and burned sixteen merchantmen, scuttled another ten, and bonded five -- all during the month of August.[75] The outcry arising from the ship owners finalized the Lincoln Administration's collective thinking that Wilmington had to be sealed off without further delay.

Rear Admiral David G. Farragut, fresh from his well heralded triumph at Mobile Bay, was scheduled to relieve Rear Admiral S. P. Lee from command of the North Atlantic Blockading Squadron. Secretary of the Navy Welles envisioned Farragut as just the man to head the Navy's role in an attack against Fort Fisher; but Farragut was not in good health, and he begged off from the assignment, requesting instead a leave of absence in order to recuperate.[76] To substitute for Farragut, Rear Admiral David D. Porter (back at New Orleans from the failed Red River Expedition) was ordered east with instructions to relieve S. P. Lee by early October.[77]

The first attempt to take Fort Fisher would fail, and the effort would become, without much doubt, the most glaring example of a lack of interservice cooperation during the Civil War. A good part of the reason for failure rested with the major players, David D. Porter representing the Union Navy and Benjamin F. Butler representing the Union Army. Both men personified the worst in overly ambitious, egocentric personalities. Grant had originally considered Butler as the one to actively lead the Army's part of the operation because of Butler's then present role as commander of the geographic region which encompassed the North Carolina coast.[78] Porter, in the company of Assistant Secretary of the Navy Fox, visited with Grant at City Point shortly after Porter arrived from the west. At that meeting, the admiral expressed to Grant his reluctance to have Butler command the Army contingent. According to Porter's later account -- written some years after the war -- Grant seemed to have appreciated Porter's sentiments, giving deference to his wishes by issuing an order for Major General Godfrey Weitzel to lead the Army's part of the operation. Grant would later claim that he never thought Butler would go on the expedition despite the fact that Weitzel and the troops he led were part of Butler's overall command. Butler undoubtedly sensed the fame and glory which would come from a successful taking of Fort Fisher, and for that reason decided to accompany Weitzel, an action which in effect removed Weitzel from making major command decisions in the days ahead.

By December 13, the transports which were to take the assault troops south were loading at Fortress Monroe. In order to confuse any enemy agents which might be observing, Butler ordered the transports to proceed up the Chesapeake Bay and into the Potomac River. As soon as darkness settled in, each transport master was told to head his ship back out of the Potomac River, down the bay, and out into the open Atlantic with a course set toward a specified rendezvous point seaward of Cape Fear.

Porter claimed some years later that he made a number of attempts to confer with Butler prior to the departure of the transports from Hampton Roads. Porter's wish at the time -- or so he would later claim -- had been to coordinate with Butler's plans. Whether either Butler or Porter had any real desire to coordinate with the other is an unresolved question.[79] Butler would later claim that he had expected

Porter to be off Cape Fear when he arrived, a claim that seems substantiated by the events which transpired prior to the fleet's departure from the Chesapeake.[80] The admiral had written to Butler prior to that departure, stating that he would rendezvous with the Army transports off Cape Fear after first stopping at Beaufort, North Carolina, to pick up ammunition for his monitors. As Butler would explain in his report, his own detour of the Army transports up Chesapeake Bay and into the Potomac before turning them seaward had given Porter "a thirty-six hour start to accomplish this," (meaning Porter's stopover at Beaufort to pick up the ammunition).[81] Butler arrived at Cape Fear and waited over the 16th and 17th and part of the day of the 18th before Porter finally showed up. The 16th and 17th of December had been days of fine weather, perfect for landing operations. But by the 18th, the weather had begun to worsen. Butler's report states that on the 19th he received a message from Porter's flagship advising him that heavy weather was on its way and suggesting that Butler proceed with the Army transports to Beaufort, there to await better conditions.[82]

An element in the planning for the attack against Fort Fisher was that a hulk was to be loaded with black powder and towed into close proximity of the fort where it would be exploded, the theory being that the explosion would flatten the place. The original idea for this seems to have had its roots in an event which occurred some years before on the Thames River in England. There, a canal boat loaded with black powder had accidentally exploded causing extensive damage to surrounding structures. Who first thought of using a similar scheme to flatten Fort Fisher is unclear and a point which was strenuously argued after the event. Those who have attributed the idea to Butler have done so without real evidence although it is certain that Butler was a strong backer. In Porter's partially autobiographical book, *The Naval History of the Civil War,* he related that all along he had considered Butler's powder vessel scheme against Fort Fisher to be unworkable. That statement is a direct reversal of the opinion he expressed in writing on December 17, 1864, which was before the explosion took place. He had then written Commander A. C. Rhind, the officer who was given the responsibility for setting off the charge, stating, "I do not anticipate such a dreadful earthquake as some suppose will take place (destroying everything) nor do I think the effect will in any way be mild." Porter went on to write Rhind that he thought the concussion would demoralize the enemy and would tumble any magazine built on framework. He stated his belief that the famous Mound Battery wound be among those things destroyed and that its guns would be buried beneath the ruins. Continuing, Porter expressed the conviction that houses in Smithville and even Wilmington "will tumble to the ground." [83] Porter's assentiveness, if not downright enthusiasm toward the scheme, had included his providing the Navy's *USS LOUISIANA*, a vessel considerably worse for the wear which was at the time being readied for retirement from the fleet. Porter ordered her to Hampton Roads, there to be loaded with powder bags provided out of both Army and Navy ordnance stores.

On December 18th, the *USS LOUISIANA* arrived off Cape Fear with Rhind in command. Rhind carried orders signed by Porter that the explosion was to be set for the next day. As far as Butler knew, that date stood despite the fact that the approaching weather front had the potential of effectively canceling any over-the-beach assault which would follow an explosion. That the explosion would not be coordinated with a beach assault made little sense either to Butler or to Weitzel. Prior to the departure of the transports to Beaufort for shelter, Weitzel went to Porter's flagship to request a delay of "several days" so as to await better weather. Porter agreed to this and sent a launch off to inform Rhind of the postponement.[84] In his prediction of approaching bad weather, Porter was right on the mark, as a heavy gale now blew in from the southeast. Although the Army transports headed in to Beaufort, Porter's squadron rode out the gale at anchor off Cape Fear.

Up to the time of the gale there had been a noticeable lack of coordination between the major players, and things did not get any better once the gale abated. Before the majority of the Army transports had returned from Beaufort, Porter ordered the *USS LOUISIANA* moored close into the beach and its powder cargo ignited. The explosion proved to be a total disappointment with the only damage occurring to the powder ship itself. She totally disappeared. The garrison at Fort Fisher felt no effects, its members merely thinking that there had been an explosion in the magazine of one of Porter's gunboats.

On his arrival from Beaufort with the van of the transport fleet, Butler asked Porter to send some of the Navy's gunboats through New Inlet so as to bring their fire against the rear of Fort Fisher, promising that once the naval vessels were in the river, the Army would supply them from over-the-beach. This assurance was, of course, based on the premise that a beachhead could be secured by Weitzel's troops. Butler later claimed to Grant that the admiral had refused outright to send any of his vessels through the inlet. Butler's contention on this point was not an accurate one since Porter did send launches in to make soundings of New Inlet, presumably in preparation for an attempt to run through some of his gunboats. The launches had been quickly driven out from Fort Buchanan by enemy fire before a survey could be made. Without adequate knowledge of the navigable depths, Porter was more than justified in not proceeding further with Butler's request.[85]

Porter now opened a bombardment against the entire seaward length of the battlements with special concentrations of the fire directed against the fort's northern face. It was the northern face against which Weitzel was to later launch his ground assault. It was by now Christmas Day. The naval bombardment kept up throughout most of that day, and observers on the Navy ships were of the belief that significant damage was being caused. Meanwhile, the remaining transports had arrived from Beaufort, and Weitzel went to Porter's flagship to confer on final arrangements for the beach assault. It was agreed that seventeen of the Navy's lighter draft gunboats would approach close in to the beach and then open fire against the battlements, a fire which was not to be lifted until the troops were all safely ashore. Porter was to send one hundred small boats with their oarsmen to help ferry the Army into the beach.[86] Besides the small boats which Porter was going to supply, Butler had brought along twenty specially designed surf boats crewed by soldiers from Graham's Naval Brigade.[87]

At 7 a.m. on the day after Christmas, the signal was sounded to begin final preparations for the landing. The light draft gunboats moved inshore to begin their covering bombardment.

Weitzel had a total troop strength of around sixty-five hundred officers and men. Five hundred of them would constitute the first landing wave. (Weitzel would later claim that this initial wave was to be for purposes of reconnaissance only and not to establish a beachhead.) A follow-up landing wave was to establish a defensive line some distance back of the beach and hold position there until the rest of the expedition had come ashore.[88]

A landing site had been chosen approximately three miles north of Fort Fisher's northern face. When the reconnaissance force came ashore there, it was not contested. After the commander of the second wave, Colonel Martin Curtis, had reached the beach, he sent a strong line of skirmishers south toward the fort. "Upon approaching to within seventy-five paces of the fort [the skirmishers] succeeded in completely silencing the guns in their front." [89] An officer was somewhat erroneously reported to have entered in through one of the fort's sally-ports, capturing and bringing out a Confederate flag, doing so without interference from any defenders, all of whom were at the time reported as cowering in their bomb-proofs.[90] As soon as Curtis was made aware that Fort Fisher could be so easily entered, he sent an officer back up the beach to bring his main body forward. The officer returned without the troops and informed Curtis, who was then up with his skirmish line, that Weitzel had just come ashore and had ordered a withdrawal back to the landing site to wait there for further orders. Weitzel's decision had been made upon his own cursory appraisal of conditions as he viewed them from 800 yards away. He was apparently unaware that Curtis's pickets had silenced the guns to their front. Following his order to Curtis to withdraw to the landing site, Weitzel had gone back offshore to confer with Butler who was then aboard the Army gunboat *CHARLES CHAMBERLAIN*.

In his report to Grant made some days following, Butler wrote that when Weitzel put in his appearance on *CHARLES CHAMBERLAIN* he gave his opinion of what he believed was the impervious appearance of the northern face of the fort. Additionally, he brought along a note from the commander of the third wave of troops (which by now was on the beach) which informed that a large enemy force consisting of two infantry brigades was supposed to be approaching from Wilmington and was thought then to be within two miles of the landing site. As deduced at the time, both by Butler and Weitzel, this development threatened to trap those ashore between the fort to their south and the enemy force reported to be approaching from the north. The information that an enemy force was approaching from the north had come from a rebel deserter who had entered the picket line that the commander of Weitzel's second wave had established a half mile or so north of the landing site.[91] No attempt seems to have been made to verify the deserter's claim that an enemy force (much less two brigades) was close. The information that Fort Fisher was about to be reinforced later proved to be correct, but contrary to what the deserter had claimed, the reinforcements were no where near at the time.[92] With only the intelligence provided from one lone enemy deserter, Butler ordered an evacuation of the beach, a move in which Weitzel at the time appears to have concurred. The order to leave the beach was acted on with such haste that over seven hundred men were stranded ashore and would not be withdrawn until late the next day.

In their decision making, neither Butler nor Weitzel seems to have taken into consideration the full firepower of Porter's fleet which was available to them. The Navy's guns could have been employed with great effect against any enemy approaching from the north along the beach strand, a strand which was in full view of those offshore. Weitzel's and then Butler's action in abandoning the solid foothold gained was carried out in direct conflict with Grant's instructions issued prior to the expedition's departure from the Chesapeake. These instructions were certainly clearly stated.

> ...Should such landing be effected whilst the enemy still hold Fort Fisher and the batteries guarding the entrance to the river, then the troops should entrench themselves, and by cooperating with the Navy effect the reduction and capture of those places." [93]

The report Butler made to Grant includes a puzzling and vague statement alleging that Grant had given Butler authorization to abort the expedition and return to Fortress Monroe.

> I lay by the shore until 11 o'clock the next day, Monday, the 26th, when having made all proper dispositions for getting the troops on board, I gave orders to the transport fleet, as fast as they were ready, to sail for Fortress Monroe, in obedience to my instructions from the lieutenant general.[94]

When sending Butler's report along to Halleck, Grant made it clear for the record that Butler's conduct in evacuating the beach had been in rank contradiction to the orders he had been given before he left Fortress Monroe.

> ...My dispatches to General Butler will show his report to be in error where he states that he returned after having effected a landing in obedience to my instructions. On the contrary, these instructions contemplated no withdrawal, or no failure after a landing was made.[95]

Grant was not the only one disturbed over Butler's conduct. A dislike of long standing which Porter held for Butler now erupted into total condemnation. The feisty admiral's prejudice over Butler's amateur standing as a general would now be replaced by a full-blown vendetta. On December 27, Porter wrote the Secretary of the Navy suggesting that Butler should be sent back to civilian life. In that communication, Porter held Weitzel blameless for what had happened at Fort Fisher, putting the entire case against Butler. Whether this was done out of ignorance of Weitzel's role in the decision to abort the landing or whether it was because of the admiral's tendency to excuse a professional soldier (Weitzel was a U.S. Military Academy graduate and a career soldier) while expecting the worst from political generals, is problematic. In all probability, a major factor in the flood of criticism against Butler which soon began to flow from Porter's pen was Porter's practice of directing the spotlight of blame upon another whenever an operation in which he (Porter) was involved had failed.

Whether the sixty-five hundred men of Weitzel's command could have held out if brought ashore and left there will forever remain a question. The Navy's supportive fire would have been a real plus toward keeping them there; however, a substantial risk would have existed in the event bad weather prevented the Navy from giving that support. Since heavy weather was a factor to be expected off the Carolinas during late December and January, there would have been the question of resupply should heavy seas have prevented over-the-beach replenishment. All this notwithstanding, had Weitzel not interfered with Curtis, and had the rest of the troops been sent ashore, and had those already there not been withdrawn, Fort Fisher might have been taken that very day. What had happened spoke of poor generalship, and Butler would pay the price for failure by being relieved of his command of the Army of the James. He was sent north to New York and placed in charge of what was virtually a paper command. Soon after, he resigned and returned to civilian life.

Quartermaster Vessels Which Participated in the Failed Attempt to Take Fort Fisher

Major General William H. C. Whiting, CSA, while reporting to Richmond about the events surrounding the attack against Fort Fisher, stated that during the landings, he counted ten or twelve transports.[96] From examination of the reports of the Union officers who were involved on the expedition, it is possible to definitively identify thirteen vessels which acted as transports to Cape Fear. They were:

ADMIRAL DUPONT	*CHARLES THOMAS*	*S. MOORE*
BALTIC	*GENERAL LYON*	*SALVOR*
C. W. THOMAS	*HAZE*	*STARLIGHT*
CHARLES CHAMBERLAIN	*IDAHO*	*WEYBOSSET*
	PERIT	

SHERMAN REACHES SAVANNAH AND
A SHIPPING SHORTAGE DEVELOPS

On December 10, 1864, Major General William T. Sherman's Army of the West reached the outskirts of Savannah. The terrain fronting Savannah's defenses appeared to Sherman to be unfavorable for a frontal assault. Sherman wrote Grant that an immediate attack did not seem necessary and that he intended to wait out the enemy. Sherman possessed a fairly substantial stock of foodstuffs at the time, the result of denuding the Georgia countryside as his army passed through it. The rice crop had also been excellent that year within the coastal belt, and Sherman's commissary officers had already added large amounts of it to the men's rations. It was estimated at the time that the bounty of foodstuffs would last another three weeks; but then supplies would have to start coming in by sea from the north. Since arriving transports would require unloading facilities accessible to good wagon roads, sea access was a priority in Sherman's planning. Toward that end, he needed to make contact with the Navy. Fortunately, a division of Sherman's XV Corps had already taken possession of Fort McAllister on the Ogeechee River, a navigable stream which runs to the south and west of Savannah before emptying into coastal Ossabaw Sound. (Fort McAllister was close to the point where that river entered Ossabaw Sound.) On the evening of December 13, Sherman boarded a small boat at Fort McAllister and headed downstream toward the sound. In no time at all, he made contact with the Navy, an event which took place when he met a Navy tug on its way upstream. The tug's skipper informed Sherman that a force of gunboats was expected at the mouth of the Ogeechee at any hour, news which soon proved accurate. On the following day Sherman met with Rear Admiral John A. Dahlgren who commanded the offshore blockading force.[97]

The original plan which had been decided upon some weeks past, and which Grant had worked out in some detail with Halleck, was that once Sherman arrived on the coast, he and his army would take ocean passage to join Grant and the Army of the Potomac in front of Richmond. However, that plan had been changed. Instead, Sherman was to undertake yet another swath of waste and desolation, this time north through the Carolinas. But before that could begin, Savannah would have to be occupied, and Sherman's army would have to be resupplied.

Taking into consideration all aspects of his army's situation, Sherman believed that the best way to force the capitulation of Savannah would be to put the city under siege. To hasten this along, Sherman ordered a train of heavy guns brought up the Ogeechee by ship from Hilton Head. Once the guns arrived, the bombardment of the city was to begin. Major General J. G. Foster, the commander of the Department of the South, notified Sherman of the progress being made to open the Ogeechee River for shipping.

> Headquarters Department of the South
> Steamer *NEMAHA*, Ogeechee River, Georgia
> December 16, 1864

Major General Sherman, Commanding:
General:

On my way up today, I sounded the [Ogeechee] river, obtained two good pilots, one of whom is on the *ISLAND CITY*, and removed a pier and the burnt rubbish of the railroad bridge so as to permit vessels to pass. Between that bridge and this point there is only seven feet of water at high water; up to the railroad bridge from the mouth of the river there is ten feet of water at low water. All the vessels with supplies may come to the railroad bridge, but from there to this point lighters must be used, except at high water, when the light draught steamers may come up. The siege battery of 30-pounder Parrotts is in the river, three pieces on the steamer *SYLPH* and three more on another steamer. Forage is also here on vessels, both steam and sailing. Two large steamers and one schooner with commissary stores are also in the river coming up. In going down, I will endeavor to pick up on the plantations pilots enough to place one on each vessel, if possible, and hurry them up. All of them should arrive at the railroad bridge at noon tomorrow. The *SYLPH* is of light draught, and can come directly here and land the 30-pounder Parrotts at the landing. I shall leave as soon as the water rises sufficiently to proceed directly to Hilton Head, to send a steamer to Fortress Monroe with Lieutenant Colonel Babcock. After that I shall return at once.

Respectfully, yours

> J. G. Foster, Major General[98]

Before the Parrott guns were landed, Sherman's advance pickets reported the surprising news that Savannah had just been evacuated. Sherman now had possession of a major port through which his army could receive its supplies. By the time Sherman's Army of the West reached the outskirts of Savannah, it totaled fifty-four thousand officers and men. That by itself, in terms of troops to be fed and otherwise provided for, was impressive.[99]

A periphery problem involving logistics was facing Sherman. It was that a host of former slaves had attached themselves to the army's columns during the march from Atlanta. Somehow these people had to be cared for, but under no circumstances could they be allowed to stay with the army. Numbering in the thousands, it was obvious that something must be done to resettle them, preferably in such a way that they could become self-sufficient and no longer a burden to the government. The answer to this was Sherman's Special Field Order No. 15. This order called for the setting aside of the Georgia and South Carolina sea islands as well as a strip thirty miles deep, extending inland from the coast. Within these areas, each Negro head of family would be granted forty acres to homestead. According to the reconstruction historian

Eric Foner, Special Field Order No. 15 resulted in "40,000 freedmen [being] settled on 'Sherman Land.'"[100]

The Army Transport Fleet on the Coasts and on the Rivers as of 1864

Within the coastal zones and on the western rivers in the summer of 1864, the Army had under its direct ownership: 39 ocean type steamers; 45 river and bay steamers; 20 steam tugs, 2 sailing barks, 2 sailing brigs, 21 sailing schooners, and 29 barges, for an owned aggregate of 48,729 tons burden. At the same time, it had under charter: 74 ocean steamers, 164 river and bay steamers, 51 steam tugs, 8 sailing ships, 4 sailing barks, 7 sailing brigs, 86 sailing schooners, and 208 barges, for a charter aggregate of 158,694 tons burden. Additionally, there were within the coastal zones and on the western rivers large numbers of vessels of varied types being employed by the Quartermaster through various affreightment (cargo space for hire) arrangements.[101]

The calls upon the Quartermaster Department's fleet (both owned and chartered vessels) serving the Atlantic and Gulf of Mexico coastal areas were considerable, not only for supplying the needs of the army then entrenched before Richmond, but also for supplying the many garrisons being maintained from Virginia to Florida's tip, as well as within the Gulf of Mexico. Additional transportation requirements cropped up in connection with serving amphibious missions being carried out rather routinely in the Carolinas, in Georgia, and in northern Florida.

The Guard Point System

As more areas within the coastal zones of the Carolinas, Georgia, and Florida came under a secure Federal occupation, so did the commercial opportunities for civilian coastal trade. This civilian trade was often in competition with the military's need for vessels, and at worst, some privately operated shipping flying the Union flag were suspected of moving illegal goods through the enemy's lines. This had become a cause of concern to the Navy. To control it, a system was put into place, beginning in 1863, whereby the Army quartermasters agreed to provide the Navy with current lists of all Quartermaster employed vessels scheduled to pass certain Navy guard points which had been established at the mouths of those rivers and bays which extended back into Confederate-held territory. If a vessel was not listed as being on legitimate Quartermaster business, the commander of the naval guard ship was to deny further passage. The guard point system soon developed problems which resulted in the exchange of some irate correspondence between the concerned military and naval authorities. The major problems came about from the failure of various quartermaster and/or commissary officers to provide up-to-date lists of their legitimately employed vessels. Irrespective of the ill feeling it caused, the guard point system did cut down on some illegal trade and the diversion from that trade had the side effect of alleviating to a degree the shortage of shipping which from time to time had cropped up to hamper the Army's movement of goods by water.[102] That shipping which had been engaged in the type of civilian trade suspected of dealing in illegal commodities would soon be diverted into the lucrative charter market which arose once Sherman's army reached the sea at Savannah. Anything which could float was to become of vital importance to the Army's needs.

Sherman Prepares to Move North

The use of the port of Savannah as a terminal for transports discharging cargo was at first prevented by obstructions which the enemy had placed to block the main ship channel in the Savannah River. These would take time to remove. In the meantime, wharfage was prepared by Sherman's engineers at Thunderbolt, a landing place approachable from the sea which was located a few miles east of Savannah. From Thunderbolt, an existing rail line connected to Savannah. This rail line had a most utilitarian advantage to Sherman since his mules and horses had come into short supply. There was, though, a handicap with Thunderbolt as a port due to the fact that only ten feet of water could be carried to the wharves there. This depth limitation excluded Thunderbolt's use by deep draft transports. To circumvent that deficit, the larger classes of ocean transports were brought to anchor at the mouth of the Savannah River where their cargoes were offloaded and taken by lighter up to Thunderbolt by way of Saint Augustine Creek.

Although Sherman would not be ready to leave Savannah for some time, he decided, with Grant's approval, that after the new year, he would send his XVII Corps to Beaufort, South Carolina, by way of Port Royal Sound. After landing at Beaufort, XVII Corps was to cross over a small river separating Port Royal Island from the mainland and take up positions along the Savannah and Charleston Railroad. This was the same railroad which Hatch's Coastal Division had earlier failed to reach. After XVII Corps had secured the rail line, it was to hold its position there until the main part of the army was ready to leave Savannah.

While making preparations to embark XVII Corps from Thunderbolt, a misunderstanding arose within the Quartermaster General's office in Washington concerning the transports which were to be used in that operation. Anxious that his buildup of supplies at Savannah would not be delayed, Sherman had earlier sent Grant a dispatch carried north by fast steamer, asking that the Quartermaster Department not reassign to the task of moving XVII Corps to Beaufort any of those vessels then being used to transport supplies down from the north. Sherman stated that the troop lift to Beaufort would be handled by light draft vessels which were already present in the Department of the South and which had already been assigned directly to that command. Grant's headquarters endorsed Sherman's message and passed it along to the quartermasters at City Point, Virginia, for their information. Meanwhile, the quartermaster at the headquarters of the Department of the South (located at Hilton Head) had been directly contacted by Sherman's adjutant who passed along Sherman's request for local vessels to move XVII Corps to Beaufort. Not having on hand at Hilton Head enough vessels to do that job, while also continuing the use of the department's shallow drafts on the Thunderbolt lighterage route, the quartermaster at Hilton Head sent a request to the Quartermaster General's office in Washington asking that a number of light draft steamers be sent south. (This request was sent without the knowledge of Sherman's headquarters.) To those in Washington, the Hilton Head request seemed to be in direct contradiction to a standing order of Grant's prohibiting the diversion of any transports -- over and above those already allocated to Sherman's supply needs -- from the supply of Grant's army in Virginia. Confusion arising over the matter was articulated within a telegram sent to Grant by Quartermaster General Meigs on December 19.

> Washington
>
> Lieutenant General Grant, Commanding, Armies of the United States
> General:
>
> Hilton Head some days since called for at least six light steamers to ply between the ocean fleet of steamers and supply vessels and Sherman's army, on the Ogeechee. I ordered the steamers to be selected from among those in the Chesapeake waters as the quickest way of supplying this necessity. I am told that yesterday verbal orders, by your authority, were given forbidding the detachment of the steamers. What shall be done?
>
> M. C. Meigs, Quartermaster General[103]

The mix-up was finally untangled; but the subject remained misunderstood by Grant for some time.

On January 3, XVII Corps began loading at Thunderbolt. A week later, it arrived at Beaufort and reassembled.[104] Only the lightest of opposition was encountered when the corps entrenched astride the Savannah and Charleston rail line.

Shipping and the priority involved with allocating it to Sherman's needs was of a dimension which seemed to require attention from the topmost echelon. At least that is how Quartermaster General Meigs saw the situation. To find out for himself where problems lay, Meigs traveled to Savannah to meet with Sherman and remained there with him until the end of January.

Ninety-nine troop and supply transports would be required for Sherman's support alone once he left Savannah. They are named below (Unless otherwise noted, those named were all steamers.)

ABBY B [d]	*GEORGE C. COLLINS*	*NELLIE BAKER*
ACHILLES	*GEORGE LEARY*	*NEPTUNE*
ACHILLES [a]	*GOLDEN GATE*	*NORFOLK*
ALBERT THOMAS [d]	*GOLIAH* [a]	*ONEONTA*
ALEXANDER YOUNG [d]	*GUIDE* *	*PARTHENIA*
ALIDA [a]	*HELEN GETTY*	*PATAPSCO*
ALLISON	*HERMAN LIVINGSTON*	*PHILADELPHIA*
ANN MARIA	*HUDSON*	*PILOT BOY*
AUGUSTA	*IDAHO*	*PLANDOME* [d]
BAZAAR [b]	*ISLAND CITY*	*PLANTER*
C. C. LEARY	*J. D. JONES* [e]	*PLATO*
C. W. THOMAS	*JAMES MURRAY* [a]	*RACHEL S. MILLER* [d]
CANONICUS	*JENNIE MORTON* [d]	*REBECCA BARTON*
CHAMPION	*JERSEY BLUE*	*RELIEF* [a]
CHARLES HOUGHTON	*JOHN FARRON*	*RESCUE* [a]
CHARLES OSGOOD	*JOHN N. JENNIN* [d]	*ROBERT PALMER* [d]
COSMOPOLITAN	*JOHN P. LEVY* [a]	*RUSSIA*
CROATAN	*LOUISA MOORE*	*SAVANNAH*
D. H. MOUNT	*LOUISBURG*	*STANDISH*
DELAWARE	*LOUISE*	*STARLIGHT* [a]
DIAMOND	*LOYALIST*	*STEPHEN DUNCAN* [c]
DUDLEY BUCK	*MARY A. BOARDMAN*	*SYLPH*
E. L. CLARK	*MARY BENTON*	*THORN*
EDWIN LEWIS	*MASSASOIT*	*TRANSIT* [d]
EL CID	*MATAGORDA*	*VANSHON*
ELIZA HANCOX	*MAYFLOWER*	*W. W. COIT*
ELIZABETH B [d]	*MAYFLOWER* [b]	*W. W. FRAZIER*
ELLA MAY	*MCCLELLAN*	*WARRIOR*
ELLEN S. TERRY	*MINGUAS*	*WIDE WORLD* [d]
FANNIE	*MONTAUK*	*WILLIAM G. AUDENRIED* [d]
FOUNTAIN	*MONTEREY*	*WILLIAM H. ASPINWALL* [e]
GENERAL HOOKER	*MYSTIC*	*WYOMING*
GENERAL HOWARD	*NANTUCKET*	

[a] tug [b] ship [c] brig [d] schooner [e] pilot boat

* The *GUIDE* appears twice in source document. No tonnage is given under second entry, nor is she identified by type. There is, however, always the possibility that there may have been two vessels named *GUIDE*.[105]

ICE CONDITIONS CREATE A SUPPLY CRISIS

The Winter's Blast

January 1865 turned out to be unusually cold along the eastern seaboard with ice conditions directly threatening the movement of shipping as far south as the Chesapeake. The impact of this was addressed to Quartermaster General Meigs by Rufus Ingalls, then at City Point.

January 10, 1865

Quartermaster General, (Through General-in-chief)

We have only some three days' grain within our reach. So far as I am informed the animals have been on half rations since the 3d instant. General Grant could not move his army, if he would, for want of forage. If there be plenty on the way here I am not informed of the fact, as ordered recently by you. Should the river close up with ice in our present situation the consequences would be fatal to our stock. Forage, particularly grain, should be sent here by steam power. Sea steamers laden with grain could tow sail crafts to this point. Our immediate necessities should be supplied in this manner. Generals Rucker or Van Vliet could have this done if so ordered.

Rufus Ingalls, Quartermaster[106]

Animal feed was not the only item about to disappear from the quartermasters' inventories at City Point. Coal supplies were also critical. Because of this, the sick and wounded in the hospitals were beginning to suffer, and many who might otherwise survive were going to die. Nineteen days later, things were much worse with the coal supply now almost gone.

City Point
January 29, 1865

General Rucker:

The *WEBSTER*[†] left here for Annapolis at 10 a.m. There are complaints that the railroad trains [from Annapolis] are insufficient and horribly slow and irregular. Can you not run a train direct between Washington and Annapolis during this cold weather? Please cause the *CITY POINT* and other vessels to be liberated from the Potomac as soon as possible. We are nearly out of coal. I had supposed General Thomas would have caused a plenty to be sent here long ago, but now the coal vessels are frozen in on the Delaware. The weather is very windy. At 12 m. today, thermometer at 38 degrees. Considerable thin ice on the river.

Rufus Ingalls, Brigadier General and Chief Quartermaster[107]

† Correct name is *DANIEL WEBSTER NO. 1*

Ice conditions, which by the end of January were beginning to block most northern harbors, were starting to impact Sherman's resupply as well as Grant's. Even in those cases where harbors were not themselves bound in, solid ice on the canals and rivers which served the major northern ports had resulted in stoppages of cargoes feeding to the seaports through those waterways. This was especially true of coal which in almost all cases was mined at considerable distances inland and which was usually transported by canals and rivers to the ports. More often than not, the masters of oceangoing steamers found themselves unable to sail because they could not obtain coal for their ship's bunkers. The crisis was summarized by Meigs in a wire to Ingalls sent at the end of January.

Quartermaster General's Office, Washington City
January 30, 1865

Brigadier General R. Ingalls, Chief Quartermaster
Armies before Richmond, City Point, Virginia

Dispatch of this date received. On my return from Savannah, I find Philadelphia, Baltimore, Washington, and Alexandria closed by ice, and these late movements of troops on an extensive scale, for which no previous notice was given, have occupied all the ocean steam vessels of the country, to the temporary interruption of most private lines. These movements have also exhausted the accumulated stock of coal at Fortress Monroe, City Point, and Annapolis, while the ice blockade of Philadelphia has prevented the shipment of the usual current supply. General Thomas informs me that coal has already been ordered to Fortress Monroe from New York. The attempt to open the port of Baltimore, and to send coal both by water and by rail from that point to Annapolis, will be made, and, if successful, this will enable the steamers now at Fortress Monroe to start from Annapolis with troops. When I left here early in January I understood that the stock at Fortress Monroe and at Washington and Alexandria was large and sufficient for all anticipated wants. I trust that the present difficulty will not continue long. There is hope that the Delaware will be opened shortly, and the present indications are that the Potomac will soon be opened again. It is of great importance that all steamers transporting troops or supplies should be unloaded as rapidly as possible and returned for further use. The supply, etc, for Sherman's army at Savannah has engaged many ocean steamers and a large fleet of sailing vessels. The steamers as they return are drawn off for coastwise expeditions, of which you doubtless have knowledge. Even in New York it has at times lately been impossible to coal steamers ordered to sea, in consequence of heavy ice in the harbor. If there has been defective supply I incline to think it has been due to want of notice of movements on a great scale, which could no more be anticipated by the Quartermaster's Department than by those who command the troops.

I am, very respectfully, your obedient servant.

M. C. Meigs, Quartermaster General, Brevet Major General[108]

Meigs's reference to the "late movement of troops on an extensive scale" related to the failed expedition to take Fort Fisher in late December and to a second expedition sent there the following month which would succeed. (That second expedition will be discussed later in this volume). There was also yet another sealift in progress at the time of Meigs's writing, that one involving the shipment of a full army corps from Chesapeake Bay to reinforce Sherman. (That troop movement will also be covered later.)

By mid February, Rufus Ingalls was located back at the War Department in Washington. On February 19, Grant notified Ingalls that City Point was out of coal.[109] Recriminations flew back and forth placing blame for the lack of sufficient supplies on hand, especially at City Point.[110] In retrospect, this criticism was probably valid, at least when it concerned most of the basic commodities, the exception being hay. Its special storage needs and the difficulties encountered during its purchase over the previous summer, would have made the stockpiling of hay difficult. The movement of hay and other vital commodities to City Point from Philadelphia (one of the few ports north of the Chesapeake that remained open in January) had also stopped, at least for barges, when the Chesapeake and Delaware Canal froze, trapping a number of barges which were then moving through the canal. Tugs tried to extract them but without success. It would not be until February 26 that the "ice blockade" in that canal was broken.[111] The number of horses and mules which either died or had to be destroyed in consequence of the shortage of hay at City Point is not of exact record; but general reference to those losses points to an extremely high tally. The hardship that the lack of coal created for the troops in front of Petersburg, especially to the sick and wounded in the hospitals, needs no superlatives to describe. That final winter of the war would long be remembered in terms of the pure misery it caused to both man and beast.

The Enemy's Gunboats Descend From Richmond

At the height of the supply crisis, line-crossers brought information to Grant's headquarters that the rebels at Richmond were preparing to launch a breakout of their gunboat fleet. The goal, as alleged by the line-crossers, was to be the destruction of the supply depots at City Point. The information was confirmed when three days later an attempt was made by enemy gunboats to run through the rapids at Trent's Reach. Six of these vessels were involved; the one in the lead got through. The second gunboat became hung up on an obstruction and blocked those coming behind it, one of them grounding hard on the upper rapids. Despite the fact that ample warning had been given to the commander of the Union Navy's James River Flotilla, none of his vessels were in the neighborhood at the time the enemy gunboats came down. This justifiably angered Grant who made his sentiments known when he described the affair to the Secretary of War.

City Point, Virginia
January 24, 1865 -- 4:30 p.m.
Honorable Edwin M. Stanton, Secretary of War:
I respectfully request that the Secretary of the Navy remove Captain Parker, US Navy, from command of the James River Flotilla tonight by telegraph. With three days' notice of his danger, and a large fleet at his command, when I sent a staff officer to him this morning before daylight, on hearing that the rebel rams were coming down the river and that two of them had passed the obstructions, he had but one gunboat, that a wooden one, and a torpedo boat above the pontoon bridge at

Aiken's Landing. On my arrival here yesterday from Washington I requested him to get to the front every boat he had in the river within reach. This he should have done two days before without notice. The rebels have suffered severely in today's operations, but with a, no doubt, gallant set of commanders for the vessels, they have been allowed to contribute but little to this result. One rebel gunboat was blown up by a shell from Battery Parsons, one other sunk, and a third disabled; the fourth, the *VIRGINIA*, was hit a great many times, but I do not know that she was injured. It is the judgment of officers who were present that had the monitor been in her place, on learning that the *VIRGINIA* and *FREDERICKSBURG* [Confederate gunboats] were aground, both vessels would have been destroyed before they could have been got off. As it is, only the weaker vessel of the two was disabled. The rebels still have five gunboats above us.

U. S. Grant, Lieutenant General[112]

Although Grant mentions two gunboats (rams) as getting through, other reports indicate only one of them succeeded in doing so.

The morning following the enemy's try at sending its gunboats down the James River, the quartermaster at City Point sent two heavily ballasted barges up the river. Tugs pushed these into the narrow channel openings at Trent's Reach, and then each barge was sunk in place, a move intended to permanently block the way downriver from Richmond. The Confederates made no further attempts to send gunboats down the James.[113]

FORT FISHER FALLS

Lieutenant General Ulysses S. Grant badly wanted to take Fort Fisher, so a second try would be made. He assigned the job of the beach assault to the commander of X Corps, Major General Alfred H. Terry.

If any project cried out for interservice cooperation, the taking of Fort Fisher was going to be it. From his experiences on the Mississippi, Grant had derived his own ideas as to how joint operations should be conducted. He was a strong believer that success in such operations called for teamwork. Grant was not going to leave the Army's role solely up to Terry (as he had done with Butler in December), nor was he about to let the naval commander independently call his shots. To ensure that the operation would be conducted as it should be, Grant received the Administration's backing in that he (Grant) would define the responsibility of each service. Grant made that amply clear, albeit with diplomacy, when communicating his views to Porter.

> City Point, Virginia
> January 3, 1865
>
> Admiral D. D. Porter, Commanding, North Atlantic Blockading Squadron:
>
> I send Major General A. H. Terry, with the same troops General Butler had, with one picked brigade added, to renew the attempt on Fort Fisher. In addition to this I have ordered General Sheridan to send a division of infantry to Baltimore to be put on seagoing transports, so that they can go also if their services are found necessary. This will augment General Terry's force from 4,000 to 5,000 men. These troops will be at Fortress Monroe, if the transportation can be obtained (there is but little doubt it can), ready to sail at an hour's notice. General Terry will show you the instructions he is acting under. My views are that Fort Fisher can be taken from the waterfront only in two ways -- one is to surprise the enemy when they have an insufficient force; then the other is for the Navy to run into Cape Fear River with vessels enough to contend against anything the enemy may have there. If the landing can be effected before this is done, well and good; but if the enemy are in very strong force, a landing may not be practicable until we have possession of the river.
>
> General Terry will consult with you fully, and will be governed by your suggestions as far as his responsibility for the safety of his command will admit of.
>
> Hoping you all sorts of good weather and success, I remain, etc.,
>
> U. S. Grant, Lieutenant General[114]

Within the instructions he sent the same day to Terry, Grant explicitly covered what Terry's upcoming relationship would be with Porter. He also laid out contingency plans should the landings fail.

City Point, Virginia
January 3, 1865

Major General A. H. Terry, Commanding Expedition:

The expedition entrusted to your command has been fitted out to renew the attempt to capture Fort Fisher, North Carolina, and Wilmington ultimately, if the fort falls. You will then proceed, with as little delays as possible, to the naval fleet lying off Cape Fear River, and report the arrival of yourself and command to Rear Admiral D. D. Porter, commanding North Atlantic Blockading Squadron. It is exceedingly desirable that the most complete understanding should exist between yourself and the naval commander. I suggest, therefore, that you consult with Admiral Porter freely, and get from him the part to be performed by each branch of the public service, so that there may be unity of action. It would be well to have the whole programme laid down in writing. I have served with Admiral Porter and know that you can rely on his judgment and his nerve to undertake what he proposes. I would, therefore, defer to him as much as is consistent with your own responsibilities.

The first object to be attained is to get a firm position on the spit of land on which Fort Fisher is built, from which you can operate against that fort. You want to look to the practicability of receiving your supplies, and to defending yourself against superior forces sent against you by any of the avenues left open to the enemy. If such a position can be obtained, the siege of Fort Fisher will not be abandoned until its reduction is accomplished or another plan of campaign is ordered from these headquarters. My own views are, that if you effect a landing, the Navy ought to run a portion of their fleet into Cape Fear River, whilst the balance of it operates on the outside. Land forces cannot invest Fort Fisher, or cut if off from supplies or reinforcements, whilst the river is in possession of the enemy. A siege train will be loaded on vessels and sent to Fortress Monroe, in readiness to be sent to you if required. All other supplies can be drawn from Beaufort as you need them. Keep the fleet of vessels with you until your position is assured. [Here, Grant was referring to the transports of the Quartermaster.] When you find they can be spared order them back, or such of them as you can spare, to Fortress Monroe, to report for orders. In case of failure to effect a landing bring your command back to Beaufort, and report to these headquarters for further instructions. You will not debark at Beaufort until so directed. General Sheridan has been ordered to send a division of troops to Baltimore and place them on seagoing vessels. These troops will be brought to Fortress Monroe, and kept there on the vessels until you are heard from. Should you require them they will be sent to you.

U. S. Grant, Lieutenant General[115]

On January 4, Grant again messaged Terry, this time changing his instructions of the day prior so as to comply with a suggestion made to Grant by Porter. Porter had recommended that when Terry arrived off Beaufort, he should keep the Army's transports far enough offshore to hide their presence from enemy agents while Terry himself went into Beaufort to meet with Porter. Grant agreed that secrecy concerning the operation was to be the order of the day. To confuse any spies which might be about, troop commanders were to pass the word among their officers that the embarkation (from Fortress Monroe) was for the purpose of reinforcing Sherman at Savannah.

For the landings on the beach in front of Fort Fisher, Terry was to use the small boats carried by the transports in conjunction with small boats which Porter would supply from the ships of his squadron.[116]   To ensure that Terry would have enough of them for use in the landings, Assistant Secretary of the Navy Fox issued instructions that any and all ships' boats the Navy had at its various shore stations from New York to the Potomac were to be delivered to Terry's custody prior to the time that the transports were scheduled to leave Fortress Monroe.

With all preparations made, Terry's adjutant issued the expedition's General Order No. 2 which stated that the expedition's transports would sail on January 6, precisely at 4 a.m.   Only when each of the transports was abeam of Cape Henry was the senior troop commander aboard to open his sealed orders which disclosed the true destination; he was then to inform the master of the vessel.[117]   Nineteen Army transports left the Chesapeake that morning.[118]

ATLANTIC	EUTERPE	PROMETHEUS
BLACKSTONE	GENERAL LYON	RUSSIA
CALIFORNIA	H. LIVINGSTON [1]	THAMES
CHAMPION	IDAHO	TONAWANDA
COMMODORE DUPONT	MCCLELLAN [2]	VARUNA
DE MOLAY	MONTAUK	WEYBOSSET
	NORTH POINT	

[1] HERMAN LIVINGSTON   [2] Terry's command ship

A heavy gale was in full force by the time the transports arrived off Beaufort, North Carolina.   Terry left the assemblage at sea and went into Beaufort to meet with Porter.   At that meeting, the admiral made a forecast of heavy weather for the next four or five days and because of that advised Terry to order all of his transports into the port.   Terry turned down the suggestion, citing Grant's instructions for the need to maintain secrecy.   Their general's decision would not have been well received by the men on the transports who already were suffering the ravages of mal de mer.   Presumably, security was the least of their concerns in light of the pummeling they were receiving.   As the weather grew worse, Terry changed his mind and sent word out by signal to the transport masters that they could enter port.   On arrival, the troop commanders board each transport were put under orders that no one -- not officers, or men, or members of the civilian crews -- was to go ashore.   Terry hoped that through confinement to the vessels the purpose of the expedition would be kept from enemy ears; however, the newspapers had received the news of the expedition's purpose even before the fleet had cleared Hampton Roads.   That is what Terry was told when he went ashore that evening to visit some friends.[119]

At the onset, Terry's meeting at Beaufort with Porter was somewhat strained, both officers being reluctant to allow the other a place of dominance during the final planning for the attack.   Terry's ego was, however, not as self-dominating as was Porter's. After the initial verbal jockeying, Terry stated that he was at the admiral's disposal.   This seemed to delight Porter, and he then offered Terry a landing force of bluejackets and marines to assist in the assault. Terry accepted, and from that point on until the end of the operation, both officers seem to have gotten along famously.

During the early evening of January 12, Fort Fisher's defenders became witness to fifty-nine naval warships and nineteen Army transports offlying the beach. The over six hundred guns of the naval fleet would soon join together in bombardment. Aboard the transports there were close to nine thousand troops consisting of the Second Division of the XXIV Corps; a brigade from the First Division of the XXIV Corps; the Third Division of the XXV Corps; two reinforced batteries of field artillery; a company of engineering troops; and some light siege guns with their artillerists.[120] The lateness of the hour would give cause for a postponement of the landing until the next day by which time it was hoped the heavy seas from the recent storm would have laid down.

At the first glimmer of dawn's light on January 13, and in accordance with a plan which had been worked out between Terry and Porter, a line of gunboats moved in toward the beach and went into parallel firing position. These gunboats were charged with delivering a close-in fire to cover the landings. As soon as they commenced fire, the Army transports moved in to anchor in two separate groups, the first group just north of the gunboats. The second group took up position about three and a half miles to the north. The first group of transports carried those troops scheduled to make the actual assault against the fort. The second group of transports carried troops which would prepare defensive positions at the head of Myrtle Sound and then hold there against any reinforcing enemy which might come onto the scene from the direction of Wilmington. If Fort Fisher could not be successfully stormed, it was this defensive line which would maintain the foothold ashore as Grant had instructed. At 8 o'clock, small boats began gathering at the lee sides of the transports, ready to load the men who were to go ashore in the first wave.

The first wave from each of the two transport groups were landed at approximately the same time. Outside of some light picket firing, the Confederates did not contest either of the landings. The commander of the group assigned to establish the defensive line at the head of Myrtle Sound made an initial examination of the terrain and decided that a better location for his line would be more to the south at a point about two miles up the beach from Fort Fisher's northern face. The main reason for this change in location was that the new location was at the peninsula's narrowest point, thus allowing for a heavier linear concentration of defenders. Meanwhile, Terry, accompanied by his senior engineering officer, was making a close examination of the fort's northern face. From that reconnaissance, he decided that one more day of bombardment was needed to soften the fort's defenses. He so advised Porter. Following that further softening up, Terry's men were to storm the western side of the fort's northern face while Porter's naval landing force would storm the eastern (seaward) end of the northern face.

Current doctrine at that juncture of the war dictated that when making a frontal assault against fixed works, the attacker was to employ half of his force to lay down covering rifle fire; the remaining half would advance against the works to be taken. If the men making the advance were forced to take to the ground, they would then commence their own fire against the enemy. The half which initially had been laying on the protective fire would then rise from their positions and advance on the works. This process would be successively repeated until the enemy's positions were entered. Such tactics naturally meant that all factions involved in such assaults should be equipped with long arms. Porter's bluejackets were, however, to go into action armed only with cutlasses and revolvers. This was unavoidable since few naval vessels carried enough long arms to equip more than a small landing party. The naval force Porter was now about to send into battle was no small group. It numbered close to two thousand officers and men. One can only guess as to whether Porter appreciated the inadequacies of the firepower with which his landing force was equipped. Comprising less than a fifth of the naval landing force were about four hundred marines who were the only ones supplied with rifles. Their task would be to provide covering fire while the sailors charged against the fort. This was, however, not the same thing, either proportionately or tactically, as the established doctrine for assaulting fixed works.

Porter's knowledge of infantry tactics may have been lacking, but that he had his blood up cannot be denied. An element of savagery was contained in the orders Porter issued to the commander of the naval landing force.

> ...If when our men get into the fort, the enemy commences firing on Fort Fisher from the Mound, every three men will seize a prisoner, pitch him over the walls, and get behind the fort for protection, or into the bomb-proofs...[121]

When Porter's bluejackets arrived on the beach, their officers began organizing them into infantry companies. Terry's assault troops were already assembled for the attack and were waiting at a distance of about 900 yards from the fort. The bombardment laid down by the gunboats was now being buttressed by fire from the more offlying ships of the line. It was obvious that the enemy was in his bombproofs as no living thing could have withstood such a fire while atop the battlements. The assault was scheduled to begin around 3 p.m., the exact moment to be announced by whistle signal from the fleet. At that signal, the bombardment was to be immediately lifted. Despite the thoroughness of the preparations, something seemed to be missing, an omission which at the time puzzled more than one observer. Contrary to Grant's request, none of Porter's vessels had yet attempted to run over the New Inlet bar into the river so as to bring the Navy's gunfire against the fort from its western side. The possible seriousness of that omission seemed apparent when a number of steamers were spotted on the inner side of the barrier beach coming down the Cape Fear River. (Information later received disclosed that these steamers were carrying troops as reinforcements to Fort Fisher.) Fortunately, the beach dunes separating the ocean and the Cape Fear River were sufficiently low to allow Porter's ships a relatively clear field of fire across the barrier beach. This fire forced all but one of the steamers to turn back. The experience made it apparent that as long as daylight remained, the Union Navy had dominance over anything coming down the river. The absence of Porter's gunboats within the Cape Fear River did, however, mean that the western side of the fort remained free from bombardment. On the basis that the assault about to take place had a reasonably good chance of success, Porter may have rationalized that there was no demanding reason to risk any of his vessels by attempting to cross over the New Inlet bar.[122]

When the signal for the assault finally came, a wild enthusiasm took hold of Porter's cutlass-wielding bluejackets. As they charged, the Confederates poured a withering fire against them. This stopped all but a few of the sailors at the outer palisades. Meanwhile, the marines began receiving fire which was directed against them from the fort. They panicked and withdrew to safety, deserting the sailors who they were supposed to support. Those sailors not already dead or incapacitated by wounds were forced to retreat.

In the interim, Terry's men succeeded in gaining the fort's parapet on their first rush. Once inside the fort, they began the slow but deadly process of fighting their way south down the length of the parapet's long face. It was tough going, as they were contested at each of the fort's traverse positions. Porter's gunners on the ships excelled in laying down a protective bombardment just ahead of the advancing infantrymen as they worked their way down the parapet. In that age of limited communication, this was no mean feat, especially since the fire from the ships had to be lifted just ahead of the troops as they advanced. The reason this coordinated fire was so successful was that prior to the expedition's departure from the Chesapeake, a number of junior officers and enlisted men detailed from Porter's fleet had been trained in the Army's method of flag signaling by the signal section at Fortress Monroe. This enabled communication between the Navy flagmen on the ships and the Army flagmen on the battlements which in turn allowed Porter's gunners to walk their covering fire at a close but safe distance ahead of Terry's advancing infantry.

The last enemy traverse of Fort Fisher was occupied at 9 o'clock that evening. Fort Buchanan, located on New Inlet to the south of the main fort, was still held by the Confederates; but by the time Terry's troops crossed the open ground separating it from Fort Fisher's southern traverse, Fort Buchanan's gunners had fled to the mainland by steamboat. This left only the Confederate gun positions guarding the Main Ship Channel. These had now become untenable, and they were abandoned by the enemy during the night.

Union losses had proven lighter than expected. Terry's regimental commanders reported only 119 men killed and 540 wounded. Porter's landing force suffered proportionately a much higher loss with 88 killed, 271 wounded, and 34 missing.[123] Confederate losses were estimated as 500 dead and wounded. Nearly 1500 Southerners were taken prisoner.[124]

~

With the mouth of the Cape Fear River and its subsidiary inlet now securely in Union hands, the blockade runners' access to Wilmington was closed off. The city of Wilmington would remain in Confederate hands for a few weeks; however, since its use by blockade runners was now denied by Union control of its river approach, it was no longer of any value to the Confederate cause.

With Wilmington out of the strategic picture for the Confederacy, the logistical noose had tightened sharply around Robert E. Lee's Army of Northern Virginia. Only one point of usable access remained open on the coasts for enemy blockade runners. This was Saint Mark's, Florida; but even that small port was soon closed down when, during the first week in March, a joint Army- Navy expedition was launched against its defenses.[125]

THE FINAL MONTHS

Reinforcements to Sherman

Grant had decided that the most provident course of action -- in terms of saving Union lives -- would be for Sherman to drive up through North Carolina and come against Richmond from the south and west. Directly contesting Sherman in such a movement would be the remnants of what once had been the Confederate Army of the Tennessee. That army -- under the command of Joseph E. Johnston -- was still a potent force and one which Sherman would have to take seriously. If Sherman found it necessary to divide his force, he would need reinforcements. Grant would order them sent from the western theater. Major General John M. Schofield's reinforced XXIII Corps was the body of troops tapped for this duty. Schofield's corps was to be routed through the Ohio Valley by steamer and then over the Baltimore and Ohio Railroad to Washington and then on to Annapolis. From there, they would travel by sea to North Carolina. This troop movement would involve a steamboat lift at both ends, a complexity in planning which would require careful coordination since the movement was to take place at the worst possible time of the year.

Up to that point in the war, the only shift of a full Union corps from one theater to another had taken place during 1863 when Hooker's XI and XII Corps were shipped from the east to assist in the Chattanooga Campaign. That move had, though, taken place during much better weather conditions, and except in the most minor way, it had not involved coordination with steamships, having been conducted almost entirely by rail. Although Hooker's command had encompassed two corps, in actuality, Schofield's reinforced XXIII Corps was almost as large. It had recently been reorganized from two reduced army corps and had been heavily beefed up by the addition of a number of support elements.

The man who would hold responsibility for transporting XXIII Corps was Colonel Lewis B. Parsons. (For a general discussion of the Civil War responsibilities of Lewis B. Parsons, the reader is referred to Appendix B.) In August 1864 Parsons was transferred to Washington and had been placed in charge of the Army's overall transportation system. On January 11, Assistant Secretary of War Charles A. Dana informed Parsons of the need to move the XXIII Corps to the east. Both men then agreed that the most efficient way to manage such an undertaking would be to locate the man in charge of the movement (Parsons) at some strategic point along the route where telegraph connections were good. The most practical location for this would be at the point where maximum activity was taking place. Parsons could then move his location as that point of activity shifted.

On the eve of his departure for the west, Parsons telegraphed the various railroad executives whose jurisdictions would be impacted, stating that between twelve and twenty-four hours after being notified, the needed rail cars should be assembled at the towns of Evansville, Louisville, and Cincinnati -- all places located on the Ohio River. Parsons had chosen these places as likely ones where ice conditions encroaching from upstream might block the Ohio for further steamship movement toward the east. The country was by this time experiencing frigid weather, but there was no sure way to determine where an ice blockage of the Ohio River might occur. Grant, whose knowledge of the area went back some years, predicted to Parsons that the point of blockage would be at Parkersburg. Parsons believed from his own experience that it might reach much farther west and that it could happen without much warning. To cover any eventuality, Parsons sent telegrams off to the quartermasters and commissary officers regularly stationed along the Ohio River, alerting them to have rations stockpiled at points approximately every one hundred miles along the entire river. Thus, no matter where transfers from steamer to rail might take place, adequate rationing would be available. Whenever the transfers from the steamers to the rail cars took place, it would automatically bring with it a slowdown in the flow of troop movement. Such a slowdown would come as the result of the lesser capacity of rail carriage on a per-train basis when measured against the much greater carrying capacity of individual steamboats. Dana had expressed speed as being of the essence, so Parsons ordered that if ice conditions allowed, the transports were not to stop until they reached Cincinnati.

Despite his best attempts to garner information from Schofield's staff, Parsons had not been given an even close to exact estimate of the number of men or the amount of equipment to be sent east, nor was he informed of Schofield's scheduling as to when the XXIII Corps would be ready to start its move. (As later to be reported, the total manpower of XXIII Corps was close to 20,000 officers and men.)

In order for travel on the Ohio River leg of the trip to be handled with efficiency, Parsons selected an initial assembly point at which all of Schofield's incoming troops would board steamers for transport up the Ohio. He designated Paducah as that place. Instructions were issued to all subordinate quartermaster commands located on the Ohio, the Cumberland, the Tennessee, and on the Mississippi anywhere in proximity to Cairo, ordering every available steamer deemed adequate for carrying troops to assemble at Paducah. Parsons's own arrival at Paducah coincided with the appearance of the first of Schofield's divisions, that division having come down the Tennessee by steamboat from Johnsonville.

Leaving Paducah, Parsons went to Louisville where on January 20, he awoke to gaze upon a severely shallowed Ohio River. A drop in temperature had iced over the small streams feeding into the Ohio, slowing their discharge into the main river. The result was a drop of twenty feet in the Ohio's level. This had shallowed the Falls of the Ohio enough to halt all passage over the rapids there. The only steamers which were still able to get above were those small enough to pass through the adjacent bypass canal. Parsons wired his quartermasters to begin gathering together steamers of limited draft and width which could pass through the canal. From that time forward in the operation, all troops coming up the Ohio by steamer from Paducah were transferred either to steamboats located above the Falls of the Ohio or to those steamers below the falls which were able to pass through the canal. The Ohio River was still reasonably ice free to Cincinnati where the troops were to be offloaded onto rail cars. (Above Cincinnati, the river was reported to be clogged with floating ice.)

While there may have been more, fifty-two steamboats are named within the orders and the related correspondence concerning the movement of XXIII Corps on the Ohio River during January 1865. These steamers were:[126]

A. BAKER	*FLORENCE*, tug	*NIGHTINGALE*
ALEXANDER SPEER	*HAVANA*	*NORA*
BALTIMORE	*HUNTSMAN*	*NORMAN*
BERTHA	*IMPERIAL*	*OMAHA*
BRILLIANT	*IRON CITY*	*PALESTINE*
BURD LEVI	*IZETTA*	*R. J. LOCKWOOD*
CAROLINE	*J. G. BLACKFORD*	*ROSE HITE*
CHAMPION	*J. H. BALDWIN*	*SAINT PATRICK*
CHARMER	*KATE ROBINSON*	*SCIENCE NO. 2*
CLARA POE	*L. M. KENNETT*	*SHERMAN*
CORA S	*LENI LEOTI*	*STEPHEN DECATUR*
ECHO NO. 2	*MAJESTIC*	*SWALLOW*
EMERALD	*MARMORA*	*TARASCON*
EMPEROR	*MERCURY*	*TELEGRAPH*
FANNIE BRANDIES	*MINNEHAHA*	*TYRONE*
FANNY GILBERT	*MORNING STAR*	*VICTORY*
FINANCIER	*NASHVILLE*	*W. F. CURTIS*
	NAVIGATOR	

By January 21, the first contingent of Schofield's corps had reached Cincinnati and had already been transferred to rail cars. This first contingent numbered around three thousand officers and men.

On January 22, a dense fog set in along the Ohio River, beginning at Cincinnati and reaching westward along the river. It was thick enough to temporarily stop all steamboat movement. By the following day, the fog had cleared so another four thousand troops could be brought upriver and transferred to waiting cars. Meanwhile, ice blockages were clearing on the upper reaches of the Ohio so steamers could continue on past Cincinnati. This would decrease the distance by rail, a piece of good luck for Parsons since, as stated earlier, steamers were so much more efficient when judged on a capacity-per-mile basis. This also would translate into a faster turnaround of the trains between Washington City and the movement's western terminus. In order to take advantage of this unexpected good fortune, Parsons ordered all steamboats then above the Falls of the Ohio to take aboard extra coal so they could proceed above Cincinnati. On January 23, after most of the steamers had started upriver, the news was telegraphed that an ice blockage was now well established a short distance upstream of Wheeling, West Virginia, but this was a good 330 statute miles above Cincinnati. Wheeling would now become the western terminus for the rail part of the trip.

From the standpoint of the difficulties with which Parsons would have to deal, the rail part of the journey became the most troublesome. Yet, despite the severity of the weather in the Appalachian Mountains through which the troop trains had to pass, things went more smoothly than might have been expected. The primary credit for this belongs to Assistant Secretary of War Dana who established that control of all facets of the movement -- be they of a military or of a civilian nature -- would be under one single officer, namely Parsons. Parsons's authority was to extend to matters involving the management of the troops while in transit.

What Parsons asked of the railroad executives was certainly beyond anything in previous experience. One example which can be pointed to was the demand placed against the rail superintendent of the Little Miami Railroad (a feeder line of the Baltimore and Ohio system). This official was told to expect a capacity of ten thousand men on the first day of the movement alone, a passenger capacity no doubt beyond what that man's wildest fantasies could envision. Everything that could roll on a track and which could be shunted over to the Baltimore and Ohio was put to use. Rail superintendents were instructed that whenever freight cars had to be substituted for regular passenger cars, they were to be insulated by placing heavy layers of straw over the flooring.

The first day of the rail part of the operation became witness to an unexplained delay. This was finally traced to orders given by the senior troop commander aboard the lead train. He had instructed the train's engineer that the train should be stopped so the troops could dismount to cook rations. Parsons ordered that such practices must immediately cease. Instructions were wired to all concerned quartermasters that precooked hot food would meet the trains at selected stops and would be loaded aboard with minimal delays. Arranging for the food was to be the responsibility of either quartermaster or commissary officers whenever such officers were located along the route. Otherwise, this would become the responsibility of railroad company personnel.

In a number of instances, it seems that troop officers were not as cooperative as they could have been, a matter often made worse whenever a source of liquor was to be found. One Baltimore and Ohio official wired Parsons that a train had become overdue in leaving a siding because the troop commander and some of his officers were sampling the flesh pots in a nearby town, and their enlisted men were nearly all drunk. The men had even threatened to shoot the impatient and irritated train crew if their officers were left behind.[127] By this point, the field command of XXIII Corps had passed from Schofield to Major General Darius N. Couch, as Schofield had gone east to prepare for his takeover of the regional Department of North Carolina. At Parsons's urgent request, orders went out from Couch discouraging future party-going along the right of way.

Headquarters XXIII Army Corps; Columbus, Ohio
January 25, 1865.
All commanding officers of trains will have company officers in the trains with
their men. All commanding officers of trains will have established guards at

stopping places, and see that no depredations are committed by the troops, and that all liquor shops are closed. Railroad officers are expected to report to me the regiment guilty of depredation.

D. N. Couch, Major General, Commanding XXIII Army Corps[128]

Legitimate delays were also occurring, these were generally the result of loaded trains being shunted to sidings to allow passage of westward moving locomotives pulling empty cars. When the move had first begun, empties rolling westward as single train units were widely separated. The result was the constant and often prolonged need to hold trains over at sidings so empties could pass. This problem was corrected through Parsons's telegraphed instructions ordering that after trains delivered their troops on the Potomac, they were to be held over at Washington until a number of such trains arrived and had been unloaded. Then, as a group, they were to be sent back west. That measure substantially reduced the time in which eastward moving troop trains were forced to lay over at sidings.

As the troops of XXIII Corps detrained at Washington, they went into temporary camp before being sent on by train to Annapolis. By the time they had finally disembarked from the rail cars, each and every soldier had traversed in total over 1500 miles, a considerable part of that trip having been made by rail over mountainous terrain and in the worst of winter weather. Despite the difficulties encountered, all accidents to personnel (except one) were suffered by the train crews, a result of their exhaustion from working inordinately long hours.

The total time elapsed for the entire movement -- including the steamboat leg of the trip and the time spent in layovers awaiting transfer from steamboat to rail car, was seventeen days. It was a remarkable feat. In his post-operation analysis, Parsons figured that the time spent for the movement of the 20,000-man command to Washington never exceeded ten days when calculated upon a per-man basis, and for most of the men, the time spent in transit was considerably less. In some newspaper accounts of the movement, reporters alluded to cases of deaths by freezing among the troops; but these stories later proved to have no substantive basis.[129]

By the beginning of the first week in February, the troops of XXIII Corps began boarding transports at Annapolis for the sea voyage south to the Carolinas. During the assembling of the transports at Annapolis, a major problem was discovered. A number of the transports were found to be ill-equipped to carry troops, prior employment having been as cargo carriers. A mistake of this sort so late in the war is hard to explain. There was justifiable criticism, a substantial part of it coming from the suffering troops. At least one loud protest reached an assistant adjutant of Halleck's staff who was sent to Annapolis to investigate. He reported his findings in a letter to Halleck dated February 3, 1865.

Annapolis, Maryland
(Received 9 a.m. 4th)

Major General H. W. Halleck, Chief of Staff:

One of General Schofield's brigades arrived at 5:30 p.m., and is being embarked. I understand from here that this command was to be shipped separate from any of Meagher's troops, and I so informed Captain Blodgett. Many of these transports have no bunks, and I do not think they can carry the number of men estimated; for example the *CREOLE* and *NEVADA*, estimated to carry one thousand men each, are very much crowded with seven hundred men each. Those ships were selected for Schofield's troops. The steamer *JOHN RICE* has not arrived. Colonel Casement, commanding brigade of Schofield's corps, expected orders as to his movements after embarkation. His troops will be on board by 12 o'clock tonight.

Robert N. Scott, Major and Assistant Adjutant General[130]

The ships selected for the voyage may not have been up to normal troop-carrying specifications, but the regime under which the luckless passengers were to live while at sea was as well regulated as any quartermaster's thinking could conceive. It is probable that the orders posted aboard the *ATLANTIC* had been the standard for some time for vessels employed in coastal troop service.

Headquarters, Third Division, XXIII Army Corps
Steamship *ATLANTIC*, February 4, 1865

SPECIAL ORDERS No. 9

The following regulations will be strictly observed by the officers and men of this command during the present voyage:

1. No open lights will be allowed in any part of the ship occupied by troops. The ship's lanterns will be arranged by the officers of the vessel in such way as to light the decks during the night, and must not be opened or interfered with by the men.

2. No smoking will be allowed in any part of the vessel used for sleeping, except the open decks. The men may smoke in the open air upon the upper decks, and the brigade commander will provide for giving proper airing and opportunity to smoke to the men quartered below. Officers will smoke either upon deck or in the smoking room near the water closets.

3. The division and brigade commissaries will make arrangements with the steward of the ship for cooking the men's coffee and doing other necessary cooking for the command, and for serving the same out at regular hours.

4. The canteens of the men may be filled with drinking water once each day, the men being marched by companies under their proper officers to the pump in the fore part of the ship for that purpose.

5. The brigade commander, in consultation with the commander of the ship, will arrange for the perfect and regular policing of the quarters, sinks, etc.

6. The starboard side of the upper and main decks, abaft the engine will be kept clear of men and reserved for the use of officers, both of the command and of the ship, during the day, and such portion of this space as may necessarily by occupied by the men for sleeping at night will have a passage kept entirely clear for the use of the officers and crew of the vessel in working her at night. No men will at any time be allowed to go upon the roofs of the houses on the upper deck.

7. Proper roll calls will be established, and the line officers will be strictly required to attend them to make close personal inspections daily of the condition of their men, and to be personally in command of them when marched out for water or coffee, or when on duty.

8. An officer of the day will be daily appointed by the brigade commanders, and shall have full charge of the execution of this order and supervision of all the police arrangements of the command. Proper line officers will be detailed on guard duty, and sentries will be regularly posted at the bulkhead of the ship storeroom on the forward lower deck, at the sinks, over the lights at night, and on the middle line of the decks reserved under paragraph 6.

9. The officer of the day, after reporting at brigade headquarters each day, will report to the captain of the ship, in order that the ship's officers may know to whom to apply for any enforcement of these regulations.
By command of Major General [Jacob D.] Cox:
Theodore Cox, Captain and Assistant Adjutant General[131]

Departure of XXIII Corps from Annapolis was being waited upon anxiously by Schofield. Schofield had just been given command of the Department of North Carolina, and XXIII Corps would become an organizational part of that department once it reached the Carolinas. (The Department of North Carolina and the Department of the South in turn had become subordinate to the overall command jurisdiction of Sherman at the time he reached Savannah.) News had just been received of Sherman's departure from Savannah, and Schofield was impatient to move inland in compliance with Sherman's instructions which he had received in a communication sent by Major General John G. Foster.

> Headquarters, Department of South, Hilton Head, South Carolina
> February 4, 1865
>
> Major General John M. Schofield; Beaufort, North Carolina
> General:
> I have the honor to inform you that General Sherman with the Right Wing of his army, moved from Pocotaligo on the morning of the 1st instant, the VII Corps taking the road to the right, nearest the Salkehatchie, and the XV Corps the road to the left. This wing made thirty-two miles in two days, and on the evening of the 2d instant General Sherman's headquarters were at The Store, [located] at the cross roads near Duck Bridge, over the Coosawhatchie. General Slocum, who had marched from Savannah with the Left Wing had not, up to yesterday (the 3d), succeeded in completing his bridge across the Savannah River at Sister's Ferry, for the purpose of advancing by the way of Robertsville and Duck Bridge. This may delay General Sherman somewhat. He will, however, in a day or two strike the railroad west of Branchville, and after destroying it will cross the Edisto. There he will probably meet with opposition, and it is possible that he may find a portion of Hood's army in his front. General Sherman desires me to press upon you again the necessity of carrying out your part of the programme as soon as you can do so effectively. He wants you to take Goldsborough and hold it if possible. If you cannot do this, to hold Kinston and as much of the railroad beyond as possible. Circumstances favoring you, he hopes you may be also able to take Raleigh and Wilmington. He does not want you to wait on his movements in your advance, but to commence your movements as soon as you can get ready. General Sherman attaches great importance to the effect that your advance will produce.
> Very respectfully, your obedient servant,
> J. G. Foster, Major General, Commanding Department of the South[132]

By grace of the regional command he held, Schofield now commanded all troops, including Terry's then waiting at Cape Fear, and he would shortly report a relatively bloodless occupation of Wilmington. With the Cape Fear River now open up to Wilmington, Union shipping could soon begin using that port. The result would be a marked improvement in Sherman's supply situation.

Schofield would begin planning to comply with Sherman's instructions for an advance toward Goldsborough and a link up with Sherman as soon as Sherman's army reached North Carolina. In line with this, Schofield established his personal headquarters at Beaufort-Morehead City, leaving Terry in charge of the Wilmington garrison. The link-up with Sherman was to be launched from both Wilmington and Beaufort-Morehead City.

Sherman Moves North

By February 17, Sherman's army had reached Columbia, South Carolina. Following its arrival, a good part of the city burned to the ground. The city's residents attributed the fire to Sherman's torch men; however, according to those senior officers who investigated, the destruction was the result of a fire which was started in warehoused cotton by retreating Confederates and which spread. That contention has been hotly argued ever since.

~

The city of Charleston, being practically undefendable from its land side, was evacuated by Confederate troops at about the same time that Sherman took Columbia. Fort Sumter in Charleston's outer harbor would hold out until early April, mainly because no effort was put into play to force its surrender.

~

On February 22, the day that Wilmington fell, Jefferson Davis ordered Joseph E. Johnston to coordinate all Confederate forces in the Carolinas. The job facing Johnston was not easy to carry out as Confederate commands were widely spread out and communications were in disarray.

The capitulation of the Southern army in North Carolina and southern Virginia seemed inevitable, a fact known to every rebel soldier from general officer down to private. One Southern private put his feelings of demoralization into a letter he sent to a friend.

> My shoes are gone; my clothes are almost gone. I'm weary, I'm sick, I'm hungry. My family has all been killed or scattered and I have suffered all this for my country. I love my country, but if this war is ever over, I'll be damned if I'll ever love another country.[133]

The collapse of morale within Lee's army at Petersburg and on the Chesterfield Peninsula was mounting. The hunger, misery, and casualties from the trench warfare, now into its ninth month, were taking their toll. Sizable groups of Lee's men were deserting on a nightly basis. At the same time, Federal activities were increasing as Grant ordered Meade to lengthen his lines toward the south and west. These extensions meant more ground for Lee to defend, and it threatened a severe logistical strain for him since the right of way of the South Side Line was uncomfortably close to being encroached upon. The South Side Railroad remained the sole major element of the lifeline supplying both Petersburg and Richmond.

Sherman's Communications in the Carolinas

The strategy which Sherman had developed for his projected march through the Carolinas toward Richmond had as its initial objective the occupation of Goldsborough, North Carolina. Goldsborough was of particular importance because of the two railroads which came together there, one line coming in from New Berne and another from Wilmington. To Sherman, these same rail lines had the potential for becoming extremely useful. Before Sherman left Savannah, he had sent Colonel W. W. Wright to New Berne with instructions to begin repair of the railroad right of way between New Berne and Goldsborough. This was to start as soon as construction crews could be moved up.

On Sunday March 12, Sherman arrived at Fayetteville where he was greeted by the sound of a steamboat whistle on the Cape Fear River. The whistle turned out to be from the tug *DAVIDSON* whose master presented Sherman with a mail bag containing dispatches from General Terry who was by now in occupation at Wilmington.[134] The arrival of the *DAVIDSON* meant that a logistical link between Sherman and the sea was once again in place. Sherman sent a dispatch back downriver with the *DAVIDSON*, explaining his favorable situation and giving his prognosis for the immediate future. That prognosis was based upon the enemy not being allowed to concentrate his forces. It was also based upon the ability of Sherman's own quartermasters to keep supplies flowing to him.

In the Field, Fayetteville, North Carolina
March 12, 1865

Major General Terry, Commanding US Forces, Wilmington
General:

I have just received your message by the tug which left Wilmington at 2 p.m. yesterday, and arrived here without trouble. The scout who brought me your cipher message started back last night with my answers, which are superseded by the fact of your opening the river. General Howard just reports that he has secured one of the enemy's steamboats below the city, and General Slocum will try and secure two known to be above, and we will load them with refugees, white and black, that have clung to our skirts, impeded our movements, and consumed our food. We have swept the country well from Savannah here, and my men and animals are in fine condition. Had it not been for the foul weather, I would have caught Hardee at Cheraw or here. But at Columbia, Cheraw, and here, we got immense stores, and have destroyed machinery, guns, ammunition, and property of inestimable value to our enemy. At all points he has fled from us, "standing not on the order of his going." The people of South Carolina, instead of feeding Lee's army, will now call on Lee to feed them. I want you to send me all the shoes, stockings, drawers, sugar, coffee, and flour you can spare; finish the loads with oats and corn. Have the boats escorted, and let them run at night at any risk. We must not lose time for Joe Johnston to concentrate at Goldsborough. We cannot prevent his concentrating at Raleigh, but he shall have no rest. I want General Schofield to go on with his railroad from New Berne as far as he can, and you do the same from Wilmington. If we can get the roads to and secure Goldsborough by April 10, it will be soon enough, but every day now is worth a million of dollars. I can whip Joe Johnston provided he don't catch one of my corps in flank, and I will see that my army marches hence to Goldsborough in compact form. I must rid my army of from 20,000 to 30,000 useless mouths, as many to go down Cape Fear [River] as possible, and balance will go in the vehicles, and captured horses via Clinton to Wilmington. I thank you for the energetic action that has marked your course, and shall be most happy to meet you.

I am, truly, your friend,

W. T. Sherman, Major General, Commanding[135]

Terry put his chief quartermaster, Brigadier General George S. Dodge, to the immediate task of complying with Sherman's requests, instructing that Dodge report progress directly to Sherman. The next day, Dodge sent off his first report.

Chief Quartermaster's Office, Department of North Carolina
Wilmington, March 13, 1865

Major General W. T. Sherman
General:

I send the steamer *HOWARD** with commissary stores and forage. I will send other boats with supplies as soon as possible, and will come myself and see what you require. General Easton is at Beaufort [North Carolina]. I am not able to state the amount of supplies he has. I ordered from Washington 20,000 pairs of shoes, which have arrived at Beaufort; also forage for your army. I will push everything we have here to Fayetteville with the greatest possible dispatch, and will explain the state of affairs as soon as I can reach you. I send a box of cigars, and will select some other articles to send you by the next boat.

Very respectfully, your obedient servant,

George S. Dodge, Brevet Brigadier General and Chief Quartermaster[136]

* *GENERAL HOWARD*

On March 14, Schofield messaged Grant that he had taken Kinston, a town above New Berne on the Neuse River. The Neuse would be the water leg of a new supply route from New Berne. New Berne was reached by vessels transiting through the North Carolina sounds or more directly by rail from the deep water twin ports of Beaufort- Morehead City. With the Neuse River now open all the way to Kinston, it became a primary supply route which in its usefulness rivaled the Cape Fear River. Initially, the use of the Neuse River seemed a provident blessing since the recent period of dry weather had brought about a lowering of the Cape Fear River above Wilmington, making that river difficult for passage by all but the shallowest draft steamers. However, within a day or so from the opening of the Neuse, spring rains caused the Cape Fear to rise rapidly, putting it back into operation as far upstream as Fayetteville. The coming of the rains had a disagreeable aspect, though, as expressed by Sherman when he wrote Terry on March 16.

In the Field, 13 Miles on Raleigh Road
Out of Fayetteville

Major General Terry
Wilmington, North Carolina:

...Tell General Dodge to keep boats running up Cape Fear until he knows I am at my new base. This rain, so damaging to my land transportation, is a good thing for the river, which had fallen very much. He can use the rebel captured boats, which, if lost, are of no account. Each of those boats should be supplied a good barge that can hold all the crew in case the boat is caught by a fall in the river. Captain Young agreed to keep his gunboats running busy and as high up as possible. I want to keep up the impression that I am using the Cape Fear River for supplies, for our foolish Northern journals have published the fact that I am aiming for New Berne, a fact that I had concealed from everybody not necessarily in my confidence. These fellows [the newspaper reporters] discovered it by the course taken by the supply boats from Port Royal.

Hoping to meet you soon, I am, etc.

W. T. Sherman, Major General, Commanding[137]

When Goldsborough was occupied on March 19, the movement of supply was accelerated to a marked degree since it lengthened the upstream navigation limits on the Neuse. Goldsborough also had direct rail connection to New Berne, and from Goldsborough, other rail lines potentially reached west and north. This entire track system would become available once reconstruction work was completed on the railroad bridges which the enemy had destroyed upon making its withdrawal.[138] When the time came that the spring runoff subsided and water levels dropped on the Neuse and on the Cape Fear, movements of war materiel by rail from Beaufort- Morehead City, via New Berne, would replace entirely that which was now being moved by water. The potential for the fast movement of materiel by rail with no time lost in cargo transfer would be possible since at Goldsborough rail cars could be easily switched over to the track running to the north. One major flaw with this promising situation was a severe shortage of rolling stock. Almost all locomotives and cars had been removed by the retreating Confederates. To counter that shortage, Sherman requested that locomotives and cars be sent south by sea. Grant, who Sherman had copied, instructed Quartermaster General Meigs to be sure that the request was expedited and that sufficient rolling stock was sent south.

City Point, Virginia
March 21, 1865 -- 9 a.m. (Received 3 p.m.)
Major General Meigs, Quartermaster General, Washington

Has rolling stock sufficient to supply an army of 100,000 men, with the usual proportion of cavalry, transportation, and artillery, over a distance of 130 miles, been sent to New Berne? If not, more should be sent at once.

U. S. Grant, Lieutenant General[139]

The shipment of the locomotives and cars not only put an additional strain on the current demands for ocean shipping, but it presented a special difficulty due to limited heavy lift loading facilities available at northern ports. Meigs explained that to Grant.

Washington, March 21, 1865 -- 5 p.m.
Lieutenant General Grant at City Point:

Dispatch of 9 a.m. received. Rolling stock is being sent to New Berne. General [Daniel C.] McCallum, who received his instructions directly from General Sherman, is attending to this. It is not going forward as fast as I could wish. Its embarkation is confined to certain docks at New York and Wilmington, Delaware, where alone the facilities are to be found, and where the wide gauge engines and cars are collected. General McCallum was here last week, and has gone back to New York to urge it forward. It requires many vessels, and the ice interfered with the earlier shipments. Whatever is possible is being done to get forward a sufficient supply of rolling stock. Your dispatch will be sent to him.

M. C. Meigs, Quartermaster General and Brevet Major General[140]

With Goldsborough established as his forward base of supply, Sherman was in the position where he could consolidate his forces for the drive into southeastern Virginia; but that movement could not begin until the railroad equipment arrived. McCallum was doing all he could to fill Sherman's needs.

> Washington, March 22, 1865
>
> Frederick Leach, Military Railroad Agent at No. 29 Nassau Street, New York:
>
> Report at once the number of locomotives and cars sent to North Carolina. If practicable, let cars be taken to pieces, and running gear and platforms only shipped for the present. Every minute is of the utmost value. Answer.
>
> D. C. McCallum, Brevet Brigadier General
> and General Manager Military Railroads[141]

Until the rolling stock was on hand, Sherman's supply continued to depend on the shipping coming up the Neuse River. The enemy appreciated that fact as exemplified by the instances of partisan attacks being made against steamers in the area between New Berne and Kinston. On that section of the river, the heavy tree cover along the banks made excellent cover for attackers.

> Headquarters, District of Beaufort, New Berne, North Carolina
> March 23, 1865
>
> SPECIAL ORDERS, No. 3
>
> Colonel Charles H. Stewart, 3rd New York Artillery, commanding defenses of New Berne, will direct the commanding officer US [Army] gunboat *SHRAPNEL* to constantly patrol the Neuse River with his gunboat for the purpose of protecting Government vessels engaged in conveying supplies to Kinston for the army of General Sherman. Colonel Stewart will see that the boat is well armed and equipped and kept fully stocked with coal.
>
> By command of Brigadier General I. N. Palmer:
>
> J. A. Judson, Assistant Adjutant General[142]

While the subsequent efforts of the *SHRAPNEL* were no doubt helpful in keeping the Neuse secure, the enemy continued its depredations with substantial success. The steamer *MYSTIC* was burned by a Confederate detachment on April 5, and two days later, the *MINGUAS*, with two barges in tow, was put to the torch.[143]

Schofield had begun to concentrate his troops in the vicinity of Goldsborough, preparatory to joining Sherman's main army for the drive to Richmond. Sherman had already ordered that any remaining regiments located at Savannah and Wilmington be brought by steamer to the twin port towns of Beaufort- Morehead City from where they would be sent by rail to New Berne where waiting river steamers would take them upriver to Goldsborough. Sherman wanted his strength to be decisive should Johnston decide to stand and fight.

A Noose To Wrap Around Richmond

On March 22, a dispatch reached Sherman from Grant, laying out Grant's overall plan for choking off Robert E. Lee by moving against Lee's lines of communication feeding into Petersburg and Richmond. From City Point, Grant was to send a cavalry force under Major General Philip H. Sheridan around Lee's defenses. The aim was to cut the South Side and the Richmond and Danville railroads and close off the James River and Kanawha Canal.[144] If Sheridan was successful, he would totally isolate Lee from his supply. Once Sheridan had started from Goldsborough, Grant's plan was to move a strong attacking force around to the south of Lee's entrenchments in front of Petersburg. This was designed to constrain Lee from moving to block Sheridan. Grant had expressed to Sherman the possibility that the Confederates might evacuate Richmond and the Petersburg defenses and move toward Lynchburg before Sheridan could begin his sweep. To add substance to that concern, recently received intelligence reports told of a considerable amount of military equipment having been recently shipped out of the Confederate capital to Lynchburg.[145] If Lee should evacuate his positions before Sheridan started, then Grant in Virginia, and Sherman in North Carolina, would both have to react quickly to counter whatever Lee might do next.

~

Before Sherman would start his move against Johnston, he believed it was time to iron out a number of details with Grant, not the least of which was the policy to be followed once Johnston had been brought to the point of surrender. Grant agreed and invited Sherman to come north to City Point for a conference. Unbeknown to Sherman until the day he arrived at City Point was that President Lincoln would also be at the meeting.

The President, Sherman, Grant, and Rear Admiral David D. Porter would confer for two days on Grant's floating headquarters, the transport *RIVER QUEEN*. On the second day of the meeting, Sherman pointedly asked how the Confederate armies were to be treated insofar as the terms to be offered for their surrender. According to the memoirs of both Sherman and Porter, Lincoln stated by way of reply that once the enemy army laid down its arms, its officers and men should be allowed to return to their homes with the right of full citizenship promised them. These conditions pleased both Grant and Sherman, as both men had come to fear that if surrender terms were made too harsh, the enemy armies might disintegrate into guerrilla bands and carry on the war indefinitely. With the meetings over, Sherman returned by ship to North Carolina and prepared to move out against Johnston.

~

Refitted and rested, Sherman's Army of the West, once joined by XXIII Corps, consisted of over eighty-eight thousand troops. Scheduled to march on April 10 from Goldsborough, the Army of the West would take the field in three columns. The left column would follow the path of the Neuse River until it was northeast of Raleigh. There, it would turn in the direction of Warrenton, Virginia. The center column would march in direct support to the left column until reaching Smithfield. It would then leave the Neuse and proceed northward, roughly paralleling the left column's route of march but keeping some twenty miles eastward of it until a point was reached near Warrenton where the two columns would again converge. The right column would operate separate and apart, moving out in a northward direction from Goldsborough to follow the tracks of the Wilmington- Weldon Railroad. The major supply depot to support the campaign was to be relocated to a point yet to be selected on either the Pamlico or Albemarle sounds. Forward depots would be established at Kinston on the Neuse River and on the Chowan River at Murfreesborough or, if provident, at Winton.

All plans were set aside when on April 6, four days before he had scheduled the columns to start, Sherman received word that Lee had abandoned Richmond and was now thought to be heading southwest toward Danville. If unchallenged, this would put Lee and Johnston in uninterrupted access to each other. Sherman immediately moved to place his entire force in interception. When the lead elements of Sherman's army reached the town of Smithfield (a place midway between Goldsborough and Raleigh), they found the town had been recently vacated with the enemy retreating in the direction of Raleigh while burning all bridges behind him.

A message from Grant caught up with Sherman on April 12 to announce that Lee had surrendered at Appomattox Court House on April 9.

Upon receiving the news of Lee's capitulation, President Lincoln breathed a sign of relief; but he would not live to hear of Johnston's surrender nine days later.

Johnston Surrenders

On April 18, William T. Sherman's army was in position in front of Joseph E. Johnston's Confederates at Durham Station, North Carolina. Realizing that to fight would be useless, Johnston asked for surrender terms.

Major General J. M. Schofield, representing Sherman in preliminary discussions with Johnston, agreed to provide, among other things, Federal transportation for those Confederate personnel whose homes were outside the Carolinas. The final surrender agreement, which was signed on April 26, included by its fourth article the use of Union transports in the repatriation of Confederates troops.

> The commanding general of the Military Division of West Mississippi, Major General Canby, will be requested to give transportation by water, from Mobile or New Orleans, to the [Confederate] troops from Arkansas and Texas.[146]

A few days after the final surrender was signed, Sherman received orders to start moving his army north preparatory to its demobilization.

> Headquarters, Armies of the United States
> Washington, April 29, 1865 - 11:30 a.m.
> Major General Halleck; Richmond, Virginia
> Four corps of the army in North Carolina will march to Alexandria, [Virginia] passing near Richmond, leaving Raleigh probably on the 1st of May. You may order the Army of the Potomac and all the cavalry, except such as you think necessary to retain in Virginia, overland to the same place, starting as soon as they can be got off.

Let them leave all ammunition and stores of every kind, except provisions and forage, behind, or to be sent by water.

U. S. Grant, Lieutenant General[147]

For all practical purposes, the Civil War had ended; but it would be some weeks before the last Confederates proffered their swords or otherwise disbanded.

On May 13, the last blood spilled in actual battle was at Palmetto Ranch, Texas. The last forces to surrender were located in the Confederate Trans-Mississippi Department where some units held out until the latter part of June 1865.

Lincoln Assassinated

The death of Lincoln on April 15, the result of a bullet fired by John Wilkes Booth, was a tragedy felt nationwide, but especially by the officers and men of the Union Army. On the probability that Booth would try to make his escape into Virginia, Quartermaster General Meigs ordered the establishment of a picket patrol of small steamers to search the shore from Point Lookout south to the Rappahannock. Seven steamers were assigned, each carrying a detail of soldiers. They were:[148]

ELLA, tug	*JAMES JEROME*	*UNITED STATES*
ELLA KNIGHT	*PATUXENT*	*WAWASSET*
	PUTNAM	

An overland search was also launched. Army shipping played its part here as well, transporting one of the search groups, a 26-man cavalry detachment, from the Washington docks to the Rappahannock River on the steamboat *JOHN S. IDE*. Landed on the banks of the Rappahannock, this detachment cornered Booth in a barn near Bowling Green, Virginia. Refusing to surrender, Booth was killed. His body was transported back to Washington on the *JOHN S. IDE*.[149]

Jefferson Davis Is Taken

Jefferson Davis, president of the now defunct Confederacy, feared the worst. With some of his staff he fled south into Georgia where the group was captured.

Army steamers played a prominent role in the transportation of Davis and his staff members after their capture on May 10 near Irwinville, Georgia. They were first taken from Irwinville to Atlanta and then by train to Augusta at the navigable headwater of the Savannah River. There, on May 13, they were put aboard the Quartermaster owned steamer *STANDISH* for the downriver trip to Savannah. Upon arrival there, Davis and the other prisoners were transferred to the Quartermaster owned steamer *EMILIE* which took them to Hilton Head under a heavily reinforced guard. At Hilton Head another transfer was accomplished, this time to the chartered sea steamer *WILLIAM P. CLYDE* which was initially scheduled for Washington. But on arrival off Fortress Monroe, the destination was changed, and Davis was taken into the fort's casements in irons. Although his irons would be removed within time, Davis would spend the better part of the next two years at Fortress Monroe before he was released.[150]

A Triumphant Army

Mourning over the departed president was not allowed to mar the triumphant arrival of the Union armies at the nation's capital. The armies' entries into Washington occurred by stages over the next five weeks.

A few regiments were mustered out near to where they were located at the time of the surrenders and were then transported either by ship or rail to their home states. These were in large part cavalry units released early because of the high expense of maintaining such units on active duty. One unit demobilized at an early date was Graham's Naval Brigade.

Headquarters, Department of Virginia; Army of the James
Richmond, Virginia, May 7, 1865

Brevet Brigadier General J. C. Kelton
Assistant Adjutant General, Division of the James
Sir:

There is a brigade serving in this department and on the coast of North Carolina, called the Naval Brigade, with an eccentric organization. The men are volunteers, principally the 13th New York Heavy Artillery. They are on board the following vessels, all but one of which, the CHAMBERLAIN,[1] belong to the United States, and are stationed as specified: Steamers BURNSIDE,[2] FOSTER,[3] RENO, MOSSWOOD, and JESUP;[4] all serving or rather laying at anchor in and around Norfolk, Virginia. The BURNSIDE[2] is just back from the Rappahannock. The SHRAPNEL and PARKE, steamers, light draft, belong to Government and serving in the waters of the coast of North Carolina. The CHAMBERLAIN,[1] chartered steamer, used as a headquarters boat by General Graham at Portsmouth. The troops of all these vessels should be put ashore for discharge at Portsmouth, Newport News, or some convenient point, and the Government vessels turned over to the Quartermaster's Department to be used as transports. The CHAMBERLAIN[1] should be discharged [from charter] at once.

Very respectfully, etc.

E. O. C. Ord, Major General, Commanding[151]

[1] CHARLES CHAMBERLAIN [2] GENERAL BURNSIDE [3] GENERAL FOSTER [4] GENERAL JESUP

[1]   If called up under the draft act of March 3, 1863, mariners were to be given the option of enlisting in the Navy.

[2]   Frank Wilkeson, *Recollections of a Private Soldier in the Army of the Potomac,* (New York: G. P. Putnam's Sons, 1887), pp 16-19.

[3]   After the occupation of New Berne in 1862, John G. Foster, then a brigadier general, remained headquartered at New Berne as the senior Army commander for the North Carolina region. When the Department of North Carolina was formed in December of 1862, Foster was given that command and with it a promotion to major general. In July of 1863, the Department of North Carolina was enlarged by that part of Virginia under Union occupation, and Foster became head of the enlarged command. He would retain command of the Department of Virginia and North Carolina until relieved by Major General Benjamin Butler on November 11, 1863. When Butler took over from Foster, Foster's department had a troop presence of the IV Corps and VII Corps. The IV and VII corps were discontinued the following month as organizational designations, and the divisions of those two corps, along with some independent regiments that were stationed within the Department, were merged into the XXIV and XXV Corps. During this same time, the X Corps, which had been operating within the Department of the South, was discontinued. Its various elements were joined to the XXIV Corps. The XXIV Corps and XXV Corps, together with other troop elements (including an independent cavalry division), then became the Army of the James under the jurisdiction of Butler. The Army of the James had been specifically organized for participation in the campaign against Richmond, scheduled to commence in the Spring of 1864. Source for these 1862-1863 organizational descriptions is Frederick H. Dyer, *A Compendium of the War of the Rebellion.* (Reprint. Dayton, OH: The Press of Morningside Bookshop, 1978), p 390.

[4]   *Official Records of the Union and Confederate Navies in the War of the Rebellion,* (Washington, DC: Government Printing Office, 1894 - 1917), Series I, 5, pp 487, 488; *War of the Rebellion: Official Records of the Union and Confederate Armies,* (Washington, DC: Government Printing Office, 1880 - 1900. Facsimile Ed: Harrisburg, PA: National Historical Society, 1971. Reprint. Historical Times, Inc., 1985), Series I, 46, Part II, p 196; *ORA,* I, 40, Part I, p 745.

[5]   *ORA,* I, 35, Part II, p 145.

[6]   Earlier (1861), *VIDETTE* was armed and employed as a gunboat during the Butler expedition of 1861 as well as during the Burnside expedition of 1862. Whether she retained her gunboat status past 1862 is not certain from the records. See *VIDETTE* and *VEDETTE, ORA,* I, 9; 29; 46, Part II; ORA III, 4.

[7]   *BOMBSHELL* was sunk by enemy shellfire at Plymouth, North Carolina, but was immediately raised by the Confederates. She was employed by them until recapture by Union forces the following month when she was put back into service by the Union Army.

[8]   See Charles Dana Gibson and E. Kay Gibson, *Dictionary of Transports and Combatant Vessels, Steam and Sail, Employed by the Union Army, 1861 - 1868,* The Army's Navy Series, (Camden, ME: Ensign Press, 1995). This work provides a brief operational accounting for each vessel, giving its dates of acquisition, charter, or other hire by the Army during the period covered. Also see *ORA,* I, 46, Part II, p 196, for a report by Brigadier General Charles K. Graham which lists Army gunboats which were then located as serving in the Department of Virginia and North Carolina. Also see *ORA,* I, 29, Part I, pp 206, 207 for a report referencing the gunboats *SAMUEL RUATAN* and *YOUNG ROVER.* The Army gunboat *YOUNG ROVER* should not be confused with a steam powered brig of the same name and which was a commissioned naval vessel. See *ORA,* I, 33, p 51 for mention of the gunboat *SEYMOUR* which was engaged in picket guard duty at Plymouth, North Carolina, in February of 1864. For reference to the gunboat *ALLISON* during 1862, see *ORN,* I, 8, pp 283-292 and *ORN,* I, 9, p 38 for later operations in which she was engaged during the spring of 1863.

[9]   *ORA,* III, 4, pp 891, 892.

[10]   *ORA,* I, 48, Part II, p. 908.

[11]   The disbandment of the 1st New York Marine Artillery "Naval Brigade" came as a direct result of a mutiny of 150 of its enlisted men during December of 1862. While at Roanoke Island, the men had attempted a takeover of the Army gunboat *PIONEER.* Although the mutiny was solely the action of enlisted personnel, a number of the officers of the 1st New York Marine Artillery were held to account for it. One of the officers, a company commander, was subsequently convicted by court-martial for neglect of duty. The organization's lieutenant colonel -- brought up on related charges -- was dismissed from the service. Despite the scandal which resulted over the mutiny, the organization's commander, Colonel William A. Howard, was not himself held at fault.

[12]   Letter sent to senior author from B. Livingston; Military Service Branch; National Archives, dated November 18, 1987.

[13]   See *Compendium* for 13th New York Heavy Artillery. Also see *ORA*, I, 35, Part II, p 145 for communication of J. G. Foster to H. W. Halleck relative to manning the *SAVANNAH* and *AUGUSTA*.

[14]   *ORA*, I, 33, p 542.

[15]   *ORA*, I, 42, Part II, p 619.

[16]   See Appendix I for a condensed history of the 99th New York Infantry. Officers from other regiments were at times attached to the New York 99th. Among them was Lieutenant C. D. Willard from the 19th Wisconsin who was given command of the Army gunboat *GENERAL JESUP*.

[17]   Returns of July 10, 1864. *ORA*, I, 40, Part I, p 267.

[18]   *ORA*, I, 35, Part II, p 145.

[19]   *ORA*, I, 40, Part II, p 371.

[20]   *ORA*, I, 42, Part I, p 969.

[21]   The practice of partially crewing Army craft with civilians had a certain counterpart with the Confederates who used civilians to officer and crew a few seagoing blockade runners which were under the ownership of the Confederate Army. *ORN*, I, 9, p 282.

[22]   *ORN*, I, 9, pp 382-384.

[23]   *ORA*, I, 46, Part II, pp 196, 197.

[24]   Howard C. Westwood, "Benjamin Butler's Naval Brigade," (unpublished monograph) held by the Naval History Center, Department of Navy. Westwood's fn 101 cites the Naval Brigade endorsement book, pp 8, 65, 66, regarding correspondence concerning civilian crew personnel.

[25]   Appendix E of this volume, "Civilian Manned Transports, 1861-1865...An Overview of Crew Status," includes a full discussion of the status of civilian employees of the Union Army when they were taken as prisoners of war by the Confederacy.

[26]   *ORA*, I, 33, pp 827, 828.

[27]   *ORA*, I, 36, Part I, pp 15, 16.

[28]   *ORA*, I, 33, p 886.

[29]   *ORA*, I, 33, p 915.

[30]   *ORA*, III, 4, pp 614-617. It would not be until 1897 that the United States Congress passed legislation which provided for collision avoidance regulations on the inland waters of the United States (7 June 1897, §1, 30, Stat. 96). In 1890, essentially the same rules were put into international practice, to become known as the International Rules of the Road. The wording of the Navy's General Order No. 34 for meeting and overtaking vessels can now be found in the present day rules with but slight alteration.

[31]   *ORA*, I, 36, Part II, p 432. Mines would continually plague Union efforts on the James River. Many of them were moored by the Confederates prior to the landings at Bermuda Hundred but were not discovered on the initial sweep by the Navy. Fortunately, these were later swept before harm was done. Some mines were laid from the shore after the landing at Bermuda Hundred, this being done practically under the noses of the Federals. Other mines were set adrift to float down the river in the hopes that they would collide with a Union vessel. An excellent account of mine warfare as practiced by the Confederates in the eastern theater can be found in J. Thomas Sharf's *The Confederate States Navy from Its Organization to the Surrender of Its Last Vessel*, (New York: Rogers and Sherwood, 1887. Facsimile Reprint. New York: Crown Publishers, Fairfax Press, 1977).

[32]   *ORN*, I, 9, pp 690, 691.

[33]   Postwar research would show that as of the beginning of May 1864, the Confederate government at Richmond had one iron sheathed sloop of antique genre, four lightly armored gunboats, one naval training vessel of four guns, one mine detonation boat, and a number of launches equipped for laying mines. Then fitting out, but still a long way from completion, were two ironclad gunboats, two lightly armored steamers (which presumably were to serve as gunboats), and around four mine barrier service boats.

[34]   See *ORN*, I, 9, pp 721, 722 for memorandum of Major General Butler which gives the order of movement of the invasion fleet up the James River and lists the units involved at the Bermuda Hundred landings.

[35]   *ORN*, I, 10, p 11.

[36]   William Glenn Robertson, *Back Door to Richmond: The Bermuda Hundred Campaign, April - June 1864*, (Newark, DE: University of Delaware Press, 1987), p 61.

[37]   *ORA*, I, 36, Part III, pp 598, 599.

[38]   *ORA*, I, 36, Part III, p 312.

[39]   *ORN*, I, 10, p 46.

[40]   *ORN*, I, 10, pp 51, 52.

[41]   A curiosity of the battle of May 15-16 was the use by the Federal troops of wire entanglements which they strung out in front of their positions. The wire used was telegraph wire. (Barbed wire had not yet come into use.) The tangled wire funneled the Confederate attackers into narrow approach paths making them much easier targets for the Union defenders. This helped immeasurably to dampen the Confederate assault. It is believed that

this was the first instance in warfare where wire of any description was employed to construct entanglements. See Robertson, p 193.

[42] *ORA,* I, 36, Part III, p 665.

[43] *ORA,* I, 36, Part III, p 769.

[44] *ORA,* I, 40, Part II, p 27.

[45] *ORA,* I, 40, Part II, pp 115, 116.

[46] *ORA,* I, 40, Part II, p 121.

[47] *ORA,* I, 40, Part I, p 38.

[48] Returns of June 30, 1864, from *ORA,* I, 40, Part I, p 177.

[49] The numbers of horses used by the artillery was not specifically covered by reference in Ingalls's July 1, 1864, inventory of horses and mules.

[50] Risch, p 435.

[51] *ORA,* I, 46, Part II, pp 39, 82.

[52] Risch, p 435.

[53] *ORA,* III, 5, p. 293.

[54] Mary C. Gillett, *The Army Medical Department, 1818-1865,* Washington, DC: Government Printing Office, Center of Military History, 1987), p 239.

[55] *ORA,* I, 40, Part II, p 432.

[56] *ORA,* I, 40, Part II, p 32.

[57] *ORA,* I, 40, Part III, p 4.

[58] *ORA,* I, 40, Part III, p 90.

[59] *ORA,* I, 40, Part III, p 106.

[60] *ORA,* I, 40, Part III, p. 106.

[61] *ORA,* I, 42, Part III, p 3

[62] *ORN,* I, 15, pp 622-624.

[63] *ORN,* I, 15, p 648.

[64] *ORN,* I, 16, pp 63, 66, 67.

[65] Another organization composed of units put together by Major General Ambrose Burnside for his expedition against the North Carolina coastal region during early 1862 had carried the temporary title "Coast Division," an identification which became blurred over time as its regiments were merged into other commands.

[66] *Compendium,* pp 373, 374.

[67] The 54th Massachusetts Infantry (colored) had been virtually decimated during the failed attack against Battery Wagner at Charleston harbor in the summer of 1863. Since that time, the 54th had received replacements but by late 1864, it was still no where near full strength.

[68] *Atlas to Accompany the Official Records of the Union and Confederate Armies,* (Washington, DC: Government Printing Office, 1891-1895), Plate XCI-4, shows the area of Hatch's Coastal Division's zone of operations off the Broad River.

[69] The force opposing Hatch included regular troops as well as Georgia and South Carolina militia. There was also a body of "state cadets". See *ORA,* I, 44, pp 936, 937. These cadets, who up to that point in the war had not seen combat, conducted themselves with distinction. On the other hand, the militia troops proved to be unsteady under fire until they were interspersed with the regulars, an action which helped put spine into the enemy line.

[70] Rowena Reed, *Combined Operations in the Civil War,* (Annapolis: Naval Institute Press, 1978), pp 328, 329.

[71] Stephen R. Wise, *Lifeline of the Confederacy -- Blockade Running During the Civil War,* University of South Carolina Press, 1988; appendices 5, 6, 7, 8, 19.

[72] Richard D. Goff, *Confederate Supply,* (Durham: Duke University Press, 1969), p 120.

[73] Some years later, the peninsula on which the remnants of Fort Fisher now rest was separated from the mainland by a canal which connects Myrtle Grove Sound to the Cape Fear River.

[74] For detailed descriptions of the Cape Fear River fortifications, the reader is referred to: *Atlas, ORA,* Plate LXXV; Robert B. Roberts, *Encyclopedia of Historic Forts* (New York: MacMillan Publishing Company, 1988); Also Rod Gragg, *Confederate Goliath: The Battle of Fort Fisher,* (New York: Harper Collins, 1991), pp 18-21. An 1860 era federal government chart of the Cape Fear River area can be viewed on Plate LXXVI of *Atlas, ORA.* Comparing this to a modern chart of the same area (such as *Ocean Survey Chart Number 11534*), Federal Point is today much as it appeared in the 1860s; however, New Inlet is now blocked off. Dry land in the form of a low dune beach is now present (1994) in the location where New Inlet was positioned in 1865. The present New Inlet, some two miles south, is so shoaled as to be inaccessible except to the smallest of craft, and

then only in the best of sea and tidal conditions. The chart no doubt used by those who planned the attack against Fort Fisher was dated September 6, 1864, which is the chart reproduced within *Atlas, ORA,* Plate LXXVI.

[75]   Sharf, pp 806-808.

[76]   *ORN,* I, 10, p 473.

[77]   *ORN,* I, 10, p 563.

[78]   Major General Benjamin Butler, in addition to being the commander of the Army of the James, had command of what had been the Departments of North Carolina and Virginia. As of the reorganizations of late 1863, these two geographic departments were assimilated to the Army of the James which in essence became a regional command.

[79]   Admiral David D. Porter, *The Naval History of the Civil War,* (Facsimile reprint, Secaucus, NJ: Castle, 1984), p 693. A reading of the operational reports as they were separately written by both men a short time after the expedition ended indicates an animosity between them which was present from the beginning and which sharpened as events progressed. Although each seems to have gone his separate way, the evidence seems to point toward Porter as the worst of the two, both in his lack of cooperation and in the vitriol shown to the other.

[80]   *ORN,* I, 11, p 191.

[81]   *ORA,* I, 42, Part I, p 966.

[82]   Here Butler was probably referring to a letter from Porter dated December 18, 1864. See *ORN,* I, 11, pp 223, 224.

[83]   *ORN,* I, 11, pp 222, 223.

[84]   See attest of Fleet Captain K. R. Breese, January 11, 1865, as contained within *ORN,* I, 11, p 224.

[85]   Surveys of New Inlet made after Fort Fisher was finally taken in January 1865 indicated that New Inlet did not have enough water in the entrance channel to have floated the heavier gunboats of Porter's squadron. The enemy blockade runners which had been using this inlet drew considerably less water than the Union gunboats.

[86]   Porter, pp 697, 698.

[87]   *ORA,* I, 42, Part I, p 969.

[88]   Report No. 5, "Expedition to and Operations Against Fort Fisher, North Carolina, December 7-27, 1864," located within *ORA,* I, 42, Part I, p 985.

[89]   *ORA,* I, 42, Part I, p 983.

[90]   The report that an officer had entered the battlement and removed a Confederate flag later proved to be a incorrect. The reality is that a Lieutenant Walling of the 142nd New York had pressed up close to the ditch at the outer side of the fort's face and retrieved a Confederate flag which had been shot away by the naval gunfire and which had fluttered down to rest in the bottom of the ditch. *ORA,* I, 42, Part I, p 968.

[91]   Report of Brigadier General Adelbert Ames, *ORA,* I, 42, Part I, p 981.

[92]   Correspondence dated December 30, 1864, written by Major General William H. C. Whiting, the senior Confederate officer who was at Fort Fisher during the attack of December 1864. Writing to the assistant adjutant general of the Confederate Department of North Carolina, Whiting stated that a division of reinforcing troops was then on its way to help in the defense of the fort and that among other factors, "...the advance of Hoke's division complete their discomfiture." Apparently Whiting was referring to the alarm experienced by Weitzel and Butler which had led to their decision to break off the attack and then order a complete evacuation from the beach. Source: *ORA,* I, 42, Part I, pp 993-997.

[93]   Grant to Butler, December 6, 1864; found within *ORA,* I, 42, Part I, pp 971, 972.

[94]   *ORA,* I, 42, Part I, p 969.

[95]   *ORA,* I, 42, Part I, p 270.

[96]   *ORA,* I, 42, Part I, p 995.

[97]   Report of Sherman to Halleck, January 1, 1865. *ORA,* I, 44, p 11.

[98]   *ORA,* I, 44, pp 735, 736.

[99]   *ORA,* I, 44, p 16, for returns of Sherman's force as of December 20, 1864.

[100]   Eric Foner, *Reconstruction -- America's Unfinished Revolution, 1863 - 1877,* (New York: Harper and Row, 1988), p 71. One of the tragedies of the Civil War was that following the war, the Federal courts disallowed the legitimacy of Sherman's Special Field Order No. 15, and the involved lands were returned to their original owners. In the majority of cases, this resulted in the eviction of those Negro families which Sherman's order had settled back in 1864.

[101]   *ORA,* III, 4, p 890.

[102]   *ORN,* I, 8, pp 542, 543; *ORN,* I, 10, p 608; *ORA,* I, 18, pp 490, 541-543.

[103]   *ORA,* I, 44, p 755.

[104]   William Tecumseh Sherman, *Memoirs of General W. T. Sherman.* (New York: The Library of America, 1990), p. 721. Also *ORA,* I, 47, Part II, pp 9, 10.

[105]   Ninety-eight of the vessels which supported Sherman are named on "List of Vessels in Service of the Quartermaster Department Supplying Sherman's Army," *Report of the Quartermaster General for the Year 1865-1866,* Document 20, Quartermaster Records. One more, *WARRIOR,* is referenced in *ORA,* I, 47, Part II, p 127, as being part of the troop lift from City Point to North Carolina in late January 1865.

[106]   *ORA,* I, 46, Part II, p 82.

[107]   *ORA,* I, 46, Part II, p 288.

[108]   *ORA,* I, 46, Part II, p 298.

[109]   *ORA,* I, 46, Part II, p 593.

[110]   *ORA,* I, 46, Part II, p 298.

[111]   Report of D. H. Rucker to the Quartermaster General, see *ORA,* III, 5, pp 387-393.

[112]   *ORA,* I, 46, Part II, pp 218, 219.

[113]   *ORA,* III, 5, p 384. From Quartermaster records, it appears that at one point in time, at least five schooners were ballasted down and sunk to act as blocking vessels somewhere in the James River. The probability is that these were sunk following the placement of the two barges. There is also a possibility that the two "barges" mentioned in the reports were really dismasted schooners which had been incorrectly identified within the report as barges.

[114]   *ORA,* I, 46, Part II, pp 19, 20.

[115]   *ORA,* I, 46, Part II, p 25.

[116]   *ORA,* I, 46, Part II, p 35. Graham's Naval Brigade had become heavily committed in operations aimed at containing guerrilla activities which had sprung up along the Rappahannock River; therefore, Graham's men were not available to man small boats as they had done in the first Fort Fisher expedition.

[117]   *ORA,* I, 46, Part II, p 46.

[118]   *ORN,* I, 11, p 431 and *ORA,* I, Part II, p 90.

[119]   Correspondence of Assistant Secretary of the Navy Fox to U. S. Grant relates that the January 4, 1865, issue of the newspaper the *Philadelphia Inquirer* carried a story of the impending attack. *ORA,* I, 46, Part II, pp 29 and 79 speak to a related communication from C. B. Comstock to John A. Rawlins.

[120]   *ORA,* I, 46, Part I, p 395.

[121]   *ORN,* I, 11, pp 429, 430.

[122]   As footnote 84 relates, soundings of the inlet made some days after Fort Fisher was taken disclosed that there was not enough water over the bar to have floated the heavier gunboats which would have been required. Only the heavier gunboats had sufficient armor to withstand the cannon fire that would have been directed against them during a passage through the inlet.

[123]   *ORN,* I, 11, p 444. *ORA,* I, 46, Part I, p 401.

[124]   Gragg, p. 235.

[125]   No Army transports were used in the Saint Mark's operation as all troops used in the attack were transported aboard the vessels of the Navy's Gulf Blockading Squadron. Although the Army elements of the attacking force were withdrawn, the mouth of the Saint Mark's River remained closely covered by the Navy's blockade vessels which effectively sealed off any entry. *ORN,* I, 17, pp 812-819.

[126]   Vessels listed as troop carriers which carried XXIII Corps up the Ohio River during January of 1865 have been identified either from orders or correspondence found within *ORA,* I, 47, Part II, pp 236, 237, 243, 250, 257.

[127]   *ORA,* I, 47, Part II, p 261.

[128]   *ORA,* I, 47, Part II, p 262

[129]   Parsons to Quartermasters McKim and Lewis, January 30, 1865. *ORA,* I, 47, Part II, pp 278, 280-282

[130]   *ORA,* I, 47, Part II, p 294.

[131]   *ORA,* I, 47, Part II, pp 303, 304.

[132]   *ORA,* I, 47, Part II, p 302.

[133]   Attributed to a "Confederate soldier." From the PBS video series *The Civil War,* produced by Ken and Rick Burns, Public Broadcasting Service, 1990.

[134]   Sherman, p 777.

[135]   *ORA,* I, 47, Part II, p 803. By his mention of "20,000 to 30,000 useless mouths," Sherman was in large part referring to another host of liberated slaves which had attached itself to the army as it progressed northward from Savannah.

[136]   *ORA,* I, 47, Part II, p 807.

[137]   *ORA,* I, 47, Part II, p 867.

[138]   Dispatch of Major William M. Wherry, aide-de-camp to Colonel W. W. Wright, Chief Engineer at New Berne, North Carolina. *ORA,* I, 47, Part II, p 944.

[139]   *ORA,* I, 47, Part II, p 929.

[140]   *ORA,* I, 47, Part II, p 930. Sherman had placed his order for locomotives and rail cars directly with Brigadier General Daniel C. McCallum who was the Director of the US Military Railroad Service. A copy of that request went to Grant from Sherman's headquarters.

[141]   *ORA,* I, 47, Part II, p 951.

[142]   *ORA,* I, 47, Part II, pp 977, 978.

[143]   *ORA,* I, 47, Part I, p 1134.

[144]   The Richmond Canal, which served to bypass the rapids of the James River above Richmond, was more correctly known as the James River and Kanawha Canal. The canal's route started at Richmond and ended at Buchanan in central Virginia, for a length of 196 miles. It was fifty feet wide and five feet deep throughout its length and was served by ninety locks. By 1860, over four hundred canal boats had become employed year round. Normally, the canal was ice free even in the coldest month of the year. Ronald E. Shaw, *Canals for a Nation; The Canal Era in the United States, 1790-1860,* (Lexington, KY: University of Kentucky, 1990).

[145]   Lieutenant General U. S. Grant to Major General W. T. Sherman dated March 22. See Sherman, pp 806 -809.

[146]   Military Convention of April 26, 1865 -- Supplemental Terms, Fourth Article, *ORA,* I, 47, Part III, p 321.

[147]   *ORA,* I, 46, Part III, p 1005.

[148]   *ORA,* I, 46, Part III, p 821.

[149]   *ORA,* I, 46, Part I, pp 1318, 1321.

[150]   ORA, I, 49, Part I, pp 537, 538.

[151]   *ORA,* I, 46, Part III, p 1108.

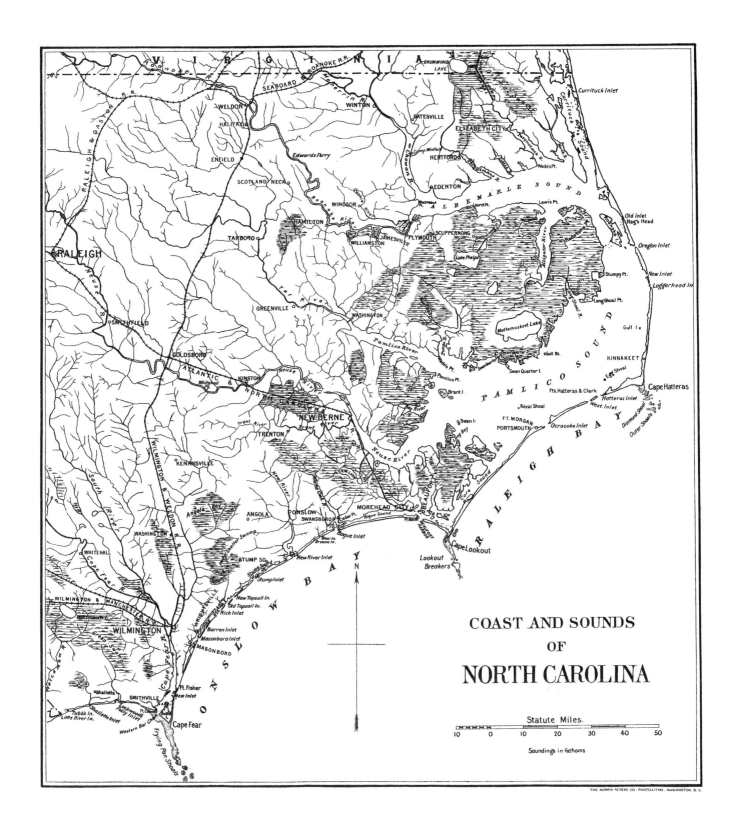

Operational Area: Sherman's Campaign in the Carolinas
Reproduced from *Official Records of the Union and Confederate Navies in the War of the Rebellion*, Series I, Volume 8.

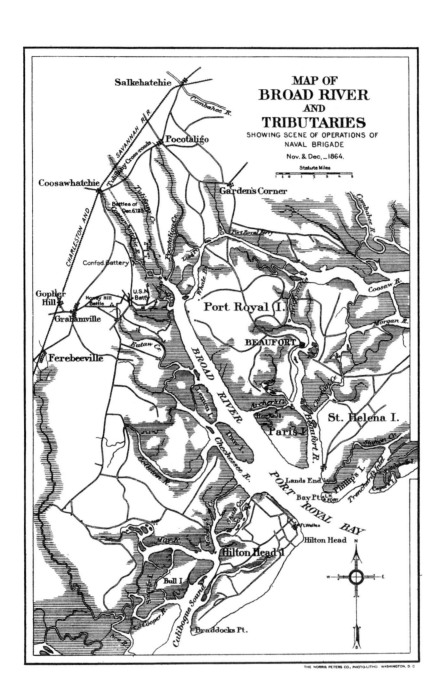

MAP OF
BROAD RIVER
AND
TRIBUTARIES
SHOWING SCENE OF OPERATIONS OF
NAVAL BRIGADE
Nov. & Dec., _1864.

Salkehatchie

Pocotaligo

Coosawhatchie

Garden's Corner

Gopher Hill

Grahamville

Ferebeeville

Confed. Battery

Honey Hill Battle

U.S.N. Batt'y

Port Royal I.

BEAUFORT

St. Helena I.

Paris I.

Lands End

Bay Pt.

PORT ROYAL BAY

Hilton Head

Hilton Head I.

Bull I.

Braddocks Pt.

Calibogue Sound

BROAD RIVER

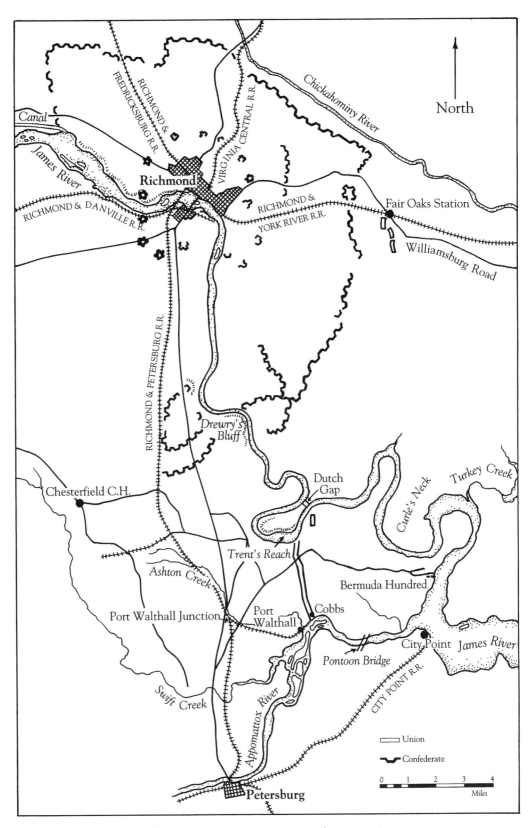

North

Chickahominy River

VIRGINIA CENTRAL R.R.

RICHMOND & FREDRICKSBURG R.R.

Canal

James River

Richmond

RICHMOND & DANVILLE R.R.

RICHMOND & YORK RIVER R.R.

Fair Oaks Station

Williamsburg Road

RICHMOND & PETERSBURG R.R.

Drewry's Bluff

Dutch Gap

Curle's Neck

Turkey Creek

Chesterfield C.H.

Trent's Reach

Ashton Creek

Bermuda Hundred

Port Walthall Junction

Port Walthall

Cobbs

City Point   James River

Pontoon Bridge

CITY POINT R.R.

Swift Creek

Appomattox River

Union

Confederate

0 1 2 3 4

Miles

Petersburg

Richmond — Petersburg Area

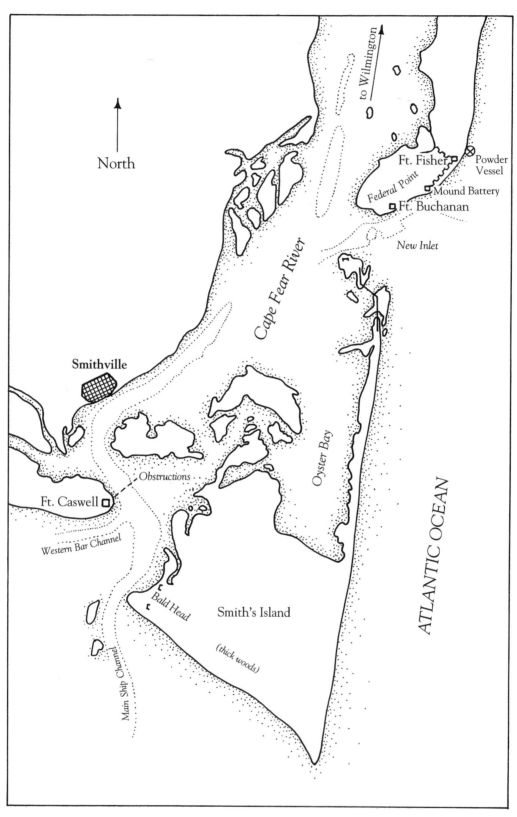

North

to Wilmington

Ft. Fisher

Powder
Vessel

Federal Point

Mound Battery

Ft. Buchanan

New Inlet

Cape Fear River

Smithville

Oyster Bay

ATLANTIC OCEAN

Obstructions

Ft. Caswell

Western Bar Channel

Bald Head

Smith's Island

(thick woods)

Main Ship Channel

Cape Fear, North Carolina
Showing Fort Fisher

EMPIRE CITY, chartered first in 1861. Sold to Quartermaster in 1865. She became the subject of considerable scandal in 1865.

From collection of the National Archives.

Army gunboat *GENERAL JESUP* which operated in the eastern theater. In his depiction, the lithographer may have inflated the size of the vessel, as in reality she was small enough to operate within the Dismal Swamp Canal of Virginia. From collection of the Mariners' Museum.

Landing Army wagons; purported to be somewhere on the James River, Virginia. Note bales of hay in center of picture and on the barges to the left.

From collection of the National Archives.

Piers near City Point, Virginia. Artillery caissons have recently been unloaded. The sail vessel appears to be discharging coal. Sidewheel steamer SILVER STAR is to the left of the sail vessel. To left of SILVER STAR is a typical steam lighter. Photo 1864 or 1865. From collection of the National Archives.

Schooners and a steamer loading or unloading rail cars; purported to be at "Rocketts" on the James River at Richmond after the evacuation of the city by the Confederates. Steamer is the SAVANNAH, ex blockade runner HOPE. Most probably the rail cars on the decks were the property of the U. S. Military Railroad.
From collection of the National Archives.

Mid-deck of small transport (river class). James River. Passengers appear either unhappy or very bored. Note stenciling on box which originally contained boots but now appears to contain a cavalry saddle. From collection of the National Archives.

Location uncertain but probability is that the scene may be on the Appomattox River near City Point. The long section of pontoon bridging shown here being used as a pier for unloading supply vessels may be one of the sections of the 2100 foot pontoon bridge which was used in crossing the Army of the Potomac over the James River in June 1864. After the crossing, the bridge was broken into three sections and towed to City Point. Another possibility is that this may be one of the pontoon bridges put in place by Butler's engineer between the Chesterfield Peninsula and City Point in June 1864. From collection of the National Archives.

Servicing the supply of Grant's army before Petersburg. Note derrick "A"-frame arrangement at end of dock used to offload railroad equipment and other heavy items from supply vessels. Track extended to the end of the dock directly below the derrick. From collection of the National Archives.

Dutch Gap canal, cut by soldiers under Butler's orders. Canal was not opened in time to serve its purpose of bypassing the Confederate batteries above Trent's Reach on the James River. (1865) From collection of National Archives.

PART IX

AFTER THE SURRENDERS
1865 - 1866

THE GRAND REVIEW

Toward the middle of May, Sherman's Army of the West and Meade's Army of the Potomac were encamped outside of Washington where planning was being finalized for a military review, the likes of which in magnitude had never before been seen and no doubt will never be seen again.

Orders were cut for Meade's Army of the Potomac to prepare to pass down Pennsylvania Avenue on May 23. Sherman's Army of the West would follow the next day. The review came off as expected for the troops of the Army of the Potomac -- its men in perfect step, its columns straight and well aligned. Almost everyone had expected Sherman's westerners to appear sloppy and ill-disciplined in their march order, but that did not prove to be the case. Sherman described what he saw as he led his men down the parade route.

> When I reached the Treasury Building and looked back, the sight was simply magnificent. The column was compact, and the glittering muskets looked like a solid mass of steel, moving with the regularity of a pendulum...I then took my post on the left of the President [Andrew Johnson], and for six hours and a half stood, while the army passed in the order of the XV, XVII, XX, and XIV Corps. It was in my judgment the most magnificent army in existence -- sixty-five thousand men, in splendid physique, who had just completed a march of nearly two thousand miles in a hostile country, in good drill...The steadiness and firmness of the tread, the careful dress on the guides, the uniform intervals between the companies, all eyes directly to the front, and the tattered and bullet-riven flags, festooned with flowers, all attracted universal notice.[1]

As Sherman's men passed the reviewing stand, they, like the Army of the Potomac the day before, passed into history. The long years of war were over.

DEMOBILIZATION

From the Eastern Theater

During the process of demobilization of the volunteer army, two hundred and twenty-three thousand men and twenty-seven thousand horses were transported from the Washington area alone. The magnitude of the movement, together with the short time frame over which it took place, was never paralleled at any time during the war. Planning for the demobilization had begun in early May.

Quartermaster General's Office; Washington, DC
May 10, 1865

Brevet Brigadier General D. C. McCallum,

Director and General Manager Military Railroads, United States (Through Colonel Parsons, Division of Rail and River Transportation.)

General:

A very large number of troops will be sent within the next twenty days from this vicinity to their respective states to be there mustered out of service. The several railway companies should be advised to prepare for the movement.

Troops for the west and southwest will probably move by the Baltimore and Ohio Railroad to the Ohio River, which will be used as far as possible for transportation by steamboat of troops destined for the country bordering on the Ohio and for points south of the Ohio.

Troops for Saint Louis, Missouri, and Kansas will probably go down the Ohio to Lawrenceburg, and then take the Ohio and Mississippi Railroad west.

Troops for central Ohio, Indiana, and Illinois will go by Bellaire, Columbus, Indianapolis, and so on west.

Troops for the northwest, by Harrisburg, Pittsburgh, Chicago, or Cleveland, Lake Erie, and Detroit.

Troops for central Pennsylvania and New York, by the North Central Railroad to Harrisburg and Elmira.

Troops for eastern New York, New Jersey, and New England, by Baltimore, Philadelphia, New York, Albany, or New Haven, Hartford, and Springfield.

The sound and river boats should be used wherever possible, as affording a relaxation and rest to the troops crowded in cars, and as being cheaper generally than railroad transportation.

Troops for the Northeast will go by way of New York, and the most direct routes thence to their respective destinations.

It is important that in this movement, which will be large and continue for some time, every possible precaution to insure the safety and comfort of the men should be observed.

For this purpose you will put yourself in communication with the several railroad lines. You will insist upon the orders of this department, requiring cars used for transportation of troops to be carefully fitted up and provided with water and other necessary conveniences, being fully observed and enforced.

Halts of the trains at proper points, to enable the soldiers to attend to the calls of nature, should be arranged.

Proper stoppages for meals; in short, everything should be done to enable those soldiers who have survived the dangers of four years of warfare to reach their homes with the least inconvenience, fatigue, suffering, and danger.

Orders for the movement will be given by the military commanders. It is desired that it be as rapid as is consistent with safety.

I have recommended that troops going north and northeast be marched to Baltimore, believing that the single railroad from this point to Baltimore will be fully occupied with the movement of troops going west from the Relay House, and that for any large body of troops the quickest movement for forty miles will be made on foot.

I am, very respectfully, your obedient servant,

M. C. Meigs, Quartermaster General, Brevet Major General[2]

In order to facilitate the departure of such a large group of men and to avoid congestion, especially at the minor rail heads and river ports, the quartermasters established major staging points, their locations depending on the routes to be traveled and the mode of transport which was to be used. By way of example: Troop units bound from Washington for New York were scheduled to go by rail from a staging point near Baltimore. New York regiments still located in the tidewater areas of Virginia were to be staged at Fortress Monroe and there were to board transports bound for New York.

Those scheduled to go from the east to the west of the Appalachians numbered 96,796 men, together with 9,896 animals. They (presumably the animals as well) were to travel by rail until they reached Parkersburg on the upper Ohio River. The river stage was low by the time the first troop elements arrived at Parkersburg, so light draft steamers were used from there to Buffington Island which was about 35 miles downstream on the Ohio. From Buffington Island westward, the river was deeper and therefore navigable by larger steamers, so there a transfer was made from the small steamers to larger ones. The steamboat trip continued either to a final destination or to ports on the Ohio or on the Mississippi River from where rail service was made available to inland destinations. The first contingent of west-bound troops detrained at Parkersburg late in the day on May 27; the last contingent arrived there on July 6.

Lewis B. Parsons would later calculate that moving these men to the west from Washington had cost a total of $328,205 for the water transportation leg of that journey. Parsons also computed that had the movement westward from Parkersburg been made by rail, the cost would have been $746,964, or $418,759 more than the cost of using steamers. Not a single loss of life or bad accident occurred either on the rail portion of the trip to Parkersburg or on any of the steamers which traveled westward from there. That same good fortune did not hold true on the eastern seaboard. On March 4, prior to the Confederate surrender, the ocean steamer *THORN*, on charter to the Quartermaster Department, was en route down the Cape Fear River from Wilmington, North Carolina. She was loaded with sick Union soldiers recently released from prisoner of war pens in Georgia and South Carolina. *THORN* struck a moored torpedo (mine) and sank while about midway between Wilmington and the inlet, taking with her a number of her unfortunate passengers.[3]

From the Western Theater

During May of 1865, Vicksburg would become the rendezvous point where troops from along the southern Mississippi corridor were staged preparatory for passage to their homes. From Vicksburg, they were allotted transportation space on steamers to northern and eastern destinations. Many of the Union soldiers who were being released from southern prisoner of war camps were also handled through Vicksburg. It appears that whenever practicable, released prisoners were given priority over others for transportation. The first group of ex-prisoners routing through Vicksburg consisted of around thirteen hundred men who were sent north on the steamer *HENRY AMES*. These were followed shortly by a second group of around seven hundred who were loaded aboard the steamer *OLIVE BRANCH* for the trip up the Mississippi. The next steamer scheduled to take on ex-prisoners was the *SULTANA* which was alleged to have had a passenger list of 1,886 when she left the docks at Vicksburg. In addition to the ex-prisoners, there were a number of independently traveling Army officers and at least one woman. Without question, *SULTANA* was dangerously overloaded for a vessel of her class. During the loading of the *SULTANA*, another steamboat, the *PAULINE CARROLL*, was moored nearby and standing empty, so there seems to have been no rational reason why the ex-prisoners were crammed as they were aboard the *SULTANA*.

After leaving Vicksburg, *SULTANA's* trip upriver was uneventful until shortly after passing Fort Pickering (near Memphis). There, her boilers exploded with extraordinary violence, immediately setting the vessel on fire. The fire spread so rapidly that the captain ordered her abandoned while in mid-stream. Of the military personnel aboard, 1,101 were lost, either killed by the explosion and fire or by drowning after taking to the water. *SULTANA* had carried a crew of 155. Of those, 137 were lost, bringing the total known deaths to 1,238 persons. It was one of the worst maritime disasters in American history; yet it went virtually unnoticed at the time, having been overshadowed by media attention given to the funeral arrangements for President Lincoln.

During the investigation which followed the loss of *SULTANA*, a general officer, who had himself interviewed some of the survivors, told an investigating officer that the men aboard had complained to the local quartermaster of the overcrowded conditions, but their complaints were to no avail.

One quartermaster officer who was directly involved with the loading was Captain Frederick Speed, later to be court-martialed on charges that he acted incorrectly in authorizing such a large passenger list. Speed was convicted and dishonorably dismissed from the service; but the finding of guilt was later overturned by order of the Judge Advocate General on the grounds of faulty evidence. Out of the court-martial of Speed came the decidedly incorrect statement made by the reviewing Judge Advocate General "...that in shipment of troops by steamer, no attention was paid throughout the war to the legal carrying capacity of the ships..." Whether the Judge Advocate General's statement referred solely to the *SULTANA* or was a general comment made in reference to quartermaster shipping practices in general is not clear. If made as a general statement, it was seemingly incorrect since limits on a transport's carrying capacity was a practice carried out by most quartermasters, both on the rivers and on the coasts throughout the war. There are, in fact, numbers of documents within *Official Records...Armies* that substantiate the fact that troop transports on the Atlantic coast and on the western rivers were rated by the numbers of persons each vessel was safely capable of carrying. It seems quite probable that bribe money may have played a major part in the *SULTANA's* overloading. That the vessel had probably never been loaded as heavily in the past should have been evident to the members of the court-martial because the trial evidence had brought out that prior to the beginning of *SULTANA's* fatal voyage it was found necessary to place extra stanchions between the decks to hold the great weight of men above, and even then the deck beams were noted to have badly sagged.[4]

THE TEXAS EXPEDITION
(May 1865 - November 1866)

No sooner had Lee and Johnston surrendered than Texas again threatened to become a powder keg. A number of Confederate units had broken away from their parent commands at the war's end, refusing to surrender. Other Confederates, either in unit strength or as individuals, had crossed over into Mexico. Reportedly, as many as four thousand of them had crossed the border by the end of May. Numbers such as this could provide a significant reinforcement for the French under Maximilian who, with the encouragement and military expertise of these veterans, might decide that the time was right to move north and take Texas.

The very presence of the French in Mexico constituted a violation of the Monroe Doctrine. Now that the war between the states was over, President Andrew Johnson decided to affirm the determination of the United States that its southwestern borders were not to be violated by a foreign presence. He also wanted to make it clear that further rebellion on the part of the Texans would not be tolerated. If there was a final catalyst for the president's decision to order United States troops to Texas, it probably came from the sympathy being shown for Maximilian in the Southern press and by the reports that a Maximilian- American political party was being organized in some parts of the south.

To command the troops being ordered to Texas, Grant selected Major General Philip H. Sheridan. The most immediate problem facing Sheridan was the assignment of the necessary transportation. Most of the transports which had previously been operating on the Gulf of Mexico coast and which had open water capabilities were homeported out of New Orleans. These had been gathered up some weeks back for service on the east coast in support of Sherman's Carolina campaign. Vessels left in the Gulf were of a class mostly unfit for open sea voyages. Making Sheridan's transportation problems even more vexing were reports that the Confederates had destroyed the wharves at all the ports west of Galveston. This would mean that once vessels reached Texas, troops and supplies would have to be taken by lighter into the beach, a process which would take time and which would seriously lower the efficiency and therefore add to the cost of the sealift. Sheridan's only other option, besides going by sea, was to march his divisions overland into southwest Texas, but that would be a slow and difficult process because of the distances and the inhospitable terrain along parts of that inland route. Accordingly, Sheridan's decision was to move the majority of his force by sea, that is, as soon as he could obtain the necessary shipping.

By the third week in May, the Quartermaster Department had assembled enough vessels to send from XXV Corps a reinforced division which embarked at City Point. These troops were ferried down the James River to Hampton Roads where they boarded the transports which were to take them on to Texas. Fifteen large transports were involved in this initial sealift.[5]

CASSANDRA	*NIGHTINGALE*	*UNITED STATES*
DANIEL WEBSTER	*PROMETHEUS*	*VICTOR*
HERMAN LIVINGSTON	*THETIS*	*WARRIOR*
ILLINOIS	*THOMAS A. SCOTT*	*WILLIAM KENNEDY*
MONTAUK	*TRADE WIND*	*WILMINGTON*

Two brigades, one of cavalry and one of artillery, sailed in early June from City Point, Virginia, routing to Brazos Santiago, Texas, but with a stopover at the South West Pass of the Mississippi River to take on coal and water. The transports were:

ASHLAND	*GENERAL MCCLELLAN*	*NEPTUNE*
BEAUFORT	*H. S. HAGAN*	*RAPPAHANNOCK*
DUDLEY BUCK	*METEOR*	*SUWANEE*

A few regiments of infantry went to Texas by way of the Red River on steamers. The assignments given these regiments were to occupy the northeastern part of the state. Another small force was sent by ship to Galveston with orders to secure the railroad leading inland from that port to Brenham.

At New Orleans and while awaiting the arrival of the main body of the expedition coming to him from the east coast, Sheridan dispatched two cavalry columns to move overland into east central Texas. One column consisted of five thousand troopers under Major General Wesley Merritt; the other of about forty-five hundred troopers was commanded by Major General George A. Custer. Both of these commands went by inland steamers up the Red River to a point somewhat eastward of Shreveport were they disembarked. Wesley then started his ride toward San Antonio while Custer's column rode toward Austin.

The extraordinary conditions of Texas coast service called for specialized types of vessels, a lack of which caused Sheridan considerable difficulty once his army arrived off Texas. In a communication to Sheridan, Meigs outlined what was being done in the way of shipping for the Texas expedition and announced that the ocean leg part of the movement of Sheridan's troops was close to being complete.

> Quartermaster General's Office
> Washington, DC
> June 17, 1865

Major General P. H. Sheridan; New Orleans, Louisiana
I have your dispatch of 14th. That of 12th June was received here 14th, and answered fully by telegraph and mail 15th. I sent with the XXV Army Corps

[Weitzel] six steamers specially adapted to Texas trade -- *MATAGORDA*, *REBECCA CLYDE*, *COSSACK*, *TONAWANDA*, *REBECCA BARTON*, and *CRESCENT*. The twin screw Government transports and lighters -- *STANTON*, *WELLES*, *FOOTE*, and *PORTER* -- were ordered, but, though on duty on the south Atlantic Coast, reported certain alterations and repairs indispensable before sailing on the long voyage to the Gulf. Three of them have been repaired and sailed some time since. You have at Mobile the *TAMAULIPAS*, iron sternwheel, bought and sent South expressly for Texas service. I regret much any inconvenience or delay, but could only send such steamers as were in existence, and could not order the vessels to sea until repairs reported necessary were made. There are few steamers fitted for the Texas coast in existence. Remember that ocean steamers are built on a different plan from the western river steamers, and the Texas trade, never very large, had built up a few, and only a few, light draft ocean steamers of special models, some of which have been destroyed during the war, and nearly all that remain have been taken into Government service, and all are now, I believe, in Weitzel's fleet. The four twin-screws were built by the Quartermaster's Department specially for this service, and were gathered from the Atlantic Coast and sent to you with all speed. Replacing the *PORTER's* donkey pump still detains her [sic]. This Department, when Weitzel sailed, had more than thirty-three thousand soldiers afloat in ocean steamships, besides Steele's corps. No great nation ever before put such a transport fleet on the ocean. It has been a great and costly effort. Nine light draft steamers have been sent to you. In such an expedition some disappointed expectations and delays of some few vessels are unavoidable. I trust that all will yet work well.

M. C. Meigs, Quartermaster General and Brevet Major General[6]

As soon as he had received word that the transports which were to carry XXV Corps had begun to load at City Point, with their destinations set for Corpus Christi, Brazos Santiago, and the Rio Grande River, Sheridan had left New Orleans for the Texas coast. He was to later complain of the difficulties encountered in landing the troops after they arrived. This was largely the result of a lack of lighters to ferry the men in from the transports which, because of their deep drafts, had to lay offshore to unload. This lack of sufficient lighters resulted in bottlenecks which were aggravated by the simultaneous arrival of other transports carrying the ten thousand troops from IV Corps which had been embarked at New Orleans.[7]

Planning by the quartermasters responsible for that part of the sealift which originated at New Orleans had been inexcusably poor. The most essential of items, drinking water, a commodity normally in short supply on the arid Texas coast, had not been provided for in enough quantity. Consequently, some ships had to be sent back to New Orleans with their troops still aboard so that enough water could be put aboard to handle initial requirements.

Before adequate amounts of supply for Sherman could be handled through Brazos Santiago, dockage had to be provided. This meant that construction material to build the docks had to be brought all the way from New Orleans, something else which had not been properly planned. The troop ships destined for the Rio Grande sector had an especially difficult time unloading. Even with the help of a handful of shallow draft river steamers sent west from the Mississippi, weather conditions often precluded even these shallow drafts from crossing over the bar into the Rio Grande River. This held up discharge of troops and incoming supplies for up to ten days at a stretch.

The number of oceangoing transports which were utilized in the Texas operations is not discernible; but it can be established that just the movement from City Point required a total of fifty-seven steamers. (One of those steamers made two trips.) In a report to the Secretary of War, Meigs would later claim that even though the fifty-seven vessels left for Texas in increments, all were actually en route during the same span of time. All told, from troop commands in the east and from the western theater, approximately fifty-two thousand troops were sent to Texas, slightly over ninety percent of that number having come from volunteer regiments.

The morale of the troops which had been selected for the Texas operation was at a low ebb from the onset. Those from the volunteer regiments had expected to return to civilian life soon after the surrenders in Virginia. Although open discontent was common in all the units, it only reached mutinous proportions within Custer's cavalry command. One episode handled by Custer resulted in a drum head court-martial which led to two convictions with one sentence of execution carried out on-the-spot by firing squad. A death sentence, if carried out without higher review, was actually illegal under United States military law, and Custer's actions solidified his reputation as a harsh disciplinarian.

When the threat of French involvement appeared to be lessening, the volunteer regiments were sent back east for demobilization. Most of the regular Army units remained in the state for some time, being employed in both reconstruction tasks and in containment of the Indian menace.

DISPOSAL OF THE ARMY'S FLEET

It does not appear that during the final months of the war much thought had been given as to the methodology by which the Quartermaster's fleet would be reduced in size once hostilities ended. At one point during the war, Lewis B. Parsons had suggested to Quartermaster General Meigs that the most economical course to follow would be to dispose of the entire fleet, after which time the Army could secure its waterborne transportation needs either through time charter or space (affreightment) hire from the private sector.[8] However, it was probably reasoned that to make early plans in this regard would be impractical in light of the difficulty to forecast troop strengths required for occupation forces. The number of occupation troops would depend on the cooperation of the Southern populations and whether or not scattered enemy units might continue hostilities. As it would turn out, the South's population adapted quite passively to the changes in their fortunes, and in most areas -- Texas being the one notable exception -- occupation garrisons would be maintained at relatively low levels.

When the decision was finally made as to the policies to be followed in disposing of the Army's holdings of vessels, the man given the responsibility was Parsons. Recovering from an operation at the time of Appomattox, Parsons had intended to return to civilian life; but the pleas of Quartermaster General Meigs, who related the far reaching importance to the government of properly disposing of its fleet, prevailed in changing Parsons's mind, and he told a relieved Meigs that he would see the job through.[9]

By the war's end, the inventory of vessels owned by the Army just on the western rivers enumerated nearly six hundred units.

Inventory of steamers and other vessels at Mobile and on the Mississippi River and its tributaries, belonging to the United States on June 30, 1865[10]

Sidewheel steamers	34	
Sternwheel steamers	37	
Center wheel steamers	3	
Screw tugs	16	
Ferryboats	1	
Total steamers		91
Steamboat hulls		2
Model barges	74	
Gunwale barges	226	
Small wood barges	26	
Box barges	3	
Barges not classified	23	
Total barges		352
Wharf boats	18	
Canal boats	3	
Coal boats	60	
Yawl boats	56	
Sailboats	1	
Metallic boats	1	
Total boats		139
Skiffs		9
Floating docks		1
Small flats		2
Sectional docks		3
TOTAL		**599**

In contrast to the river fleet, the numbers of vessels owned by the Army which were in the coastal service was comparatively small, although most of them, by merit of their larger size and greater sophistication, represented a far greater investment than did the average river steamer.

Inventory of vessels owned by the United States and employed on oceans and lake service for the fiscal year ending June 30, 1865[11]

Sidewheel steamers	75
Propellers	40
Tugs	28
Schooners	12
Canal barges	22
TOTAL	**177**

All but three of the vessels listed as being in ocean and lake service were employed upon coastal routes or in the sounds and bays contiguous to the sea. The excepted three were employed on the Great Lakes.

In addition to those vessels owned at this time by the Quartermaster, both on the rivers and in the coastal service, there were hundreds of others employed under various forms of charter.

Any prior thought which might have been given toward the disposal of the Quartermaster Department fleets at war's end would have turned out to be premature, as once the war ended, a huge need developed to transport demobilized troops and to send the occupation force to Texas. Yet another demand on shipping came from the requirement to shift around regular Army regiments which were to remain on active service. In fact, there was as much demand for shipping in the first three or four months following the close of hostilities as there had been at any time during the war.[12] The need to move men and their equipment by water was only part of the Quartermaster's transportation tasks. It was also necessary to transfer the Army's surplus hardware and other supplies from locations where they had been situated at the time of the surrenders. A certain amount of this materiel was sent to depots for storage. Other items were scheduled to be sold off; but before they could be sold, they first had to be transferred to assembly points from which sales could be conducted.

The first steps put in place toward reduction of the Quartermaster's fleet came from instructions issued by Parsons stipulating that wherever practical, vessels under charter were to have their charters terminated. This practice was to apply on the coasts as well as on the western rivers. Subsequent to this taking place, the Army's transportation requirements would be handled on the Army's own vessels. When shipping needs began to slacken, then sales of Army owned vessels would commence.

The officer who became most heavily involved with the disposals was Colonel Arthur Edwards. This was the same Edwards who had been such an important factor in constructing the *"Cracker Line"* which had resolved the supply crisis at Chattanooga during 1863. Parsons delegated Edwards as his most immediate subordinate to deal with the sale of the western rivers fleet. At the end of July 1865, Edwards wrote to the officer in Washington who was charged with Quartermaster accounting procedures.

> I conceive it the best policy to at once and promptly dispose of every steamer and barge on the Mississippi and its tributaries, first at private sale, afterward at public auction.[13]

As far as the western rivers were concerned, this comment by Edwards reinforced the opinions being developed by Parsons. Despite the Army's continued heavy employment of shipping on the rivers which continued well past the mid months of 1865, Parsons viewed the matter of vessel retention there to be quite different than the situation on the coasts. Quartermaster operations on the rivers required the services of a large number of officers serving as shipping agents due to the number of river ports which were involved. Personnel were needed at each river port in order to keep the Army's shipping moving efficiently. The management of the coastwise fleet was quite a different matter. The ships on the coast were usually routed from one port, returning to that same port upon the completion of each voyage. Since the ports the Army used on the coasts were quite limited in number as compared to those which the Army utilized on the rivers, this required a corresponding lesser number of supervisory officers. Just from an officer personnel standpoint, there was therefore a less urgent fiscal need to reduce the Army fleet on the coasts than was the case on the rivers.

The first vessels which Edwards decided to sell on the Mississippi system were the coal barges. Most of these barges were now moored along the banks or tied to wharves, and most of them were loaded down with reserve supplies of coal. The loaded barges had very limited buoyancy and were therefore in danger of sinking whenever the slightest leak developed to their hulls. Edwards estimated that about two million bushels of coal was being stored on the Army's barges along the Ohio and Mississippi rivers and their respective tributaries. With a reduced movement of Army traffic on the rivers, the service no longer had a need for coal in such quantities.

Although Parsons was the one who developed the overall policy under which sales would be conducted in the west, it was Edwards who had charge of making the required pre-sale appraisals. At the beginning, the sales system called for sealed bids which were to be invited from the public. No bid was to be accepted unless it was at least 25% of the appraisal value established by Edwards. (Edwards's valuations were to be kept secret to all but those officers presiding at the opening of the bids.) The first bid sale occurred on Monday, August 28, 1865. It did not go at all well. Most of the offerings went unsold because few of the bids came up to the minimum 25% of the appraised values. It was apparent that the prospects for this method of disposal were not promising. Parsons ordered that a public auction method be substituted. No sooner had the public auctions started than a lack of cooperation began to show on the part of some quartermaster officers who had come to realize that once the Army owned shipping was gone, so would be their own chances for retention in what would be a rapidly shrinking Quartermaster Department. Probably on the theory that financial hay should be made while the sun was still shining, a few of these officers had begun to utilize quartermaster steamers to ship their own and their friends' freight. Edwards put an immediate stop to this whenever he discovered it taking place. The same dishonest practice, or worse, was reported to Edwards to be occurring at Gulf Coast ports. In a letter dated during October of 1865, Edwards wrote Parsons:

> Government owned ships operating in Texas between Mobile, Fort Morgan, and Fort Gaines are carrying private freight and passengers and [are] running off or causing to be seized, private boats running on the same route. This looks bad and is bad.[14]

Upon being informed of what was going on, Quartermaster General Meigs foresaw the emergence of a fertile field for scandal, one which would hover over the Quartermaster Department as long as the Army maintained even a small portion of its wartime fleet. Neither Parsons nor Edwards wanted to be smeared with the dirty brush that could develop from such a scandal. Both officers were also impatient to retire from the Army and get back to their civilian pursuits, Edwards even more so, and he insisted upon submitting his resignation immediately. Morally, Parsons felt he could not bind Edwards in the service, so he reluctantly recommended to Meigs that the resignation be accepted.

Previously unforeseen by Parsons was the circumstance under which if steamers were offered for sale and then sold to a shipping conglomerate or to members of a close trade association, then a monopoly could be set into place which would adversely impact the shipping business. Ultimately this could not help but impact the Army's own transportation costs. Parsons began suspecting that the establishment of shipping cartels was already beginning to occur throughout the Gulf of Mexico region as well as on the lower Mississippi. Collusion dealing with other facets of the shipping industry was also coming to light. One of the most flagrant situations resulting in high costs came from unnecessary pilotage and lighterage fees charged to the Quartermaster Department. Most of these problems were occurring with the movement of ships engaged in support of Sheridan's expedition to Texas. Parsons believed that the operation of ships, owned or otherwise controlled by the Army, was costing the government nearly double of what the cost would have been if the same ships had been commercially owned and operated with the Army's shipping needs carried on either through time charter or, preferably, through some form of affreightment basis. Parsons expressed a caveat to this within a letter he sent to Meigs.

> It certainly would not seem to me safe to sell our Texas steamers without first obtaining some reliable arrangement with private parties for the services; otherwise, you would be thrown entirely upon their mercy.[15]

In the late fall, Parsons discovered a major reason for the glutted market which was starting to depress the Army's sales prices even lower than the prices experienced during the earlier summer sales. It was that the Navy, starting in November 1865, had begun unloading its own river fleet and had disposed of nearly two hundred vessels, the majority of them being suitable for use in the commercial trades. Compounding this was the fact that the shipping business by volume was already seriously depressed from what it had been during the war. Parsons found himself selling into a market with very little demand. He did manage to sell off forty-nine river class steamboats by December 1865, but at a hugely deflated value. A sale scheduled on February 28, 1866, for river class vessels turned out to be an even greater disappointment. Some of the offerings were withdrawn because the bids did not meet an established minimum. Only sixteen of the offered river craft could be sold.

Following the February 28th sale, Parsons was approached by a New Orleans shipping merchant who proposed what seemed to be a reasonable plan for encouraging buyers with an interest in the Gulf of Mexico coastal trade. The merchant's idea was to provide a mechanism which would protect the interests of the private ship owner as well as the government's interests as a shipper. Under this proposition, a special sale would be held whereby a successful buyer of any Quartermaster vessel which was suitable for the coastal trade within the Gulf of Mexico would simultaneously be awarded a contract by the Quartermaster Department for the carriage of the government's personnel and cargo on Gulf of Mexico routes. Such carriage would only be on an affreightment basis. Safeguards would be written into the contracts to prevent price gouging by those ship owners carrying passengers and freight for the account of the government. Following this sale, those vessels remaining would be sold elsewhere, and only to companies or individuals operating on routes outside of the Gulf of Mexico. Parsons worked this proposal into contractual form, and when the documents were ready, he placed into auction practically all of the Army's coastal class vessels then located along the Gulf coast. As the shipping merchant had forecast, the results of this sale were good.

Parsons's next task was the sale of coastal and inland class vessels at Atlantic ports as well as the completion of the disposal of remaining vessels on the Mississippi River system. The only Quartermaster vessels to be excepted from these close-out sales were local service craft still employed by the Army at its garrison points on the coast and on some of the western rivers. With the sales program nearly completed, Lewis B. Parsons submitted his resignation from the Army. It was accepted by Quartermaster General Meigs on April 10, 1866.

An important era of the Army's involvement with marine transportation had come to a close.

EPILOG TO THE CIVIL WAR

For the next three decades following 1866, the United States Army was to find itself reduced in numbers and mission to what amounted to a mere constabulary force. For its transportation requirements, a part of which continued to be carried on by vessels traveling coastal and river routes, the Army mainly used commercial carriers on an affreightment basis.[16]

It would not be until the War with Spain in 1898 that marine transportation would again become of any significant importance to the United States Army. Following the War with Spain, and as a direct result of that war, the United States became a world power with significant overseas holdings. To maintain those holdings, the Army's navy would be reborn -- this time as the Army Transport Service, a permanent subsidiary agency of the Quartermaster Corps.

Volume III of *THE ARMY'S NAVY SERIES* will be an accounting of the men and the ships which made up the Spanish-American War sealifts to Cuba, Puerto Rico, and the Philippine Islands during 1898, inclusive of the Army Transport Service, organized in the Fall of 1898 and which continued in existence through the First World War and into the Second World War.

[1]   William Tecumseh Sherman, *Memoirs of General W. T. Sherman.* (New York: The Library of America, 1990), pp 865, 866.

[2]   *War of the Rebellion: Official Records of the Union and Confederate Armies,* (Washington, DC: Government Printing Office, 1880 - 1900). Facsimile Ed: (Harrisburg, PA: National Historical Society, 1971. Reprint. Historical Times, Inc., 1985), Series III, 5, pp 301, 302.

[3]   A diligent search of *ORA* and *ORN* disclosed no specifics on the sinking of *THORN* or of the exact casualties which were incurred in that sinking. Only one item, a Confederate intelligence communication found within *ORA* even mentions the *THORN's* loss. The Quartermaster General's office comment on the sinking, which is to be found within the *HR-337* listing of "Ocean and Lake Vessels," gives only the place and date of the loss. A brief description of *THORN's* sinking and mention of the ex-prisoners she carried (mostly sick men) may be found within the wartime memoirs of John McElroy who had been a prisoner at Andersonville. While being transported on another vessel which was traveling in the wake of *THORN*, McElroy claimed to be an eye witness to the sinking. John McElroy, *This Was Andersonville* Roy Meredith, ed., (New York: Bonanza Books, 1957), pp 282, 283.

[4]   *ORA,* I, 48, Part I, p 215.

[5]   *ORA,* I, 48, Part II, p 1141.

[6]   *ORA,* I, 48, Part II, p 908.

[7]   Report of Major General Philip H. Sheridan to Major General John A. Rawlins, Chief of Staff at Washington, November 14, 1866. See *ORA,* I, 48, Part I, pp 297-303.

[8]   Schottenhamel citation: Parsons to Meigs, August 17, 1864, Loose Letters, Parsons collection.

[9]   On March 17, 1865, a general officer's opening occurred in the Quartermaster Department. This gave Meigs the authority to promote Parsons to the rank of brigadier general, an action which was confirmed shortly afterward by the Senate.

[10] *ORA,* III, 5, p 295.

[11] *ORA,* III, 5, p 292. This inventory done in 1865 took place at a time when some vessels, probably all sail, had already been sold.

[12] Report of Colonel George D. Wise to the Quartermaster General, dated August 31, 1865, as taken from *ORA,* III, 5, p 287-291.

[13] Schottenhamel citation: Edwards to Bliss, July 26, 1865, Loose Letters, Parsons Collection.

[14] Schottenhamel citation: Edwards to Parsons, October 3, 1865, Loose Letters, Parsons Collection.

[15] Schottenhamel citation: Parsons to Meigs, February 4, 1866, Copy Book January 19, 1866, to June 20, 1866, Parsons Collection.

[16] The Quartermaster charter records, as they were reported within Executive Document No. 337, House of Representatives, 40th Congress, 2nd Session, show a number of Quartermaster charters extending into 1867. A few were entered into during 1868. In almost all such cases, these late charters involved schooners.

PART X

APPENDICES

APPENDIX A
THE ARMY'S PROCUREMENT OF VESSELS IN THE EAST FOR COASTAL AND GULF OF MEXICO SERVICE: 1861-1865

The Union's maritime position at the outbreak of the war was vastly superior to that of the South. The North had within its boundaries the bulk of the nation's merchant marine, both on the coasts and on the western rivers. (In 1861, the total tonnage of United States ocean shipping was 2,496,894 tons.)[1] Almost all of the larger shipbuilding and repair facilities were located in the northern states. This advantageous situation did not, though, mean that the North had everything it needed in the way of shipping. On the contrary, there was a shortage of large steam-powered passenger ships. In the early 1850s, thanks in part to large government mail subsidies, the New York based Collins Line had built up a transatlantic steamship service to Europe. When war clouds began to threaten near the end of the 1850s, Southern Congressional interests, in an attempt to create a counter irritant to Northern agitation against the slavery issue, forced through an end to the mail subsidies. The result of this was that the Collins Line, faced with competition from the strongly subsidized British steamship companies, was forced to give up its transatlantic service and sell its ships. By 1860, the United States had in regularly scheduled service only two transatlantic passengers vessels.[2] With but few exceptions, the Union controlled steam merchant fleet consisted of coastal class vessels, not the most perfect bottoms for bulk transportation of troop units, together with their organizational impedimenta. Many of the better coastal class steamers were picked up by the Navy, leaving the War Department with the remnant second best.

During the early months of the Civil War, the Union War Department played only a partial role in arranging troop movements by sea. Instead, the government empowered New York's governor as well as a New York City consortium of businessmen to make arrangements for the transportation of troops and military supplies which were to be sent to Washington City from New York.

War Department
Washington, April 23, 1861

Governor Edwin D. Morgan; Honorable Alexander Cummings:

In consideration of the extraordinary emergencies which demand immediate and decisive measures for the preservation of the national capital and defense of the National Government, I hereby authorize Edwin D. Morgan, Governor of the State of New York, and Alexander Cummings, now in the city of New York, to make all necessary arrangements for the transportation of troops and munitions of war in aid and assistance of the officers of the Army of the United States until communication by mails and telegraph is completely re-established between the cities of Washington and New York. Either of them in case of inability to consult with the other may exercise the authority hereby given.

Simon Cameron, Secretary of War[3]

Governors of other states such as Massachusetts, acting on their own without waiting for federal authorization, chartered ships to move state volunteer units south to the Chesapeake. This informal method of hiring vessels for military use continued for some time before the War Department took over full control and arrangements for troop movements by sea. Erna Risch, in her *Quartermaster Support of the Army: A History of the Corps, 1775*-1939 quoted one J. Edgar Thompson who worked directly for the Pennsylvania Railroad system and who, acting under the authority of "...the power invested in me by the Secretary of War," set up a system under which he signed charters for the use of twenty-four steamers, all of which were to be utilized in the transportation of troops. The extent of power actually granted to Thompson by the Secretary of War remains vague to this day; however, to Thompson's credit, he got the job done. At that juncture of the war, that in itself was enough.

On April 22, the first steam transport known to have been directly chartered by the War Department for service in the Civil War brought New York's 7th Regiment to Annapolis, Maryland.[4] The regiment was rushed from there to Washington over the rail spur of the Little Elk Ridge line which connected to the Baltimore and Ohio from Annapolis Junction.

Not much is known of the identity of particular ships used to carry troops during the first two or three months of the war. One early-on charter- this one arranged directly through the Quartermaster Department-was for the *CATALINE*. This ship was purchased by speculators for $18,000 and then time chartered to the Army for $10,000 a month with a guarantee that in the event she was lost during this period, her compensated value would be $50,000. The agent for that pork barrel prime cut was one Richard E. F. Loper who as a chartering agent had previously been associated with the aforementioned J. Edgar Thompson. Loper, apparently sensing a fertile field for profit-making, established his own shipping agency which became devoted solely to the chartering of vessels to the War Department. According to Risch, Loper was the same person who the Quartermaster General had selected in 1846 as the government's agent for the construction of nested-type barges which Winfield Scott had utilized during his landing operations at Vera Cruz.[5] Now, fifteen years later, in addition to running his new agency, Loper was also the owner of a fleet of ships under the corporate name, Philadelphia Steam Propeller Company. Prior to the war, the return of profit on Loper's fleet was reported to be around 10%. By 1862, Loper was getting a return of 50% for the same ships.[6] Loper's reputation in his dealings with the Army soon degenerated to the point that it was deemed best to distance him from any direct War Department connection. The record shows that he was officially terminated as an agent before the beginning of 1862; however, as a commercial middleman, Loper continued on, his name cropping up from time to time in Army correspondence. He was a prime mover, for instance, in obtaining the shipping for the 1862 Burnside Expedition to North Carolina, and again, he is known to have been a factor in the assemblage of shipping for the 1862 Peninsular Campaign.

In an attempt to put some order into what had become an unmanageable situation, Secretary of War Simon Cameron appointed John Tucker as general transportation agent to handle the needs of Army shipping. The Secretary also assigned to Tucker the duties of arranging land transport.

War Department
Washington, May 8, 1861

John Tucker, Esq.
Sir:

In the present exigencies of public affairs and the requirements of the military branch of the public service it has become imperatively necessary to appoint a general agent of transportation for the Government, to whom shall be confided the duties consequent upon the transportation of men, supplies, and munitions of war.

Relying on your well-known integrity and high character, you have been selected, and are hereby appointed, as such general agent of transportation, and you are requested to enter upon the duties thereof at the earliest day practicable. Being thus appointed, you are hereby desired to proceed forthwith to Philadelphia and New York, and hold yourself subject to any orders of the Secretary of War, communicated to you either direct or through the proper officers.

It is the purpose of this Department that you provide, and you are hereby authorized to purchase (with the sanction of the Department), charter, or in such manner as may be the best for the public interests, the speediest means of transportation for all troops and those connected with the Army, all munitions of war, and all supplies of whatever nature of which you may be informed by this Department, using every economy in procuring such necessary means of transportation, whether in so purchasing, chartering, or hiring water conveyance or in engaging transportation by land, whatever the character of such conveyance.

You will keep the Department advised of your movements, that communications by mail or by telegraph may reach you without delay. You will keep a careful record of your proceedings, and report to the Department from time to time your action under this authority.

Simon Cameron, Secretary of War[7]

Tucker wasted little time in shearing off some of the dead wood which had already been accumulated by Loper and others. On May 14, he reported that progress to Secretary Cameron.

Philadelphia
May 14, 1861

Honorable S. Cameron
My Dear Sir:

I am earnestly devoting my energies to saving money for the Government, and you may depend upon it that there is occasion for it.

Owing to the sickness of Mr. Thompson and the absence of Captain Loper (at Washington), I could not till today obtain a list of the vessels chartered by them, and it may now be incomplete. In it I find nine charters "by the day," and fifteen "by the month or as long as wanted," beginning from April 20 to May 7. Of these chartered by the day I have already got rid of all but two, besides having ordered some of the others to return here before I could get the information as to the terms of the contract. I will see that all of them are discharged before their term expires, except such as are absolutely required, which in my judgment can be reduced for the transportation between Perryville and Annapolis to two steamers for passengers and three good propellers. Some of the charter party are at enormous prices.

I shall go to New York tomorrow night if necessary, to discharge all vessels engaged by parties there that can be dispensed with. I hear of parties who have gone to Washington to sell their vessels. I assure you with the utmost confidence that for transportation purposes there is no occasion for you to be in haste about buying anything. Anything that is required for this purpose can be bought or chartered without any difficulty and at fair prices.

As to gunboats or steamers for blockading purposes, the case may be different. I enclose a description of a new propeller, *LA UNION*, which I should think would be about what is wanted for blockading small ports. She is entirely new, the price about $25,000, which, I suppose, means something less. I will have an exact description of another smaller propeller tomorrow, also entirely new. I find that I can have a large number built of any description of gunboats in sixty days. Unless the emergency is great, do not buy old ones, which will be constantly out of order. I will send plans and bids in a day or two from experienced and honest contractors.

I am most anxious to protect you from imposition, and if you will refer the parties who have vessels for sale or charter to me, the Government interests shall be protected.

Yours, very respectfully,

John Tucker[8]

Of some curiosity is Tucker's mention of "gunboats and steamers for blockade purposes." Even at this early stage of the war, that activity had been assigned to the Navy Department thus seemingly making Tucker's interest in vessels for blockading somewhat beyond the interest of the Secretary of War. At the end of 1861, John Tucker was appointed Assistant Secretary of War. In that capacity, he would retain the responsibility for ocean shipping procurement until that function was transferred to the Office of the Quartermaster General. The reforms put in place by Tucker in the matter of handling the Army's shipping were not completely foolproof. A Congressional committee which was convened in late 1862 with the intent of investigating the Army's policies in the hiring of shipping, and which ended up by centering its focus on the affairs of Richard E. F. Loper, accused Tucker of tolerating Loper's behind-the-scenes activities even after Tucker had been appointed Assistant Secretary of War.[9]

The costs for obtaining vessels during the first year of the war remained extremely high. Before the war, whenever obtaining the use of vessels on a charter basis, the Quartermaster Department had routinely advertised for bids. But during the shipping crisis which continued through the 1862 Peninsular Campaign, the needs were generally met in a spirit of exigency, all bidding being laid aside allegedly in the interest of getting the job accomplished. When the Congressional investigation of 1862 was convened, a case was put forth that there had been in general an inordinately high gouging of the government; but even when it came to Loper's dealings, the evidence was not strong enough-- at least by the rather loose standards of that day-- to enable criminal prosecutions.

The Quartermaster General's own investigations uncovered a number of different ways the ship owners could cheat and found that all of them had been put into practice at some point or another. These practices continued to a degree throughout the war but lessened as the various scams were exposed. One method for cheating, and perhaps the most common of all, was to falsify the net tonnage of vessels.[10]

Misrepresentations of tonnage, if left undiscovered, resulted in the government paying thousands of dollars for cargo space that in fact did not exist.

Fiscal order began to come to the marketplace when a clause was inserted into Quartermaster charter agreements that gave the government the right to purchase any vessel which it had taken under charter whenever the accumulated charter rate, together with any fixed operating costs, reached a predetermined amount. The vessel's conversion value under this system was based upon the appraised value of the vessel plus 33% of that appraisal-- this to be factored together with any repair costs that the owners had paid during the period of the charter. Of course to make this work to the government's advantage, appraisals had to be reasonably and honestly applied. That was mostly taken care of when the Navy agreed to make ship appraisals for the Army although some commercial appraisals are on record as having been made after that point.

There were apparently enough gaps left in the system of appraisals that Congress, in 1864, passed Public Law No. 212 entitled *An Act for Better Organization of the Quartermaster Department*. Its Section 9 specified that all steam and sail vessels in the coastal service were henceforth to be inspected prior to purchase by "one or more naval officers." The legislated requirement of naval inspection related only to the coasts. Upon the western rivers, the law merely said that inspections would be by "competent persons."

Brigadier General Montgomery C. Meigs, who became the Quartermaster General of the Army in May of 1861, had the Army's charter forms refined from time to time as experience pointed out where improvements were needed. A notable example of such a change was the insertion of a provision which provided that the Army could retain a vessel's service past the expiration of the charter and at the original daily rate. Under another added clause, a ship could be returned to her owner's custody whenever the quartermaster on the scene felt the vessel was no longer required.

A method the Army developed that enabled it to utilize the merchant marine fleet without overly disrupting commercial service routes was the creation of affreightment charters. These were agreements by which vessels operating under regular commercial schedules could be utilized by the Army for all or part of her cargo or passenger capacity, that on the basis of a predetermined passenger or freight rate.

The Quartermaster Department's policies, as they were eventually improved by way of charter formats and through the exercise of outright ship purchases, removed much of the potential for corruption that had existed early-on. Reforms appear to have taken place first on the Atlantic coast and then later on the western rivers. The reason that reforms took hold earlier in the east seems to have been the result of a more centralized control by the Quartermaster Department than that which was initially in place in the western commands. Even in the east, though, some questionable practices continued right up to the war's end. Two of the most flagrant examples where political influence played a part involved the coastal steamers *EMPIRE CITY* of 1751 tons and the *ILLINOIS* of 2123 tons. Both vessels were owned by Marshall O. Roberts of New York. Roberts had dealings with the War Department even before the surrender of Fort Sumter when his vessel the *STAR OF THE WEST* was chartered in January 1861 by the Quartermaster Department to take troops and supplies from New York to Fort Sumter for the reinforcement of the garrison there. The trip was to be made in secret and it was a risky undertaking, a factor of which Roberts seems to have taken advantage. His chartering of *STAR OF THE WEST* to the government does not seem to have been motivated by patriotism, a factor which is brought to light within War Department correspondence.

New York
January 4, 1861

Lieutenant General Winfield Scott
    Washington, DC
Dear General:
    I had an interview with Mr. Schultz at 8 o'clock last evening, and found him to be, as you supposed, the commission, and together we visited Mr. M. O. Roberts. The latter looks exclusively to the dollars, whilst Mr. S. is acting for the good of his country. Mr. R. required $1,500 per day for ten days, besides the cost of 300 tons of coal, which I declined; but, after a long conversation, I became satisfied that the movement could be made with his vessel, the *STAR OF THE WEST*, without exciting suspicion. I finally chartered her at $1,250 per day. She is running on the New Orleans route, and will clear for that port; but no notice will be put in the papers, and persons seeing the ship moving from the dock will suppose she is on her regular trip. Major Eaton, commissary of subsistence, fully enters into my views. He will see Mr. Roberts, hand him a list of the supplies with the places where they may be procured, and the purchases will be made on the ship's account. In this way no public machinery will be used.
    Tonight I pass over to Governor's Island to do what is necessary, i.e., have 300 stand of arms and ammunition on the wharf, and 200 men ready to march on board. Mr. Schultz's steam tugs about nightfall tomorrow, to go to the steamer, passing very slowly down the bay. I shall cut off all communication between the island and the cities until Tuesday morning, when I expect the steamer will be safely moored at Fort Sumter.
    I have seen and conversed with Colonel Scott, and also saw your daughter at your house. After leaving you, I obtained the key of the outer door of the office, but could nowhere find the key of your door or of mine, so failed to get the chart. This is of little moment, as the captain of the steamer is perfectly familiar with the entrance of Charleston.
    I telegraphed you this morning, as follows: *Arrangements made as proposed; to leave tomorrow evening; send map.* I will now leave the office, where I am writing, to proceed to the island.
    Very sincerely, General, your obedient servant,
L. Thomas, Assistant Adjutant General[11]

STAR OF THE WEST was fired upon when it became apparent that she was attempting to approach Fort Sumter. She returned to New York with her troop passengers still aboard.[12]
    At the outbreak of the war, sensing an opportunity for high profits, Roberts purchased the *EMPIRE CITY* for $12,000. Throughout the war, without counting in a series of short trip charters to the Navy, Roberts received from the Army a total of $833,000 for various time charters for *EMPIRE CITY*. His other vessel, the *ILLINOIS*, earned between $1000 and $1600 a day for a grand total of $414,000 in charter fees through to January of 1865. At that time (January 1865), upon what

seems to have been the direct instructions of President Lincoln, the *ILLINOIS* was sold to the Army for $400,000, an amount well in excess of what the Army had originally set as the vessel's maximum worth. On the same day, and by the same order, *EMPIRE CITY* was sold to the Army for $225,000.[13] There is little doubt that those representing the government were in collusion with Roberts. The circumstances were so flagrant that to conclude anything but willful wrongdoing is impossible. In the case of Roberts's two vessels, the evidence indicates with clarity that Lincoln was himself a willing participant in what went on. Quartermaster General Meigs was so opposed to these two sales that despite pressures from the White House, he protested not only the amounts involved but also what were clearly irregularities insofar as the methods used in making the required appraisals-- and well he might have. Through the direct act of Assistant Secretary of War Charles A. Dana, an appraisal committee had been specially appointed to handle these particular sales. Two members of that committee were New York businessmen, Moses Taylor and William E. Dodge, Taylor being designated as chairman of the board doing the appraisals. The Congress, no doubt acting on a tip, began looking into the matter; but this did not deter President Lincoln from ordering the Army to purchase the ships on the basis of the appraisals made by the Taylor board. Thirteen years later, in 1878, a Congressional committee again took up the issue, this time highlighting for the hearing record more of the particulars than were known earlier. What was not brought out, however, during either of the Congressional inquiries, were the shipping and other business connections that existed between Moses Taylor and Marshall O. Roberts, connections which, according to Taylor's biographer Daniel Hodas, started as early as 1837 when Taylor began making business loans to Roberts in support of the latter's United States Mail Steamship Line. These loan transactions continued on a fairly regular basis, at least until 1860. (In 1857, Roberts expressed his gratitude to Taylor by naming one of the United States Mail Steamship Line's vessels after Taylor.)[14] During part of the time that Taylor made these loans to Roberts, Taylor also served as Roberts's business agent. In addition to their close relationship in the shipping industry, Taylor and Roberts were involved in other enterprises, including the ownership of substantial real estate holdings on the Hudson River. When Roberts chartered one of his vessels to the Quartermaster during the opening month of the war, he assigned that charter to Taylor and instructed that the Quartermaster Department send all subsequent payments directly to Taylor.[15] William E. Dodge, the other member of the appraisal committee, had been involved with both Taylor and Roberts in a coal mining partnership in Pennsylvania during 1852. We find yet another compromising connection over the *ILLINOIS* and *EMPIRE CITY*, this one involving one Percy Rivington Pyne. Pyne was Taylor's long-standing partner in many of his affairs and the husband of Taylor's daughter. Pyne was also Roberts's operating agent in the matter of War Department charters involving both the *ILLINOIS* and the *EMPIRE CITY*. Considering Taylor's position as chairman of the government's appraisal board and his close business and personal ties to Roberts, collusion seems too mild a word to attach to the matter of those vessels. Under the laws that we have today, criminal indictments almost certainly would have resulted; and with the type of media scrutiny that we enjoy today, the press almost surely would have uncovered that the moneys paid for the *ILLINOIS* and the *EMPIRE CITY* were meant as the repayment of an obligation the Lincoln Administration owed to Taylor at al. At the start of the war, the government had come close to economic disaster-- a disaster narrowly averted by loans arranged by the business leaders of New York City. Moses Taylor and his colleagues were prominent not only in promoting those loans but also two large Treasury bond issues which followed.

~

There is one other factor to be considered when speculating upon the reasons for Army charter rates being at times inordinately high. The government's agreement to such high rates may have in part been the Administration's attempts to keep American vessels under the US flag and thus available for military needs. At the beginning of the war, there had been a threat of Confederate privateers and later in the war there had been the acts of Confederate naval raiders, particularly the *CSS ALABAMA*. The *CSS ALABAMA* created such a panic among Union ship owners that an exodus of US-owned shipping to foreign registry came uncomfortably close to decimating the north's standing as a shipper in the world market. By the summer of 1863, insurance rates involving war risk in the Atlantic had climbed to as high as 4% of ship value. Transpacific insurance was even higher, rising during that June to 7 1/2% on average. The owners of one merchant ship, *ONEIDA*, on a run scheduled from China to New York, were forced to either pay a rate of 12% or lose their entire insurance. Although only 105 United States oceangoing merchant ships were actually captured by Confederate raiders during the Civil War, the threat of capture was as effective as if the numbers of captures had been three times higher. It was that fear which drove the owners of over nine hundred American flag vessels (almost all of them sail) to transfer over to foreign flags during the period of the Civil War. (The majority of these were outright "sold foreign" transactions.)[16]

The United States coastal fleet of steam powered shipping had not been noticeably impacted by sales to foreign owners due in main to the fact that Army and Navy charters provided a lucrative wartime market. Under the terms of those charters, the government underwrote war losses. Additionally, the Union Navy provided a protection to coastal shipping which was not present on the high seas. During the war, the number of coastal class steam vessels actually increased through new constructions.

~

The question remains as to why Lincoln did not nationalize the shipping industry thus making it illegal for ship owners to sell their vessels to foreign buyers. After all, there had been no hesitation on the part of the Lincoln Administration concerning nationalization of the nation's railroads. In January of 1862, the Congress, at Lincoln's request, authorized the President to seize any or all of the railroads and their equipment and to make the "officers and agents and employees of the railroads a part of the military establishment of the United States." This authority was to apply in those cases whenever the government had to transport troops or their arms or other supplies by rail. In May of 1862, the Lincoln Administration began exercising that power. In actual practice, what this amounted to was an injunction issued to the railroad companies to hold them in readiness for those times when the needs of the military arose, and to further establish that military traffic was to be a priority matter over any other railroad business, no matter what that business might be. As the history of the war tells us, there were only a few examples of railroad companies which found their assets taken under full military operation. (One railroad which did go to military operation was that part of the B & O which ran within the state of Maryland and the District of Columbia.) As the war progressed, military rail operations came into being in those enemy areas which came under occupation by the Union Army, such as in Virginia and some parts of the western theater. The organizational structure for the military's rail operation was formally designated the United States Military Railroad. Before the war ended, that organization directly controlled 2100 miles of track, 6330 railroad cars, and 419 locomotives.

The closest the government came to nationalizing shipping was through the exercise of temporary requisitions, usually done only in cases of military exigency and where an owner was reluctant to charter his ship to the government. The power of requisition was practiced more often on the western rivers than it was in the east. From a legal and political standpoint, the situation in the western theater of war provided a more likely scenario for such takeovers since in many of the cases, the vessels involved were located within a forward area subject to what amounted to martial law.

It appears shortsighted that the Lincoln Administration did not requisition the shipping industry through charter, particularly that part of it consisting of the larger seagoing vessels which were the ones most likely to be sold foreign. The initial requisition could have been followed up by a system of lease-backs or subcharters which would have allowed the owners the commercial utilization of their ships until such times when the vessels were needed for military or naval service. If such a system had been put into place, and if it had been used in conjunction with across-the-board federally subsidized war risk insurance similar to the programs developed during the later 1917-18 war and again in 1941-45, it would have provided a mechanism for placing a cap on charter rates, both on the oceans and on the rivers; and it almost certainly would have prevented the heavy exodus of sail tonnage out from under the flag.

At the time the war started, shipping along the east coast was concentrated out of a relatively few northern ports, namely Annapolis; Baltimore; Philadelphia; New York; Boston; and Portland. By mid-1862 when the Quartermaster Department began getting a better handle on the management of its shipping needs, the quartermasters working at each of these ports were in constant telegraphic communication with the Office of the Quartermaster General. The quartermasters at these ports developed ongoing lists of available shipping, and they were tasked to work out standardized procedures dealing with methods for chartering, loading cargoes, routings, etc. The identification of shipping and its capabilities which resulted from those listings (which were fairly well developed by late 1862) could have provided the basic information for a speedy government takeover of the industry.

A possible caution toward a takeover of the shipping industry, at least early in the war, could have been the lack of enthusiasm on the part of some ship owners for the Union cause. Would the threat of a federal takeover have caused these owners to take their vessels south? To ponder over the Lincoln Administration's decision not to take over the merchant marine can only be a problematical exercise as no records appear to exist regarding such deliberations, although almost surely they must have taken place.

APPENDIX B
LEWIS B. PARSONS, UNION QUARTERMASTER, AND THE SYSTEMS IN PLACE ON THE WESTERN RIVERS, 1861-1866

In James A. Huston's fine work *The Sinews of War: Army Logistics, 1775-1953,* which is part of the US Army's Official Historical Series, there is only one minor reference to Lewis B. Parsons-- and this within a volume which spans 789 pages. We found that surprising since it would be accurate to say that it was Parsons who wrote the original rules on the subject of the military's management of marine transportation. Huston has not been the only one who has overlooked the performance of Parsons. Of the hundreds of vessels which the US Army has named over the years in honor of those whose contributions have been significant to the Army, not one has been named for Parsons. Nor, during the huge sealift of World War II, when it became increasingly difficult to come up with names for the liberty ship program, was one of those liberties named for him. The first time that Parsons's memory came even close to receiving recognition was in 1901 when an historian named John Fiske wrote to Parsons stating that he hoped to make use of Parsons's papers so as to be able to treat the story of the Civil War in a comprehensive fashion. Fiske died a few months after he wrote that letter, and that was the end of that. The only known work done on Parsons is a doctoral dissertation by George Carl Schottenhamel which examined Parsons's wartime career.

In preparing this monograph on Lewis B. Parsons, we have utilized the following sources:

War of the Rebellion, Official Records of the Union and Confederate Armies: Series I, volumes 8, 13, 16, 17, 22-24, 29-31, 34, 39, 41, 45, 47, 48, 52, 53; Series II, volumes 3, 4, 7; Series III, volumes 3-5.

George Carl Schottenhamel, *"Lewis Baldwin Parsons and the Civil War Transportation,"* thesis, Doctorate of Philosophy in History (University of Illinois, 1954), available through University Microfilms International, Order Number 00-10542.

House Executive Documents, 37th Congress, Second Session, Volume VII, 1862.

Records of Third Auditor's Office for 1865, Treasury Department.

~

Lewis B. Parsons began his career as a school teacher and then later became an attorney. As an attorney, he gained a well regarded reputation throughout the midwest, a reputation which in 1853 led to his appointment as general manager of the western section of the Ohio and Mississippi Railroad (later to become known as the Baltimore and Ohio). The president of that railroad system at the time was George B. McClellan. It was through Parsons's friendship with McClellan, along with Parsons's own solid record of getting things done, that Parsons developed wide business contacts throughout the midwest. These contacts were to stand him in good stead during the Civil War.

At the outbreak of the Civil War, Parsons was 43 years of age. He entered military service in May of 1861 as a volunteer aide to Nathaniel Lyon during operations in Missouri. It does not appear that he held any type of commission, militia or otherwise, while serving with Lyon. Shortly after the campaign in Missouri slowed down, Parsons applied for a volunteer commission in the Union Army. It was granted, and as his first assignment, he was detailed to Brigadier General George McClellan's staff at Saint Louis. The Parsons's collection as examined by Schottenhamel at the Illinois State Historical Society Library, contains a recommendation on Parsons signed by Abraham Lincoln and addressed to Secretary of War Cameron. This states: "I personally know Mr. Parsons and have no doubt he would make a good paymaster, quartermaster, or commissary officer." The recommendation was apparently the result of Parsons having known Lincoln earlier when they were both practicing lawyers in Illinois.

After a short stint on McClellan's staff, Parsons, who by then held the rank of captain, was transferred to Saint Louis which was the headquarters for the Western Department under Major General John Charles Fremont. The only way to describe the running of that department under Fremont is to say that it resembled chaos, well salted with corruption. Parsons was one of those assigned to clean up what was becoming a fiscal scandal. Specifically, he was given the task of auditing claims against the government. In great part, these claims-- legitimate or otherwise-- were for stores and other materiel provided to the Army; however, claims for transportation services were also involved. The senior Army quartermaster in the west at that time was Colonel Robert Allen. In a telegraph sent that summer to Quartermaster General Meigs, Allen said, "I have been here but a few days but long enough to tell you that unless the wanton, reckless expenditure in this command is arrested by a stronger arm than mine, the Quartermaster Department will be wrecked in Missouri along with Fremont." In that same message to Meigs, Allen directly accused Fremont of making a joke of the Army's regulations and "a contemptible farce" of the laws of Congress. The frauds which Parsons would uncover became factors leading toward Fremont's removal from command.

In December of 1861, Colonel Allen notified Parsons that in addition to his other duties he was to take charge of dispatching all river transportation pertaining to the Department of the Mississippi. There was then no centralized command or method for allocating transportation within the department, whether by rail, steamship, or wagon. Parsons wrote at the time, "Every man with a gun or a sword [could] order transportation and railroads...." Literally, no system existed at all. Not only did this result in an open invitation for corruption, but it also had the effect of bilking railroad and steamship operators out of what was due them simply because there was no method for establishing that services had been provided by the carrier. Parsons would discover that the local quartermasters attached to Fremont's command had stopped seeking competitive bids, particularly as the bids dealt with transportation. In fairness, this had not been entirely the fault of Fremont's local administration. The Congress was to discover during an investigation it would later conduct on Fremont's tenure at Saint Louis that a circular had been sent to Fremont's headquarters command from the War Department (subsequently approved for action by Fremont) allowing 2¢ per mile for the transportation of troops. A follow-up War Department circular had stated that the 2¢ per mile, as well as a pointed reference that quartermasters were to be guided by "local freight rates," was for guidance as to the maximum rates to be paid by the quartermasters. Quartermasters in the field were advised to negotiate lower rates if possible. That last advice does not seem to have been put into practice. If anything, the records indicate that rates paid by quartermasters during 1861 and early 1862 were higher than the commercial norm. As an example, Parsons was to discover that in the case of the transportation of horses, at least one quartermaster had actually paid 80% more than the local going rates. In order to try to put a stop to all this, as a starter Parsons ordered that competitive bids were to be invited whenever dealing for rail transportation, thus lessening chances of monopolistic rate setting between the railroads. He also recommended to Quartermaster General Meigs that whenever possible, bids were to be solicited from other operators of modes of transportation such as wagon freighters and steamship owners. Parsons would inaugurate a system which required that any voucher issued by troop commanders for railroad passage must indicate the exact mileage traveled and the number of men that had been involved. Vouchers were to be signed personally by the troop commander or his quartermaster officer. In putting through such reforms, Parsons made enemies of railroad officials, steamboat operators, and of course a few quartermaster officers who had been skimming off government funds. As a result of his reforms, complaints and innuendoes directed against him found their way to Washington. Investigations by Meigs upheld both Captain Parsons's practices and his personal integrity.

As War Department confidence grew over Parsons's performance so, did his reputation for fairness, particularly among railroad company executives. One of the many difficulties the railroads faced during the war was the destruction of their property by newly recruited troops who quite often made their initial trips to the scene of war in a state of advanced intoxication, "behaving in a most violent manner, assaulting the conductors, and destroying the furniture of the cars." Parsons fully admitted that in such cases the railroads were being asked to perform, "a service of peculiar difficulty, and as such, it was almost impossible to have the receipts in such order as they should be." By this, he was referring both to the collection of transportation vouchers by the railroad conductors as well as claims made by the railroad companies for damages.

In attempting to straighten out those problems inherent to the utilization of steamboats, Parsons discovered that under the Fremont administration, all such vessels had been hired on a time charter arrangement which usually meant hire by the day. As a result, each owner received the same daily rate whether his vessel was gainfully employed or merely lying at the dock awaiting the Army's convenience. There was little reason under such a system for captains or owners to expedite shipments. The system was doubly marred in that under the time charter formats, the owners were to pay for any fuel consumed. This resulted in owners keeping their vessels as idle as possible since obviously at such times no fuel was consumed. As Parsons would discover, abuses if not outright fraud were far more prevalent on the part of the steamboat operators than had been the case with the railroads. The Congressional committee which investigated what had happened at Saint Louis during the Fremont tenure, reported that the captain of the steamer *NEW SAM GATY* had offered the use of his ship to the Army through a charter agent named John H. Bowen. After the first trip which Bowen arranged with the Army, the captain (as the owner's representative) submitted through Bowen a bill for $400. Bowen then advised the captain that this was not enough-- that the trip was easily worth $500. When the captain received payment, he discovered that the extra $100 had gone directly into Bowen's pocket as an adjunct to his regular agent's fee.

Under the new system which Parsons established, all prior contracts dealing with time charters were immediately canceled. Requests for bids were then put out for the carriage of supplies either by the piece or by bulk-- the latter on the basis of per hundred weight. But even that system did not work too well- at least in the beginning. On one section of the river (upper Mississippi), Parsons was to discover that the successful bidder on an inordinately high volume of Army business was one Barton C. Able. Originally, Able had been the Superintendent of Steamboat Transportation under Fremont. Neither Able or his partner, a man named Mitchell, owned any steamboats. An inquiry by Parsons was to bring out that after winning a bid, the two partners would advertise for steamboat operators to work for them as subcontractors. Once the subordinate role of the steamboat owners had been set into being, Able and Mitchell went ahead to underbid all competition hoping to establish a monopoly and thus set the stage for price fixing in their dealings with the Army. As soon as Parsons discovered their scheme, he gave notice to Able and Mitchell that any contracts awarded to them would be annulled immediately.

As he gained experience, Parsons discovered that a certain leeway to accommodate varying situations would have to be made. For instance, at times when the rivers were low, and in order to get freight forwarded quickly to where it was needed, steamboats could only be partially loaded if they were to pass over shoal spots in the rivers. There were also cases where certain specific items were needed immediately, yet steamboat operators were reluctant to transport them on a rate-per-mile basis, that is if the steamboat did not have other goods aboard so as to make a full payload. In those circumstances, Parsons's quartermasters were instructed to pay by the trip.

Despite the many new reforms which on face value should have put the Army's transportation requirements into a semblance of order, some major stumbling blocks remained. There was the problem of obtaining funds for use by local quartermasters, particularly moneys needed for reimbursing labor bills at the various subdepots. Labor was at this time in short supply, particularly for stevedore services.

(This would change for the better when escaped Negro slaves began to make their way north during 1863.) Slow payments had a tendency to dry up labor supplies. On January 21, 1862, Parsons received a letter from A. S. Baxter, Assistant Quartermaster at Cairo.

> Captain:
>
> What does Government intend to do? This Department has been neglected in every way. No funds; no nothing, and don't seem as though we ever would get anything. Everybody, high and low, in this District is discouraged, and I assure you I would rather be in the bottom of the Mississippi than work night and day without being sustained by Government. I have written to Saint Louis and Washington, and it avails nothing, and if my whole heart and soul was not in the cause, I would never write another word on the subject, but let matters float, I assure you; and a few days will prove by ascertation [sic] that unless Government furnishes this Department with funds, transportation, and et cetera, the whole concern will sink so low that the day of resurrection will only raise it. Laborers have not been paid a dime for six or seven months; don't care whether they work or not. If they do, don't take any interest in anything. Government owes everybody and everything, from small petty amounts to large. Liabilities more plenty than Confederate scrip and worth less. Regiment after regiment arriving daily. Nothing to supply them with and no funds [with which] to buy or men to work. No transportation for ourselves or anyone else.
>
> To tell you the truth, we are on our last legs, and I have made my last appeal on behalf of Government unless it's to a higher power, for it will kill any man and every man at the head of departments here the way we are now working. Is it possible that General Halleck does not know the situation of affairs here? If you think not, I hope you will inform him at once for if he should come here, he will be astonished and annoyed to find us in such a condition. The General commanding and myself have done our best to bring about better results, but our wants are not supplied or even noticed.

That letter and others much like it were passed on by Parsons for endorsement by the department area commander, Major General H. W. Halleck. Parsons's attached his own comment, to wit: "These letters show the condition of affairs not only at Cairo but throughout the Department." Parsons's complaints seem to have had some effect, as funding began to loosen up. Then there were problems of security to deal with. Initially, it had been thought that those steamboat operators who had previously operated on the Mississippi south of Cairo, but who had come north to Union-held territory at the onset of the conflict had been motivated by loyalty to the Union. In general, this may have been true, but among them were some who were motivated solely by economics, and there were those who held political sympathy toward the Southern cause. Parsons soon realized the necessity for running checks on not only the owners of the steamboats but also on the backgrounds of their captains as well. On January 7, 1862, he wrote the draft of a bulletin which was to be issued to quartermasters at the various river ports. It stated that when any vessel is owned in whole or part by citizens of secessionist states, both the captain and pilot must be checked for proven loyalty before the boat could be allowed to leave a quartermaster's jurisdiction. This applied whether or not the steamer carried Army cargo. Enclosing a copy of the draft, Parsons wrote to Halleck:

In view of the fact that very many of the pilots and engineers on our rivers are unquestionably disloyal, and of the great importance of their position as our army advances south, we deem it essential that something like the enclosed order be made as being the only practical way of securing safety.

A reworded version of the original draft included the framework for a plan by which the licenses of all engineers and pilots would be revoked; new licenses were to be granted only to, "persons of approved loyalty." In the event the loyalty of a pilot or engineer could not be established with complete certainty, then the steamboat inspector issuing the license was to require a bond in security for the conduct of that particular engineer or pilot. Another problem Parsons had to resolve concerned wage demands by the pilots. The hazards these pilots faced from the enemy could be unusually severe as in order to properly navigate a steamboat, pilots had to have a full range of visibility. This meant that they had to position themselves atop the wheel house where their vision would not be obscured by protective housing. Thus they became prime targets for any partisan snipers hiding on the river banks. Not liking the odds, the pilots began negotiating for higher wages in early 1862. Parsons did not believe in collective bargaining, at least not in time of war. An order was issued over his signature stating that anywhere on the Mississippi system-- that is between Saint Louis and Memphis-- if a pilot demanded wages exceeding $200 a month, his pilot's license was to be revoked immediately. Although to an extent this order dampened wage demands, the pilots found subtle ways to press their case, one ploy being to ask for an extra day's pay for those months which had thirty-one days. Whether Parsons's policy in regard to the pilots was really justified is open to question. According to John J. Morrison, in his *History of American Steamboat Navigation*, there was a certain substance behind the pilots' complaints on wages. Morrison wrote that as far back as 1837, when wages and prices in general were far lower than they were in the 1860s, pilots were regularly obtaining $300 a month on the Mississippi.

Problems over payment of crews cropped up in a somewhat different form during 1863. Captain G. O. Fort, who had been appointed assistant quartermaster in charge at Vicksburg, wrote Parsons that something had to be done in a hurry in order to retain the crews of those steamboats which were under charter to the Army. "Money has not, and I feel will not be promptly furnished to pay them." The non payments to the crews was in such cases the blame of the owners as in most charter arrangements (time charter formats), the responsibility to pay the crews was an obligation of the vessel's owner(s). Fort claimed that some of the crews had not been paid for up to three months. This had resulted in a condition, as Fort put it to Parsons, "...to make the officers and crews of boats dilatory and sometimes almost mutinous, and some deck hands are deserting the boats."

As time went on, most of the problems were worked out, and the organization which Parsons oversaw was truly remarkable for what it accomplished. Although in most cases the Army's hiring of steamboats on the western rivers was accomplished through negotiation, there were numerous circumstances when Parsons's subordinate quartermasters had to take what vessels they needed by impressment. Impressment was usually employed during times of heavy troop movements when the increased demand for vessels could have brought about considerable price gouging and other finagling on the part of the operators. At such times, affreightment contracts (meaning established prices for shipment of goods based either upon cubic measurement or tonnage of the cargo to be moved) could not be continued since the needs of the Army were such that the sole use of the vessel was required at the pleasure of the government for indefinite periods. To meet such conditions, Parsons set up a mechanism whereby local committees of "well informed and influential citizens" could establish the daily rates which were to be paid to the owners of the vessels which were impressed. We have little detail as to how the quartermasters were to organize these committees, nor do we know if they were put into use on any sort of regular basis. In the Shiloh campaign of 1862 when 174 steamers were utilized for transporting Grant's army up the Tennessee (most of those steamers had been impressed), Parsons reported to General Meigs that the daily rates the boats were to be paid had been fixed by "four influential men." Apparently the rates which were established by those four men were not universally accepted as fair since at the end of that campaign, Parsons was forced to make adjustments. To have assembled that many vessels and coordinated their utilization with the rather limited staff that Parsons had was a monumental undertaking, one that was unprecedented up to that time. It was especially impressive when one realizes that at the same moment in time, another major military effort was underway which also involved the use of transports. That second undertaking was the operation against the Confederate fortifications at Island No. 10 on the Mississippi below Cairo.

Policies on Charters and Dealings with Steamboat Owners

Generally speaking, during the first year and a half of the war, when the Army had a vessel under hire on the western rivers, it assumed all of the risk, both from enemy action and marine peril. This covered boats under charter as well as those impressed for specific operations. Such does not seem to have been the case on the east coast. There, the War Department, from the beginning to the end of the war, assumed risk for war peril but left the matter of marine peril up to the owners. In a late 1862 letter addressed to the Third Auditor of the US Treasury, Parsons explained that since almost all of the boats on the western rivers were normally insured by private companies, his policy would henceforth be to only place the government under responsibility for damages specifically related to war risk. In reality, Parsons's policy in this regard does not seem to have been applicable universally on the western rivers since in a few instances, War Department charter records into 1864 and 1865 show owners being paid in full for losses which appear to have been marine peril.

Impressment of vessels was continually a sore point between the government and the steamboat operators. It was, of course, the simplest and most convenient solution to be followed by quartermasters whenever the Army needed river transportation in large quantities without the luxury of giving advance notice. However, the taking was often done in a most arbitrary manner. For instance, it was not unusual for quartermasters to actually stop boats on the river. In the case of vessels which at such a time were carrying private freight, they would be ordered to unload, and the vessels then put to the task of transporting troops or military equipment. What happened to that private freight left unattended on docks or upon levies can only be imagined. In June of 1863, a group of steamboat owners met in Cincinnati to protest against impressment. They lodged specific complaints over the methods established by the Quartermaster Department through which rates were established. The owners called for a policy prohibiting impressment except in cases of genuine emergency. They asked for a universal system on the rivers whereby at the time when a vessel was impressed, a price would be agreed upon between the government's agent and the owner (or his representative). In lieu of that, they asked for the appointment of a representative to arbitrate between the two factions. When meeting with the owners, Parsons came on strong, clearly giving them the impression that he would not knuckle under. He stood firm against the Quartermaster Department settling on prices at the time of impressment, arguing that such negotiations would result in serious delay to troop movements. There is no record to show that the owners succeeded in any of their demands.

One of Parsons's major perplexities was the corporate structuring inherent to the western rivers' steamboat industry. Unlike the nation's railroads which were operated by large companies with sophisticated management, steamboats on the western rivers were usually separate units of ownership. Seldom would an owner possess more than two or, at the most, three vessels. Very few companies of any size had been developed by the 1860s; and when large companies did exist, they often proved to be nothing more than a combination of boat owners banded together for purposes of providing economic leverage in the marketplace. The nature of such marketing organizations usually resulted in short-lived alliances. As Parsons was to find out, any agreement made with those companies would only last for the short time that the individual owners were combined for mutual advantage. Any manner of circumstances could cause an abandonment of these mergers. When mergers were dissolved, all corporate agreements entered into with outside parties automatically became null and void. Schottenhamel, whose studies encompassed the history of such mergers during the Civil War, concluded that for the Army's quartermasters, working with these corporate entities was "like dealing with a ghost."

The steamboat operators often by-passed Parsons with their complaints, taking them instead to the senior troop commanders in the region or directly to Washington. One more or less typical case came up during 1863 at a time when Parsons's responsibilities had been enlarged to cover the entire Mississippi system. It was filed by the owners of the steamer *DILIGENT*. The vessel had been part of field operations which had taken place within the jurisdictions of both General Grant and General Sherman. Over time, both generals developed a personal relationship with the *DILIGENT's* captain and went to bat for him when Parsons refused to pay the rate of $175 a day asked for by the owners. The rate request (which was inordinately high when compared against the standard) was endorsed by both Grant and Sherman on the premise that the service provided by the *DILIGENT* had been exceptional and that her captain had shown extraordinary efficiencies. Even though the interference by these two general officers put Parsons in an awkward position, he still refused to pay the amount asked. When pressure continued, Parsons finally settled at $135 a day, but he had the last word which he addressed to both Sherman and Grant, stating that this was about $15 to $20 a day more than it should have been. Such a blunt sentiment by

Parsons who was by this date a colonel, was not geared toward enhancing a junior officer's relationships with his seniors; however the generals overlooked it.

Parsons and Grant would later have a more serious disagreement as evidenced from a letter Grant wrote on August 15, 1863, to Parsons's superior Brigadier General Robert Allen. At the time, Grant's father was employed as a commercial steamboat agent. In that capacity, the senior Grant had been championing a claim against the Quartermaster Department on behalf of the owners of the steamboat *SUNNY SOUTH*. Taking on his father's cause, General Grant wrote:

> My father has come down here on the insistence of the owners of the *SUNNY SOUTH* to effect a settlement for her services. I know nothing of the merits of the case, or what the services of the boat ought to command. This I do know, however, the course pursued by Colonel Parsons in taking up boats without any agreement and settling with them arbitrarily, and in annulling charters and not paying for services already rendered has resulted in very great dissatisfaction and constant reference to me of matters which I really have nothing to do with.
>
> I hope you will give the matter a few moments of your time and enable my father to transact all he has to do on the matter.

Grant's letter was referred directly to Parsons by Allen for answering. Writing Grant, Parsons explained that the *SUNNY SOUTH* was an example of one of those vessels where the owners were clearly attempting to obtain far more than the services were worth. As to the other matters to which Grant had referred, Parsons replied,

> Waving the injustice of condemning one unheard, I will only seek to correct erroneous impressions produced by the misrepresentations of others. I have very seldom taken boats without agreement except in three instances: once on orders of Major General Halleck to send twenty-seven boats without delay to move General Pope's army up the Tennessee, and in both the other cases, on your order...In each of these cases, I think you will admit that in all of these cases, there was no time for negotiation of regular charter, and even if there had been, it must be plain that negotiation would simply end in extortion, aside from these the cases of seizure to me amount to nothing, and have never been made when they could reasonably be avoided. These are the facts and who inform you differently informed you falsely.

Grant's interpretation of Parsons's letter was that a slur had been cast, at least indirectly, toward his father. Grant assigned an officer on his staff to further investigate the matter. This resulted in the following memo:

> Whilst Colonel Parsons may be working zealously for the interests of the public service, I think many of his efforts tend to no good results and in some instances amount to impertinent interference.

At this point, things were becoming somewhat uncomfortable for Parsons, and Quartermaster General Meigs, made aware of the situation, was moved to come to the aid of his transportation officer. In a letter to Grant, Meigs wrote:

In his zeal to conduct the affairs of the Transportation Branch of the service with economy, he [Parsons] has drawn down upon him the whole power of the steamboat interests, and by those representing this interest he has been vilified and abused without stint...It is not justified that he should be rewarded by a sneer from his commanding officer? I ask my dear general, your reconsideration of this subject, satisfied that you have pronounced a hasty judgment, and knowing that you will not deliberately do injustice to a highly meritorious officer and personal friend.

At about the same time, in a letter to Major General Sherman who had also forwarded the criticisms of various steamboat operators on to Washington, Parsons wrote:

You have no idea how much these men have made-- every man owning an old tub is richer. I have been lied about by them without stint. Why should I wish to defraud them? It would be infinitely easier for me to settle to please them-- it would not have involved the patient examination for days and days of their accounts to get a just settlement-- and then instead of unmeasured denunciation, they would all have joined in hosanna and in furnishing me with horses and perhaps made a Brigadier of me. I have not for a moment allowed such consideration as to influence me, and I will never do so. I have and will act as near as I can the part of a just arbiter-- and allow neither too little or too much. And I will get out of this damnably [sic] laborious perplexing thankless position just as soon as I can. PERIOD.

Sherman wisely decided to bow out of the controversy. Beginning to realize that Parsons was in all probability being unfairly judged, Sherman wrote to Parsons.

I construe General Grant's endorsement [meaning the letter from Grant's staff officer claiming impertinence on Parsons's part] which gives you so much concern into an impatience at having cases referred back to him with which he should not be bothered. Take example of some of the old Army quartermasters who are as insensible to the grumblings and growlings of others as a patient Army mule.

At this point, Grant must have come to the conclusion that the matter was getting out of hand. In a letter to Brigadier General Allen, Grant wrote:

Perhaps the remark I made was rather hasty. I have always esteemed what Colonel Parsons did while he was with me, and have always looked upon him as an officer who had his whole heart in the cause and cannot say that I have had reason to change my opinion of him. If I have done him injustice, and I think I did in using the term 'impertinent,' I should be happy to correct it and shall take pains to do so.

~

Although ship owners often did try to take unfair advantage of the government, it is clear that some injustices did occur. One clear case which had nothing to do with Parsons or even with the Quartermaster Department, concerned the steamer *IDAHO* (also spelled *IDAHOE* in some records). While the saga of *IDAHO* was perhaps not especially typical, it is attention getting by its circumstance. On May 18, 1863, the *IDAHO*, a brand new sidewheel steamer built for John M. Newcombe, was chartered by the Quartermaster Department at the rate of $175 per day for service on the Tennessee River "and elsewhere." The *IDAHO* was the pride and joy of Newcombe who was also her captain. Fitted out for passenger service, *IDAHO's* cabins were comfortable and well appointed.

On July 6, 1863, Special Order No. 29 was issued by Headquarters, US Forces, Nashville, Tennessee. Through the content of that order, fate dealt a hand which would adversely impact Newcombe's hopes and dreams for his new vessel.

> Lieutenant Colonel Spalding, Provost Marshal, is hereby directed without loss of time to seize and transport to Louisville all prostitutes found in this city or known to be here. The Provost Marshal will give personal attention to this matter. The prevalence of venereal disease at this post has elicited the notice of the general commanding the department who has ordered a preemptory remedy.

Two days later, the commander of a detachment of military guards appeared at the foot of the gangway of the *IDAHO* to announce that he would soon bring aboard one hundred soiled ladies for immediate transport. He handed Newcombe a letter which read:

> From the Provost Marshal
> Nashville, July 8, 1863
>
> To Captain, Steamer *IDAHO*
> Sir:
> You are hereby directed to proceed to Louisville, Kentucky, with the one hundred passengers put on board your steamer today, allowing none to leave the boat before reaching Louisville.
> George Spalding, Lieutenant Colonel and Provost Marshal

Newcombe strongly protested, arguing that his boat was only three months old; all her furniture was new; and she was a fine passenger boat. If the one hundred prostitutes were dumped upon him, the reputation ensuing to his boat would ruin him. His protests got him nowhere. The girls were then herded up the gangway. In a letter written two years later which he sent to the Secretary of War, Newcombe described what happened next.

> I asked Captain Stubbs how these women were to be subsisted. He told me I would have to see General Morgan about that. I saw General Morgan, and he told me to subsist them myself. I entreated to let the government subsist them that it would do so [for] much less than I could. His reply was, 'You subsist them.' When I found General Morgan determined that I should subsist them, I had to buy meat and vegetables at enormous high prices from store boats along the river, and in addition at many places to buy ice and medicines, these women being diseased and more than one half of them sick in bed. I applied to Commissaries of Subsistence along the route, for Commissary stores, to feed these women; but at each place was refused by the officers in charge, and the civil as well as the military authorities would not allow my boat to land, and put guards along the shore to prevent me from doing so. When leaving Nashville, I applied for a guard to be put on board. General Morgan told me I did not need any but to take charge of them myself. Having no guard, I could not keep men along the route from coming on board to these women, when at anchor and being angered because I strove to drive them away, both themselves and these bad women both destroyed and damaged my boat, and the furniture to a great

extent. When I arrived at Louisville, I stated my grievances to General Boyle, and he gave me a guard and ordered me to proceed to Cincinnati and await further orders there. I remained in the stream opposite Cincinnati, Ohio, because I would not be allowed to land for thirteen days, when I was ordered to Nashville again with my cargo of prostitutes.

I wish to say to Your Honor that I was compelled to subsist these women that it cost me all that I have made charge for, to do so, that this claim is merely a reimbursement of my money which I had to expend which complying with the orders of the Officers of the United States Government... I had to leave my business and travel from Cincinnati to this place to see if I could collect it, it being over two years due me. I am here now one week, going from one office to another, to see to get my papers, and to effect a settlement, which I have not yet done, nor likelihood to have done, unless Your Honor will please to direct payment of this account so justly due me and for so long a time....

Finally, in October of 1865, Newcombe's claim was honored to the amount of $1,000. This was for damages done to his boat by the prostitutes and their unauthorized customers and an additional $4,316.04 for "subsistence and medicines furnished to one hundred eleven prostitutes on board the steamer *IDAHO* at the rate of $1.50 per day for each while being transported."

Unfortunately, Newcombe's prediction that the *IDAHO* would be a ruined vessel was correct. The *IDAHO* came to be known upon the river as "the floating whorehouse."

Demand for River Transport Increased After June of 1862

Prior to the taking of Memphis in June 1862, heavy usage of steamboats by the Army had been rather spasmodic. While abnormally large numbers of boats were needed for specific operations such as those against Fort Henry and Fort Donelson and later at Shiloh, these would be followed up by an abrupt slackening in demand. As more of the Mississippi was opened through Union conquests, the need for steamers became heavier since garrisons had to be supplied and side expeditions up rivers such as the Arkansas and the Yazoo became a fairly regular thing. As the penetration of the Mississippi continued south to Vicksburg and beyond, there developed a need for steamboats and barges as floating warehousing, a direct result of the swampy and often completely flooded terrain which bordered the river banks and which made storage ashore unfeasible.

It was becoming increasingly evident to Parsons that although he had the overall responsibility for obtaining steamboats and for initially moving troops forward on those boats, he had no real control over the steamers once they arrived in the operating areas at which time they came under the jurisdiction of the field commanders. These commanders would also hold vessels as insurance against the possibility that they might be needed to move troops to another location. The problem of holding over vessels became evident as early as the spring of 1862 when, following the Battle of Shiloh, arrangements were made to ship to Pittsburg Landing weekly consignments of two hundred head of cattle. During the same time frame, another forty head per week had been scheduled to be shipped to one of the garrison posts on the Mississippi.

Parsons could not meet the order because so many boats had been held over for use as warehouse vessels. To the field commanders responsible, Parsons wrote, "If the Army gets out of beef, it will not be our fault."

It was not just food supplies for the troops that had to be shipped by river. Forage for the cavalry and artillery horses was a major user of river transportation. One cavalry commander wrote to Parsons on August 31, 1862. "We must have forage. There is not enough in the country within twenty miles of Helena [Arkansas] to subsist our animals for a week." A cavalry division which had been assembled at Columbus, Kentucky, soon exhausted all locally available hay and grain, resulting in an urgent appeal for at least five hundred tons a day which would have to be sent to that place for the next three or four days and perhaps longer. The problem with commodities like grain and forage was not their availability. Headquarters at Cairo announced that it had sufficient hay and grain to supply the whole army on the river. The problem was in getting it to the units in the field.

The Peculiar Needs of the Steamboats

Fuel for the steamboats was a problem all along the Mississippi system. It was a problem which called for a two-fold solution: first, to arrange for a supply, and next to get the fuel distributed to the right places. Before the war, a system had evolved for servicing commercial steamboats. Stockpiles of wood or coal were assembled at various pickup points along the rivers, the quantity usually enough to take care of the river's normal traffic. But by late 1862, there was nothing normal about steamboat volume on the rivers. On short notice, entire Army corps were being loaded aboard any and all steamboats that could be gathered up. Obviously, during such periods of high demand for steamboat fuel, the system previously in place could not work. In December of 1862, Parsons advised his quartermasters:

> ...large movements are in prospect, and you will require very soon a large supply of coal...You will have to propose for and had best take such as comes to Cairo at once, unless you can purchase at fair rates. You will give this your prompt attention-- I have advertised for propositions [bids] for five hundred thousand bushels to be opened on the 15th instance, but it will not do to rely very much on that as I fear there will be little competition.

The steamboat operators joined Parsons in the worry about the supply of fuel, both wood and coal. They believed, and with justification, that if a system could not be evolved to guarantee the supply of fuel, river transportation could become unreliable and prohibitively costly to the Army. Such a circumstance could cause the quartermasters to begin relying more on rail than on river steamers, something which the steamboat operators did not wish to see happen. Planning was formulated so that coal would be provided at main departure points-- places such as Cairo. Along the river south of Cairo, wood was to be stockpiled for replenishment. As in the prewar period, the wood at these pickup points was supplied by transient wood cutters who in turn relied on the local areas to supply them with meat and other foodstuffs. Game was usually plentiful, but salt for its preservation often was not. In order to help guarantee a steady supply of wood, the steamboat operators suggested to Parsons that boats under Army charter be allowed to sell salt and/or salted beef to the wood cutters. Parsons agreed but with the provision that the steamboat operators were only to sell to those from whom they directly purchased wood. The salt was to be sold at cost. The system worked for a while although there was often difficulty in obtaining salt. There were certain areas, though, where wood cutters could not be influenced to work-- salt or no salt. These were locations where Confederate guerrillas and just plain bandits were operating. The only way to keep the wood cutters on the job in those areas was to assign protective detachments of infantry. But the problems did not end there. In a number of instances, after the wood cutters and their guards had moved on, the stockpiled wood was discovered and burned by guerrillas. Parsons's agents were able to locate some land owners who held woodland on islands in the Mississippi. These locations had the advantage of offering relative safety for both the cutters and their wood.

By the spring of 1864, the difficulty of fueling steamboats was still very much a factor. The longer the war went on, the harder it became to find good stands of wood which were easily accessible from the rivers. On the Mississippi system, the wood that was found was located mostly on the branch streams lying to the west of the main channel of the Mississippi. Most of that was green and thus not the best material for firing steam boilers. Laborers to cut the wood were also becoming increasingly scarce as more and more men were taken into the Army. The old system of relying on entrepreneurial wood cutters was clearly outdated. The task soon fell to big business. The scope of contracts given out is a good indication of how big that business became. For instance, one contract called for up to one hundred fifty thousand cords to be stockpiled between Memphis and New Orleans. In large part, woodcutting laborers were former slaves who had escaped from Confederate territory. For such people, cash was secondary to maintaining a reasonable subsistence. This need was satisfied through the vehicle of providing access to commissary stores signed out by the Army to the wood contractors.

Because of guerrilla activity, some areas continued to present special wood gathering problems. The Arkansas River, particularly the upstream sections of it, was one of the more troublesome. A more or less typical trip on the Arkansas River was described by one infantry officer who had been placed in charge of the guard on a steamer named *POCAHONTAS*, then engaged by the Quartermaster Department to take supplies upriver. He described the difficulties, not the least of which was a shortage of fuel coupled to the particular inefficiencies of the captain of the steamer.

> ...only 518 barrels of pork were on board which he [the captain] had left there on her previous trip, for some cause or another. She [*POCAHONTAS*] had taken on only wood, to run her on the upriver trip for two days, when it was evident she could not make the trip up in less than four or five days. First class boats can run it in about two days with good fuel. It was ascertained that with green wood, she could not keep up with the fleet; the *THOMAS J. PATTIN* [*T. J. PATTEN*] took her in tow. The next morning, the *HOMEYER* [*HENRY A. HORMEYER*] took from the *POCAHONTAS* 200 barrels of pork (offering to take the whole load but was refused) and after spending three or four hours wooding her took her in tow. The third morning before we started, and again during the day, the crews of all the boats, and

all soldiers on board were ordered out to carry rails for the *POCAHONTAS*. And so it went. Nearly one third of the running time was spent during the first three days wooding the boat. On the third day, the *PATTIN* sprung a leak and would have capsized and sunk in a very short time if the *HOMEYER* had not went to her assistance with a steam pump... I have partially examined the hull of the *PATTIN* and do not think she is fit to use on another trip... On the morning of the fourth day, the *POCAHONTAS* having found good wood (rails) during the night was able to keep up with *PATTIN* and *HOMEYER*, they running slow time. But the *GILLUM* which had only been able to keep up with the *POCAHONTAS* when she was towed was taken in tow by the *GUNBOAT NO. 37* (under Captain Rodgers) first and as it made them fall behind, she was turned over to the *HOMEYER* which boat towed her nearly to the bluffs. The *GILLUM* is not in the government service and by what authority she is convoyed, or how much she pays for being towed and delaying the fleet is more than I know. Colonel, any man who has traveled on this river will tell you that there is something wrong somewhere...he would come to the conclusion that the only remedy is to employ boats to freight by the pound. It is after all the difference between private and government enterprise. In all other matters, the government is supposed to have the best of everything. With boats, it is too often the case of only the worst. So bad indeed that no insurance company would take a dime of risk on them.

Severe Shortages Develop

Shipping volume increased as Federal troops continued their southward advance on the Mississippi. A report of the Office of Transportation, Quartermaster Department at Saint Louis which was prepared for the Quartermaster General for the fiscal year ending June 30, 1863, enumerated the total amount of materiel transported from Saint Louis to the Vicksburg area during that year.

Subsistence, ordnance, medical stores	491,014,463 pounds
Troops (in number)	328,932
Horses and mules (in number)	82,681
Cattle (in number)	25,540
Wagons and ambulances (in number)	4,348
Cannon and caissons (in number)	274
Locomotives, railroad cars (in number)	178
Bricks	8,000 tons
Board feet (in number)	2,314,619
Shingles	461 packages

In transmitting that report to the Quartermaster General, the Saint Louis office commented that the report addressed only the shipments from Saint Louis. It was then explained that to get a correct volume of all troops and materiel shipped to Vicksburg would require adding in the reports of the other quartermasters at Pittsburgh, Cincinnati, Louisville, Cairo, and Memphis.

The Parson papers contain a breakdown of commissary supplies which were received at Vicksburg during this same period. That list purported to represent incoming shipments from all sources.

Ale	5,000	gallons
Beans	2,500	bushels
Cabbage and Onions	20,000	gallons
Candles	43,750	barrels
Coffee	150,000	pounds
Dried Apples	50,000	pounds
Flour	1,500	barrels
Hominy	20,000	pounds
Molasses	10,000	gallons
Pepper	5,000	pounds
Pickles	10,000	gallons
Rice	170,000	pounds
Rice	20,000	pounds
Salt	1,000	bushels
Salt meat	2,000,000	pounds
Soap	100,000	pounds
Sugar	375,000	pounds
Tea	8,100	pounds
Vinegar	20,000	gallons
Whiskey	20,000	gallons

It seems that the quartermasters were continually faced with new reasons for shortages in the supply of available steamboats. One of the more annoying was the habit of field commanders along the Mississippi who appropriated entire vessels for the personal use of themselves and their staffs. Brigadier General William Orme was one such offender. In a letter to his wife, written after the fall of Fort Hudson and which is now contained within the Parsons Collection, Orme wrote:

On last Thursday night at 12 o'clock, with the kind offer of General Herron, I dropped silently out of the fleet at Port Hudson on my boat the *DES ARC* and steamed down the river to New Orleans-- we reached there at 11 o'clock Friday morning. I immediately took rooms at the once famous Saint Charles Hotel and prepared for a short season of rest and quiet. I brought no one down with me but my staff. On Saturday morning, I ordered my horses (they were brought down on the boat with us) and at 4 o'clock in the morning, myself and staff started for a ride on the famous Shell Road to Lake Pontchartrain. After a delightful ride of about an hour in the cool morning air, we reached the lake-- a distance of six miles-- we soon dismounted and bathed in the pleasant waters of a lake I longed to see. After leaving the water, we ordered a nice fish breakfast at the hotel on the lake shore.

Parsons stated that the *DES ARC* had a 345-ton cargo capacity for which the Army paid a charter rate of $250 a day.

As the cotton producing regions came under occupation, a demand arose for the use of steamboats to move cotton into the northern economy. This new commercial use for steamboats only added justification for the demands from boat owners asking for higher charter and affreightment rates for Army hire.

Although Parsons and his subordinate quartermasters felt that the affreightment method for hiring vessel space was the most economic from the Army's standpoint, Quartermaster Department policy began moving away from the affreightment hire system, going instead to time chartering. The department did this in order to hold vessels in the government's service rather than having them seek commercial business. One problem over resuming a wider use of the charter system was that demurrage charges added heavily to overall costs, particularly so in periods of low water when river conditions often necessitated that steamers tie to the bank and wait for the next freshet. During such times, the government was paying for vessels that were doing absolutely nothing.

Transportation on the Western Rivers Consolidated Under A Single Director

The biggest challenge that Parsons probably faced at the onset of his taking over transportation responsibilities on the upper Mississippi was that of developing an organization that could exercise a centralized control and yet which at the same time would not become so bureaucratically complex as to hamper initiative on the part of subordinate quartermasters. In December of 1862, Parsons issued a circular to all quartermasters in his jurisdiction, the content of which tells us quite a bit about his management style.

> In order to furnish the necessary information by which to render the river transportation of the Mississippi and its tributaries more efficient, uniform, and economical, you will please immediately forward to this office a list of all boats of every kind in Government service under your order or control,.... You will also furnish like information until further orders, at the end of each week. You will also advise this office of such transportation as you are likely to receive. Also, whether any change can be made in the way of wharf or other boats whereby expenses can be diminished and of any accidents in transportation by which Government property has been lost or damaged. Also of any wrecked or damaged property in your vicinity requiring attention. Also the amounts paid or expended by you for, and on account of, Government transports, and on what boats. Also relative to fuel expended or received.

In the summer of 1863, Parsons made his bid for a central control of all western river shipping. He put this forth within a draft recommendation sent to Brigadier General Allen recommending that an officer with the rank of brigadier general be assigned as superintendent for all steamboat transportation west of the Allegheny Mountains. Parsons summarized his recommendation by stating that the "rivers of the west and the government transportation on them should be regarded as a unit." He recommended in the same letter that assistant quartermaster officers should be stationed at all the important ports so that the proposed general superintendent could coordinate with them. Parsons reiterated the reporting system he had earlier inaugurated within his present area of responsibility: "The post of Superintendent should have as its function that of receiving precise reports from all assistant quartermasters at the out-ports at least weekly for all boats chartered or impressed, all contracts made or rates paid for transportation."

On December 9, 1863, Meigs cut orders appointing Parsons as the Chief of River Transportation on the western rivers. That appointment carried with it the full authority that Parsons had suggested, less one provision. Parsons had requested the rank of brigadier general but he would remain a colonel for some time into the future. Although Parsons was still under the overall jurisdiction of Brigadier General Allen, he was now to report directly to General Meigs in Washington. It is probably accurate to state that it was Parsons's appointment to head up river transportation that marked the keeping of accurate charter and hiring records on the river. Prior to that time, the records at some out-ports were extremely sketchy if not in many cases entirely nonexistent.

For the new Chief of River Transportation, things did not go smoothly at first. Parochial interests had to be overcome. Perhaps the worst of the fiefs was that held by Captain J. H. Ferry, the quartermaster officer at Louisville, Kentucky. Ferry had been using the charter system exclusively despite the previous policy of utilizing affreightment contracts whenever possible. In Ferry's jurisdiction there had been no shortages of steamers which would otherwise have justified a practice of chartering in lieu of an affreightment system. Ferry's ongoing excuse for noncompliance had been that the affreightment method had not been in the best interest of the Louisville area. Why?, he never explained. In truth, his own self interest had been involved. It was alleged in reports that found their way to Parsons's desk that Ferry had close ties with the steamship interests and that he had developed a profitable skimming operation. In any event, costs at Louisville had been exorbitant. Ferry had consistently claimed that the high costs of operation were in part the result of the Navy's interference with Army supply movements on the river. Parsons found this an excuse without substance.

Despite Parsons's appointment as Chief of River Transportation, local quartermasters were still appointed through the Quartermaster General in Washington. Parsons therefore had to request to Meigs that Ferry be fired rather than executing that authority himself. For some reason Meigs vacillated on the issue. Parsons resolved this problem by physically moving himself to Louisville and once there, he went about assembling sufficient depositions to be able to formally charge Ferry with corruption. Meigs then had no choice but to remove Ferry.

Innovations on the White River- Arkansas System
        The transport system on the Arkansas had certain unique aspects which had to be overcome if the river was to be used in a satisfactory manner. A great part of the freight destined for Little Rock and other locations on the Arkansas came in from the Mississippi by way of the White River. Some distance up the White at a place called Devall's Bluff, steamers were offloaded. Their cargoes were transferred to a single track railroad for transit overland to Little Rock. (The single track appears to have been constructed in 1862.) At Little Rock, shallow draft steamers would pick up cargoes offloaded from the trains and continue upriver on the Arkansas to the consigned destination. This river-rail transfer worked fairly well, but there were times when serious bottlenecks developed because of the one-way rail track from Devall's Bluff. To solve that problem, Parsons recommended that a second track be installed. This was completed sometime prior to August of 1864.

Partisan forces were constantly troublesome on both the Arkansas River and the White River. That menace was not alleviated until late 1864 which in part explains the absence of proper wooding facilities during the fall of 1863, a deficiency which the infantry officer on the *POCAHONTAS* had complained of.

A Dynamic Logistics System Leading to Victory in 1865

Writing to his mother on February 26, 1864, Parsons summed up his feelings of optimism that at long last, the various parts of the transportation matrix were beginning to come together. Increasing demands did not, though, allow for relaxation.

> I hope soon to get the vast transportation of all the rivers into a good condition. Its vastness is little understood. Only think of one point-- I have nearly 200,000 tons of supplies and say 10,000 animals to transport to Nashville for General Grant's army from January 1 to May 1. [This materiel was being sent east to the Virginia campaign.] I have in the last three weeks had requisitions for forty boats from General Banks, twenty from General Sherman, and nearly one hundred boats for the Cumberland. A fleet up the Arkansas for Little Rock, Fort Smith and the Cherokee country. Boats for up the Tennessee. Large supplies, say at least 35,000 tons and 6,000 animals to Memphis and various points down the river and the general management of all the government railroad business in the northwest.

When Grant was called east as General-in-Chief of the Union Army, it would fall to Sherman to penetrate the heart of the southern Confederacy by striking at Atlanta and then marching to the sea. Until Sherman reached Atlanta, he would depend on Nashville for his logistics. Assistant Quartermaster Winslow, one of the officers who worked under Parsons during the last part of the war, summed up in retrospect the movement of supplies as the problems became ever more complex.

> The greatest problem to be solved was how during the short period in which the Cumberland was navigable to Nashville, say from February to May, to throw such an amount of supplies into Nashville, with more than 200,000 men and 50,000 animals to be subsisted during a whole summer's campaign, without relying on substance or forage in the enemy's country.

In the Annual Report of the Quartermaster General dated November 3, 1864, Quartermaster General Meigs discussed the logistical achievements of that year, mentioning Parsons as being one of those to whom the country owed a debt of gratitude for the outstanding way he had contributed to the campaign which led up to the capture of Atlanta.

> All accounts of charter of steamers in the western rivers were ordered to his [Parsons's] office for examination and settlement. Under his just and energetic control, uniform rates for transportation of troops and freight were soon established, and all the resources of the immense steamboat interests in the west were brought to contribute to the regular, prompt, and abundant supply of the armies operating on the Mississippi and its tributaries. Availing himself of the high water in the Cumberland [River], he pushed forward to Nashville vast stores of supplies at moderate rates and effected great economies in their transportation.

To the energy, intelligence, and zeal of General Allen at Louisville; Colonel Donaldson at Nashville; Colonel Easton at the Headquarters in the field; Captain Arthur Edwards in charge of construction and management of steamers on the Tennessee; Colonel Lewis B. Parsons, in charge of steamboat transportation on the western rivers; and Colonel D. C. McCallum in charge of the 930 miles of military railways which it became necessary to repair and manage, the country owes a debt of gratitude for the brilliant success of the campaign resulting in the capture of Atlanta, and relieving the hearts of the people of the United States of all fears as to the final victory of our cause and re-establishment of our united country. Three of these officers have been rewarded by brevet promotion for their services. I respectfully recommend that the services of the others be likewise recognized.

One of the three breveted officers was Parsons. In the summer of 1865, Parsons was promoted to brigadier general of volunteers.

~

Following the surrender of the Confederate armies in the spring of 1865, Parsons remained in the Army until such time that he was able to complete the disposal of the wartime fleet. With that task completed, his resignation from the Army was accepted as of April 10, 1866. When viewed from the standpoint of the management of marine transportation in modern warfare, Brigadier General Lewis B. Parsons, did indeed write the original book.

APPENDIX C
THE ARMY'S OFFICE OF THE GUNBOAT FLOTILLA
(WESTERN WATERS)

Organization of the Flotilla

Separate and apart from what was later to become Lewis B. Parsons's transportation organization on the western rivers was a subcommand of the Quartermaster Department called "Office of the Gunboat Flotilla." The commanding officer of this subcommand reported directly to Brigadier General M. C. Meigs. Captain George D. Wise, Assistant Quartermaster, was appointed as the Army's representative to work with Commander Andrew H. Foote, the naval officer who was placed in tactical command of the flotilla. (Commander John Rodgers, had held command during the early construction phase of the flotilla.)

Captain Wise was appointed to his responsibility on September 28, 1861. Captain Wise's report to Quartermaster General Meigs, dated two years later is, in the authors' opinions, the best description available of the organizational composition of the Western Gunboat Flotilla while it was under the aegis of the Army. That report, found in *ORA*, III, 5, pp 476, 477, is reproduced below.

Office of Gunboat Flotilla
Saint Louis, Missouri, September 14, 1863

Brigadier General M. C. Meigs, Quartermaster General

General:

In accordance with General Orders, No. 13, I have to report as follows:

I received my appointment as captain and assistant quartermaster on the 28th of September, 1861, and was ordered to report for duty to Captain A. H. Foote, US Navy, commanding gunboat flotilla on the western waters.

The flotilla was under the command of naval officers and subject to naval rules, while at the same time its whole organization was a part of the Army and its expenditures paid from that department.

Being the only representative of the Army with the flotilla, all requirements for the service were made through me, and I performed the various duties of naval paymaster, storekeeper, and commissary beyond the general duties of an Army quartermaster. In addition, I was required to audit the accounts of each acting assistant paymaster of the gunboats, involving an examination into their expenditures for a year-- a duty which under other circumstances would belong to the Fourth auditor.

By act of Congress of July 16, 1862, the Western Gunboat Flotilla was transferred from the War to the Navy Department, but the final transfer was not made until September 30, 1862, and I was not relieved from duty until the 1st of December following, since which time I have been constantly engaged in settling the accounts of the flotilla and making the necessary reports required by the War Department.

Before leaving I transferred a large amount of property to the naval authorities, estimated in the aggregate to be $1,869,574 in value, comprising gunboats, tugs, transports, and captured steamers and their equipment, clothing, provisions, small stores, coal barges, naval wharfboat, and general quartermaster stores.

The total amount received from the US Treasury and other officers in money was $2,920,147.24; add to this estimated value of stores, &c., received from other officers, $226,385; in all, $3,146,532.24.

There were captured at different times from the enemy five gunboats, fifteen transport steamers, and five wrecks, which, including other property, amounts to $450,000, estimated value. There has been paid in the aggregate for transportation of ordnance and quartermaster stores, as follows: express companies, $25,325; railroad companies $25,381; river, $10,187; and for mileage of officers, $3,161; in all, $64,054.

While under the Army the flotilla, commencing with three small, improvised, wooden gunboats, hardly able to keep the river open between Saint Louis and Columbus, Kentucky, increased to ten ironclads, eleven wooden gunboats, two large ammunition steamers, thirteen tugs, a hospital boat with everything requisite for the sick and wounded, and a fleet of fifteen chartered and captured transports. There was also attached to the flotilla a floating blacksmith shop and a distributing commissary steamer. Large depots of coal were kept at convenient places on the rivers, and at Cairo, Illinois, a new large and superior wharfboat was purchased, which answered as a general depot for most of the requirements of the flotilla, including offices for the transaction of business.

While every assistance possible was extended by other branches of the Government to the flotilla, yet the officers necessarily were thrown upon their own resources, and a Navy had to be formed from new materials, far from what was generally considered its proper element. Officers, sailors, and gunboats had to be made to suit the exigencies of the times. How well all this was performed history will tell, and the flotilla under the Army will have had a most important bearing upon the final result of the rebellion.

I would refer to the reduction of Forts Henry and Donelson, the evacuation of Columbus, Kentucky, Island No. 10, Fort Pillow, and the destruction of the rebel fleet off Memphis; in addition, the important part taken by the flotilla in the sanguinary fight at Belmont and the great battle of Shiloh. League after league of the great Mississippi was opened to commerce, until the name of a gunboat became a terror to the rebels.

For a more detailed account in relation to the above, I would refer you to the accompanying papers, comprising a "Tabular list of gunboats, transport steamers, and wrecks, captured from the enemy," "Names, tonnage, and earnings of the steamboats chartered and employed," and "Statement of cash received and disbursed, on what account, together with balance remaining on hand June 30, 1863." All of which is respectfully submitted.

Very respectfully, your obedient servant,

George D. Wise, Captain
and Assistant Quartermaster with Gunboat Flotilla

As the Wise report indicates, the list of gunboats, transports, steamers, wrecks, etc., captured from the enemy by the Western Gunboat Flotilla only applies to the period of Army control over that flotilla, that is, up to the point when the flotilla went to the Navy. That transfer took place on September 30, 1862, although the vessels themselves were not physically transferred until well into the following month.

LIST OF GUNBOATS, TRANSPORTS, STEAMERS, WRECKS, &c.
CAPTURED FROM THE ENEMY BY THE GUNBOAT FLOTILLA
From *ORA,* III, 5, p 478

Gunboats	Where captured	Estimated Value
EASTPORT[1]	Savannah, Tennessee	$20,000.
GENERAL BRAGG[1]	Memphis	$50,000.
GENERAL PRICE[1] *	Memphis	$10,000.
LITTLE REBEL[1]	Memphis	$20,000.
SUMTER[1]	Memphis	$50,000.

Steamers		
ADMIRAL[3]	Island No. 10	$10,000.
ALFRED ROBB[1]	Tennessee River	$ 8,000.
CATAHOULA[4]	Memphis	$10,000.
CLARA DOLSON[1]	White River	$60,000.
DESOTO[1]	Island No. 10	$30,000.
FAIR PLAY[1]	White river	$ 8,000.
GENERAL PILLOW[1]	Fort Pillow	$ 1,000.
H. R. W. HILL[2]	Memphis	$ 8,000.
KENTUCKY[8]	Island No. 10	$ 5,000.
MARS[3]	Island No. 10	$ 5,000.
NEW NATIONAL[1]	Memphis	$30,000.
OHIO BELLE[6]	Island No. 10 or New Madrid	
RED ROVER[1]	Island No. 10	$30,000.
SALLIE WOOD[5]	Island No. 10	$ 6,000.
SOVEREIGN[1]	Island No. 10	$10,000.
VICTORIA[1]	Island No. 10	$15,000.

Wrecks		
GRAMPUS[7]	Island No. 10	$ 5,000.
JOHN SIMONDS[7]	Island No. 10	$ 6,000.
MOHAWK[7]	Island No. 10	$ 500.
PRINCE[7]	Island No. 10	$15,000.
WINCHESTER[7]	Island No. 10	$ 5,000.
YAZOO[7]	Island No. 10	$ 8,000.

Total value of vessels captured: $425,500.00

[1]	Transferred to Navy, September 30, 1862	[4]	Taken immediate possession of by Army.
*	Correct name is *GENERAL STERLING PRICE*	[5]	Recaptured from flotilla; destroyed by enemy.
[2]	Transferred for commissary use at Cairo	[6]	Unknown (may have been wreck).
[3]	Remained in possession of Army	[7]	Rebel gunboat. Sunk at Island No. 10.
		[8]	Returned to owners.

VESSELS ACQUIRED BY ORDER OF THE QUARTERMASTER FOR THE OFFICE OF THE GUNBOAT FLOTILLA (Western Waters), 1861 and 1862

From report by Captain G. D. Wise, Assistant Quartermaster, when vessels of the Western Gunboat Flotilla were transferred from Army to the Navy's Upper Mississippi Squadron, September 30, 1862. Lists compiled from *ORA,* III, Volume 2, pp 832, 833.

GUNBOATS

A. O. TYLER   wooden gunboat; received June 1, 1861, by purchase

ALFRED ROBB   wooden gunboat; received February 28, 1862, possession by capture

BENTON   ironclad gunboat; received December 5, 1861; purchased and rebuilt by United States

CAIRO   ironclad gunboat; received December 5, 1861; built by United States

CARONDELET   ironclad gunboat; received December 5, 1861; built by United States

CINCINNATI   ironclad gunboat; received December 5, 1861; built by United States

CONESTOGA   wooden gunboat; received June 1, 1861, by purchase

EASTPORT   ironclad ram and gunboat; received February 7, 1862, possession by capture

ESSEX   ironclad ram and gunboat; received December 5, 1861; purchased and rebuilt by United States

FAIR PLAY   wooden gunboat; received September 5, 1862, possession by capture

GENERAL BRAGG   wooden ram and gunboat; received June 6, 1862 possession by capture

GENERAL PILLOW   wooden gunboat; received July 3, 1862, possession by capture

GENERAL STERLING PRICE   wooden gunboat; received June 6, 1862, possession by capture

LEXINGTON   wooden gunboat; received June 1, 1861, by purchase

LITTLE REBEL   wooden ram and gunboat; received June 6, 1862, possession by capture

LOUISVILLE   ironclad gunboat; received December 5, 1861; built by United States

MOUND CITY   ironclad gunboat; received December 5, 1861; built by United States

PITTSBURG   ironclad gunboat; received December 5, 1861; built by United States

SAINT LOUIS   ironclad gunboat; received December 5, 1861; built by United States

SUMTER   wooden gunboat; received June 6, 1862, possession by capture

AUXILIARIES

CLARA DOLSON	receiving ship; received June 10, 1862, possession by capture
DAUNTLESS	steam tugboat; received January 1, 1862; either purchased or built by US
DESOTO	transport; received April 3, 1862, possession by capture
EREBUS	steam tugboat; received January 1, 1862; either purchased or built by US
FIRE FLY	steam tugboat; received January 1, 1862; either purchased or built by US
GREAT WESTERN	ordnance steamer; received February 10, 1862, by purchase
H. R. W. HILL	transport; received June 6, 1862, possession by capture
INTREPID	steam tugboat; received January 1, 1862; either purchased or built by US
JESSIE BENTON	steam tugboat; received May 5, 1862; either purchased or built by US
JUDGE TORRENCE	ordnance steamer; received February 10, 1862, by purchase
KENTUCKY	transport; received June 6, 1862, possession by capture
MALFORD	steam tugboat; received February 10, 1862; either purchased or built by US
NEW NATIONAL	transport; received June 6, 1862, possession by capture
RED ROVER	hospital steamer; received April 3, 1862, possession by capture
RESOLUTE	steam tugboat; received January 1, 1862; either purchased or built by US
RESTLESS	steam tugboat; received January 1, 1862; either purchased or built by US
SALLIE WOOD	transport; received February 20, 1862, possession by capture
SAMSON	steam tugboat; received January 1, 1862; either purchased or built by US
SOVEREIGN	storeship; received June 6, 1862, possession by capture
SPITEFUL	steam tugboat; received January 1, 1862; either purchased or built by US
SPITFIRE	steam tugboat; received January 1, 1862; either purchased or built by US
TERROR	steam tugboat; received January 1, 1862; either purchased or built by US
VICTORIA	store ship; received June 6, 1862, possession by capture
W. H. BROWN	transport; date received is unknown; by purchase
WONDER	steam tugboat; received January 1, 1862; either purchased or built by US

38 mortar boats (box barge types), attached to the fleet. Built at Eads's yards on the Ohio River; received December 5, 1861. Eleven were known to have been in the Island No. 10 action. These were Nos. 5, 7, 11, 12, 13, 19, 22, 23, 36, 38. Source: *ORN,* I, 22, pp 769-772.

Large (unnamed) wharf boat; used as a depot ship; received January 1, 1862; either purchased or built by US

CHARTERED AUXILIARIES

Chartered to Western Gunboat Flotilla during 1861 and 1862 by Captain George D. Wise. From Report of G. D. Wise for *Report of Secretary of War to the Congress for the Year 1865-1866*, reporting the year 1862 for the Quartermaster, page 883.

ALPS	towboat and transport for mortar boat crews
CHAMPION NO. 3	transport, towing, wrecking boat
DAN POLLARD	transport
EMERALD	receiving ship based at Saint Louis
G. W. GRAHAM	towboat for mortar boats and gunboats
GRAY FOX	transport and towboat
IKE HAMMIT	towboat for mortar boats and transports
ILLINOIS	ammunition boat
J. H. DICKEY*	storeship with flotilla
KEYSTONE	transport
LADY PIKE	towboat and transport for mortar boat crews
LAKE ERIE NO. 2	towboat and transport for mortar boat crews
MARIA DENNING	receiving ship based at times either at Saint Louis or Cairo
MOSES MCCLELLAN	towboat for mortar boats
RED FOX	transport and towboat
SHINGIS	transport and dispatch boat
SUBMARINE NO. 8	used as crane vessel in service to mortar boats
V. F. WILSON	towboat for mortar boats and transports
WISCONSIN NO. 2	towboat and transport for mortar boat crews

*JOHN H. DICKEY

APPENDIX D
ELLET RAM FLEET and MISSISSIPPI MARINE BRIGADE

A ram fleet was organized in April of 1862 as a separate Army command under the jurisdiction of the Western Department. It reported directly to the Secretary of War. In November of 1862, it was reorganized as the Mississippi Marine Brigade. It still remained under Army command but was placed under the tactical control of the Navy's Upper Mississippi Squadron. When the personnel of the Mississippi Marine Brigade were ordered from their vessels in August of 1864, the rams and support vessels were handed over to the Quartermaster, either for general transport use or for disposal. From August 1864 until January of 1865, the military personnel of the Brigade were assimilated to a shore-based regiment called the Consolidated Marine Regiment.

RAMS
Purchased by Charles Ellet, Jr., during April-May of 1862 for inclusion in his ram fleet.
From *ORA,* III, 2, pp 834, 835

DICK FULTON*	sternwheel
LANCASTER NO. 3*	sidewheel
LIONESS*	sternwheel
MINGO†	sidewheel
MONARCH*	sidewheel
QUEEN OF THE WEST*	sidewheel
SAMSON†	sternwheel
SWITZERLAND*	sidewheel
T. D. HORNER*	sternwheel
Three "battery barges"‡	

*   Incorporated into the Mississippi Marine Brigade in early 1863.
†   Turned over to Quartermaster in September 1862
‡   These were flat-deck barges designed to be towed alongside the rams to protect the rams against gunfire. At times, they were employed to carry coal. One was sunk in Mississippi River, June 20, 1862; two were turned over to the Quartermaster during June 1862.

AUXILIARIES
Purchased by Quartermaster in November and December of 1862
for Support Use by the Mississippi Marine Brigade

ALF CUTTING; tug	*CLEVELAND*; tug
AUTOCRAT; steamer	*DIANA*; steamer
BALTIC; steamer	*E. H. FAIRCHILD*; steamer
BEN J. ADAMS; steamer	*JOHN RAINE*; steamer
BELLE DARLINGTON; [1] tug	*WOODFORD*; hospital steamer

[1] Appears in some lists as *BILL DARLINGTON*

APPENDIX E
CIVILIAN MANNED ARMY TRANSPORTS, 1861-1865...
AN OVERVIEW OF CREW STATUS

The subject of transport vessels and crews thereon and their legal role, when viewed by friend and foe, was a matter seriously considered by Francis H. Upton, LL.D., as early as 1861. Upton, a practicing admiralty attorney in New York, was approached at the time by Samuel R. Betts, Judge of the District Court of the United States (District of New York) and asked to prepare an updated analysis of international laws and practices concerning sea warfare in its application to the developing contest against the Confederacy as it might impact the merchant marine as well as any privateers operating under letters of marque. The status of merchant ships employed directly as carriers for the military was one of the concerns Upton was to cover.

In compiling his treatise-- actually a 304-page tome entitled *The Laws of Nations...Affecting Commerce During War.* Upton leaned heavily on the opinions of two admiralty jurists who, up to that time, had been considered the experts on the issues. Lord Stowell was from Britain; Justice Joseph Story had been appointed to the US Supreme Court by President James Madison.[1] Renowned for his specialty in maritime and international law, Justice Story had been particularly recognized for his paramount role in establishing federal jurisdiction over individual states in matters of admiralty. He was known as the foremost American authority on prize law.

The Rights of Ships To Be Legally Engaged in Warfare
Upton had argued strongly in his thesis that such a right-- that is when judged by the then current practices of international law-- is restricted to the sovereign power. In other words, it is restricted to those ships under the direct employment of, and under the full control of the sovereign, meaning, in the context of US law, the Government.

> Lawful captures can only be made by national vessels of war, or vessels commissioned for that purpose...."In order to support that averment," said Lord Stowell, "it must be shown either that there has been some express designation of her in that character, by the orders of the admiralty, or, that there has been a constant employment and occupation, equivalent to an express designation and sufficient to impress that character upon her."

Upton further explained:

> The right of making war, as we have seen, is a right of appertaining exclusively
> to the sovereign power of the state; and this right necessarily carries with it, as an
> incident, that of directing and controlling all its operations. Private citizens cannot,
> of themselves, and without commission from the supreme power, take any steps in
> relation to the perpetration of acts of hostility...[2]

From the above, it would appear that transports in the employ of and under the control of the Army become sovereign ships; and they are legal ships of war if ordered by their government to perform a warlike function.

The Law and Policies of Armament

In 1861, it was clear to most experts in admiralty that under international law, only naval ships and military transports could engage in an armed attack against a declared enemy's vessels. Privateers could also attack the enemy, but only under a formal letter of marque. This did not mean that an ordinary peaceable merchant ship could not carry armaments to enable its crew to put up a defense against attack. That right clearly did exist under United States law by a statute of March 3, 1819, entitled *An Act to Protect the Commerce of the United States and Punish Acts of Piracy*. The impetus for the 1819 law seems to have come about following depredations which were at that time being waged by pirates against merchant vessels (including American vessels) within the Bahama Channel and the Caribbean Sea. The 1819 Act has continued within the statutes under successive recodification up to the present day.[3] Its present language still reads in the 1990s as it did in 1819, stating to the effect that merchant ship crews can defend their vessels by use of force if they are attacked. The act is quite specific in allowing force to prevent boarding by persons from other vessels, provided that such vessels are not either US public vessels or public vessels belonging to parties with which the United States is at peace. The law also allows merchant crews to take any action necessary to retake vessels previously captured "by pirates." It does not, though, allow armed action by merchant crews unless they are attacked on the initiative of another or are engaged in the act of retaking a vessel previously seized "by pirates." Case law dealing with such limitations was extant and quite recent to the time of Upton's study:

> To make the fire of one vessel into another a piratical aggression within this
> section must be a first aggression unprovoked by any act of hostility or menace from
> the other side.[4]

The first indication of a ship owner's concern over arming his vessel during the 1861-1865 war appears to have been when Cornelius Vanderbilt wrote to the Secretary of the Navy requesting the arming by the Navy of certain merchant ships in which he and some of his colleagues had financial interests. Vanderbilt cited precedence for this request by explaining that in the Mexican War, the government had supplied defensive cannon for ships of the Pacific Mail Steamship Company. Vanderbilt stressed to the Secretary that merchant ships required armament to be used in defense against Confederate commerce raider attacks.[5] Although nothing direct seems to have developed that year from the Vanderbilt request, the Navy did conceive of an imaginative solution for arming at least certain merchant ships during August of 1861. Under a plan put into place, two ships belonging to the firm of Spoffard, Tileston, and Company were supplied with naval guns and the naval personnel to man those guns. These ships, the *MARION* and the *COLUMBIA*, were operating on the New York to Cuba run. The civilian masters of the ships were commissioned by the Secretary of the Navy as acting masters, US Navy, without pay. The rationale behind this plan was threefold:

First, that by commissioning the masters into the Navy, the connotation of armed privateers could not be attached to the ships. (At this juncture of the war, the Lincoln Administration was considering that the South's issuance of letters of marque constituted a policy of piracy; therefore, Lincoln was keen on avoiding any accusation of the use of privateers under Union authorization.)

Second, that the crewmembers, consisting of the ships' regular merchant mariners and now the naval gunners, would be under one single commander and therefore subject as a whole to naval discipline.

Third, that if as an incidental byproduct of the normal commercial voyage, enemy vessels (blockade runners) should be taken, the crews as a whole would be legitimately eligible for the award of prize money under the acts governing the Navy. This of course provided an incentive to the civilian crewmembers, and it gave a justification for the Navy in supplying its armament and its personnel.[6]

Vanderbilt's plea for armament, which had been requested to protect those vessels in which he had interest and which were bringing valuable cargoes from California via the Panama Isthmus route, seems to have been finally met in 1862, the year following the request. On June 5 of 1862 the Secretary of the Navy, in writing to the agent for the California Mail Steamship Company, stated the Navy's willingness to supply guns and gunners and to commission the masters (without pay) as was done the year before in the case of the Spoffard, Tileston, and Company ships[7].

A unique case of arming a commercial ship is evident within the circumstances surrounding the *HENRY W. JOHNSON*, a vessel owned by New York insurance underwriters. Prior to the outbreak of the war, this vessel had been employed as a standby salvage ship working upon the Bahama Banks. By the summer of 1861, Nassau had become a virtual headquarters for blockade runners outbound from there for southern ports. Many of the blockade runners were suspected of being armed as privateers under letters of marque issued by the government at Richmond. Consequently, the New York Underwriters (with US Navy acquiescence) armed the *HENRY W. JOHNSON*, its mission being to protect Union shipping. The instructions issued by the New York Underwriters to its captain were clear in that the vessel was to use its armament for its own defense as well as in those cases where it might become engaged in assisting a vessel under piratical (privateer) attack, or when attempting to recover a vessel previously captured by an enemy privateer. These orders were seemingly structured upon the strictures established by the act of 1819 (*An Act to Protect the Commerce of the United States and Punish Acts of Piracy* as further reinforced by a recodification of August 5, 1861.) The record also shows that the *HENRY W. JOHNSON's* master, one Moses Hoyt, was commissioned by the Navy as an "acting master" and that his crew was subsequently placed under naval discipline (July 1862).[8]

The Navy was not the only Federal service which armed merchant vessels. There is considerable material in the way of reports and correspondence to show that the Army supplied guns (and the gunners to serve them) to river boats in commercial service which operated upon certain of the western rivers which were subject to Confederate partisan activity. The same type of arming policy was also in effect for vessels employed upon the sounds of the Carolinas as well as for canal boats transiting the Albemarle and Chesapeake Canal and the Dismal Swamp Canal. The arming of Army owned transports or those transports under charter to the Army was an even more prevalent practice. The pictorial record, as well as commentary found within numerous dispatches and reports, indicates that such arming became relatively standardized during 1862-1864 on the lower Mississippi, and in the Union zones within the coastal regions of the Carolinas where the Army, starting with the Burnside Expedition of early 1862, also employed a number of gunboats and attack transports. A report of November 3, 1864, contained in *Official Records...Armies* states:

> The larger and more powerful steamers owned or chartered by the department, and employed in the transport of troops and supplies along the coast, have been generally armed sufficiently to enable them to defend themselves against privateers, or to capture such blockade runners as in their cruises they may overhaul. Several captures have been made by these vessels. Upon the bayous of the Southwest, where transports are constantly liable to attacks by partisans, or even by large detachments of the rebel forces, the transport steamers have also been generally provided with guns and arms. In these waters, and at the mouths of the Mississippi River, several of the department vessels have been surprised and captured. This misfortune is less frequent since the habit of arming them and of holding the commanders and crews to a rigid accountability, has been established by Colonel Holabird, Chief Quartermaster, Department of the Gulf, under authority from the War Department.[9]

In the summer of 1862, Army transports in coastal service were formally authorized-- in a like manner to that of naval vessels-- to take Confederate prizes. Gideon Welles, then Secretary of the Navy, in correspondence dated August 5, 1863, cited the *Act for the Better Government of the Navy of the United States,* as the authority under which armament could be provided to the Army's transports.[10] That statute contained the provision that "any armed vessel in the service of the United States which shall make a capture, or assist in making a capture, under circumstances which would entitle a vessel of the Navy to prize money, shall be entitled to an award of prize money in the same manner as if such vessel belonged to the Navy;..."[11] This provision was interpreted to encompass ships of the Army Quartermaster Department as well as the Revenue Service. Army transports did capture blockade runners during the war. The top score in that regard went to the transport *FULTON* which during November of 1863 brought in the runner *MARGARET AND JESSIE* and during the following month, the runner *G. O. BIGELOW*. The next year, *FULTON* gave chase to (but missed capturing) yet a third runner. The capture of blockade runners by Army transports was, of course, only done as the opportunity presented itself, as it was considered but an adjunct to a transport's primary mission, that being the carriage of troops and supplies.

Some uncertainty revolves around those who usually manned the cannon and other weaponry placed aboard Army transports. One report compiled by the master of the Army transport, *W. B. TERRY*, tells us that his vessel carried "two 6-pounder rifled cannon and billeted aboard a number of military sharpshooters as guards." The report implies that the military guards, and, one would presume, military gunners as well, were under the civilian master's direct command.[12] On other ships, it would appear that the guns were served by the civilian crew. The type of command arrangement where overall command was vested to the master was probably the norm on ordinary Army transports in the coastal service. Conversely, aboard Army gunboats and rams, a military officer (or naval officer loaned to the Army) was often designated as vessel commander holding tactical authority over a civilian master.[13] There were, though, some exceptions to this last. Daniel Ammen, who was privy to the operational orders for the attack on Roanoke Island in February of 1862, listed in his writings the armed assault vessels of the Army's floating contingent used in that operation. According to Ammen, all had civilian commanders. Although gunboats on paper, these were in truth an assortment of odd craft, mainly tugs, upon which field guns were mounted. Ammen lists them by name.[14]

CHASSEUR	Captain John West
HUSSAR	Captain F. Crocker
LANCER	Captain M. B. Morley
PICKET	Captain T. P. Ives
PIONEER	Captain C. E. Baker
RANGER	Captain S. Emerson
VIDETTE	Captain I. L. Foster

In the coastal sounds, the Army maintained gunboats under its own manning up through the last year of the war. Army gunboats were being operated on the Ohio River, the Tennessee River, and the Cumberland River during 1864 in order to counter the threat of Confederate cavalry raids. The Army had under construction that same year, at a Philadelphia shipyard, four shallow draft assault ferries capable of making short sea voyages but which were designed specifically for estuary work along the Atlantic and Gulf coasts. These were to be heavily armed and were to have as crew the Army's uniformed personnel, both for operating personnel and for gunners.[15]

Military Control Exercised Over Civilian Crewmen

There does not seem to have been any hesitation-- at least on the part of Union forces-- to utilize the Quartermaster Department's civilian employees as combatant personnel. This practice applied both on land and on the steamboats of the western rivers. One case of major note-- this particular one having taken place on land-- was in the fall of 1864 during a Confederate cavalry raid against the quartermaster depot at Johnsonville, Tennessee. In a report to Brigadier General J. L. Donaldson, Captain Henry Howland reported that the infantry commander at

Johnsonville, Colonel Charles R. Thompson, directed that the quartermaster there arm and place in the defensive works five hundred of the Quartermaster Department's civilian employees. These employees were immediately sent into the entrenchments and placed under the command of Captain J. E. Montandon. It is believed that most of those employees were Negro laborers normally used in the handling of supplies at the depot.[16]

When the status of a ship was that of a military transport, as the matter was discussed by lawyer Upton, the vessel became a *sovereign's ship* and therefore was considered to be under the government's authority. Under the force of such circumstances, her crew could, without much question, be brought under naval or military discipline. The particular circumstances which could place a vessel under the identity of a *ship of war*, (again we reference lawyer Upton's thesis) was whenever she went under a service which provided support to naval or military operations. Whenever determining such status, some elasticity is always present, and it clearly was during the early months of the Civil War. Things become clearer whenever the privately employed ship is seen as being directly supportive of the war-fighting, war-sustaining efforts of the military.[17] In the Civil War campaigns on the western rivers, the Confederates assumed that craft operating within a contested area were supportive of the Union's military effort, and they treated such vessels as military craft and targeted them accordingly. The legality of that status as it involved civilian crews became clarified by the *Lieber Code* which will be discussed later.

Theoretically, at least as it was understood by Upton in 1861, the status of a ship doing service with the military could be determined in large part by the control the military exercised over the crew. This control as exercised in the form of military discipline was applied between 1861 and 1865 to civilian members of military transport crews on the western rivers. Control by the military over civilians was not, however, unique to seamen. The imposition of military law against certain civilians had been the American military commander's birth right inherited from a British Army regulatory article that had been incorporated almost verbatim into the Continental Army Code of 1775. The spirit of that article was written into the United States Army Articles of 1806 which stated, "All sutlers and retainers to the camp, and all persons whatsoever serving with the armies of the United States in the field, though not enlisted soldiers, are to be subject to orders, according to the rules and discipline of war."[18] The early records of military discipline as it was applied against civilians do not show any marked difference in application regardless of whether the offender was an employee of the military force or merely a hanger-on within a military operational area. Within his book *Summer Soldiers, A Survey and Index of Revolutionary War Courts-Martial*, James C. Neagles lists 3,315 cases out of which 56 or 01.7% were trials of civilians. The civilian miscreants ranged widely in their occupations and in their affiliation to the military and included, to give but a few examples: the Deputy Commissioner of Military Stores, a vessel's boatswain, a number of sailors on one of the courier sloops serving with the Army's fleet on Lake Champlain in 1775, a transient Negro, a number of civilian cattle drovers, a wagon master, a superintendent of pack horses, a civilian express rider, and a civilian quartermaster employee. It is of some interest to note that although commissioned military officers were not given sentences involving flogging or switching, (there is one exception to this rule in Neagles's study) such was not the case in sentences handed out to civilians in management positions. To their discomfort, civilians were liberally allotted their share of the lash, laid on, it seems, without deference to the job they may have held. A case in point was that of a civilian in a high position. The man, who had been made the custodian of $300,000 in Army payroll funds, appropriated a portion of it to his own use. The penalties the court martial assessed was: an order to repay; then one hundred lashes; then dismissal from employment. Another case involved a civilian seaman of General Richard Montgomery's Lake Champlain fleet. During 1775, he was tried for mutiny. He received the relatively light sentence of seventy-eight total lashes to be administered "around the fleet."[19]

By the time of the Civil War, it had generally come to be recognized that a certain distinction should be drawn by commanders between *retainers*, usually meaning employees of other than the Army itself, but who accompanied military forces on campaign, as against those civilians directly employed by the Army, the latter being considered to be "serving with the armies in the field."[20] In the general application of military discipline, those civilian "retainers" who were guilty of crimes or who were merely making nuisances of themselves were expelled from areas of military jurisdiction. On the other hand, those who were direct employees and who were "serving with the Army in the field" were generally tried under military law and punished in like manner to the soldiery. William Winthrop, in his authoritative work *Military Law and Precedent*, further defined civilians serving with the Army during the Civil War, describing them as "civilians in the employment and service of the government." Winthrop classified all other civilian personnel as "retainers."[21] For guidance, Winthrop gives examples of those who were directly employed by the government, e.g., guides, scouts, spies, and men employed on transports and military railroads. He also delineates those types of employees who most frequently were known to have been subjects of courts martial: *teamsters; employees of the Provost Marshal; surgeons and nurses;* and further includes through citation *officers and men employed on steam transports.*[22] General Order No. 175, issued April 22, 1864, removed all doubt as to the military's authority over its employees while in the field when it stated, "Employees of the Quartermaster, if refusing to obey military orders, are to be subject to arrest and trial before a military tribunal."[23]

From the onset of the Civil War, the Army utilized civilians on its vessels in the capacity of masters, pilots, mates, engineers, firemen, and deck hands. One wide utilization of civilian crews occurred within the Ellet Ram Fleet organized by Colonel Charles Ellet, Jr., during the spring of 1862. This unit started out as a separate command involved only with steamers which were converted into rams. The unit was later assimilated as the transport element of the Mississippi Marine Brigade which was organized in the fall of 1862 under the command of Charles Ellet Jr.'s brother, Lieutenant Colonel (later Brigadier General) Alfred W. Ellet. The Mississippi Marine Brigade's floating equipment, in addition to the vessels which previously had belonged to the Ram Fleet, included troop transports, a hospital steamer, and an assortment of supply vessels. The Brigade's function was to provide the means for fast deployment of amphibious landing parties consisting of infantry units buttressed by cavalry and artillery detachments-- all such units having been assigned as permanent parts of the brigade.[24]

According to Warren D. Crandall, who served with the Brigade and later became senior editor for its published history, discipline-- particularly concerning the civilian crewmembers-- was "a subject of great perplexity." The disciplinary problems first surfaced prior to the Ram Fleet's baptism of fire at Fort Pillow (May of 1862) when Colonel Charles Ellet, Jr., "encountered a reluctance and opposition on the part of several civilian boat officers which gave him much uneasiness for the success of his enterprise." It was this "reluctance" which created the need to impart a sense of obligation within the civilian component of the crews, and also to establish some fixed period of tenure in order to hold the crews on the vessels. Prior to June of 1862, crewmembers could resign at will, hardly a desirable arrangement within an outfit organized to fill what essentially was a combatant role. Ellet developed an oath of obligation which each civilian had to sign upon his taking employment in the fleet. It read:

MILITARY OBLIGATION

I, David L. Southwick, Do Solemnly Swear. That I will bear true allegiance to the United States of America, and that I will serve them honestly and faithfully against all their enemies or opposers whatsoever, and observe and obey the orders of the President of the United States, and the orders of the officers appointed over me, according to the rules and articles for the government of the forces of the United States, and all Government business entrusted to me shall be strictly and sacredly confidential, and I will use my influence to have good discipline in the service to which I belong, and continued well and truly to serve until I am discharged, provided the term of service shall not exceed six months from the date hereof. SO HELP ME GOD.

(Signed)   David L. Southwick.
(X) his mark

Dated and subscribed at Cairo, Ill., May 16th, 1862.[25]

That Southwick used his "mark" to sign the oath indicates an obvious illiteracy. How typical the inability to read (or write) was among the civilian boatmen is another unknown; but if it was extensive, it would tell us that the signers may not have completely understood the position that they had placed themselves in, namely that they would be subject to the Army's disciplinary code and its attendant punishments. Later related circumstances bear out the conclusion that this factor was not fully understood, at least up to the end of 1862.

When Colonel Charles Ellet, Jr., died of wounds in June of 1862, the command of the Ram Fleet was then assigned to his brother, Lieutenant Colonel Alfred W. Ellet. Promoted to the rank of brigadier general, Alfred W. Ellet was to spend most of the remainder of 1862 near Saint Louis recruiting and training the infantry, cavalry, and artillery components of what was to become the Mississippi Marine Brigade. While in Saint Louis, Alfred W. Ellet also recruited many of the fleet's civilian crewmembers. Ellet would later be accused of having contributed to the disciplinary problems of the civilians by promising them certain safeguards which could not, at least with practicality, be carried out. During Brigadier General Ellet's absence, the Ram Fleet remained operationally active, participating in expeditions within the

Mississippi River system north of Vicksburg. When he left for Saint Louis, Brigadier General Ellet arranged for the command of the rams to go to his 19-year-old nephew, Charles Rivers Ellet. Prior to this appointment, nephew Ellet had held the rank of medical cadet although he had actually been performing line officer duty on the rams. In an almost unprecedented move, Charles Rivers Ellet was propelled from medical cadet to the rank of full colonel (staff) and placed in charge of all the vessels then operating. Along with the burden of command went the responsibility for administering discipline, a subject about which young Ellet knew virtually nothing. That deficiency, when coupled with what was probably the ignorance of the civilian crewmembers as to the basic obligations laid down by the oath they had signed, resulted in a state within the fleet which at times resembled anarchy. At any rate, that is how the naval commander on the upper Mississippi (Rear Admiral David D. Porter) would describe the state of discipline when he visited Ellet's command in March of 1863. Although an Army unit, the Mississippi Marine Brigade had been attached to the Navy's Upper Mississippi Squadron. Tactical authority over the Mississippi Marine Brigade was vested to Rear Admiral Porter; but that authority did not, as it was to turn out, extend to the exercising of disciplinary authority over Ellet's civilians. A letter written by Porter describes the dilemma.

> Mouth of Yazoo River
>
> In the case of Josiah V. Reeder, pilot [civilian] on board the ram *QUEEN OF THE WEST*, on whom a Court of Inquiry was held, for refusing to perform the duty for which it was supposed he enlisted, the charges were all sustained, but the court find: (1). That the accused was discharged by Colonel Charles R. Ellet after the offense was committed-- Colonel Ellet taking no steps in the matter, except to complain to the Admiral. (2). It appears that the accused received assurances from General Ellet, [Alfred W. Ellet] at Mound City, Illinois, that the accused would not be required to run heavy batteries, if he shipped in the Ram Fleet. (3). That as shown by the evidence of G. W. Lindsay, Second Master in the Ram Fleet, pilots, engineers, firemen, and men on board the Ram Fleet, do not consider themselves as belonging to either Army or Navy. (4). That there is an ignorance existing as to what laws and regulations they are subject to. (5). That some have been allowed to disobey orders and others have been punished for it. (6). That the discipline of the Ram Fleet was not very good. (7.) That pilots, engineers, and boatmen in the Ram Fleet are subject to the orders [only] of the Colonel commanding the Ram Fleet. (8). That all officers and men have to obey orders emanating from their superior officers. (9). That Colonel Charles R. Ellet did, on 1st February, 1863, give to three of his engineers the privilege of going on the *QUEEN OF THE WEST*, past the Vicksburg batteries and they went. (10). That a discharge from a ram is the order from the commanding officer to the paymaster to pay the person the money due him. In consideration of the imperfect understanding with the immediate commanders of the Ram Fleet and (the) apparent irregular manner of doing things on those vessels, the accused is hereby released from any further proceedings, and is at liberty to go when he pleases.
>
> David D. Porter, Admiral, USN [26]

The major cause for the problem over Reeder and some of the other brigade seamen was not one which either Ellet, their subordinate officers, or even Rear Admiral Porter seemed to initially comprehend. Simply put, the Navy was not vested with disciplinary authority over Army personnel-- be they military personnel or civilian employees. This applied even when such persons were operationally assigned to a Navy command and even when on a Navy mission. Brigadier General Alfred W. Ellet, having been urged by his nephew, solicited guidance over what to do through correspondence dated March 31, addressed to the Army's adjutant general, Lorenzo Thomas. Thomas in turn bucked the question up to the Secretary of War who passed it on for answer by the Army's Judge Advocate General's office. The Judge Advocate's reply, dated June 11, 1863, should have settled the question, once and for all.

> Judge Advocate General's Office
> Respectfully returned to the Secretary of War. The question raised by the within paper is: How shall pilots, engineers, etc., of the Ram Fleet be prosecuted and punished for offenses committed, while on duty. In the first place it is to be remarked that the force under Colonel Ellet, on duty in the Ram Fleet, is understood to be a special contingent and portion of the Army, and not of the Navy of the United States. Persons therefore employed upon these rams are to be punished, if at all, under the law which governs the discipline of the Army. These pilots, etc., are neither officers nor enlisted men and can not, therefore, be tried under those articles, which concern only officers and soldier. By a special article, however (Article 60) these persons, specified as "All persons whatsoever serving with the armies of the United States in the field, though not enlisted soldiers...[are]...made subject to orders, according to the rules and discipline of war." DeHart (p 25) in commenting upon the phrase p*ersons serving with the armies*, holds that it includes *those that serve in the Army by engagement for public hire or pay*, and this is precisely the case of the pilots, engineers, etc., on the rams, who are hired by the commanding officer of the fleet, to perform the duties of their profession, for a certain period, receive as a final discharge, an order from that officer upon the paymaster for their pay. Article 60 was the result of a "necessity" felt among armies in the field. (see DeHart, p 23, and Benet, p 29), and is especially applicable to the present case. The persons in question, therefore, should be tried by court martial under this article.
> J. Holt, Judge Advocate General[27]

From an historical perspective, the disciplinary control advised by the Judge Advocate General appears to provide the first good example of the Army's Civil War policy involving civilians aboard military vessels. In turn, it stands as precedence for military control and the exercise of discipline over civilians who are employed by an armed force and who are serving with such a force "in the field." The jurisdiction of the military over civilians during the Civil War was generally applicable, as it still is today, to those circumstances wherein the civilian in question was actively participating in military operations. In the case of civilian employees serving on the Ellet vessels, this was thought of as applying during the entire period of a seaman's contractual obligation.

In exercising their authority over civilians, Union Army quartermasters within the western theaters of operation used that authority quite freely. This included implementing control over pilots and engineers including the prohibition of collective bargaining over wage rates. Colonel Lewis B. Parsons, the Army's quartermaster officer then in charge of all wartime river transportation on the Mississippi and its tributaries, issued an order during 1862 stating, "...if anywhere on the Mississippi, that is between Saint Louis and Memphis, if a pilot demanded wages exceeding $200 a month, he was to immediately have his pilot's license revoked." By the law of the land, the issuance and/or revocation of pilot licenses was under the direct authority of steamboat inspectors operating as part of the civilian sector through inspector appointments dispensed by federal judicial districts. There does not, therefore, seem to have been a legal basis through which the Army could revoke such licenses.[28]

Prisoners of the Enemy

In late 1862, Major General Henry W. Halleck, then General-in-Chief of the Union Army, requested Francis Lieber, Professor of Law at Columbia University, to draw up a set of guidelines to deal with the subject of prisoners of war. Lieber's completed work underwent review by a group of Army officers headed by Major General E. A. Hitchcock before getting final approval by Halleck and by the Secretary of War. The guidelines were officially endorsed by President Abraham Lincoln and entitled, *Instructions for the Government of the Armies of the United States in the Field (The 'Lieber Code')*. They were published as regulations under *General Orders 100*, dated April 24, 1863. Under these instructions, the definition was determined as to under what circumstances enemy captives were to be considered as eligible for the status of a prisoner of war. In other words, who was to be held as a military prisoner subject both to the attendant restraints put against such persons as well as to their protections.

> A prisoner of war is a public enemy armed or attached to the hostile army for active aid, who has fallen into the hands of the captor, either fighting or wounded, on the field or in the hospital, by individual surrender or by capitulation.
> All soldiers, of whatever species of arms; all men who belong to the rising en masse of the hostile country; all those who are attached to the army for its efficiency and promote the object of the war, except such as are hereinafter provided for; all disabled men or officers on the field or elsewhere, if captured; all enemies who have thrown away their arms and asked for quarter, are prisoners of war, and as such exposed to the inconveniences as well as entitled to the privileges of a prisoner of war.[29]

In dealing with civilians attached to or serving with an army, the status of prisoners was generally decided by utilizing the same basis as the Army generally used toward its establishment of disciplinary jurisdictions- that is, a distinction was made between "retainers" and direct employees of the government. In *General Orders 100* (derived from Lieber's work), Section III, it was stated "Citizens who accompany an army and who are of benefit to the army may be considered as prisoners of war. This does not apply to medical personnel or medical aids." In practice then, those civilians who were taken captive while performing a military type function were to be handled as prisoners of war until properly exchanged. On the other hand, "retainers" to the army were only held "as long as may be necessary."[30]

The exchange of prisoners during the Civil War was very much of an on-again, off-again affair. It ceased almost entirely during the last part of the war. During the Civil War's first two years, exchanges were made in large volume. A good part of these exchanges followed an agreement established during July of 1862 between the principles. The terms were specified within the *'Dix-Hill Cartel' for the General Exchange of Prisoners of War Entered into Between the Union and Confederate Armies (July 22, 1862).*[31] Article I of that document stipulated that all prisoners of war held by either party, "including those taken on private armed vessels known as privateers," should be handled as any other military prisoner including the status given them for purposes of exchange. The terms of the cartel were understood by all parties in that civilian crewmembers taken from any armed vessel of the enemy's fighting fleets or from its armed transports and supply vessels were to be looked upon by the enemy as part of the military force in the same fashion as regular military or naval personnel. Civilian crews of unarmed private vessels which were employed contractually on troop or animal transports or on supply vessels were placed into a category classified as, "all those who are attached to the army for its efficiency and [who] promote the object of the war" thus directly correlating such persons with the category of persons who could legitimately be detained as prisoners of war.[32]

The *Dix-Hill Cartel's* wording specifically mentions "masters of merchant vessels and commanders of privateers," as being equal in exchange value to midshipmen and warrant officers of the Navy. They were to be, "exchanged for officers of equal rank, or three privates or common seamen." Other exchange formulae were provided for those of lower grades captured while serving on privateers or merchant vessels.

No separate tabulation seems to have been maintained by either Union or Confederate authorities as to the number of transport crews or merchant crews or, for that matter, the number of civilians as a whole who were captured by each side. There are, however, a number of references within the *Official Records...Armies* and *Official Records...Navies* which concern transport and gunboat crews which had been taken captive. Captures of such crews appeared to have been quite common on the western rivers. On the east coast, one well-documented instance of capture took place during the expedition to Port Royal Sound in late 1861. A number of transports then under charter to the Army encountered heavy weather off Cape Hatteras while on their way south to Port Royal Sound. One of them, the *OSCEOLA*, foundered but not before most of her crew made it off the wreck and into the ship's boats. Upon landing on the beach near Georgetown, South Carolina, they were spotted by a Confederate patrol and taken prisoner. In a report to the Secretary of War dated February 26, 1862, the *OSCEOLA's* master, J. T. Morrill, writing from a prison in Charleston, South Carolina, related that his crew was being held in the Marion Court House Jail, being detained there as prisoners of war while he was incarcerated in Charleston in company with Union Army officers. Captain Morrill was finally exchanged for a Confederate sympathizing merchant marine master who had allegedly thumbed his nose (in the literal sense) while passing his vessel out of Charleston, South Carolina prior to the surrender of the Fort Sumter garrison in 1861. Later, he was arrested and accused of sedition by the Union authorities. The "nose thumbing" mariner had been held under house arrest in a northern port until the time when he was exchanged for Morrill. While in the Charleston jail, Morrill met another ship master, one "Captain Nichols," of the merchant brig *E. K. EATON*.[33] During 1864, the Army gunboat *SMITH BRIGGS* was sunk while on an operation up one of the rivers in Virginia. Her crew included a number of civilians who, along with military personnel who had been aboard, were made prisoners of war. According to Robert G. Albion and Jennie Barnes Pope writing in *Sea Lanes in Wartime, The American Experience, 1774-1945,* another group of civilian seamen held as prisoners of war were from a merchant vessel carrying-- again according to Albion and Pope-- an Army owned cargo. After being captured by the Confederate naval raider *CSS OLUSTEE,* Confederate authorities denied civilian status for them, claiming that the crew had a military character because of the ship's cargo. They were incarcerated as prisoners of war.[34]

In November of 1861, the steamer *UNION* was driven ashore in a gale on the North Carolina coast, south of Morehead City. The *UNION* had been recently purchased by the Quartermaster Department, and her crew were civilian employees of that department. Taken prisoner, the ship's crew was taken to Salisbury, North Carolina. The ship's officers were thereafter removed to Raleigh. Held as prisoners there, the officers were finally exchanged and repatriated to the north in September of 1862. There is no record as to the disposition of the remainder of the *UNION's* crew.[35] As a general practice, crews of whalers as well as crews of merchant ships not carrying military materiel were released when taken by Confederate raiders on the high seas.

Military Pensions Awarded Civilians

In 1862, the Congress of the United States recognized the service of civilians who were employed aboard gunboats by encompassing them under the Military Pension Act of July 14, 1862. These people were described within the act as "those pilots, engineers, sailors, and crews upon the gunboats and war vessels of the United States who have not been formally mustered into the service of the United States." The 1862 act, in addition to providing the basis for granting military pensions to this class of civilians, also authorized that military bounties be paid to them as incentives toward signing them up for such employment. Insofar as the pensions, the law contained a stipulation that unless disabled by wounds, these persons must have continued their employment through to the conclusion of the war.

It is not clear as to how the term service on *war vessels* was to be defined in order to establish eligibility under the 1862 pension act. The evidence suggests-- but only suggests-- that it was originally designed to encompass the crews of armed assault ships, such as gunboats, rams, and assault transports. Civil War pension records are not in a format which would allow any practical determination to be made as to the status of the Civil War pensioners, i.e., civilian or military. Therefore, it becomes next to impossible to find out to what extent the Military Pension Act of 1862 was applied to civilians who were eligible under it.

Pay

Pay for crewmembers on Army transports in coastwise service seems to have been on a par with the merchant marine. On the western rivers, though, the pay was less than for those crews serving in commercial vessels upon the rivers.

An order signed by Lieutenant General Ulysses S. Grant in January of 1865, and which was apparently applicable to both the western rivers and to the eastern theater of operations, established a wage of $300 for pilots working on transports. (This constituted a raise in wage rates from the ceiling of $200 per month that was established by the Army in 1862 for the Mississippi.) The discussion that arose at the time over Grant's order relates that pilots serving in the merchant service received a higher salary ranging anywhere from $450 up to $750 a month.[36]

The Draft

Conscription of those working for the Army on both its transports and its gunboats seems to have been a problem to the quartermasters throughout much of the war. (The Navy also employed civilians, both on its supply vessels and as pilots on its gunboats and had the same problem.)

As late as June of 1864, Rear Admiral David P. Porter of the Navy's Mississippi Squadron transmitted by endorsement a petition of the Western Boatmen's Benevolent Association asking for a Congressional order to give pilots immunity from the military draft. This seems to have been quickly granted. On June 29, 1864, in correspondence to Secretary of the Navy Gideon Welles, Porter wrote, "Owing to the necessity that exists for having the pilots on the Mississippi tributaries ready at all times to serve the government, all registered pilots are exempt from conscription in the Army." However, going along with that freedom from the draft was a certain coercion. As Admiral Porter described it, "A fine of $1,000 will be imposed on all who neglect a summons [to pilotage duty] and such punishment as a naval or military tribunal may impose."[37] Congressional order or no, the problem of losing crewmen to the draft continued to persist from time to time-- especially on the lower Mississippi. One naval officer operating there recommended in 1865 that pilots, already drafted, be released from their regiments so they could return to river service.[38] The same naval officer, two months later, complained of yet more cases of pilots being ordered into military service by Army provosts. He decried that the provost marshal did not have the right to conscript, claiming instead that the pilots were already in the military service due to their employment as pilots.[39]

It is probable that military conscription of civilian crewmembers was not universally widespread but rather that it occurred in more of a happenstance manner peculiar to certain Army provosts on the Mississippi River. Where it was prevalent, it often produced serious consequences to the operation of the government's vessels.

Use of Contrabands on Army Vessels

There is considerable evidence that the Union Army made extensive use of escaped slaves as roustabouts and stokers on not only its supply vessels, but on Army gunboats as well. This took place both on the western rivers and in the eastern sounds.

We have located crew lists of seven gunboats which were attached to Burnside's Coast Division and which, as early as the fall of 1862, all had large contingents of Negroes in the crews. Whether these Negroes were impressed or volunteered is not certain. They were paid $10 a month which appears to have been the standard paid all Negroes, inclusive of contrabands, throughout most of the war.[40]

The rosters of the Mississippi Marine Brigade contain listings of well over one hundred Negroes (unnamed) who were employed as coal passers and deck hands on the Brigade's rams and on its transports. Fourteen Negroes on the Brigade's vessels were women who were listed in the rosters as *chambermaids*.

Policies Developed Following the Civil War

Difficulties over the utilization of civilian crews by the military in the fields of discipline, pay, the handling of prisoners, eligibility for pensions, and a myriad of other aspects, were worked out and reconciled by the time the Civil War ended. The lessons on the subject which were learned during the Civil War were soon forgotten. During the War with Spain, World War I, and World War II, all of the same problems resurfaced, in one form or another. How to deal with them was addressed as if little precedence existed for a solution. One exception to this ignoring of lessons from the past may have been an act of the Congress passed in 1896 which covered, among other things, the conscription of merchant marine personnel during times of war.

> ...draft in time of war, except for the performance of duties such as are required by his licenses; and while performing such duties in the service of the United States every master, mate, pilot, or engineer shall be entitled to the highest rate of wages paid in the merchant marine of the United States for similar services; and if killed or wounded while performing such duties under the United States, they, or their heirs, or their legal representatives, shall be entitled to all the privileges accorded to soldiers and sailors serving in the Army or Navy under the pension laws of the United States.[41]

APPENDIX F
THE BURNSIDE EXPEDITION and CONFEDERATE ESPIONAGE
(December 1861- January 1862)

During the preparations for departure of the Burnside Expedition to Roanoke Island in late 1861, a bit of intrigue was taking place ashore. Rose O'Neil Greenhow (the same Mrs. Greenhow who in July of that year had alerted Confederate General Beauregard that McDowell was advancing toward Manassas Junction) seemingly again became a key player in events. She, or perhaps somebody representing to be her, authored a series of secret dispatches which were smuggled out of Washington addressed to reach Jefferson Davis's Secretary of War, J. P. Benjamin. The first of these dispatches was written three months following Mrs. Greenhow's imprisonment in a Washington jail where she was being held by Federal authorities under suspicion of having conducted espionage. That alone has led to a contention held by many historians that even while under imprisonment, Greenhow continued her role as mastermind of a spy ring operation which fed to the Confederates information on Union plans and movements.[1] A critical examination of the circumstances could indicate that such a theory may have had as its basis a scheme put into play by Union authorities as a counter-intelligence ploy to lead the Confederates astray. If there was such a scheme, it seemed to have been a clumsy one. For instance, the November 30 dispatch attributed to Mrs. Greenhow and which is reproduced below appears-- even when judged by the overblown writing style of that day-- to be almost too dramatic and overly vitriolic to be taken seriously. On the other hand, it could indicate a somewhat neurotic woman's acid hatred directed toward the Yankee oppressors of her beloved Southland. (Rose O'Neil Greenhow was a native of Maryland.)

> I have every reason to believe, from all I can hear, that McClellan will certainly make a bolt at you next week. Watch him on every hand. Every device will be used to deceive you. An impression will be made on every hand that no advance will be made; that the Army will go into winter quarters, etc. Pay no attention to such reports. I say, watch by land and by water. I also caution you to look to the several fleets now being fitted out-- Butler's and Burnside's; they will make a demonstration soon. Watch Norfolk and York rivers. A meaner set of devils never lived than Butler and Burnside. They would do anything to succeed. Burn cities, murder men, women and children, and do every other wicked thing they can, if by so doing they can raise themselves a buttonhole higher with the Northern Yankee devils. Kill the devils incarnate wherever you find them. Watch your batteries on the Potomac by day and by night. The darkest night may be selected to attack your batteries. I expect to send you a dispatch in a day or two from a lady friend, 'Mrs. Argie.' You know she received your letter and was more than delighted to hear from you.[2]

The above represents but one of a series of informational items that had arrived on Confederate Secretary of War Benjamin's desk during that month, all alluding to Federal fleets preparing to disgorge their troop passengers onto Southern shores. A prior intelligence dispatch, dated on October 27, had reported that twenty-five thousand men were to be landed somewhere on the Rappahannock River. Benjamin at first had some reservation that the Greenhow dispatch might be a plant, but he finally decided it was genuine. Another message had been smuggled through the Union lines at about the same time, this one, "from an informant in Washington," and addressed to President Davis. It imparted the news that the expedition then making ready to sail was "aimed at Cape Fear River, North Carolina, with the intention of occupying Wilmington, Smithville, and Fayetteville arsenal." In early November, Benjamin received a long letter from Assistant Adjutant General Thomas Jordan specifically discussing the dispatch which was dated October 27 and which was thought by Benjamin to have come from Greenhow. Benjamin's assistant adjutant general cast doubt that Greenhow had actually written the note, but rather thought it was a Union device "to deceive." The same officer then counseled Benjamin that since Mrs. Greenhow had been detected and arrested, "it would be ill-advised to take her communication seriously."

Another note incoming to the Confederate War Department and signed by Greenhow was dated December 28. It was sent through the lines directly to General Beauregard who immediately passed it along to Secretary Benjamin. It in part stated: "Burnside's fleet is to engage the batteries on the Potomac, and McClellan and company will move on Centerville and Manassas. The move will be made next. The information comes from Fox of the Navy Department." The "Fox" mentioned probably referred to Gustavus Vasa Fox who was then the Assistant Secretary of the Navy under Gideon Welles. The writer warned, "...Look out for a large army and tell your men to cut and slay until the last man is destroyed.... My God!, General, give them the most awful whipping that an army ever received."[3] Whether Mrs. Greenhow wrote this last note-- or if she did, whether she was acting as a double agent-- will probably never be known. She was soon afterward brought to trial in Washington and found guilty; but instead of further imprisonment, she was deported to Richmond. She was then sent to Europe by Jefferson Davis, there to gather intelligence of British intentions toward the Confederacy. She was recalled from Europe by Davis in 1864. En route home, Greenhow drowned off Cape Fear when the blockade runner on which she was a passenger foundered while attempting to evade capture. Mrs. Greenhow attempted to escape the wreck in a small boat while carrying dispatches and $2,000 in gold. The boat overturned, and ironically, the weight of the gold bore her to the bottom.

Posthumously, Mrs. Greenhow became a heroine throughout the Confederacy.

APPENDIX G
THE SIOUX UPRISINGS OF 1862 THROUGH 1864 AND THE ROLE OF RIVER TRANSPORTATION IN THEIR SUPPRESSION

1862

During early 1862, Minnesota's resident Santee Sioux Indians went on the war path, terrorizing that state's population. The Indians tortured and raped their way from settlement to settlement, slaying in all four hundred whites. When finally put down by Army units and state militia, two thousand of the hostiles either surrendered or were captured. Those of the hostile tribesmen who escaped capture were pushed westward, migrating into the Dakotas to join in alliance with the Yanton and the Yanktonnaise Sioux. The joining together of tribes with histories of violence against whites naturally provoked alarm on the part of settlers and traders residing in the Dakotas. In Minnesota, the settlers feared a return of the Santee Sioux, this time perhaps in company with their new found allies.

Even before the Santee Sioux moved west, the situation had been tense along the Missouri River. In 1862, Yanktonnaise Sioux had attacked a steamer carrying miners up the river. An editorial written at the time in a Dakota Territory newspaper challenged the government as to whether it was going to support white settlement then taking hold along the Missouri River, or was it going to stand by and let the frontier white population be pushed back by the threat of the Indians?

1863

In the early spring of 1863, a large force of Sioux (thought to have been Santee Sioux) were reported to have gathered together near former Fort Pierre on the Missouri. One estimate considered to be fairly reliable pegged the number at nearly five hundred warriors. Adding to the worries of the settlers along the Missouri was the news that the by-now very nervous Minnesotans had successfully pressured the government for the westward removal of remnant bands of Sioux which still remained in Minnesota but which had not participated in the uprising of the year before. Such a removal would add almost three thousand more Indians to the strength of the Sioux already along the Missouri. The rather rational theory offered by those whites in the Dakotas was that once those peaceable bands were forced to move west, their previously friendly attitude toward settlers would be friendly no more.

Gold had recently been discovered on the upper Missouri, and on March 23, 1863, the Congress had passed a military conscription act. Together, these two factors exacerbated what was already a dangerous situation. The news of the conscription act had immediately produced a horde of draft dodging prospectors who began ascending the Missouri at ice out in the spring of 1863. The journey of the gold-seekers up the Missouri had an ironic twist to it since the trip began taking on much of the same dangers that these men would have faced had they stayed home to await call-up into the Army. Instead of the Confederates, they would now face an even more unforgiving enemy. The steamboats *SHREVEPORT* and *ROBERT CAMPBELL NO. 2* were both fired upon by Indians who followed up with sustained attacks when the steamers grounded out on a sandbar. The Indians, numbering around two hundred warriors, then began to smell blood. Fortunately, both of the steamboats were equipped with cannon, and most of the miners were armed. The Indians were finally driven off, but it had been a close call. Reports soon began coming in from trappers and from squaw men (whites married to Indian women) that the Sioux were planning a blockage that summer of all westward migration, whether by prospectors or by settlers, even if the latter were just passing through on their way to a more westward destination.[1]

The situation in the Northwest Territories was considered serious enough that Major General Henry Halleck thought it necessary to create a Military Department of the Northwest. He placed Major General John Pope in command of it. Pope, in conference with his subordinate commanders, Brigadier General Henry Hastings Sibley and Brigadier General Alfred Sully, planned a campaign which called for Sibley to move north from Fort Ridgely following the banks of the Minnesota River to the northern shores of Big Stone Lake. From there, Sibley would cut westward toward Devil's Lake, this being the general area where it was believed the tribes would be concentrated by early summer. Sibley's strength would consist of two thousand infantry and eight hundred cavalry, reinforced by two sections of mountain howitzers. A second column under Sully and consisting of two thousand cavalry would ride up the banks of the Missouri. Their advance would be paced by steamboats carrying the supplies needed to keep the column in the field. Sully was not to leave the river bank until he was near the Devil's Lake region at which point he would strike overland to meet up with Sibley.[2]

The concentration of Indians expected near Devil's Lake did not materialize, the Indians having departed on their annual buffalo hunt well prior to Sibley's arrival. Sibley eventually came on the bands after a week of following their trail. In the action which followed, the Indians were forced into retreat. Sibley again followed, but it was not long before there was a question as to who was following who. The Indians started harassing Sibley on his flanks, a matter that become increasingly serious when the Sioux were reinforced by a band of Blackfoot. On July 27, a major action was fought. The Indians, seemingly quite confident of being able to overpower the soldiers, charged Sibley en masse. Such a direct charge against a strong force of troops was a rare occurrence in the Indian wars of the nineteenth century. Had it not been for Sibley's mountain howitzers, the Indians would probably have carried the field, a circumstance which, had it happened, would have made the 1876 Battle of the Little Big Horn pale by comparison. Instead, the Indians retreated with heavy losses.

Sully had meanwhile encountered a separate group of hostiles at Whitestone Hill, a rolling hill area about halfway between the Missouri and the James rivers. There, Sully's soldiers killed between two hundred fifty and four hundred warriors. (The body count varied, depending on which of Sully's officers reported the episode.)

After these actions, Sibley and Sully returned east. The 1863 campaign against the Sioux had come to a close.

1864

In the winter of 1863-1864, reports began coming out of Indian country alluding to a resurgence of hostilities planned against the whites in the spring. Pope faced a dilemma. Should he merely try to keep the Missouri open to immigration and trade through the establishment of garrison points, or should he make another attempt to subjugate the Sioux? The Army's urgent needs elsewhere precluded the kind of large scale campaign which would be required to completely conquer the tribes. Nevertheless, Pope was also aware that any show of weakness could be an invitation for the Sioux to totally close down traffic on the Missouri-- a happening which a few isolated garrison posts could not prevent. Although Halleck tended to understand Pope's dilemma, he wrote Pope explaining the difficulties he was facing from various political factions:

> General:
>
> Your letter of March 30 [1864] is just received. You probably are not fully aware of the difficulty of ascertaining and counteracting the baneful influence upon military operations exercised by speculators, through members of Congress and the civil departments of the Government. More especially is this the case in regard to Indian affairs, when dishonest men are continually intriguing to use the military for their individual purposes. As soon as I explained to the Secretary of War the real conditions of affairs in your department, he ordered me to suspend his order in regard to sending the 6th Minnesota Regiment to the Army of the Potomac. Your alacrity in sending troops to other departments whenever you could spare them has been most praiseworthy.
>
> H. W. Halleck, General-in-Chief [3]

The Sioux, in fact all of the tribes east of the Rocky Mountains, were well aware of the war then going on between the Union and the Confederacy. Some of the tribes had been witness to the warfare that was taking place within the Mississippi corridor. Indian tribes within the designated Indian Territory (now the state of Oklahoma) had in fact been formed into voluntary regimental units that were fighting on both sides of the white man's war. Farther to the west, contact with white traders kept those Indians abreast of what was going on in the east. The Indian tribes were as a whole therefore thoroughly aware of the Army's limited abilities to respond to threats of uprisings, and they were consequently emboldened. [4]

In early April, Pope began to receive reports that warriors were beginning to again show aggressiveness against steamboats ascending the Missouri. Were the Indians testing the Army's ability and its determination, or were they out to make serious trouble? [5] The strategy that was finally decided upon by Pope was a blend of containment and punitive action. The Army would garrison points on the Missouri, and it would conduct a limited offensive campaign tailored to Pope's available troop strength. Sibley was to construct a fortified post on the upper James river. Sully was sent to construct a post near the headwaters of the Missouri and a second post on the Yellowstone near the mouth of the Powder River. (The location of the second post was later to be changed.)[6] While these fortified posts were being built, mounted columns were to strike consolidations of Indians whenever they could be found.[7] Steamers would be the supply umbilical for the posts as well as for the operations in the field.

The steamboat season on the upper Missouri was fairly short, usually beginning just after ice-out and lasting only until mid-July when the river became too shallow for navigation. This meant bringing everything needed upriver before mid-summer. Since the troops assigned to the punitive columns were to be mounted, there was a need for considerable quantities of grain for the horses. Unlike Indian ponies which could subsist nicely on grasses, the more finely bred mounts used by the Army required grain when on active campaign.[8]

Gathering together enough steamers to serve the needs of Pope's 1864 campaign was to prove difficult. The short season and the special risks which were involved with navigation on the upper Missouri made chartering unattractive for steamboat owners who were at the time enjoying a "sellers' market." The demand for steamers on the Mississippi and elsewhere was extremely heavy that season. Nevertheless, the needed boats were finally located.

By July 28, Sully's men had established a post on the upper Missouri at that river's junction with the Cannonball River. Sully named it Fort Rice. From there, Sully led twenty-two hundred mounted troops on a search for hostiles. When he finally located them, the Indians' strength was more than he had bargained for. Scouts later estimated that the bands numbered between five and six thousand warriors; however, most historians of the Indian wars think that this was an overestimate. The fact that Sully's presence was known to the Indians left him without option. He had to attack. At the beginning of the action, it appeared that the Indians would gain the upper hand, but as with Sibley the season before, artillery decided things in the Army's favor. When the Indians broke under the fire of Sully's field pieces, they abandoned their tepees and most of their supplies of food which they had gathered to see them through the coming winter. Sully followed up the Indian's retreat to the area known as the Badlands and again attacked. This time he broke the tribesmen into small and scattered units. A number of those smaller groups fled north toward Canada.

Returning to the Missouri, Sully established his second post where that river joins with the Yellowstone. He also left a garrison at Fort Berthold, an established trading post located somewhat downstream from the junction of the Missouri with the Little Missouri.

Eight steamboats supported Sully in the 1864 campaign. They were the *MARCELLA, SAM GATY, CHIPPEWA FALLS, GENERAL GRANT, ISABELLA, TEMPEST, ALONE*, and *ISLAND CITY*. In close proximity to the location of Fort Union on the upper Missouri, *ISLAND CITY* hit a snag and sank. Five of the remaining steamers then waited at Fort Union while the *ALONE* and *CHIPPEWA FALLS* went up the Yellowstone in support of Sully's cavalry column which by then was moving against the hostiles. These two steamboats were the first to ever navigate the Yellowstone River.[9]

An important side benefit coming out of the 1864 campaign against the Indians was the locating of coal deposits on the bluffs overlooking the Missouri River a short distance upstream from Fort Rice. By 1864, most of the original cottonwood groves adjacent to the river had been cut, and steamboat captains were having increasing difficulty in obtaining fuel for their boilers. The only wood supplies left were to be found up a few of the side streams which were too shallow to be navigable. In a country infested with hostile Indians, the risk to woodcutting parties became a serious consideration once the wood cutters were out of sight of the fire support offered by their vessels. Now, with the discovery of coal in veins which reached the surface, steamboat pilots could anticipate non-stop travel while both ascending and descending the Missouri.

In his report of the 1864 campaign in which he touched on the discovery of the coal deposits, Pope expressed his belief that the discovery would be the catalyst for opening the northern prairies to the railroads once the Confederacy was defeated. In that, he proved to be correct. In that same report, Pope told Washington that the major danger from the Sioux seemed to be over; but he qualified this somewhat by cautioning that this prognosis would depend upon reforms in the policies exercised toward the tribes. Up to that time, treaties had promised annual annuities. In other words, the Indian were "paid to be good." Pope now advocated an entirely different approach. He felt that the tribes should be moved east well away from the frontier. Once they were relocated into permanent settlements and trained in sedentary agricultural pursuits, they would no longer pose a danger. A companion reform, and one equally important in Pope's thinking, was that the Indians should be administered under a format designed to destroy their existing tribal structure.[10] Despite Pope's urging, this idea was never implemented except perhaps in the sense that reservation life, as it came to exist following the Indian wars of the 1870s, had the end effect of disrupting tribal hierarchies. Politically, it is doubtful that moving the tribes east, if it had been attempted, would have been acceptable to the established white communities or, for that matter, any state governments which by necessity would have become involved in such a plan. The Sioux uprising of 1862 had wrecked so much havoc in Minnesota that it hardened white attitudes against the red man. It would be difficult for such people to think of the Indian as a close neighbor.

Pope's subordinate commanders also had recommendations. In a report sent to the Assistant Adjutant General, Department of the Northwest, dated September 11, 1864, Sully broached what he believed would be an improvement in control by the Army over the immigrant wagon trains. To date, a number of incidents involving friction with the Indians stemmed from the poor handling of situations by wagon train masters. Under the system in effect during 1864, men given territorial commissions were placed in command of all immigrant wagon trains scheduled to pass through the Northwest Territories. These temporary officers were usually either not knowledgeable of Army doctrine or else not amenable to it. Sully backed his plea for a change in this policy by telling of the lack of know-how of at least one such territorial officer. The man referred to in Sully's report as "Captain Fisk" had recently been the cause of a near disaster. Fisk had corralled his wagons when harassed by an insignificant number of hostiles and had decided to stay put until reinforced, a rider having been sent out for help. This brought about rescue by a cavalry column called out especially for the "emergency." The rescue column consisted of convalescent men otherwise confined to garrison duty because of poor health. Pulling Fisk's chestnuts from the fire had been the cause of much suffering, all totally unnecessary. Sully opined in his report that one of the major causes of the Indian problem, a factor to which Pope had also added a voice, was the trade carried on with the Sioux from across the Canadian border. Through that trade, the Sioux were receiving most of their weapons and ammunition without which they would not have constituted the threat that they had become.[11]

~

The contest with the Sioux would accelerate following Appomattox and would impact the postwar careers of many of the officers and men who had served in the war against the Confederacy.

APPENDIX H
Excerpt From UNITED STATES ARMY REGULATIONS

Containing the Changes and Laws Affecting Army Regulations
and Articles of War to June 25, 1863 (as affecting troops on transports)
(Article XXXVII)
and The Content of *General Order 276,* August 8, 1863

Article XXXVII   Troops on Board of Transports

851.   Military commanders charged with the embarkation of troops, and officers of the Quartermaster Department entrusted with the selection of the transports, will take care that the vessels are entirely seaworthy and proper for such service, and that suitable arrangements are made in them for the health and comfort of the troops.

852.   If, in the opinion of the officer commanding the troops to be embarked, the vessel is not proper or suitably arranged, the officer charged with the embarkation shall cause her to be inspected by competent and experienced persons.

853.   Immediately after embarking, the men will be assigned to quarters, equal parties on each side of the ship, and no man will be allowed to loiter or sleep on the opposite side. As far as practicable, the men of each company will be assigned to the same part of the vessel, and the squads, in the same manner, to contiguous berths.

854.   Arms will be so placed, if there be no racks, as to be secure from injury, and enable the men to handle them promptly-- bayonets unfixed and in scabbard.

855.   Ammunition in cartridge boxes to be so placed as to be entirely secure from fire; reserve ammunition to be reported to the master of the transport, with request that he designate a safe place of deposit. Frequent inspections will be made of the service ammunition, to insure its safety and good condition.

856.   No officer is to sleep out of his ship, or to quit his ship, without the sanction of the officer commanding on board.

857.   The guard will be proportioned to the number of sentinels required. At sea the guard will mount with side arms only. The officer of the guard will be officer of the day.

858.   Sentinels will be kept over the fires, with buckets of water at hand, promptly to extinguish fires. Smoking is prohibited between decks or in the cabins, at all times; nor shall any lights be allowed between decks, except such ship lanterns as the master of the transport may direct, or those carried by the officer of the day in the execution of his duty.

859. Regulations will be adopted to enable companies or messes to cook in turn; no others than those whose turn it is, will be allowed to loiter around or approach the galleys or other cooking places.

860. The commanding officer will make arrangements, in concert with the master of the vessel, for calling the troops to quarters, so that in case of alarm, by storm, or fire, or the approach of the enemy, every man may repair promptly to his station. But he will take care not to crowd the deck. The troops not wanted at the guns or to assist the sailors, and those who cannot be advantageously employed with small arms, will be formed as a reserve between decks.

861. All the troops will turn out at   , A.M., without arms or uniform, and (in warm weather) without shoes or stockings; when every individual will be clean, his hands, face, and feet washed, and his hair combed. The same personal inspection will be repeated thirty minutes before sunset. The cooks alone may be exempted from one of these inspections per day, if necessary.

862. Recruits or awkward men will be exercised in the morning and evening in the use of arms, an hour each time, when the weather will permit.

863. Officers will enforce cleanliness as indispensable to health. When the weather will permit, bedding will be brought on deck every morning for airing. Tubs may be fixed on the forecastle for bathing, or the men may be placed in the chains and have buckets of water thrown over them.

864. Between decks will not be washed oftener than once a week, and only when the weather is fine. The boards of the lower berths will be removed once or twice a week to change the straw. Under the direction of the Surgeon and the officer of the day, frequent fumigation will be performed between decks. The materials required are-- common salt, four ounces; powdered oxide of manganese, one ounce; sulfuric acid, one ounce, diluted with two ounces of water. The diluted acid is poured over the other ingredients in a basin placed in a hot sand-bath. Solutions of chloride of lime and chloride of zinc are excellent disinfecting agents.

865. During voyages in hot weather, the master of the vessel will be desired to provide wind sails, which will be kept constantly hung up, and frequently examined, to see that they draw well and are not obstructed.

866. During cooking hours, the officers of companies visit the camboose [sic], and see that the messes are well prepared. The coppers and other cooking utensils are to be regularly and well washed, both before and after use.

867. The bedding will be replaced in the berths at sunset, or at an earlier hour when there is a prospect of bad weather; and at tattoo every man not on duty will be in his berth. To insure the execution of this regulation, the officer of the day, with a lantern, will make a tour between decks.

868. Lights will be extinguished at tattoo, except such as are placed under sentinels. The officer of the day will see to it, and report to the commanding officer. The officers' lights will be extinguished at 10 o'clock, unless special permission be given to continue them for a longer time, as in case of sickness or other emergency.

869. For the sake of exercise, the troops will be occasionally called to quarters by the beat to arms. Those appointed to the guns will be frequently exercised in the use of them. The arms and accouterments will be frequently inspected. The metallic parts of the former will be often wiped and greased again.

870. The men will not be allowed to sleep on deck in hot weather or in the sun; they will be encouraged and required to take exercise on deck, in squads by succession, when necessary.

871. At morning and evening parades, the Surgeon will examine the men, to observe whether there be any appearance of disease.

872. The sick will, as far as practicable, be separated from the healthy men. On the first appearance of malignant contagion, a signal will be made for the hospital vessel (if there be one in company), and the diseased men removed to her.

873. A good supply of hospital stores and medicines will be taken on each vessel, and used only for the sick and convalescent.

874. The Surgeon will guard the men against costiveness [sic] on approaching a hot climate. In passing through the West Indies, to the southern coast for instance, and for some weeks after landing in those latitudes, great care is required in the use of fruit, as strangers would not be competent to judge of it, and most kinds, after long voyages, are prejudicial.

875. In harbor, where there is no danger from sharks, the men may bathe; but not more than ten at a time, and attended by a boat.

876. In fitting up a vessel for the transportation of horses, care is to be taken that the requisite arrangements are made for conveniently feeding and cleaning them, and to secure them from injury in rough weather by ropes attached to breast-straps and breeching, or by other suitable means; and especially that proper ventilation is provided by openings in the upper deck, wind sails, etc. The ventilation of steamers may be assisted by using the engine for that purpose.

877. Horses should not be put on board after severe exercise or when heated. In hoisting them on board, the slings should be made fast to a hook at the end of the fall, or the knot tied by an expert seaman, so that it may be well secured and easily loosened. The horse should be run up quickly, to prevent him from plunging, and should be steadied by guide ropes. A halter is placed on him before he is lifted from the ground.

878. On board, care is to be taken that the horses are not overfed; bran should form part of their ration. The face, eyes, and nostrils of each horse are to be washed at the usual stable hours, and, occasionally, the mangers should be washed and the nostrils of the horses sponged with vinegar and water.

879. In loading vessels with stores for a military expedition, the cargo of each should be composed of an assortment of such stores as may be available for service in case of the non-arrival of others, and they should be placed on board in such a manner that they may be easily reached, in the order in which they are required for service. Each storeship should be marked, at the bow and stern, on both sides, in large characters, with a distinctive letter and number. A list is to be made of the stores on board of each vessel, and of the place where they are to be found in it; a copy of this list to be sent to the chief officer of the proper department in the expedition, or at the place of destination.

~

To provide an implementing mechanism for the regulations dealing with the conduct of troops embarked aboard transports, *General Order No. 276* was issued.

War Department, Adjutant General's Office
Washington, August 8, 1863

General Order, No. 276

To secure and preserve discipline, provide against disaster from the elements or attack by the enemy, the senior officer in the military service of the United States present with troops upon any transport will assume command, unless he finds, on going on board, a commander already designated by proper authority.

All troops on board the transport will at the earliest moment after embarking be inspected and organized into detachments or companies. The senior officer will assign officers to each detachment or company and take all measures necessary to put his command into the best state of efficiency to meet any emergency.

This order applies to all troops on board of transports, whether on duty or furlough or in separate detachments; and the senior officer on board will be held responsible for any failure in the performance of the duties above imposed upon him, and for the enforcement in his command of strict observance of the Article XXXVII, Revised Army Regulations, for the government of troops on transports.

He will require, when arriving in sight of port, a report of the voyage from the senior officer or acting officer of each staff department on board, and will transmit it with his own report, through the proper channel, to the Adjutant General of the Army.

These reports should give any facts of interest touching the accommodation and health of the troops, the manner in which the officers and crew of the transport have performed their duties, and the length of the voyage, and any observations which may enable the War Department to detect and correct abuses and punish neglect.

This order will be placed in a conspicuous position in every chartered or purchased transport.

By order of the Secretary of War.

E. D. Townsend, Assistant Adjutant General

APPENDIX I
ARMY SAILORS THE 99th NEW YORK INFANTRY REGIMENT

Initial Union Army recruitment of what would eventually become the 99th New York Infantry Regiment took place during April of 1861 at New York City. Its organizer and chief recruiter was Colonel Washington A. Bartlett.[1]

According to its recruitment announcements in the New York newspapers, Bartlett's organization was to consist of mariners and fishermen. It would have the purpose, as envisioned by Bartlett, of operating as an amphibious attack force along the coast from North Carolina south to Florida. It was to be equipped with its own vessels on which it would cruise the coast and then make landings to take temporary possession of installations "such as bridges and even towns." Anything of value to the enemy was to be destroyed before withdrawal. The organization's vessels were to be light draft gunboats. These were to be mounted with portable cannon for use aboard the gunboats or as mobile artillery for use by the landing parties once ashore. The theory behind these coastal forays was that they would compel the Confederates to guard their entire coast, never knowing when or from where the next strike might appear. Bartlett announced publicly that he envisioned his organization as eventually growing to brigade size. Once reaching that strength, it was to be known as the "Naval Brigade." Although Bartlett's full ambitions for the organization would never be realized, it did become the only Army unit possessed of an amphibious mission which operated continuously throughout the entire period of the conflict. There were other organizations within the Union Army which had either maritime or amphibious functions during the war, but none of these organizations had a tenure as long lasting as that of the 99th New York.

On May 2, 1861, Bartlett's organization, although still considerably short of even regimental strength, was ordered to Virginia to report to the commander of Fortress Monroe. Upon arrival, the officers and men were to be mustered into federal service.

No sooner had the organization arrived in Virginia than Colonel Bartlett fell off some stone riprap and laid open his skull. His lieutenant colonel, a man named Whitmore, thinking Bartlett was about to die, started for Washington to gain the colonelcy before someone else could beat him to it. Shortly after Whitmore left, Bartlett regained consciousness. When told what Whitmore was up to, Bartlett started for Washington, and once there, put an end to his lieutenant colonel's ambitions. Whitmore's attempted power grab appears to have contributed to a total breakdown in morale among the regiment's enlisted men who-- apprehensive of the quality of their leadership-- collectively announced that they had decided to decline entry into the federal service. The commander of Fortress Monroe then tried to enter them on the roles as civilian laborers, threatening not to feed anyone who did not sign up for that duty. The men reacted with a "To Hell with you," and strolled down to the beach where they scratched around for clams and oysters on which to subsist. Although it took some doing on the part of Colonel Bartlett and his officers, the difficulties were eventually resolved, and the majority of the men expressed a willingness to be sworn into the Federal Army. A few remained reluctant and presumably were returned to New York.

What the novice soldiers of the 99th New York had first anticipated of military life did not jibe with the reality of what now followed. They were first put to work repairing and improving Fortress Monroe's battlements-- this in early summer heat that was debilitating to men accustomed to a northerly climate. To make matters worse, their living conditions were just short of primitive. Uniforms had yet to be issued, and when they finally arrived, the ensemble consisted only of one hickory flannel shirt, one pair of white duck pants, and a straw hat.

In July, the unit received orders to proceed to Washington to assist in that city's defense. As defenders of any place, the unit's worth was at best questionable since the men had yet to be issued arms. When rations were handed out for the trip, there were no haversacks in which to carry them. To make up for that inadequacy, the men were told to "carry them [the food rations] in your pockets;" but their white duck pants had no pockets. At the last minute, the Washington order was canceled, and the unit was ordered to remain in garrison at Fortress Monroe awaiting further assignment. They eventually received their rifles; but it was found that over two-thirds of the weapons in that initial issue were in such bad condition that they would not fire.

At the time the unit was entered into federal service, it had received the designation of "Union Coast Guard." A few weeks later, at a time when it was at last being equipped for what held the promise of becoming a combatant force, it was renamed the "New York and Virginia Coast Guard." That designation was short-lived, though, when it was decided that it should instead be known as the "99th New York Infantry Regiment." The designation stuck, and following that point, all records for the command can be found under that regimental designation.

Although the regiment's duties varied after this point, they were substantially of a maritime nature. The regiment appears to have rarely served together as an integral unit. In fact, in its 4-year history, a substantial part of its officers and men were continuously on "detached service," being assigned to shipboard duty either in the estuaries off Chesapeake Bay or on the rivers contiguous to the North Carolina sounds. According to the unit's history (which was written in 1905 by one of its veterans), some of the companies of the 99th New York served as detached infantry. One example of the regiment's dual functioning took place during Major General Benjamin Butler's expedition to Hatteras Inlet. Two of the 99th New York's companies were joined as infantry to the assault landing force while those members of another of its companies were assigned as boatmen to handle the landing craft which one participant described as "unwieldy iron boats." After the Hatteras Inlet area was secured, the personnel from these three companies returned to Fortress Monroe to await another assignment.

Recruiting for the 99th New York continued as an ongoing effort throughout 1861 and into 1862, but the regiment never reached its full authorized strength.

The regiment's companies often found themselves widely separated, and even the companies were sometimes divided into smaller detachments. In February of 1862, Company B found itself split into three sections. One of the three sections was loaned to the Navy to help man the naval gunboat *USS SOUTHFIELD;* another was loaned to the *USS HUNCHBACK*.[2] It appears that Company B's people acted as gunners on both of these gunboats although some of the men may have been assigned to seamen duties. After the capture of New Berne, North Carolina, and the subsequent occupations of the nearby joint ports of Beaufort-Morehead City, a third section of Company B was employed as crewmen aboard launches utilized for patrolling the inland sounds north and south of those ports.

D. W. Wardrop who was Company D's original commander (and who later became colonel of the 99th New York) related for the regiment's history the circumstance under which Company D became assigned to the Navy's man-of-war, *USS CONGRESS* in January of 1862. Wardrop stated that when the Navy had earlier paid off the ship, it had issued discharges to three hundred men. Lacking enough new recruits with which to fill these open positions, the Navy requested the Army's assistance. As a temporary measure, Company D was asked to make up for the crewing deficits. To a man, the company volunteered. Reporting to the *USS CONGRESS*, the officers and men acted both as marines and as sailors working the ship under the direct orders of her naval officers. As a result of that assignment, Company D was serving aboard the *USS CONGRESS* at the time of the action against the *CSS VIRGINIA* (ex *USS MERRIMAC*) which took place in Hampton Roads on March 8. During that action, the *USS CONGRESS* was forced aground and burned by *CSS VIRGINIA*. Of the eighty-nine men of Company D who were aboard, the company lost one sergeant, one corporal and eight privates. Nine others were wounded and seven more were reported missing.

In the early fall of 1862, the 99th New York shifted its regimental headquarters from Fortress Monroe to Deep Creek, Virginia, a hamlet located along the Dismal Swamp Canal, a waterway which connects the port of Norfolk with North Carolina's Albemarle Sound. From Deep Creek, infantry elements of the regiment made frequent raids into the surrounding countryside. These raids were carried out from small shallow draft transports.

During the summer of 1863, Brigadier General Henry M. Naglee ordered that an inland blockade be established to stop the flow of enemy infiltrators and illegal commerce into the Dismal Swamp Canal and its adjacent waterways from Confederate-held Virginia. The blockade line was to commence on the Elizabeth River at the outskirts of the city of Norfolk, thence to run by the course of that river to its navigable head, thence to the head of Deep Creek and through the Dismal Swamp Canal to Lake Drummond. From Lake Drummond, the line would follow the Dismal Swamp Canal to the western branch of the Pasquotank River and on that river to its discharge into the Albemarle Sound.[3] The enforcement of the blockade was to be conducted by the Army's gunboats and its armed tugs. The manning of these craft became the responsibility of the 99th New York. One of the assignments went to Captain John C. Lee who was to take over the armed tug *CURRITUCK* and another went to Lieutenant C. D. Willard who was to command the gunboat *GENERAL JESUP*. (It appears that at the time Willard had been assigned to service with the 99th New York.) The orders given both officers were explicit as to the rigidity of the blockade. The orders given Willard are descriptive of that intent.

> Headquarters, Department of Virginia, VII Army Corps
> Norfolk, August 14, 1863
>
> Lieutenant C. D. Willard, 19th Regiment Wisconsin Volunteers
>
> You will forthwith assume command of the Army tugboat *GENERAL JESUP* and proceed to the Albemarle Sound, where you will watch constantly and closely the water courses that flow into it from Princess Anne, Currituck, and Camden Counties of this department. You will burn all boats that you find upon the Pasquotank River, and seize and destroy or send to this place all boats or other vessels that you find engaged in contraband trade. No fisheries will be allowed unless by special permission from these headquarters, and then you will satisfy yourself that all the restrictions that may be imposed are complied with. You will enforce the provisions of the special orders hereunto attached, for which purpose you will communicate as often as necessary with the United States forces on the Pasquotank River. You will report, via the land forces above referred to, once a week to these headquarters, and more frequently if you have any important information to communicate.
>
> By command of Brigadier General Naglee:
>
> Signed George H. Johnston, Assistant Adjutant General[4]

The regimental headquarters returned to Fortress Monroe from Deep Creek during the late summer of 1863. It was around then that many of the original terms of enlistment in the regiment began to expire. Those men who did not choose to reenlist were sent to New York and mustered out. Those who reenlisted were reorganized, together with recruits, into new company designations. After this reorganization, those units of the regiment which were not on detached vessel service were ordered to New Berne, North Carolina, where they remained on garrison duty until June of 1864.

An article entitled "Army Gunboat Service," written for the unit's history by Lieutenant Frank B. Lawrence, relates directly to some of the ongoing gunboat duty as it continued to be performed by members of the 99th New York. (Lawrence began his gunboat service in August of 1863.) The gunboat of which he was given command was the *FLORA TEMPLE*. At the time Lawrence took her over, she was armed with Navy type howitzers. Lawrence turned these howitzers back to the Navy and in return was supplied with two 20-pound Parrotts. While aboard *FLORA TEMPLE*, Lawrence and his all-Army crew worked with Navy gunboats in combined operations on the Virginia estuaries offlying the Chesapeake Bay. Most of the operations consisted of landing reconnaissance patrols. Lawrence was next given command of the armed tug *C. P. SMITH* ; and following that, he received command of the *SMITH BRIGGS* which was an attack transport. During amphibious operations being conducted in Virginia waters, the *SMITH BRIGGS* was lost by enemy action. Reports prepared at the time of the vessel's loss state that thirty crewmen from the *SMITH BRIGGS* were taken prisoner. The enlisted men, as well as some civilian personnel who were serving with them as crewmen, ended up at Andersonville Prison.[5]

During the time frame of 1864, officers and enlisted men of the 99th New York were also detached for crewmen duty on the Army vessels *WEST END, C. P. SMITH, SWAN,* and *COMMERCE.* These four were all armed and employed as light gunboats and attack transports in Virginia waters.

When Sherman reached North Carolina in early 1865, units of the 99th New York, minus those men then on detached duty, were joined to Sherman's army. They participated in the campaign in North Carolina which led to the Confederate surrender at Durham Station. It is a reasonable assumption that during this period, the regiment's personnel participated as guards or gunners on supply vessels operating on the Cape Fear and Neuse rivers. These rivers became primary routes for Sherman's resupply after he left Savannah.

The 99th New York Infantry Regiment was mustered out of federal service on July 15, 1865, at Salisbury, North Carolina. During the war, it lost two officers and thirty-seven enlisted men who were either killed in action or who died from fatal wounds. The regiment additionally lost three officers and one hundred sixty-one men from disease either while on active service or while being held by the Confederates as prisoners of war.

Other Army units which were in the eastern theater during 1864 and 1865, and which for a period of time had individuals or groups detailed as crewmen or gunners to the Army's gunboats or its armed transports, were the 4th Rhode Island Infantry, the 9th New Jersey Infantry, the 13th New York Heavy Artillery, the 20th New York Cavalry, the 9th New York Infantry, the 19th Wisconsin Infantry, and the 3rd Pennsylvania Heavy Artillery. These units were all attached to the Army of the James.[6] It is probable that most of these detached persons were assigned to the 99th New York Infantry Regiment for their tenure as crewmen or gunners, and that as such, during 1864 and 1865, they were integrated into Graham's Naval Brigade.

APPENDIX J
THE MILITARY TELEGRAPH SERVICE DURING THE RICHMOND
CAMPAIGN, 1864-1865

During the Civil War, a Military Telegraph Service was organized as part of the Army's Quartermaster Department. Its telegraph operators were civilian employees working under the supervision of Army officers.

Initially, the Army's telegraph system on the lower Chesapeake Bay served only the base area of the James and York river's operational sector. The more forward areas were served by a system of visual flag communication. At the time of Major General Benjamin Butler's amphibious movement up the James River which resulted in the occupation of Bermuda Hundred and City Point, each troop commander, down to the division level, had been assigned at least one trained flagman. Flag signaling in the Civil War differed from the semaphore method developed in later years. In the 1860s, military flag signaling was carried out by waving a flag to the right or to the left, or straight up and down, each movement representing a numerical value which was then decoded into word sequence. During the hours of darkness, torches were substituted in place of flags, using the same side and vertical movements.

After the Bermuda Hundred and City Point landings, telegraph lines were extended to these forward areas, and communication by flag was phased out.[1] Following the occupation of Bermuda Hundred and City Point, a total of 546 miles of telegraph wire was in place for communication between Fortress Monroe and the various Federal installations located on both the York and James rivers. From there, telegraph communication was maintained with the War Department in Washington.

To have run telegraph wire directly overland to Washington would have meant extending it across the Virginia countryside, a vulnerable situation since enemy infiltration was commonplace over the entire stretch. Instead, it was decided to extend the line to Washington via the Delmarva Peninsula. That of course meant crossing under the bay from Fortress Monroe by the use of submarine cable. In the mid-1860s, the dependability of submarine cable had yet to be proven. The first attempt to lay a telegraph cable under a sizable span of water had been in New York harbor from "The Battery" at the end of New York's Manhattan Island to Governor's Island in 1843. Seven years later a cable was laid by the British between Dover, England, and Calais, France. The short time that these early cables remained in service had not offered encouragement. In June 1858, a joint American-British naval expedition tried laying a cable between the British Isles and North America; but that effort failed when the cable parted. In August of that year, a second attempt succeeded, but service lasted only a month due to a failure of the cable's insulation.[2] In May of 1864, the Union Army telegraph system employed a cable running under the Potomac River from the Maryland shore to Pope's Creek on the Virginia side.[3] However, the Chesapeake Bay, because of its size and unique current conditions, created special problems. It was decided that running a cable under such a wide expanse of open water would not be practical. To facilitate transmissions, a tug ran closely scheduled dispatch service from Fortress Monroe to Cherrystone, a hamlet located on the bay's eastern side near Cape Charles.[4] At Cherrystone, a telegraph station was established, and from there a line ran up the length of the western shore of the Delmarva Peninsula to a point near Crisfield, Maryland. Directly opposite from Crisfield, was Point Lookout at the entrance to the Potomac River. Reports and correspondence contained within *Official Records...Armies* are silent as to whether there was a submarine cable link between Crisfield and the opposite shore at Point Lookout. Because of the bay's strong tidal flow in this area, it is quite possible that the Army used a courier vessel to handle this cross-bay communication in the same fashion as was done in the lower bay between Fortress Monroe and Cherrystone. From Point Lookout, a telegraph line ran directly to the War Department.

Inaugurated as part of the military's utilization of telegraph during the Civil War was the Beardslee magneto-electric machine, a device which used a paper disc to automatically transmit and receive Morse code. At one time or another, the Beardslee machine was widely used by the Union Army in both the eastern and the western theaters. However, Major T. T. Eckert, Assistant Superintendent of the United States Military Telegraph Service and the person in direct charge of the James and York River communication sector, came to find the Beardslee machine "inefficient for speedy communication." The rapid transmission of messages was a necessity, especially in the 1864-1865 Richmond campaign during which an extraordinarily high volume of messages emanated to and from the various field commands.[5] In the interest of speedy transmission, Eckert preferred the manually operated telegraph key in the hands of experienced operators[6].

While discussing the telegraph's utilization within all the theaters of war during 1864, the Chief of the Military Telegraph Service stated in a post-war report that 1,800,000 telegrams dealing with military business had been transmitted. It is fair to presume that well over half of that traffic was generated by Grant's campaign to take Richmond. It is also a reasonable assumption that the communication traffic generated during 1865 increased in volume from that of the year before.

~

The American Civil War is generally considered to be the first major conflict in the world's history where coordination of widespread armies in the field was orchestrated through a centralized national command. Telegraphy was the medium which had made this possible.[7]

APPENDIX K
EMIGRATION TO HAITI, 1863
THE ILE A VACHE COLONIZATION SCHEME AND THE ROLE OF THE ARMY QUARTERMASTER

When the Civil War began, little thought was given by Union planners as to any potential problem arising over slaves escaping from their southern masters. The full emancipation of Negroes held in bondage within the new Confederacy was still a long way into the future and was a concept considered at the time as far too radical, that is, if the South was ever to be coaxed back into the Union.

Hostilities had hardly started when a slow but steady trickle of slaves began crossing through Confederate lines to what they hoped would be freedom. In the war's early weeks, those escaping from northern Virginia found their way to Fortress Monroe, a Union stronghold on the lower Chesapeake Bay. The number arriving there at first was not of a quantity considered burdensome to the Federal commander. He merely ordered the males put to work at heavy labor on the battlements while the women were put to the tasks of cooking and laundering for the garrison. Any questions which arose over the legal status of these people does not seem to have resulted at the time in any serious discussions within the Lincoln Administration. The situation would change with the advent of a Union expedition launched against Port Royal, South Carolina (Hilton Head). This was shortly followed by a Union occupation of a rather substantial strip of coastal Georgia and South Carolina. Throughout this area, hundreds of Negro refugees who had evaded the inland exodus of their owners begged to be sent north, pleading a fear that if they were ever retaken, their punishments for escaping would be severe.

The attitude of the Union commanders on the scene in Georgia and South Carolina became that of treating these people as prizes of war to be utilized as labor in support of the Army. Huge refugee camps were established near Hilton Head and elsewhere in the coastal zone as even more Negroes found their way to the coast.

To more or less formalize what had virtually been a labor impressment of Negro males, the War Department issued an order dated October 1, 1861, which specifically allowed commanders holding territory in those coastal zones bordering Confederate-held territory to enlist Negroes as "soldiers;" however, none would be issued arms, as their sole purpose was employment as military laborers. The theory was that as "soldiers," such Negroes would be subject to military discipline and the punishments under that discipline which enforced order and effectively prevented any refusals to work. They were to be paid, but at only half the rate of white soldiers.[1]

It appears all too clear that by early 1862 the Lincoln Administration was beginning to take a rather hard look at what was becoming an overwhelming problem with Negroes coming across from the Southern lines, not only in the coastal zones but elsewhere as well. Feeding and housing these escapees, who by now had come to be known as contrabands, was only acceptable to the administration as long as a benefit resulted to the Union Army's labor needs. But as the influx mounted, it became obvious that the number of laborers needed by the Army had its limitations. To send these people north to enter the civilian labor market in competition with white workers would almost certainly produce a political backlash, something which Lincoln wished to avoid. To force them to go south again was unthinkable, both morally and politically. Colonization, at least for some of these contrabands, to somewhere outside of the United States seemed a partial solution, one worthy of investigation.

In April of 1862, President Lincoln met with representatives of the Chiriqui Improvement Company, a firm with holdings in what is now the Republic of Panama. This company owned coal deposits in the northern part of that Central American region, and the company had earlier expressed interest in employing free Negroes from the United States to work there as miners.

Helping to set the stage for any such emigration, Congress passed an act in July.[2] This act, which had been proposed to the Congress by the President, allowed the slaves of owners who supported the rebellion to legally gain their freedom once they crossed over into Union lines; and it formally authorized such ex-slaves to be employed toward suppressing the rebellion. Additionally, the act authorized the President to provide for colonization "in some tropical country beyond the limits of the United States of such persons of African race, made free by the provisions of this act, as may be willing to migrate." (It would not be until January 1863 that full emancipation was granted those of the Negro race still held in slavery and with that emancipation the War Department orders allowing the enlistment of Negroes into the Union Army as armed fighting men.)

Shortly after the signing of the act of July 1862, Lincoln hosted at the White House a deputation of Negro leaders to whom he urged colonization, putting the reasons for it rather bluntly. "But for your race among us there could not be war... It is better for us both, therefore, to be separated." Advocating Central America as the destination for such separation (with the Chiriqui Improvement Company mines probably in mind), the President promised the government's help toward affecting any migration[3]. On December 1, 1862, in a speech to the full Congress, Lincoln urged the funding of a colonization program for Negroes. There was little adverse reaction to the idea, either in Congress or in the press, due in part, it would appear, to the work of a private organization of long standing which had been transporting to Africa those free Negroes who wished to migrate. The African colonization movement to what was termed Liberia had exported a total of 15,386 free American Negroes between the years 1817 and 1860, the last date marking the time that the program had virtually ceased. Only a few of those who migrated had asked for repatriation thus presumably indicating some measure of success with that colonization. The voluntary migration of American Negroes to Liberia had radically altered the socio-political makeup of that part of west Africa. Before long, these former American Negroes had established a political structure completely alien to the native African scene in that the place became modeled after the United States. This was considered, of course, as a great plus on the part of those favoring the idea of colonization for Negroes.[4]

Following Lincoln's speech to the Congress, a study committee of the House was formed under the chairmanship of Albert S. White of Indiana. That committee requested $20 million "for the purpose of acquiring overseas territory and of transporting any Negroes willing to migrate."[5] White's committee did not get the $20 million it had asked for, but rather had to settle for $100,000 from an earlier appropriation, plus the addition of $500,000 especially set aside for the project. A Commission of Emigration was appointed to select possible sites. Under that commission's review, the Chiriqui idea died a rather abrupt death because of the suspicion that it would encourage a plan (long advocated by a strong political ally of Lincoln's) to make the Caribbean 'our India'. Secretary of State William H. Seward agreed with this concern, adding to it the warning that unless colonization was carefully monitored, it could provide a scenario for reducing the new freed man back into a state of slavery. In Seward's opinion, the Chiriqui mines had all the earmarks of doing just that. Putting the final squelch on the Chiriqui idea were the protests of the by then alerted Central American nations which were strongly opposed to receiving American Negro migrants into their Hispanic social structure.

Entering now upon the scene appeared an entrepreneur named Bernard Kock who in early 1862 had leased from Haiti's all-Negro government an island called Ile a Vache lying off Haiti's southern coast. Under the terms of Kock's leasehold with the Haitian government, 35% of the timber cut on the island would be delivered to the Haitian capital of Port-au-Prince and turned over to the government. Further, any labor force imported for employment on the island was to be of the Negro race; and before their arrival, such persons would show advanced willingness to become naturalized Haitians.[6]

To Lincoln's Secretary of the Interior, Caleb B. Smith, colonization to Ile a Vache had considerable merit, and he believed, as did Secretary Seward, that it was certainly less complex than the diplomatic problems posed by pushing the idea of emigration to Central America. To begin with, there was no native population on the island to be economically displaced; and secondly, the host government seemed in perfect accord. Kock was asking the United States government for very little, i.e., only transportation south for the colonists and just enough supplies to see them through until the first food crop could be harvested. As the matter was being taken under study by the Lincoln cabinet and supposedly by the Commission of Emigration established by Representative White, Kock followed up with the news that he had already purchased material for a sawmill, considerable farm equipment, and a number of cotton gins. He also claimed that supervisory personnel had been hired and that they were standing by awaiting orders to start south.

At Fortress Monroe, Virginia, six thousand Negroes-- all ex-slaves-- were living in badly crowded, squalid conditions. These people who had continued to come into Federal lines from Confederate-held Virginia expressed little interest in going north, and so it was from this particular group that it was thought the colonization volunteers could most likely be recruited.

Meanwhile, rumors began to reach Washington that Kock was not all that he professed to be. One report had it that the man had been involved in a business fraud some years back. In another report, the resident United States Minister to Haiti wrote that he had been to Ile a Vache and had seen no activity being made in the way of preparations for colonists-- that, despite Kock's contradictory claim that such preparations had already taken place. The minister's further inquiries made around the Haitian capital brought forth a number of opinions that Kock was "an adventurer and a rascal."[7] Obviously Kock was not projecting the kind of image thought necessary for such a politically sensitive undertaking. Fortunately, or so it was considered by the administration at the time, two New York City businessmen who had earlier invested in the Kock scheme, Paul S. Forbes and Charles K. Tuckerman, offered to take over the project. They promised that Kock would no longer be involved. The administration's investigations of Forbes and Tuckerman came up with a clean bill of health for both men.

At this point the original idea of transporting the six thousand ex-slaves at Fortress Monroe was downgraded to a pilot group of about five hundred people. Satisfied that everything was now on the up and up, Lincoln authorized transportation for five hundred would-be colonists along with the sum of $50 per person to subsist them while en route and for their provender during the first weeks after arrival on the island.[8] The vessel chosen to take these people was the merchantman *OCEAN RANGER* .[9]

Shortly after the colonists arrived, they were visited by an American vice-consul stationed at Port-au-Prince. He reported back to the State Department that the fledgling colonists appeared healthy and happy and that they were flourishing under the guidance of none other than Bernard Kock. This information, when passed along to the White House, created an instant stir since Forbes and Tuckerman had promised to be completely divorced from association with Kock. When these two were asked about the matter, they replied that the use of Kock on the scene at Ile a Vache was necessary since among other factors, he alone had been party to the lease with the Haitian government. Apparently Lincoln accepted the explanation as a fait accompli not to be undone at this late date.

Not many weeks had passed when rumors began to reach the Secretary of the Interior that the colony was being impacted by death and disease caused by considerable deprivations suffered by the inhabitants. (The Interior Department had been charged by Lincoln with monitoring progress on Ile a Vache.) Next, word arrived that Kock had suddenly appeared on the Haitian mainland claiming that a civil insurrection was underway on Ile a Vache and asking for military aid to put it down. The Haitians had sent a contingent of troops back with Kock. The officer in charge discovered that the population was in dire straits, subsisting on a diet of moldy corn and salt pork. Forty people had already died from illnesses. Not one dwelling for the colonists was in evidence, and it was apparent that they were sleeping on the open ground. Complaints were made to the soldiers that Kock had earlier confiscated or "borrowed" United States currency from those colonists who had any, with the pledge that it would be immediately paid back-- a promise not kept. When the United States Consul was told by the Haitian government of the conditions existing on Ile a Vache, he personally journeyed to the island to be confronted with the sight of the people reduced to the most miserable of states.

For the emigrants, things were apparently getting worse instead of better. Conversely, Kock and his white assistants were reported to be living in the fashion of plantation aristocracy. When the Secretary of the Interior received the news, he sent a special agent south to further investigate. The agent, when later stating what he had found, painted a picture of complete neglect by Kock reporting that little if any improvement had been made to the original wild state of the island. Many of the colonists had expressed to the agent an eagerness to return to the United States. Before the investigator left the island, he had personally dismissed Kock from any further participation in the colony.

In February 1864, the White House instructed the Army Quartermaster Department to charter a suitable vessel to go to Ile a Vache and pick up the surviving colonists. The vessel chartered was the *MARCIA C. DAY*.[10] The instructions given by the White House to the Quartermaster Department were that the purpose of the voyage was to return the colonists to Washington. The voyage and its purpose was to be kept completely secret since quite obviously the whole matter had the potential of becoming a huge political embarrassment to Lincoln if word got out. The quartermaster officer placed in charge of the evacuation was to accompany the relief vessel. In the interest of secrecy, he would tell the captain prior to sailing nothing of the real purpose of the voyage, only that the outbound destination was to be Aspinwall (now Panama). When the ship had reached a point east of the Bahamas at latitude 26 degrees, the quartermaster officer would give the captain the true destination.

Returning from Ile a Vache (none of the colonists refused repatriation) the passengers were unloaded onto the wharves at Washington City. Fortunately for all those in the Lincoln government who had been involved, the sad conclusion of the enterprise eluded the attention of the press.

~

EPILOG

The Ile a Vache fiasco effectively ended the Lincoln government's enthusiasm for any re-colonization of Negroes. A few Negroes found their own way to Liberia following the end of the Civil War, but they were an insignificant number. Some migration schemes developed in the post war period involving separate Negro communities. These enterprises were generated by Negroes themselves, and were restricted to the United States, mainly in the west (Kansas and Arkansas), where settlements became established during the time frame of 1866 to 1880.

APPENDIX L
HAY: ITS IMPORTANCE TO THE CONDUCT OF THE CIVIL WAR

The supply of hay in its importance to an American army in the field became focal as early as the Revolutionary War when in 1777 Washington's cavalry regiments had to be detached from the rest of the Continental Army. This separation was necessary in order that the cavalry commander could find hay and pasture for his mounts. During the winter of 1779, Pulaski's Legion (a cavalry command) was moved south to Delaware for the same reason. In both instances, without a cavalry screen, Washington and his senior commanders became virtually blinded as to British intentions.[1]

Animal forage became even more of a vital commodity for the conduct of operations during the 1861-1865 American Civil War. Its relationship to the support of an army in the field during the Civil War was articulated by the nineteenth century historian Louis Philippe d'Orleans in a study drawn upon his observations of the Union Army and the problems that army encountered once it distanced itself from its primary supply base.

The American [army] wagon, drawn by six mules, carries a load of two thousand pounds, sufficient, therefore, to supply five hundred men, provided it can make the trip daily, going and returning, between the army and its depots. If the distance to be traveled is such as to require a whole day's march, one day being lost in returning empty, it will only be able to supply five hundred men every other day, or two hundred fifty daily. To go a distance of two days' march from its base of operations is a very small matter for an army that is maneuvering [sic] in front of the enemy, and yet, according to this computation, it will require four wagons to supply five hundred with provisions, or eight for one thousand, and consequently eight hundred for one hundred thousand men.

If this army of one hundred thousand men has sixteen thousand cavalry and artillery horses, a small number comparatively speaking, two hundred more wagons will be required to carry their daily forage, and therefore, eight hundred to transport it to a distance of two days' march. These sixteen hundred wagons are, in their turn, drawn by ninety-six hundred mules, which, also consuming twenty-five pounds during each of the three days out of four they are away from the depot, require three hundred sixty wagons more to carry their forage; these three hundred sixty wagons are drawn by twenty-four hundred animals, and in order to transport the food required by the latter, ninety-two additional wagons are necessary. Adding twenty wagons more, for general purposes, we shall find that two thousand wagons, drawn by twelve thousand animals, are strictly necessary to victual an army of one hundred thousand men and sixteen thousand horses at only two days' march from its base of operations. In the same proportion, if this army finds itself separated from its base of operations by three days' march, three thousand seven hundred sixty wagons, drawn by twenty-two thousand animals, will be found indispensable for that service.[2]

Dry forage was near the top of the list of critical supply commodities for the Union armies. Only the smallest of cavalry or artillery units could place any reliance on grazing while in nightly bivouac. During operations in the field, horses and mules were, for reasons of security as well as for purposes of simple management, placed upon picket lines, meaning that whatever grass was available was only within the arc of the individual animal's short tether. While an army was in encampment or located on a static line of defense, any grazing that might at first have been available was usually consumed within the first few days or even in hours. What grass was not immediately eaten was soon ground into the dust or mud. The presence of hundreds and often thousands of hoofed animals would, within a short time, turn lush meadows into moonscapes. Under such a typical scenario, everything an animal needed had to be brought to it in the form of grain or dry forage. The volume of dry forage required was tremendous.[3] Without its horses, the Army could not carry out far ranging reconnaissance, nor could it strike at the enemy's flanks or his rear through the use of the cavalry arm. The mobility of field artillery depended entirely on its dray animals. Besides all this, there were the beef herds which the Commissary Department provided for the subsistence of the troops. The beef cattle were maintained entirely upon hay until ready for slaughter. Except in the coolest of weather, beef had to remain on the hoof until the very day of its issue to the cooks. Robert M. Browning, Jr., in his work *From Cape Charles to Cape Fear: The North Atlantic Blockading Squadron During the Civil War*, relates that during the Civil War the Navy utilized steamers filled with large ice compartments to transport slaughtered beef to its vessels on blockade duty. There is, however, nothing which we could find within the Army's Commissary reports or correspondence to indicate that the Union Army transported beef by any method other than on the hoof.[4] In her exhaustive work, *Quartermaster Support of the Army: A History of the Corps, 1775-1939*, Erna Risch, states that it was Army policy to purchase cattle from contractors and then herd them to the armies where they would remain on the hoof until ready for consumption. At one point during 1864, the beef animals for the Army of the Potomac in front of Petersburg numbered 3,000 in a single corralled herd. While on the march, the soldier's ration was normally "one pound of hard bread; three-fourths of a pound of salt pork or one and one-fourth pounds of fresh meat; sugar, coffee, and salt....Butchers connected with the brigade organization slaughtered the animals at night, and the meat was then cooked." Salt beef was rarely if every issued although salt pork was a regular and well received ration.[5]

Transportation of Hay

Although attempts were made during the war to limit the high tonnage of hay required to subsist the Army's horses and other livestock through the substitution of more easily transportable grains, such substitutions could only be limited. Horses and cattle can, it is true, do well on grain, but without the additional bulk provided by hay (or straw if hay is not available), digestive troubles will soon take their toll.

Since the armies of 1861-1865 could not shift location to where the forage was grown, transportation became a critical item in the logistical matrix. A review of the Union Army's statistical shipping records establishes with some certainty (at least for the years 1864-1865) that the hay and straw which was shipped to field commands was sent by barge under tug assist or upon sailing vessels[6]. The voyages were not entirely uneventful. One shipload of hay which left New York in July 1864, consigned to the Army quartermaster at Fortress Monroe, Virginia, was on the sail bark *GENERAL BERRY*. That vessel and its cargo of hay would never arrive at their destination. When eastward of Hampton Roads, the *GENERAL BERRY* was overtaken by the Confederate sea raider *CSS FLORIDA*. After the crew was removed to the raider, *GENERAL BERRY* was destroyed by fire.[7]

The large majority of the hay as well as a large proportion of the straw which went to the Army of the Potomac during the period was shipped through the port of New York. So important had the hay shipments become that a special division of the Army Quartermaster Department was established to handle its procurement. Heading that division was Colonel S. C. Brown who, during 1864 and well into 1865, headquartered at New York City.

Between 1861 and 1865, the quartermasters signed receipts for 491,000 tons of hay shipments incoming to Washington City alone. The value of shipments of hay and straw sent from the northern seaports just to City Point, Virginia, amounted to nearly $1,000,000 a month during the winter period of 1864-1865.[8] The cost of the individual shipments to City Point varied widely-- anywhere from $2 to $28 a ton within the time frame of the same month. This variance in cost can be explained in a number of ways: The primary factor was the quality of the hay since that which had been badly damaged by rain while curing or which had molded while in storage would have been of considerably less value than bright, undamaged hay. A second reason would have been the type of hay. Newly seeded timothy hay, for instance, brought more money than long-stand weedy hay. Although we have no figures on variety price differentials for the port of New York, in the Chicago market the top price during the decade of the 1860s for loosely baled timothy was $18 to $19 a ton; for tightly baled timothy, $19 to $20 a ton; and for loosely baled prairie hay, $11 to $12 a ton.[9] A third reason for the wide cost differentials seems to have been that some shipments were purchased directly from the vessel masters at the point of delivery to the Army, while other shipments were F.O.B. without the cost of transportation factored in at the time of sale. When forage was purchased by the Army at a point near to its origin, the transaction was conducted with a commission agent acting on behalf of a farmer or with a wholesale dealer who had earlier purchased the hay directly from a farmer.

Hay As a Farm Crop in New York State

The demand for hay created by the Union Army's needs came at a time when hay production had developed into a prime market crop in New York State, having peaked in that respect during the late 1850s. This production peak stemmed from a series of circumstances: botanical, economic, and mechanical.

During the first decade of the nineteenth century, New York State had garnered the reputation of being the granary of the nation, especially in wheat production. Then in 1820 the scourge of the Hessian fly hit the wheat crop. This disaster was followed a year or so later by what was then called "the midge fly." These happenings impacted both the Hudson Valley and the Mohawk Valley. Fortunately for the hard hit farmers of that period, expanding urbanization on the island of Manhattan as well as at the city of Albany provided a developing market for rye grain which was used for breadstuff and the production of beer. A valuable by-product of rye production was the straw left over from threshing. This straw made excellent animal bedding, and to some extent straw, although far less nutritious, could be used as a substitute for hay in the feeding of animals.[10] There was also born out of urbanization a strong market for grass and legume hay to feed the cities' horses, an equine population used then for carriage and dray purposes, a usage which continued to expand with the increase in human population. By 1840, New York State was leading the nation in hay production, most of which was consumed within the state itself.[11] Paul W. Gates makes the claim that by the eve of the Civil War, three-fourths to four-fifths of the cultivated land of New England and northern New York was in hay.[12]

Keeping pace with the increasing demand for hay were new inventions in harvesting equipment. Although the horse drawn rake was in fairly common use by the mid 1820s, it was not until the 1850s that the revolving horse rake equipped with sulky seat became standard on almost all farms. Horse drawn mowing machines were first seen on some farms at about the same time as the early horse drawn rake, but the early models were clumsy affairs, and their adoption was not widespread. The first practical horse drawn mower, invented by William F. Ketchum of Buffalo, New York, was patented in 1847. That invention was followed up by others, the best of which was a floating cutter bar type which went on sale in the mid-1850s. Mowers and hay tedders were common on most farms by the early 1860s, the most popular models of mowers being the "*Buckeye*," the "*Cayuga Chief*," and the "*Bull*." Getting the cured hay from field to barn remained pretty much of a pitch fork effort. (Mechanical hay loaders would not appear until after the Civil War.) However, for unloading from wagons into the barn, the harpoon hay fork, operated by pulleys and horsepower, was in use by the 1860s.[13]

By the mid nineteenth century, two forms of improved transport-- rail and water-- had become available to the farmers of the Hudson and Mohawk valleys. The Erie Canal, which in part traversed the Mohawk Valley, had been completed in 1825, and its usage by canal boats drawn by horses from the banks was heavy from the onset.[14] The development of the Erie Canal was followed shortly by the railroads. By 1851 the Hudson River Railroad had opened service between Manhattan Island and Albany with its tracks paralleling the east bank of the Hudson River. The following year, the New York and Harlem Valley Railroad extended its right of way northward through the Harlem Valley to Chatham, a town about 20 miles south of Albany. (The Harlem Valley of New York State, which is a north-south geographic feature, lies midway between the Hudson Valley and the New York State border with Massachusetts and Connecticut.) The coming of the New York and Harlem Valley

Railroad opened yet another rich agricultural region to market access with New York City.[15]

By 1861, a large proportion of New York State's agriculture had evolved toward forage production. New York's improved transportation system made the task of getting this commodity to market a much easier proposition than had been the case in the past. From the standpoint of the Union Army's needs in the conduct of its operations bordering on Chesapeake Bay and points southward, transshipment of forage through the port of New York made for a most adaptable situation due to the fine cargo handling facilities that the port offered.

A number of physical transfers were involved with each shipment of hay which went to the Army. The producer had to first move the hay from his farm to a rail siding for loading onto rail cars or to a point on a waterway for loading aboard canal boats or barges. Whether initially transported to the port of New York by rail or by water, the hay would next have been offloaded for transfer to seagoing vessels (usually either a schooner or tug-assisted barges). At the port of destination in the south, it would be offloaded onto wagons or to rail cars for its final movement to the point of consumption.

Packaging of Hay for Shipment

In only a very few instances do Army records specify the form in which hay or straw was shipped. What records there are all relate to the hay being in "bales." There is also considerable photographic evidence which shows bales of hay stacked or lying about at Army supply depots. Since the shipment of hay or straw in anything but baled form would have been very labor intensive and prohibitively expensive, not to mention the waste of shipping space that would have been involved, it is reasonable to conclude that all the hay or straw which was moved south to the armies in the eastern theater (and within the western theaters as well) was shipped in the baled (or pressed) form.[16]

The earliest known hay press was advertised for sale in 1836. It was in that year that mention of one such device appeared in the *Annual Catalogue of the Agricultural Warehouse and New England Seed Store* of Boston.[17] Another hay press, the "Dederick Patent Parallel Lever Hay Press," manufactured at Albany, was being marketed by 1857. The Dederick Hay Press was described by its makers as operating in the following fashion:

> The principle improvement of the above Hay Press, over all others, lies in the absolute impossibility of the Follower canting, or in any measure binding against the sides of the machine during its operation of pressing the hay. It is operated...by two parallel toggle joints and levers, so arranged that one lever is near one end, and the other near the end of the follower; and as the arms of each set of these parallel toggles are exactly the same length, and connected together at the same distance on the Follower, it will be understood that the press works with entire accuracy[18]...

The Dederick Hay Press could be purchased in any one of five models to make bales in weights of from 150 pounds to 500 pounds. Albany, New York, seems to have become a major center of hay press manufacturing, as another firm located there was the H. L. Emery Company. Emery had begun to manufacture his press by 1853. With Emery's press, at least according to its manufacturer's claim, "two men and a horse could make five 250 pound bales in one hour, each bale measuring 24 x 24 x 18 inches." After the farmer had loaded his hay into the Emery press, "wires were fed through slots at each end, and the bales tied together." [19]

The use of a press for hay that was to be sold into the New York marketplace was well established by the late 1850s. Unlike the modern mobile hay baler which picks hay up from windrows and bales it in the field, the hay press of the 1850s and 1860s was a stationery machine with the hay being transported to it in loose form for pressing. Such baling, or pressing, took place either at the farm or somewhere fairly close to the farm. It is probable that many hay presses were set up at or near rail depots or at river and canal ports to which farmers would have brought their loose hay by wagon. The loose hay would have been sold directly to wholesale dealers who would have supervised its pressing before loading on the train cars or canal barges, or else the farmer would have paid a fee to the owner of a press for baling the hay prior to shipping the product to a hay broker in the city.[20]

Economic Variables of Hay Production

The production of hay had become a profitable enterprise to New York farmers well prior to the outbreak of the Civil War. In terms of cash value per crop acre, grain crops such as rye and barley were financially more rewarding when looked upon solely from the standpoint of gross returns. However, hay farming was far less labor intensive since hay fields needed plowing and reseeding only every few years. The labor saving advantages of hay over grain production became ever more attractive once the Civil War started. By 1861, voluntary enlistment into the Union Army began taking large numbers of farm hands from the rural labor pools. As the war dragged on, the bounty system which paid volunteers for enlisting, and later the military draft, would seriously deplete the remaining labor force. At the same time, the demand for hay was increasing as the Army grew in size. By early 1863, the raising of market hay became a highly lucrative business on those farms located within transportation access to the port of New York.[21]

To give one example of a New York farmer who prospered with hay as his main market crop during the Civil War, we have singled out the circumstance of Anthony Christopher Michael who was born in the Harlem Valley of New York during 1825. He married in 1850 and in that year moved to a cleared farm at Martindale in the township of Claverack, Columbia County, New York. The farm then consisted of 165 acres. (Martindale is located halfway between the city of Hudson, New York, and the state line at Egremont, Massachusetts. The Michael farm bordered on a road that is today known as Route 23, and was adjacent to where that modern highway now crosses over the Taconic State Parkway.) When farmer Michael purchased his farm, he took on a debt load of $8,000, a heavy fiscal burden for that day and age. However, Michael had chosen his location well, as in 1852, the tracks of the New York and Harlem Valley Railroad had reached north to Martindale. The following year would see Martindale become a scheduled rail stop. The advantage of the railroad to Michael was considerable. Not only did it provide him with a ready access to the New York City market, but the effort needed to reach the depot was minimal since the Michael farmstead was only a 10-minute wagon haul to the depot.[22] A ready transportation access to markets, coupled with a soil type well suited for hay production and a demand for hay which was accelerated by the military needs of the Civil War, enabled Michael to pay off his farm mortgage and amass considerable savings by the war's end in 1865. By then, he was in the position to afford an attractive home which he built to replace the original farm dwelling he and his bride had moved to as newlyweds.[23]

The Hay Crisis During Grant's Final Campaign to Take Richmond

By mid-1864, the Union Army of the Potomac, then located on the James River of Virginia, had sixty thousand horses and mules. In terms of hay consumption at 25 pounds a day on average for the various classes of livestock, this translated into hay needs of around 750 tons a day.[24] That December, serious hay shortages began to develop. In trying to meet the need, Quartermaster agents were scouring not only the usual forage markets such as New York and Pennsylvania, but even those markets as far away as the northernmost New England states. The shortage had been created by a combination of events. One was the ever worsening farm labor shortage, a direct result of the manpower demands made on behalf of the Army. For instance, Claverack Township (where Michael had his farm) was credited for enlistment bounties on 256 men, most of them probably agricultural workers. Although some of the bounty fund was raised through bond issues, a good part of it was raised by taxation. There was also a problem of weather. In the summer of 1864, farms throughout the central Atlantic states suffered an abnormally poor harvest brought about because of drought. This had virtually eliminated a second cutting in most areas. Contributing to the production problems caused by drought and the labor shortages was the need that farm owners had for immediate cash to satisfy taxation demands. (The Township of Claverack's share as paid into the Columbia County Treasurer for enlistment bounties had been $86,473.16.) The abnormally high taxes forced many farmers to sell off their hay into the civilian hay market soon following the harvest, thereby lowering inventories much earlier in the year than would have normally been the case.

The hay shortage which began occurring during the early winter of 1864-1865 not only affected the Army of the Potomac but it also was threatening the northward movement of Sherman's Army of the West from Savannah. After his arrival at Savannah, Sherman, through a series of urgent dispatches, had been pressing the Quartermaster Department to replenish his supplies, generally all of which, once he reached the sea, had to come from the north by ship. Forage for his artillery horses and his cavalry mounts was near the top of Sherman's shopping list. The Quartermaster General explained to Sherman the difficulties over getting the requested amount of forage south, offering a partial remedy, albeit a rather severe one.

> Quartermaster General's Office, Washington City
> December 19, 1864
>
> Major General Sherman, Commanding, at Savannah
> General
>
> I wrote you fully a day or two since in regarding to supplies. As it is reported that you will not find light steamers enough on the coast to supply you up the Ogeechee, I have ordered six of the most suitable to be sent from the Chesapeake. The *LOUISE*, a very fine iron steamer, goes this morning, and I write by her unless my other dispatch may miscarry. I see you are aware of the importance of stripping your army of all useless mouths. The only supply about which I have any anxiety is hay; this we have not been able to procure in sufficient quantities. [emphasis added] There is no difficulty, so long as the credit of the government holds out, in sending on everything else in abundance. But I hope that you will get rid of every mule and horse not absolutely needed about Savannah.
>
> Wishing you continued success, I am, very truly, your friend.
>
> M. C. Meigs, Quartermaster General, Brevet Major General[25]

Hay supplies at the Union Army depots in northern Virginia became dangerously short when, starting around the New Year (1865), ice conditions sealed up many coastal seaports as far south as Philadelphia. The freeze-up stopped shipments of everything going south to the Army. Hay inventories at City Point, Virginia, were at one point down to a half ration 5-day supply. The animals had already been restricted for some weeks to half of their normal forage requirements, and many of them, drawn down badly in physical condition, had already died of disease. Now it looked like the rest faced an almost certain death from starvation. The situation had reached the point by January 19 that Grant's quartermaster, Brigadier General Rufus Ingalls, stated in his official correspondence that the Army of the Potomac had become an army totally incapable of movement.[26]

The crisis surrounding the shortage of forage was somewhat relieved by mid-February through the breakup of the ice which had been blocking the northern ports. Although the hay situation remained of concern to the Union command, the tonnage which began coming south during the remainder of that winter and into the spring was sufficient to maintain the army's mobility once Grant forced Lee from his entrenchments in front of Petersburg.

~

The productivity of New York State farmers and their utilization of up-to-date harvesting and packaging equipment, when joined in equation with the efficiencies in rail and water transportation which had developed within New York State by the 1860s, were essential to the successes of the Union Army. As petroleum was vital to the Allied victories during the Second World War, animal forage was the energy source which fueled the military juggernaut which finally brought about the Confederate surrenders of April 1865.

~

During the 1960s, the senior author served as a commissioner on the New York State Agricultural Resources Commission.

APPENDIX M
UNITED STATES v 269½ BALES OF COTTON

A federal court case relating to cotton seizures on the Mississippi River was tried in the Circuit Court for the District of Missouri during October of 1868. The subject of the case was the seizure of cotton by Union Army troops during the month of September 1862. (*United States v 269½ Bales of Cotton.*) The circumstances of the case revolved around a cavalry force which had been transported on steamers chartered by the Army Quartermaster. The cavalry force had been landed from the transports onto the banks of the Mississippi from whence the cavalrymen rode some miles inland on a routine search mission. During that mission, 269½ bales of cotton were seized and carted by wagon back to the transports. The government's attorneys claimed that the cotton was a prize of war since the cavalry unit was operating from vessels which were on navigable waters. (There was no question here of prize law awards for the cavalrymen. Only the government had presented itself as the party in the case.) In its decision, the Circuit Court opined that the Mississippi River (per se), being navigable, was an area of admiralty prize jurisdiction. The Court questioned whether prize status could be claimed for seized commodities when the location of the actual seizure was completely remote from those navigable waters. As part of its ruling, the Court summarized:

> 6) The prize jurisdiction has been sustained only when the naval arm has made, or cooperated in making, or, by its presence and active assistance, contributed immediately in effecting the capture...and...
> 8) The capture has been of some place used in naval warfare, as an island, and etc...

The Court ruled negatively against the government, stating that the vessels from which the cavalry had operated were not armed "nor were they commissioned." Rather, they were merely a means of transport for the troops which then operated from the transports in a remote fashion unrelated to normal maritime employment.

We would ourselves comment that in making its 1868 ruling the Circuit Court was seemingly incomplete in its knowledge of the statutes governing prize law. To explain:

An Act for the Better Government of the Navy, as that act was incorporated into the federal statutes during 1862, had allowed the award of prize money to any vessel's crew as long as the vessel was "armed" and in the "service of the United States." The Circuit Court stood, therefore, incorrect in stating that eligibility for prize money was dependent on the "commissioned" status of the vessel. Under the act of

1862, prize money had been awarded to the crews of at least two Army transports, neither of which were commissioned, but whose crews captured Confederate blockade runners off the Atlantic coast.

~

One can only speculate as to how the same Circuit Court would have viewed the case of Rear Admiral David D. Porter's "liberation" of cotton during the Red River Expedition in the spring of 1864. Before leaving Alexandria, Porter had commandeered wagons which his men, on their search for cotton, took a considerable distance inland. This in effect made the scene of the seizures somewhat removed from admiralty jurisdiction. Nevertheless, Porter's circumstances differed considerably from the circumstances of the cavalrymen as described in the transcript of the case *United States v 269½ Bales of Cotton* in that Porter's men were all integral to the crews of commissioned naval vessels, therefore meeting the Circuit Court's admiralty jurisdiction theory in that respect. This is not to say, though, that there was anything legally or morally defensible in Porter's alleged instructions to his men that they were to falsely mark the seized cotton bales with the symbol "*CS*" so as to give the impression that the cotton had been enemy property when discovered.

APPENDIX N
THE NAVY'S MISSISSIPPI SQUADRON ON THE RED RIVER EXPEDITION: (March-May of 1864)

# *USS BENTON*	*USS JULIET*
USS BLACK HAWK (Porter's flagship)	*USS KENWOOD*
* *USS CARONDELET*	# *USS LAFAYETTE*
* *USS CHILLICOTHE*	* *USS LEXINGTON*
# *USS CHOCTAW*	* *USS LOUISVILLE*
USS COVINGTON (lost)	* *USS MOUND CITY*
USS CRICKET	* *USS NEOSHO*
USS EASTPORT (lost)	* *USS OSAGE*
# *USS ESSEX*	# *USS OUACHITA*
USS FOREST ROSE	* *USS OZARK*
* *USS FORT HINDMAN*	* *USS PITTSBURG*
* *USS GAZELLE* (dispatch boat)	*USS SAINT CLAIR*
USS GUNBOAT NO. 13	*USS SIGNAL* (lost)

BENEFIT (supply vessel)
BROWN (coal transport)
† *CHAMPION NO. 3* (pump boat, lost)
CHAMPION NO. 5 (pump boat and transport, lost)
GENERAL STERLING PRICE (armed supply vessel)

‡ *BROWN* (tug)
‡ *DAHLIA* (tug)

Vessel was sent out of the Red River to the upper Mississippi (Fort Pillow) during first week in April; Source, *ORN,* I, 26.

*   Vessel reported "above the falls of Alexandria" (dam sites) as of April 28. Source, *ORN*, I, 26, page 94.

†   In a report by Porter found in *ORN,* I, 26, *CHAMPION NO. 3* is mistakenly referred to by Porter as "*NEW CHAMPION*," that being a nickname.

‡   Tugs not named either in reports or in correspondence found within *ORN*, however the work of Ludwell H. Johnson names these tugs as having gone up above the falls of Alexandria in service to Porter's fleet. See Johnson, *Red River Campaign: Politics and Cotton in the Civil War,* p 207, fn. 6.

APPENDIX O
WESTERN RIVER SYSTEMS ON THE EVE OF THE CIVIL WAR

This appendix is a repeat, with some slight modification, of Appendix 7 of Volume I of The Army's Navy Series. At the risk of some redundancy, it is reproduced here because of the importance of the western rivers and their navigation to the conduct of military operations as they took place between 1861 and 1865.

The Mississippi

The Mississippi River formed the main trunk of the system known as the Mississippi basin. On the Mississippi, navigation could be carried on during the spring and early summer past the junction with the Saint Croix River up to the falls near Stillwater in western Wisconsin. The drop in river depths normally occurring in summer and lasting to ice-up became the limiting factor to navigation. On the upper tributary known as the Des Moines River, traffic extended to the town of Des Moines on the northern border of Missouri. Steamboat navigation in a direct connection to New Orleans from the most northern points is recorded as early as 1823, but traffic had not reached any commercially dependable level until well into the late 1840s. According to George Armroyd writing in *A Connected View of the Whole Internal Navigation of the United States,* navigation extended 2,250 miles from the Gulf of Mexico to the Falls of Saint Anthony, but this was reflective only of keelboat use. For steamboats, it can be generally stated that the Mississippi was regularly navigated, once the ice was out, for approximately 1,400 miles.[1]

Of great import to the carriage of commerce were the tributary systems offlying the Mississippi River within the state of Mississippi. The Sunflower and Yazoo river drainage networks, which flowed into the Mississippi north of Vicksburg, became the scenes of a number of amphibious type operations in 1862 and 1863 during the campaign to take the fortress of Vicksburg. To a substantial degree, the Yazoo and the Sunflower were navigationally independent of the Mississippi. As discussed extensively by Harry P. Owens in *Steamboats and the Cotton Economy: River Trade in the Yazoo- Mississippi Delta,* the Yazoo steamboat trade interconnected directly to railroads which in turn exported the region's goods to outside markets.[2] There was also direct steamboat connection between the Yazoo region and New Orleans. The river trade to New Orleans was a recognized fact of commerce by around 1830; but according to Owens, steamboats may have penetrated the Yazoo system prior to that time.

<u>The Ohio River, Its Interconnection with the Cumberland and the Tennessee Rivers;</u>
<u>and The Rivers' Interrelationships with the Existing Railroad Networks</u>

At Cairo, Illinois, the Mississippi River forms a triple boundary. The state of Illinois is to the north of the river; Kentucky is on the south and east. The angle is completed by the state of Missouri to the west. It is at this point that the Ohio River meets the Mississippi along the Mississippi's eastern bank. During the Civil War, Cairo became a place of particular strategic significance in the control of the river systems.

The Ohio River had been navigated by flatboats since the earliest settlements. That navigation initially had started at Pittsburgh in western Pennsylvania, continuing on to the junction with the Mississippi and then on that river all the way downstream to New Orleans. However, major natural barriers existed for steamboats on the Ohio. Proceeding upstream on the Ohio from Cairo, the first was the "Falls of the Ohio" at Louisville. Another obstruction consisted of shallow rapids known as the "Ohio Piles" which were in proximity to Wheeling. Only at the periods of highest water could steamboats negotiate either of these obstructions. In 1831, a canal was constructed at Louisville to bypass the Falls of the Ohio. In 1860, a total of 1,520 steamboats in addition to 1,299 other types of craft passed through that canal.[3] It is not known for certain whether a War Department report written in 1853 was correct when it estimated that only 43% of the steamboat tonnage on the Ohio could use the canal. The figure was close enough, though, to make Louisville the main terminus on the Ohio for direct steamboat connection to the Mississippi. (It would be five years following the Civil War before the canal at the Falls of the Ohio was improved through widening.)

During the Civil War, Louisville became an important railroad spur terminus, served, as it was, by the east-west line of the Baltimore and Ohio Railroad where the latter line passed through Seymour, Indiana (45 miles to the north of Louisville). To its south, Louisville had a direct rail connection to Bowling Green, Kentucky. From Bowling Green, people and goods could make direct rail connection to Memphis, Tennessee.

<u>The Tennessee River</u>

On its downstream course, the Tennessee River wound westward from the mountain gaps at Chattanooga, radically changing direction at Florence, Alabama (a place nearly on the Alabama-Mississippi state line). There, the river makes a ninety degree course change to the northward, running through the states of Tennessee and Kentucky until it meets with the Ohio River near Paducah located on the northern boundary of Kentucky. According to Armroyd, the Tennessee's navigation limits in 1830 encompassed a distance of 250 miles from its mouth at the junction of the Ohio River, proceeding from there upstream to the rapids at Muscle Shoals near Florence; and from the upstream end of the Shoals, another 625 miles to the head of navigation at Tellico Block House.

The Tennessee had had a long standing history of steamboating prior to the decade of the 1860s. The first steamer to traverse its full length, was the *ATLAS* in 1828. The *ATLAS* was a small but powerful craft which made her historic trip from the river's mouth at Paducah on the Ohio, upriver to the junction of the French Broad and Holston Rivers near Knoxville, Tennessee. That first upstream journey was made under the best of seasonal river conditions, not ordinarily easy to duplicate. During most of any year, as Armroyd tells of it, the natural obstructions of Muscle Shoals, made the upper sections of the river generally impossible to reach by through traffic coming from the Ohio. Prior to around 1840, steamer traffic was only practical on a seasonal basis. According to Henry S. Tanner, in his book *Canals and Railroads of the United States,* by 1840, a canal to by-pass Muscle Shoals was in the process of completion. Tanner describes the work so far completed and already in use as, "a section 35.75 miles in length" and having dimensions of "60 feet wide at top and 42 feet wide at bottom, 6 feet deep; 16 lift and 2 guard locks overcoming an ascent of 96 feet." [4]

The town of Tuscumbia was situated at Muscle Shoals, across the river from Florence. (Tuscumbia was to become an important supply point during the Civil War.) In 1840, a Memphis and Charleston Railroad Company siding was located there. With the coming of the railroad, cargo was off-loaded there from river steamers coming up from the Ohio. The Muscle Shoals canal became obsolete when the Memphis and Charleston siding took over for most of the freight going either east to Chattanooga or west to Memphis. That railroad connection passed over the Tennessee about fifteen miles down river from Chattanooga. At the crossing of the Tennessee, a small town called Bridgeport had grown up. Even before the coming of the railroad and the partial obstruction of the channel by the bridge, navigation beyond Bridgeport toward Chattanooga was never very practical. It required considerable vessel power, accompanied by steam jenny warping, to pull vessels upstream through the fast currents racing in rock-lined flumes known as the "Boiling Pot"; "Tumbling Shoals" and "The Suck," the latter the most difficult of all. By the late 1850s, the Memphis and Charleston Railroad had pre-empted almost all commercial river traffic which previously had operated on the fifteen mile stretch of the Tennessee from Bridgeport to Chattanooga.

Upstream from Chattanooga, to Knoxville, a certain amount of river commerce was still being carried on as late as 1860, but it was not of any great significance. Above Knoxville, the French Broad River provided limited draft navigational access as far as Danbridge (about forty-five miles above Knoxville); however, very little of that took place following 1855. [5]

By 1860, waterborne transport on the Tennessee River served the economy of the area from the mouth at the Ohio upstream to Muscle Shoals. From there, for about 140 miles eastward to Chattanooga, the railroad held sway, although the river remained an ancillary mode of travel for all its length.

The Cumberland

The Cumberland River meets the Ohio at the latter's southern bank at a point fifteen miles upstream on the Ohio from where the Ohio joins with the Tennessee. On its upstream course, the Cumberland trended southward on a near parallel course with the Tennessee to a spot where both rivers approached to within a mile of each other at a narrow neck of land. Prior to the twentieth century when manmade alterations were made in the Tennessee system, this constriction was at a place on the Cumberland River referred to as "Kelly's Landing."

> Note: The Louisville-Bowling Green rail connection known as the right of way of the Memphis, Clarksville, and Louisville Railroad, crossed the Cumberland River by bridge at Clarksville and later crossed over the Tennessee River near Dover, Tennessee. Clarksville and Dover, because of the dual importance of rail and river, were to take on great strategic significance during the war. The points commanding the two mentioned bridge approaches became strong holds of the Confederate Army in their 1862 attempt to prevent Union penetration upstream on either river. Control of these points could deny access to the Memphis, Clarksville, and Louisville Railroad and to its interconnecting systems. These Confederate strong points came to be known as Fort Henry and Fort Donelson.

Upstream of Dover, the Cumberland veered away from the Tennessee, taking a course to the eastward toward Nashville.

Except during periods of low water, the head of steamboat navigation on the Cumberland at the eve of the Civil War was considered to be the town of Carthage which lays a few miles upstream from Nashville; however, during low water, moderate draft navigation on the Cumberland was limited by shoal spots located not far from Eddyville, a town quite close to the river's junction with the Ohio.

For purposes of military transportation, as it would be carried out by the Union command during the Civil War, the Cumberland was looked upon as an adjunct to the railroads. Additionally, the security of the river from Nashville downstream to Dover (near Fort Donelson) would become essential in order to safeguard the Memphis, Clarksville, and Louisville Railroad whose right-of-way paralleled and was in close proximity to the river bank between the towns of Clarksville and Dover.

The interrelationship of the Ohio River with the Cumberland and the Tennessee and their interlocking rail systems illustrates, as nothing else can, the military importance of these networks to the conduct of the Civil War west of the Allegheny Mountains.

An historian cannot adequately discuss the riverine warfare aspects of the Civil War in the west without orienting that discussion to the direct relationship that the railroads had upon the rivers. Complete military control of the rivers and of the corridors along their banks was to become essential if the railroads which penetrated the region were to be of use either to invading or to defending armies. The Tennessee and the Cumberland rivers not only complemented the railroad systems that joined Memphis, Saint Louis, Louisville, and Chattanooga, but often times, the rivers and railroads substituted one for the other. Whenever enemy cavalry raids or the activity of partisans cut the rails or destroyed the railroad bridges, as they were to do on countless occasions, the steamboats served as a substitute means of transportation for movement of troops and supplies. Only the full control of both modes, river and rail, enabled the Union armies to operate in anything but the most static of fashions. Achieving control of these lines of communication would become a major consideration as the war progressed.[6]

The Missouri System

By 1860, the head of commercial navigation on the Missouri had become Fort Lewis (later known as Fort Benton). As the river flowed, this was thirty-one hundred miles from Saint Louis.[7] From a practical standpoint, though, reliability of travel could not be counted upon upstream of Fort Pierre. By 1860, the Missouri River had become the sole logistical artery for the Army in maintaining its presence on the northern plains.

When the Civil War started, the Missouri River was sealed off from Confederate utilization by Union control of the northern Mississippi River. For the Union, the river continued to be important throughout the entire four years of war. It was the major conduit for commerce from the northwest, including the transport of gold from the newly developed Montana lodes, and would provide a means by which the Union Army could maintain its garrisons on the northern plains. The Indian problem did not diminish during the Civil War. Although there were only a few cases where the tribes developed a partisan attitude toward either side, the Indians were sophisticated enough to realize their advantage in starting offensive action when Federal troops were involved elsewhere. Actions against the eastern Plains Indians took place intermittently between 1862 and 1865; these episodes would have been far more serious had the Union Army not maintained garrisons on the Missouri River.[8]

The Arkansas River

The mouth of the Arkansas River enters the western bank of the Mississippi at a point roughly halfway between Memphis and Vicksburg. Prior to 1824, steamer penetration of the Arkansas had gone no farther than Fort Smith; however, in the spring of that year, service was extended to Three Forks, near where the Grand River and the Verdigris River met the Arkansas, this being where Cantonment Gibson was established. (Cantonment Gibson was close to what is now the city of Muskogee, Oklahoma.) The steamer *FLORENCE* had made the first trip to Three Forks carrying recruits for the Seventh Infantry Regiment.[9] By 1827, steamers were in regular use, bringing in the Indian immigrants relocated from the east.

During 1832, Congress approved an appropriation of $15,000 to improve the navigation of the Arkansas River.[10]

When the campaigns of the Mississippi basin began in 1861, most of the watershed of the Arkansas was held by the Confederacy. From the onset, it was deemed necessary to control any direct Confederate access from the Arkansas into the Mississippi. Union efforts to that end were the basis for considerable activity on the

Arkansas River in the form of expeditions conducted as early as 1861 and which continued into 1864.

The White River

The White River was often used as a substitute route for the Arkansas, the Arkansas presenting more navigational problems at times of low water than the White. During the Civil War, steamboats were able to ascend the White River to Devall's Bluff where unloading would take place onto a rail spur connecting with a river terminus near Little Rock on the Arkansas River, thus bypassing entirely the use of the Arkansas River from its mouth to Little Rock. It is unclear whether this rail spur was in place prior to 1861.

The Red River

The Red River enters the Mississippi on the latter's western bank at a point 179 miles above New Orleans and 113 miles below Vicksburg.

In its upstream course the Red River wends to the northwest diagonally bisecting the state of Louisiana. As a pathway of commerce to the west, the Red River, as early as the first decade of the 1800s, was navigable as far as Shreveport near the Texas border. North of Shreveport, there were literally miles of uprooted trees which snarled the river at its every bend. In the late 1820s, Captain Henry M. Shreve, a commercial riverboat pilot and a man with no limit of enterprise and energy, began work removing the snags. Before he was done, he had opened navigation to what is now southeastern Oklahoma.

By 1860, thanks to Shreve's efforts, the river could be navigated at high water for nearly 720 miles from its junction with the Mississippi upstream to Fort Towson in the Indian Territory.[11]

Following the Union's seizure of New Orleans in 1862, the control of the lower section of the Red River was considered to be of vital importance to Union operations since the Red River country provided a substantial amount of the supply going to besieged Vicksburg. Confederate presence, if allowed to hold sway on the lower Red River, carried with it the high probability that raids would be made into the main river by southern gunboats, a situation which clearly could not be tolerated. Union control of the Red River from Shreveport down to the river's junction with the Mississippi, would provide the key to Union domination of Louisiana and a stoppage of the flow of Confederate supply emanating out of Texas. Subsequent to the taking of Vicksburg, an expedition would be launched to accomplish that goal. That attempt, which came to be known as the Red River Expedition of 1864, would fail. The Red River country would remain in Confederate hands until the final surrenders in 1865.

APPENDIX P
SEALIFT REQUIREMENTS FOR THE INITIAL MOVEMENT OF MAJOR GENERAL GEORGE McCLELLAN'S TROOPS DURING THE 1862 PENINSULAR CAMPAIGN

A Memorandum of the different classes of vessels required for the projected expedition with the freight, passengers, etc., of each, based mainly on Mr. Tucker's Calculation, prepared by Lieutenant Colonel Rufus Ingalls, Aide de Camp and Quartermaster (as dated February 27, 1862) and sent out under the signature of the Quartermaster General.

Class of vessel	Directions for Loading
100 Barges	Each to carry 12 wagons and 200 men, with their equipment; five days rations in haversack; 1000 rations in bulk without pork - put on board where chartered; and 2000 gallons water in cask and tanks.
	Twenty-four 4-horse ambulances with horses, teamsters, etc., to be put on the schooners and barges.
150 Schooners	Each to carry 76 horses on deck, a few additional if required; under deck 20 teamsters with five days rations cooked; 9500 lb. grain; 11,000 lb. hay and 3,000 gallons water in casks and tanks. Forage and water to be put on board at place of charter; teamsters and horses at Perryville. Rendezvous at Annapolis.
16 Propellers. 200 tons each	Each to carry a battery, unlimbered on deck if possible, and 400 men; five days rations for men in haversack; five days rations, except pork, in bulk; 2,000 rations; 4,000 gallons water. The 2,000 rations and water to be put on board at place of charter.
12 Propellers	Each to carry 600 men, equipment, with five days rations in haversack; five more in bulk, say 3000 rations; 6000 gallons water. Provisions and water to be put on board at place of charter. Men, etc. at Annapolis. The 28 propellers to tow the barges to their destination.
10 Propeller - tugs	Each to assist in towing schooners with sidewheel tugs - and to act as omnibus boats to fleet.
6 large sidewheel steam tugs	Each to assist in towing schooners and to carry 400 men with equipment and five days cooked rations in haversacks; five more days in bulk, or 2000 rations, except pork; 4000 gallons water, the latter two items to be put on board at place of charter.
30 Steamers	Each to carry 700 men, their equipment; five days rations in haversacks; 3500 more in bulk, except pork; 7000 gallons water, the latter two items to be put on board at place of charter; men, etc., at Annapolis. Coal for the voyage must be provided, and on board each steam vessel. Beef on hoof for five days rations, to be shipped from Baltimore. If provisions cannot be put on each vessel as herein indicated, the amounts can be more consolidated on selected vessels of the fleet. If forage be not put on board at place of charter, it will be obtained at Perryville where the horses and wagons are now collected. All to rendezvous at Annapolis and report to Colonel Ingalls, Quartermaster.

Recapitulation: 324 vessels*; 54,828 men; 11,416 animals; 1200 wagons; 24 ambulances.

Estimated capacity of the vessels, 60,000 men. The Commissary General has today telegraphed to the Commissary at New York to deliver to the vessels as chartered in New York, and Philadelphia, 540,000 rations on your requisition.

Communicate this to Mr. Tucker and if not able to carry it out exactly, keep me informed of the necessary changes and the progress made. Colonel Ingalls will go to Annapolis today or tomorrow probably.

Respectfully, Your obedient servant.

M. C. Meigs, Quartermaster General

Source: Military History Institute; Carlisle Barracks, PA. Call No. UC323.3 - A3 (1861 - 1865).

[*An additional sixty-nine vessels were later added to meet needs.]

NOTES: ALL APPENDICES

Appendix A

[1]   George Weiss, *America's Maritime Progress,* (NY: New York Marine News Company, 1920), p 18.

[2]   Cedric Ridgely-Nevitt, *American Steamships in the Atlantic,* (Newark, DE: University of Delaware Press, 1981. The two vessels in transatlantic service were *FULTON* and *ARAGO* operated by the Havre Line.

[3]   *War of the Rebellion: Official Records of the Union and Confederate Armies,* (Washington, DC: Government Printing Office, 1880 - 1900) Facsimile Ed: (Harrisburg, PA: National Historical Society, 1971. Reprint. Historical Times, Inc., 1985), Series III, Volume 1, p 104.

[4]   The officers and men of the New York Seventh Regiment were transported for the defense of Washington but were never sworn into Federal service for that duty. Shortly thereafter, they returned to New York.

[5]   Charles Dana Gibson with E. Kay Gibson, *Marine Transportation in War, 1775- 1860,* (Camden, ME, Ensign Press, 1992), pp 89 and 99, fn 8.

[6]   Erna Risch, *Quartermaster Support of the Army: A History of the Corps 1775-1939,* (Washington, DC: Office of the Quartermaster General, 1962), p 371.

[7]   *ORA,* III, 1, p 175.

[8]   *ORA,* III, 1, pages 196, 197.

[9]   *Public Ledger,* (Philadelphia, February 12, 1863).

[10]   The net tonnage of a vessel is a volume (cubic) measurement indicating the vessel's carrying capacity. Charter rates were generally promulgated on that capacity. The foreword to Gibson and Gibson, *Dictionary of Transports and Combatant Vessels, Steam and Sail, Employed by the Union Army, 1861 - 1868,* (Ensign Press, 1995), discusses in some depth the subject of tonnage as it was applied to the chartering of vessels by the Army's quartermasters during the Civil War.

[11]   *ORA,* I, 1, pp 130, 131.

[12]   *STAR OF THE WEST* was later placed under charter to evacuate Federal troops from Texas. She was captured by the Confederates and renamed *CSS SAINT PHILIP.* She sank in the Yazoo River during 1862.

[13]   See Executive Document HR-337, *Quartermaster list, Ocean & Lake Vessels, Chartered or Otherwise Hired, pp* 149, 150 and HR-337, *Quartermaster List, Ocean and Lake Vessels, Purchased, pp* 144 and 148; Also House of Representatives Document 92, 45th Congress, 2nd Session.

[14]   Moses Taylor was the great, great grandfather of the senior author who has in his personal collection a watercolor painting of the steamship *MOSES TAYLOR* which presumably was painted shortly after that vessel's launching in 1858. Heyl (Vol. I), lists the *MOSES TAYLOR.* Eric Heyl, *Early American Steamers,* (Buffalo, NY: privately printed, 1953).

[15]   Daniel Hodas, *The Business Career of Moses Taylor,* (New York: New York University Press, 1976), pp 42, 87, 138, 191.

[16]   George W. Dalzell, *The Flight From the Flag,* (Chapel Hill: The University of North Carolina Press, 1940), pp 244-247.

Notes for Appendices B, C, and D are self contained

Appendix E

[1]   Francis H. Upton, *The Laws of Nations Affecting Commerce During War.* (New York: John S. Voorhies Law Bookseller and Publisher, 1861).

[2]   Upton, p 118.

[3]   Act of March 3, 1819- Chapter LXXVII, Recodified as of this writing as §383 *Title 33, United States Code Annotated.*

[4]   1860, 9 Op. Atty. General 455. See §383 Historical Notes, Title 33, *United States Code Annotated.*

5   *Official Records of the Union and Confederate Navies in the War of the Rebellion,* (Washington, DC: Government Printing Office, 1894 - 1917), Series I, Volume 1, p 8.

6   *ORN,* I, 1, p 85. Under this plan, each of the Spoffard, Tileston, and Company ships was to be provided with naval gun crews consisting of a gunner's mate, one quarter gunner, four able seamen, four ordinary seamen, and four landsmen.

7   Whether this offer was actually acted upon cannot be determined from a search of the records. See *ORN,* I, 1, p 393.

8   *ORN,* I, 1, pp 31, 37, 203.

9   Quartermaster General's Report of November 3, 1864, as reproduced within *ORA,* III, 4, p 891.

10   *ORN,* I, 14, pp 417, 418.

11   *Act for the Better Government of the Navy of the United States,* Chapter CCIV, Thirty-seventh Congress, Session II, July 17, 1862.

12   *ORN,* I, 23, pp 332, 333.

13   *ORN,* I, 4, p 314.

14   Daniel Ammen, *The Atlantic Coast,* (New York: Charles Scribner's Sons, 1883. Reprint, *Campaigns of the Civil War Series,* Wilmington, NC: Broadfoot Publishing Company, 1989), p 179.

15   *ORA,* III, 4, pp 891, 892.

16   *ORN,* I, 26, pp 620-623.

17   In the years following the Civil War, definitions specifically explaining the term *warship* were placed into the regulations of some governments. British Naval Regulations published in 1912 contained definitions which included the term, *ship of war,* to be understood as including all ships designated as such in the "accepted sense of the term and also auxiliary vessels of all descriptions." See Naval War College, Blue Book Series, *International Law Situations, 1930* (Washington: Government Printing Office, 1931), p 10. The United States Navy has since helped define the point when a merchant ship's status changes to one which can be considered similar to a warship. "Merchant vessels acquire enemy character and are liable to the same treatment as enemy warships when engaged in the following acts: 1.) Taking a direct part in the hostilities on the side of an enemy. 2.) Acting in any capacity as a naval or military auxiliary to an enemy's armed force." See *Law of Naval Warfare, NWIP 10-2,* Department of Navy, Office of the Chief of Naval Operations, September 1955, §501 and §503. Also, see *Law of Naval Warfare, NWP (Revision A), 1989,* Department of the Navy, for definition of naval auxiliary. *NWP (Revision A)* was released in November 1989 and was later published as part of the International Law Studies Series. See Robert J. Grunawalt, *Law of Naval Warfare-- Targeting Enemy Merchant Shipping,* (Newport, RI: Naval War College, 1993). Vol. 65.

18   Article 60, *Articles of War,* enacted April 10, 1806, by the Senate and House of Representatives.

19   James C. Neagles, *Summer Soldiers, A Survey and Index of Revolutionary War Courts Martial* (Salt Lake City, Utah: Ancestry, Incorporated, 1986).

20   See Judge Advocate General's Opinion, *Civilians Employed With Troops,* XXIII, 331. Major William Winthrop, editor, *Digest of Opinions of the Judge Advocate General of the Army,* (Washington, DC: Government Printing Office, 1868), p 84.

21   Colonel William Winthrop, USA, *Military Law and Precedent,* 2nd Edition (Washington: Government Printing Office, 1920), p 99, fn 97.

22   Winthrop, *Military Law and Precedent,* p 100, fn 4: "G.O. 7, Dept. of the Ohio 1863; Do. 126, Dept. of the South, 1864; Do. 88, Div. West Miss 1864; G.C.M.O. 26, Army of the Potomac 1864; G.O. 40, Dept. of LA. 1865."

23   *ORA,* III, 5, p 241.

24   Warren D. Crandall, editor, *History of the Ram Fleet and the Mississippi Marine Brigade in the War for the Union on the Mississippi and its Tributaries-- the Story of the Ellets and Their Men,* (St. Louis: Privately published by Society of Survivors, 1907). The history, consisting of 465 pages, was primarily the work of Crandall who was the senior editor. Crandall saw service as a commissioned officer, first becoming associated with the Ram Fleet in 1862 and then later with the Mississippi Marine Brigade beginning in late 1862 and up through most of 1864. His final service during 1865 was with the Consolidated Infantry Regiment (Army) an offshoot remnant of the by-then disbanded Mississippi Marine Brigade. While with the ram fleet and later the Brigade, Crandall served as assistant adjutant. His last assignment with the Consolidated Marine Regiment was as a company commander. Crandall's history of these organizations relates mainly to the Brigade's operations and to the personalities involved with the organization. Considerable attention is given to organizational detail including those factors dealing with the civilians who made up the crews which served on the rams as well as on the various transports and support vessels. Crandall's work includes much official correspondence concerning

control exercised over the crews. His source for this was individual officers' files which were retained by those officers. This is fortunate since, as Crandall tells us, most of the unit's records were misplaced and/or lost when the organization was disbanded at Vicksburg in 1865. As a result, little of that type of correspondence remains remnant within the *Official Records...Armies* or within National Archives Record Groups. Crandall's work is invaluable to researchers.

[25] Crandall, pp 239, 240. What position Southwick held in the Ram Fleet is unknown. The records of the Ellet Ram Fleet and of the Mississippi Marine Brigade (Record Group 92, National Archives) unfortunately hold few of the names of the civilian boatmen. Crandall's history mentions only a small part of them by name and then only in those circumstances which related to specific events which are described in his text, e.g., those in command positions during a particular action as well as some of those killed during those actions. The Crandall history contains a photographic section which portrays some of the ram fleet and Brigade veterans; but only one of the photographic montages depicts civilian boatmen, and that montage merely includes fifteen men-- those fifteen being but a very small representation of the large number of civilians who were employed in that fleet.

[26] Crandall, pp 237, 238.

[27] Crandall, p 239. *DeHart* and *Benet* who are cited in the Judge Advocate General's correspondence, refer to legal experts of that day. Also relevant to the Judge Advocate General's position on the case of the ram fleet's civilian crewmembers is II, 570 of Judge Advocate General's Opinions as published in Winthrop, *Digest of Opinions of the Judge Advocate General of the Army.*

[28] Schottenhamel cite, Copy book, Parsons Collection.

[29] General Orders 100, Article 49.

[30] Winthrop, *Military Law and Precedents*, pp 789-794.

[31] *ORA*, II, 6, p 266.

[32] *Instructions for the Government of the Armies in the Field,* General Orders, April 24, 1863. Although the April 1863 order was put into effect some months following the creation of the July 1862 cartel, before that time, it had been generally understood by both sides that those captured while performing a service in direct support of the other side's military or naval activity were considered as serving with those forces.

[33] *ORA*, II, 3, pp 241, 279, 320, 784, 826.

[34] Robert G. Albion and Jennie Barnes Pope, *Sea Lanes in Wartime, The American Experience, 1774-1945,* 2nd Edition, (Hamden, CT: Archon Books, 1968), p 166. The name of this vessel is not known, her identity by Albion and Pope given only as a "bark." Only one bark is listed in the Confederate records as taken by *CSS OLUSTEE*, that being the *EMPIRE CITY*. *EMPIRE CITY* is not listed by the Union Army Quartermaster in Executive Document HR-337 as being under quartermaster charter. It could therefore be presumed that the *EMPIRE CITY* must have been carrying Army cargo on an affreightment (space for hire) basis when she was taken by *CSS OLUSTEE*. There is also the possibility that Albion and Pope may have been mistaken and were instead referring to the crewmen off the bark *TEXANA* who were captured during 1863 and held as military prisoners in Libby Prison at Richmond. *ORA*, II, 6 has numerous entries concerning that case. *TEXANA* was a commercially employed merchant ship.

[35] There are a number of items of correspondence on the *UNION* and her crew within *ORA*, II, volumes 2, 3, and 4.

[36] *ORN*, I, 27, p 32.

[37] *ORN*, I, 26, pp 448-450.

[38] *ORN*, I, 27, pp 31, 32.

[39] *ORN*, I, 27, p 126.

[40] For reference on the employment of contrabands and other Negroes by the US Army, see: Order of the War Department, Adjutant General's office, Washington, December 10, 1863; Order signed by E. D. Townsend, Assistant Adjutant General, to be found in *ORA*, III, 3, p 1162; also *ORA*, III, 4, pp 893, 894. Vessel muster lists indicating Negro labor and their pay are contained within Quartermaster Records for 1861-1862: Record Group 92, "Burnside's Coast Division-- Vessels on North Carolina Sounds, 1861-1862." Record Group 92, Quartermaster Records: 8W2A/3/3/D/Box 6; 8W2/34/3/H; 8W2/38/9/H; 8W2/35/25/A; 8W2/34/7/ (New Berne, NC, 1 Nov. 1862). Also crew list, *J. H. BALDWIN*, at Nashville, Tennessee, Box 6.

[41] Act of May 28, 1896, entitled, *License to Officers of Vessels of the United States; Exemption from Draft, Pay, and Pensions* (c255 ,29, Stat 188). We found nothing within the legal history to indicate that the provisions of the 1896 act were employed either during the War with Spain or in any other of our subsequent wars. The Congressional Research Service, at the request of a Congressman, did a research study on the law but could find no evidence of any individual or any group applying under its provisions. There is one item of case

law in the USCA relating to a seaman attempting relief from Selective Service following World War II, but the court denied him relief since his petition involved a period when the United States was not at war.

Appendix F
1   Patricia L. Faust, Ed., *Historical Times Illustrated Encyclopedia of the Civil War*, (New York: Harper and Row, 1986), p 324.
2   *ORA*, I, 5, p 979.
3   *ORA*, I, 5, p 1038.

Appendix G
1   Robert G. Athearn, *Forts of the Upper Missouri*, (Englewood Cliffs, NJ: Prentis Hall, 1967.)
2   *ORA*, I, 22, Part II, pp 304, 305.
3   *ORA*, I, 34, Part III, p 33.
4   Besides trouble with the Sioux, hostilities were also erupting with the Cheyenne tribe on the Southern Great Plains. *ORA*, I, 34, Part III, pp 218, 219.
5   Report of H. H. Sibley, dated April 3, 1864, from *ORA*, I, 34, Part III, pp 33, 34.
6   Robert M. Utley, *Frontiersmen in Blue; The U. S. Army and the Indian, 1848-1865*, (New York: MacMillan Publishing Co., 1967).
7   *ORA*, I, 34, Part II, pp 109, 110.
8   The necessity to provide grain for cavalry mounts restricted the Army's mobility against the Great Plains Indians. Once cavalry columns had absented themselves from the support of steamboats, grain had to be transported with the columns by wagon. Wagons badly slowed cavalry on the pursuit, making it nearly impossible for the Army to overtake retreating bands of Indians. On more than one instance during the long years of the Indian wars, cavalry units were rendered ineffective as the horses progressively gave out through lack of adequate nutrition.
9   The loss of *ISLAND CITY* had taken the entirety of the corn supply that had been brought upriver as feed for the cavalry mounts. That loss severely shortened Sully's time in the field. Sources: *ORA*, I, 41, Part I, p 147. Joseph Mills Hanson, *The Conquest of the Missouri*, (New York and Toronto: Murray Hill Books, Inc., 1909).
10   *ORA*, I, 41, Part I, p 139.
11   *ORA*, I, 41, Part I, pp 152-155, contains Sully's full report.

Appendix H has no notes

Appendix I
1   Bartlett's organization should not be confused with another Army unit which had amphibious employment around this time, namely, the 1st New York Marine Artillery "Naval Brigade", which was mustered into federal service on November 12, 1861. Detachments of both of these organizations were assigned to Army gunboats on the Carolina sounds, a circumstance which has been the main reason for confusion between the two organizations. The 1st New York Marine Artillery was, however, short-lived, being disbanded in March of 1863 following some severe disciplinary problems on the part of its enlisted members. On the other hand, the 99th New York Infantry served throughout the war, doing so with relative distinction.
2   The Navy converted the *USS SOUTHFIELD* and *USS HUNCHBACK* from civilian ferryboats into gunboats.
3   *ORA*, I, 29, Part II, pp 58-60.
4   *ORA*, I, 29, Part II, p 48.
5   If the unit history is correct, and "25 or 30" of those taken prisoner from the *SMITH BRIGGS* actually died at Andersonville Prison, this would have meant a near total mortality of those men taken prisoner.
6   *ORN*, I, 8, pp 104,109, 129, 250; also *ORN*, I, 7. Also see Frederick H. Dyer, *A Compendium of the War of the Rebellion*, (Dayton, OH: The Press of Morningside Bookshop, 1978), which references detached duty personnel from the 4th Rhode Island Infantry and the 9th New Jersey Infantry.

Appendix J
1   *ORA*, I, 51, Part I, pp 197-200. The basic material for a telegraph network, namely the wire itself, seems to have been made available in such abundance that superfluous coils of it were used to form an entanglement in front of Butler's defensive positions on the Chesterfield Peninsula. This was done with the aim of funneling

attackers into narrow approach paths, increasing their vulnerability to defensive fire. (At this time, barbed wire had yet to be invented.) Robertson, p 193.

[2] It would not be until following the Civil War in 1866 that a reliable underwater telegraph system would span the Atlantic.

[3] *ORA*, I, 36, Part 2, pp 800, 830, contains mention of the Potomac underwater telegraph cable that was in use by May of 1864.

[4] *ORN*, I, 10, pp 279, 280.

[5] The Navy also had a strong presence within the Chesapeake Bay estuaries, and its use of the military telegraph added significantly to the volume of wireless messages flowing back and forth to Washington.

[6] The 63rd Congress recognized the contribution of the civilian operators of the Military Telegraph Service by awarding to surviving telegraphers (or their widows) military pensions for Civil War service.

[7] For a detailed discussion of the use of telegraphy by both sides during the Civil War, see William R. Plum, *The Military Telegraph During the Civil War in the United States*, (2 volumes; Chicago: Jansen McClurg and Company, Chicago, 1882). Plum included a section on cryptography systems then in use.

Appendix K

[1] *ORA*, I, 6, pp 176, 177.

[2] Act of July 17, 1862.

[3] E. B. Long with Barbara Long, *The Civil War Day by Day - An Almanac, 1861-1865*, (New York: DaCapo under arrangement with Doubleday, 1971), p 251.

[4] P. J. Staudenraus, *The African Colonization Movement, 1816-1865*, (New York: Columbia University Press, 1961). The political structure in Liberia, as established by the American Negro migrants, remained in place until the 1970s when a military junta overthrew the establishment. Since that time Liberia has degenerated, both socially and economically, through a series of blood baths which have returned the nation to something akin to the primitive tribal structure in place prior to the beginning of colonization in 1817.

[5] *House Report of the Committee on Emancipation and Colonization*, House Report 148, 37th Congress, 2nd Session.

[6] Willis D. Boyd, "Ile a Vache Colonization Venture, 1862 - 1864." *Americas*, Vol. 16, July 1959 p 47.

[7] Boyd, p 50.

[8] Four hundred fifty-three Negroes would actually be shipped to Ile a Vache. Most were in their twenties with males outnumbering females three to one.

[9] Nothing could be found by the authors to indicate which department of the government chartered *OCEAN RANGER* to transport the Ile a Vache colonists. Presumably, the responsibility would have fallen on the Quartermaster Department of the Army, but that is only conjecture.

[10] In the Army orders cut to charter the *MARCIA C. DAY*, the vessel was incorrectly identified as the *MARIA L. DAY*. See *ORA*, III, 4, pp 75-77.

Appendix L

[1] John A. Lynn, editor, *Feeding Mars, Logistics in Western Warfare from the Middle Wages to the Present*, (San Francisco and Oxford: Westview Press, 1993), 167.

[2] Louis Philippe d'Orleans, *History of the Civil War in America*, (Philadelphia: Porter and Coates Publisher, 1875), vol. 1, 212, 213. Reproduced in Huston, p 216.

[3] *ORA*, III, 5, p 314.

[4] Robert M. Browning, Jr., *From Cape Charles to Cape Fear. The North Atlantic Blockading Squadron During the Civil War* (Tuscaloosa: University of Alabama Press, 1993) 177.

[5] Risch, pp 384, 385, 449.

[6] "Document 56," Quartermaster Records, Record Group 92, National Archives.

[7] George W. Dalzell, *The Flight from the Flag*, (Chapel Hill, NC: University of North Carolina, 1940), 119.

[8] James A. Huston, *The Sinews of War: Army Logistics, 1775 - 1953*, (Army Historical Series. Washington, DC: Office of the Chief of Military History, 1966), p 230.

[9] Paul W. Gates, *Agriculture and the Civil War*, (New York: Alfred A. Knopf, 1965), p 135.

[10] John H. Thompson, ed, *Geography of New York State*, (Syracuse, NY: Syracuse University Press, 1966).

[11] William P. Hedrick, *A History of Agriculture in the State of New York*, (Albany, NY: New York Agricultural Society, 1933), p 344

[12] Gates, p 235.

[13]   R. Douglas Hurt, *American Farm Tools: From Hand-Power to Steam-Power,* (Manhattan, KS: Sunflower University Press, 1982), pp 84-95. Also Gates, p 236.

[14]   In the early 1850s, steam tugs were introduced on the Erie Canal, but their use was not extensive since a 4-mile per hour speed limit was enforced in order to prevent damage to the canal's banks. Speed averages for horse drawn canal boats was 2-miles per hour, so to a limited extent, steam towboats did increase efficiency, but not to an extent where the economics balanced out since steam towboats of that era were capable of far greater speeds. George E. Condon, *Stars in the Water, The Story of the Erie Canal,* (Garden City, NY: Doubleday and Co., 1974), p 230.

[15]   By 1861, the upper Hudson Valley and the Harlem Valley together were providing Manhattan not only with animal forage and grains for its breweries, but with livestock for slaughter, dairy products, assorted market garden items, not to mention huge quantities of ice which had been cut from upstate lakes and ponds and then stored during the cold months of winter. Louis V. Grogan, *The Coming of the New York and Harlem Valley Railroad,* (Pawling, NY: privately published, 1989), pp 14-21.

[16]   Gates pp 132, 133, states that the many advantages of baling hay and the higher prices received for it resulted in the hay press being widely adopted prior to the beginning of the Civil War. On his page 134, in regard to the use of hay presses in the west, Gates states that in 1861 flat boats loaded with baled hay were regularly arriving at New Orleans from upriver. Hay arrivals in two days alone amounted to nineteen hundred tons of baled hay. On a nationwide basis, Gates concludes that by 1861 the demand for hay (civilian and military demand) was well over "half a million tons.

[17]   Correspondence with senior author from Frank G. White, Curator of Mechanical Arts, Old Sturbridge Village, Sturbridge, MA, February 2, 1993. Mr. White enclosed p 61 of this catalog.

[18]   *Nourse, Mason and Co.'s Illustrated Catalog of 1857*, pp 14, 15, from the collection of the library at Old Sturbridge Village.

[19]   Hurt, pp 95, 96.

[20]   One system employed in the baling (pressing) of hay-- at least in northern New England-- is described by Eleanor M. Richardson in her book *North Haven Summers, An Oral History* (Andover, MA: privately published). On page 96, she quotes from an interview with one "Garry" [sic]. Norton who remembered that as late as the First World War, farmers producing hay on the Maine islands would bring wagon loads of loose hay to wharves to await schooners which were equipped with "balers." The schooner captains would pay cash to the farmers for the wagon loads of hay which the schooner crews would then bale. The bales would then be transported to urban areas for sale. Whether buyers of hay whose places of business were canal or river boats traveling the New York waterways employed a similar purchasing method during the 1860s is not known, but it is probable that some of them did.

[21]   Gates, while attempting to arrive at the wartime hay production of Hudson Valley farms, complains of the difficulty of arriving at such figures through the Census. However, utilizing as his sources the agricultural magazine *Country Gentleman* of March 1862 and the *New York State Business Directory* of 1864, he estimates that seven Hudson and Catskill counties produced 712,000 tons of hay in 1863.

[22]   *Biographical Review, The Leading Citizens of Columbia County, New York,* (Boston: Biographical Review Publishing Company, 1894), p 188.

[23]   After the Civil War, Michael continued to grow hay as one of his primary cash crops in company with crops of rye and buckwheat. The Michael house, still in excellent repair, is no longer in the Michael family. Its new owners operate it as a bed and breakfast. The original farm lands have been broken up over the years and are now in a number of separate parcels, being utilized as residential properties. Kenneth Piester, "Winter 1890 - A Columbia County Farmer's Diary," *Roe Jan Independent*, December 1986. Also personal observations made in 1994 by the author.

[24]   *ORA,* I, 40, Part II, p 463.

[25]   *ORA,* I, 44, p 75.

[26]   *ORA,* I, 46, Part 2, p 82.

Appendix M has no notes.

Notes for Appendix N are self contained

Appendix O
[1]   George Armroyd, *The Whole Internal Navigation of the United States,* (New York: Burt Franklin, 1830, reprint Lenox Hill, 1971).

[2]   Harry P. Owens, *Steamboats and the Cotton Economy,* (Jackson, MS: University Press of Mississippi, 1990).

[3]   Erik Haites, James Mak, and Gary Walton, *Western River Transportation, The Era of Early Internal Development, 1810-1860,* (Baltimore, MD: The Johns Hopkins University Press, 1975), p 92.

[4]   Henry S. Tanner, *Canals and Railroads of the United States,* (reprint, New York: Augustus M. Kelley Publishers, 1970) We could find no evidence that this canal was still in use, or even in existence, by the time the Civil War began. During the war, there was little through-steamboat traffic over the Muscle Shoals, especially in an upstream direction..

[5]   J. Haden Alldredge, Mildred Burnham Spottswood, Vera V. Anderson, John H. Goff, Robert M. LaFarge, *A History of Navigation on the Tennessee River System,* (Washington: Transportation Economics Division, Tennessee Valley Authority, Government Printing Office, 1937), p 9.

[6]   The dual utilization of river and rail was of special value during Sherman's invasion into Georgia up to the point when he took Atlanta. His march to the sea was independent of a logistical tail. Sherman's subsequent thrust northward through the Carolinas, obtained almost all of its provender from an armada of transports which offloaded at various ports along the Carolina coasts.

[7]   William E. Lass, *Steamboating on the Upper Missouri River* (Lincoln, NE: University of Nebraska Press, 1962), p 19. Lass's source was a report of Charles P. Chouteaux contained within Contributions to the Historical Society of Montana, VII, p 256. The steamers that established the then historic head of navigation had been the *CHIPPEWA* and the *KEY WEST* which reached that place on July 2, 1860.

[8]   The worst of the Indian troubles took place in Minnesota during 1862 when the Sioux rose en masse, inflicting high casualties against white settlers. Later, during 1864, campaigns would take place involving troop and supply movement. These relied heavily on the Missouri River.

[9]   Brad Agnew, *Fort Gibson,* (Norman, OK: University of Oklahoma Press, 1980), p 33. Agnew's source was the *Arkansas Gazette,* May 11, 1864.

[10]   Agnew, p 39. By 1832, the Army had its own steam vessel on the Arkansas. It was described as "a red colored craft" used to patrol against the traffic in illegal whiskey flowing to the Indians.

[11]   In 1827, President John Quincy Adams appointed Henry Miller Shreve to the position of "Superintendent of Western River Improvements." Shreve developed a steam powered snag-pulling device which he then mounted on the snag boat *HELIOPOLIS.* Michael Allen, *Western Rivermen, 1763 - 1861* (Baton Rouge: Louisiana State University Press, 1990), p 158.

Notes for Appendix P are self contained.

BIBLIOGRAPHY UTILIZED IN THE PREPARATION OF
ASSAULT AND LOGISTICS

PRIMARY

Battles and Leaders of the Civil War. Being for the most part contributions by Union and Confederate officers. Based upon the Century War Series. 4 volumes. New York: The Century Company, 1884-1888.

Bellard, Alfred. *Gone For a Soldier: The Civil War Memoirs of Private Alfred Bellard.* From the Alec Thomas Archives, edited by David Herbert Donald. Boston: Little, Brown, and Co., 1975.

Civil War Letters of Sergeant Onley Andrus. Fred L. Shannon, editor. Urbana, IL: Illinois Studies in the Social Sciences, 1947.

Civil War Reminiscences of General M. Jeff Thompson. Donald J. Stanton, Goodwin F. Berquist, and Paul C. Bowers, editors. Dayton: Morningside, 1988.

Crandall, Warren D. *History of the Ram Fleet and the Mississippi Marine Brigade in the War for the Union on the Mississippi and its Tributaries: The Story of the Ellets and Their Men.* St. Louis: Privately published by the Society of Survivors, 1907. (Crandall, a former officer of both the Ram Fleet and the Mississippi Marine Brigade, was given access to the Ellet papers then being held by the Ellet family.)

Higginson, Thomas W. *Army Life in a Black Regiment.* Republished Boston: Beacon Press, 1962.

History of the 99th New York Volunteers. Philip Corell, editor. (Corell was the unit's historian.) New York: Regimental Veterans Association, 1905. Monograph held on microfilm at Brown University Library, Providence, RI.

LeDuc, William G. *Recollections of a Civil War Quartermaster.* St. Paul: North Central Publishing Co., 1963.

Selfridge, Thomas O. *Memoirs of Thomas O. Selfridge.* New York and London: G. P. Putnam, Sons, 1924.

Sherman, William Tecumseh. *Memoirs of General W. T. Sherman.* Literary Classics of the United States. New York: The Library of America, 1990.

Stein, Douglas L. *American Maritime Documents, 1776 - 1860.* Mystic: Mystic Seaport Museum, 1992.

The Conduct of Federal Troops in Louisiana During the Invasions of 1863 and 1864: Official Report. Compiled from sworn testimony, under direction of Governor Henry W. Allen, Shreveport, April 1865. David C. Edmonds, editor. Reprint, Lafayette, LA: Acadiana Press, 1988.

Warfare Along the Mississippi: The Letters of Lieutenant Colonel George E. Currie. Norman E. Clarke, Sr., editor. Clarke Historical Collection. Ann Arbor: Edwards Brothers, 1961.

Welles, Gideon. *Diary of Gideon Welles, Secretary of the Navy Under Lincoln and Johnson.* 3 vols. Boston: Houghton Mifflin Company, 1911.

Welles, Gideon. *Diary of Gideon Welles.* Beale, Howard K., editor. 3 vols. New York: W. W. Norton and Company, Inc., 1960.

Note regarding the Welles diary: In the 1870s, Welles revised his original circa 1860s diary entries, making comments in retrospect. The 1960 Beale edited publication reproduces the original diary entries as well as those retrospective addenda made in the 1870s.

Wilkeson, Frank. *Recollections of a Private Soldier in the Army of the Potomac.* New York: G. P. Putnam's Sons, The Knickerbocker Press, 1887.

GOVERNMENT DOCUMENTS

Act for Better Government of the Navy of the United States. Chapter CCIV, Thirty-seventh Congress, Session II, July 17, 1862.

American State Papers. Naval Affairs, i. (Relative to legal precedents, status of civilian seamen.)

Articles of War enacted April 10, 1806. (Relative to legal precedents, status of civilian seamen.)

Davis, Major George B., Leslie J. Perry, Joseph W. Kirkley. *Atlas to Accompany the Official Records of the Union and Confederate Armies.* Washington, DC: Government Printing Office, 1891-1895. Published in facsimile as *The Official Military Atlas of the Civil War.* New York: Fairfax Press, 1983.

Executive Document 337, House of Representatives, 40th Congress, Second Session.

Executive Document 92, 45th congress, Second Session.

General Orders 100, April 24, 1863. *Instructions for the Government of the Armies of the United States in the Field (The 'Lieber Code')*

House Executive Document, 37th Congress, Second Session, Vol. VII, No. 94.

Indexes to Compiled Service Records of Volunteer Union Soldiers Who Served in Organizations Not Raised by States or Territories. Microfilm: NEPS-1W1, National Archives. (1st New York Marine Artillery; 99th New York Infantry, Union Coast Guard; 3rd Pennsylvania Heavy Artillery).

Judge Advocate General of the Army. *Military Laws of the United States.* 8th edition, annotated. Washington, DC: Government Printing Office, 1940.

Log of the DIANA. On microfilm, held by Clarke Historical Library, Central Michigan University, Mt. Pleasant, MI.

Message of the President of the United States to the Two Houses of Congress at the Commencement of the Third Session of the Thirty-seventh Congress. Executive Document No. 1. Volume III. Washington: GPO, 1862.

Mississippi Marine Brigade and Ram Fleet, RG 94, Records of the Office of the Adjutant General, Microfilm 1290, Rolls 33, 34, 35

Mississippi Marine Brigade Records, Microfilm ID No. 63-08-12-63, Order Book Correspondence for August 12, 1863. National Archives

Mississippi Marine Brigade, Regimental Order Book, Rosters, Miscellaneous Record Group 94, Microfilm 231, Roll 56 held by National Archives.

Official Records of the Union and Confederate Navies in the War of the Rebellion. Series I and II, 31 vols. Washington, DC: Government Printing Office, under the Supervision of the Secretary of the Navy, 1894 - 1917.

Preliminary Inventory of the Textual Records of the Office of the Quartermaster General. National Archives, Record Group 92, Compiled by Maizie H. Johnson, May 1967. (A listing by file numbers of Quartermaster records, inclusive of related shipping during period 1861 - 1868 which was used to locate specific records, the further identification of which is reflected in our notes.)

Quartermaster General's Office, Washington, DC, August 1865 Introduction for report of the fiscal year ending June 30, 1865, relative to the operations of the three division in charge of the ocean and lake transportation of the Quartermaster Department.

Quartermaster Records for 1861-1862. National Archives, Record Group 92, "Burnside's Coast Division -- Vessels on North Carolina Sounds, 1861-62," 8W2A/3/3/D/Box 6; 8W2/34/3/H; 8W2/38/9/H; 8W2/35/25/A; 8W2/34/7/ (New Bern, NC, 1 Nov 1862). Also crew list, *J. H. BALDWIN*, at Nashville, Tennessee, Box 6.

Report of the Joint Committee on the Conduct of War. 38th Congress, 2nd Session. Washington: GPO, 1865.

Report of the Joint Committee on the Conduct of War, in 3 parts. House of Representatives, 37th Congress, 3rd Session. Washington: GPO, 1863.

Report of the Quartermaster General (Report No. 28). Executive Documents, House of Representatives, First Session, 39th Congress.

Reports of the Committee on the Conduct of the War on the Attack on Petersburg on the 30th Day of July 1864. Report No. 114. Senate, 38th Congress, 2nd Session. Washington: GPO, 1865.

Reports of the Committee on the Conduct of War. "Fort Pillow Massacre: Returned Prisoners." Report No. 63. Senate, 38th Congress, 1st Session. Washington: GPO, 1865.

Revised United States Army Regulations of 1861. Washington: GPO, 1863.

Special List No. 22, List of American-flag Merchant Vessels that Received Certificates of Enrollment or Registry at the Port of New York, 1789-1867. Volumes I and II. Washington: National Archives, 1968.

Steamboats Built in the United States During and Including the Year 1807-1856. Washington: Compiled by the U. S. Department of Commerce, Bureau of Navigation, 1931.

Supplemental Report of the Joint Committee on the Conduct of War, Volume II. Supplemental to Report No. 142, 38th Congress, 2nd Session. Washington: GPO, 1866.

Trial of the Officers and Crew of the Privateer SAVANNAH on the Charge of Piracy. U. S. Circuit Court for Southern District of New York (Judges Nelson and Shipman, presiding). New York: Baker and Goodwin, 1862.

U. S. Congress. *House Journal*, 20th Congress, 1st Session.

U. S. Congress. *Senate Document, i.* No. 1, 21st Congress, 1st Session.

U. S. Congress. The Reports of the Secretary of War for the Civil War Period. Attachments of the Report of the Quartermaster to the Secretary of War.

U. S. *Congressional Record.* House 5375, May 18, 1896. (Relative to Appendix E.)

U. S. *Statutes at Large*: i, ii, iv, xxvii.

United States v Winchester. Supreme Court of the United States (99 U.S. 372; 25L Ed. 479) Also (174 U.S. 778; 43 L Ed. 1169) Also *United States vs 269 ½ Bales of Cotton,* Woolworth 236.

War of the Rebellion: Official Records of the Union and Confederate Armies. Series I - IV. 70 vols., 130 bindings. Washington, DC: Government Printing Office, under supervision of the Secretary of War, 1880 - 1900.

Winthrop, Colonel William. *Military Law and Precedents.* 2nd edition. Washington: Government Printing Office, 1920.

Winthrop, Major W. *Digest of Opinions of the Judge Advocate General of the Army.* Washington, DC: Government Printing Office, 1868.

SECONDARY

Abdill, George B. *Civil War Railroads.* New York: Bonanza Books, 1961.

Agnew, Brad. *Fort Gibson.* Norman, OK: University of Oklahoma Press, 1980. (Relative to Appendix O.)

Albion, Robert G. and Jennie Barnes Pope. *Sea Lanes in Wartime, The American Experience, 1774 - 1945.* 2nd edition. Hamden, CT: Archon Books, 1968.

Alldredge, J. Haden; Mildred Burnham Spotswood; Vera V. Anderson; John H. Goff; Robert M. LaFarge. *A History of Navigation on the Tennessee River System.* Washington: (Tennessee Valley Authority), Government Printing Office, 1937.

Allen, Michael. *Western Rivermen, 1763-1861.* Baton Rouge, LA: Louisiana State University Press, 1990. (Relative to Appendix O.)

Ammen, Daniel. *The Atlantic Coast.* New York: Charles Scribner's Sons, 1883. Reprint, *Campaigns of the Civil War Series,* Wilmington, NC: Broadfoot Publishing Company, 1989.

Armroyd, George. *The Whole Internal Navigation of the United States.* Reprint, New York: Lenox Hill, 1971.

Assault From the Sea: Essays on the History of Amphibious Warfare. Lt. Col. Merril L., Bartlett, editor. Annapolis: Naval Institute Press, 1983.

Athearn, Robert G. *Forts of the Upper Missouri.* Englewood Cliffs, NJ: Prentiss Hall, 1967.

Baldwin, Leland D. *The Keelboat Age on Western Waters.* Pittsburgh: University of Pittsburgh Press, 1980. (Relative to Appendix O.)

Barriger, John W. *Railroads in the Civil War* (an address). Reprinted from the Bulletin of the National Railway Historical Society, Vol. 31, November 6, 1966.

Barton, O. S. *Three Years with Quantrill.* Norman, OK: University of Oklahoma Press, 1992.

Bearss, Edwin C. *Hardluck Ironclad: The Sinking and Salvage of the CAIRO.* Baton Rouge: Louisiana State Univ. Press, 1980.

Black, Robert C., III. *The Railroads of the Confederacy.* Wilmington, NC: Broadfoot Publishing Co., 1987.

Boorstin, Daniel J. *The Americans: The National Experience.* New York: Random House, 1965.

Boykin, Edward. *Ghost Ship of the Confederacy: The Story of the Alabama and Her Captain, Raphael Semmes.* New York: Funk & Wagnall's, 1957.

Brown, Alexander Crosby. *Juniper Waterway: A History of the Albemarle and Chesapeake Canal.* Charlottesville: University Press of Virginia, 1981.

Brown, Alexander Crosby. *The Dismal Swamp Canal.* Chesapeake, VA: Norfolk County Historical Society, 1970.

Brown, Dee. *The Galvanized Yankees.* Lincoln: University of Nebraska Press, 1963.

Browning, Robert M., Jr. *From Cape Charles to Cape Fear: The North Atlantic Blockading Squadron During the Civil War.* Tuscaloosa: University of Alabama Press, 1993.

Bukar, George E. *Blockaders, Refugees, and Contrabands. Civil War on Florida's Gulf Coast.* Tuscaloosa: University of Alabama Press, 1993.

Burchard, Peter. *We'll Stand By the Union: Robert Gould Shaw and the Black 54th Massachusetts Regiment.* New York: Facts on File, Inc., 1993.

Carroll, John M. *Custer in Texas: An Interrupted Narrative.* New York: Sol Lewis and Liveright, 1975.

Carse, Robert. *Hilton Head Island in the Civil War: Department of the South.* Columbia, SC: Hilton Head Historical Society, 1976.

Carter, Samuel, III. *The Final Fortress: The Campaign for Vicksburg, 1862 - 1863.* Wilmington, NC: Broadfoot Publishing, 1988.

Catton, Bruce. *A Stillness at Appomattox.* Garden City, NY: Doubleday & Co., 1956.

Catton, Bruce. *Glory Road: The Bloody Route From Fredericksburg to Gettysburg.* Garden City, NY: Doubleday & Co., 1952.

Catton, Bruce. *Grant Takes Command.* Boston: Little, Brown & Co., 1968.

Catton, Bruce. *Never Call Retreat.* The Centennial History of the Civil War, vol. 3. Garden City, NY: Doubleday & Co., 1965.

Catton, Bruce. *Terrible Swift Sword.* The Centennial History of the Civil War, vol. 2. Garden City, NY: Doubleday & Co., 1963.

Catton, Bruce. *The Coming Fury.* The Centennial History of the Civil War, vol. 1. Garden City, NY: Doubleday & Co., 1961.

Catton, Bruce. *This Hallowed Ground: A Story of the Union Side of the Civil War.* Garden City, NY: Doubleday & Co., 1956.

Cist, Henry M. *The Army of the Cumberland.* New York: Charles Scribner's Sons, 1882. Reprint, *Campaigns of the Civil War Series*, Wilmington, NC: Broadfoot Publishing Company, 1989

Civil War Naval Chronology 1861 - 1865. Compiled by Naval History Division, Navy Department. Washington, DC: U. S. Government Printing Office, 1971.

Civil War Papers of George B. McClellan: Selected Correspondence, 1860-1865. Stephen W., Sears, editor. New York: Ticknor & Fields, 1989.

Civil War Times in St. Augustine. Jacqueline K. Fretwell, editor. St. Augustine, FL: St. Augustine Historical Society, 1988.

Condon, George E. *Stars in the Water, The Story of the Erie Canal.* Garden City, NY: Doubleday and Co., 1974. (Relative to Appendix L.)

Cooling, Benjamin Franklin. *Forts Henry and Donelson: The Key to the Confederate Heartland.* Knoxville: University of Tennessee Press, 1987.

Cornish, Dudley Taylor. *The Sable Arm: Black Troops in the Union Army, 1861 - 1865.* Reprint, Modern War Studies, Lawrence: University Press of Kansas, 1987.

Cox, Jacob D. *The March to the Sea -- Franklin and Nashville.* New York: Charles Scribner's Sons, 1882. Reprint, *Campaigns of the Civil War Series*, Wilmington, NC: Broadfoot Publishing Company, 1989

Dalzell, George W. *The Flight From the Flag.* Chapel Hill: The University of North Carolina Press, 1940.

Davis, Burke. *Sherman's March.* New York: Random House, 1980.

Davis, Nora M. *Military and Naval Operations in South Carolina, 1860-1865.* Columbia, SC: South Carolina Archives Department, South Carolina Confederate War Centennial Commission, 1959.

Dictionary of American Naval Fighting Ships. 8 vols. Washington, DC: Naval Historical Center, Department of the Navy, 1969 through 1981.

Donovan, Timothy H., Jr.; Roy K. Flint; Arthur V. Grant; Gerald P. Stadler. *The American Civil War.* The West Point Military History Series. Wayne, NJ: Avery Publishing Group, 1987.

Dufour, Charles L. *The Night the War Was Lost.* Lincoln NE: University of Nebraska Press, 1990.

Dyer, Frederick H. *A Compendium of the War of the Rebellion.* 1908. Reprint. Dayton, OH: The Press of Morningside Bookshop, 1978.

Elliot, James W. *Transport to Disaster.* New York: Holt, Rinehart, & Winston, 1962.

Feeding Mars: Logistics in Western Warfare From the Middle Ages to the Present. John A. Lynn, editor. San Francisco and Oxford: Westview Press, 1993.

Fellman, Michael. *Inside War: The Guerrilla Conflict in Missouri During the American Civil War.* New York: Oxford University Press, 1989.

Foner, Eric. *Nothing But Freedom: Emancipation and its Legacy.* The Walter Lynwood Fleming Lectures in Southern History, Louisiana State University. Baton Rouge: Louisiana State Univ. Press, 1983.

Foner, Eric. *Reconstruction: America's Unfinished Revolution, 1863-1877.* New York: Harper and Rowe, 1988.

Force, M. F. *From Fort Henry to Corinth.* New York: Charles Scribner's Sons, 1881. Reprint, *Campaigns of the Civil War Series*, Wilmington, NC: Broadfoot Publishing Company, 1989

Frassanito, William A. *Grant and Lee: The Virginia Campaigns 1864 - 1865.* New York: Charles Scribner's Sons, 1983.

Freeman, Michael. *Inside War.* New York: Oxford University Press, 1989.

Gates, Paul W. *Agriculture and the Civil War.* New York: Alfred A. Knopf, 1965. (Relative to Appendix L.)

Geography of New York State. Edited by John H. Thompson. Syracuse: Syracuse University Press, 1966. (Relative to Appendix L.)

Gibson, Charles Dana and E. Kay Gibson. *Dictionary of Transports and Combatant Vessels, Steam and Sail, Employed by the Union Army, 1861 - 1868.* Camden, ME: Ensign Press, 1995.

Gibson, Charles Dana. *Boca Grande, A Series of Historical Essays.* St. Petersburg, FL: Great Outdoors Publishing Co., 1982.

Gibson, Charles Dana. *Merchantman? Or Ship of War.* Camden, ME: Ensign Press, 1986. (Relative to Appendix E.)

Gillett, Mary C. *The Army Medical Department, 1818 - 1865.* Army Historical Series. Washington, DC: Center of Military History, 1987.

Glasson, William H. *Federal Military Pensions in the United States.* 1918 Washington, DC: U. S. Navy Library, Old Navy Yard. Recopied.

Glatthaar, Joseph T. *Forged in Battle: The Civil War Alliance of Black Soldiers and White Officers.* New York: MacMillan, The Free Press, 1990.

Glatthaar, Joseph T. *The March to the Sea and Beyond: Sherman's Troops in the Savannah and Carolina Campaigns.* The American Social Experience Series, vol. 1. New York: New York University Press, 1986.

Goff, Richard D. *Confederate Supply.* Durham: Duke University Press, 1969.

Gosnell, H. Allen. *Guns on the Western Waters: The Story of River Gunboats in the Civil War.* Baton Rouge: Louisiana State University Press, 1949.

Gragg, Rod. *Confederate Goliath: The Battle of Fort Fisher.* New York: Harper Collins, 1991.

Greene, Francis Vinton. *The Mississippi.* New York: Charles Scribner's Sons, 1882. Reprint, Campaigns of The Civil War, Wilmington, NC: Broadfoot Publishing Co., 1989.

Grogan, Louis V. *The Coming of the New York and Harlem Railroad.* Pawling, NY: Louis V. Grogan, 1989. (Relative to Appendix L.)

Grunawalt, Robert J. *The Law of Naval Warfare: Targeting Enemy Merchant Shipping.* International Law Studies, Vol. 65. Newport, RI: Naval War College, 1993. (Relative to Appendix E.)

Haites, Erik; James Mak; Gary Walton. *Western River Transportation, The Era of Early Internal Development, 1810-1860.* Baltimore, MD: Johns Hopkins University Press, 1975. (Relative to Appendix O.)

Hanson, Joseph Mills. *The Conquest of the Missouri.* 1909. Reprint. New York: Murray Hill Books, 1946.

Haythornthwaite, Philip Jr. *Uniforms of the Civil War.* MacMillan Color Series. New York: MacMillan Publishing Co., 1975.

Hedrick, Ulysses Prentiss. *A History of Agriculture in the State of New York.* Albany: The New York State Agricultural Society, 1933. (Relative to Appendix L.)

Heyl, Eric. *Early American Steamers.* 6 volumes. Privately published, Buffalo, NY, 1953-1969.

Hilliard, Sam Bowers. *Hogmeat and Hoecake: Food Supply in the Old South, 1840 - 1860.* Carbondale: Southern Illinois University Press; Feffer and Simons, 1972.

Historical Times Illustrated Encyclopedia of the Civil War. Patricia L. Faust, editor. New York: Harper and Row, 1986.

History of the Confederate States Navy from Its Organization to the Surrender of Its Last Vessel. Thomas J. Sharf, editor. New York: Rogers and Sherwood, 1887. Facsimile Reprint. New York: Crown Publishers, Fairfax Press, 1977.

Humphreys, A. A. *The Virginia Campaign of 1864 and 1865.* New York: Charles Scribner's Sons, 1883. Reprint, *Campaigns of the Civil War Series*, Wilmington, NC: Broadfoot Publishing Company, 1989

Hurt, R. Douglas. *American Farm Tools: From Hand-Power to Steam-Power.* Manhattan, KS: Sunflower University Press, 1982. (Relative to Appendix L.)

Huston, James A. *The Sinews of War: Army Logistics, 1775 - 1953.* Army Historical Series. Washington, DC: Office of the Chief of Military History, 1966.

International Law Situations, 1930. Blue Book Series. Washington, DC: Naval War College; Government Printing Office, 1931.

Johns, John E. *Florida During the Civil War.* Gainesville: University of Florida Press, 1963.

Johnson, Ludwell H. *Red River Campaign: Politics and Cotton in the Civil War.* Baltimore, MD: Johns Hopkins University Press, 1958.

Jones, Robert Huhn. *The Civil War in the Northwest: Nebraska, Wisconsin, Iowa, Minnesota, and the Dakotas.* Norman, OK: University of Oklahoma Press, 1960.

Josephy, Alvin M., Jr. *The Civil War in the American West.* New York: Alfred A. Knopf, 1991.

Lass, William E. *Steamboating on the Upper Missouri River.* Lincoln, NE: University of Nebraska Press, 1962.

Leech, Margaret. *Reveille in Washington 1860 - 1865.* New York: Harper and Brothers, 1941.

Lewis Gene D. *Charles Ellet, Jr.,....The Engineer as Individualist, 1810-1862.* Urbana, IL: University of Illinois Press, 1968.

Linderman, Gerald F. *Embattled Courage: The Experience of Combat in the American Civil War.* New York: MacMillan, The Free Press, 1987.

Logan, John A. *The Great Conspiracy: Its Origin and History.* New York: A. R. Hart and Co., 1886.

Long, E. B with Barbara Long. *The Civil War Day by Day: An Almanac 1861 - 1865.* New York: Doubleday and Co., DaCapo Press, 1971.

Lord, Francis A. *Uniforms of the Civil War.* South Brunswick: Thomas Yoseloff, 1970.

Lowry, Thomas P. *The Story the Soldiers Wouldn't Tell.* Mechanicsburg, PA: Stackpole Books, 1994.

MacDonald, John. *Great Battles of the Civil War.* New York: MacMillan Publishing Co., 1988.

Mahan, Alfred Thayer. *The Gulf and Inland Waters.* New York: Charles Scribner's Sons, 1883. Reprint, Campaigns of the Civil War Series. Wilmington, NC: Broadfoot Publishing Co., 1989.

Marvel, William. *Andersonville, The Last Depot.* Chapel Hill, NC: The University of North Carolina Press, 1994.

McElroy, John. *This Was Andersonville.* Edited by Roy Meredith. New York: Bonanza Books, 1957.

McKay, Ernest A. *The Civil War and New York City.* Syracuse: Syracuse University Press, 1990.

McPherson, James M. *Battle Cry of Freedom: The Civil War Era.* The Oxford History of the United States, vol. 6. New York: Oxford University Press, 1988.

Merchant Steam Vessels of the United States, 1790-1868. "The Lytle-Holdcamper List" Staten Island, NY: The Steamship Historical Society of America, Inc., 1975.

Merill, James M. *Battle Flags South: The Story of the Civil War Navies on Western Waters.* Rutherford, NJ: Fairleigh Dickinson University Press, 1970.

Milligan, John D. *Gunboats Down the Mississippi.* U. S. Naval Institute Press, 1965. Reprint. New York: Arno Press, 1980.

Mitchell, Reid. *Civil War Soldiers: Their Expectations and Their Experiences.* New York: Viking, The Penguin Group, 1988.

Modelski, Andrew M. *Railroad Maps of North America, The First Hundred Years.* Washington: Library of Congress, 1984.

Moe, Richard. *The Last Full Measure: The Life and Death of the First Minnesota Volunteers.* New York: Henry Holt and Company, 1993.

Monaghan, Jay. *Civil War on the Western Border, 1854 - 1865.* New York: Bonanza Books, 1955.

Morrison, John J. *History of American Steamboat Navigation.* New York: Stephen Daye Press, 1958.

Nathaniel, Richard. *Atlas of American Wars.* Greenwich, CT: Arch Cape Press, 1986.

Nicholay, John G. *The Outbreak of Rebellion.* New York: Charles Scribner's Sons, 1881. Reprint, *Campaigns of the Civil War Series*, Wilmington, NC: Broadfoot Publishing Company, 1989

Nichols, James L. *The Confederate Quartermaster in the Trans-Mississippi.* Austin: University of Texas Press, 1964.

Nolan, Dick. *Benjamin Franklin Butler: The Damnedest Yankee.* Novato, CA: Presidio Press, 1991.

Owens, Harry P. *Steamboats and the Cotton Economy: River Trade in the Yazoo - Mississippi Delta.* Jackson: University Press of Mississippi, 1990.

Phisterer, Frederick. *Statistical Record of the Armies of the United States.* New York: Charles Scribner's Sons, 1883. Reprint, *Campaigns of the Civil War Series*, Wilmington, NC: Broadfoot Publishing Company, 1989

Porter, Admiral David D. *The Naval History of the Civil War.* Facsimile reprint, Secaucus, NJ: Castle, 1984.

Ransom, John. *John Ransom's Andersonville Diary.* 1881. Reprint. Middlebury, VT: Paul S. Eriksson, 1986.

Reed, Rowena. *Combined Operations in the Civil War.* Annapolis: Naval Institute Press, 1978.

Ridgeley-Nevitt, Cedric. *American Steamships on the Atlantic.* Newark, DE: University of Delaware Press, 1981.

Risch, Erna. *Quartermaster Support of the Army: A History of the Corps 1775 - 1939.* Washington, DC: Quartermaster Historian's Office, Office of the Quartermaster General, 1962.

Roberts, Robert B. *Encyclopedia of Historic Forts: The Military, Pioneer, and Trading Posts of the United States.* New York: MacMillan Publishing Co., 1988.

Robertson, William Glenn. *Back Door to Richmond: The Bermuda Hundred Campaign, April - June 1864.* Newark: University of Delaware Press, 1987.

Robinson, William Morrison, Jr. *The Confederate Privateers.* Columbia, SC: University of South Carolina Press, 1990.

Robinton, Madeline Russell. *An Introduction to the Papers of the New York Prize Court, 1861 - 1865.* Studies in History, Economics, and Public Law, No. 515. Edited by the Faculty of Political Science of Columbia Univ. New York: Columbia University Press, 1945.

Roske, Ralph J., and Charles Van Doren. *Lincoln's Commando: The Biography of Commander William B. Cushing, USN.* New York: Harper and Brothers, 1957.

Schiller, Herbert M., MD. *The Bermuda Hundred Campaign: Operations on the South Side of the James River, Virginia, May 1864.* Dayton: Morningside House, 1988.

Schlesinger, Arthur M. Jr. *The Almanac of American History.* New York: G. P. Putnam's Sons, 1983.

Shaw, Ronald E. *Canals For a Nation; The Canal Era in the United States, 1790 - 1860.* Lexington: University of Kentucky, 1990.

Short, Lloyd M. *The Bureau of Navigation: Its History, Activities, and Organization.* Institute for Government Research: Service Monographs of the U. S. Government, No. 15. Baltimore: Johns Hopkins Press, 1923.

Sifakis, Stewart. *Who Was Who in the Civil War.* New York: Facts on File Publications, 1988.

Silverstone, Paul H. *Warships of the Civil War Navies.* Annapolis: Naval Institute Press, 1989.

Soldier Life in the Union and Confederate Armies. Edited by Philip Van Doren Stern. New York: Bonanza Books, 1961.

Standenraus, P. J. *The African Colonization Movement, 1816-1865.* New York: Columbia University Press, 1961. (Relative to Appendix K.)

Still, William N. Jr. *Iron Afloat: The Story of the Confederate Armorclads.* Columbia, SC: University of South Carolina Press, 1985.

Symonds, Crag L. *A Battlefield Atlas of the Civil War.* 1983. Second edition. Baltimore: The Nautical and Aviation Publishing Co. of America, 1985.

Tanner, Henry S. *Canals and Railroads of the United States.* Reprint, New York: Augustus M. Kelley Publishers, 1970.

The Maple Leaf: An Extraordinary American Civil War Shipwreck. Keith V. Holland; Lee B. Manley; James W. Towart, editors. Jacksonville, FL: St. Johns Archeological Expeditions, Inc., 1993.

Thomas Wentworth Higginson, *Army Life in a Black Regiment,* 1869. Reprint Beacon Press, Boston, 1962.

Thomas, Emory M. *The Confederate Nation, 1861 - 1865.* The New American Nation Series. New York: Harper and Row, 1979.

Trotter, William R. *Ironclads and Columbiads: The Civil War in North Carolina: The Coast.* Winston-Salem, NC: John F. Blair, 1989.

Trudeau, Noah Andre. *The Last Citadel: Petersburg, Virginia, June 1864 - April 1865.* Boston: Little, Brown and Co., 1991.

Upton, Emory. *The Military Policy of the United States.* (Reprint of 1904 edition) New York: Greenwood Press, 1968

Upton, Francis H. *The Laws of Nations Affecting Commerce During War.* New York: John S. Voorhies Law Bookseller and Publisher, 1861.

Utley, Robert M. *Frontiersmen in Blue: The United States Army and the Indian, 1848 - 1865.* New York: MacMillan Publishing Co., 1967.

Vandiver, Frank E. *Their Tattered Flags: The Epic of the Confederacy.* New York: Harper's Magazine Press, 1970.

Way's Packet Directory 1848 - 1983: Passenger Steamboats of the Mississippi River System Since the Advent of Photography in Mid-Continent America. Compiled by Frederick Way, Jr. Athens, OH: Ohio University Press, 1983.

Webb, Alexander S. *The Peninsula.* New York: Charles Scribner's Sons, 1881. Reprint, *Campaigns of the Civil War Series,* Wilmington, NC: Broadfoot Publishing Company, 1989

Weber, Thomas. *The Northern Railroads in the Civil War, 1861 - 1865.* New York: Columbia University, King's Crown Press, 1952.

Weigley, Russell F. *History of the United States Army.* New York: MacMillan Co., 1967.

West Point Atlas of American Wars, 1689 - 1900. vol. 1: Compiled by the Department of Military Art and Engineering, West Point. Edited by Colonel Vincent J. Esposito. New York: Frederick A. Praeger, 1959.

Wheeler, Richard. *Sword Over Richmond: An Eyewitness History of McClellan's Peninsula Campaign.* New York: Harper and Row, 1986.

Wiener, F. B. *Civilians Under Military Justice.* Chicago: University of Chicago Press, 1967.

Wilkinson, Warren. *Mother, May You Never See the Sights I Have Seen: The Fifty-seventh Massachusetts Veteran Volunteers in the Army of the Potomac, 1864 - 1865.* New York: Harper and Row, 1990.

Wise, Stephen R. *Lifeline of the Confederacy: Blockade Running During the Civil War.* Columbia, SC: University of South Carolina Press, 1988.

UNPUBLISHED SECONDARY

Westwood, Howard C. *Benjamin Butler's Naval Brigade.* Monograph held by the Naval History Center, Department of the Navy, Washington Navy Yard, Washington, DC.

THESES

Marvin, Thomas Eugene, III. *Prisoner of War Exchange During the American Civil War.* Ph.D. dissertation, Auburn University 1976. Available through University Microfilms Incorporated; Ann Arbor, Michigan.

Schottenhamel, George Carl. *Lewis Baldwin Parsons and Civil War Transportation.* Ph.D. dissertation, Department of History, University of Illinois. Available through University Microfilms Incorporated; Ann Arbor, Michigan. Schottenhamel's primary source was the University of Illinois's collection of papers of Lewis Baldwin Parsons.

PICTORIAL

Divided We Fought: A Pictorial History of the War, 1861 - 1865. Edited by David Donald. New York: MacMillan & Co., 1953.

Gardner, Alexander. *Gardner's Photographic Sketchbook of the Civil War.* 1866. Reprint. New York: Dover Publications, 1959.

Gibbons, Tony. *Warships and Naval Battles of the Civil War.* New York: Gallery Books, 1989.

Guernsey, Alfred H. and Henry M. Alden. *Harper's Pictorial History of the Civil War.* New York: Harper's, 1866. Reprint by Fairfax Press.

Jordan, Robert Paul. *The Civil War.* Washington, DC: National Geographic Society; Special Publications Division, 1969.

Katcher, Philip. *American Civil War Armies.* vol. 3: Staff Specialists and Maritime Services. Men at Arms Series. Edited by Martin Windrow. London: Osprey Publishing, 1986.

Photographic History of the Civil War. 5 volumes. Reprint, Secaucus, NJ: The Blue and Grey Press, 1987.

Photographic Portraits of American Ocean Steamships, 1850 - 1870. Providence: The Steamship Historical Society of America, 1986.

Roberts, Bobby and Carl Moneyhon. *Portraits of Conflict: A Photographic History of Mississippi in the Civil War.* Fayetteville, AR: University of Arkansas Press, 1993.

Touched by Fire: A Photographic Portrait of the Civil War. vol. 1. A Product of the National Historical Society. Edited by William C. Davis. Boston: Little Brown & Co., 1985.

BIBLIOGRAPHIC REFERENCES

Civil War Books, A Critical Bibliography. 2 volumes. Allan Nevins, James I. Robertson, Jr.; Wiley Bell, editors. Baton Rouge: Louisiana State University Press, 1970.

Civil War Books, A Priced Checklist. Wendell, NC: Broadfoot Publishing Co., 1983.

Civil War Manuscripts. A Guide to Collections in the Manuscript Division of the Library of Congress. Compiled by John R. Sellers. Washington: Library of Congress, 1986.

Mullins, Michael and Rowena Reed. *The Union Bookshelf: A Selected Civil War Bibliography.* Wendell, NC: Broadfoot's Bookmark, 1982.

Munden, Kenneth W. and Henry Putney Beers. *Guide to Federal Archives Relating to the Civil War.* Washington: The National Archives, 1962.

ARTICLES

Abbott, John S. C. "Charles Ellet and His Naval Rams," *Harpers New Monthly Magazine,* XXXII, New York, 1866.

Bailey, Anne J. "The Mississippi Marine Brigade: Fighting Rebel Guerrillas on Western Waters." *Military History of the Southwest,* vol. 22, Spring 1992.

Boyd, Willis D. "Ile a Vache Colonization Venture, 1862 - 1864." *Americas,* Vol. 16, July 1959.

Civil War Prisons. William B. Hesseltine, editor. Kent, OH: Kent State University Press, 1962.

Day, Lieutenant Harry E. "Ellet's Horse Marines." *The Marine Corps Gazette.* vol. 23, no. 1. March, 1939.

Gordon, Cmdr. Arthur. "The Great Stone Fleet, Calculated Catastrophe." U. S. Naval Institute *Proceedings.* December 1968.

Hurst, T. M. "The Battle of Shiloh," *Tennessee Historical Magazine,* July 1919.

Rasmussen, Wayne D. "The Civil War: A Catalyst of Agricultural Revolution." *Agricultural History: The Quarterly Journal of the Agricultural History Society.* Champaign, IL: Garrard Press, 1965. (Relative to Appendix L.)

GENERAL INDEX

VESSEL INDEX

OCEAN EMPRESS, 36
OCEAN EXPRESS, 18, 36
OCEAN QUEEN, 15, 18, 218
OCEAN RANGER, 599, 624
OCTORARA, 394
OHIO, 79
OHIO BELLE, 79, 87, 152, 557
OHIO NO. 3, 79
OLIVE BRANCH, 508
OLUSTEE, CSS, 574, 622
OMAHA, 153, 469
ONEIDA, 532
ONEIDA, USS, 117
ONEONTA, 455
ORIENTAL, 79
OSAGE, USS, 355, 360, 611
OSCEOLA, 17, 19, 20, 573
OSGOOD, SEE CHARLES OSGOOD
OTSEGO, USS, 336
OTTAWA, USS, 22, 23
OUACHITA, USS, 611
OZARK, USS, 611
PAINT ROCK, 376, 379, 380, 401
PALESTINE, 469
PALMER, SEE EDWARD PALMER
PALMER, SEE ROBERT PALMER
PARKE, 411, 414, 482
PARKERSBURG, 15, 18
PARTHENIA, 228, 229, 455
PARTRIDGE, SEE A. H. PARTRIDGE
PATAPSCO, 455
PATROON, 394
PATTEN, SEE THOMAS J. PATTEN
PATUXENT, 481
PAULINE, 368
PAULINE CARROLL, 508
PEABODY, SEE GEORGE PEABODY
PEERLESS, 17, 19, 20
PEKIN, SEE CITY OF PEKIN
PEMBINA, 153
PENSACOLA, USS, 89, 93
PEORIA, SEE BELLE PEORIA
PERIT, 449
PERRY, SEE COMMODORE PERRY, USS
PETREL, USS, 268
PHANTOM, 79
PHILADELPHIA, 455
PICKET, 28, 29, 412, 566
PIKE, SEE LADY PIKE
PILLOW, SEE GENERAL PILLOW
PILOT BOY, 455
PINK VARBLE, 79
PIONEER, 28, 419, 483, 566
PITTSBURG, 70-73, 86, 87, 104, 111, 558
PITTSBURG, USS, 150, 277, 283, 611
PLANDOME, 455
PLANET, 79, 153, 271
PLANTER, 79, 299, 419, 455
PLATO, 455
PLATTE VALLEY, 79
POCAHONTAS, 30, 336, 548, 549, 553
POE, SEE CLARA POE
POE, SEE JACOB POE
POLAND, 79
POLAR STAR, 153, 368
POLK, 136
POLLARD, SEE DAN POLLARD
PONTCHARTRAIN, 122
PORT ROYAL, USS, 193
PORTER, 413, 512

PORTSMOUTH, 419
POST BOY, 245
POTOMAC, 18
POWELL, SEE JONAS POWELL
PRAIRIE ROSE, 67, 79
PRICE, SEE GENERAL STERLING PRICE
PRINCE, 87, 557
PRINGLE, SEE J. S. PRINGLE
PROMETHEUS, 462, 511
PUTNAM, 481
PUTNAM, USS, 35
QUEEN OF THE WEST, 98, 100, 108, 109, 112-115, 123, 138, 139, 141, 142, 149, 150, 154, 162, **179, 181,** 240, 243, 244, 253-261, 278, 289-291, 334, 345, 561, 570
R. B. HAMILTON, 231
R. J. LOCKWOOD, 469
R. M. PATTON, 67
RACHEL S. MILLER, 18, 455
RAINE, SEE JOHN RAINE
RAMM, SEE JOHN RAMM
RANGER, 28, 37, 566
RAPPAHANNOCK, 511
RATTLER, USS, 266
REBECCA, 79
REBECCA BARTON, 419, 435, 455, 512
REBECCA CLYDE, 394, 512
RECRUIT, 28, 37
RED CHIEF, 368
RED FOX, 560
RED ROVER, 87, 121, 165, 557, 559
REINDEER, 18
RELIEF, 455
RENO, 411, 414, 482
RESACA, 380
RESCUE, 455
RESOLUTE, 559
RESTLESS, 559
RICE, SEE JOHN RICE
RIVER QUEEN, 479
ROANOKE, 15, 17, 18
ROB ROY, 65, 67, 350, 351, 355, 368
ROBB, SEE ALFRED ROBB
ROBERT ALLEN, 153
ROBERT CAMPBELL NO. 2, 580
ROBERT CAMPBELL, JR, 152, 245
ROBERT J. MERCER, 18
ROBERT PALMER, 455
ROBINSON, SEE KATE ROBINSON
ROBINSON, SEE SALLIE ROBINSON
ROCKET, 28, 79
ROCKLAND, 419
ROE, SEE JOHN J. ROE
ROGERS, SEE JENNIE ROGERS
ROMEO, USS, 266
ROSE, SEE JOHN ROSE
ROSE HAMBLETON, 79
ROSE HITE, 469
ROTARY, 220
ROVER, USS, 165
RUATAN, SEE SAMUEL RUATAN
RUSSIA, 455, 462
RUTH, 271
S. MOORE, 449
S. R. SPAULDING, 27, 219, 412, 435
S. W. THOMAS, 79
SABINE, USS, 17
SACHEM, USS, 95
SAINT CHARLES, 394
SAINT CLAIR, 79
SAINT CLAIR, USS, 611

Mississippi Valley Theater of Operations